Developing
Arguments

Developing

Arguments

STRATEGIES FOR REACHING AUDIENCES

KATHLEEN BELL
OLD DOMINION UNIVERSITY

WADSWORTH PUBLISHING COMPANY
BELMONT, CALIFORNIA
A DIVISION OF WADSWORTH, INC.

93

\# 20390982

English Editor: Angela Gantner
Editorial Assistant: Julie Johnson
Production Editor: Patricia Brewer
Managing Designer: Donna Davis
Print Buyer: Barbara Britton
Designer: Christy Butterfield
Copy Editor: Carolyn McGovern
Art Editor: Irene Imfeld
Compositor: G & S Typesetters, Austin, Texas
Cover: Paula Shuhert

Acknowledgements begin on p. 718.

Printed in the United States of America   19

  2 3 4 5 6 7 8 9 10—94 93 92 91 90

Library of Congress Cataloging-in-Publication Data

Bell, Kathleen L, 1946–
    Developing arguments : strategies for reaching audiences / Kathleen Bell.
        p.   cm.
    ISBN 0-534-12192-6
    1. English language—Rhetoric.   2. Persuasion (Rhetoric).   3. College readers.   I. Title.
PE1431.B45   1990
808'.0427—dc20   89-38577
                                                                              CIP

Contents

PART V   EVALUATING ARGUMENTS   487

Preface

When the artist Renoir reached the age of ninety, his arthritis was so severe that his paintbrush had to be strapped to his hand. Asked how he could paint in such an awkward and painful state, Renoir replied, "But I don't paint with my hand."

Writers and teachers of writing have come to realize the significance of Renoir's words: Effective writing is built on effective thinking—a recursive process of discovering choices, making decisions, and evaluating choices made. This book guides students in using this critical thinking and writing process in developing effective arguments.

Any book on how to write poses a conceptual problem: Writing is an interactive process, but only one feature can be discussed at a time. With that problem in mind, I used three levels of organization for this text: the stages of writing, a whole-to-parts rhetoric, and critical thinking strategies. This organization will help students focus simultaneously on the *what* of their purpose for writing, the *how* of developing their writing, and the *why* of making and evaluating their decisions. Structurally these emphases are interwoven in the following ways.

STAGES OF WRITING

Each part of the text represents a different stage of the composing process: discovering, investigating, planning, writing, and evaluating. While these stages progress in a natural order from generating ideas and collecting information to shaping and refining ideas, writing full essays is *not* delayed until the fourth stage. The exercises in each chapter include all stages of the composing process.

In their broadest sense the stages are meant to serve as reference points for students as they compose arguments in or out of class. The ongoing nature of the writing stages means they will allow flexibility in instruction; the methods used here can be adapted to the needs of individual students.

WHOLE-TO-PARTS RHETORIC

The chapter titles within each part identify rhetorical concerns. This emphasis leads students from what they already know to what they determine they need to know. From there, students learn to analyze what their audiences know, what they need to know, and how they will best understand the argument. This strategy assumes that once students have an overall sense of purpose for their writing—once they can define the context and the direction of the claim—they will be more strongly motivated to investigate their assumptions and take the risk of experimenting with ways to share those beliefs. In advocating this assumption, the text focuses in every chapter on the relationship between the writer and the audience so that students will write *real* arguments for *real* audiences.

CRITICAL THINKING LEVELS

The presentation of the material within each chapter follows the hierarchy of the critical thinking strategies. The rhetorical principles—the focus of each chapter—are introduced at the discovery level using heuristics and often diagrams to assist students in visualizing the range of available choices. From that point the actual decision-making process is illustrated with varied examples that require choosing among several alternatives. Students find that they cannot apply formulas in making decisions. An array of audiences and contexts expands students' understanding of why and how choices are made and prepares them for the next level of critical thinking, evaluating the choices they make. Arguments are evaluated in each chapter, each of which focuses on one principle but builds on all principles presented in previous chapters. The evaluations are designed to emphasize how the choices made and the effects of those choices are unique to the context of the argument being evaluated. This organizational level strives to reinforce the value of choosing and of making effective and responsible decisions rather than following prescribed formats.

Combined, these three organizational designs put students at the center of the decision-making process, a process that can be used beyond the writing class in making responsible judgments on what they hear or read, as well as on what they present to others. Argument, then, becomes an individualized means of seeing and shaping ideas for oneself and generating structures for sharing those ideas as beliefs. The dialogue that emanates from this relationship between writer and reader requires the critical inquiry and reasoning this book hopes to provide.

ACKNOWLEDGEMENTS

Thanks to the following reviewers for their comments and suggestions on the manuscript: Chris Anderson, Oregon State University; Josephine Bloomfield, University of California, Davis; Carol Ann Britt, University of Texas, San Antonio; Ed Corbett, Ohio State University; Linda D. Doran, Volunteer State College; Linda R. Eastburn, Linn-Benton Community College; John Hagaman, Western Kentucky University; Susan S. Harland, University of Pittsburgh; Gail Hemmeter, Mary Washington College; Sharon Hockensmith, University of Texas, San Antonio; Palma Lower, California State University, Sacramento; Larry McDoniel, St. Louis Community College; George Miller, University of Delaware; Susan Miller, University of Utah; Denise E. Murray, San Jose State University; Sara Murray, University of Texas, San Antonio; John Price, California State University, Sacramento; Jeanne Simpson, Eastern Illinois University; M. Clare Sweeney, Arizona State University; and Victor J. Vitanza, University of Texas, Arlington.

Kathleen Bell

PART I

Discovering Arguments

There is a great deal of difference in believing something still, and believing it again.

W. H. AUDEN

Has anyone ever challenged your belief in something? When was the last time you examined your reasons for believing in something? This examination of beliefs to understand *why* you believe what you do is the distinction Auden implies between "believing something still" and "believing something again."

The process of determining why you believe in something begins with the process of discovering arguments that exist on the subject in question. An **argument** is the position or conclusion a person reaches based on supportive reasons and examples.

Who are the people who are taking a position on a particular subject?

What caused them to formulate an argument?

What is their position in that argument?

When and for whom did they state this position?

The answers to these questions provide the **context** for an argument: the people involved, the occasion for involvement, the purpose of the argument, and the audience to whom the argument is directed. Chapter 1 shows you how to discover the available arguments on a subject by analyzing these context features.

Once you determine the range of arguments that exists, you can begin to examine the claims of each position—the reasoning that informs the argument. Chapter 2 demonstrates the thinking that underlies making a claim and the relationship the claim builds with the audience to gain acceptance. This process guides you in determining the clarity and credibility of others' arguments and your own.

Chapter 1

THE CONTEXT
FOR DISCOURSE

Discourse is language in use, spoken and written. When people use language together on a regular basis, as a group they have an identity as a **discourse community.**
Although you have more than likely never thought of yourself as a member of a discourse community, you could easily name half a dozen or more that you belong to—
family, church group, athletic team, car pool, roommates, performance group, social
club, professional or political organization, work shift, calculus study group.

The activities of a discourse community distinctly shape its use of language. For
example, a theater group is likely to use specialized language, such as "Clear the apron
and put the palms by the proscenium before we run through," during a rehearsal but
personalized, telegraphic language, such as "Dan's—7:30!" when informing other
members of their whereabouts. The shape of the discourse, then, will be characterized
by a distinct level of usage that depends on the purpose of the community's activity.
You can use the range of discourse levels shown in Figure 1 to identify the language
use of different community activities.

Looking carefully at each type of activity and its corresponding level of discourse,
you can see that the *purpose* of the activity, the *occasion* of the activity, and the *people*
involved in giving and receiving the information influence the shape of the discourse.
These features—the who, what, when, and why—form the **context** for discourse.
And it is the context in which discourse takes place that will guide you in discovering
the available arguments on a subject and in forming your own arguments.

Figure 1 *Activities for a theater group*

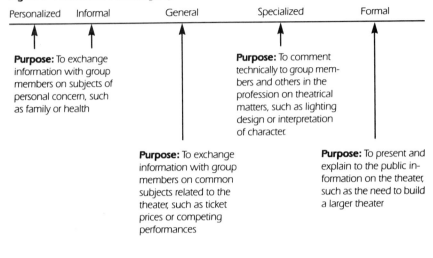

Personalized   Informal   General   Specialized   Formal

Purpose: To exchange information with group members on subjects of personal concern, such as family or health

Purpose: To comment technically to group members and others in the profession on theatrical matters, such as lighting design or interpretation of character.

Purpose: To exchange information with group members on common subjects related to the theater, such as ticket prices or competing performances

Purpose: To present and explain to the public information on the theater, such as the need to build a larger theater

ANALYZING CONTEXT

THE PEOPLE: THE *WHO* OF AN ARGUMENT

The context for argument requires at least two people: the producer (writer/speaker) and the receiver (audience). One discourse community might present an argument to another discourse community, or two or more members within the same discourse community might discuss an issue. In each case, the *function* of each community involved will affect how the members perceive an argument and how they relate their position to others.

Discourse communities have a primary function that unifies their members. Figure 2 presents a range of function categories for certain discourse communities. Naturally, the function of a discourse community defines the main interests of the group—what subjects they discuss, read about, and write about. Let's say, for instance, that all people are concerned about available sources of energy. After all, most of us would have difficulty living without electricity, gasoline, and heating fuel. But, even though this issue affects all people, few communities are likely to *discuss* the problem of available energy sources, *read* about it, and *write* about it as part of their primary function. Thus, if you were searching for arguments on available energy sources, you would use primary group functions related to the issue as starting points for discovering the arguments that exist. For instance, you might begin with groups of geologists and oceanographers who locate mineral sources for energy; nuclear physicists and engineers who create processes for developing energy; public utility and petroleum companies that finance the development, research, and distribution of energy sources; or the U.S. De-

Figure 2 *Function categories of discourse communities*

Private	Social	Educational	Professional	Public
Family	Bridge club	Calculus study group	Geologists' association	Environmental organization

partment of Energy and the Environmental Protection Agency, which initiate laws and guidelines to protect the people and the environment. Even this general range of discourse communities related to the issue of available energy sources illustrates the diverse perspectives you are likely to find.

Once you determine the community whose arguments you want to study, you need to consider one more level of *who:* the **audience** for whom the arguments were written. The audience could be people in the *same* community, *related* communities, or *unrelated* communities. Each of these audiences will have a different degree of understanding of the issue and will require different kinds of information before accepting the position. For example, geologists within the same company share a technical understanding of the subject and a company direction for their work. This closeness in thinking relieves them of the need to define terms and purpose; instead, they can get right to the particulars of their position. If the same geologists wanted to present their position to the geophysicists of another company, they could rely on the other community's technical understanding of the subject. However, in this case the geologists would need to provide more information to explain the purpose for their position. The differences in their specialties and their companies would create just enough distance in understanding for an explanation of the rationale to be necessary. Even more distance would be present if the geologists wanted to present their position to the general public. Imagine how they would need to simplify their language, define terms, and provide background information to make their point.

Knowing *who* the audience for an argument is not only helps you to evaluate someone else's argument but also directs you in shaping your own arguments. As you review the potential audience groups listed here, notice that, as the nature of the group moves from personal to public, a greater distance in shared knowledge occurs.

GROUP: KNOWN PEERS	DISTANCE FEATURES
People you know well socially	Common concerns
Your professional colleagues	High degree of specific knowledge shared

EXAMPLE: Convincing your roommates to share the expense of buying a VCR.

Living together, you already know the amount of money each person has to spend and the level of interest in making the purchase.

EXAMPLE: Persuading coworkers to endorse a new software program.

Working together, you recognize the features and capacities a software program should have for the particular work you do.

GROUP: KNOWN AUTHORITY

People you know personally who make decisions that directly affect your life

DISTANCE FEATURES

Common concerns
Selective degree of shared knowledge

EXAMPLE: Persuading your parents to buy you a computer system.

Having lived together, you know your parents' financial status and they know your level of responsibility and appreciation.

EXAMPLE: Convincing your adviser that you should change your major.

Your adviser knows what course work you have taken, what your goals are, and how to distribute credit for the work completed; you know the adviser wants you to succeed.

GROUP: SPECIALISTS

Teachers in specific content areas
People in your profession who have more expertise and whom you know and admire

DISTANCE FEATURES

Assumed mutual interest in content
Shared knowledge of basic content information

EXAMPLE: Convincing your physics professor that you understand entropy.

Your professor already understands *entropy* but does not know if you understand the principles and their application.

EXAMPLE: Persuading the leader of your research team to accept your grant proposal.

As an expert in the field, your leader knows more than you do and can judge the acceptability of your idea.

GROUP: UNKNOWN AUTHORITY

A person, company, or institution whose decisions and actions affect your life but with whom you do not have a personal relationship

DISTANCE FEATURES

Reciprocal personal concern
Highly selective shared knowledge that is issue specific

EXAMPLE: Convincing the governor of your state to upgrade literacy programs.

Neither you nor the governor are experts, but the governor's decisions affect the quality of your life just as your support can affect the governor's elected position.

EXAMPLE: Persuading the Federal Aviation Administration (FAA) to increase the number of airport security checkpoints.

Although the FAA may know more about airport security measures, it must be concerned about your feelings of safety. If you do not feel safe, you may choose to use another form of transportation.

GROUP: GENERAL PUBLIC

A large, diverse group with generalized characteristics. You may be a part of this audience. The audience may be local, national, or global

DISTANCE FEATURES

Assumed mutual concerns but an anonymous personal relationship
Often less informed on specific issues

EXAMPLE: Convincing parents of 9 to 11-year-olds that children in this age group should take music lessons.

These parents may or may not have experience with this issue, but they are likely to question your credibility in giving them advice.

EXAMPLE: Persuading the people of all countries to support an international law against terrorism.

These people may have different levels of knowledge on the subject; this knowledge may be country specific rather than international, but their concerns may be similar.

The potential audiences for your arguments are likely to share the characteristics of one of these audience groups. The more personal the audience, the closer your sharing of specific knowledge will be; the more distant and public your audience is, the more generalized your sharing of knowledge will be. This means that each audience requires you to use different types of information in shaping your argument. And how do you decide what information to use? The best way to begin is with these two questions:

What does the audience *already* know?

What does the audience *need* to know?

When you have answered these two questions, you will be well on your way to shaping a convincing argument.

THE OCCASION: THE *WHEN* OF AN ARGUMENT

Whatever event brings people together may serve as an **occasion,** the *when,* for a potential difference in opinion. As you read through this list of occasions, think about the features that make them different or similar.

A. A community theater group meets to decide which plays to perform for the season.

B. Students from Professor Harvey's political science class attend with their professor a public forum on nuclear disarmament.

C. An advertising agency presents a revised ad campaign to company executives.

D. An employee receives a negative performance evaluation in writing from his supervisor.

E. A consumer buys a toaster that breaks the first time he uses it.

F. *Time* publishes an article on the merits of legalizing drugs.

G. A bank rejects a couple's loan application for a new house.

One of the first features you will notice is that for some occasions the interaction between people is *direct* while for other occasions it is *indirect*. In A, B, and C, for example, the participants can state their positions directly to one another. But in D, E, F, and G, a physical distance between the people involved makes the interaction indirect, at least initially. As the distance between you and your audience increases, your personal control over reaching your audience becomes more difficult.

Another feature you are likely to notice is the relationship between the people involved. Just how well do the participants know each other, and how is that relationship likely to affect the occasion? In A the participants' familiarity makes their interaction informal and personal, but in B the students' role as part of a larger, public group makes their relationship to the group more formal. Some of the same features occur in occasions C and D but with a different intensity. Occasion C is not exactly a public event, but the participants do not know each other well, so it becomes more formal. In D, although the employee and the evaluator probably know each other, the difference in their status makes the occasion one of formal interaction. This distance in relationship widens in occasions E, F, and G where the consumer, the *Time* readers, and the couple applying for the loan have to relate to a corporation. The greater the distance in the relationship of the participants, the more formal the interaction that takes place.

Knowing the levels of interaction and formality of an occasion can help you determine what kind of information you need and how to present it. As the relationship between you and your audience becomes less personal and more public and the level of your expression becomes more formal, the need to go beyond yourself as a resource—to use more content-centered information—increases.

THE SUBJECT: THE *WHAT* OF AN ARGUMENT

Once an occasion provokes a strong response in you on a particular subject, you need to discover the focus of your acceptance or rejection. A good way to do this is to brainstorm from the perspective of different audiences. This brainstorming process will help you to see the many parts of the issue and to learn which communities would be the best audience for your argument. The example that follows illustrates how this process takes place.

OCCASION: Dave has just voted in his first local election. Feeling rather proud of himself, he asks his friends and classmates if they voted. Dave is shocked that most of them didn't vote. His outrage is confirmed by the next morning's headline: "43% Voter Turnout Disappointing."

BRAINSTORMING: The occasion raises several immediate questions in Dave's mind, so he writes them down and begins to focus on his main concerns.

QUESTIONS	POSSIBLE FOCUS
Why don't more people vote?	
Why don't they care?	*What causes voter apathy?*
Don't people have faith in the electoral system?	
Is ours a representative government if less than half the people vote?	*Does voter apathy threaten our democracy?*
How did it get this bad?	
Why don't federal or city officials do something about it?	*Who's responsible?*

Dave has found a preliminary focus: voter apathy. Now he needs to find out who is apathetic and why, so he looks at the focus from the perspective of different audiences to discover how they relate to the issue.

AUDIENCE COMMUNITIES	RELATED CHARACTERISTICS
Peers (ages 18–22)	May not be registered to vote
	Are inexperienced voters
	Say they are too busy
	Are uninformed about candidates
	Don't believe their vote can make a difference
	Don't realize the consequences
	Haven't anything to lose yet
Parents and other experienced voters (ages 40 and up)	Have established party loyalty
	Show patriotism more openly (flags, bumper stickers)
	Are war veterans
	Want their vote to make a difference, believe in system
	Stay informed on issues
	Don't want to lose what they have achieved
Businesses and institutions	Form special interest groups (lobby power)
	Are politically dependent (research, grants, trade)
	Desire to control
	Show open support for candidates (contributions, fund raisers)
General Public Local	Are uninformed and uninvolved
	Are media saturated, suffer information burnout
	Do not believe their vote will make a significant difference
	Are not fully aware of consequences

AUDIENCE COMMUNITIES	RELATED CHARACTERISTICS
National	Are more interested in presidential elections
	Are too busy struggling
	Lack initiative and faith in change
	Are cynical about what can be accomplished
Global	Could see us as fragmented, weak, and vulnerable
	Might question the democratic system if so few support it

This process of brainstorming preliminary issues in relation to different audiences generates a wide range of connections between the writer and his or her subject. From these kinds of connections, writers can discover their major concerns or focuses. The connections Dave has generated, for example, might reveal three concerns he can use to develop an argument.

FOCUS ONE: Age and level of accomplishment have the strongest effect on voters' participation in the electoral process.

FOCUS TWO: Voter apathy is threatening the balance of representation in the democratic process.

FOCUS THREE: Continued voter apathy will weaken the global image of the United States.

Dave can now decide which point he is most concerned about and which audience needs the information most.

THE PURPOSE: THE *WHY* OF AN ARGUMENT

Once you determine a focus for your subject, you will need to find a direction for presenting it. Who needs to know your position on the issue and why? By answering these questions, you establish your purpose. Basically the **purpose** expresses the relationship you hope to develop between the audience and the focus of your argument. Here are some examples:

To convince Chesapeake Bay area residents that their pollution control efforts can reverse the environmental damage that has already taken place.

To persuade the city council to enact a law banning smoking in all enclosed public buildings.

Choosing a worthwhile audience-purpose relationship requires another level of brainstorming. On the first brainstorming level Dave generated the relevant characteristics of the different audiences. This information helped him to find a potential focus based on what the audiences *already* know. Now, by determining what each audience *needs* to know, Dave can discover potential purposes for his argument—ways of reaching each audience. Here is how that process would work:

POTENTIAL FOCUSES:
The causes of voter apathy
The threat to the democratic process
The vulnerability of the U.S. image

AUDIENCE COMMUNITIES	AUDIENCE INFORMATION NEEDS	POSSIBLE PURPOSE
Peers (ages 18–22)	Their vote can make a difference. It is easy to stay informed on candidates and issues. The process is valuable. Their future accomplishments need to be protected.	To convince them that by choosing strong leaders they can protect their future
Parents and other experienced voters (ages 40 and up)	Their accomplishments and belief in the power of voting can influence others. Patriotism can be shown in many ways. If others don't vote, their accomplishments and future can be jeopardized.	To persuade them to influence others to vote, especially young people
Businesses and institutions	Their special interests affect more than their profit margin. Their lobbying efforts and contributions are threatening our system of equal representation. Their established power base can help more people.	To persuade them to use their influence to decrease voter apathy and establish fairer representation
General Public Local	They need to stay informed. They are affected greatly by the outcome of local elections. Their vote can make a difference.	To convince them that being involved in local politics will protect their future
National	They can protect their right to vote by voting. Local involvement in politics affects national politics. Not voting aggravates their struggle to get ahead.	To convince them that voting on a local level protects their rights and the possibility for a successful future

AUDIENCE COMMUNITIES	AUDIENCE INFORMATION NEEDS	POSSIBLE PURPOSE
Global	They need to understand the total process. They need to get their information from reliable sources. By supporting our democratic process, they are more likely to benefit from our strengths.	To convince them that when the democratic process is strong, they benefit

Using this brainstorming technique helps you not only to specify your purpose more clearly but also to discover *how* to provide an audience with what it *needs* to know to accept your position on the issue. From this point you can begin to research and collect data for presenting and supporting your argument.

Arguments are important to the intellectual and social growth of all communities: they test our beliefs, promote understanding, and help us plan for the future. But arguments do not exist without a context. Knowing the relationship of the people involved, what brought them together, and what prevents their having the same point of view is the first step toward developing a well-reasoned position that others can accept.

EXERCISES: DISCOURSE COMMUNITIES

1. Make a personal inventory of each discourse community you are a member of. Under each community, list the primary function of the group, your role in the group, and the range of occasions that bring you together. Then identify the discourse that characterizes your communities: what you read, what you discuss, and what you write. Keep a copy of this inventory for future reference for your writing.

2. For each of the following discourse situations, identify the context features important for understanding the meaning of what is taking place and what needs to be accomplished. Specify the level of interaction and the level of formality.

a. You are interviewing your grandfather about his views on and participation in World War II for a report assigned by your history professor.

b. A student receives what she considers an unfair grade on an essay exam in biology.

c. You are reading a newspaper analysis of the president's televised press conference that you viewed the night before.

d. The student senate at your college has given its support to the university president's suggestion for a new school logo. Since you and many of your friends do not agree with the decision, you decide to write a letter to the editor of the school newspaper.

e. At their monthly meeting, faculty committee members from several departments present individual recommendations for scholarship awards.

f. You would like to get a part-time job while at school, so you write to your previous employer requesting a letter of recommendation.

3. Reconstruct an argument you heard or were a part of. Identify the context. After writing out the main parts of the dialogue, analyze how the participants attempted (or failed) to recognize what the audience already knew and what it needed to know.

4. Tell what discourse communities you would contact to discover the available arguments on the subjects listed below. For each community you identify, state how its primary function will limit the arguments.

the greenhouse effect   tuition increases
safe drinking water   movie ratings

5. Describe an occasion that provoked a strong response in you for or against a particular subject. Then, use the process demonstrated earlier in this chapter for finding a focus and establishing a purpose to explore an argument you would be interested in developing.

Chapter 2

THE CLAIM
OF AN ARGUMENT

What *do* people argue about?

As members of a discourse community, people argue about their roles, beliefs, procedures, and status: those factors that determine the identity, behavior, and function of the group and the individuals within the group:

Should we require a minimum grade point average for membership?

Should we openly endorse one of the mayoral candidates?

Should our officers serve two-year terms?

Should we change the format of our publication?

Because the members of a community interact on a regular basis, they share rules governing the conditions for their actions, such as how often they meet and who makes the decisions. These shared understandings, whether written or unwritten, constitute the community's view of reality—that is, the point of view the community uses to determine the rightness and wrongness of ideas and actions. So, when a member presents a new idea or when new information intrudes on this shared understanding, the beliefs of the group are challenged. The group then uses its view of reality—how the members believe things *should be*—to determine whether to accept and incorporate an idea or reject it. This process of comparing the beliefs of one point of view to the beliefs of another point of view is an **argument.**

Argument, then, is a kind of verbal dueling by which an individual or community can *test* new ideas and information. And, by testing these ideas, people discover where they are willing to draw the boundaries for their beliefs and actions. When you examine the beliefs stated below, you can see that the boundaries are indicated clearly:

ISSUE: *Who should teach children about sex?*

Community A: Sex education should be taught in the schools, so students have a chance to discuss issues openly with their peers.

Community B: The parents have the responsibility to teach their children about sex, because it is a personal, intimate subject.

Using argument to test your beliefs keeps you on guard—intellectually and socially alert to what constitutes meaning for you and the communities you belong to. In this respect, the function of language is not simply to duplicate reality but to recall it, comment on it, and make predictions about it.

STATING THE CLAIM

The claim, also called a *proposition,* serves as the *thesis* for your argument. The **claim** of an argument is the conclusion you reach after testing the evidence that supports your belief. It contains your **assertion,** or the idea you propose for the reader's acceptance. Before you state your claim to your audience, you need to test the reasoning that led you to that conclusion.

After studying the way professionals in many disciplines present arguments to one another, philosopher Stephen Toulmin designed a model that will help you to diagram the reasoning of your argument.[1] The Toulmin model, shown in Figure 1, has three primary elements: data, warrant, and claim.

The **claim** or conclusion is an assertion based on the **data** or verifiable evidence. The **warrant** is the major assumption you expect to share with your audience. This shared assumption connects the data and claim. In other words, in the example below, the audience must believe that anyone who can win a marathon is healthy before accepting the claim that Clara is healthy because (data) she won the marathon.

You might need to explore the soundness of your argument further to test your

Figure 1 *The Toulmin model*

Data (Because) ⟶ **Claim** (Therefore)
Clara won the marathon.   Clara is healthy.

Warrant (Since)
Anyone who can win a marathon is healthy.

---

[1] Stephen Toulmin, *The Uses of Argument* (Cambridge: Cambridge University Press, 1958).

Figure 2 *The expanded Toulmin model*

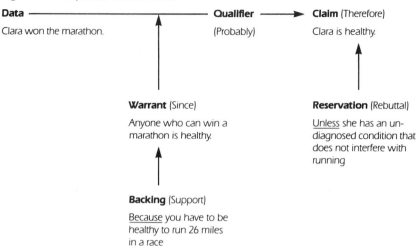

Data ——————————————— Qualifier ——▶ Claim (Therefore)

Clara won the marathon.   (Probably)   Clara is healthy.

Warrant (Since)   **Reservation** (Rebuttal)

Anyone who can win a   <u>Unless</u> she has an un-
marathon is healthy.   diagnosed condition that
does not interfere with
running

Backing (Support)

<u>Because</u> you have to be
healthy to run 26 miles
in a race

reasoning and the assumption you expect your audience to share. The Toulmin model includes three additional elements for this purpose: the backing or support, the qualifier, . and the reservation or rebuttal. In Figure 2, you can see how they work. A **qualifier,** commonly represented by words such as *probably, usually,* and *in most cases,* limits the claim in some way, thereby changing the formality of the claim from absolute to probable. The **reservation** states the circumstances for the qualification of the claim. Under the conditions of the reservation the claim would not be valid. A reservation is characterized by the word *unless.* The **backing,** characterized by the word *because,* provides the support that strengthens the reasoning of the data and the warrant.

Together the six elements of the Toulmin model help you to make logical connections between ideas, to determine what level of confidence you can use in stating your argument, and to identify the assumptions you share with your audience. In some cases you will not need to use all six elements, nor will you need to state the ones you do use in determining the connections. If the argument diagrammed above were presented to a general public audience of people who had never run a marathon, the warrant would not have to be stated. But suppose the argument were presented to experienced marathon runners. Would they unconditionally accept the assumption underlying the warrant? Perhaps their years of running have actually jeopardized their health. The reservations of your audience would lead you to explore your own reservations further. Of course, if your claim has too many reservations, then your argument won't be strong enough to present. But the reservations of your audience might also lead you to a revision of your warrant. Perhaps a different *kind* of warrant would make your claim acceptable to the audience.

The type of warrant an audience is willing to unconditionally accept represents *why* the members of the audience believe what they do. Most warrants fall into one of three categories: *authoritative, substantive,* or *motivational.*

For you and your audience to share the assumption of an **authoritative war-rant,** you must both respect the same authorities used to support your claim. Historical figures, currently well-known personalities in their fields, people of high stature with recognizable titles, institutions, and legal documents convey a commonly accepted level of expertise. Researchers, unknown authors of books, unfamiliar experts in various fields, and your own experience, among other sources, will need to have their credibility established firmly before you can assume that the audience will accept their authority as support for your claim.

For you and your audience to share the assumption of a **substantive warrant,** you must both have a high level of confidence in the reliability of the evidence presented. Are there sufficient and representative examples? Are comparisons superficial or thorough? Have dissimilarities been overlooked? Do causes account entirely for the effects? Is the documentation accurate and convincing?

And for you and your audience to share the assumption of a **motivational warrant,** both of you must recognize the needs and values associated with your claim as important. Equal opportunity, a sense of fair play, self-esteem, safety, recognition, and freedom of choice—these along with many other needs and values can establish the relevancy between your claim and the goals and standards of the audience (see also the discussion on using appeals in Chapter 8).

Overall, the Toulmin model gives you the structure for testing the informal logic or reasoning of your claim and the flexibility to shape your argument for a particular audience and a particular context. And by relying on the knowledge and beliefs of your audience as part of your argument, you interact more closely with the audience, allowing them to provide, in effect, much of the necessary persuasion.

In the article, "Courting Clients: What Limits on Ads for Lawyers?" from the *Christian Science Monitor* of February 25, 1988, Curtis J. Sitomer presents the conflict among lawyers on advertising their services. His use of informal logic to explain the arguments on both sides of the issue provides the reasoning his audience needs to make an informed decision. As you read the article, use the Toulmin model to diagram each argument.

Courting Clients: What Limits on Ads for Lawyers?

CURTIS J. SITOMER

Warren Burger, former chief justice of the United States, has likened it 1 to selling cereal or dog food.

Some critics call its practitioners "ambulance chasers" and insist 2 that, at the very least, they are undignified.

But the courts have sanctioned the advertising of legal services as 3 a proper exercise of free expression—at least to a degree.

And that's the rub: degree. How far may American lawyers go in 4
hawking their wares?

Display ads in newspapers, magazines, and professional jour- 5
nals, offering expertise in a range of specialties from product liability
to environmental regulations, have so far passed muster. And radio and
television commercials promoting the services of Black, Black, White &
Brown—if in good taste—generally win bar association approval.

But what about letters from Lawyer Grey to a prospective local 6
client telling him that he can get big bucks for a whiplash claim?

This is going too far, some state lawyers' groups insist. Individual 7
legal practitioners, however, defend the practice as professional promotion and a legitimate way to let would-be clients know just what
individual lawyers have to offer.

The issue of direct mail solicitation by lawyers goes before the 8
U.S. Supreme Court on March 1. The justices are faced with deciding
whether Kentucky has the right to ban this type of advertising. And
their ruling may well affect the way the lawyering business is carried
on in all states.

Legal advertising was considered a taboo until 1977, when the 9
Supreme Court termed it commercial speech and narrowly ruled that
lawyers have a constitutional right to publicize their services. By a 5 to
4 vote, the court rejected the notion that allowing lawyers to compete
in the marketplace would "tarnish the dignified public image of the
profession."

The high court, however, left it to the states to regulate advertis- 10
ing by lawyers that they believed might deceive the public. Commercial speech that is false or misleading enjoys no blanket constitutional
protections.

Later the Supreme Court further clarified its stand in this area, 11
stating that lawyers may not be disciplined for soliciting legal business
"through printed advertising containing truthful and nondeceptive information and advice regarding legal rights of potential clients."

An American Bar Association (ABA) poll indicates that these high 12
court edicts have prodded 25 percent of the nation's 600,000 lawyers
to hawk their wares. Most do this through newspapers and professional journal displays.

Now in the current matter before the Supreme Court (*Shapero v.* 13
Kentucky Bar Association), the justices will specifically address direct
mail solicitation—a type of advertising that is highly controversial
even among those who approve advertising.

ABA's model rules recommend that offering of services through 14
promotional letters to specific prospective clients be banned "when
a significant motive for the lawyer's doing so is the lawyer's pecu-
niary gain."

Kentucky is among six states that have adopted these standards 15 and banned legal advertising along ABA guidelines. A dozen other states allow the practice but with strict regulations.

State courts are often influenced, but not bound, by bar associa- 16 tion resolutions. Massachusetts and New York, for example, have ruled that some form of direct mail solicitation must be allowed. California and Maine, on the other hand, have upheld bans.

The Kentucky case involves a Louisville lawyer who wanted to 17 solicit by mail potential clients against whom foreclosure lawsuits had been filed. He was told that such action would violate the state's lawyer-ethics rules. And he took the matter to court.

Legal advertising is just part of an on-going debate over legal eth- 18 ics. Responding to public pressures including opinion polls that indicate that respect for lawyers' honesty and ethical standards runs extremely low, the ABA has adopted several moral conduct codes and established a commission on professionalism.

Recommendations to state bars include strengthening law school 19 ethics courses, reporting misconduct to disciplinary bodies, increasing *pro bono,* or unpaid legal work by lawyers, encouraging written fee agreements for attorneys and clients, and placing public service above the acquisition of wealth.

As a foundation for understanding the conflict, the writer presents the argument that led to the 1977 Supreme Court decision giving lawyers the right to publicize their services. Using the Toulmin model, we would express that argument as in Figure 3.

Figure 3 *Toulmin model of argument supporting lawyer advertising*

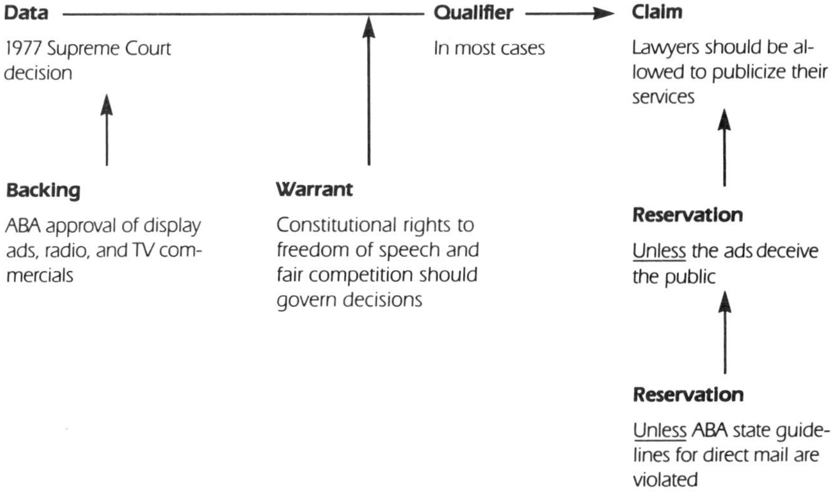

| **Data** ———————————————— **Qualifier** ————▶ **Claim** |
| 1977 Supreme Court decision   In most cases   Lawyers should be allowed to publicize their services |
| **Backing**   **Warrant** |
| ABA approval of display ads, radio, and TV commercials   Constitutional rights to freedom of speech and fair competition should govern decisions   **Reservation** — Unless the ads deceive the public |
| **Reservation** — Unless ABA state guidelines for direct mail are violated |

Figure 4 *Toulmin model of argument opposing lawyer advertising*

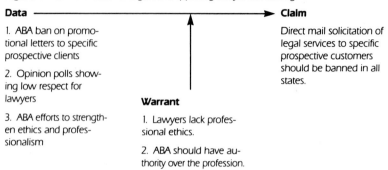

Data

1. ABA ban on promotional letters to specific prospective clients

2. Opinion polls showing low respect for lawyers

3. ABA efforts to strengthen ethics and professionalism

Claim

Direct mail solicitation of legal services to specific prospective customers should be banned in all states.

Warrant

1. Lawyers lack professional ethics.

2. ABA should have authority over the profession.

Using the law as the basis for understanding, the reader can then explore the opposing arguments of the conflict, as shown in Figure 4. The advantage of diagramming the informal logic of an argument is the discovery of the possibilities the argument holds for different audiences. The warrants in the examples clearly identify audiences with a strong respect for authority (support for the ban) and those with strong advocacy for individual rights (against the ban). Just as important is the indication that the audiences hold strong views on lawyers' ethics. When your audience contributes a strong opinion as a causal link between the data and the claim, as in Figure 5, your argument becomes more forceful and your need to provide support for the warrant less arduous.

Figure 5 *Toulmin model of argument with causal link between data and claim*

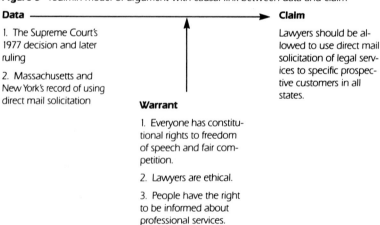

Data

1. The Supreme Court's 1977 decision and later ruling

2. Massachusetts and New York's record of using direct mail solicitation

Claim

Lawyers should be allowed to use direct mail solicitation of legal services to specific prospective customers in all states.

Warrant

1. Everyone has constitutional rights to freedom of speech and fair competition.

2. Lawyers are ethical.

3. People have the right to be informed about professional services.

KINDS OF CLAIMS

CLAIMS OF FACT: WHAT IS IT? DOES IT EXIST?

When you hear statements such as "Her dress is red," "Yucatan is a peninsula in southeast Mexico," "Pet store owners feed mice to snakes," or "Entropy is the second law of thermodynamics," you have no need to question their truth. Why? Because each of these statements can be tested by a widely accepted means of verification: the first statement by simply observing; the second by referring to an atlas; the third by asking a pet store owner; and the fourth by referring to a dictionary, textbook, or encyclopedia. When you and your audience agree on the means of verifying a claim, then that claim can be accepted as fact; it is not arguable. But, if your intended audience does *not* accept the means of verification you choose, or if they define the key terms of the claim differently, then your **claim of fact** *is* arguable.

Let's examine the arguability of the following claims of fact by asking two questions: (1) Would a general audience be likely to agree on a definition of terms? and (2) Would a general audience agree on a means of verification?

Soccer is growing in popularity in America.

The meaning of the term *soccer* should be easy to agree on. The rules of the game can be used to define it. The term *popularity,* however, can be defined from several points of view using different means of verification, such as number of teams, attendance at games, or news coverage. Once *popularity* is defined, the means of measuring its growth would also need to be agreed upon. These two levels of disagreement or uncertainty make the claim arguable.

Each year the number of street people increases.

Defining the commonly accepted terms of this claim would not be difficult, but the means of verification could create a level of uncertainty. Still, whether the figures are collected through interviews, actual head counts, or surveys of shelters, an educated audience aware of the economics of the times probably already accepts the claim as true. The low degree of uncertainty makes this a less arguable claim.

Being on welfare suppresses the personal initiative of the poor.

A general audience with little or no experience with welfare would probably need the terms *welfare* and *initiative* defined before a relationship between the two could be established. In addition, the probable lack of agreement on how to verify *initiative* would make this claim highly arguable.

If you look carefully at the terms that need to be defined in the examples above, you will notice that *the more abstract the term is, the more uncertainty it produces.* Claims of fact express their terms on one of three category levels: specific/concrete, general, or universal/abstract. This is why claims of fact are often called **categorical propositions.** Here are some examples:

Specific/concrete:	*My tennis coach, Jan Stevenson,* is a fair disciplinarian.
	The *Oak Park* recreation center is undersupported financially.
General:	*Some* tennis coaches are fair disciplinarians.
	Some city recreation centers are undersupported financially.
Universal/abstract:	*All* tennis coaches are fair disciplinarians.
	City recreation centers are undersupported financially.

By noting the differences in these categorical propositions (CP's), we can draw an important conclusion about stating claims of fact: *The higher the level of uncertainty, the greater the degree of evidence and verification the audience will require.* For instance, on the specific/concrete level, the subjects in the claim are limited to *one individual* item to be defined. By reducing the uncertainty in defining the subject term, the writer can shift the focus quickly to the abstract quality being applied to the subject (*fair disciplinarian* and *undersupported financially*). On the general level, the subjects include several members of a large group. The uncertainty increases at this level because each example presented must be accepted by the audience. If one of the examples is not acceptable, the audience will not be persuaded to believe the claim. Naturally, the risks of overcoming uncertainty increase at the universal/abstract level. In order to define *all* the members in one category well enough to gain the audience's acceptance, the writer will need impressive evidence to demonstrate the characteristics all of the members share.

Claims of fact need some level of uncertainty to be considered arguable. The category level you choose for expressing the terms in your claim will depend on what you intend your argument to do and on what your audience already knows and what they need to know.

As you read the essay "Everyday Drugs" by Adam Smith (from his 1975 book, *Powers of Mind*), written for a general public audience, notice the categorical levels used and the degree of evidence needed to verify the claim for audience agreement.

Everyday Drugs

ADAM SMITH

Americans take xanthines at the rate of 100 *billion* doses per year. 1
Xanthines are alkaloids which stimulate portions of the cerebral cortex. They give you "a more rapid and clearer flow of thought, allay drowsiness . . . motor activity is increased. There is a keener appreciation of sensory stimuli, and reaction time to them is diminished." This description, again from the pharmacology textbook, is similar to de-

scriptions of cocaine and amphetamine. Of course, the xanthine addict pays a price. He is, says Sir Clifford Allbutt, Regius Professor of Medicine at Cambridge, "subject to fits of agitation and depression; he loses color and has a haggard appearance. The appetite falls off; the heart suffers; it palpitates, or it intermits. As with other such agents, a renewed dose of the poison gives temporary relief, but at the cost of the misery."

Xanthines are generally taken orally through "aqeous extracts" of 2 the plants that produce these alkaloids, either in seeds or leaves. In the United States the three most common methylated xanthines taken are called caffeine, theophylline and theobromine. The seeds of *Coffea arabica* contain caffeine, the leaves of *Thea sinensis* contain caffeine and theophylline, and the seeds of *Theobroma cacao* contain caffeine and theobromine. In America the three are known as "coffee," "tea" and "cocoa," and they are consumed daily, at the rate of billions of pounds a year. They are generally drunk as hot drinks, but Americans also drink cold drinks containing caffeine from the nuts of the tree *Cola acuminata*. The original drinks ended in the word "cola," but now there are many "colas" which do not bear that name in the title. The early ads for Coca-Cola said it gave you a lift.

Coffee, tea, cocoa and cola drinks are all drugs. Caffeine is a cen- 3 tral nervous system stimulant, theophylline less so, and theobromine hardly at all. All xanthines increase the production of urine. Xanthines act on smooth muscles—relaxing, for example, especially in the case of theophylline, bronchi that may have been constricted. Like the salicylates—aspirin—xanthines can cause stomach irritation. Caffeine can cause sleeplessness, and researchers have found that it causes chromosome breaks.

Maxwell House, meet the Regius Professor of Medicine. Is the 4 stuff good to the last drop, or another dose of the poison? Is it a food, to be sold in supermarkets, or a stimulant to the central nervous system like the amphetamines? "The popularity of the xanthine beverages depends on their stimulant action, although most people are unaware of any stimulation," says the giant pharmacology text.

It is surprising to find substances we think of so cheerfully, 5 perkin' in the pot, listed as drugs. That's the point. In our society, there are some drugs we think of as okay drugs, and other drugs make us gasp. A coffee drinker who drinks coffee all day and cannot function without it is just a heavy coffee drinker, but someone using a non-okay drug is a "drug user" or an "addict."

Smith chooses to present his evidence first and lead inductively to his claim or CP: "In our society, there are some drugs we think of as okay drugs, and other drugs make us gasp." The terms in the claim are on a general categorical level: "*some* drugs"/"*okay* drugs"; "*other* drugs"/"gasp." As part of the intended audience, you understand these terms, but they are hardly specific enough to convince you to accept the claim as fact. Does Smith present enough evidence to define the terms and verify his claim for you?

Smith begins his definition of drugs by using their scientific names and quotes from a pharmacology textbook to verify the drugs' effects on the body. The professional text is a credible source for explaining the effects scientifically, but what the drugs are is still uncertain at this point. When Smith compares the effects of the drugs to cocaine and amphetamines, the nature of the drugs becomes more familiar. Next he introduces expert testimony from a professor of medicine who describes the characteristics of a xanthine addict. This source is also credible, and the specific description in the quote helps to further define the drugs and their effects. Finally, Smith identifies the drugs by their commonly known names and sources. Now the audience is able to fully under-stand the terms of Smith's claim.

Smith's claim is not one that any of us wants to accept, but the evidence is con-vincing and the warrants Smith relies on reflect accurately the shared beliefs of the writer and audience.

You can check Smith's reasoning by diagramming his argument using the Toulmin model, as in Figure 6. If you question the evidence Smith presents or if you do not share the assumptions Smith relies on in the warrants, you are not likely to accept his claim.

Strategies for Definition.   Composing an effective argument depends a great deal on your ability to define terms and concepts. Although your readers' famil-iarity with the subject may contribute to the overall understanding of your argument, you cannot take for granted that you define key terms in exactly the same way. By as-suming that the readers are interested in how *you* define terms, you will be more care-

Figure 6 *Toulmin model of argument using claims of fact*

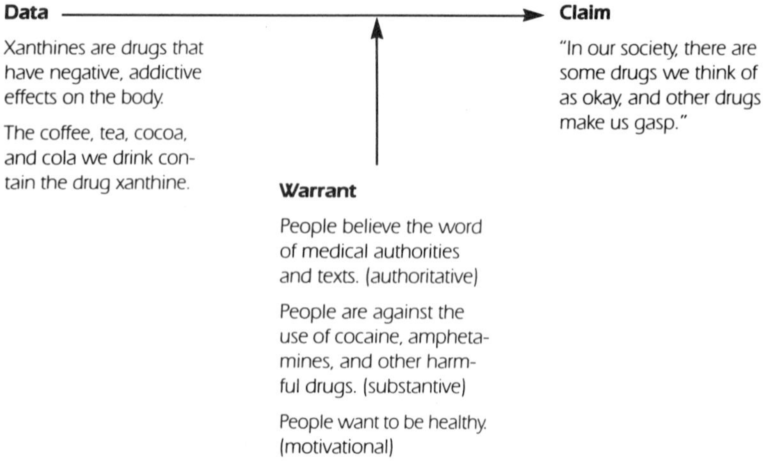

Data ————————————————————→ **Claim**

Xanthines are drugs that have negative, addictive effects on the body.

The coffee, tea, cocoa, and cola we drink con-tain the drug xanthine.

"In our society, there are some drugs we think of as okay, and other drugs make us gasp."

Warrant

People believe the word of medical authorities and texts. (authoritative)

People are against the use of cocaine, ampheta-mines, and other harm-ful drugs. (substantive)

People want to be healthy. (motivational)

ful to provide clear, precise definitions that specify the significance associated with the claim of your argument.

While many definitions can be explained in a sentence or a paragraph, definitions for words or concepts that are complex because of their abstract, emotional, or evaluative dimensions often need to be presented in greater detail. What is discrimination? Obscenity? Confidentiality? Censorship? Because terms such as these convey a range of meanings to different audiences, you would need to use an **extended definition** to explain the term as *you* see it in relation to the significance of your argument.

An extended definition can be presented in several paragraphs or it might constitute the main topic of your argument. Extended definitions usually begin with a *formal* or *essential definition* in three steps: (1) state the term to be defined, (2) name the class to which it belongs, (3) show its differences from other members of its class. A simple example would be

Term: A shareholder

Class: is a person

Differences: who owns a share or shares of stock.

After the formal definition, an extended definition would develop the implications of the word in detail. Each of the following means of defining will help you explore your term more thoroughly before choosing the most effective sequence for shaping the definition for your argument.

A **synonym** is one of the most common, unobtrusive ways to define a word, but make sure the synonym you choose is familiar to your readers. The easiest way to include a synonym is in an appositive: His was the scowl of a misanthrope, *a hater of mankind*.

Using the historical roots of a word, its **etymology,** to clarify meaning can often reveal a level of intensity or progression of development that gives the word a new dimension. Consider the word *plagiarism*, which in its original Latin form meant *plunderer* and *hunting net*. Both terms emphasize the intentionality of the plagiarist.

Stipulation can be helpful when a term has a number of commonly accepted meanings. You stipulate the particular meaning that you are using in your argument. The word *endowment*, for example, can be the *act* of enriching something; the thing received; or a natural capacity, power, or ability. The difference between something that is given and something that is natural or already present can lead to a significant difference in interpretation.

An **example** applies a definition to a specific situation, producing an image that lessens the distance between words and what they stand for. But one example may be too limiting or confusing for the reader. If in defining *expatriates,* for instance, you cited only the most celebrated Americans who lived in Paris following World War I, your American readers would not realize that some writers and artists—for instance, the English poet W. H. Auden—were expatriates in America. Always provide enough examples to represent the full dimension of the definition.

Explaining what a word is *not,* the technique of **negation,** gives you the opportunity to eliminate qualities that could interfere with the definition you are trying to develop. A negative definition helps to isolate the meaning you want. For example, "A diploma is not an education, but the process a person goes through to receive a diploma is" uses negation to isolate the importance of process in education.

Using a figure of speech, primarily metaphor, to produce a creative comparison between the word being defined and a normally unrelated thing or quality can make a memorable impression on your readers. **Figurative comparison** has the power to convey emotion and attitude as well as meaning. The writer Stephen Crane left such lasting impressions when he defined war as "the red animal—war, the blood-swollen god" and a wound as "a red badge of courage."

What is it for? What does it do? The answers to these questions of **function** can clarify the meaning and explain the significance of some terms. A definition of a familiar term such as *loyalty* can be significantly broadened by demonstrating its function in relation to people, ideals, and country.

Using **comparison and contrast,** or demonstrating the similarities and differences between two closely related terms, people, theories, or governments can emphasize important shades of meaning. Consider the terms *libel* and *slander.* Both are acts that damage another's reputation, but *libel* is a written, usually published, statement and *slander* is an oral utterance.

A variation of this method is the **analogy,** a point-by-point comparison in which *possible* similarities are inferred on the basis of *established* similarities. Analogies can provide persuasive illustrations, especially in comparing past events with the present to predict the future. The Prohibition laws of the 1920s are often used as an analogy to new legislation under consideration to dramatize the possible effects of passing such a law. As persuasive as some analogies appear on the surface, however, fundamental differences are often suppressed, limiting the usefulness of the analogy. In the Prohibition example, for instance, the differences in demographics and economics that have developed between the 1920s and the 1990s would indicate that the effects of a prohibitive law could be considerably different today. Before using an analogy in your extended definition, be sure to think through both the similarities *and* differences.

You will notice that this list of defining methods excludes a common method— the dictionary definition. The dictionary is a good place to review the commonly accepted definitions of a word. However, unless you have an *uncommon* point to make by quoting from the dictionary, there is no need to include wording your readers have direct access to. Instead, use the dictionary as a source for synonyms, etymologies, and historical insights into how the word has changed in meaning.

There is no formula for writing an extended definition, but the principle of beginning with what your audience already knows will guide you in choosing your methods of defining. Your definition will build—extend—from your audience's frame of reference to the underlying meaning that is essential to understanding your argument. Your definition needs to build in meaning and force if it is to both clarify *and* persuade.

In the following excerpt, "Gumption: The Psychic Gasoline," from Robert M. Pirsig's 1974 book, *Zen and the Art of Motorcycle Maintenance,* the author accepts the difficult challenge of defining an attitude. His extended definition is personal and quite informal, and he interacts well with the audience through his use of common examples and in his use of the word *you*. But, more importantly, he uses a variety of defining methods, each providing the reader with a deeper insight into the significance of the word *gumption*. While reading the selection, keep a list of the defining methods Pirsig uses.

Gumption:
The Psychic Gasoline

ROBERT M. PIRSIG

I like the word "gumption" because it's so homely and so forlorn and 1 so out of style it looks as if it needs a friend and isn't likely to reject anyone who comes along. It's an old Scottish word, once used a lot by pioneers, but which, like "kin," seems to have all but dropped out of use. I like it also because it describes exactly what happens to someone who connects with Quality. He gets filled with gumption.

The Greeks called it *enthousiasmos,* the root of "enthusiasm," 2 which means literally "filled with *theos,*" or God, or Quality. See how that fits?

A person filled with gumption doesn't sit around dissipating and 3 stewing about things. He's at the front of the train of his own awareness, watching to see what's up the track and meeting it when it comes. That's gumption. . . .

The gumption-filling process occurs when one is quiet long 4 enough to see and hear and feel the real universe, not just one's own stale opinions about it. But it's nothing exotic. That's why I like the word.

You see it often in people who return from long, quiet fishing 5 trips. Often they're a little defensive about having put so much time to "no account" because there's no intellectual justification for what they've been doing. But the returned fisherman usually has a peculiar abundance of gumption, usually for the very same things he was sick to death of a few weeks before. He hasn't been wasting time. It's only our limited cultural viewpoint that makes it seem so.

If you're going to repair a motorcycle, an adequate supply of 6 gumption is the first and most important tool. If you haven't got that you might as well gather up all the other tools and put them away, because they won't do you any good.

Gumption is the psychic gasoline that keeps the whole thing 7
going. If you haven't got it there's no way the motorcycle can possibly be
fixed. But if you *have* got it and know how to keep it there's absolutely
no way in this whole world that motorcycle can *keep* from getting fixed.
It's bound to happen. Therefore the thing that must be monitored at
all times and preserved before anything else is the gumption.

This paramount importance of gumption solves a problem of for- 8
mat of this Chautauqua. The problem has been how to get off the gen-
eralities. If the Chautauqua gets into the actual details of fixing one individual machine the chances are overwhelming that it won't be your
make and model and the information will be not only useless but dangerous, since information that fixes one model can sometimes wreck
another. For detailed information of an objective sort, a separate shop
manual for the specific make and model of machine must be used. In
addition, a general shop manual such as *Audel's Automotive Guide*
fills in the gaps.

But there's another kind of detail that no shop manual goes into 9
but that is common to all machines and can be given here. This is the
detail of the Quality relationship, the gumption relationship, between
the machine and the mechanic, which is just as intricate as the machine itself. Throughout the process of fixing the machine things always come up, low-quality things, from a dusted knuckle to an accidentally ruined "irreplaceable" assembly. These drain off gumption,
destroy enthusiasm and leave you so discouraged you want to forget
the whole business. I call these things "gumption traps."

There are hundreds of different kinds of gumption traps, maybe 10
thousands, maybe millions. I have no way of knowing how many I
don't know. I know it *seems* as though I've stumbled into every kind of
gumption trap imaginable. What keeps me from thinking I've hit them
all is that with every job I discover more. Motorcycle maintenance gets
frustrating. Angering. Infuriating. That's what makes it interesting. . . .

What I have in mind now is a catalog of "Gumption Traps I Have 11
Known." I want to start a whole new academic field, gumptionology, in
which these traps are sorted, classified, structured into hierarchies
and interrelated for the edification of future generations and the benefit of all mankind.

Gumptionology 101—An examination of affective, cognitive and 12
psychomotor blocks in the perception of Quality relationships—3 cr,
VII, MWF. I'd like to see that in a college catalog somewhere.

In traditional maintenance gumption is considered something 13
you're born with or have acquired as a result of good upbringing. It's a
fixed commodity. From the lack of information about how one acquires this gumption one might assume that a person without any
gumption is a hopeless case.

In nondualistic maintenance gumption isn't a fixed commodity. 14 It's variable, a reservoir of good spirits that can be added to or subtracted from. Since it's a result of the perception of Quality, a gumption trap, consequently, can be defined as anything that causes one to lose sight of Quality, and thus lose one's enthusiasm for what one is doing. As one might guess from a definition as broad as this, the field is enormous and only a beginning sketch can be attempted here.

As far as I can see there are two main types of gumption traps. 15 The first type is those in which you're thrown off the Quality track by conditions that arise from external circumstances, and I call these "setbacks." The second type is traps in which you're thrown off the Quality track by conditions that are primarily within yourself. These I don't have any generic name for—"hang-ups," I suppose. . . .

In the first paragraph Pirsig uses three definition strategies to introduce the term *gumption*:

figurative description:	"it's so homely and so forlorn and so out of style it looks as if it needs a friend"
historical context:	"an old Scottish word, once used by a lot of pioneers . . . all but dropped out of use"
function:	"what happens to someone who connects with Quality"

The four paragraphs that follow contain five additional strategies:

etymology:	"*enthousiasmos,* the root of 'enthusiasm'"
negation:	"A person filled with gumption doesn't sit around dissipating and stewing about things."
metaphor:	"He's at the front of the train of his own awareness, watching to see what's up the track"
process:	"The gumption-filling process occurs when one is quiet long enough to see and hear and feel the real universe"
analogy:	"You see it often in people who return from long, quiet fishing trips."

By this point Pirsig has used enough definition strategies to make most readers comfortable with this seldom used term. Now as he applies the term to the art of motorcycle maintenance, he explains the relationship of *gumption* to *Quality.* Notice how, beginning in paragraph 9, he presents the two terms *gumption* and *Quality* as synonomous. From that point on, Pirsig concentrates on the interrelationship between the two that is necessary for a person to feel a sense of achievement. While this excerpt cannot give a complete picture of Pirsig's purpose, it does illustrate how definition can develop a claim of fact.

EXERCISES: CLAIMS OF FACT

1. For each of the following claims of fact, evaluate its level of arguability (fact, arguable, or very arguable) on the basis of the definition of terms and the certainty of the means of verification. Write a brief rationale for your decision. Assume that the claim is directed toward a general public audience.

    a. Vertebrae are distinct elements that never unite.
    b. Pets provide emotional security.
    c. Private colleges have fewer students than public colleges.
    d. John F. Kennedy was the most dynamic president of this century.
    e. Good samaritans are an endangered species.

2. For each subject listed below, write an arguable claim of fact and designate an audience that would benefit by accepting the claim.

      music   traffic   discipline
      vitamins   vacations   hunger

3. After reading "Culture Gives Us a Sense of Who We Are" by Robert C. Solomon (*Los Angeles Times*, January 25, 1981), written for a general public audience, write out the CP, list the type of evidence he presents, and comment on how the evidence persuades you to accept or reject Solomon's proposition.

Culture Gives Us a Sense of Who We Are

ROBERT C. SOLOMON

In our aggressively egalitarian society, "culture" has always been a sus- 1 pect word, suggesting the pretentions of an effete and foolish leisure class, like the grand dames spoofed in Marx Brothers' films. But the pretentions of a self-appointed cultural elite notwithstanding, "culture" actually refers to nothing more objectionable than a system of shared symbols and examples that hold a society together. Within a culture we are kindred spirits, simply because we understand one another.

    A recent and somewhat frightening Rockefeller Foundation study 2 on the state of the humanities in American life reported that the vast majority of even our most educated citizens are ignorant of the common literature and history that reinforce not only cultural identity but also moral choices. Doctors, lawyers and business executives are in positions of great responsibility, but often have little or no training in the ethical background that makes their critical choices meaningful.

Across our society in general, we find ourselves increasingly fragmented, split into factions and "generation gaps"—which now occur at two- or three-year intervals—just because the once-automatic assumption of a shared culture, something beyond shared highways, television programming and economic worries, is no longer valid. 3

In our schools, according to the Rockefeller report, the problem lies largely in what has recently been hailed as the "back to basics" movement, which includes no cultural content whatsoever, just skills and techniques. Reading is taught as a means of survival in the modern world, not as a source of pleasure and of shared experience. The notion of "great books" is viewed by most educators as an archaic concept, relegated to the museum of old teaching devices, such as the memorization in Greek of passages from Homer. 4

But are "great books" (and legends, poems, paintings and plays) indeed the only conduit of culture, or have they been replaced by more accessible and effortless media of transmission—television, for example, and films? 5

Films, to be sure, have entered into our cultural identity in an extremely powerful way; indeed, it is not clear that a person who knows nothing of Bogart or Chaplin, who has never seen (young) Brando or watched a Western could claim to be fully part of American culture. But these are classics, and they have some of the same virtue as great books; their symbols, characters and moral examples have been around long enough to span generations and segments of our population, and to provide a shared vocabulary, shared heroes and shared values. No such virtue is to be found in television series that disappear every two years (or less), films that survive but a season or "made-for-TV" movies with a lifetime of two hours minus commercial breaks. 6

Television culture is no culture at all, and it is no surprise that, when kids change heroes with the season, their parents don't (and couldn't possibly) keep up with them. The symbolism of *Moby Dick* and *The Scarlet Letter*, however much we resented being force-fed them in school, is something we can all be expected to share. The inanities of *The Dukes of Hazzard*, viewed by no matter how many millions of people, will not replace them. 7

The same is true of our musical heritage. The Beatles are only a name to most 12-year-olds. Beethoven, by contrast, continues to provide the musical themes we can assume (even if wrongly) that all of us have heard, time and time again. This isn't snobbery; it's continuity. 8

A professor recently wrote in the *Wall Street Journal* that he had 9
mentioned Socrates in class (at a rather prestigious liberal arts college)
and had drawn blanks from more than half the students. My colleagues and I at the University of Texas swap stories about references
that our students don't catch. Even allowing generous leeway for our
own professional prejudices and misperceptions of what is important,
the general picture is disturbing. We are becoming a culture without a
culture, lacking fixed points of reference and a shared vocabulary.

It would be so easy, so inexpensive, to change all that; a reading 10
list for high school students; a little encouragement in the media; a bit
more enlightenment in our college curricula.

With all of this in mind, I decided to see just what I could or 11
could not assume among my students, who are generally bright and
better educated than average (given that they are taking philosophy
courses, hardly an assumed interest among undergraduates these
days). I gave them a name quiz, in effect, of some of the figures that, on
most people's list, would rank among the most important and often
referred to in Western culture. Following are some of the results, in
terms of the percentage of students who recognized them:

Socrates, 87%; Louis XIV, 59%; Moses, 90%; Hawthorne, 42%; John 12
Milton, 35%; Trotsky, 47%; Donatello, 8%; Copernicus, 47%; Puccini,
11%; Charlemagne, 40%; Virginia Woolf, 25%; Estes Kefauver, 8%;
Debussy, 14%; Giotto, 4%; Archduke Ferdinand, 21%; Lewis Carroll,
81%; Charles Dodgson, 5%; Thomas Aquinas, 68%; Spinoza, 19%;
Moliere, 30%; Tchaikovsky, 81%; Darwin, 56%; Karl Marx, 65%; Faulkner,
43%; George Byron, 18%; Goethe, 42%; Raphael, 17%; Euripides, 8%;
Homer, 39%; T. S. Eliot, 25%; Rodin, 24%; Mozart, 94%; Hitler, 97%;
Wagner, 34%; Dante, 25%; Louis XVI, 25%; Kafka, 38%; Stravinsky, 57%;
John Adams, 36%.

A friend who gave the same quiz to his English composition class 13
got results more than 50% lower on average.

I suppose that many people will think the quiz too hard, the 14
names often too obscure—but that, of course, is just the point. The
students, interestingly enough, did not feel this at all—not one of
them. They "sort of recognized" most of the names and felt somewhat
embarrassed at not knowing exactly who these people were. There
was no sense that the quiz was a "trivia" contest (as in, "What's the
name of Dale Evans' horse?") and there were no accusations of elitism
or ethnocentrism. The simple fact was that they knew these names
were part of their culture, and in too many cases they knew that they
weren't—but should be—conversant with them. Maybe that, in itself,
is encouraging.

4. Keeping in mind Solomon's view of what constitutes culture, respond to him in an essay presenting your generation's view of the meaning of culture. Before you begin writing your essay, diagram your argument using the Toulmin model to check your reasoning.

5. J. B. Priestley in "Wrong Ism" (from *Essays of Five Decades*, 1968) uses several definition strategies to inform and persuade his intended audience to accept the claim of his argument. List the defining methods used and the sequence in which they occur; identify the term being defined in each method. At the end of each sequence, write a paragraph analyzing the effectiveness of the definition sequence in relation to the writer's claim.

Wrong Ism

J. B. PRIESTLEY

There are three isms that we ought to consider very carefully— 1
regionalism, nationalism, internationalism. Of these three the one there is most fuss about, the one that starts men shouting and marching and shooting, the one that seems to have all the depth and thrust and fire, is of course nationalism. Nine people out of ten, I fancy, would say that of this trio it is the one that really counts, the big boss. Regionalism and internationalism, they would add, are comparatively small, shadowy, rather cranky. And I believe all this to be quite wrong. Like many another big boss, nationalism is largely bogus. It is like a bunch of flowers made of plastics.

The real flowers belong to regionalism. The mass of people every- 2
where may never have used the term. They are probably regionalists without knowing it. Because they have been brought up in a certain part of the world, they have formed perhaps quite unconsciously a deep attachment to its landscape and speech, its traditional customs, its food and drink, its songs and jokes. (There are of course always the rebels, often intellectuals and writers, but they are not the mass of people.) They are rooted in their region. Indeed, without this attachment a man can have no roots.

So much of people's lives, from earliest childhood onwards, is 3
deeply intertwined with the common life of the region, they cannot help feeling strongly about it. A threat to it is a knife pointing at the heart. How can life ever be the same if bullying strangers come to

change everything? The form and colour, the very taste and smell of dear familiar things will be different, alien, life-destroying. It would be better to die fighting. And it is precisely this, the nourishing life of the region, for which common men have so often fought and died.

This attachment to the region exists on a level far deeper than 4 that of any political hocus-pocus. When a man says "my country" with real feeling, he is thinking about his region, all that has made up his life, and not about that political entity, the nation. There can be some confusion here simply because some countries are so small—and ours is one of them—and so old, again like ours, that much of what is national is also regional. Down the centuries, the nation, itself so comparatively small, has been able to attach to itself the feeling really created by the region. (Even so there is something left over, as most people in Yorkshire or Devon, for example, would tell you.) This probably explains the fervent patriotism developed early in small countries. The English were announcing that they were English in the Middle Ages, before nationalism had arrived elsewhere.

If we deduct from nationalism all that it has borrowed or stolen 5 from regionalism, what remains is mostly rubbish. The nation, as distinct from the region, is largely the creation of power-men and political manipulators. Almost all nationalist movements are led by ambitious frustrated men determined to hold office. I am not blaming them. I would do the same if I were in their place and wanted power so badly. But nearly always they make use of the rich warm regional feeling, the emotional dynamo of the movement, while being almost untouched by it themselves. This is because they are not as a rule deeply loyal to any region themselves. Ambition and a love of power can eat like acid into the tissues of regional loyalty. It is hard, if not impossible, to retain a natural piety and yet be forever playing both ends against the middle.

Being itself a power structure, devised by men of power, the na- 6 tion tends to think and act in terms of power. What would benefit the real life of the region, where men, women and children actually live, is soon sacrificed for the power and prestige of the nation. (And the personal vanity of presidents and ministers themselves, which historians too often disregard.) Among the new nations of our time innumerable peasants and labourers must have found themselves being cut down from five square meals a week to three in order to provide unnecessary airlines, military forces that can only be used against them and nobody else, great conference halls and official yachts and the rest. The last traces of imperialism and colonialism may have to be removed from Asia and Africa, where men can no longer endure being condemned to a permanent inferiority by the colour of their skins; but even so, the modern world, the real world of our time, does not want and would be far better without more and more nations, busy creating for themselves the very paraphernalia that western Europe is now trying to abolish. You are compelled to answer more questions when trying to spend half a day in Cambodia than you are now travelling from the Hook of Holland to Syracuse.

This brings me to internationalism. I dislike this term, which I 7 used only to complete the isms. It suggests financiers and dubious promoters living nowhere but in luxury hotels; a shallow world of entrepreneurs and impresarios. (Was it Sacha Guitry who said that impresarios were men who spoke many languages but all with a foreign accent?) The internationalism I have in mind here is best described as world civilisation. It is life considered on a global scale. Most of our communications and transport already exist on this high wide level. So do many other things from medicine to meteorology. Our astronomers and physicists (except where they have allowed themselves to be hush-hushed) work here. The UN special agencies, about which we hear far too little, have contributed more and more to this world civilisation. All the arts, when they are arts and not chunks of nationalist propaganda, naturally take their place in it. And it grows, widens, deepens, in spite of the fact that for every dollar, ruble, pound or franc spent in explaining and praising it, a thousand are spent by the nations explaining and praising themselves.

This world civilisation and regionalism can get along together, 8 especially if we keep ourselves sharply aware of their quite different but equally important values and rewards. A man can make his contribution to world civilisation and yet remain strongly regional in feeling. I know several men of this sort. There is of course the danger—it is with us now—of the global style flattening out the regional, taking local form, colour, flavour, away for ever, disinheriting future generations, threatening them with sensuous poverty and a huge boredom. But to understand and appreciate regionalism is to be on guard against this danger. And we must therefore make a clear distinction between regionalism and nationalism.

It is nationalism that tries to check the growth of world civilisa- 9 tion. And nationalism, when taken on a global scale, is more aggressive and demanding now than it has ever been before. This in the giant powers is largely disguised by the endless fuss in public about rival ideologies, now a largely unreal quarrel. What is intensely real is the glaring nationalism. Even the desire to police the world is nationalistic in origin. (Only the world can police the world.) Moreover, the nation-states of today are for the most part far narrower in their outlook, far more inclined to allow prejudice against the foreigner to impoverish their own style of living, than the old imperial states were. It should be part of world civilisation that men with particular skills, perhaps the product of the very regionalism they are rebelling against, should be able to move easily from country to country, to exercise those skills, in anything from teaching the violin to running a new type of factory to managing an old hotel. But nationalism, especially of the newer sort, would rather see everything done badly than allow a few non-nationals to get to work. And people face a barrage of passports, visas, immigration controls, labour permits; and in this respect are worse off than they were in 1900. But even so, in spite of all that nationalism can do— so long as it keeps its nuclear bombs to itself—the internationalism I have in mind, slowly creating a world civilisation, cannot be checked.

Nevertheless, we are still backing the wrong ism. Almost all our 10 money goes on the middle one, nationalism, the rotten meat between the two healthy slices of bread. We need regionalism to give us roots and that very depth of feeling which nationalism unjustly and greedily claims for itself. We need internationalism to save the world and to broaden and heighten our civilisation. While regional man enriches the lives that international man is already working to keep secure and healthy, national man, drunk with power, demands our loyalty, money and applause, and poisons the very air with his dangerous nonsense.

CLAIMS OF CAUSE AND EFFECT: WHY DOES IT HAPPEN? WHAT ARE THE CONSEQUENCES?

When you want to know *why* something happened, you naturally retrace the events that led to the occurrence. For instance, you flip on the wall light switch, but the lamp doesn't go on. You try again. Still nothing. You tighten the light bulb. Still nothing. You replace the light bulb. Finally, light! By retracing the sequence of events needed to make the lamp work, you discover the cause. Most people would follow the same sequence to determine the cause of this problem. But what if you wanted to know the cause of the Watergate scandal or why the number of teenage suicides has increased? Such complex problems have diverse causes—social, political, psychological—and a variety of sequences to retrace.

It is likely, then, that you might see the cause of a problem from one point of view while someone else sees it from another. Let's say that Karen was put on academic probation. You think Karen has poor grades because she doesn't study. Karen says the work is too hard. Her parents say it's because her teachers don't care. Her advisor thinks Karen is not psychologically ready for college; she has no goal for being there. Which view is right? All of these views contribute to understanding what happened to Karen, but none is in itself sufficient to explain her poor grades.

The multiple causes that contribute to an occurrence and the multiple effects that can result make understanding the relationship between cause and effect complex. So, before you can claim a direct cause-effect relationship with confidence, you need to systematically examine the possibilities that might exist.

Claims of cause may focus on the retracing of events to establish clearly why something happened, but they may also focus on the *effect*. The cause is the *before*, the effect is the *after*. To establish cause you look *backward* to *explain* and to establish effect you look *forward* to *predict*. As you can see, causes and effects form a unified view in the eye of the arguer. A caused B to happen; if A happens again, B may happen again or may continue. In this way an effect presupposes the existence of a cause and vice versa. The cause-and-effect relationship appears deceptively simple, but because most occasions include multiple causes, multiple effects, or both, the arguer's task of reaching consensus with the audience becomes increasingly difficult.

To determine whether or not your cause-effect claim is arguable, you need to analyze all the causes that might contribute to the problem and all the possible effects that might occur. Causes and effects fall into two basic categories, immediate and ultimate. *Immediate causes and effects* are those encountered first. Although these may be the most obvious, they may also be the most superficial. Immediate causes and effects provide the starting point from which you can go backward to retrace the sequence of causes or project forward to predict a sequence of effects. Retracing and projecting will lead you to the *ultimate causes and effects,* the basic, underlying factors that help to explain the more apparent ones. Looking at both the immediate and ultimate factors of your claim helps you to understand the complexity of the situation and to better identify the arguable issues.

Retracing Causes.   To establish cause you look *backward* to *explain*. In retracing the sequence of events, begin with the immediate causes, those that are most apparent.

ISSUE: *Why did Japan bomb Pearl Harbor?*

Immediate causes: Retaliation for the U.S. embargo on the sale of oil Japan needed to sustain her military forces

Consolidation of all American warships in one harbor

The immediate causes are absolutely necessary to the occurrence of the effect (the bombing). Without the motivation and opportunity present, the Japanese would not have planned the event. But what ultimate causes or underlying factors led the Japanese to the point of acting on the immediate causes?

ISSUE: *Why were the Japanese willing to wage war against the United States?*

Ultimate causes: Influenced by their previous relationships with the United States and Britain, they were willing to fight for a higher standard of living.

They had fought a world power (Russia) and won (in Korea).

As an island nation with a growing population, they needed more land and natural resources.

This brief and incomplete retracing of ultimate causes begins to uncover an important link between economic need and the willingness to declare war. Whether or not war was the only means by which the Japanese could fulfill their economic needs leads the analysis to an arguable focus.

Projecting Effects. To establish effect you look *forward* to *predict*. In projecting a sequence of possible effects, begin with the immediate effects, those that are most apparent. Then explore the ultimate effects, those that might occur over a period of time, perhaps as a result of the immediate effects.

ISSUE: The effect of the automatic teller on people's behavior

Immediate effects:	Depersonalization
	—no contact with another human when banking
	—behavior determined by buttons
	—person using machine represented by plastic card and secret number
Ultimate effects:	Reliance on machines, not people
	Atrophy of decision-making skills
	Lack of concern for individuality
	Willingness to conform
	Loss of identity

Notice that as the ultimate effects are projected, they become more remote from the original situation, and perhaps more arguable. By sequencing the possible predictions first, you can test whether one effect logically leads to another.

Retracing causes and projecting effects give you a more unified view of the issue. The more you know about why something happened and what consequences are likely to result, the less likely you are to oversimplify the cause-effect relationship. Once you have determined your claim, you can test how arguable it is by examining it from several points of view. Consider how those involved in the issue might respond to your claim. This exploration might also help you to select the most appropriate audience for your argument—the one that would benefit most from understanding your claim. Here is how that process would work:

TENTATIVE CLAIM: Increased television viewing continues to keep SAT scores at a historic low.

High school senior:	"I rarely have time to watch TV except on the weekends when I deserve a break from my part-time job."
High school freshman:	"What do you expect? I'm not old enough to drive and my parents won't let me go out."
High school teacher:	"When I make references to TV shows and characters the students seem more interested in the material."
College freshman:	"My SAT scores weren't the best, but I was admitted

	to college, probably because of my grades and activities."
Parent:	"The teachers don't assign enough homework to keep my daughter busy at night, so she talks on the phone or watches TV."
University professor:	"Research has demonstrated that many items on tests such as these are culturally biased."
Admissions director:	"Although SAT scores have not risen, our standards for admission have. Even if SAT scores are not the only criterion for admission, students are fooling themselves if they think they are not important."
Television producer:	"Every year we add more documentaries and education programs to our program list."

Looking at the responses from the people most directly involved, you find some support for the arguability of the claim. The high school students admit to watching TV, and the parent and high school teacher confirm the students' behavior. But none of the responses specifies a direct connection between watching TV (the cause) and low SAT scores (the effect). Is there evidence to support this cause-effect relationship, or does the claim confuse *conditions* and *influences* with cause?

Generally you think of conditions as passive, the setting for the action. A condition may be so closely connected to the sequence of causes that you mistake it for a cause. For example, to say, "If he hadn't registered for the course, he never would have failed," is to confuse a condition with a cause. The student did not fail the course *because* he registered for it, but registering for the course was a *necessary condition* of failing something he made a commitment to.

In a similar way, an influence can determine the rate at which an effect takes place or the degree to which it happens. This close connection to cause can make for an incorrectly stated claim. For instance, if a bank employee allegedly embezzled funds, the proof that he spent a great deal of money on gold-plated fixtures for his bathroom *heightens the probability* of his conviction, but it is not responsible for the effect.

When stating your claim, remember that identifying something as a cause or effect does not make it so. You actually have to *prove* the relationship you claim. Several factors influence how you present your proof: the level of uncertainty in your claim (Are your terms and means of verification acceptable?); the audience's familiarity with the issue (How knowledgeable are they? What is their attitude toward the issue?); your purpose (Are you trying to change people's behavior or get them to see new possibilities?); your resources (Do you have first-hand experience? Have you consulted experts? Is your data current?).

The following essay, "Fear of Dearth" by Carll Tucker (*Saturday Review,* 1979) was written for the general, well-educated reading public. Look for the author's use of immediate and ultimate causes and effects. Is his purpose to explain and establish causes so that the effect can be repeated or stopped? Or is he more interested in getting people to think more consciously about their behavior?

Fear of Dearth

CARLL TUCKER

I hate jogging. Every dawn, as I thud around New York City's Central 1
Park reservoir, I am reminded of how much I hate it. It's so tedious.
Some claim jogging is thought conducive; others insist the scenery relieves the monotony. For me, the pace is wrong for contemplation of
either ideas or vistas. While jogging, all I can think about is jogging—or
nothing. One advantage of jogging around a reservoir is that there's no
dry shortcut home.

From the listless looks of some fellow trotters, I gather I am not 2
alone in my unenthusiasm: Bill-paying, it seems, would be about
as diverting. Nonetheless, we continue to jog; more, we continue to
choose to jog. From a practically infinite array of opportunities, we select one that we don't enjoy and can't wait to have done with. Why?

For any trend, there are as many reasons as there are partici- 3
pants. This person runs to lower his blood pressure. That person runs
to escape the telephone or a cranky spouse or a filthy household. Another person runs to avoid doing anything else, to dodge a decision
about how to lead his life or a realization that his life is leading nowhere. Each of us has his carrot and stick. In my case, the stick is my
slackening physical condition, which keeps me from beating opponents at tennis whom I overwhelmed two years ago. My carrot is
to win.

Beyond these disparate reasons, however, lies a deeper cause. It 4
is no accident that now, in the last third of the twentieth century, personal fitness and health have suddenly become a popular obsession.
True, modern man likes to feel good, but that hardly distinguishes him
from his predecessors.

With zany myopia, economists like to claim that the deeper 5
cause of everything is economic. Delightfully, there seems no marketplace explanation for jogging. True, jogging is cheap, but then not jogging is cheaper. And the scant and skimpy equipment which jogging
demands must make it a marketer's least favored form of recreation.

Some scout-masterish philosophers argue that the appeal of jog- 6
ging and other body-maintenance programs is the discipline they
afford. We live in a world in which individuals have fewer and fewer
obligations. The work week has shrunk. Weekend worship is less com-
pulsory. Technology gives us more free time. Satisfactorily filling free
time requires imagination and effort. Freedom is a wide and risky river;
it can drown the person who does not know how to swim across it.

The more obligations one takes on, the more time one occupies, the less threat freedom poses. Jogging can become an instant obligation. For a portion of his day, the jogger is not his own man; he is obedient to a regimen he has accepted.

Theologians may take the argument one step further. It is our 7 modern irreligion, our lack of confidence in any hereafter, that makes us anxious to stretch our mortal stay as long as possible. We run, as the saying goes, for our lives, hounded by the suspicion that these are the only lives we are likely to enjoy.

All of these theorists seem to me more or less right. As the growth 8 of cults and charismatic religions and the resurgence of enthusiasm for the military draft suggest, we do crave commitment. And who can doubt, watching so many middle-aged and older persons torturing themselves in the name of fitness, that we are unreconciled to death, more so perhaps than any generation in modern memory?

But I have a hunch there's a further explanation of our obsession 9 with exercise. I suspect that what motivates us even more than a fear of death is a fear of dearth. Our era is the first to anticipate the eventual depletion of all natural resources. We see wilderness shrinking; rivers losing their capacity to sustain life; the air, even the stratosphere, being loaded with potentially deadly junk. We see the irreplaceable being squandered, and in the depths of our consciousness we are fearful that we are creating an uninhabitable world. We feel more or less help-less and yet, at the same time, desirous to protect what resources we can. We recycle soda bottles and restore old buildings and protect our nearest natural resource—our physical health—in the almost super-stitious hope that such small gestures will help save an earth that we are blighting. Jogging becomes a sort of penance for our sins of glut-tony, greed, and waste. Like a hairshirt or a bed of nails, the more one hates it, the more virtuous it makes one feel.

That is why *we* jog. Why *I* jog is to win at tennis. 10

Using personal observation, Tucker begins his essay on why people jog by quickly re-viewing the immediate, obvious reasons (to lower blood pressure, avoid decisions, and escape the telephone) so he can concentrate on the ultimate causes. In this way Tucker focuses on what his audience *needs* to know rather than on what they *already* know. And, by sequencing the ultimate causes using theoretical categories (economics, phi-losophy, and theology), he appeals to his audience's intelligence, prodding them to consider their behavior in new ways.

Does Tucker persuade the audience to accept his claim? His use of *we* in the final paragraph indicates that by aligning himself with the audience he anticipates their acceptance. And further, by stating his personal reason in the final sentence, he encour-

Figure 7 *Toulmin model of argument using claims of cause*

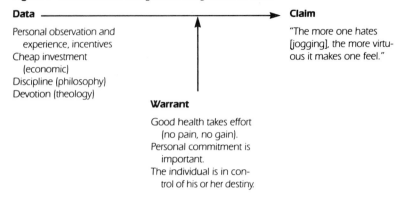

Data ————————————————————→ **Claim**

Personal observation and
 experience, incentives
Cheap investment
 (economic)
Discipline (philosophy)
Devotion (theology)

"The more one hates
[jogging], the more virtuous it makes one feel."

Warrant

Good health takes effort
 (no pain, no gain).
Personal commitment is
 important.
The individual is in con-
 trol of his or her destiny.

ages members of the audience to maintain their individual reasons while understanding and accepting the ultimate cause for their behavior.

A diagram of Tucker's reasoning, using the Toulmin model as in Figure 7, shows
that his audience—well-educated, goal-oriented professionals—are likely to accept
his claim.

Like Tucker, you can better understand what you do and what you know by analyzing the cause-effect relationships of events and decisions that involve you. The responsibility you take in formulating the claim and shaping your purpose becomes an
act of deciding how others can benefit from the same analysis.

EXERCISES: CLAIMS OF CAUSE AND EFFECT

1. For each of the following, retrace an immediate and an ultimate cause and project
an immediate and ultimate effect.
   a. teenage pregnancy
   b. the increase in the number of private high schools
   c. the election of a particular president
   d. urinalysis for drug testing
   e. decisions in football based on instant replay

2. To practice discovering the arguable points of a claim, write responses from three
different points of view for each claim below. Identify the point of view for each
response.
   a. A high percentage of teenage marriages results in divorce.
   b. Coffee consumption has declined in the United States.
   c. Businesses are hiring more liberal arts majors.
   d. Making it harder to get married would lower the divorce rate.
   e. Economic instability has reduced the average size of today's family.

3. After reading Pico Iyer's essay, "How Paradise Is Lost—and Found," written in 1986 for the readers of *Time,* list the sequence of causes, from immediate to ultimate, that he presents in support of his claim. Identify the immediate and ultimate effects he leads to. In a paragraph, explain why you accept or reject Iyer's claim.

How Paradise Is Lost—
and Found

PICO IYER

Every month, it seems, brings news of another paradise lost, and every 1
year new Edens fall like palm trees before a hurricane—first Tahiti,
then Bali, then Hawaii, Mykonos, Sri Lanka. The process is, in a sense,
irresistible: after all, paradises cannot get better any more than children can grow purer. Each passing season (and each passing tourist)
can only bring to the world's forgotten areas new developments—and
in a never-never land, any development is a change for the worse.
Elysium cannot be universally enjoyed until it has been discovered,
and once it is discovered, it is lost.

Sometimes an Eden is brought down by the quite literal invasion 2
of the real world, as even the most faraway places get placed in the
sights of the superpowers. Tibet was stormed by the Chinese, and now
the dreamed-of Shangri-La is vanished forever. Cambodia was caught
in a cross fire, and an earthly paradise so gentle that ricksha drivers
were said to tip their passengers is now a land of skulls: Afghanistan
was overrun by Soviet tanks, and now a book of photographs remembering its fugitive beauties is subtitled, mournfully, *Paradise Lost.* In an
age when airlines and satellites are rapidly turning the global village
into the smallest of small worlds, no man can be an island. These days,
not even an island can be an island.

Usually the spoiling of paradise comes more gently, and more 3
gradually, at the hands of individuals. The trouble with paradise is that
it is almost made to be lost: as fast as idyls seduce visitors, visitors reduce idyls. And as soon as a new last paradise has been found, so
many people hurry to make claims on it that it becomes, almost instantly, a lost paradise. With crowds of strangers flocking together
to escape the crowds, last year's lotus land becomes this year's tourist trap.

The mere presence of visitors, moreover, inevitably strips perfec- 4
tion of its most distinctive blessing: its innocence of self-consciousness.
As soon as Eden is told that it is Eden, it becomes something else.
These days every Arcadia is tempted to regard itself as a potential
commodity, and paradise is less often lost than remaindered. The visitor to Nepal, which was long known as the Forbidden Land and closed
to foreigners until as recently as 1951, can now stay comfortably at the
Hotel Eden in Katmandu. Just around the corner, he can dine at the
Paradise Restaurant or the Earth's Heaven Restaurant; after dinner,
he can stroll to Nirvana Tours, the Hotel Shangri-La or a host of other
50¢-a-night flophouses and cappuccino houses. There, the locals are
sure to remind him that the real paradise is that great American city
across the sea, rich with Cadillacs and videos and fast-food joints. By
now, even New York, least otherworldly of cities, lists in its phone
books 27 Edens, nine Arcadias and almost 100 Paradises (including the
Paradise Memorial Pet Crematory and Paradise Guard Dogs, Inc.).

A deeper reason for the steady decline of idyls, though, may be 5
that travelers love to report that paradise is lost. If it is the first secret
conceit of every voyager to imagine that he alone has found the world's
last paradise, it is the second to believe that the door has slammed shut
right behind him. A paradise is by its nature a fine and private place, a
deserted island or a solitary glade. Adam and Eve would have seemed
considerably less charmed had they been surrounded by squawking
kids, knickknack vendors and a row of time-share condos. Every visitor
hopes to keep his idyl to himself; he's in heaven, and hell is other
people. "The place is a Utopia," he's likely to tell his friends, "but
there's no point in your going there. I saw it pristine, but now it's
spoiled forever."

In a sense, paradise *is* precisely what's lost. Nothing is more in- 6
corruptible than what is irretrievable. And just as a good man, once
dead, becomes a saint, so a nice place, once quit, becomes an Eden. As
the years slide by, the places we have visited are steadily pushed back
to an enchanted distance, and memory, the mind's great cosmetician,
begins to remove wrinkles, soften edges, touch up the past in a golden
glow. The 26-hour bus trip, the simultaneous swarm of hucksters and
mosquitoes, the revolutions of the stomach are all forgotten or, better
yet, transfigured into the unforgettable adventures with which we
can impress our friends. Paradise's loss is our gain. Small wonder that
Proust, great poet laureate of reminiscence, wrote, "*Les vrais paradis
sont les paradis qu'on a perdus.*" Nothing is ever what it used to be.

That kind of plangent wistfulness is hardly confined to Mother's 7
account of her honeymoon or Grandpa's homesickness for his youth.
The tug and ache of nostalgia pull even at the hardiest of travelers. The
caustic Evelyn Waugh introduces his collection of travel essays, *When
the Going Was Good,* with a heartbroken valedictory to a vanished

Golden Age of travel that is, in effect, a valentine to his own lost youth. In every traveler's eulogy there is a strain of elegy, and every traveler hearkens to the raven's knelling cry of "Nevermore."

So it is, perhaps, that the world's most fabled paradises are being 8 lost each day yet never seem to lose their paradisiac allure. Take Bali, for example, the Indonesian tropical garden visited this spring by President Reagan and the world. Every intruder on the island quickly registers its palm-fringed beaches, magical dances and golden native beauties out of Gauguin and then remarks that all these delights are being corrupted by a camera-toting crush of alien surfers, satyrs and souvenir hunters. The single most changeless feature of Bali, indeed, is this litany of laments. "'Isn't Bali spoiled,' is invariably the question that greets the returned traveler," wrote Miguel Covarrubias. That was in 1937. "This nation of artists is faced with the Western invasion, and I cannot stand idly by and watch their destruction," wrote André Roosevelt, introducing a book titled—what else?—*The Last Paradise.* That was in 1930. Fifty years later, thousands of visitors continue to "discover" Bali each year, acclaim it as a paradise and, once home, mourn that it is lost forever.

All this suggests that paradise may ultimately lie more in the eye 9 of the beholder than the heart of the beheld. That is the secret of its beauty, and its poignancy. For paradise must always, in a sense, be a creation of the imagination, must always, if it is to be worth seeking, be unattainable, just around the corner or behind us in the past. To find perfection is to bring it down to earth and make it mortal. We want, we need to be taken in—both welcomed and illusioned. And in the end, perhaps, the search for paradise may really come down to nothing more than a search for a paradise within. If only we can rediscover Eden, we imagine, we will recover our unfallen selves, and so lead simpler lives with happier hearts and consciences unsullied. That may be why some shrewd paradise seekers never leave home at all.

---

4. Iyer's essay on paradise has probably made you think in Technicolor about the places you would like to visit. Or perhaps you have already had the opportunity to travel and feel as Iyer does about the search for paradise. Use your travel experience or your imagination to write a short essay on one of the topics below, demonstrating how to develop and support claims of cause.

    a. Choose a paradise you have *not* visited but want to and explain what has caused you to accept it as a paradise.

    b. Using a historical view, as Iyer does in paragraph 8, demonstrate how the view of a particular paradise has diminished or become stronger.

    c. Has your concept of what constitutes paradise changed over the years? If so, explain what has caused your view to change. If not, explain why your view has remained constant.

CLAIMS OF VALUE: WHAT IS GOOD OR BAD, RIGHT OR WRONG?

Who your friends are, what you wear, where you eat, how you spend your leisure time, what music you listen to—all are results of value judgments you have made. And although each choice reflects your personal taste, the *value* you attribute to each is determined by generally accepted standards. Both personal taste and value judgments express approval or disapproval, but the purpose and audience for each differ.

Statements such as "I like water skiing better than snow skiing," "Jazz is my favorite kind of music," and "Old westerns are really fun to watch" express personal preference, but the speaker does not anticipate having to defend these statements. The purpose and audience for statements of personal taste are *informal;* the writer or speaker wants only to share an opinion, not to convince others that they should value something in a different way.

Value judgments, on the other hand, intend to persuade an audience to accept the writer's view—to value something differently. Both the purpose and the audience for value judgments is *formal.* When you make a value judgment, or a **claim of value,** you *expect* to defend it and are prepared to do so. For instance, if someone were to claim, "John Updike ranks as America's most versatile living writer," you would expect the writer to demonstrate Updike's versatility to *your* satisfaction. To gain your acceptance, the writer needs to apply criteria or standards that you both accept to demonstrate how well Updike meets those criteria. Supporting a value judgment, then, depends on the knowledge and values of the audience and on the writer's ability to establish mutually acceptable criteria for evaluation.

Selecting and Supporting Criteria. When you make a value judgment about a common, constructed object—such as a camera, dishwasher, or piano—the criteria are readily defined and agreed to by your audience. Such practical evaluations are generally based on how well the object fulfills its function. If a washing machine uses water efficiently, has settings to match the needs of your clothes, and gets your clothes clean, it fulfills its function. To judge a particular object, you have only to measure it against the easily defined criteria of its class. But when you make value judgments about aesthetics (what constitutes beauty and pleasure) and ethics (what constitutes right and wrong), you are dealing with abstractions that can be evaluated by varying sets of criteria. As a writer, your first task in supporting an aesthetic or ethical value judgment is to determine what systems of values your audience holds on the subject. If you can show that your standard of evaluation complements your audience's basic assumptions about what has value, then you have supported your criteria for that audience.

How do you anticipate what your readers' assumptions are? You examine the experiences, training, and heritage that have shaped their beliefs. The more specifically you can define your audience, the more precisely you can anticipate their assumptions. In Figure 8 the writer anticipates how various audiences might value the space program. From each response the writer has estimated the audience's assumed value to-

Figure 8 *A writer's anticipation of audiences' evaluations*

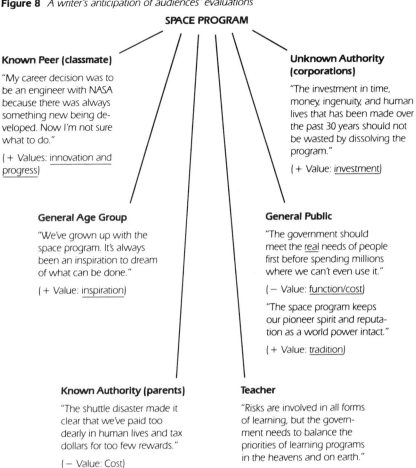

SPACE PROGRAM

Known Peer (classmate)

"My career decision was to be an engineer with NASA because there was always something new being developed. Now I'm not sure what to do."

(+ Values: <u>innovation and progress</u>)

Unknown Authority (corporations)

"The investment in time, money, ingenuity, and human lives that has been made over the past 30 years should not be wasted by dissolving the program."

(+ Value: <u>investment</u>)

General Age Group

"We've grown up with the space program. It's always been an inspiration to dream of what can be done."

(+ Value: <u>inspiration</u>)

General Public

"The government should meet the <u>real</u> needs of people first before spending millions where we can't even use it."

(− Value: <u>function/cost</u>)

"The space program keeps our pioneer spirit and reputation as a world power intact."

(+ Value: <u>tradition</u>)

Known Authority (parents)

"The shuttle disaster made it clear that we've paid too dearly in human lives and tax dollars for too few rewards."

(− Value: <u>Cost</u>)

Teacher

"Risks are involved in all forms of learning, but the government needs to balance the priorities of learning programs in the heavens and on earth."

(+ and − <u>conditional value:</u> Priorities needed)

ward the subject and identified this value as positive (+) or negative (−). By doing this, the writer can determine which audience would most benefit from her argument and how to select an agreed-upon set of criteria. Although many more opinions exist on the space program, this brainstorming cluster provides a sufficiently broad and specific range of values to begin some tentative planning.

POSITIVE VALUES	NEGATIVE VALUES
Innovation and progress	Cost in money and human lives
Investment in the future	Needs on earth—poverty, education, drugs, hun-
Tradition of pioneer spirit	ger—neglected
Inspiration	

POTENTIAL AUDIENCES

1. Students planning to be engineers or those in fields directly related to the space program

2. Members of the general public who don't believe the space program benefits social or educational needs

From this preliminary information the writer gains a more balanced view of the values associated with the issue and the audiences that might benefit the most from a persuasive discussion of those values.

In assessing *why* people hold the values they do, you need to keep in mind that often people's personal interests during a particular time in their lives influence the assumptions they hold toward specific subjects. When the stock market plummeted in October 1987, for instance, investors' lives were more affected than were those of noninvestors. But the return of a healthy stock market in October 1988 was likely to have changed the assumptions of both investors and noninvestors. This likelihood of change is what you depend on when supporting your criteria for evaluation. If you find that you and your audience hold different assumptions toward the same subject, you can use three tactics to convince them to accept your criteria for evaluation: an appeal to authority, an appeal to consequence, or a comparison.

Aesthetic judgments generally require an **appeal to authority,** to the testimony of those considered experts in the field. While most people have an opinion about what they like and dislike in the arts, from painting and dance to music and theater, few people actually have the training to develop a standard set of criteria for evaluation. Consequently, you need to refer to the respected critics and authorities in the field to establish credible and acceptable criteria. In the same respect, laws and documents, such as the Constitution, can be used as authority in establishing and supporting criteria for ethical evaluations. An authority has the advantages of (1) knowing the subject well enough to identify what aspects need to be considered, such as techniques and quality of materials; and (2) having the training and experience to establish the ideal definition against which an individual case can be measured objectively, without the interference of emotion.

An **appeal to consequence** appeals to the cause-effect relationship between the value and the audience. Consequence predominates in evaluating actions, useful objects, and many ethical judgments. If you claim, for example, "Shopping malls are detrimental to society because they suppress cultural diversity," you are appealing to consequence. But your audience will not be convinced of that consequence unless you both agree on the value of and criteria for cultural diversity. In this way, consequence provides the motivation and leverage for the audience to accept your criteria for evaluation.

You can also persuade your audience to accept your claim by using a **comparison** of whatever is being judged to something similar that the audience has already judged as good or bad. For example, if you think people should value active military service as an accepted ritual, then you could prepare your audience to accept your claim by comparing it to a similar ritual they already respect or at least accept. Paying taxes, for instance, is a ritual citizens of this country must accept. And even though people may not enjoy paying taxes, they accept the ritual as necessary to the state and federal governments' ability to benefit *all* the people in a democracy. Similarly, even though people may not enjoy serving in the military, they may be able to accept the service as necessary in a democracy. If the points of comparison are *parallel*, this approach can be particularly convincing in establishing a common ground for acceptance with your audience.

While reading the movie review, "Sea Shepherd from Outer Space," written by *Time* movie critic Richard Corliss in 1986, note the criteria he uses for supporting his claim of value.

Sea Shepherd from Outer Space

RICHARD CORLISS

Star Trek IV: The Voyage Home
Directed by Leonard Nimoy
Screenplay by Steve Meerson,
Peter Krikes, Harve Bennett
and Nicholas Meyer

Trekkies are the Moonies of pop culture. Since the tatty sci-fi series *Star* 1
Trek went off the air in 1969, they have devoted themselves with canonical fervor to annotating and explicating the 79 episodes. To Trekkies it matters not that the show was bad science and worse fiction, or that its actors, outfitted in futuristic Dr. Dentons, read their portentous lines with nitwit solemnity. The show's only soaring spin-off was *Star Trek: The Motion Picture* (1979), in which the cast took a back seat to a splendid special-effects light show that made an eloquent case for the fusion of art and technology, man and machine. Trekkies, of course, consider it anathema—too much hardware, not enough kitsch.

Still, the movie was popular enough to tag the property as a solid 2
box-office attraction. And gradually, the films' creators managed to beam the series up to competence, even to emotional resonance. In 1982 *The Wrath of Khan* brought Admiral Kirk (William Shatner) back from the executive junk heap to conquer both an old nemesis and a

mid-life crisis. In 1984 *The Search for Spock* resurrected Mr. Spock (Leonard Nimoy) for a reunion with Kirk that was tender enough to make a Vulcan almost cry. Now comes *The Voyage Home*—and a radical, canny shift of moods. This time, if you laugh at *Star Trek*, you are in good company. The whole starship *Enterprise* crew is giggling up its polyester sleeves.

The plot could be torn from yesterday's headlines: SEA SHEPHERD 3 FROM OUTER SPACE. Imagine that the environmental activists who recently sank two Icelandic whaling vessels were the rulers of a 23rd century planet, and that they had sent to earth a probe with signals that could be answered only by humpback whales—a species that had been hunted to extinction by blubber-lusting 20th century man. If the whales don't talk back, the earth blows up. So the *Star Trek* crew must become time travelers. They must boomerang their stolen Klingon warship around the sun, land in San Francisco in 1986, steal a whale or two and transport their precious cargo . . . *back to the future!*

Take one more ride in Hollywood's favorite pop-satirical time 4 machine, while the *Enterprisers* try to pass themselves off as primitive earthlings. With the help of Co-Screenwriter Nicholas Meyer (who, in *Time After Time*, propelled H. G. Wells and Jack the Ripper into San Francisco in 1979), they do just fine. Dr. "Bones" McCoy (DeForest Kelley) brazens his way through a little miracle surgery; Chekov (Walter Koenig), the Russian, has to explain his way out of an American nuclear submarine; Scotty (James Doohan) brings postmodern plastics to Marin County. And Spock, wandering around Golden Gate Park in a Vulcan bathrobe and proving his ineptness with the local slang, must be passed off as a casualty of the '60s free-speech movement. "He did a little too much LSD," Kirk explains helpfully.

It is familiar stuff, and even a die-hard *Star* Trasher may regret 5 that these stolid figures of fun have decided to have a few laughs at their own expense, as if they were doing a turn for some intergalactic David Letterman. Still, the film should have appeal—skin-deep but worldwide—for novices and exegetes alike. Watch it make a bundle.

As a writer for a magazine intended to inform the general public, Corliss is well aware of his readers' interest: they want to know if the movie is worth their time and money. As a movie critic, Corliss is more interested in the movie's artistic quality. The problem, then, is how to satisfy the readers' interest *and* his own claim of value. Corliss chooses a comparative historical approach to merge the two interests. His criteria focus on plot, characterization, special effects, and entertainment value.

His opening commentary on the TV show and the four spin-off movies makes clear that as an authority in the field he found only the first movie to have any artistic quality: "a splendid special-effects light show that made an eloquent case for the fusion

Figure 9 *Toulmin model of argument using claim of value*

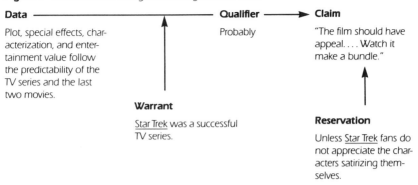

Data ──────────────────────── Qualifier ────▶ Claim

Plot, special effects, char-   Probably   "The film should have
acterization, and enter-   appeal. . . . Watch it
tainment value follow   make a bundle."
the predictability of the
TV series and the last
two movies.

Warrant

Star Trek was a successful   **Reservation**
TV series.
                                 Unless Star Trek fans do
                                 not appreciate the char-
                                 acters satirizing them-
                                 selves.

of art and technology, man and machine." But, he points out, the fans wanted more emphasis on the characters—the television series in movie form. And that's what they got in the next two movies. The question now is, How does *Star Trek IV* compare? Noting what moviegoers have previously valued, Corliss assures readers that they can expect the same attention to predictable plot, special effects, and entertainment value. In characterization they can expect the added twist of satire—that is, the characters' making fun of themselves. This satirical twist, in Corliss's judgment, may not amuse all fans. However, his claim, stated in the final sentence—"Watch it make a bundle"— cleverly reveals his sentiments about its commercialism while endorsing its popularity. By using criteria that merge his authority with the interests and values of his audience, Corliss presents a balanced claim of value for his readers' consideration.

Using the Toulmin model, we can diagram Corliss's argument as in Figure 9.

EXERCISES: CLAIMS OF VALUE

1. For each of the following subjects, analyze audience assumptions toward the subject by anticipating their responses. Use a diagram similar to Figure 8.
  a. Urban renewal
  b. Banning smoking from public buildings
  c. A recent movie
  d. Sex education in the schools
  e. Planned parenthood clinics

2. Choose two of the subjects below or two of interest to you and formulate a claim of value. For each you should designate an appropriate audience and list the criteria you would use to support your claim.
  a. Neighborhood crimewatch
  b. Home computers
  c. A sports hero

d. Your favorite form of music

e. Environmental laws

3. In the following essay from the *New York Times* (August 31, 1986), "No More Zero-sum Game," Arthur Ashe evaluates the success and new legacy of his generation of black men since the passage of the civil rights laws. His claim, however, is implied rather than stated. After reading the essay, state what you believe to be Ashe's claim and list the criteria he uses to develop his support. Then diagram Ashe's argument using the Toulmin model. In a paragraph explain why you think *New York Times* readers will accept or reject the argument.

No More Zero-sum Game

ARTHUR ASHE

There are a bunch of us black men between the ages of 39 and 45 who   1
share the bond of being in the first generation that took full advantage
of the civil rights laws of 1963–65. Few of us felt genuinely comfortable
with that new privilege, because, from birth, we were conditioned to
feel that life would be a zero-sum game.

Early on, I learned that white society would tolerate only so   2
many of us in one group at any one time: only so many—or none in
some places—"nice Negro families" in a previously all-white suburban
neighborhood; only so many in certain public schools; only so many
in white colleges. When I got in any of these, I was supposed to feel
lucky. My self-confidence was constantly being tested, but it was exhilarating just the same. Not that I was among the very first, mind you.

The first black college graduate received his diploma back in   3
1826, at Bowdoin College. Yet, even today I can count on two hands the
number of my childhood friends whose parents were both college
graduates. So what made us different from those black men before us
who got degrees? Simply that our expectations were much higher. Our
predecessors knew they could go only so far. But America was telling
us, "The sky's the limit!"

I have kept up with my friends, and some have done very well.   4
The smartest in our class has lived up to his potential and is the con-
ductor of a Northern symphony orchestra. Another became the president of the National Bar Association. Still another friend, from Little
League baseball, heads Trans-Africa, black America's first foreign-
policy lobby.

But my 39- to 45-year-old black professional buddies have paid a very heavy emotional toll. Divorce is the norm rather than the exception. Nearly everyone is hypertense. The stress is barely bearable most of the time, but it is hidden behind ingenious subterfuges. I am not the only one to have had a heart attack before age 40—and I was in excellent physical condition. Most of my friends are frustrated, and some are now visiting shrinks—something our older black professionals almost never did. Black shrinks themselves are grossly overscheduled.

In the corporate world, few white superiors will risk running interference for us. Our white peers—men more than women—generally think we got to where we are because of a quota. That notion rankles more than anything else. They are still stuck with the idea that though we make great entertainers and athletes, we do not have the right stuff for the business world.

Fortunately for me, I can now kid my buddies from grade school who told me that tennis was a sissy sport. They are now frantically taking tennis lessons to help them adjust socially as they aspire to be senior vice presidents. Some may be aiming higher, but no one really thinks he will be president of a multibillion-dollar corporation. In public, we say, sure, we'll do it, but few of us really believe it will happen, because "these things take time."

Some of us have gone out on our own and tried the entrepreneurial route. However, not many black banks are willing to risk much on a man with no track record who wants to run a business outside the big corporate womb. Can you blame the banks? I have done well as a tennis player and as an investor. Yet a black bank turned me down for an uncollateralized loan—I wanted to sign a note—for a purchase of land even though my net worth was 52 times the amount of the loan. The fact that I still understand the bank's conservatism says a lot.

Once we are in business, I'm told, some of us are forced to do some things we could never tell our mothers about. The teachings of the traditional black church on morality, honesty and a good name have always been clear. They begin with the Ten Commandments. Black media preachers like the Reverend Ike aside, our churches still stress the biblical passages "Lay not up for yourselves treasures upon earth . . ." and "It is easier for a camel to go through the eye of a needle than for a rich man to enter into the kingdom of God." The messages connect. Most black children are officially classified as poor. But the consensus now among most of us professional blacks is that such rules have to be bent to get ahead.

Still, we sometimes laughingly imagine how America would react if someone like T. Boone Pickens were black. Not that Pickens has done anything illegal. Hell, he is genuinely admired, but quite a few black deacons would wonder how much is enough. The closest analogy to him we can think of in our world is Muhammad Ali, who stood up to the Federal Government and won.

Our primary worries now, though, are the young black males be- 11 tween 16 and 24 years old who were so dramatically highlighted during Bill Moyers's "Vanishing Family" documentary a few months ago. Their condition has reached crisis level as a result of their woeful upbringing in mostly-fatherless homes. They see no need to study hard to get ahead. Drugs, high dropout rates in school, petty crimes and teen-age pregnant girlfriends mark their passage to young adulthood. Some have succeeded, despite all this, and are doing well at college. I was lucky, I guess. Even though my mother died when I was only 6, I grew up with a strong father.

My generation was supposed to feel grateful for the opportunity 12 to be able to choose between Howard and Harvard Universities. Still, I did not have nearly so much daring as these young men have today. The black college freshmen of today have grown up without the psychological burdens of the black social revolution of the 1960's or the Vietnam War, and they see the choice between Howard and Harvard as routine—their right. If we dared to hope for the good life, most of them unabashedly demand it. They do not even mind telling you they like President Reagan. A large proportion of the one in six black college men who eventually will graduate will become Republicans. My generation, burdened as it was by being in the first wave, admires their spunk, even envies the fact that they are unbridled.

Most of my buddies certainly have changed from the days of the 13 sit-ins. A mortgage, two or three kids, a couple of cars and college to pay for make you sober up real fast. I now look forward to the first black C.E.O. of a Fortune 500 company. That day is not too far off, in spite of our doubts. But I know she will be up to it.

---

4. Are you representative of the whole or of a segment within your generation? Write a short essay in which you evaluate the actions of your generation with respect to the opportunities available. You may wish to choose a particular segment of people (those attending college) or a particular subject (choice of career, dress, attitude toward authority) as your focus.

CLAIMS OF POLICY: WHAT SHOULD BE DONE?

You are frustrated at being unable to find a parking place on campus even as early as 8:30 A.M. Fear of being mugged is a concern when attending the movie theater downtown. And whenever you get a glass of water from the kitchen faucet, you think about buying bottled water. "Something must be done about this!" you tell yourself. These feelings of frustration and dissatisfaction over persistent problems are what motivate you to develop an argument that proposes action.

Claims of policy advocate adoption of policies or courses of action because there are problems that demand solutions. And because you as the writer feel that the need for a solution is a crucial one, your language will reflect the intensity of the need: *should, ought to,* and *must* are usually expressed or implied in the claim.

To persuade an audience to accept your claim and take action, you first have to convince them of two points: (1) that something is wrong and needs to be righted; and (2) that the remedy you propose is a feasible solution to the problem. How you balance these two sections in your argument depends on the knowledge and sentiments of your audience about the problem.

Demonstrating the Problem.   Implied in your claim of policy is the existence of a problem. "A dress code should be mandated for all public high schools," implies that the way students currently dress interferes with their education. Your first responsibility, then, is to prove the existence of the problem. To do this, you follow the same strategies for establishing definition as you did for claims of fact. How extensive your definitions and means of verification are will depend on the audience's level of awareness of the problem.

If the audience is not aware of the problem, you will need to make the demonstration a highly informative part of the argument to convince them of its existence. For example, with respect to the need for a dress code in public schools, a person who has not been inside a school for a long time or who does not have children attending school may have no idea how students dress when they are there. These people would need very specific descriptions of the clothes. Neighbors of schools may have a general idea of how students dress and act outside the school but little or no understanding of the problem taking place inside the school. Administrators and teachers would need only a brief reminder of the problem, while students, who would probably be hostile to the idea, would more than likely deny the problem. This last audience would need special, diplomatic handling to convince them of the problem's existence. A reasonable tone of voice, then, is more likely to convince your audience to consider your claim with an open mind.

As in developing claims of fact, the specific data and means of verification fulfill two purposes: to inform the audience and persuade them to accept the problem. Then you can demonstrate the negative consequences of the problem. This is a crucial, transitional section in your argument, for by convincing the audience to agree on the extent of the undesirable consequences, you arouse in them the incentive to change and act.

To demonstrate the consequences of the effects, you follow the same strategy you used in developing a claim of cause: retrace and verify the cause in a logical sequence. An audience can have the same range of awareness about effects as it did about the nature of the problem. For instance, people may not approve of the way teenagers dress at the mall or on the way to school, but they may have never considered how dress can affect the quality of education. Point of view may also be a factor. Consider the person who doesn't approve of the dress but who thinks conformity in dress may produce static conformity in thinking as well. The audience may also be unaware of the extent of the consequence. Using prediction from immediate to ultimate effects will arouse them even more to action. If they discover, for instance, that the lack of a dress code is causing students to act in such undisciplined ways that not only are they not learning anything but incidents of vandalism have increased and more tax money will be needed to repair damage, their incentive to pay close attention to your proposal will increase.

Presenting the Proposal. Once you have convinced the audience that the problem exists and the consequences need their attention, you can assume they are ready for the proposal. The proposal must bring about a reversal: from the negative effects of the problem to the positive effects of the solution. To do this, your proposal must be both practical and feasible.

Designing a practical proposal requires thinking carefully about human nature. While the audience may want easy and efficient methods to solve the problem, they may suspect that something too easy will not be successful. And, if the problem is so easy to solve, why hasn't it been done before and why do you need their help? Direct your proposal to an audience that has the ability and influence to participate and convince them that the success of the solution depends on their participation. If they feel that their participation is necessary, they will be more willing to expend the time, energy, and money that most proposals require.

Feasibility takes the proposal one step further in persuading the audience to participate. By suggesting a sequence of steps they can follow to obtain the desired solution, you can demonstrate that the proposal is attainable. This use of logic shows the audience that even if they must sacrifice in terms of time, money, or energy, they will be compensated by the benefits of the proposal's outcome, whether directly or indirectly.

While reading Fred Powledge's essay, "Let's Bulldoze the Suburbs," from *Penthouse* (1981), pay particular attention to the balance of demonstrating the problem and proposing the solution. How does this balance indicate the awareness level of his audience? Who is the audience, and what tone has Powledge chosen to use in addressing them?

Let's Bulldoze the Suburbs

FRED POWLEDGE

For almost 30 years now, America has been systematically destroying 1
the centers of her cities. In the name of urban renewal, we have declared choice parcels of downtown real estate to be slums and then

forced their rightful owners—often stable but poor families and small businesses—to move away. We have sent bulldozers in at taxpayers' expense to flatten the old housing, and then we have given the cleared land away at bargain prices to the operators of parking garages, over-priced hospitals, and chain hotels, to the developers of high-rise bank buildings and luxury housing.

The downtowns thus "renewed" have become cold, juiceless 2 mausoleums that the more well-to-do office workers pass through nervously when heading to and from their homes in the suburbs—suburbs that were built simultaneously with the urban-renewal program and at the expense of the cities and city-dwellers. For while our politicians were giving the downtowns away, they were also encouraging the construction of suburban rings (some call them nooses) around the cities to house the Americans who, to them, count: the white, young, middle- and upper-income citizens who fear and despise the black, the poor, the city.

Who despise *some* of the city. The suburbanites like to come 3 downtown to collect their paychecks, to take advantage of the cultural offerings, to cruise for interracial sex, to go to the ballgames. So the politicians have built a series of interstate highways and peripheral expressways to serve the suburbanites. The incredible rationale was that the roads were essential for our civil defense.

The white, better-off Americans are still there in the suburbs, and 4 the poor and black and despised are still there in the central cities. Discrimination and exclusion, far from abating, have only gotten worse. It is time, now, that the nation undertook a massive new effort to renew its citizens' lives and surroundings. It is time to systematically destroy suburbia.

The need for suburbia's annihilation should be obvious to any 5 reasonable person who has the stomach to pass through its sacred precincts. Suburbia is, first of all, ugly—physically, socially, politically, intellectually, and emotionally ugly.

It is, and of right ought to be, an embarrassment to its residents. 6 No one, to my knowledge, has ever bragged about living in suburbia.

Suburbia is where the police commit the grossest sins against the 7 Constitution and where the seamiest political corruption may be found. It is the place where school board members routinely burn the "obscene" or "controversial" books by honored authors and then admit that they have never read them. Suburbia has a peculiar talent for bringing out the dumbest and worst in people.

Suburbia is as culturally alive as a turnip. It has no great mu- 8 seums or libraries of its own, and so its residents must go to the cities to keep their brains from ossifying. There are no great restaurants in suburbia. The only social institution that it *has* developed is the giant shopping center, our most fitting possible memorial to greed and bad taste. Suburbia's young people may be seen loitering day and night at these Eastgates and Westgates and asphalt-encrusted Green Acres, their glassy eyes reflecting the vacuity of the suburban landscape, their brains forever soft-boiled by the Muzak that issues from endless chains of K-Marts and Woolcos. Some young people manage to escape into the real world, but many do not. The only salvation for many of them is rock music and killer weed.

Suburbia is racist, and so most of those young people will never 9 know contemporaries who are not socioeconomic duplicates of themselves. Suburbia was conceived largely as a place in which better-off whites might escape confrontations with blacks; so it is not surprising that even now Negroes make up a tiny portion of the suburban population. Similar exclusion prevails in religious and economic matters; such time-honored schemes as requirements that housing be built on minimum-sized plots of one or two acres make it certain that communities will be homogenized into lifelessness.

Suburbia is supremely wasteful at a time when civilization simply 10 cannot afford to throw its resources away. Because there is no adequate public transportation and because suburban housing is largely single-family and one-story, it squanders and taints vast quantities of fragile land, air, water, and energy. It removes enormous areas of cropland from cultivation and replaces them with large numbers of people who have been trained to consume highly processed foods. Suburbia is parasitic, draining both the cities and the surrounding farmlands and forestlands of their resources and vitality and giving nothing in return.

And, as is the case with most shoddily built contraptions, sub- 11 urbia is falling apart before its time. No one is surprised that the housing is disintegrating, but there's more: suburbia is discovering that there's no place to dump the sewage and garbage. The water's starting to taste funny, the kids have strange scars on their arms, crime is rampant, taxes are sky-high, transportation is an ordeal, and it takes half an hour to get out of Eastgate's parking lot. Education is becoming a joke, politics are corrupt, and the pollution is often worse than in the hated city. Surely it's time to do something swift and lasting to this slumland that festers out there beyond the city limits.

The obvious solution is a giant slum-clearance program similar 12 to the one by which the central cities were stripped, flattened, and resold. Suburbia—its houses and highways and shopping centers— must be leveled to the ground from which it so recently oozed. But this time the profiteers must not be the bankers and builders and other special interests. This time the American public in general must benefit.

I propose a program by which almost all suburban land will be 13 returned to its former state of wildness or agriculture. The people who live in suburbia will be paid equitable sums for their homes and carports, of course, and they will be free to move wherever they want, as long as it is outside of the officially designated Suburban Clearance Agency Region (SCAR). Some might want to establish totally new cities. Those who agree to return to the decaying central cities will receive the best deal: relocation incentives and technical assistance in rehabilitating abandoned urban housing.

This time the relocation will take place on a strictly nondiscrimi- 14 natory basis. It is certain that once the suburbanites move into the city, the concern and solicitude of the politicians and bankers will quickly follow them, as will adequate social services and other amenities. Thus *two* sets of slums simultaneously will be eradicated—the ones left behind in the suburbs and the ones that have existed all along in the cities.

Overnight the inner-city blocks will develop into solid, attractive 15 housing stock. The cities will regain their financial stability. Mortgage money will finally become available inside the city limits. Employment rates will climb, since everyone who wants a job will be able to find one in either the construction or demolition industries. America will be on the move again.

In the territories that once were known as suburbia, the land will 16 be encouraged to return to forest and pasture for the refreshment, recreation, and nutritional improvement of all Americans. It shouldn't take long to recrown these parks and woodlands with more fitting names: the New Rochelle Natural Area, for example, or Scarsdale National Forest. Maybe we'll discover a silver spring under the asphalt and aluminum siding of Silver Spring, Md., or sand in Sandy Springs, north of Atlanta. The names of all those suburban condotheques will finally start to reflect some reality—the Quail Hollows and Forest Hills and Hickory Groves. Maybe Deer Park will actually become a deer park, and perhaps that ominous split down Southern California's middle will miraculously heal once the weight of so much suburban excess is removed.

I don't think suburbia should be *completely* dismantled. Small 17 tracts of housing should be offered free to poor, black, brown, red, yellow, and tan urban Americans as temporary vacation lodgings—as *pieds-à-terre*, literally, for people whose feet seldom have had opportunities to touch real earth. Some of the shopping centers can be retained for use as prisons or museums or educational institutions where the newly reemerging environment might be studied. Some of the more garish shopping malls might serve especially well as grain silos or chicken coops or indoor feedlots.

And there should be a few suburban preserves—places where 18 the suburban environment as we now know it can be retained for the enlightenment and amusement of posterity. These preserves will contain real, live suburban homes and suburban people, who go through their daily routines while their visitors—curious city residents out for the weekend, schoolchildren on field trips—look on. There they'll be: staggering home from the bar car, watching television with single- (not to mention simple-) minded devotion, wolfing down their Frozen Entrees and Tuna Helper and Kraft Miniature Marshmallows, riding around out front on their nasty little lawnmowers. These living museums will help future generations understand, better than any history book or television documentary could, why it was so necessary that the suburban slums be eradicated.

In contrast to the outrageous idea the title suggests, Powledge uses a rational, controlled tone to establish the existence of the problem and lead to his claim of policy: "It is time to systematically destroy suburbia." Notice that Powledge's use of *we* and *our* in this section makes him part of the audience; consequently, he shares the guilt of having let this problem develop. This tactic creates the incentive to work together toward a solution. But in paragraph 8, Powledge changes his tone dramatically as he begins his condemnation of suburbia to demonstrate the effects of the problem. By reversing his tone, Powledge risks alienating his audience, many of whom probably live in suburbia; however, if they are the intelligent, caring people he assumes them to be, they will understand the irony of his tone.

Powledge's argument would look like the Toulmin model in Figure 10.

Powledge devotes the greatest portion of the essay to the effects section, indicating to his audience the need to be more aware of the consequences. The exaggeration and insulting tone he uses to demonstrate the extent of the effects are designed to produce both humor and concern, literally provoking the audience to ask, "Are things

Figure 10 *Toulmin model of argument using claim of policy*

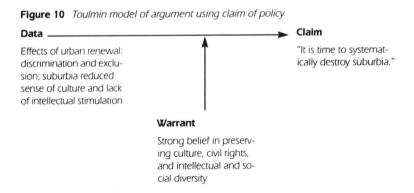

Data

Effects of urban renewal: discrimination and exclusion; suburbia reduced sense of culture and lack of intellectual stimulation

Claim

"It is time to systematically destroy suburbia."

Warrant

Strong belief in preserving culture, civil rights, and intellectual and social diversity really this bad? Am I willing to let it continue?" At this point Powledge has achieved his purpose of getting the audience to lift their complacent heads out of the suburban sand to recognize the problems that exist around them. Now that they are ready for action, Powledge sets forth his proposal, an ironic plan that systematically parallels the urban renewal that initially caused the conditions giving rise to the problem. Obviously he does not expect his audience to follow the plan, but he does expect them to take action to solve the problem.

EXERCISES: CLAIMS OF POLICY

1. For each of the following subjects, identify a possible problem that needs a solution to remedy its consequences:

   a. Thirty-eight percent of Chicago public school teachers send their own children to private or parochial schools.

   b. Changing your major is not a simple matter.

   c. Approximately 122 million Americans have not been to a dentist in over a year.

   d. Forty percent of federal prison inmates are serving sentences for drug dealing.

   e. A single course can entail a crushing amount of work.

2. For each problem you identified in exercise 1, assess the awareness level the following audiences have concerning the problem and its effects.

   a. Teachers

   b. Parents

   c. Friends

   d. Federal government agencies

   e. The general public

3. For each of these claims, state a proposal that might solve the problem and name the audience you would address on the issue.

   a. The library should be open on Friday and Saturday evenings.

   b. Multilevel parking garages must be built on campus.

   c. The homeless people who are crowding our streets and parks should have a place to sleep and eat.

   d. All cities should have recycling garbage pickup.

   e. Companies should provide day care for their employees' children.

4. After reading the essay, "How to Fix the Premedical Curriculum," by Lewis Thomas (from his book *The Medusa and the Snail*, 1978), analyze the four components of the argument by (1) stating the claim of policy and identifying the audience, (2) listing the causes for the problem, (3) listing the effects of the problem, and (4) identifying each point of the proposal. Include a paragraph on why you think the intended audience will or will not accept and act on the proposal.

How to Fix
the Premedical Curriculum

LEWIS THOMAS

The influence of the modern medical school on liberal-arts education   1
in this country over the last decade has been baleful and malign,
nothing less. The admission policies of the medical schools are at the
root of the trouble. If something is not done quickly to change these,
all the joy of going to college will have been destroyed, not just for that
growing majority of undergraduate students who draw breath only to
become doctors, but for everyone else, all the students, and all the faculty as well.

The medical schools used to say they wanted applicants as   2
broadly educated as possible, and they used to mean it. The first two
years of medical school were given over entirely to the basic biomedical sciences, and almost all entering students got their first close
glimpse of science in those years. Three chemistry courses, physics,
and some sort of biology were all that were required from the colleges.
Students were encouraged by the rhetoric of medical-school cata-
logues to major in such nonscience disciplines as history, English,
philosophy. Not many did so; almost all premedical students in recent
generations have had their majors in chemistry or biology. But anyway,
they were authorized to spread around in other fields if they wished.

There is still some talk in medical deans' offices about the need   3
for general culture, but nobody really means it, and certainly the premedical students don't believe it. They concentrate on science.

They concentrate on science with a fury, and they live for grades.   4
If there are courses in the humanities that can be taken without risk to
class standing they will line up for these, but they will not get into anything tough except science. The so-called social sciences have become
extremely popular as stand-ins for traditional learning.

The atmosphere of the liberal arts college is being poisoned by   5
premedical students. It is not the fault of the students, who do not
start out as a necessarily bad lot. They behave as they do in the firm
belief that if they behave any otherwise they won't get into medical
school.

I have a suggestion, requiring for its implementation the follow-   6
ing announcement from the deans of all the medical schools: hence-
forth, any applicant who is self-labeled as a "premed," distinguishable
by his course selection from his classmates, will have his dossier
placed in the third stack of three. Membership in a "premedical so-

ciety" will, by itself, be grounds for rejection. Any college possessing something called a "premedical curriculum," or maintaining offices for people called "premedical advisers," will be excluded from recognition by the medical schools.

Now as to grades and class standing. There is obviously no way of ignoring these as criteria for acceptance, but it is the grades *in general* that should be weighed. And, since so much of the medical-school curriculum is, or ought to be, narrowly concerned with biomedical science, more attention should be paid to the success of students in other, nonscience disciplines before they are admitted, in order to assure the scope of intellect needed for a physician's work. 7

Hence, if there are to be MCAT tests, the science part ought to be made the briefest, and weigh the least. A knowledge of literature and languages ought to be the major test, and the scariest. History should be tested, with rigor. 8

The best thing would be to get rid of the MCATs, once and for all, and rely instead, wholly, on the judgment of the college faculties. 9

You could do this if there were some central, core discipline, universal within the curricula of all the colleges, which could be used for evaluating the free range of a student's mind, his tenacity and resolve, his innate capacity for the understanding of human beings, and his affection for the human condition. For this purpose, I propose that classical Greek be restored as the centerpiece of undergraduate education. The loss of Homeric and Attic Greek from American college life was one of this century's disasters. Putting it back where it once was would quickly make up for the dispiriting impact which generations of spotty Greek in translation have inflicted on modern thought. The capacity to read Homer's language closely enough to sense the terrifying poetry in some of the lines could serve as a shrewd test for the qualities of mind and character needed in a physician. 10

If everyone had to master Greek, the college students aspiring to medical school would be placed on the same footing as everyone else, and their identifiability as a separate group would be blurred, to everyone's advantage. Moreover, the currently depressing drift on some campuses toward special courses for prelaw students, and even prebusiness students, might be inhibited before more damage is done. 11

Latin should be put back as well, but not if it is handled, as it ought to be, by the secondary schools. If Horace has been absorbed prior to college, so much for Latin. But Greek is a proper discipline for the college mind. 12

English, history, the literature of at least two foreign languages, and philosophy should come near the top of the list, just below Classics, as basic requirements, and applicants for medical school should be told that their grades in these courses will count more than anything else. 13

Students should know that if they take summer work as volun- 14
teers in the local community hospital, as ward aides or laboratory assistants, this will not necessarily be held against them, but neither will
it help.

Finally, the colleges should have much more of a say about who 15
goes on to medical school. If they know, as they should, the students
who are generally bright and also respected, this judgment should
carry the heaviest weight for admission. If they elect to use criteria
other than numerical class standing for recommending applicants,
this evaluation should hold.

The first and most obvious beneficiaries of this new policy would 16
be the college students themselves. There would no longer be, anywhere where they could be recognized as a coherent group, the "pre-
meds," that most detestable of all cliques eating away at the heart of
the college. Next to benefit would be the college faculties, once again
in possession of the destiny of their own curriculum, for better or
worse. And next in line, but perhaps benefiting the most of all, are the
basic-science faculties of the medical schools, who would once again
be facing classrooms of students who are ready to be startled and excited by a totally new and unfamiliar body of knowledge, eager to
learn, unpreoccupied by the notions of relevance that are paralyzing
the minds of today's first-year medical students already so surfeited by
science that they want to start practicing psychiatry in the first tri-
mester of the first year.

Society would be the ultimate beneficiary. We could look forward 17
to a generation of doctors who have learned as much as anyone can
learn, in our colleges and universities, about how human beings have
always lived out their lives. Over the bedrock of knowledge about our
civilization, the medical schools could then construct as solid a structure of medical science as can be built, but the bedrock would always
be there, holding everything else upright.

---

5. As students following a specifically designed curriculum, you may have questions about why you need to take certain courses or how well prepared you will be to handle the responsibilities of your profession when you graduate. Write an essay pro-posing a change in your curriculum or in a university policy. The most likely audiences for either of these subjects would be school administrators, faculty, or students, so plan your strategies accordingly: What does your audience already know and value? What does your audience need to know and value if you expect them to act on your pro-posal? How will the audience's participation help to effect change? Before writing your essay, test your reasoning by diagramming your argument using the Toulmin model.

PART II

Investigating

E very day your brain is literally bombarded with information from various sources—conversations, class lectures, observations, radio, television, newspapers, books, magazines, and movies. Have you ever thought about what your brain does with all these facts, figures, feelings, and opinions? Swiss psychologist Jean Piaget used the terms *assimilation* and *accommodation* to explain how the brain processes information. When you assimilate information, you integrate new perceptions and experiences into preexisting categories of memory and knowledge. This process increases the *quantity* of information you have about a particular subject. But when you accommodate information, you must create new categories or modify old ones for the information to fit or be understood. This process, then, increases the *quality* of what you know.

To demonstrate this process, let's say that after reading two of Shakespeare's plays in your literature class, you read several of his sonnets for the first time. Discovering that Shakespeare wrote poetry in addition to plays increases the quantity of your knowledge about Shakespeare (assimilation) just as learning that a sonnet is a form of poetry increases the quantity of information you have about poetry. However, once you determine that a sonnet has a special form distinct from all other poetry, you modify the quality of what you know by creating a new category within your general knowledge about poetry (accommodation).

Using your abilities to assimilate and accommodate helps you determine the need for investigation. When you are introduced to something new—an activity, a person, a theory, or even an old idea in a new context—your brain automatically notes similarities and makes associations with what you already know, and your brain seeks to accommodate whatever information is not assimilated. This is the beginning of your search to make distinctions—going from what you already know to what you need to know. This is where your investigation begins.

To investigate is to consciously select information and the source of your information. To make these choices you have two routes to follow: primary sources and secondary sources. As the term implies, a **primary source** is the most immediate and direct source available, one that represents an "eyewitness" account. While primary sources may take the form of written documents, such as the Constitution or diaries of pioneers who sought their fortune during the gold rush days, your own investigation may produce primary source material through interviews, planned observations, and questionnaires or surveys. In Chapter 3 you will learn how to use these data-collecting procedures in your investigation. Each procedure will bring you closer to understanding a problem you need to resolve. In fact, once you have explored the primary sources related to what you need to know, you may search for secondary sources to verify what you have discovered.

Secondary sources make it possible for you to learn what many different people know about a subject. Reports and commentaries can expand and support what you already know or offer a new perspective on interpreting the data you have collected. Chapter 4 will show you how to locate these sources, plan your search in an organized way, and evaluate the use of these sources.

Knowing what information to use from a source and determining how to present information from a variety of sources are difficult when you have several sources from which to choose. Chapter 5 will demonstrate how you can make the best use of your time during the investigation by using critical reading skills to extract the most pertinent information from your sources.

Investigations can be time-consuming ventures. A scientist, historian, or anthropologist would probably consider five years a mere beginning on a project. In a semester course, however, your time is limited, so you will need an argumentative stance that is narrow enough to explore thoroughly and interesting enough to give you a burst of enthusiasm to pursue your sources with a sense of commitment.

Chapter 3

COLLECTING PRIMARY SOURCES

Diana attended the concert, Ralph heard it simulcast on his stereo, Emilio bought the group's live tour album, and Kim read a review of the concert in the newspaper. Which person would you ask about the quality of the group's performance? All four could easily give you an opinion, but notice that as each person becomes further removed from contact with the original source, fewer details will be available to you.

From the written review, Kim can tell you the details someone else saw blended with her own opinion of the group.

From the group's tour album, Emilio can comment on the recording quality and the response of the audience at a different concert site.

From the stereo simulcast, Ralph can provide details about the sound of each song performed and the audience's general response.

From the concert itself, Diana can give you hours of details—faces, colors, sounds, names, actions, special effects—from before, after, and during the event.

Selecting the source of your information will depend on the purpose that information is to serve. If you are just casually curious about the group, for instance, secondhand information might be enough to satisfy your needs. However, if you are seriously considering investing your time and money in attending one of the group's concerts, you would talk to Diana, your most primary source. Her eyewitness account would help you make a better informed decision.

Because primary sources provide the immediacy of the experience and the authenticity of numerous, specific details, the information is particularly convincing; it gains credibility through personal testimony. The level of credibility of any information, however, is only as reliable as the actual source. For this reason, it is important that you strategically plan the sources you use when conducting research.

SELECTING PRIMARY SOURCES

The first level of obtaining primary source information is your own firsthand experience. Of course, sometimes this experience is not possible or even desirable. If you wanted to better understand the apprehension your uncle is likely to experience in undergoing open-heart surgery, you certainly don't want to undergo surgery yourself. But, if you were able to talk to others who had undergone the surgery, you could anticipate the fears your uncle might have. In this case, a face-to-face interview can be a strong substitute for your own eyewitness account.

Interviews, observations, and surveys help you to gain access to primary source information. These methods of collecting data can be used for two purposes in your investigation: (1) to generate a broad range of opinions from which you can identify the main issues; (2) to focus selectively on a specific point within one of the issues. Let's look at a problem in action to see how these methods can direct and support your investigation.

> **PROBLEM FOR INVESTIGATION:** Over the past two years your college tuition has increased 16 percent and your financial aid has decreased by 50 percent. Why is this happening and how can I stop it? you wonder. The *why* should be a clue that you need to identify the issues before you can do anything about them.

USA Today (March 3, 1987) used a survey of personal opinion to generate the issues involved in this problem.

Do You Think College Tuition Costs Are Too High?

1. **Retired, male, McAlester, Okla.**
   The costs of college are not too high. People who really want an education can find a way to finance it. There is more money circulating now to help defray the costs than there was when I was a student. Most of us students, including me, had to work to help pay for our tuition. It took a strong desire to want to go.
2. **Company president, female, Los Angeles, Calif.**
   If one is motivated enough to attend college, every effort should be made to make it affordable. If costs continue to rise, the people in this country will be divided into two distinct classes: the rich and educated, and the poor and uneducated. While education is a privilege, it is not one that should be available only to the rich.

3. **Professor/department head, male, Fort Collins, Colo.**

   As a parent, I feel the high tuition costs in my pocket. As a faculty member, I recognize why my pocket is pinched. Tuition costs are rising because of the insufficient share of priority funding that is given to the institutions that educate our kids. Tuition goes up if sources of money such as endowments or grants are not available.

4. **Homemaker, female, Magnolia, Minn.**

   Looking ahead with three younger children, I am concerned about the high costs of college. I hope the high tuitions will not discourage my children from attending because I am sure they will have to pay for it themselves. Our future depends on our children, and if we cannot educate them, the future does not look bright.

5. **Student, male, West Lafayette, Ind.**

   Tuition can go as high as it wants, as long as there is financial aid to help students gain access to the institutions they desire. There is a big differential between college costs and the financial aid available, especially with the administration asking for cuts. Actual college costs are much higher than they used to be.

6. **Systems architect, male, Southport, Conn.**

   College tuition is high, but the same is true of any industry that offers a service. High costs are a general problem all around. Perhaps it would be advantageous if more money for college education—money with no commitments or obligations—were derived from federal or local funding. Scholarships do not go far enough.

7. **Music teacher, female, Vauxhall, N.J.**

   My oldest son was unable to return to college after Christmas break last year because I was putting myself too far in the hole by financing his education. The money we had put aside for college and the grants he received were not enough. Now, he's working to save enough money to attend a less expensive college.

From this variety of opinions several issues emerge:

A strong desire for a college education may not be enough to get an education at the college of one's choice. (Opinions 2, 3, 7)

As tuition costs increase, access to financial aid needs to increase. (Opinions 2, 3, 5, 6, 7)

A society that values the contributions of those who are educated must make education a priority in its funding. (Opinions 2, 3, 4, 5, 6)

The common denominator of the major issues appears to be funding. How are colleges and universities funded, and how does that funding affect tuition costs? With funding as your focus, you can begin to collect primary source data. One of the best

Figure 1 *Cluster diagram of primary source possibilities*

ways to organize the use of your sources is to use a **cluster** to diagram the sources you have access to.

Write your focus in a circle in the middle of a piece of paper, then draw a line or spoke from the center to a source related to the focus (see Figure 1). After brainstorming sources for your cluster, you can begin making preliminary plans for using interviews, observations, and surveys. Look at the example below.

PRELIMINARY PLANS

Who to interview?	Alumni association (contribution trends)
	Financial aid office (change in opportunities)
	Research office (government and corporate funding)
	Bursar (tuition support of academic program)
What can be observed?	Giving or participation, support for the college or university
	Alumni event, student scholarship fundraiser
	Newspaper coverage (number and frequency of articles)
Who can be surveyed?	Alumni
	Students
	Endowment agencies

By beginning with the interviews, you will find that your sources can direct you more specifically in your observations and surveys.

The following sections in this chapter will show you how to design each of these data-collecting procedures to gain access to the primary source information you need.

INTERVIEWS

DESIGNING THE INTERVIEW

Interviews used for daily informal purposes are similar to those used in formal research in that both require reliable sources. After all, learning something from someone who knows more than you do about a particular subject is the intention of the interview. Thus, selecting a knowledgeable source—one with close access to the information you need—is the first step in designing an interview. The more precise and detailed the source can be, the more reliable and useful the information will be.

Selecting a Source. Use your cluster of sources to determine which people or agencies will be the easiest to contact for a face-to-face interview. This type of interview has two advantages: (1) the body language the interviewee uses will indicate his or her emotional posture toward the information; and (2) it will be easier to recontact a nearby source if you need further clarification.

Formulating Questions. However knowledgeable your source may be, it is up to you to formulate in advance the kinds of questions that will elicit the information you need. This means, of course, that you must be clear about your purpose for the interview—about what information you need and why you need it. Directing the interview in this way, you will make the best use of your time by being prepared to ask more specific questions. Consequently, the more background information on the person and the issue you can gather *before* the interview, the more your questions can be directed to the person's expertise.

Generally, interview questions fall into three categories:

1. Literal questions about the facts, definition of terms, and concepts that initiated the occasion for the interview help to clarify the present state of the issue. Through these questions you establish a common ground of understanding with your source.

2. Application questions develop an understanding of how things work and what their causes and effects are.

3. Evaluation questions require the interviewee to use his or her expertise to interpret and predict.

Here is an example of how these levels of questioning can be used. When you read the following interview from the *Virginian-Pilot and the Ledger-Star* of June 8, 1987, pay close attention to the sequence of the interviewer's questions.

An Issue That
Radiates Confusion

In less than 50 years, man has learned to use atomic power in a variety of ways—from generating electricity and building bombs to diagnosing and treating disease.

But the use of nuclear power and radioactivity has outpaced man's ability to deal with the waste it generates.

Federal, state and sometimes local regulations have been structured to protect a public that fears and often misunderstands radioactivity. This web of laws and agencies that seek to prevent health hazards also make nuclear management difficult and expensive.

And this is where Diane W. Harmon makes her living.

Harmon is president of Wrightmon USA Inc., a consulting company in Alexandria that specializes in researching regulations and bureaucracies that control the transportation and storage of radioactive waste.

Harmon, who has worked for waste shipment companies since her graduation from Ohio State University with a communications degree in 1972, regards the nuclear waste field as an overregulated mess, full of emotional political battles and misinformation.

The confusion, she said, threatens both the country's and individual businesses' plans for managing waste that ranges from spent fuel from nuclear reactors to contaminated clothing and tools from hospitals and research labs.

Harmon spoke recently to staff writer Cyril Zaneski.

Q. *How much nuclear waste is produced and shipped each year in Virginia alone?* 1

A. Per reactor, the shipments of waste in regular truckloads are about 40,000 pounds. There are about 100 shipments a year. There are four reactors, so there are a total of 400 shipments a year from them alone. Of course, there are other sources of nuclear wastes—all hospitals generate nuclear waste; so do universities, science organizations and museums, which use radioactivity to find the age of fossils, for example.

Q. *Where does the waste go?* 2

A. There are three low-level waste sites now in the United States—in South Carolina, Washington state and Nevada. This waste, which includes contaminated gloves, clothing, machinery, tools and paper, is shipped in sealed 55-gallon drums.

There is no permanent disposal site for high-level wastes, which includes spent fuel from nuclear reactors. The spent nuclear fuel right now is stored at the reactor sites; all of the reactors are getting pretty full with their fuel. So this is a business now that's very competitive building different style casks for dry long-term storage and high-level waste disposal for the future.

Q. *Where will this high-level waste eventually be buried?* 3

A. Texas, Washington and Nevada were selected as waste sites in the first-round selection. The second round included Virginia as a possible site, but there was a political hoo-ha over that one.

    The Department of Energy maybe made a political mistake by backing out of selecting a second state disposal site in the East. That decision, some people are saying, may negate the Nuclear Waste Policy Act. If the Eastern states can say that we don't need a second site, then maybe the Western states can say we don't need a repository at all. It's a battle.

Q. *When will the high-level waste site be chosen?* 4

A. Well, it has all been set back five years. It's now 1993, instead of 1987 for a low-level nuclear site for each region. For high-level, the Department of Energy must be prepared to pick up and store high-level material.

Q. *How are the businesses and utilities coping with the apparent confu-* 5 *sion in the government regulation of nuclear activities?*

A. Utilities cannot sit around and wait for the Department of Energy to fight the Congress to come up with some sort of an answer. Their reactors are backing up with fuel, and they're going to come up with their own answers. They are meeting with other utilities to see how they're solving their problems, putting all their engineering heads together.

Q. *What is an example of a solution to the storage problem?* 6

A. Some are as simple as developing flotation devices to keep the waste floating in storage pools and better use of the available space. Virginia Power recently gave a $70 million contract to a Japanese firm to do supercompacting of waste for them. Now, Virginia Power saves money because storage is charged by the cubic foot. They are sending a lot of their waste to Tennessee for compacting at a 2-1 ratio. Then, of course, that cuts their need for storage space in half.

Q. *How does the federal government regulate nuclear activities?* 7

A. We have many layers of regulation. There's the Department of Energy, the Department of Transportation, there's the Federal Highway Administration, the Interstate Commerce Commission, the railways, the Federal Emergency Management Agency. And the Environmental Protection Agency is starting to get involved.

Q. *How does this layered approach complicate nuclear waste man-* 8 *agement?*

A. The cost for shipping uranium in its natural state before it goes into a reactor is about the same as it would be to ship blue jeans. You hire a truck, and you pay for mileage and time. Once it is processed, it becomes high-level waste, and the costs go up because there is escorting, there are notifications. And you have to pay fees—if you go through 50 states, you have to pay everybody as you pass a border.

Q. *Given the hazards of dealing with radioactive material, aren't the* 9 *precautions justified?*

A. Well, I would say that since in 40 years nobody's been injured through the nature of the cargo, and they keep adding regulations on top of a non-event, then it's bordering on overregulation. Even the Nuclear Regulatory Commission doesn't keep track of the layers of regulations that are being tacked on.

Q. *Are the regulations adhered to?* 10

A. The violations are small. There are some utilities or companies that may not make every single report on time, with t's crossed and i's dotted. Some of these watchdog organizations make a list of what they call nuclear transportation incidents—I remember a couple years ago they said there were 141 incidents—but on their list were broken tail lights, there were fuel lines that broke, or a broken axle. These are things that happen in trucking.

Q. *What is the greatest single obstacle that any waste management pro-* 11 *gram must overcome?*

A. Public acceptance. . . . Right now, we are dealing with a fear of the unknown. And there is overreaction. Look, if you ask 20 of your friends what industries were within a 20-mile radius of their homes, I'll bet they couldn't come up with 2 percent of them.

How many people live near a paint company? Yet the materials that go into producing paint are pretty darn toxic. How many people live near gasoline stations where it's delivered every day? These are things that are seen from the road, not to mention timber and oil refineries and other kinds of chemical plants. And just think of things you use in your own life that have toxic materials in them. It's unbelievable.

Q. *Can communities be convinced to accept disposal sites nearby?* 12

A. People don't want development. It really doesn't matter if it's a restaurant in their neighborhood or a nuclear waste site. I think it just adds a little more ammunition when it's a plant that has a stronger technological base.

But these sites might be seen in the future as a real economic benefit for the community. There is money to be made in waste disposal, and it crosses all segments of society. You'll have scientists doing geology work, hydrology work. Study organizations to provide studies. You'll have construction, you'll have fees coming into general revenue from people sending their fuel to disposal sites. You'll have administration, regulators, truckers, robotic manufacturers. It goes on and on.

Of course, if such a site is chosen in Virginia, for example, it will be over in an area where they need jobs.

The title of the article makes clear that the interviewer's purpose is to lessen the confusion his readers have about the issue of nuclear waste management. He does this systematically by using an **interview question sequence** that begins with the literal, factual level of questions and leads to application and evaluation.

LITERAL LEVEL	Question 1: How much
	Question 2: Where
	Question 3: Where
	Question 4: When
APPLICATION LEVEL	Question 5: How
	Question 6: Example of how
	Question 7: How
	Question 8: How
EVALUATION LEVEL	Question 9: Aren't the precautions justified? (opinion)
	Question 10: Are regulations adhered to? (interpretation)
	Question 11: What is the greatest obstacle? (opinion)
	Question 12: Can communities be convinced? (prediction)

Although these questions happen to be evenly proportioned among the three categories of question levels, the sequencing rather than the distribution develops the primary source information. Notice how the following interview conducted by a student uses the same sequencing of question levels to elicit evaluative opinions.

Interview with the University Parking Manager

Q. *How many parking spaces are there on campus? (literal)*   1
A. Just under 5,000.
Q. *How many parking decals are issued each semester? (literal)*   2
A. In the spring, 5,248 general parking and 947 full-time faculty decals were issued.
Q. *About how many parking tickets are issued annually? (literal)*   3

A. Last year we issued 16,000 tickets.

Q. *Do you strictly enforce towing of cars parked illegally, especially at* 4
the BAL parking lot? (application)

A. Yes, if there is a sign we will tow the car away.

Q. *Does the University have a parking problem? (evaluation)* 5

A. No, we don't. There are enough parking spaces but they are not conveniently located. In fact, a recent study by an unbiased independent consultant hired by the university showed that at any given point in time there are at least 800 empty parking spaces.

Q. *Do we need a multistory parking garage? (evaluation)* 6

A. Right now we are fine. But when construction on the new performing arts center begins in the fall, we will lose some parking spaces. These lost spaces will be more than made up by the new parking garage.

By carefully sequencing the questions, you keep your focus on the issue and purposefully develop the information to highlight the expertise of your source.

CONDUCTING THE INTERVIEW

Common courtesy is important to a successful interview. Time and place arrangements need to be made in advance, either in person or by phone. If you would like to tape-record the interview, you will need to ask for permission and, if granted, use the recorder as unobtrusively as possible. In addition to these amenities, you need to establish your credibility as a researcher.

Establishing Your Persona. As the interviewer, your role becomes one of confidant. You are expecting the interviewee to confide in you, to express his or her personal and professional opinions for public record. For this reason, the interviewee needs to have confidence in you as a researcher. Here are some ways to demonstrate the kind of competence that will instill trust in your abilities.

Explain your purpose. When you first contact the interviewee for an appointment and when you arrive for the interview, introduce yourself as a student researcher and state the purpose of your research as well as your personal interest in the research. Your interviewee will also want to know what part he or she plays in this research and what you plan to do with the information—that is, what form your presentation will take and who will read it. Knowing your intentions and commitment to the research will give the interviewee confidence in you.

Be prepared. Not only does studying background information before the interview allow you to formulate better questions, it also allows you to respond more intelligently. This sign of competence will demonstrate your ability to interpret and present the information you receive fairly and accurately.

Be flexible. Although you direct the interview with your prepared questions, you need to be open to the interviewee's responding in a direction you didn't anticipate. When this happens, allow your curiosity to show and ask for explanations of any answers that are not clear to you. Being responsive encourages the person to speak more freely and also shows that you respect his or her expertise.

Establishing Objectivity. Personal interest is essential to choosing an issue to research, but because an issue is inherently controversial, your personal interest may bias your point of view in choosing sources and asking questions. As a researcher your main concern should be with establishing the truth. Achieving this objectivity may be difficult, but there is one method of interviewing that will increase the likelihood of your producing a more objective opinion.

This method involves interviewing from multiple perspectives. Because an issue includes a basic pro and con dichotomy, you will increase the objectivity of your investigation if your questions include both views and if you choose interviewees on both sides of the issue. Even if a person from only one side is available, you will need to incorporate both viewpoints in your questions. The responses made by the interviewee will help you understand the basis for his or her rejection of the opposing view.

Observe how Philip Shenon of the *New York Times* has used this method in his 1987 interviews of two legal experts on opposing sides of the Miranda issue.

The Defendant's Rights vs. Police Efficiency

According to officials in the Justice Department, Attorney General Edwin Meese 3d might soon ask the Supreme Court to overturn its 1966 Miranda decision, which requires the police to inform criminal suspects of their legal rights to silence and to counsel before questioning.

Like other law-enforcement officials, Mr. Meese has often said that the Miranda ruling hinders police investigations and makes it more difficult to obtain confessions. Now, the Justice Department officials said, the Attorney General has endorsed a 128-page internal report, prepared a year ago, that urges the department to seek a review by the High Court. It also recommends the creation of a set of rules to uphold the rights of criminal suspects, including

*perhaps videotaping police questioning to show that
defendants have not been coerced.*

*Philip B. Heymann, a Harvard law professor who
led the Justice Department's criminal division under
President Carter, and Paul D. Kamenar, executive
legal director of the Washington Legal Foundation, a
conservative study group, talked about the Miranda
decision with Philip Shenon, a reporter in the
Washington bureau of the* New York Times. *Excerpts
from the interviews follow.*

PAUL D. KAMENAR

It Allows Guilty People to Go Free

Question. *Do you think Attorney General Meese should press the Su-* 1
preme Court to reverse the Miranda decision?

Answer. Yes. The rules as they existed before Miranda were more
than sufficient to safeguard individual rights. And since the time
of the decision, police practices have come a long way in their
professionalism.

Miranda only hurts society by allowing guilty people to go free
on technicalities.

Q. *Are there many such cases?* 2

A. What you don't see in the newspapers are the thousands of cases
that prosecutors don't pursue. They know they're not going to have
a chance in court because of violations of the Miranda warning—
even if they feel someone is guilty.

Q. *Was the Court within its authority in its 1966 decision in* Miranda v. 3
Arizona?

A. What the Court did was create a judicial rule of evidence, saying
that the confession of a person who has not been advised of his
rights cannot be introduced in the prosecution's case.

But rules of evidence are supposed to be promulgated by the
legislature, not the courts. Miranda is an artificial rule that's been
created by the Court because of its view—not the legislature's or
the executive's—that this is the way the evidentiary rule should be.

Q. *Was it appropriate for the Court to seek a specific method of pre-* 4
venting police coercion?

A. If it's coercive, a confession will not be admissible, with or without
the Miranda warnings.

Before Miranda we used the voluntariness test. It's a test used all the time to determine whether a statement was coerced from a defendant. The judge asks: What were the circumstances of the statement? Was the suspect under duress?

All of these things protect the suspect's rights. You don't need Miranda. There are other ways to deter police misconduct.

Q. *You say Miranda has been misused. An example?* 5

A. Let's assume a criminal knows very well what his rights are, perhaps better than the police, and is arrested and interrogated without them giving him his Miranda rights. He confesses to the crime. The court will throw out that confession, even though the criminal admits that he knew what his rights were, because he was not read his Miranda rights.

Now that to me and to most of the American people is totally absurd. I think it's that kind of criminal justice that is getting a lot of Americans upset with our revolving door of justice.

Q. *Many believe that the Miranda warnings offer a sense of fairness,* 6 *since all people are offered the same warning of their rights. Do you agree?*

A. It's fair in that respect. The question is if it's fair to society as a whole that the police are not able to ask questions of the people who have firsthand knowledge of the crime.

Q. *Have the police learned to live with Miranda?* 7

A. I think they generally feel that they are at a disadvantage in getting evidence. And they see case after case getting thrown out on these technicalities.

There are so many permutations on Miranda that it's almost impossible for a police officer to be up on the current state of the law.

Q. *Do you think the Supreme Court would be willing to overturn* 8 *Miranda?*

A. Over the last couple of years, the Court has trimmed away on Miranda, recognizing the absurd results that are obtained by a wooden application of the rule. I think the Court would be receptive to review and possibly to reverse Miranda.

PHILIP B. HEYMANN

An Important Symbol of Fairness

Question. *Would you support an effort to overturn the Miranda ruling?* 1

Answer. No. It would be both foolish and symbolic law enforcement.

Q. *Symbolic?* 2

A. We have to take crime very seriously. People get hurt by being mugged. People get hurt by being addicted to drugs. If you're going to deal with crime, what it takes is money and other resources.

Doing away with Miranda won't make any difference. But it has one advantage: It costs nothing. It seems to me it misleads the American people into thinking that somebody is serious about dealing with crime when all they want is to wrap themselves in the mantle of law and order.

Q. *But don't studies show that fewer criminals confess—and fewer are* 3 *convicted—because they are informed of their Miranda rights?*

A. I know of no significant study within the last decade that shows a major impact on convictions. And the earlier studies are wholly ambiguous.

Q. *But certainly there is an effect on confessions.* 4

A. Every hardened criminal, every career offender, every member of a criminal organization knows his rights and isn't about to confess.

The whole universe that is affected by Miranda are the first-time offenders—and of them, only those who are poor, ignorant and unassertive. And of them, a large percentage have always waived their Miranda rights and confessed.

There is a cost to law enforcement; some small number of those first offenders don't confess. But what you're buying for that cost is at least a plausible claim that we don't specialize in sending the poor and the ignorant and the fearful to jail on the basis of their own testimony. It's a very important symbol for fairness.

Q. *Did the Court exceed its mandate and dabble in a type of regulation* 5 *when it demanded that a rigid set of warnings be read to suspects?*

A. Before Miranda, the standard was that a confession had to be voluntary. But no one quite knew what that meant. The result was that either every court of the United States arrived at its own decision of what was voluntary, or many of those cases had to come before the United States Supreme Court, and that's obviously an impossible load on the Supreme Court.

Q. *Do you think the Supreme Court now sees Miranda as a threat to* 6 *law-enforcement efforts and would consider reversing it?*

A. No. Since 1966, the Court has decided dozens of other cases under Miranda, and they have cut back on Miranda. The most important cutback was a very early decision that the police could use a statement taken without the Miranda warnings to cross-examine a defendant if the defendant took the stand.

If Miranda ever represented a major threat to law enforcement—and I would argue that it never did—it does not now.

Q. *At the time of the Miranda decision, some police officials took it as* 7 *an insult, an indication that they were using coercive tactics. How do they view it now?*

A. Twenty times a night on television a police officer is shown arresting someone and immediately advising the suspect of his legal rights, and that seems to me to be a very professional picture. It shows a police officer who's got a bit of the judge in him.

My guess is that if you asked the police chiefs of this country, a majority would say they disapproved of Miranda. But if you asked them whether they would rather have a 4 percent increase in their budgets or a reversal of Miranda, I think they would quickly take the 4 percent increase.

As you can see, in the Kamenar interview, questions 4 and 6 require the interviewee to respond to the opposing point of view. In the Heymann interview, questions 3 and 5 require the same. Balance is created not only in the number of questions but also in the positioning of the questions. In fact, all of the questions in both interviews follow similar content patterns. This balance of content, viewpoint, and number of questions builds in the objectivity needed in attaining information.

Using this method will help you narrow the focus of your issue for more careful scrutiny and at the same time increase your objectivity. Knowing both sides increases your competence and ultimately the confidence the interviewee has in your credibility as a researcher.

PRESENTING INTERVIEW DATA

Magazine and newspaper interviews are often presented in a verbatim question/answer format. Actually, the majority of these interviews are edited to a degree to eliminate pauses, such as "uh" and "um," or repetitions and to refine the grammar, if needed or requested. In a research essay an integrated or synthesized approach is generally used.

When using the synthesized approach, you need to carefully select the information that will achieve your purpose for your intended audience. The expert testimony of primary source information is persuasive to readers, so the best place in your essay to use the interview data is where your audience needs the most convincing. Three common points in the essay where you might consider using interview data are at the factual level, the supportive evidence level, and the evaluation and prediction level. Here are some examples demonstrating how and when this information can be integrated.

> **FACTUAL LEVEL:** The main method used in the past to nourish the resort strip beach has been the reapplication of sand, according to Carl Thorn, city engineer.

> **SUPPORTIVE EVIDENCE LEVEL:** Several vans are parked in this area and do obstruct the view. . . . However, when asked if there was anything he could have done to avoid the accident, Mr. Miller replied, "No, I couldn't even see the truck because of the van parked next to my truck."

EVALUATION AND PREDICTION LEVEL: James Knoblach, manager of the heat treating department located 10 feet off the dangerous stretch of road, feels the accidents are due to employees' speeding in an attempt "to be the first one out of the parking lot at the end of the day." Knoblach further stated that, having watched the cars speeding by on numerous occasions, he was sure that once the employees killed each other, the speeding and accidents would subside.

Notice that in each example the writer clearly identifies the credentials of the interviewee to establish the reliability of the information. Whether or not the interviewee's words need to be quoted will depend on your needs in reaching your audience.

By using primary source information from interviews at crucial points in your research essay, you better inform your audience, provide them with a stronger foundation for making a judgment, and increase the credibility of your persona as a researcher.

EXERCISES: INTERVIEWS

1. Make a list of the issues that emerge from reading the opinions of people interviewed on the issue of using commercials in movies and videos (from *USA Today,* August 15, 1989). State the issues in complete sentences.

Does It Bother You to See Commercials on Videos?

1. Student, female, 16, Conn.
No, it doesn't. You see commercials all of your life on TV, so it really doesn't bother me to see them on videos. Some of them are educational, like the ones about AIDS or drunken driving. I watch them all. My favorite is the Pepsi commercial that comes on before the *Top Gun* video with Tom Cruise.

2. Hotel executive, male, 48, Texas
Yes. Where I become offended is when you think you're getting something that's commercial-free and it isn't. If consumers knew that the movies they were watching were being subsidized by advertising, it would make a good argument for the rental houses to reduce the prices of videos.

3. Photographer, male, 29, Washington, D.C.
It doesn't bother me. I know how it is to promote a product, and the

Pepsi and car people are paying big money to put their commercials on videos. I would prefer that the commercials run at the end of the movie instead of at the beginning. When you put in a tape, you want to go straight to the movie.

4. **Business owner, female, 53, N.M.**

Yes. I have seen previews of coming attractions on a video, but I haven't seen a commercial yet. I think the idea is ridiculous. We rent videos to watch the movies, not commercials. I would fast-forward through them. There are plenty of other places to advertise a product, which they do plenty of already.

5. **General manager, male, 37, Kan.**

No. This is a free enterprise system, and the advertisers are not altering the movie in any way. The video people probably recoup some of their expenses from the commercials. As a businessman, I understand that. If you go to a theater, you have to sit through the slide-show advertisements before the movie.

6. **Homemaker, female, 70, N.J.**

Yes, it does. Network television is free, so you have to put up with the commericals. But when you buy or rent a video, you're paying to watch a movie, and you shouldn't have to put up with a commercial. I buy videos for two reasons—to see a movie and to get away from all the commercials.

---

2. Carefully observe the questions, both their content and sequence, in the following interview by Steven Beschloss for the *Virginian-Pilot and Ledger-Star* (April 20, 1987). Identify the level of question and evaluate the effectiveness of the sequence. Comment on the interviewer's questioning strategy in relation to his purpose.

Working on an Acid-Rain Solution

President Ronald Reagan met with Canadian Prime Minister Brian Mulroney several weeks ago in Ottawa. Mulroney was seeking a U.S. commitment to cut acid rain-causing emissions in half by 1994. Nothing was agreed upon.

Congress is considering legislation for a $2.5

billion, five-year program for clean-coal research and related projects, although resulting answers for significantly reducing or eliminating air pollutants could be decades away.

Robert Sackett is chairman and chief executive officer of RCM Technologies Inc., a Camden, N.J.- based company that has developed a patented process to cut emissions caused by the burning of high-sulfur coal and high-sulfur oil.

Thus far the company has only built a demonstration plant to show that its desulphurization process can eliminate virtually all of the sulphur in flue gas, a major source of acid rain. Yet Sackett is counting on convincing a utility or another significant user of coal or oil to install the new technology.

By 1990, when the Clean Air Act comes up for review, RCM Technologies could be in a good position to find some takers for its process.

But Sackett is not relying on acid rain or other pollution legislation for success. He believes that companies will act to reduce pollution because they can save or make money, rather than as a matter of social responsibility—and he contends that his company's process fits that bill.

Sackett, in Norfolk recently to talk to local companies and stockbrokers, met with staff writer Steven Beschloss.

Q. *Why should the public be interested in your company's technology?*   1
A. When the Clean Air Act was passed 20 years ago, a very small portion of the utilities were required to comply. So as of this date, of the 800 utilities out there, only a little over 135 have ever put equipment in. The rest of them have never had the required equipment.

As a result you've got a tremendous amount of sulfur going into the air every single day. Unabated.

Let's assume that there's a move today in force to do something about acid rain. Congress, the administration, legislators want to do something about it. The problem is that if they enforce the laws and make it restrictive, the utilities cry that the systems that are available to them are either unacceptable, have too many problems or are too costly.

Most systems out there have tremendous disposal problems. What you're doing is solving an air pollution problem and creating a land pollution problem. The reagent that's used to attract the gas is a waste product in the systems out there. You have to haul it out to landfills, to dumps, to storage ponds, etc.

So the technology for systems that have disposals are not acceptable. No one is going to put them in.

Besides, the land pollution people are getting after them because you're creating a tremendous water quality problem with all these trace elements going into the ground. Eventually that water seeps into the ground, into the water table. Regardless of how long it takes, if the earth is 300 feet deep, that water is eventually going to go down there. It may take 20 years, but it's going to go there.

Q. *How does your process work?* 2

A. The need is for a process that has no waste product. It has nothing to haul to a landfill. It's a dry process rather than a wet process.

We have a media which, when injected into an airstream, absorbs the sulfur dioxide on contact. You can take it out of the airstream. And the sulfur becomes a saleable product.

There's nothing to haul out of a mass tonage every day. It's a dry system, therefore there's no corrision. Wet systems are very acidic and very corrosive.

Q. *Who can use this kind of system?* 3

A. Basically the power utility plants. The people who generate electricity that uses coal—the big users of coal.

Anybody who puts sulfur compound into the air. Steel mills. Paper mills. Commercial plants. Anyone who burns oil has problems. Anyone who burns gas has problems with gases coming off the gases. Just because they burn gas or oil doesn't mean it's clean fuel. There's a problem with those also.

The important thing you have to remember is, coal is our best natural resource. The coal industry is committed to stay in business. They're not going to put them out of business. There's going to be coal fire generators as long as I live, as long as you live, as long as your kids are going to be around.

It's our best natural resource. It's our cheapest source. We have an estimated 300 to 1,000 years' supply of coal, of which a good portion is high sulfur. We could create a whole new market based on high-sulfur technology.

Q. *How much is your role one of educating companies about their re-* 4
sponsibility to reduce pollution?

A. First, someone has to build the equipment and put it in. We're only an engineering company. We have to have a joint venture with a company that has that capability.

But given that installation, once we have that acceptability, then there will be a need to go to the legislative body and say to them there's now available a system that utilities can afford. It makes sense. It has no disposal problems. Therefore, given that fact, if you want to really clean up the air, it can now be enforced on a restrictive basis because utilities cannot say to you there's nothing out there I can afford.

That's what they're saying today. They're saying the technology is not affordable because it has problems and therefore we don't want to comply with anything because we don't have to. There's nothing out there we can buy.

Q. *There's a $2.5 billion program for clean-coal research before Congress now. Are you counting on participation?* 5

A. No. We don't need that. We've already done our own research and development.

The Clean Air Act is coming up for review in 1990. There are technologies out there now that in the early days, it was said if you put gas up in the tall stacks that's OK. If those tall stacks blow, it's 2,000 miles away. That's where Canada is getting a lot of their acid rain from. The mood for those things surviving 1990 doesn't look too good from where I sit. But who knows?

I can only say that, on an economic basis, if we can demonstrate the fact that you can save money (utilities will be interested). If they burn high-sulfur coal they could save $30,000, $40,000 per day per boiler by using a system like ours today. Whether the legislation is passed or not, the mood will be to put it in because it makes money for them. People do things to make money. Not to be a good Boy Scout. Industry is not a good Boy Scout unless they're made to be.

Industry only complies with something if the guy sits there and writes them a citation: "Listen, if you pollute it's going to cost you $10,000 per day. If you don't stop this, we're going to close you." Then they're going to listen.

Q. *Have you had discussions with the government?* 6

A. Not yet. . . . I can't go and talk to anybody based on the test plant and based on a study. We have to invest the time and money to take this test information, this test plant, into a working actual utility. Once we have it in the utility and it's working—when it's proven— then we can go and do a lot of talking.

My personal opinion is there's going to be a lot of things done come 1990. The Reagan administration is going to put out some money for research and development. Hopefully they may come up with some answers. I can only say our system may be one answer.

---

3. All of the people questioned for this *Psychology Today* article by the magazine's editor, Patrice Horn (May 1987), were interviewed by the same person, but the interviewer's questions were not included in the anthology of responses. After reading the responses, make a list of what you think the interviewer's questions were. State what you think the interviewer's intended purpose was and comment on how the sequence of questions achieved that purpose.

Allen Funt
Host of "Candid Camera," a popular television show
of the 1950s and 1960s

My happy childhood memories were sparse. I had a sister who was 1 infinitely more intelligent and brilliant and charming in every way than I was. I was sort of in her shadow most of my childhood. I was a terribly insecure guy; I didn't like the way I looked, I wasn't as great an athlete as I wanted to be, and there was always Dorothy, who was great in everything. My parents tried so hard to be evenhanded about it, but [I thought] I was the unfortunate one and she was the gifted one. But eventually, I grew into my own and grew away from her. My greatest memories of childhood were of summer camp. I went to all the New England camps, and it was a very important part of my growing up.

I hope this doesn't sound too childish, but I don't think I've ever 2 felt like a grown-up. I spent much of my life looking for my mother to give me the guidance and the answers that I needed. I haven't had a mother for a long, long time, but that feeling, of not being grown-up— even when good and important things happen to me—I think that I'm just playing like a grown-up, and that someday I might be a grown-up.

I have had numerous turning points in my life that stand out: my 3 second divorce, the advent of the television show [*Candid Camera*] and moving to California and becoming a rancher.

The divorce involved such a radical change in my life. I had to try 4 for the first time in my existence to be entirely alone. It took me three years to work it out; I don't think I really solved anything, but I adjusted.

The show has really been half my life. When it became a success, 5 I didn't even know what a success was. Sitting in New York and reading in *Variety* in 1960 that *Candid Camera* was the number one show in the country was [hard to relate to]. I just didn't feel a part of it. Much of my life has found me watching the parade go by. It's not me.

Moving to California and becoming a rancher, like all good things 6 in my life, was the greatest stroke of luck. I came upon this piece of land—it's a mountain on the Pacific, 1,200 acres—and I just bought it impulsively. It is probably the most beautiful piece of real estate in the world. I feel ecstatic every time I see it.

I have five kids. Each of them is so different that it makes me feel 7 that genes, inheritance and the environment are all so misunderstood. How any five people could be so different I'll never understand. The one thing that they all have in common is that nobody wants to take on where I left off in my work. I think they wisely resisted work that's too close to mine. And they're doing fine.

Joyce Carol Oates
Novelist, critic, professor of literature

I don't believe there was any precise moment when I thought of my- 8 self as an adult. Each of us carries a child within us—fortunately, or unfortunately, depending upon the circumstances. If there was a turning point of any kind, it occurred when I was about 13, with the death of my grandfather, the first death in the family for me.

Happiness tends to be generalized, unlike grief. The childhood 9 was happy in the abstract—a blurred, pleasant, perhaps dream-like memory.

F. Lee Bailey
Prominent defense attorney

I have many happy memories of my childhood. My family was rela- 10 tively poor but happy. In particular, Christmas and Christmas Eve were high points every year.

I first thought of myself as an adult in the military at 19 years of 11 age when I had my first solo flight training. The military was a turning point in my life. It was the military that first thrust me into the practice of law, as there was a shortage of lawyers in the service at that time.

Judy Goldsmith
Former president of National Organization for Women

The happiest moment of my childhood was so clearly delineated that 12 its details still live vividly in my mind.

I was 7 years old. It was a sunny, lovely day in the little Wisconsin 13 town where I was growing up.

Suddenly, bells began to ring and people came out of stores and 14 homes to talk to each other. They were all smiling (there is probably nothing that makes a child happier and more secure than to be surrounded by happy adults). The woman who ran the drugstore on the corner near our house gave out free Hershey candy bars to all the children. Everywhere there was joy and celebration.

There was no way, of course, that I could comprehend the sig- 15
nificance of what my mother told me when I asked her the reason, and
she said, "World War II is over," but I knew it had to be something
really wonderful, and I'd never forget it.

There are many moments when we come to grips with the stark 16
realities of adulthood: the first time we understand that there is no appeal to a higher authority, that we are finally responsible for ourselves;
the first time we realize that no one else will pay for our bills; when we
give birth to our own children and know that we have taken on the
profound obligation of nurturing new life.

I've had more major turning points in my life than I can recount 17
here, but two were especially important.

The first was the birth of my daughter 16 years ago. My husband 18
and I, after 11 years of marriage, decided that we wanted to have a
child, and were profoundly fortunate in the birth of Rachel.

I had two very specific reactions when the nurse first put Rachel 19
in my arms: One was absolute desperation and apprehension. Now, in
this moment of truth, there was no doubt in my mind that motherhood was *not* instinctive! There were surely no answers built into my
genetic codes. I was a novice, a beginner, no two ways about it. Fortunately, so was Rachel.

The other reaction was awe, at the sheer wonder of this little 20
creature. I believed the medical experts who said that a newborn's
eyes can't focus, but it seemed that she looked at me with a wisdom
and seriousness that underscored the responsibilities that lay ahead.
She was heart-stopping in her beauty, touching in her vulnerability,
splendid in her health and strength.

The other major turning point in my life was deciding to become 21
involved nationally in the National Organization for Women.

I knew that the decision to go would make some significant 22
changes in my life (and Rachel's): going from a quiet Midwestern town
to the accelerated pace of Washington, D.C., from a measured academic life to an intensely political one, from peripheral involvement in
issues of social and political concern to involvement that would be
central. Taking the step felt like walking off a cliff.

I decided that it would be irresponsible to pass up such a chance, 23
and I went. Although many of my apprehensions about the move did
indeed materialize, they paled in comparison with the rich and unforgettable drama. Sometimes we need to walk off cliffs.

---

4. Read the two opposing views in the following editorials from *USA Today* (July 15,
1987). Then, design a list of questions (at least five) that you would ask each of the
writers in an interview on the subject of tuition and financial aid costs.

Colleges Must Not Cut Quality to Curb Costs

SHELDON HACKNEY
President of the University of Pennsylvania

Educational opportunities should be determined by a student's abili- 1
ties and interests, not financial status. The individual student benefits,
but so does the nation if students attend the schools that can challenge them.

At Penn, we admit students on their academic qualifications, 2
then work with them to find the necessary financial support. We hold
to that policy despite the rising costs and changes in federal student
aid that have left most U.S. colleges in a financial crunch.

Higher education is a complex and expensive enterprise. It's la- 3
bor intensive, and that labor is highly specialized. Top scholars are expensive to attract and retain, especially in fields such as business, law,
medicine, science, and engineering, where we compete for employees
with the for-profit sector.

The rapid increase in knowledge also has its costs. Major new 4
disciplines are emerging, and simply keeping up with existing ones increases expenses yearly. Lab equipment is more sophisticated and
more expensive now, and computers—Penn, for example, has 10,000
computer work stations—have become an integral part of teaching,
research, and administration.

In recent years, colleges have assumed a greater burden in pro- 5
viding student financial aid, augmenting state and federal aid with
their own funds. This year, more than 40 percent of Penn's students
will receive financial aid, including more than $20 million from univer-
sity resources.

In addition, universities are as large as small cities and require 6
many of the same support services. Penn is the largest private employer in the Philadelphia region; our public safety force is larger than
most of the state's 900 municipal police departments; our annual utility costs are upward of $18 million; and insurance costs have doubled
in two years.

In response to mounting costs, universities have implemented 7
cost-saving programs, ranging from purchasing stationery at bulk rate
to generating their own electrical energy. They have more intelligently
managed their endowment portfolios to provide a more secure economic base and better endowment income, and they have approached
fund-raising more creatively.

Penn will spend $30 million in endowment income this year and 8
raise more than $140 million in research funding, and more than $50
million from alumni and friends to augment tuition revenue, which
covers less than one-half the cost of the education we provide.

Colleges must continue to hold down costs without sacrificing 9
their educational missions. But federal aid is vital both to assist individuals in reaching their potential and to ensure that society will have
an educated citizenry, a future generation of doctors, engineers, teachers, and other college-trained professionals, and the benefit of the kind
of basic research that is best done by academic institutions.

Taxpayer Subsidies Help
Fuel Tuition Hikes

WILLIAM J. BENNETT
U.S. Secretary of Education

As colleges and universities begin announcing next year's tuition in- 1
creases, many parents once again find themselves pained and baffled
by the skyrocketing costs of college education.

Many colleges have announced tuition increases for next year 2
ranging from 4 percent to, in one case, 20 percent—even though inflation in 1986 was only 1.8 percent.

In fact, tuition has risen at twice the rate of inflation since 1980. 3
No wonder that some 82 percent of the American people worry that
college costs will soon be out of reach of most families.

For a while, the higher education establishment denied that much 4
of a problem existed. Recently, though, they have switched gears. The
American Council on Education is now encouraging the higher education community to "intensify its efforts to identify the causes of tuition
inflation."

This is welcome. But it would be better still if the American Coun- 5
cil on Education also urged the higher education community to *act* to
keep tuition inflation down.

Such action is needed. As things now stand, tuition inflation 6
threatens to cancel out the beneficial effects of federal college aid
programs.

Instead of helping families meet the cost of a college education, 7 the $14 billion per year federal subsidy seems to enable college administrators to raise prices ever higher.

While the current structure of federal student aid may not cause 8 tuition inflation, there is little doubt that it helps make it possible— because when colleges raise prices, the taxpayers increase their subsidy to help families make up the difference, then colleges raise tuition again, and so on.

We have proposed reforms that would address this problem. But 9 the primary responsibility for containing education costs cannot lie with the federal government. It lies with our colleges and universities.

No one doubts that there is a lot of fat in some areas of higher 10 education—just as there has been in some areas of U.S. business.

The pressures of economic competition have forced a lot of busi- 11 nesses to slim down and become more cost-efficient. U.S. higher education needs to look to that example, rather than justifying whopping tuition increases by merely saying, as one university official recently said, that "new knowledge is inherently more expensive."

Americans have always been generous when it comes to provid- 12 ing funds for higher education. So we shall remain. But it's time for our colleges and universities to do better at living up to their end of the bargain.

WRITING SUGGESTIONS

1. Public television stations produce several programs using the forum format. Watch one of these programs and write a critique of the moderator. Note the moderator's question level and sequence and how the moderator responds to and directs the members of the group.

2. Choose a common issue, such as which are the best running shoes to buy, and interview three of your classmates on the subject. Integrate their opinions with your own in a short essay that reaches a conclusion.

3. Draw a resource cluster for one of the following subjects or for one of your own interest. Below the cluster make a preliminary list of people you could interview to begin your research. Next to each person's name describe the kind of information you would hope to receive from the interview.
   a. Use of generic drugs
   b. Organ donation
   c. Highway carpooling lanes

d. Buying American products

e. Need for graduate degree

f. Environmental protection

OBSERVATIONS

Frequently your own informal observations initiate your interest in an issue. For instance, when you voted in your first local election, you may have noticed that no one in your age group was there. Were they voting at another location? Did they vote later in the day? Are they even registered to vote? Do they care about politics at all? One way to investigate this issue is through further observation. What will differentiate the second observation from the first is the quality of your "seeing."

The purpose of planning an **observation** is to see more, to selectively narrow your focus on a subject so you can make new discoveries. Most professions require a level of trained observation that results from years of practice; knowing how to look and what to look for are just as important to an accountant as they are to a microbiologist or a civil engineer. And, while methods and criteria for observation may differ according to profession, an open attitude remains essential to conducting an effective observation in all areas.

A primary ingredient to developing an open attitude is desire: you have to care about *what* you are observing and *how* you are observing it. When you have this committed interest, you observe things with an open mind, allowing discoveries to happen.

Equally as important as the openness of your attitude is the quality of objectivity. Being objective doesn't necessarily mean distant and unfeeling. Instead, the emphasis of objectivity in observation is on fairness and accuracy. Perhaps psychoanalyst Erich Fromm explained it best: "Objectivity does not mean detachment, it means respect; that is, the ability not to distort and falsify things, persons, and oneself." To prevent the possibility of such distortion you need to conduct your observations *without* preconceived conclusions. Use your observation as a process of discovery. When you combine openness and fairness in your attitude, you will be more likely to see the rich details and complexities that exist and to report them in a meaningful way for others.

FINDING A FOCUS

From your own experience with taking photos you already know that focusing on a subject doesn't necessarily mean eliminating everything else from the picture. But focusing does mean being selective, especially when planning an observation. After all, there are a limited number of people, things, and activities a person can look at with a high degree of concentration. In this passage from *In the Shadow of Man* (1971) you can see how Jane Goodall adapts her field of vision to accommodate the movement of her focus.

The Eighth Day

On the eighth day of my watch David Graybeard arrived again, to- 1
gether with Goliath, and the pair worked there for two hours. I could
see much better: I observed how they scratched open the sealed-over
passage entrances with a thumb or forefinger. I watched how they bit
the ends off their tools when they became bent, or used the other end,
or discarded them in favor of new ones. Goliath once moved at least fifteen yards from the heap to select a firm-looking piece of vine, and both
males often picked three or four stems while they were collecting tools,
and put the spares beside them on the ground until they wanted them.

Most exciting of all, on several occasions they picked small leafy 2
twigs and prepared them for use by stripping off the leaves. This was
the first recorded example of a wild animal not merely *using* an object
as a tool, but actually modifying an object and thus showing the crude
beginnings of tool-*making*.

Previously man had been regarded as the only tool-making ani- 3
mal. Indeed, one of the clauses commonly accepted in the definition
of man was that he was a creature who "made tools to a regular and
set pattern." The chimpanzees, obviously, had not made tools to any
set pattern. Nevertheless, my early observations of their primitive tool-
making abilities convinced a number of scientists that it was necessary
to redefine man in a more complex manner than before. Or else, as
Louis Leakey put it, we should by definition have to accept the chim-
panzee as Man.

Goodall's focus is clear from the beginning of the passage. She is observing how the
chimpanzees use tools to collect their food (termites). How did she determine that this
should be her focus? Implicit in her decision is her *previous* discovery that the chimps
use tools to collect food. Thus, *how* they use the tools became the next logical focus in
the progression of her observations. And, by keeping an open attitude in her observation, even after eight days of watching the same behavior, she was able to make her
discovery.

As a student you may also use previous research to find a focus for your observation. Information from interviews, especially when combined with previous informal
observations, can be a worthwhile beginning point and can generate multiple perspectives from which you can narrow your focus. In the following article, which appeared in
the *Virginian-Pilot and Ledger-Star* of February 15, 1987, the writer has combined his

informal observations with face-to-face interviews to create interest in a particular focus—the Japanese position in the U.S. home-building market.

Japanese Poised to Enter U.S. Home-Building Market

BRADFORD W. O'HEARN
Los Angeles Times/Washington Post News Service

Your automobile, your stereo, your television, your calculator and your favorite restaurant may already be Japanese. But will your next home or office also be Japanese? 1

Do not be surprised if it happens. 2

In mid-January, over cocktails in Dallas at the nation's largest home-builders show, several U.S. builders, with typical entrepreneurial bravado, said the Japanese will never be major players in America's housing market. 3

The builders rolled out their reasons over bottles of Lone Star beer: They do not know local markets; they build houses of rice paper or steel; they will not accept the risks; they have no sense of American tastes and style in homes; and Japan is too far away economically to ship increasingly popular modular homes. 4

But many of those who have already dealt with savvy Japanese executives in other areas of business are convinced that their entry into the mammoth U.S. home-building market is not a question of whether but simply when. 5

"The only reason the Japanese aren't into homes yet," said Robert G. Johnson, executive director of the International Real Estate Institute in Scottsdale, Ariz., "is that they are now getting greater rates of return and less risk in things like commercial real estate. 6

"But there is only so much prime commercial real estate to be had, and I guarantee you that the Japanese will eventually get into housing, especially multifamily housing, in a big way." 7

The small signs are there already: 8

•Japanese businessmen—there are very few businesswomen— have been seen in steadily increasing numbers at the home-builders convention in recent years, doggedly plodding up and down the aisles of exhibits, collecting one plastic bag full of product information after another. 9

•For the first time, the National Association of Home Builders 10
held a special seminar at the convention aimed squarely at builders
from Japan. The well-attended event offered tips on the latest developments in home automation, trends in architectural and interior design, and apartment development and management.

•A press conference on Japanese investment in the United States 11
attracted as many, perhaps more, reporters and television crews than
did the association's annual housing forecast.

"The Japanese love real estate," said Leanne Lachman, president 12
of the Real Estate Research Corp. in Chicago. "There's not much of it in
Japan, and what little there is seldom changes hands. They have been
studying the U.S. market for years, and last year they started buying
and building."

Noriko Yamamoto is president of Global Link Inc., a California- 13
based company offering market research and other services to home-
building industries in the United States and Japan. She said that in
1984, Japanese investments in U.S. real estate amounted to only $680
million.

But with the yen soaring in value and an increasingly competitive 14
business climate at home, Yamamoto said Japanese investors are entering the American market in droves. Investments, primarily in commercial properties, last year totaled about $5 billion, and that figure is
expected at least to double in 1987.

Although most Japanese investors so far have been the cash-rich 15
large banks and insurance companies, Yamamoto said smaller investors are clamoring for opportunities to export their yen as well.

"The trends show a shift toward smaller investors, not just the 16
big players and institutions," the Japanese-born executive said. "Banks
in Japan have been taking out full-page ads in the newspapers asking
for $1 million investments, and they have their syndicates completed
in a very few days."

The attractions for Japanese investment are many. "There are 17
much higher yields here," Yamamoto said. "In Japan they can expect
yields of 1 to 2 percent; here they can expect 9.5 percent or higher. Also
capital-gains tax rates on property held less than 10 years in Japan are
40 percent; it's 28 percent here. And depreciation schedules are much
shorter in the U.S., even with the new tax law. You have 30-year depreciation. In Japan it's 60 years."

Yamamoto said Japanese investors are often willing to pay top 18
dollar for commercial property, because compared with prices in
Japan, it is still a bargain. "I've heard story after story of Japanese coming in and buying at retail—retail," Johnson said. "People thought they
were out of their gourds. But, with rapid appreciation, as little as three
years later those prices looked very reasonable."

Yamamoto added that some Japanese investors have been buy- 19 ing raw land in the United States for years that could be used for home development. Some companies such as Daiwa House, the fourth-largest prefabricated-housing builder in Japan, have already started learning the U.S. market by building traditional homes in Texas and California.

Most experts who have followed Japanese investment practices 20 say their entry into home-building will be similar to their entry into other businesses: first, joint ventures or partnerships with American companies, and later, solo ventures.

"They are getting their comfort levels up," Johnson said, "and 21 they will slowly branch out on their own."

James Mooney, managing director of Landauer Associates, one of 22 the nation's larger real-estate counselors, said, "All indications are that the Japanese will soon replace the British as the largest foreign owners of U.S. investment properties."

One of the first things you might notice about this article is that the writer does not reach any conclusions. He does, however, generate several focuses for further observation: Do the Japanese show this same interest at other home-building conventions? Do Americans recognize this interest by the programs they provide at the conventions? Are there signs of partnerships with American companies in the home-building industry? If so, how many and where? To what extent and where have the Japanese already started buying and building?

To discover the answers to some of these questions you can observe on-the-spot human behavior, but for other answers you might need to study documents or reports. Formulating your interests into questions will help you see the multiple perspectives from which you can observe the subject. And, as implied by both Goodall's research and our questions about the Japanese interest in home building, one observation will rarely be enough to provide the amount of primary source information you need to make a generalization or draw a conclusion.

With these features in mind, you can use a resource cluster to identify focuses for observation. Let's use the question "Do television viewing habits affect students' grade point averages (GPA)?" as a sample research problem. Figure 2 is a resource cluster that breaks down the subject—first, into its possible observable components and, second, into possible multiple perspectives.

Clustering the resource possibilities for observations demonstrates the complexity of the issue, but it can also help you plan a logical progression for your focus. In this example, while you can watch where and when students view television, you can't tell students' GPAs just by looking at them. Therefore, to observe the relationship in question you would probably narrow your focus by selecting students with specific GPA levels to observe. Then you would decide how to collect data on these students' tele-

Figure 2 *Cluster diagram of observation possibilities*

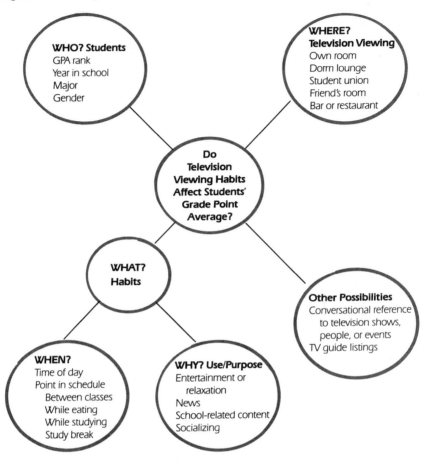

vision viewing habits and how long to observe them. The next section will give you some ideas for this stage of your research.

Finding a focus, then, should be a logical progression in the reasoning chain of what you want to know. Previous research, interviews, prior informal observations, and reading can help you identify your focus. But identifying a focus also means looking for multiple perspectives from which to observe the subject so you can preserve the objectivity and attitude of discovery required for effective observation.

COLLECTING AND RECORDING THE DATA

In research, recording observations requires some form of **systematic notation.** The key word here is *systematic.* A *system,* in its most basic sense, is a group or network of interrelated elements that form a collective unity. *Notation* itself is also a system—a system of figures or symbols used to represent meaning (as in musical notation and chemical notation).

Three forms of collecting and recording data have given us invaluable historical information: the diary, the log, and the journal. All three provide the systematic record that close observation requires, yet they differ in their use of selectivity, making them useful for different purposes.

The log is probably the most commonly used form of record keeping; it certainly is the most objective. Most businesses and organizations use logs to keep track of such daily activities as orders, deliveries, patients, employees' work hours, location of vehicles and shipments, or prescriptions. In this respect logs have a high level of focus or selectivity; that is, every time a particular "thing" occurs at a particular "place," it is logged in. And, because logs record physical events with minimal detail, the information is objective. Look for these features in the two logs presented here. The first log is from James Moffett's book *Points of Departure* (1985); the second (Figure 3) from an art supply store.

A Week in the Life

from Sheriff's Log of Madera County, California, 1983

November 10

10:45 AM *A suspicious person was reported to be at the Coarsegold Frostie. Upon officer's arrival, subject was inside drinking coffee, causing no problems.*

4:10 PM *North Fork Elementary reported a 14 year old student driving his parent's vehicle.*

November 11

1:40 AM *Ahwahnee Hills School reported a walkaway. Juvenile was later reported to be at father's home in the Bay area.*

11:15 AM *A Coarsegold man reported a young juvenile riding a motorcycle on his property.*

12:30 PM *The Narrow Gauge Inn in Fish Camp reported the theft of a sign from their driveway. $620 loss.*

2:05 PM Renata Atkins, of North Fork, was the victim of burglary to her residence. $200 loss.

8:05 PM An Oakhurst man was taken into custody for public intoxication.

November 12

12:30 AM A 20 year old North Fork woman was charged with using a false I.D. for purchasing alcoholic beverages.

10:00 AM Ellen Winston, of Ahwahnee, reported a burglary to her residence and theft of a generator from her property.

10:00 AM Bruce Patrickson, of Coarsegold, reported malicious mischief to a residence under construction. A window was broken, but no sign of theft. $50 damage.

1:04 PM Sierra Ambulance requested assistance with a woman down call. On officer's arrival, ambulance crew had everything under control. Victim was up and around.

1:45 PM A downed aircraft was reported northeast of Bass Lake on Iron Mountain. Search and Rescue (SAR) operation organized.

9:42 PM An Oakhurst man reported a prowler at his residence. Deputy unable to locate responsible.

Notice how both logs are organized by date and time. Although both record calls, they differ in how the information is recorded. While the sheriff's log reports who, what, when, and where, the art supply store phone log (Figure 3) records frequency of the type of call made. Because they are logs, neither interprets the information as it is recorded. However, the accumulation of material allows you to see the pattern of events and therefore to make generalizations about the behavior during a particular period.

Another feature of logs that you will need to consider is *who* records the data. In most cases the type of data recorded does not require a highly trained observer. However, you can collect more personalized data using a log format if you select different types of people to record similar information about themselves. For instance, several ratings companies have families and individuals keep radio and television logs for one to six months. While each participant merely logs in the station, program, and time of listening or viewing, the results are interpreted according to the participants' age, education level, profession, and socioeconomic group.

Diaries also provide a daily record but, unlike logs, diaries are neither selective nor

Figure 3 *Art supply store phone log*

Saturday, June 3

Time	Store Hrs.	Store Items & Prices	Type of Call "How To"	Questions About Local Exhibits & Classes	Personal
10:00–11:00	ЖІ III	ЖІ	I	III	
11:00–12:00	III	IIII	ЖІ III		
12:00–1:00	IIII	ЖІ	IIII	I	III
1:00–2:00		IIII	ЖІ I	III	
2:00–3:00	II	III	IIII	II	I
3:00–4:00		II	II		
4:00–5:00	IIII	I	III		
5:00–6:00	II				ЖІ

objective. Instead, they are a daily collection of personal responses, a miscellaneous mixture of thoughts and feelings. While this information can offer details about a particular era or a phase in a person's life, it lacks objectivity.

Journals, on the other hand, can be focused on a particular activity or project, giving them the selectivity needed for observational research. But because journal entries are generally made in narrative form, the recorder's subjective feelings are often included to some degree. In the journal entry below from Charles Darwin's *Voyage of the Beagle*, you can see that while Darwin focuses his observations on the land and people of Tierra del Fuego, he includes some subjective reactions as well.

Voyage of the *Beagle*

CHARLES DARWIN

January 22, 1833

22nd.—After having passed an unmolested night, in what would appear to be neutral territory between Jemmy's tribe and the people whom we saw yesterday, we sailed pleasantly along. I do not know anything which shows more clearly the hostile state of the different tribes, than these wide border or neutral tracts. Although Jemmy Button well knew the force of our party, he was, at first, unwilling to land amidst the hostile tribe nearest to his own. He often told us how the savage Oens men "when the leaf red," crossed the mountains from the eastern coast of Tierra del Fuego, and made inroads on the natives of this part of the country. It was most curious to watch him when thus talking, and see his eyes gleaming and his whole face assume a new and wild expression. As we proceeded along the Beagle Channel, the scenery assumed a peculiar and very magnificent character; but the effect was much lessened from the lowness of the point of view in a boat, and from looking along the valley, and thus losing all the beauty of a succession of ridges. The mountains were here about three thousand feet high, and terminated in sharp and jagged points. They rose in one unbroken sweep from the water's edge, and were covered to the height of fourteen or fifteen hundred feet by the dusky-coloured forest. It was most curious to observe, as far as the eye could range, how level and truly horizontal the line on the mountain side was, at which trees ceased to grow; it precisely resembled the high-water mark of drift-weed on a sea-beach. . . .

Long narrative entries provide the necessary context, but in some cases they also make it difficult to extract relevant data. To include context in the entries and still retain the objectivity and the notated form, you may want to design an entry format that directs observation more selectively in the journal. Here are examples of a log and a journal kept on television viewing for one day. Note how the journal entry format is designed to include the context of viewing.

LOG: TELEVISION VIEWING

Thursday, February 18, 1988	12:30 PM
7:00 AM	1:00 PM MTV (Cable)
7:30 AM Today Show (NBC)	1:30 PM MTV (Cable)
8:00 AM Today Show (NBC)	2:00 PM
8:30 AM	2:30 PM
9:00 AM	3:00 PM
9:30 AM	3:30 PM
10:00 AM	4:00 PM
10:30 AM	4:30 PM
11:00 AM	5:00 PM
11:30 AM	5:30 PM MASH (Ch. 11)
12:00 Noon	6:00 PM

LOG: TELEVISION VIEWING

6:30 PM National News (NBC)	10:30 PM
7:00 PM Wheel of Fortune (ABC)	11:00 PM
7:30 PM Jeopardy (ABC)	11:30 PM
8:00 PM	12:00 Midnight
8:30 PM	12:30 AM David Letterman (NBC)
9:00 PM Cheers (NBC)	1:00 AM
9:30 PM	1:30 AM
10:00 PM	2:00 AM

JOURNAL: TELEVISION VIEWING

Thursday, February, 18, 1988

What & when:	7:30–8:30 AM Today Show (NBC)
Where:	Dorm room
Why:	Hear news & weather
Comments:	Mostly listened while getting ready for class

What & when:	1:00–2:00 PM MTV (Cable)
Where:	Student union
Why:	Relax and visit with friends
Comments:	No new videos

What & when:	5:30–6:00 PM MASH (Ch. 11)
Where:	Dorm room
Why:	Relax alone
Comments:	Favorite show

What & when:	6:30–7:00 PM National News (NBC)
Where:	Dorm room
Why:	Info for political science class
Comments:	

What & when:	7:00–7:30 PM Wheel of Fortune (ABC)
Where:	Dorm lounge
Why:	See Vanna and socialize
Comments:	A real spectator sport

What & when:	7:30–8:00 PM Jeopardy (ABC)
Where:	Dorm lounge
Why:	Group competition
Comments:	I sure don't know much about art.

What & when:	9:00–9:30 PM Cheers (NBC)
Where:	Dorm room
Why:	Humor, relax
Comments:	Study break

What & when:	12:30–1:00 AM David Letterman (NBC)
Where:	Dorm room
Why:	Viewer mail night
Comments:	When is he going to read our letter?

At first glance the journal may seem to be a better form to use because it includes more information, but your decision should be based on your purpose. If you are interested only in the number of shows people watch per day or in the time of day people watch TV, the log may be the better choice. Or you may want to use both to observe different perspectives. The manageability of the form for your data should govern your choice. Both are useful because they are selectively focused, have objectivity, and do not interpret or draw conclusions.

PRESENTING RESULTS

After your observations are collected, you need to organize the data for interpretation. When observations focus on when, how frequently, where, and to what extent something occurs, you must count occurrences before you can discover what patterns emerge. If you have observed how a specific behavior changes, you will need to identify a range of details to describe those changes. And, of course, you may have a combination of both to organize. In some clear way you need to combine your data and organize it visually before you can interpret it. This is generally accomplished with charts using the criteria of your focus. The following student examples demonstrate procedures you can use.

This student was investigating student complaints about the lack of parking on campus (see Figures 4, 5, and 6).

By counting the number of occurrences for a range of behaviors and converting these numbers to percentages, the student was able to view the data proportionally as well. Percentages can be displayed visually using bar graphs or pie graphs if the representation will help your audience understand the information.

Some observations may require a different treatment. For example, another student who investigated the cause of accidents where he worked found that after his

Figure 4 *Student's observation log I*

Observation Log I

Tuesday, 7 July 1987
Time: 18:57
BAL parking lot has 20 empty spaces and there are 2 cars illegally parked.
Time: 19:10
BAL parking lot has 3 empty spaces and there are 13 cars illegally parked.

Wednesday, 8 July 1987
Time: 18:55
BAL parking lot is filled to capacity and there are 6 cars illegally parked.
Time: 19:10
BAL parking lot is filled to capacity and there are 8 cars illegally parked.

Note: On both occasions, the parking lot behind the library was 75% empty.

Figure 5 *Student's observation log II*

Observation Log II

Thursday, 9 July 1987
At 08:57 BAL parking lot has 25 spaces left and the parking lot behind it is empty.

Number of cars entering the parking lot	Time
5	09:00
5	09:05
5	09:10
20	09:15
15	09:20
3	09:25
0	09:30

At 09:11 the BAL parking lot is filled to capacity and at 09:30 there are 5 spaces left in the second parking lot. At this point there are 4 cars illegally parked at a tow-away zone next to BAL.

At 09:30 I began observing other parking lots.
Behind the library:
      8 cars present, parking lot nearly empty
Behind MGB:
      50 cars present, over 50% of lot empty
Behind chem building:
      24 cars present, over 75% of lot empty
Behind Webb Center:
      19 cars present, over 75% empty
HPE parking lot:
      10 cars, virtually empty
Beside Webb Center and Chandler Hall:
      Parking lot has 30 empty spaces and there are 6 cars illegally
      parked under the shade of some trees.
On Elkhorn Avenue between HPE parking lot and the four other parking lots:
      There are 27 cars illegally parked.

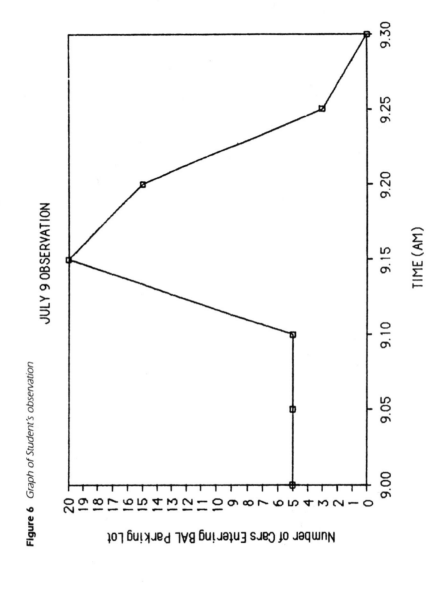

Figure 6 *Graph of Student's observation*

Figure 7 *Student's diagram of problem area between speed bumps*

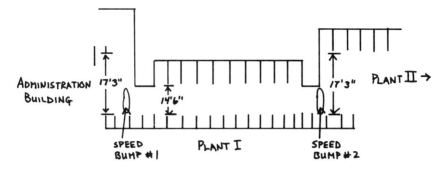

interviews he needed to study the physical dimensions of the lot more closely to understand and explain the other data he collected. Figure 7 represents those observations. He also included the diagram in his final report to clarify his references to accidents that had occurred.

Whether or not you include your observational charts depends on the needs of the audience and the complexity of the data. If combining different sources of observation into a single chart can demonstrate the relationships you discovered, visual representation could make your information clearer and more convincing. You should, however, avoid insulting your audience with pages of simplistic frequency counts.

Still, your data must be presented in your final report in some way. In presenting your observations you should emphasize the generalizations you feel confident in making from interpreting the data. Observational research is inductive: when the same behavior occurs repeatedly under the same conditions, we tend to believe that it will happen most of the time. Your confidence in your generalizations can be only as strong as the integrity of your observations. Are you sure you looked closely enough, long enough, and frequently enough? Did you examine the problem from enough perspectives? Obviously the more fully developed your observations, the more important their role in your report. If you were limited by time constraints or the availability of resources, you should state these limitations when reporting your findings and use the information in a less strategic position in your argument.

Here is how the student investigating accidents at work chose to report his findings. His generalizations are underscored.

STUDENT'S REPORT

On three different days (Friday, June 26; Monday, June 29; Wednesday, July 1), I observed the parking area to determine if speeding was indeed the problem. I expected to find Friday's speeding to be worse than the other days but instead was surprised to note the speeding was just as prevalent on Monday and Wednesday. Inspecting the stretch of parking lot in a physical sense showed that the problem area was narrower than the other parking area lanes by 2'9" and likewise was not marked with road dividers (i.e., painted lines dividing the two lanes). Two-way traffic is possible, but there is little room for error on the part of the drivers. It is ironic to note that many of the people expressing concern in the survey about the speeds driven in this area were themselves travelling well over the posted speed limit of 15 miles per hour. It was almost as if the speed bumps installed by the company became a starting and ending point where drivers would, and could, test their car's ability to accelerate.

EXERCISES: OBSERVATIONS

1. After reading this list of people who applied for marriage licenses (from the *Virginian-Pilot and Ledger-Star*), formulate a primary research question and draw a resource cluster indicating potential sources for observation of your issue.

Licensed to Wed

Ernest Lewis Jr., 55, and Ruth Hall Bandy, 35, 719 W. 27th St.

James Earl Jones Sr., 44, and Marjorie Lee Reese, 41, 600 Warwick Ave.

Johnie Ray Coffey, 22, and Patricia Dale Tate, 27, 123-D View Ave.

Joey Lewis Waugh, 19, 9516 Chesapeake St., and Michelle Elizabeth Baines, 18, 1907 Edgewood Ave.

Johnathan Michael Bigelow Jr., 23, Fairfax, and Brenda Marie Martin, 23, 5915 Appleton Drive.

Benjamin Tyrone Thompson, 32, Virginia Beach, and Phyllis Anita Moore, 31, 7244 Oakmont Drive.

Robert Eugene Pullins, 33, and Sandra Rosemary Alberta, 31, 3729 E. Ocean View Ave.

Thomas James Armstrong, 24, and Patricia Ann Wing, 29, 8141 Shore Drive.

Joseph Harold Anderson, 29, Portsmouth, and Catherine Ann Voigt, 28, 217 Bradford Ave.

George Eis, 20, USS Charleston, and Donna Mattia Trifeletti, 27, Norfolk Naval Station.

Anthony Fitzgerald Silver, 21, 6401 Partridge St., and Adrienne Gail Jackson, 18, Virginia Beach.

Joseph Woodrow Beckner Jr., 35, and Margaret Conant Oakley, 28, 338 W. Freemason St.

Stephen Russell Bobbitt, 31, 3020 Tarrant Drive, and Minnie Ann Kopp, 39, 2319 E. Ocean View Ave.

James Eddie Boone Jr., 20, and Cynthia Louise Rhem, 19, 1566 Lea View Ave.

Eugene Allen Jr., 22, and Nadine Ann Suey, 22, 523 Ashlawn Drive.

Terry Vaughn Boothe, 22, and Cheryl Denise Phipps, 19, 219 Balview Ave.

Daniel Joseph Ferrell, 27, Currituck, N.C., and Sandra Louise Jones, 26, 8141 Shore Drive.

Mitchell Erwin Crawford, 29, and Antoinette Claire Tarricone, 23, 1866 Parkview Ave.

James Michael Ten Broeck, 21, and Lorraine Elizabeth Elias, 19, 1644 W. Little Creek Road.

Abdol Hamid Shirzad, 28, and Cheryl Ann Ribblett, 25, 513-B Hicks Ave.

Daniel Kevin Taylor, 24, 9304 Mason Creek Road, and Carol Ann Dunbar, 23, 228 Maple Ave.

Gary Belmer, 19, USS Harry E. Yarnell, and Jeanette Wilson, 18, 2719 Liberia Drive.

George Frances Boucher, Jr., 24, and Diane Lynn Core, 20, 8522 Chesapeake Blvd.

Bradley Eugene Pufpaff, 21, and Kellilee Ann Campbell, 21, 4508 E. Ocean View Ave.

Randy Scott Bacon, 21, and Deborah Darlene Dow, 18, 9630 23rd Bay St.

Ronald Eugene Barrington, 30, 215 Hough Ave., and Darlene Parker, 28, 860 W. 34th St.

Gary Fred Kuester II, and Christie Joan Lammers, 18, 3814 E. Ocean View Ave.

Leonard Alan Greene, 25, and Myra Andrea Nelson, 20, 9625 28th Bay St.

Thomas Lewis Donald Jr., 21, and Monica Lynn Smith, 18, 4140 E. Ocean View Ave.

James Edward Johnson Jr., 19, Sandra Irene Paris, 20, 1426 W. Ocean View Ave.

Steven Shea Snyder, 33, Virginia Beach, and Marcia Lynn Green, 30, 107 Sinclair St.

Anthony LaMott Speights, 22, Ettrick, Va., and Zina Bethea Norman, 20, 1031 W. 36th St.

Ricky Jones, 26, and Stephanie Renee McCaw, 18, 4720 Pleasant Ave.

James Anthony Coy, 28, and Robin Annette Helms, 25, 4506 E. Ocean View Ave.

Matthew Woodard Watson, 24, and Kimberly Michelle Hunter, 22, 1404 Longdale Drive.

Jay Anthony Daigle, 21, and Tammy Kay Dobbs, 19, 9531 6th Bay St.

Michael John Krawczyk, 24, and Mary Elizabeth Keefe, 24, 5753 Don Drive.

---

2. The following article from the *Los Angeles Times* (July 31, 1987) demonstrates the natural progression of observation that produces discoveries. After reading the article, identify the various observations according to these categories: Prior to Discovery, Discovery, Future. In addition to those observations planned for the future, add those you would like to see conducted. Consider multiple perspectives in your list of future predictions.

Frog Leads Researcher to Powerful New Antibiotics

THOMAS H. MAUGH II

A chance observation by a federal researcher working with a common 1 laboratory frog has led to the discovery of a new family of naturally occurring antibiotics that kill an unusually wide variety of germs.

The discovery adds credence to the growing belief that virtually 2 all animals and insects—including humans—have previously unknown chemical defenses that provide at least some protection against many infections, said Michael Zasloff, a molecular biologist at the National Institute of Child Health and Human Development.

If so, he said in an interview Thursday, these defense systems 3 could be exploited to provide new drugs for fighting human disease. The compounds should be particularly valuable, Zasloff added, because they have a different mechanism of action than existing antibiotics and thus should kill microorganisms that have grown resistant to conventional antibiotics, such as the bacteria that cause venereal disease.

Preliminary studies in animals suggest that the new antibiotics 4 may also have fewer side effects than most antibiotics now in use.

The newly discovered agents are the third family of so-called 5 peptide antibiotics to be discovered in recent years.

Robert Lehrer, a professor of medicine at UCLA who discovered 6 one of the other families of peptide antibiotics, said the new antibiotics are particularly exciting because they kill many different germs.

"Most antibiotics are effective against either bacteria or fungi," he 7 said. "These kill both, and many other microorganisms as well."

The new discovery, to be officially announced today, is to be published in the Aug. 15 issue of the prestigious Proceedings of the National Academy of Sciences.

Zasloff, a pediatrician with a doctorate in biochemistry, made his 9 observations while working on African clawed frogs, which are widely used in biological research because they are very hardy.

For five years, he had been surgically removing the frogs' ovaries 10
to obtain their eggs, which have a high concentration of DNA, for his
studies on genetics. After the surgery, the incisions were sutured and
the frogs were placed back into a tank filled with murky brown water
teeming with bacteria, their natural environment.

Different Perspective

One day last July, Zasloff said, he suddenly viewed the frogs' re- 11
covery from surgery through new eyes. "The miracle of that healing is
that the wounds do not get infected . . . despite the very dirty environment of the tanks that they are thrown back into after surgery. Why
is that?"

Intrigued, Zasloff studied the surgical wounds under a micro- 12
scope and discovered no accumulation of white blood cells or other
evidence that the frog's immune system was fighting off infection. "If
the wound heals without any assistance from the immune system, then
it must be protected by something in the skin or circulation," he said.

Working alone and often late into the night in his narrow, clut- 13
tered laboratory on the 10th floor of the Clinical Center at the National
Institutes of Health in Bethesda, Md., just outside Washington, Zasloff
attempted to find the antibiotic that he was sure was present.

Two Peptides Identified

He skinned the frogs, ground the skin up, and then treated it 14
chemically to break it down further. He then separated the various
components and tested each one to see if it would kill bacteria.

After several false starts, earlier this year he found a component 15
that, when applied to a Petri dish coated with bacteria, left a clear
circle where all of the bacteria were dead.

Further purification led to the identification of two peptides, 16
short chains of the amino acids from which proteins are built. He
named the peptides "magainans" (pronounced ma-GAY-nins) from the
Hebrew word for "shield."

After he had identified the 23 amino acids in each magainan, a 17
biotechnology company made synthetic forms of the magainans. Zasloff found that the synthetic magainans—like the natural peptides—
killed many different bacteria, fungi and protozoa in test tubes and
that they had very low toxicity in laboratory animals. Such synthetic
agents can be produced in much greater quantities.

The test results were so promising, Zasloff said, that about 25 Na- 18
tional Institutes of Health scientists are now studying the magainans,

testing them against viruses and cancer cells in test tubes and against bacteria in animals. The government has patented them, he added, and several drug companies are negotiating with the institutes for a license.

Zasloff believes that human trials of the drugs could begin in as 19 little as two years, probably to treat burns, in which damage to the skin destroys the body's protective barrier against infection.

Zasloff is now looking for the magainans in humans and is con- 20 fident that they will be found. "Almost every substance that has been identified in the frog has had its analog found in mammals," he said. The most likely source of magainans will be the mouth or the gut, he said, so he is looking in saliva and stomach fluids.

"One of the mysteries to me is how you can live with the massive 21 amount of bacteria in your gut and your mouth and never know it," he said. "You can bite your tongue and not get an infection, but if you bite your arm you do."

The first peptide antibiotics were discovered in the late 1970s by 22 Swedish microbiologist Hans Boman, who isolated three from the Cecropium moth.

"It was thought that these were a fluke of the invertebrates," Zas- 23 loff said, and nobody thought they would be found in other organisms.

The moth antibiotics, called cecropins, contain 37 amino acids 24 and their composition is quite different from that of the magainans, Zasloff said. Nonetheless, the three-dimensional structures of the cecropins and magainans are nearly identical, he added, suggesting that they may act by the same mechanism. The cecropins are being studied by Swedish drug companies, Zasloff said.

The other peptide antibiotics were discovered in rabbits and 25 guinea pigs, also in the 1970s, by UCLA's Lehrer. They are found in neutrophils, white blood cells that surround germs identified by the immune system and destroy them. These compounds, called defensins, have since been found also in human neutrophils.

Lehrer's group is now trying to synthesize the defensins. If they 26 could be given as a drug, they could kill bacteria that the immune system could not fight off.

---

3. Assume that the birth announcements presented on the next page represent the total amount of information collected from the log of the two hospitals. Make a list of generalizations you would be willing to state from this data.

Births

General Hospital

Kathleen and Robert Cramer, 1406 Sunset Drive, a boy.

Ellen and Darnell Knight, 3241 Granby St., a boy.

Marvalene and Alexander Bethea, 6600 Chesapeake Blvd., a girl.

Patricia and Christopher Dowell, 5656 Tidewater Drive, a boy.

Robin Goodwin, 1934 Greenleaf Drive, a girl.

Anita Riggins, 9528 15th Bay St., a girl.

Kimbery Dunbar, 9660 Shore Drive, a boy.

Christina and Joey Durden, 9449 Mason Creek Road, a girl.

Michelle Hopkins, 802 Craig St., a boy.

Valerie Jones, 1368 Bolton St., a boy.

Terry and Solomon Smith, 1419 Alsace Ave., a boy.

Tracie Worrell, 442 Virginia Ave., a girl.

Hyang and Eueal Carter, 2304 Wharton Ave., a boy.

Paulette Fuller, 1511 Kile Circle, a girl.

Andrea and Tony LeSane, 7422 Gregory Drive, a boy.

Angela and Christopher Miller, 411 Birmingham Ave., a girl.

Judy and Christopher Stoll, 907 Gates Ave., a boy.

Sabrina Whaff, 2650 Ballentine Blvd., a girl.

Sandra and Albert Yarbrough, 5007 Cape Henry Ave., a boy.

Julie Dempsey, 2416 Hill St., a girl.

Cynthia and Steven McCoy, 2920 Tidewater Drive, a boy.

Katrina Williams, 2716 E. Princess Anne Road, a boy.

St. Paul Hospital

Grace and Kelly N. Parrish, 3531-H Mangrove Ave., a girl.

Cheryl and Ralph M. Watson, 8107 Old Ocean View Road, a girl.

Helen and Lawrence P. Shipp, Jr., 3752 Tait Terrace, a girl.

Teresa Marie Payne, 922 Denison Ave., a girl.

Laurie and Kevin W. Cook, 1881 Brookwood Road, a boy.

Connie and Billy Joe Cook, 9615 25th Bay St. Apt. 31, a boy.

Lisa and Joseph A. Guagenti, 5477 Bayberry Drive, a girl.

Judith Marie Beck, 119 Beechwood Ave., a boy.

Georgia and Eric A. Tyson, 2830 Somme Ave., a boy.

Cathy and William E. Lawrence, 9621 Chesapeake Blvd., a girl.

Huey-Jiuan and Chun-Neng Kuo, 1063 W. 45th St., a girl.

Linda and Felix N. Brooks, 9530-B 28th Bay St., a boy.

Elizabeth and Wayne F. Jones, Jr., 508 Connecticut Ave., a girl.

Lisa and Angel A. Burgos, Jr., 2824-B Early St., a girl.

Catherine and Jerry T. Samotis, 1713 S. Oriole Drive, a girl.

Diane and Kirby J. Van Pelt, 4-19-2B Pleasant Ave., a boy.

WRITING SUGGESTIONS

1. Choose something in your own behavior you are concerned about, such as the amount of chocolate you eat or the number of hours you study per day. Keep a log or a journal focused on this behavior for one to two weeks and write up the results. Be prepared to explain why you chose the data-collecting method you used.

2. Using the subject you clustered for the interview section or a different subject, draw a new resource cluster for possible observations (include multiple perspectives). From this cluster design a logical progression of observations and the methods you would use to collect the data. Write a memo to your teacher proposing your plans.

SURVEYS

Surveys add the dimension of community to your collection of primary source information. While interviews provide the insider's view and observations reveal general descriptions of behavior and events, surveys present a panoramic view. The survey asks, "You who are the human context of this problem, whose lives will be affected by its outcome, what do you think?"

In most cases the affected group will consist of at least thousands, perhaps millions, of people. **Surveys** have the advantage of efficiently reaching a representative sample of these people. Their opinions and attitudes give you a more comprehensive frame of reference from which to understand the extent of the conflict. Your own interest in the issue probably makes you a part of this group. Are your opinions similar to or different from those of others? In what way? The results of your survey should give you a measure of the multiple dimensions of the issue.

The most common methods for conducting surveys are polls and questionnaires. Both use a set of questions to elicit public opinion, but they are administered differently. Polls—the name accurately implies a relationship to voting—are generally conducted in person at polling places or on the phone. People cast their votes on an issue as they see it at that moment. You have noticed that, particularly in election years or other periods of controversy, polls are conducted at regular intervals to gauge the immediacy of public opinion in response to each new candidate or issue. And the results of the polls, which are usually published within days, have the effect of encouraging people to get more involved in the issue, to think about it more carefully. Polls are often conducted house to house, outside voting places immediately before or after a vote is cast, or in large public gathering places, such as malls, to achieve a range of community opinion.

Questionnaires, which are generally mailed to a representative sector of a population, give the respondent more time to contemplate the questions. But because the respondent must fill in answers and return the form, questionnaires rely more on concerned interest. The rate of return could limit your result. And, because this process is longer, time is an important factor.

The effectiveness of either method, however, depends on your identification of target groups, the reliability of your sampling, the fairness of your questions, and the interpretation of your results.

IDENTIFYING THE TARGET GROUP

Who knows the background and circumstances of the issue?

Whose opinion can make a difference?

Who will be affected?

These are the groups you need to consider in choosing who to survey. The larger the group in proportion to the whole and the more random the selection, the more reliable the results. *Size and randomness equal reliability in identifying a target group.* By using your original resource cluster or by extending it, you can begin to determine which target group or groups to survey. Let's use the television problem from the previous section as an example. While you can interview sociologists and students and observe student habits, your survey resource cluster could be expanded to include the resources shown in Figure 8. The survey cluster reveals possibilities for either several specialized surveys or one general survey that includes related groups with specialized views. To

Figure 8 *Cluster diagram of survey target groups*

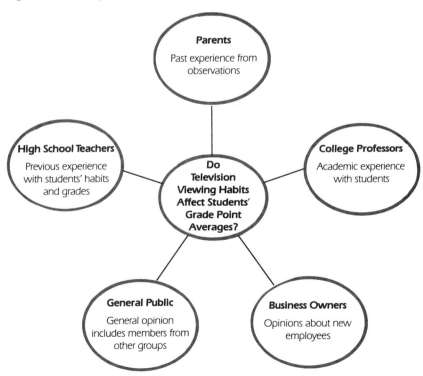

ensure randomness, each member of the groups you choose to survey should have an equal proportional chance to be questioned. In this case, you would need to determine the proportion that each specialized view represents in the total population of the group being surveyed: Do college professors constitute 10 percent of the community? Do business owners constitute 25 percent? Are these people also parents? From what point of view do you wish them to answer? Can they separate their respective viewpoints easily? To obtain results as valid as possible, you must take these considerations into account before identifying your group and designing your poll. In fact, when you plan to survey the general public, you need to allow for special characteristics that will affect your results—for instance, socioeconomic levels, geographic distribution, ethnic and racial diversity, educational background, age, political affiliation, and gender.

In addition to proportionality, size and randomness requirements must be met for your results to be valid. You need to make every effort to use as large a sample as possible with proportional representation. Randomness can be achieved by assigning a statistical random table of numbers to each potential subject and choosing numbers at regular intervals (for instance, every fifth number) or using some other method that provides anonymity and fair representation.

Here is a description of how the *New York Times* conducted a 1987 poll. Note the care with which the newspaper explains how people were chosen, how the survey was conducted, and how the results can be interpreted.

How the Poll Was Conducted

The latest New York Times/CBS News Poll is based on telephone interviews conducted May 11 through 14 with 1,254 adults around the United States, excluding Alaska and Hawaii, of whom 991 said they were registered to vote. 1

The sample of telephone exchanges called was selected by a computer from a complete list of exchanges in the country. The exchanges were chosen so as to insure that each region of the country was represented in proportion to its population. For each exchange, the telephone numbers were formed by random digits, thus permitting access to both listed and unlisted residential numbers. The numbers were then screened to limit calls to residences. 2

The results have been weighted to take account of household size and number of residential telephones and to adjust for variations in the sample relating to region, race, sex, age and education. 3

In theory, in 19 cases out of 20 the results based on such samples, as the 1,254 adults or the 991 registered voters, will differ by no more than three percentage points in either direction from what would have been obtained by interviewing all adult Americans. The error for smaller subgroups is larger. For example, for registered voters who say 4 they vote in Democratic primaries or in Republican primaries it is plus or minus five percentage points.

In addition to sampling error, the practical difficulties of con- 5
ducting any survey of public opinion may introduce other sources of error into the poll.

A clear explanation accompanying a report of the survey findings enables the reader to interpret the meaning of the results. The conditions of the poll are explained so precisely that the poll's meaning is easy to understand. Because the chart describes a subgroup, you know there is a possibility of a 5 percent difference in either direction. As a reader, you will have to determine whether that margin is acceptable and whether the exclusion of Alaska and Hawaii from the poll makes the results representative enough for your acceptance.

Democrats and the Presidency

The New York Times/CBS News Poll

How Democratic primary voters rate their party's candidates. At left is ranking of those who say they are running or considering running. At right is a ranking including other prominent Democrats.

		Cuomo	25%
Jackson	17%	Jackson	12%
		Bradley	6%
Dukakis	11%	Dukakis	6%
Simon	6%	Simon	5%
		Nunn	4%
Gore	5%	Gore	4%
Gephardt	4%	Gephardt	3%
Babbitt	2%	Babbitt	3%
Clinton	2%	Clinton	2%
Biden	2%	Biden	1%

Based on telephone interviews conducted May 11 through 14 with 453 adults around the United States, excluding Alaska and Hawaii.

The target group for the survey reported by the Associated Press (August 8, 1987) is highly specialized: the Harvard Business School class of 1961. In this case randomness is not a crucial requirement because it is assumed that all members of the class were surveyed; however, if you look carefully, you will notice that the report does not state how many of the 650 members actually responded, an exclusion that casts doubt on the proportionality of the results.

Harvard Grads Happy, Poll Shows

ASSOCIATED PRESS

More than a third of the 650 members of Harvard Business School's   1
Class of 1961 made it to the top of their companies, and most say they
are satisfied with life, a poll shows.

The poll was released at the 25-year reunion of the class, where   2
participants heard Dean John H. McArthur say he wants to add nine
tenured ethics professors.

Ninety-three percent of those responding "feel good or extremely   3
satisfied about the whole of our lives," and 7 percent are unhappy.

Members of the class defined success as "being a good parent   4
and spouse and being true to oneself rather than money and fame."

About 63 percent of them make more than $100,000 a year. Com-   5
panies in which they have risen to the top include American Express,
Equitable Life Assurance Society, Sara Lee Corp., Prime Computer and
Timken Co.

About 400 members of the class donated $3.9 million to Harvard,   6
more than twice the previous record for the 25-year reunion class.

And in the next survey, reported in the *New York Times* January 18, 1987, while the size of the sample sounds impressive, the reader is not informed of the proportionality of the response, geographically or by type of institution. If those considerations are important to the reader, the results would be limited in their influence.

Freshman Attitudes

American college freshmen are more interested in financial success, according to a new survey by the University of California at Los Angeles and the American Council on Education, and less interested than their predecessors in helping others. The study, based on responses from 204,491 students who entered college last fall, also reported less support for the preservation of the environment and a significant drop in support for the legalization of marijuana.

	Agree Strongly or Somewhat		
	Fall 1976	Fall 1985	Fall 1986
The Government is not doing enough to control pollution.	82.4%	78.0%	78.0%
Marijuana should be legalized.	48.9	21.8	21.3
It is important to have laws prohibiting homosexual relationships.	47.0	47.9	52.2
Abortion should be legalized.	55.7*	54.9	58.6
The death penalty should be abolished.	32.6**	26.6	25.4
A couple should live together for some time before deciding to get married.	48.8	47.4	51.1

	Think It Essential or Very Important		
	Fall 1976	Fall 1985	Fall 1986
To promote racial understanding	35.8*	32.0	27.2
To be very well off financially	53.1	70.9	73.2
To help others in difficulty	63.1	63.4	57.2
To be involved in environmental clean-up	27.7	20.3	15.9
To develop a philosophy of life	60.8	43.3	40.6

*1977   **1978

The proportionality and randomness of the group has become a particular problem in assessing the validity of the votes cast on the telephone polling lines television stations are using to survey response to the content of their shows. As the article from the *Virginian-Pilot and Ledger-Star* (July 11, 1987) points out, how the results are presented and how they are used to affect content of the shows, especially when the content is a national news issue, make many people uneasy: Do the responders actually represent public opinion or are their responses merely those of a special—and therefore limited—viewing audience? What do you think, and why?

Viewers "Vote" by Dialing 900, but Pollsters Call It Deceptive

LISA BELKIN
New York Times News Service

Television is using the telephone as an instrument of audience opinion, asking for votes on everything from whether Bernhard Goetz is guilty, to who will win the Super Bowl, to whether a particular television pilot would succeed or fail. But opinion among television executives is divided. 1

The ballots are cast by calling numbers with a 900 prefix; the opinion calls are counted rather than answered. To vote for the Denver Broncos, viewers dial one number. To vote for the New Jersey Giants, they dial another. There is a charge to the caller, usually of 50 cents, a percentage of which is given to the station, which pays nothing for the service. 2

Another form of 900 service is called an "information line," on which callers pay the same 50 cents a call to listen to a tape. Most of the 46,000 lines reserved for information lines (the number will increase to 80,000 this month) are used for sports highlights, financial news, weather reports and other things. 3

As the use of these numbers grows, so do the protests from pollsters—many of whom work within the television industry—who describe the results of the call-ins as misleading. "This is not a scientific poll but it is presented as a scientific poll," said the director of the election and survey unit for CBS, Warren Mitofsky. "They always put their disclaimers on, but then they go on and talk about the results if they were talking about public opinion." 4

But audiences seem to find the numbers intriguing, and stations 5 continue to use them, mostly in regard to entertainment shows. CBS, for instance, is currently presenting a series called "Summer Playhouse" every Friday night. Each of the shows is a pilot for a series the network decided not to run, and the audience is asked to vote on whether they enjoyed the pilot.

NBC used the numbers for "The Most Beautiful Girl in the World" 6 pageant two years ago and said that one million calls were received. Last April, ABC asked viewers to vote for their favorite songs of the decade during a Dick Clark music special, and received 1.3 million calls.

Many of the applications of the 900 numbers, however, are to 7 gauge audience reaction to news events. Several dozen radio stations have leased the lines full time for that purpose, according to AT&T's product manager for 900 service, Andrea West. Just before a verdict was returned in the Goetz trial, the Fox Broadcasting Co.'s "Current Affair" program asked its viewers to vote on his guilt or innocence. (They found him not guilty.)

The lines are so popular that AT&T increased the number late 8 last year, to 128,000 from 80,000. And, according to West, the phone company has developed additional services with television stations in mind and is actively promoting them.

ABC introduced Soap Talk in January, a 900 number that is an- 9 swered by the taped voice of an ABC soap-opera star. The network said the line—which is out of service until the fall—received 5 million calls in the first 11 weeks. Also being pitched to television stations is a concept called "premium numbers," which AT&T is promoting as the future of charity telethons. With this system, a number would be flashed on the screen as a low-overhead way to attract small donations; each call would cost up to $2.50 and would be billed to the charity, with a percentage taken for the telephone company and the host station.

These uses of the telephone earn profits for TV stations. A CBS 10 spokesman, George Schweitzer, stresses that the funds raised from 900 numbers are donated to charity.

More controversial is the question of whether the non-informational numbers should be used for seeking audience opinion.

"It looks like a poll, it sounds like a poll, but it isn't a poll," said 11 Richard Kaplan, executive producer of "Nightline." It was that program that first used the 900 numbers, to gauge audience reaction to the presidential debate between Ronald Reagan and Jimmy Carter in 1980. The show stopped using the lines in 1983, before Kaplan joined the staff, and he vows they will not be used again.

The results of such tallies, according to Kaplan, are skewed be- 12 cause the people who respond are not randomly selected, but choose to make the call. In addition, all phones handle the same number of calls per minute, which gives all callers from a sparsely populated state the chance to get through, whereas callers from a state such as New York are more likely to hear a busy signal.

"I think there are certain circumstances when I can see using a 13 900 number," Kaplan said. "It's great entertainment. When you're voting on football, I think you can have some fun with that. But I don't think you should use a 900 number to decide if we should go to war with Iran and I don't think we should use a 900 number to decide who won a presidential debate."

For every broadcaster who criticizes the system, however, there 14 is another who praises—and uses—it. "A Current Affair" has conducted about one telephone canvass a month in the past year, according to the show's producer, Joachim Blunck, and receives between 10,000 and 40,000 calls each time.

"As far as we're concerned, we're soliciting the opinion of our own viewers," Blunck said. "We're not saying that this is what all the people in the country or all the people in New York think. We're saying this is what the people watching the show think."

The 900 numbers, he said "promote viewer involvement in the program."

"For us," he said, "that's good."

With such a wide range of variables to control in establishing randomness and proportionality, the person who designs and conducts polls and questionnaires needs extensive training to obtain an acceptable level of validity in the results. Consequently, as a college student with limited experience in using these procedures, you must realize and state in your report the limitations of your study; and, further, you should make generalizations ONLY about the group that you survey. If, for example, you poll the students in your chemistry lab and find that they studied for the course an average of 8.25 hours that week, you cannot claim that figure to be typical of all college chemistry students in the country or of all chemistry students in your school or even of those same students during other weeks. But you can use the results to make statements about that particular group for that particular week. If you understand and accept these limitations, your surveys can serve a useful purpose in your research.

Questionnaires operate under many of the same conditions that polls do. However, because questionnaires are generally mailed to the chosen respondents, the percentage of the response may affect your results. To allow for this you need to sample a large enough group for the results to be substantial enough to report. For example, if you wanted to survey the residents of your dorm on an issue, you might choose to distribute questionnaires to 10 of the 100 people living on each of the five floors. If you selected those people randomly and if every person responded, your results would be proportional and representative of 10 percent of your total population. For some research purposes this representation might be enough for your audience to accept. But what if only 15 people returned the questionnaire and two of the floors did not respond at all? In this situation your results would not be substantial enough to use. Had the sample size been larger, the possibility of getting a representative response would have been much greater.

Rarely do large samples yield 100 percent response, even when the survey is conducted by experts. Sometimes questionnaires are lost in the mail or misplaced after they are received; other times people forget about them or choose not to participate. In the explanation of a questionnaire survey presented in *Psychology Today* (July 1987), note both the percentage of response and the means by which the target group was selected.

Survey Facts and Figures

Surveys were sent to three groups: members of the American Produc- 1
tivity Center (APC), a nonprofit organization based in Houston, Texas, that includes more than 300 business, labor, government and academic organizations; members of the American Compensation Association, a nonprofit group based in Scottsdale, Arizona, that includes nearly 10,000 individuals in business, government, public service, education, and consulting; and additional firms that use gain-sharing plans. In all, surveys were sent to about 4,500 locations. APC received 1,598 responses from 40 industry groups that employ nine million people. Among the 1,598 organizational units, 741 produce goods, 741 services and the rest are either government facilities or unclassified operations.

The APC believes these organizations' experiences with reward 2
and human resource systems are typical but points out that the sample has three characteristics that prevent it from being a cross section of businesses. First, it includes many large organizations that are probably more concerned than are smaller companies with issues of productivity, quality and compensation. Second, firms interested enough to respond to this survey are more likely than most to be using innovative approaches. And finally, the APC specifically sought out companies using gain sharing.

Is the 40 percent response rate acceptable for the survey explained above? Although some audiences may need a stronger response rate to accept the data, the first question to ask is "Forty percent of what?" Without a well-defined target group appropriate to the purpose of the survey, the reliability factors of size, proportionality, and randomness are meaningless. The limitations listed in the survey explanation relate to the problem of bias in selecting a target group. If the issue at hand were whether or not the university should improve facilities for fraternities and sororities, members of those organizations would surely be biased. But, if you want to know whether or not artificial turf is easier to play on, you would survey those who actually play on the turf. When you select a group to be surveyed, you expect their combined opinions to register a *balanced* view of the issue. You survey a group because you *need* to know something, not because you already know it.

DESIGNING SURVEYS

The two primary factors that govern the design of an effective survey are *reliability* and *efficiency*. Just as a biased target group will produce skewed or slanted results, so too will a biased question. Consider the differences in these pairs of questions: Should the state be licensed to kill? / Are you for or against capital punishment?; Should teenagers really be allowed to vote? / Should the 18-year-old vote be continued? The first question in each set imposes the questioner's point of view on the respondent. Some respondents may be intimidated into changing their opinions; others may get perturbed and vote in the opposite direction; and still others may be insulted and refuse to answer the question. Any of these reactions will make your results unreliable.

Using absolutes in the wording of your questions or statements can also confuse a person's response and contribute to invalidating your results. Words like *all, none, always,* and *never* allow no room for the one exception in a person's experience; they often force people to think in extremes and respond in a direction contrary to their usual inclination. For example, if you were polling people on their experience with American and foreign cars, you would have to consider choices in wording such as these:

I have never had any problems with the American cars I have owned.   _____ Yes   _____ No

OR

I seldom (or rarely) had any problems with the American cars I owned.   _____ Yes   _____ No

All of my foreign cars got excellent gas mileage.   _____ Yes   _____ No

OR

The foreign cars I owned had good gas mileage records.   _____ Yes   _____ No

The point is to allow the respondent to make his or her own decision rather than imposing your judgment or forcing a particular response.

Another way to eliminate absolutes from your questions and at the same time provide choices for your respondents' consideration is to use a *Likert scale*. This scale also allows for easy tabulation of results. Here are two examples:

My high school English courses prepared me for writing on the college level.

___ Strongly   ___ Agree   ___ Undecided   ___ Disagree   ___ Strongly
    agree   disagree

	Always	Almost always	Sometimes	Seldom	Never
I like to write.	5	4	3	2	1

If you use this approach, your results will be a measurement of your respondents' point of view rather than your interpretation. If the respondent selects an absolute answer, it will be his or her choice, not yours.

Another problem in wording questions is clarity. The respondents should be able to understand all of the terms used. Keeping your statements and questions short and to the point will help, but each term used needs to be checked carefully as well. A question such as the following might cause confusion in two cases:

Should song lyrics be more conservative?　　　　_____ Yes　　_____ No

Song lyrics to what kind of music? What do you mean by *conservative*? When the terms of your question are vague, your respondents may not interpret the content the same way, making the responses useless.

The design of your survey will also contribute to its clarity and efficiency. A limited number of concise questions arranged for easy response and tabulation should be your goal. Your questions may ask for limited personal data, such as age of respondent; they may also include information on the background and current status of the issue and provide choices predicting outcome or action to be taken. With each type of question, the response should require the person being surveyed to merely check or circle one of the choices. Observe how easily the following questionnaires can be completed:

QUESTIONNAIRE A

Directions: Check the answer that best reflects your experience with parking on campus.

1. Do you use a car as a means of transport to the university?

   Yes _____　　　　　　No _____

2. Do you believe the university has a parking problem?

   Yes _____　　　　　　No _____　　　　　　Don't know _____

3. Has there ever been an occasion when you did not find a parking space on campus?

   Yes _____　　　　　　Never _____

4. If you answered "Yes" in question three (3), how often has this occurred?

   Frequently _____　　　　Rarely _____

5. Does the university require a new parking lot in the form of a multistory garage?

   Yes _____　　　　　　No _____　　　　　　Don't know _____

Thank you for your help and cooperation.

QUESTIONNAIRE B

I am conducting a questionnaire as part of a research project for my composition class and would appreciate your taking a few minutes to answer the questions below. Your responses will be kept anonymous.

Related Personal Data

1. Are you a business major?

   _____ Yes   _____ No   _____ Undecided

2. What is your class standing?

   _____ Freshman   _____ Sophomore   _____ Junior   _____ Senior

3. Have you ever worked in a retail establishment?

   _____ Yes   _____ No

Select the choice that most accurately reflects your opinion of the following statements:

4. In a retail establishment, customer service should come before the convenience of the employees.

   ____ Strongly ____ Agree ____ Undecided ____ Disagree ____ Strongly
         agree   disagree

5. Personal phone calls do not interfere with the employees' ability to serve customers.

   ____ Strongly ____ Agree ____ Undecided ____ Disagree ____ Strongly
         agree   disagree

6. Personal phone calls by employees should be restricted to emergency situations.

   ____ Strongly ____ Agree ____ Undecided ____ Disagree ____ Strongly
         agree   disagree

Notice that both examples include clear directions, a courteous statement expressing gratitude for the person's participation, and an efficient method for completing the form. Also observe that neither requests the person's name. Remember that in conducting a survey you are interested in collecting *group* data.

Before conducting your survey, whether it is a poll or a questionnaire, you should review it carefully to make sure it has the following features:

- Explanation of your purpose

- Clear, concise directions

- Attractive, professional appearance

- Questions or statements that are free from personal bias and slanted terms that would influence responses

- Questions and statements whose terms are understood in a similar way by the group
- Clear range of choices and efficient means of responding

PRESENTING RESULTS

You can use your survey results to provide background information, illustrate major points, or serve as the central focus of your research. But the more important the position your survey information serves, the more confident you need to be about the reliability of the results. While determining your results depends initially on computing responses, you must present the statistical results in a carefully controlled way to represent them with integrity.

Quite often a reader can be misled by the use of the word *average* in a presentation, because the word can have three legitimate meanings—the *mean*, the *median*, and the *mode*. Each kind of average has its own value.

The *mean* is the total number of responses divided by the number of responders or items.

The *median* is the middle value in the series of responses.

The *mode* is the number that appears most frequently.

Let's look at two examples to see how differently these values can interpret the meaning of survey results.

Survey A: You surveyed 13 high school drivers, all 16-year-olds, on what speed they drive on open roads. Here are their responses:

80, 70, 70, 70, 70, 70, 65, 65, 60, 60, 60, 55, 55

Results: mean = 67 mph
median = 65 mph
mode = 70 mph

Survey B: You surveyed 13 students in your dorm on how many times per week they eat pizza. Here are their responses:

28, 22, 20, 16, 14, 8, 8, 7, 7, 4, 4, 4, 2

Results: mean = 11.11
median = 8
mode = 4

While the results of Survey A do not vary much, it is obvious that the results of Survey B could distort the interpretation of the information if the values of the figures were not clearly identified.

As a reader and as a researcher you need to be discriminating in your assessment of statistical language. In the following excerpt from a *Los Angeles Times* article of August 5, 1987, the lack of precise language combined with percentages evokes alarm and confusion in the reader.

10-State Survey Finds
Radioactive Gas
in Fifth of Homes

LARRY B. STAMMER

The U.S. Environmental Protection Agency said Tuesday that health- 1
threatening levels of radon gas have been found in one of every five
homes tested in a 10-state survey. . . .

The EPA study, which involved 11,600 homes, was the largest of 2
its kind to date. The 10 states were Alabama, Colorado, Connecticut,
Kansas, Kentucky, Michigan, Rhode Island, Tennessee, Wisconsin and
Wyoming. . . .

The percentage of homes that exceeded the 4 picocurie action 3
level in each of the 10 states were Alabama, 6%; Colorado, 39%; Connecticut, 19%; Kansas, 21%; Kentucky, 17%; Michigan, 9%; Rhode Island, 19%; Tennessee, 16%; Wisconsin, 27%, and Wyoming, 26%.

In this excerpt from an Associated Press story that appeared in the *New York Times* May
17, 1987, the term *average* is used frequently, but the value the term represents is never
clarified and the number of institutions surveyed in each division is not specified.

Survey Finds Major Gaps
in College Salaries

The presidents of the nation's major private research universities were 1
paid an average of $153,400 in 1986, nearly $50,000 more than their
counterparts running the largest public universities, an administrators' group says.

Over all, presidents, chancellors and other top officials on cam- 2
puses earned 7.3 percent more in 1986 than they had a year earlier,
according to the survey by the College and University Personnel
Association.

The group canvassed 1,429 colleges and universities for the sur- 3
vey, which was co-sponsored by the American Council on Education
and a trustees' organization, the Association of Governing Boards of
Universities and Colleges.

The report did not disclose top administrators' salaries by in- 4
stitution. But using the Carnegie Corporation's standard definitions
for various types of colleges, it offered this breakdown of the average
salaries for the chief executive officers at the largest institutions in
each group:

- Major research universities: $103,600 public, $153,400 private.
- Other doctoral institutions: $89,600 public, $111,300 private.
- Comprehensive: $98,900 public, $119,900 private.
- Baccalaureate: $71,800 public, $95,100 private.
- Two-year: $78,680 public, $125,000 private.

The survey figures cover major research universities with enroll- 5
ments of more than 15,000 students if public, or more than 10,000 if
private; doctoral institutions with more than 10,000 if public, or more
than 3,500 if private; comprehensive schools with more than 15,000
students if public, or 4,000 if private; baccalaureate schools with more
than 4,000 students if public, or more than 2,000 if private, and two-
year campuses with more than 10,000 if public, or more than 1,000 if
private.

When the value of an average is specified, the reader has a fuller understanding of
the data. The following excerpt from a *Los Angeles Times* article of July 31, 1987,
demonstrates how the term *median* gives the reader a clearer frame of reference for
interpretation.

Poverty Rate Drops
to Lowest Since 1980

TOM REDBURN

The percentage of Americans living below the poverty line dropped 1
last year to the lowest level since 1980, the Census Bureau reported
Thursday. It shrank from 14% in 1985 to 13.6%.

But although it dropped for the third year in a row, the poverty rate remained well above the levels of the 1970s. And, the new figures disclosed, the income of the poor fell further behind the income of the rest of the country, widening the gap between haves and have nots. 2

There was no significant change in the number of Americans living in poverty, the Census Bureau said. It estimated the number at 32.4 million last year compared with 33.1 million in 1985. The income at which the poverty level is set varies by family size; for a family of four it was $11,203 last year. 3

While the poor made only modest gains last year, the average American family enjoyed one of the largest increases in real income in the last 15 years as median family income rose 4.2% to $29,460. When adjusted for inflation, the median family income remained below the peaks of $29,734 in 1973 and $29,647 in 1978, but it is finally likely to surpass those levels this year, the Census Bureau said. 4

Real median family income—the point that divides the top half of all family incomes from the lower half—has risen 10.7% since 1982, when the country was in the midst of one of its worst recessions of the last 40 years. 5

Continuing a recent trend, the gap between the most affluent and the poorest Americans reached its widest point in decades. The top 20% of all households, which represented those with incomes above $45,980, collected 46.1% of all household income, an increase from 44.2% in 1980 and 43.3% in 1970. Meanwhile, the lowest 20%— those with incomes below $10,250, collected just 3.8%, a decrease from 4.1% in both 1970 and 1980. 6

Still, while the *Los Angeles Times* excerpt explains the value of the median, its presentation of data points out another common problem in presenting results—the use of comparative statistics and comparative populations. When you compare data from one year to another, your reader needs to know if there was a difference in the characteristics of the sample, such as size, age, or geographic location. If, for example, only 50 percent of the graduating seniors in engineering passed the writing proficiency exam last year and 80 percent passed this year, the results would imply a marked improvement. But were the same number of students sampled in each group? If there were only two people in the group and one passed, the pass rate would be 50 percent, making the figure seem better than it was. The reader has the right to the most accurate information you can provide.

There are several ways to integrate the results of your data into your presentation. The reliability of your results, your research purpose, and the needs of your audience will determine whether or not you should present statistical charts or focus more on the concepts of the issues, using numerical data only when support is needed.

In an article by the Knight-Ridder News Service that appeared in the *Virginian-Pilot and Ledger-Star* July 12, 1987, the emphasis is on the issues. Note how the report ranks the issues using terms such as *most, finished second,* and *followed by.* The only figures included serve to characterize the group surveyed.

Parents Recall Happily Child's First Steps, Fear Substance Abuse

KNIGHT-RIDDER NEWS SERVICE

Parents remember most fondly their babies' first steps, according to a 1 recent national poll by Louis Harris and Associates. Among parental highlights of their kids' early years, babies' first words finished second, followed by the first day of school and a good report card. On the list of also-rans were such auspicious occasions as reading for the first time, making a first friend, growing up to be pretty or handsome and having a wonderful birthday party.

What parents recalled most happily about the lives of their older 2 children was when they finally demonstrated an ability to think for themselves. This was particularly important to college-educated parents and those earning more than $50,000 per year. Among blacks, Southerners and those earning less than $15,000 per year, developing a belief in God and discovering a deep religious meaning in life ranked high. Other highlights for parents of older children included getting into a good college, economic success, graduation day and artistic, athletic or romantic prowess.

What parents feared most, the Harris poll showed, were drug 3 abuse, alcohol abuse, sexual promiscuity and unwanted pregnancy, in that order. Not much further down the list of perils, however, was the fear that kids would watch too much TV.

On balance, though, the poll of 3,001 households, conducted for 4 Philip Morris Companies, revealed American families generally at peace with one another and their circumstances.

The writer of "Bigger Pay for Better Work" (*Psychology Today*, July 1987) has chosen to include charts that highlight specific issues to support his discussion. In the beginning he uses general terms, such as *most, nearly half,* and *only about a third* to orient the reader to the findings. When the writer does use statistics, he is careful to explain how to interpret them. In fact, he demonstrates how some of the percentages are misleading. By being as accurate as possible, the writer strengthens his credibility with the reader.

Bigger Pay for Better Work

The Problem: More Foreign Competition and Stagnant Production. The Answer: Increase Worker Involvement and Reward Performance.

JACK C. HORN

For years we've been reading newspaper stories and watching televi- 1 sion programs on the struggling state of American industry. Hampered by stagnant productivity, companies have been looking for better ways to motivate employees and cut costs to meet increasingly strong foreign competition.

Last year the American Productivity Center (APC) and the Ameri- 2 can Compensation Association (ACA) surveyed 1,598 firms and organizational units to see what methods were being used to meet these goals and how well they were working. (See "Survey Facts and Figures," this article, for details about the survey and the companies involved.) [p. 123]

The researchers found that what the companies were doing fell 3 into two broad areas: innovative reward systems and more supportive human resource practices. The specific objectives varied from company to company, but overall the systems and practices were designed to tie pay closer to performance, improve productivity and quality and increase employee involvement. Three-quarters of the companies that responded used at least one innovative system.

Most of the programs have been adopted quite recently. For ex- 4 ample, more companies have installed gain sharing and small-group incentive plans since 1980 than in the previous 20 years. In both of these programs, everyone in a work unit receives a bonus when the unit meets preset goals.

Other popular reward systems include profit sharing and individual incentives or bonuses, still used mainly for managers and professional employees, and pay-for-knowledge plans, used for both salaried and hourly workers. In these plans, what an employee earns is determined by the number of jobs he or she can do, rather than the job actually done on a given day. Pay for knowledge, which gives a company greater production flexibility and broadens a worker's skills, is used chiefly in work units that rely on the team concept rather than traditional job classifications.

Nearly half the firms reported that their reward systems included at least one recognition program—employee of the month, best service team or the like. The payoffs are often merchandise or travel awards; symbolic rewards such as banquets or trophies; or status awards such as club memberships or designated parking spaces. The aware criteria are usually subjective, matters of supervisory nomination or managerial decision rather than objective standards such as surpassing assigned goals.

Despite the prevalence of recognition programs, most companies don't consider them very successful in encouraging better performance. Only about a third rate them as effective or very effective—perhaps, the report speculates, because the standards are subjective, the rewards are usually small and only 5 percent of the employees, on the average, win awards.

"Recognition does have a role," the report concludes, but mainly as one element "of a larger performance improvement effort such as gain sharing or other incentive-based plans." In short, money talks much more persuasively than plaques or certificates.

The bottom line, of course, is how well these reward systems increase productivity and improve employee relations. The table, "Impact of Reward Systems," this article, shows that most of the firms were well-satisfied; from 66 percent to 89 percent rated all but one of the systems they used as effective in achieving these objectives. Only recognition programs did poorly.

Reward systems are just part of the package many companies use to improve their competitive position. Human resource programs designed to make the reward systems more effective by increasing employee involvement, job security and information sharing have also become more popular.

Fifty percent of the firms have at least one involvement program, most of which are fairly new (see "Employee Involvement Practices,"

Impact of Reward Systems

Type of System	Percent*
Pay for knowledge	89
Earned time off	85
Gain sharing	81
Small-group incentives	75
Profit sharing	74
Individual incentives	73
All salaried	67
Lump sum bonus	66
Recognition	30

*Firms reporting that the system was effective or very effective had a positive or very positive impact on performance

Employee Involvement Practices

Involvement Practice	Percent*	Mean Years in Use
Small problem-solving groups	23	6.8
Quality circles	22	3.7
Team or group suggestions	21	7.9
Cross-functional employee task forces	20	7.0
Other employee involvement efforts	12	6.4
Labor/management participation teams	10	7.0
Quality of work life programs	8	5.1
Self-directed, self-managed or autonomous work teams	8	9.4
Total using at least one employee involvement practice	50	

*Percentage of firms using this practice

this article). This percentage is misleading, however. The researchers found "a disappointing level of active participation" in the programs. More than half of the organizations that have programs such as quality circles and small problem-solving groups "report less than 15 percent of their employees are active involved." Some employees are "skeptical of the real importance of the program to the organization." Others see each of them as simply another "program of the month," one that has little real support from supervisors and managers.

About 32 percent of the organizations have programs to increase 12 job security. More than 20 percent of these rely on informal means such as reassigning workers to new jobs, retraining them or bringing work that had been subcontracted to other firms back in-house. The other 10 percent have installed formal programs such as written commitments to no layoffs or guarantees of a minimum number of hours of work per week.

More than 40 percent of the companies share information about 13 job performance, quality of work and corporate financial matters with nonmanagement employees, usually through newsletters, bulletin boards, regular meetings and mailings. Companies that have programs for employee involvement, job security and information sharing are also more likely to offer gain sharing and other innovative reward systems.

At present, such reward systems and human resource programs 14 are much more common in organizations that produce goods than they are in the service sector. An important reason for this difference is competition. The researchers found that 48 percent of the goods-producing firms reported an increase in foreign and domestic competition recently, compared to only 19 percent of the service firms.

But the situation seems to be changing. Anticipating stronger 15 competition, service firms report that they expect to introduce more of these programs soon. During the next five years, for example, they expect to increase gain-sharing plans by 168 percent, pay for knowledge by 122 percent and small-group incentives by 93 percent.

The report suggests that companies encourage their different 16 departments and organizations to learn from each other. Sales and marketing people who have always used incentives and bonuses can benefit by examining gain sharing and other group rewards used by production people that don't encourage destructive internal competition.

Conversely, production people may learn to use incentive pro- 17 grams more effectively by calling on sales and marketing's experience in this area. "Throughout the organization," the report notes, "systems that focus hourly and salaried employees on the same objectives would greatly reduce the adversarial relations that are a drag on our economic system."

The report also stresses that incentive systems tied to productiv- 18
ity work best in combination with supportive human resource practices to "provide greater compensation flexibility without layoffs" and
"increase commitment to performance improvement. . . . Without adequate and timely information sharing, employee involvement and assurance of some employment stability," the report concludes, "compensation plans will not be effective."

EXERCISES: SURVEYS

1. As a college student affected by the results presented in the following Associated
Press article (*Los Angeles Times,* August 7, 1987), assess how well the survey design
and the interpretation and presentation of results serves your needs as an audience.
What *average* do you think is being used?

College Costs Expected to Climb 6% to 8%, Top $18,000 at Some Schools

College tuitions will continue to climb faster than the inflation rate this 1
fall, and total student expenses at some elite institutions will top
$18,000, the College Board said Thursday in its annual survey of col-
lege costs.

The average annual tuition and fees for the 1987–88 school year 2
will climb 8% from last year's level at private four-year colleges and 6%
at public institutions, the report said.

It will be the seventh straight year that the increase exceeds the 3
rate of inflation. So far this year, the consumer price index has risen at
an annual rate of 5.4%.

The most expensive school in the nation, the report said, is Ben- 4
nington College in Bennington, Vt., where total estimated costs will be
$19,390.

Average total estimated costs at four-year private schools will be 5
slightly less than $12,000 and at public schools will be almost $5,800.

"There They Go"

Education Secretary William Bennett, a frequent critic of in- 6
creases in college costs, said of this latest survey: "There they go again,
and again, and again. When will they ever stop?"

Still, this fall's increases are well below the peak reached in the 7
1982–83 academic year, when tuitions rose an average 20% at public
colleges and 13% at private schools at a time when the inflation rate
was just 3.8%.

"The College Board does not collect data on why tuition and fees 8
are rising, but other investigators point to the considerable increase in
the price of goods and services purchased during the 1980s, such as
books, faculty salaries and scientific equipment," said board President
Donald M. Stewart.

Using a new method of calculating average college costs, which 9
takes each school's enrollment into account, the board estimated that
average "fixed charges" at private four-year institutions—tuition, fees,
room and board—will hit $10,493 for 1987–88. Counting such inciden-
tal expenses as books, supplies and transportation, estimated annual
costs rise to $11,982 for students living on campus and to $10,173 for
commuting students.

At four-year public institutions, tuition, fees, room and board will 10
average $4,104 for in-state students. Adding incidental expenses in-
creases the estimate to $5,789 for resident students and $4,554 for
commuters.

The basic annual fee at the California State University's 19 cam- 11
puses will be up 10% from last year, from $573 to $630. Adding in room
and board, the total cost ranges from $3,730 at the Stanislaus campus
to $4,861 at Cal State Long Beach. Students who are not California resi-
dents must pay $147 more per unit, a slight increase over the $141
charged last year.

At the nine University of California campuses, tuition has been 12
raised 9% and ranges from a low of $1,431 at UCLA to a high of $1,615 at
UC Santa Cruz. Room and board charges vary from campus to campus, with the highest apparently at UC San Diego, where the College
Board said the total estimated cost for a year is $8,400 for state residents.

Non-Resident Surcharges

Besides Bennington, schools where the total estimated cost for 13
the year for undergraduates will exceed $18,000 include Sarah Law-
rence College, University of Chicago, Columbia University, Harvard
University, Dartmouth College, Tufts University and the Massachusetts
Institute of Technology.

Average surcharges for out-of-state students attending four-year 14
public institutions will rise 7% to $2,367 and 10% at two-year public
colleges to $1,811. Out-of-staters attending some top public universi-
ties thus face expenses rivaling those at many private colleges.

Estimated total costs at the Colorado School of Mines, for ex- 15
ample, will be $8,274, and $13,796 for out-of-state students. UC San
Diego will cost $12,690 for non-Californians, and the University of
Michigan $13,098 for out-of-state students.

The New York-based College Board is a private, nonprofit organi- 16
zation whose members include more than 2,500 educational institutions and associations.

---

2. The information presented in the chart from *Changing Times* (August 1987) was
designed to interest a large, general adult audience. Analyze the criteria used for the
survey, the group surveyed to collect the information, and the presentation of the data
in chart form. Would you be willing to base your decisions on the information presented? Explain why or why not.

The Pain and the Gain

*Before You Decide Which Sport Will Be
the Centerpiece of Your Fitness Program, Weigh
the Benefits Against the Costs*

After you've made the commitment to fitness, it's time to choose your 1
method. Running or aerobic dance? Cycling or rowing machine? How
you invest your time, sweat and money may mean the difference between crossing the threshold to lifelong fitness and dropping out because of boredom, lack of time or injury. Drawing on expert advice,
Changing Times created this at-a-glance format for sizing up the benefits and costs of a dozen activities—not only the dollar cost but also
injury rates and the time you'll have to work out each session to benefit.

Most important is the contribution to your cardiovascular health. 2
Strength, endurance and flexibility, though necessary for well-rounded
fitness, are less crucial in preventing life-threatening disease. This is

| | Benefits | | | | | | Costs | | |
Activity	Aerobics	Fat Loss	Strength	Muscle Endur-ance	Flexi-bility	Total	Injury Rate	Workout Time (Min.)	Start-up Cost
Swimming	●●●●●	●	◗	●	●	9½	low	30	$30–$750*
Cross-country skiing (outdoor)	●●●●●	●	◗	●	◗	9	medium	25	$130–$180
Aerobic dance	●●●●	●	◗	●	◗	8	high	35	$200–$350*
Rowing machine	●●●●	●	◗	●		7½	medium	35	$250–$450
Running	●●●●●	●		◗		7½	high	25	$35–$65
Cycling (outdoor)	●●●●	●	◗	◗		6½	high**	35	$350–$550
Racquetball/squash	●●●●	●	◗	◗		6½	medium	35	$350–$600*
Tennis (singles)	●●●●	◗		●		5	medium	45	$110–$650*
Walking	●●●	◗		◗		5	low	45	$35–$65
Calisthenics	●●		◗	◗	●	4	low	60	$40–$55
Weight training†	●●		●	●		4	medium	60	$120–$500*
Golf	●					1	low	75	$300–$1,050*

*Upper range includes club fees.   **Includes collisions.   †Not aerobic circuit training.

reflected in the ratings: The aerobics segment of each activity gets one to six symbols. The more symbols, the greater the benefit. In each of the other categories under benefits, the sport earns a single symbol if it significantly contributes to that part of fitness or half a symbol if it contributes somewhat (all ratings assume average levels of intensity and competence). "Fat loss" means how well the activity burns fat; "strength" is how the sport contributes to your muscles' ability to lift, push or pull against resistance a single time; "muscle endurance" is how it helps you repeat the same activity over and over; "flexibility" rates how the sport helps limber your muscles and joints.

The totals for each are revealing—swimming wins as the best all- 3 around fitness enhancer, golf loses big. But that's not the whole story; the costs are important, too. Is one activity more likely to sideline you with an injury? Is another too pricey? (Prices assume shoes and necessary equipment.) Will it take too much time?

Developing a sounder cardiovascular system means working out 4 at your target heart rate for 20 to 30 minutes three or four times per week. But to be certain you're getting maximum benefit, you should burn at least 300 calories each time you work out. This expenditure shows up in the "time" column.

Our ratings were based on recommendations from six experts: 5 Edward Howley, Ph.D., professor of human kinetics, University of Tennessee, Knoxville; David Johnson, M.D., National Swimming Team physician; Robert Nirschl, M.D., orthopedic consultant to the President's Council on Physical Fitness and Sports; Michael Pollock, Ph.D., director of the Center for Exercise Science at the University of Florida at Gainesville; Paul Ribisl, Ph.D., former chairman of the preventive and rehabilitative programs committee of the American College of Sports Medicine; Thomas Whitehead, M.S., director of health and fitness programming, National Institute for Fitness and Sport.

---

3. The following charts from the *Los Angeles Times* (July 31, 1987) were presented as results from the same survey. For each chart, make a list of from three to five generalizations based on the information presented. After each set of generalizations, state any reservations you might have about the reliability of the chart as a source of information.

These are results of a Los Angeles Times Poll of 2,095 residents nationwide between July 24 and July 28.
Percentage who said AIDS had an almost total or large impact on their life style.
Black represents July, 1987, responses; hatched bars are December, 1985, responses.

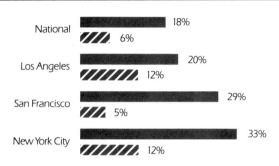

Percentage concerned about AIDS as a problem for their personal health		
	July, 1987	**Dec., 1985**
National	46%	42%
Los Angeles	49%	49%
San Francisco	44%	33%
New York City	57%	56%

Percentage who felt knowledgeable about AIDS		
	July, 1987	**Dec., 1985**
National	52%	35%
Los Angeles	60%	43%
San Francisco	63%	56%
New York City	50%	43%

Percentage who know someone who has tested positive for the AIDS virus, developed AIDS or died of AIDS		
	July, 1987	**Dec., 1985**
National	11%	5%
Los Angeles	15%	14%
San Francisco	25%	15%
New York City	20%	16%

Percentage who would befriend a person who tested positive for AIDS antibodies		
	July, 1987	**Dec., 1985**
National	42%	35%
Los Angeles	53%	35%
San Francisco	54%	43%
New York City	36%	37%

These are results of a Los Angeles Times Poll of 2,095 residents nationwide between July 24 and July 28.

"Should we place most emphasis on educating the public about how to avoid the AIDS virus, or should we place our greatest effort into testing potential AIDS patients, or should we be spending more time and money to find a cure?"

Education 46%

Research 42%

Testing 6%

Other steps 2%

Not sure 4%

"If you suspected that you had been exposed to AIDS, would you feel that you had a duty to find out if you test positive to the AIDS virus?"

Duty to find out 90%

Right to refuse 9%

Not sure 1%

"If you were infected by the AIDS virus, would you want to know about it?"

Yes 96%

No 3%

Not sure 1%

"Do you think people with a high risk of acquiring AIDS should be made to take the AIDS antibodies test?"

Made to take test 49%

Voluntary testing only 47%

Not sure 4%

"Which if any of the following groups of people do you think it would be most useful to test for the presence of the AIDS virus?"

All citizens 29%

Drug abusers 16%

Known homosexuals 16%

Prostitutes 14%

Food service employees 4%

Applicants for insurance 4%

All employees 1%

None 6%

Not sure 8%

"Do you think public agencies should be allowed to use test results to trace the sexual partners of people who have tested positive for AIDS antibodies?"

Yes 70%

No 24%

Not sure 6%

"If you had reason to know that someone had tested positive to the presence of AIDS antibodies, do you think you would have a duty to inform past or present sexual partners about the person's condition?"

A duty to inform 69%

Keep confidential 24%

Not sure 7%

WRITING SUGGESTIONS

1. Choose one of the issues listed below or one of your own choice, to use as the base for brainstorming a survey resource cluster. After drawing your cluster, choose the group to survey and design a possible questionnaire to use with the group. Use the guidelines in the Designing Surveys section in this chapter to critique the effectiveness of your design.

    a. A smoking ban in a specific public place
    b. Controlling the price of concert tickets
    c. Drinking problems among college students
    d. Gun control
    e. Building a performing arts center in the community
    f. Preservation of a historic building
    g. Problems of air traffic controllers
    h. Concern for the preservation of the environment

2. Using information presented on the following pages from the *Chronicle of Higher Education* (January 11, 1989) from a survey of 209,000 freshmen entering college in 1988, write a three- to five-page report focusing on a particular issue. Before deciding how and when to integrate the statistical data, identify the audience for the report. Also determine what their needs will be to accept your point of view.

Age on December 31, 1988:

16 or younger	0.1%
17	2.6%
18	73.3%
19	18.8%
20	1.7%
21–24	1.6%
25–29	0.7%
30–39	0.8%
40–54	0.2%
55 or older	0.0%

Racial/ethnic background:

White	83.2%
Black	9.5%
American Indian	0.8%
Asian-American	2.9%
Mexican-American	1.8%
Puerto Rican-American	1.4%
Other	2.2%

Average grade in high school:

A or A+	11.0%
A−	12.6%
B+	18.5%
B	24.8%
B−	14.2%
C+	11.5%
C	7.0%
D	0.4%

Year of high-school graduation:

1988	93.6%
1987	2.3%
1986	0.7%
1985 or earlier	1.9%
H.S. equivalency (G.E.D. test)	1.3%
Never completed high school	0.2%

Have met or exceeded recommended years of study, as proposed by the National Commission on Excellence in Education, in:

English (4 years)	94.9%
Mathematics (3 years)	91.5%
Foreign language (2 years)	78.6%
Physical science (2 years)	49.5%
Biological science (2 years)	34.7%
History, American government (1 year)	99.1%
Computer science (.5 years)	58.1%
Art or music (1 year)	66.8%

Number of honors courses taken in high school:

None	50.0%
One	12.3%
Two or more	37.7%

Number of Advanced Placement courses taken in high school:

None	60.8%
One	17.4%
Two or more	21.8%

Racial composition of high school:

Completely white	16.0%
Mostly white	59.1%
Half white	17.5%
Mostly non-white	5.6%
Completely non-white	1.8%

Racial composition of neighborhood:

Completely white	41.2%
Mostly white	42.4%
Half white	6.2%
Mostly non-white	6.2%
Completely non-white	4.1%

Disabilities:

Health-related	1.2%
Hearing	0.8%
Learning	1.2%
Orthopedic	1.0%
Speech	0.3%
Visual	1.9%
Other	1.4%

Current religious preference:

Baptist	13.4%
Buddhist	0.4%
Congregational	1.2%
Eastern Orthodox	0.6%
Episcopal	2.5%
Islamic	0.3%
Jewish	3.2%
Latter Day Saints	0.3%
Lutheran	6.2%
Methodist	8.7%
Presbyterian	4.5%
Quaker	0.2%
Roman Catholic	36.2%
Seventh-Day Adventist	0.3%
Other Protestant	4.8%
None	11.6%
Other	5.5%

Residence planned during fall term:

With parents or relatives	30.4%
Other private home or apartment	6.8%
College dormitory	59.3%
Fraternity or sorority house	0.6%
Other campus housing	2.3%
Other	0.6%

Residence preferred during fall term:

With parents or relatives	14.9%
Other private home or apartment	32.3%
College dormitory	37.6%
Fraternity or sorority house	7.3%
Other campus housing	5.7%
Other	2.1%

Miles from college to home:

5 or less	8.7%
6 to 10	9.4%
11 to 50	26.8%
51 to 100	14.7%
101 to 500	29.3%
500 or more	11.2%

Father's occupation:

Artist (incl. performer)	0.9%
Businessman	29.8%
Member of clergy or religious worker	0.9%
Engineer	8.2%
Farmer or forester	2.9%
Lawyer	1.8%
Military career officer	1.7%
Physician or dentist	2.4%
Other health professional	1.3%
Research scientist	0.6%
Teacher or administrator, college	0.9%
Teacher or administrator, elementary school	0.9%
Teacher or administrator, secondary school	3.9%
Worker, skilled	10.1%
Worker, semi-skilled	4.1%
Worker, unskilled	2.9%
Other occupation	24.2%
Unemployed	2.3%

Father's education (highest level):

Grammar school or less	4.1%
Some high school	7.3%
High-school diploma	26.9%
Postsecondary other than college	4.8%

Some college 14.5%
College degree 21.1%
Some graduate school .. 2.8%
Graduate degree 18.6%

Mother's occupation:
Artist (incl. performer) ... 1.6%
Businesswoman 14.2%
Member of clergy or
  religious worker 0.1%
Clerical worker 11.1%
Engineer 0.2%
Farmer or forester 0.3%
Homemaker (full-time) .. 18.0%
Lawyer 0.3%
Nurse 7.6%
Physician or dentist 0.4%
Other health
  professional 1.9%
Research scientist 0.1%
Social, welfare, or
  recreation worker 1.4%
Teacher or administrator,
  college 0.4%
Teacher or administrator,
  elementary school ... 6.7%
Teacher or administrator,
  secondary school 4.0%
Worker, skilled 2.1%
Worker, semi-skilled 2.6%
Worker, unskilled 1.8%
Other occupation 19.1%
Unemployed 6.1%

Mother's education (highest level):
Grammar school or less 3.1%
Some high school 6.1%
High-school diploma ... 34.3%
Postsecondary other than
  college 8.0%
Some college 16.7%
College degree 19.1%
Some graduate school .. 3.0%
Graduate degree 9.7%

Students estimate chances are very good that they will:
Change major field 14.4%
Change career choice ... 13.1%
Fail one or more courses 1.4%
Graduate with honors .. 11.9%
Be elected to student
  office 3.4%
Get a job to pay college
  expenses 35.4%
Work full-time while
  attending college 3.5%

Join a social fraternity or
  sorority 18.2%
Play varsity athletics 14.8%
Be elected to an honor
  society 7.2%
Make at least a
  B average 41.7%
Need extra time to
  complete degree 7.1%
Need tutoring in some
  courses 12.7%
Work at outside job 20.0%
Seek vocational
  counseling 5.0%
Seek personal
  counseling 3.8%
Participate in student
  protests 5.4%
Transfer to another
  college 12.0%
Drop out permanently .. 0.9%
Drop out temporarily ... 1.1%
Get bachelor's degree .. 71.3%
Be satisfied with college 51.3%
Find employment in
  preferred field 70.7%
Marry while in college .. 4.4%
Marry within a year after
  college 15.8%

Student rated self above average or in highest 10 percent in:
Academic ability 56.1%
Artistic ability 24.7%
Competitiveness 54.2%
Drive to achieve 63.7%
Emotional health 56.1%
Foreign language ability 31.4%
Leadership ability 51.6%
Mathematical ability 40.6%
Physical health 58.4%
Popularity 43.5%
Popularity with opposite
  sex 41.9%
Public speaking ability .. 29.5%
Self-confidence
  (intellectual) 49.7%
Self-confidence
  (social) 43.8%
Writing ability 39.8%

Number of other colleges applied to for admission this year:
None 31.2%
One 15.0%
Two 16.6%

Three 15.2%
Four 9.2%
Five 5.7%
Six or more 7.0%

Number of other college acceptances this year (of those with multiple applications):
None 15.1%
One 27.9%
Two 24.5%
Three 17.1%
Four 8.4%
Five 3.7%
Six or more 3.4%

College attended is student's:
First choice 67.9%
Second choice 23.0%
Third choice 5.8%
Other 3.3%

Prior credit at this institution:
No 96.5%
Yes 3.5%

Reasons noted as very important in selecting college attended:
Relatives' wishes 7.1%
Teachers' advice 4.1%
Good academic
  reputation 56.0%
Good social reputation .. 22.6%
Offerred financial
  assistance 21.4%
Offered special education
  programs 22.0%
Low tuition 21.3%
Advice of guidance
  counselor 7.5%
Wanted to live near
  home 19.2%
Friend's suggestion 8.2%
Recruited by college 3.7%
Recruited by athletic
  department 4.4%
Graduates get good
  jobs 33.5%
Not offered aid by first
  choice 4.6%

Highest degree planned at college attended:
None 3.7%
Vocational certificate ... 0.8%
Associate (or equivalent) 16.1%

Bachelor's	58.4%
Master's	14.8%
Ph.D. or Ed.D.	2.0%
M.D., D.O., D.D.S., or D.V.M.	1.3%
LL.B. or J.D.	1.1%
B.D. or M.Div.	0.2%
Other	1.6%

Highest degree planned anywhere:

None	1.8%
Vocational certificate	0.6%
Associate (or equivalent)	3.9%
Bachelor's	33.1%
Master's	36.3%
Ph.D. or Ed.D.	11.7%
M.D., D.O., D.D.S., or D.V.M.	5.7%
LL.B. or J.D.	5.0%
B.D. or M.Div.	0.4%
Other	1.5%

Probable major field of study:
Arts and Humanities

Art, fine and applied	2.1%
English	1.3%
History	0.8%
Journalism	1.6%
Language or literature	0.6%
Music	1.0%
Philosophy	0.2%
Speech	0.1%
Theater or drama	0.7%
Theology or religion	0.1%
Other	0.8%

Biological Science

Biology (general)	1.8%
Biochemistry or biophysics	0.5%
Botany	0.0%
Marine science	0.4%
Microbiology or bacteriology	0.2%
Zoology	0.3%
Other	0.5%

Business

Accounting	6.1%
Business administration (general)	7.3%
Finance	2.0%
Marketing	2.9%
Management	4.9%
Secretarial studies	0.8%
Other	1.6%

Education

Business education	0.3%
Elementary education	4.9%
Music or art education	0.3%
Physical education or recreation	1.0%
Secondary education	1.7%
Special education	0.6%
Other	0.5%

Engineering

Aeronautical engineering	1.7%
Civil engineering	0.9%
Chemical engineering	0.6%
Electrical or electronic engineering	2.9%
Industrial engineering	0.3%
Mechanical engineering	1.8%
Other	1.3%

Physical Science

Astronomy	0.1%
Atmospheric science	0.1%
Chemistry	0.6%
Earth science	0.1%
Marine science	0.1%
Mathematics	0.6%
Physics	0.4%
Statistics	0.0%
Other	0.1%

Professional

Architecture, urban planning	1.2%
Home economics	0.4%
Health technology	1.0%
Library science	0.0%
Nursing	2.5%
Pharmacy	1.0%
Pre-dental, pre-medical, pre-veterinary	2.8%
Therapy (physical, occupational, etc.)	2.0%
Other	1.3%

Social Science

Anthropology	0.2%
Economics	0.5%
Ethnic studies	0.0%
Geography	0.0%
Political science	3.2%
Psychology	4.1%
Social work	0.9%
Sociology	0.4%
Women's studies	0.0%
Other	0.2%

Technical

Building trades	0.2%
Data processing, computer programming	1.1%
Drafting or design	0.4%
Electronics	0.2%
Mechanics	0.2%
Other	0.4%

Other Fields

Agriculture	1.2%
Communications	2.9%
Computer science	1.7%
Forestry	0.5%
Law enforcement	1.6%
Military science	0.1%
Other	1.4%
Undecided	6.8%

Probable career occupation:

Accountant or actuary	5.9%
Actor or entertainer	1.0%
Architect or urban planner	1.7%
Artist	1.7%
Business (clerical)	1.0%
Business executive	12.4%
Business proprietor	3.9%
Business salesperson or buyer	1.4%
Clergy (minister or priest)	0.1%
Clergy (other)	0.1%
Clinical psychologist	1.7%
Computer programmer or analyst	2.7%
Conservationist or forester	0.7%
Dentist	0.5%
Dietitian or home economist	0.2%
Educator (college)	0.4%
Educator (elementary)	5.6%
Educator (secondary)	3.2%
Engineer	8.6%
Farmer or rancher	0.5%
Foreign-service worker	1.1%
Homemaker (full-time)	0.1%
Interior decorator	0.5%
Interpreter	0.2%
Journalist or writer	2.5%
Lab technician or hygienist	0.5%
Law-enforcement officer	1.2%
Lawyer or judge	5.4%
Military service	1.1%

Musician	1.1%				
Nurse	2.5%				
Optometrist	0.3%				
Pharmacist	1.1%				

Musician 1.1%
Nurse 2.5%
Optometrist 0.3%
Pharmacist 1.1%
Physician 3.7%
Research scientist 1.6%
School counselor 0.3%
School principal 0.0%
Social, welfare, or
  recreation worker 1.4%
Statistician 0.1%
Therapist 2.3%
Veterinarian 0.9%
Skilled trades 0.7%
Other occupation 6.8%
Undecided 11.5%

Estimated parental income:
Less than $6,000 .... 3.7%
$6,000–$9,999 .... 2.9%
$10,000–$14,999 ..... 5.1%
$15,000–$19,999 ..... 5.4%
$20,000–$24,999 ..... 6.9%
$25,000–$29,999 ..... 7.0%
$30,000–$34,999 ..... 9.1%
$35,000–39,999 .... 9.1%
$40,000–$49,999 ..... 12.4%
$50,000–$59,999 ..... 11.6%
$60,000–$74,999 ..... 10.7%
$75,000–$99,999 ..... 7.0%
$100,000–$149,999 .... 4.8%
$150,000 or more 4.3%

**Concern about financing
college:**
None 36.7%
Some 49.0%
Major 14.3%

Received any aid from:
Parents, relatives 78.2%
Spouse 1.2%

Savings from summer
  work 54.4%
Other savings 28.6%
Part-time job on campus 19.4%
Part-time job off campus 23.3%
Full-time job while in
  college 2.1%
Pell Grant 15.6%
Supplemental
  Educational
  Opportunity Grant ... 3.7%
State scholarship 9.7%
College Work-Study 6.6%
Other college grant 20.0%
Other private grant 9.1%
Other govt. aid (ROTC,
  GI, etc.) 2.4%
Guaranteed Student
  Loan 20.1%
National Direct Student
  Loan 2.4%
Other college loan 5.8%
Other loan 5.4%
Other source 2.8%

**Received $1,500 or more
from:**
Parents, relatives 52.4%
Spouse 0.3%
Savings from summer
  work 6.7%
Other savings 5.0%
Part-time job on campus 0.8%
Part-time job off campus 1.3%
Full-time job while in
  college 0.5%
Pell Grant 2.5%
Supplemental
  Educational
  Opportunity Grant ... 0.5%
State scholarship 1.5%
College Work-Study 0.3%
Other college grant 8.2%

Other private grant 2.1%
Other govt. aid (ROTC,
  GI, etc.) 1.4%
Guaranteed Student
  Loan 7.3%
National Direct Student
  Loan 0.5%
Other college loan 2.4%
Other loan 2.6%
Other source 1.1%

**Number of hours per week in
the last year spent on these
activities:**
None:
Studying or doing
  homework 1.4%
Socializing with
  friends 0.3%
Talking with teachers
  outside of class 7.7%
Exercising or sports 4.0%
Partying 12.5%
Working 24.9%
Volunteer work 56.8%
Student clubs or groups 30.5%
Watching television 5.0%
Hobbies 9.1%

6 or more hours:
Studying or doing
  homework 41.9%
Socializing with
  friends 78.2%
Talking with teachers
  outside of class 9.0%
Exercising or sports 47.9%
Partying 35.5%
Working 63.2%
Volunteer work 5.1%
Student clubs or groups 14.9%
Watching television 32.4%
Hobbies 27.7%

	All Institutions			2-year Colleges	
	Men	Women	Total	Public	Private
Activities in the past year:					
Used a personal computer*	30.1%	25.1%	27.4%	23.2%	22.1%
Attended a religious service	78.3%	84.5%	81.7%	79.4%	84.2%
Was bored in class	93.3%	93.8%	93.5%	88.5%	93.1%
Participated in demonstrations	32.4%	37.4%	35.1%	33.7%	42.8%
Won a varsity letter in sports	55.2%	39.2%	46.6%	36.6%	49.0%
Didn't complete homework on time ...	73.0%	65.1%	68.8%	65.8%	73.8%
Tutored another student	44.7%	45.1%	44.9%	36.5%	29.0%
Discussed religion*	18.3%	23.1%	20.9%	15.8%	21.4%
Did extra course work or reading*	9.0%	12.6%	10.9%	9.5%	10.3%
Copied homework from another student	58.8%	55.6%	57.1%	54.5%	57.3%
Studied with other students	85.9%	88.5%	87.3%	82.2%	87.6%
Was a guest in teacher's home	30.1%	30.5%	30.3%	25.5%	34.8%
Smoked cigarettes*	8.2%	11.8%	10.1%	14.0%	15.3%
Discussed sex*	35.3%	26.8%	30.7%	27.5%	28.9%
Cheated on a test in school	38.7%	34.8%	36.6%	35.6%	37.6%
Drank beer	72.1%	59.5%	65.3%	66.0%	63.9%
Drank wine or liquor	63.5%	69.4%	66.7%	65.0%	64.8%
Discussed politics*	22.0%	15.5%	18.5%	12.5%	13.8%
Stayed up all night	80.9%	81.1%	81.0%	79.2%	82.6%
Spoke a language other than English at home*	6.7%	7.1%	6.9%	8.0%	6.9%
Felt overwhelmed*	14.9%	27.2%	21.5%	16.2%	24.2%
Felt depressed*	7.4%	13.2%	10.5%	10.1%	13.0%
Discussed sports*	58.8%	29.0%	42.7%	37.8%	43.9%
Worked in political campaign	8.7%	8.6%	8.7%	5.6%	7.7%
Reasons noted as very important in deciding to go to college:					
Parents' wishes	18.9%	19.8%	19.4%	18.2%	21.6%
Could not find job	3.2%	3.3%	3.3%	5.0%	3.4%
To get away from home	11.6%	10.9%	11.2%	8.1%	12.6%
To be able to get a better job	82.7%	82.4%	82.5%	86.1%	83.5%
To gain general education	53.6%	65.6%	60.1%	58.2%	61.3%
To improve reading and study skills ...	35.6%	42.7%	39.4%	41.8%	46.7%
Nothing better to do	3.4%	2.4%	2.9%	3.8%	3.0%
To become a more cultured person ...	29.2%	40.7%	35.4%	31.2%	35.6%
To be able to make more money	76.5%	69.2%	72.6%	77.5%	75.0%
To learn more about things	69.3%	77.6%	73.8%	72.2%	75.7%
To prepare for graduate school	46.1%	53.1%	49.9%	46.5%	55.0%
Political views:					
Far left	2.7%	2.1%	2.3%	2.7%	2.3%
Liberal	20.5%	23.2%	22.0%	18.5%	19.9%

| 4-year Colleges | | | | Universities | | Predominantly Black Colleges | |
Public	Pvt. non-sectarian	Protestant	Catholic	Public	Private	Public	Private
28.1%	30.3%	28.4%	26.1%	30.3%	36.2%	26.4%	30.7%
84.0%	79.1%	88.9%	89.3%	79.5%	82.2%	88.2%	93.3%
95.6%	95.4%	95.3%	96.0%	96.6%	96.4%	90.3%	92.0%
38.0%	36.1%	36.0%	36.5%	32.7%	29.6%	48.5%	47.9%
51.2%	50.1%	51.9%	53.6%	50.3%	52.1%	44.1%	42.6%
70.5%	72.1%	70.7%	68.4%	68.6%	68.2%	69.0%	72.3%
43.9%	49.6%	47.8%	46.8%	54.3%	62.2%	41.1%	53.9%
20.5%	25.1%	32.7%	24.6%	20.9%	28.7%	25.6%	33.1%
10.5%	12.7%	12.4%	10.8%	11.9%	13.4%	14.9%	18.7%
59.4%	54.9%	55.3%	60.5%	59.9%	54.5%	53.9%	55.2%
88.6%	89.0%	90.1%	89.3%	90.5%	91.0%	86.1%	89.0%
32.0%	34.5%	38.2%	29.7%	29.6%	34.2%	30.8%	32.3%
8.7%	9.9%	6.0%	8.6%	7.3%	7.0%	4.7%	2.5%
32.9%	33.8%	28.1%	30.4%	32.6%	32.2%	33.4%	38.9%
38.5%	34.2%	33.3%	39.5%	38.4%	32.6%	33.5%	38.4%
63.9%	64.8%	52.2%	71.6%	68.2%	68.9%	36.5%	35.9%
66.5%	67.4%	57.3%	72.8%	70.0%	71.5%	39.5%	45.7%
16.6%	25.5%	24.1%	19.9%	22.3%	32.1%	15.5%	24.7%
81.3%	82.4%	80.2%	81.8%	82.5%	81.4%	79.9%	84.8%
4.3%	7.7%	4.4%	8.2%	7.5%	10.8%	4.6%	4.1%
22.2%	24.4%	25.7%	23.9%	24.4%	25.2%	20.4%	23.2%
11.1%	10.9%	11.3%	10.8%	10.0%	9.3%	15.3%	13.8%
45.8%	40.5%	45.6%	46.1%	45.3%	44.6%	43.5%	43.5%
9.0%	10.9%	11.6%	10.1%	9.8%	13.3%	11.9%	16.7%
20.3%	19.7%	20.6%	19.8%	19.1%	19.6%	34.4%	32.4%
3.2%	2.2%	2.4%	2.2%	2.0%	1.5%	8.2%	5.4%
12.5%	12.4%	12.4%	10.9%	12.9%	12.6%	19.4%	17.8%
83.7%	76.2%	77.4%	80.6%	81.4%	77.3%	89.7%	90.6%
56.8%	65.2%	61.9%	62.5%	60.8%	69.3%	76.0%	73.7%
39.1%	39.4%	40.6%	41.8%	35.4%	35.1%	71.6%	64.4%
2.7%	2.5%	2.5%	1.9%	2.2%	2.3%	8.0%	4.5%
32.5%	42.7%	39.8%	40.0%	37.2%	45.7%	54.0%	61.6%
74.9%	63.7%	62.8%	67.9%	71.9%	62.5%	85.5%	84.9%
71.7%	77.8%	74.1%	72.7%	75.2%	78.4%	78.7%	80.2%
46.4%	50.2%	50.1%	51.5%	54.8%	59.3%	69.1%	74.6%
2.3%	2.9%	2.3%	1.6%	1.8%	1.9%	5.5%	4.6%
21.1%	28.0%	22.0%	21.6%	25.0%	25.7%	26.4%	35.4%

	All Institutions			2-year Colleges	
	Men	Women	Total	Public	Private
Middle of the road	49.5%	57.6%	53.9%	59.7%	57.2%
Conservative	24.8%	16.2%	20.2%	17.4%	18.9%
Far right	2.5%	0.9%	1.6%	1.8%	1.7%
Agree strongly or somewhat that:					
Government isn't protecting the consumer	61.0%	69.1%	65.4%	69.0%	67.3%
Government isn't promoting disarmament	56.9%	75.2%	66.7%	65.9%	66.6%
Government isn't controlling pollution	82.3%	85.3%	83.9%	83.6%	82.8%
Taxes should be raised to reduce the federal deficit	32.0%	24.1%	27.8%	23.6%	22.6%
There is too much concern for the rights of criminals	72.7%	66.0%	69.1%	71.1%	66.0%
Military spending should be increased	33.1%	20.5%	26.3%	30.2%	29.7%
Nuclear disarmament is attainable	59.5%	61.2%	60.4%	59.5%	59.7%
Abortion should be legal	56.8%	57.2%	57.0%	52.6%	54.2%
The death penalty should be abolished	19.6%	26.0%	23.0%	21.6%	24.8%
It is all right for two people who like each other to have sex even if they've known each other for a very short time	65.1%	37.1%	50.0%	51.0%	45.7%
Women's activities should be confined to the home	32.1%	20.1%	25.6%	30.5%	30.4%
Couples should live together before marriage	57.3%	46.3%	51.3%	53.1%	48.7%
Students might appreciate the value of college more if they had to pay a greater share of the costs	56.2%	50.8%	53.3%	51.7%	55.0%
Marijuana should be legalized	22.8%	16.4%	19.3%	18.0%	20.1%
Busing to achieve racial balance in schools is all right	52.3%	54.9%	53.7%	54.9%	57.8%
Homosexual relations should be prohibited	59.7%	39.9%	49.0%	53.9%	57.2%
Colleges should divest of South African investments	51.4%	42.1%	46.4%	41.7%	39.2%
The chief benefit of college is that it increases one's earning power	73.9%	64.7%	69.0%	75.4%	71.9%
Employers should be allowed to require employees or job applicants to take drug tests	69.8%	72.0%	71.0%	72.4%	70.4%
The best way to control AIDS is through widespread, mandatory testing	67.7%	67.7%	67.7%	73.2%	72.6%
Just because a man thinks that a woman has "led him on" does not entitle him to have sex with her	75.3%	91.0%	83.8%	80.4%	82.3%
Only volunteers should serve in the armed forces	52.7%	53.9%	53.4%	53.0%	53.5%

4-year Colleges				Universities		Predominantly Black Colleges	
Public	Pvt. non-sectarian	Protestant	Catholic	Public	Private	Public	Private
55.7%	45.8%	47.2%	54.7%	50.5%	44.1%	47.7%	42.1%
19.4%	21.6%	26.6%	20.7%	21.1%	26.5%	17.9%	16.4%
1.5%	1.8%	1.9%	1.4%	1.5%	1.7%	2.5%	1.5%
65.7%	66.0%	63.9%	64.9%	61.2%	59.5%	75.8%	76.0%
66.7%	69.5%	66.6%	69.6%	66.4%	66.1%	74.5%	82.1%
82.7%	86.3%	84.7%	84.1%	84.0%	86.6%	80.3%	86.0%
26.5%	31.6%	28.5%	26.2%	32.9%	34.8%	22.4%	25.1%
70.1%	65.8%	67.5%	67.3%	68.8%	65.8%	57.3%	62.4%
27.9%	23.2%	23.7%	21.0%	22.5%	21.5%	30.9%	21.4%
61.1%	61.7%	59.8%	62.3%	61.0%	58.7%	56.6%	59.4%
56.0%	64.4%	49.4%	46.6%	64.8%	61.5%	57.0%	63.3%
21.7%	27.0%	25.1%	28.4%	21.9%	27.3%	35.8%	36.4%
49.4%	52.5%	37.5%	44.0%	53.9%	49.3%	42.0%	42.4%
25.5%	23.5%	23.8%	23.4%	21.3%	19.8%	37.3%	29.0%
49.8%	54.1%	37.8%	45.8%	55.0%	50.9%	52.2%	49.1%
54.5%	54.1%	53.5%	54.1%	53.1%	54.4%	50.5%	51.2%
18.1%	23.5%	15.6%	17.4%	21.6%	21.1%	21.8%	16.3%
53.8%	55.8%	53.8%	54.7%	50.5%	51.8%	62.3%	64.1%
53.2%	41.3%	50.3%	44.2%	42.7%	36.4%	51.3%	47.1%
43.9%	54.3%	47.5%	46.7%	50.8%	57.9%	50.9%	64.9%
72.1%	60.4%	61.2%	64.8%	65.9%	55.6%	76.2%	75.5%
73.3%	67.8%	73.6%	69.4%	68.3%	67.4%	69.8%	73.8%
70.3%	62.0%	63.4%	66.0%	62.9%	56.8%	72.4%	67.0%
84.3%	84.5%	87.4%	84.6%	86.1%	86.6%	79.5%	82.7%
54.1%	55.8%	52.0%	51.4%	53.3%	51.6%	58.6%	60.7%

	All Institutions			2-year Colleges	
	Men	Women	Total	Public	Private
Objectives considered essential or very important:[†]					
Becoming accomplished in a performing art	9.8%	11.3%	10.6%	8.7%	11.5%
Becoming an authority in his or her field	73.6%	70.6%	72.0%	69.1%	70.6%
Obtaining recognition from colleagues	56.9%	53.6%	55.1%	52.0%	51.8%
Influencing the political structure	19.8%	14.2%	16.8%	13.3%	14.2%
Influencing social values	32.7%	40.7%	37.0%	32.7%	39.9%
Raising a family	66.5%	67.3%	67.0%	66.1%	66.6%
Becoming an expert on finance and commerce	32.0%	20.8%	25.9%	26.3%	25.0%
Having administrative responsibility ...	42.9%	37.3%	39.8%	39.8%	38.0%
Being very well-off financially	77.8%	69.7%	73.4%	76.3%	74.7%
Helping others who are in difficulty ...	46.3%	65.0%	56.4%	53.7%	59.5%
Participating in such organizations as Peace Corps or VISTA	6.3%	8.0%	7.2%	6.1%	8.2%
Making a contribution to scientific theory	15.6%	8.8%	11.9%	10.8%	8.0%
Writing original works	12.7%	13.3%	13.0%	10.5%	11.6%
Creating artistic work	11.9%	13.0%	12.5%	11.3%	18.0%
Keeping up to date with political affairs	38.2%	29.4%	33.4%	24.3%	26.2%
Being successful in own business	56.8%	48.2%	52.1%	54.2%	60.6%
Developing a meaningful philosophy of life	49.4%	51.4%	50.5%	44.4%	50.3%
Participating in a community-action program	18.8%	24.2%	21.7%	18.0%	23.2%
Promoting racial understanding	29.8%	34.2%	32.2%	26.4%	31.2%
Getting married	66.0%	68.4%	67.3%	64.9%	67.5%

4-year Colleges				Universities		Predominantly Black Colleges	
Public	Pvt. non-sectarian	Protestant	Catholic	Public	Private	Public	Private
10.4%	13.9%	12.6%	10.2%	10.9%	12.9%	14.3%	12.9%
72.7%	72.2%	70.3%	71.2%	75.5%	74.9%	80.2%	83.3%
55.8%	55.8%	50.2%	57.3%	59.4%	58.2%	63.8%	65.0%
16.1%	20.0%	18.5%	18.6%	18.8%	24.1%	28.7%	30.8%
37.4%	40.4%	43.8%	41.5%	37.2%	40.5%	51.5%	55.0%
66.4%	66.6%	69.6%	70.7%	66.9%	70.2%	61.6%	67.5%
26.9%	22.9%	23.1%	27.4%	26.3%	26.1%	44.1%	37.7%
41.9%	35.8%	35.3%	40.7%	40.8%	40.0%	55.8%	50.2%
75.0%	68.1%	62.4%	71.6%	74.4%	68.7%	84.9%	88.2%
56.8%	58.5%	63.4%	60.2%	55.2%	59.0%	65.3%	73.9%
6.1%	10.1%	8.7%	8.7%	7.4%	9.4%	11.7%	10.5%
10.2%	13.4%	10.0%	9.9%	15.8%	14.7%	15.2%	18.7%
12.0%	16.7%	15.0%	13.5%	14.6%	17.3%	15.6%	15.6%
10.8%	17.7%	11.6%	12.6%	12.8%	13.0%	14.6%	11.1%
30.5%	41.8%	38.2%	37.3%	40.3%	52.0%	36.5%	46.3%
51.4%	50.5%	45.9%	52.3%	51.4%	49.5%	70.4%	68.5%
49.9%	56.6%	54.9%	52.6%	53.1%	59.7%	85.9%	67.3%
21.6%	25.6%	25.8%	24.1%	22.1%	27.5%	35.7%	44.2%
31.7%	41.1%	37.1%	33.9%	33.4%	40.7%	63.8%	74.1%
67.2%	67.1%	70.1%	72.0%	68.4%	71.6%	55.5%	61.8%

Note: Because of rounding or multiple responses, figures may add to more than 100 per cent.

*Frequently only; all other activities frequently or occasionally.

†Comparisons with previous years not recommended due to change in item order.

Source: "The American Freshman: National Norms for Fall 1988," by Alexander W. Astin, published by American Council on Education and University of California at Los Angeles.

3. Choose a local problem that interests you, one on your campus or in your home community. Follow the procedure below, using primary sources to develop a research essay for an audience of people who share your concerns.

- Describe the problem as you and your audience commonly know it. This should lead to a tentative hypothesis that you want to explore using the primary sources. (Example: It would appear, then, that if students had a vote on issues before the board of regents, the board's decisions would be more representative and would be adhered to.)
- Closely observe the problem—its components, movement (past and present), and operation.
- Interview those directly involved and those who can offer expert insight.
- Survey the opinions of others to inform your own view and to present a representative response to the issue.
- Test your hypothesis using the data you collect and formulate a conclusion.

Chapter 4

SELECTING SECONDARY SOURCES

- 65 percent of all Brazilians suffer from malnutrition.
- 33 percent of newspaper stories quote an unnamed source.
- 85 percent of elementary schoolchildren are characterized as hyperactive by their teachers.
- $8,000,000,000 is spent annually on pornography.
- One-fifth of the world's population lives under military-controlled government.
- Workers in France receive a minimum of 25 paid vacation days after one year of service; American workers receive 8.7 days.
- A single parent heads 26 percent of American families.
- Advertising time costs $12,700 per second on "The Cosby Show."
- There is a ratio of one physician to every 549 inhabitants in the United States.
- 720,000 Americans have surgery each year solely to improve appearance.
- 26,000 American-style homes were built in Japan in 1985.
- Twelve corporate mergers occurred per business day in 1986.
- 2,242,602 U.S. government employees have authority to classify documents as secret.
- 450,000 Americans were conceived by artificial insemination.
- 70 percent of fathers who contest child custody cases win custody of their children.[1]

Where would you go to find such information? Collecting such comprehensive data on your own, using primary source collection methods, would take a great deal of

---

[1] Lewis H. Lapham, Michael Pollan, and Eric Etheridge, *The Harper's Index Book* (New York: Henry Holt, 1987).

time and expertise. However, you can use the reference materials, periodicals, and books in your college library to lead you to the primary sources that others have gathered and the secondary sources that interpret and evaluate those sources for *your* assessment.

The diversity of sources and sheer volume of material that the library contains often make investigating appear to be an overwhelming task. But organized researchers don't spend days rummaging through one floor at a time, hoping to stumble upon some worthwhile information. The kinds of materials that libraries house make it possible to design a search strategy that will give you the balanced view of your subject that you need to write knowledgeably.

DESIGNING A SEARCH STRATEGY

A search strategy enables you to make a systematic search of the library's diverse resources. Beginning with reference works (encyclopedias, dictionaries, and bibliographies) and proceeding to more specific sources (abstracts, articles, and books), you will build the informational foundation needed to address your research to a variety of audiences; viewing the issue from a variety of perspectives will enable you to present your own view with confidence. A search strategy helps you to discover the issues, select the most relevant material for your needs, and make the best use of your time.

1. GATHERING GENERAL BACKGROUND AND SOURCE INFORMATION

Encyclopedias. Encyclopedias provide background information on people, places, subjects, events, and ideas. When using general encyclopedias, be sure to look in the encyclopedia's index for references to related subtopics and articles within the encyclopedia. Specialized encyclopedias cover information in particular fields or disciplines, providing more technical information and more thorough treatment of a topic. In addition, specialized encyclopedias often contain bibliographies that can lead you to other sources.

GENERAL ENCYCLOPEDIAS

Academic American Encyclopedia. Danbury, Conn.: Grolier, 1983.

Colliers Encyclopedia. New York: Macmillan, 1977.

Encyclopedia Americana. New York: Americana, 1977.

Encyclopaedia Britannica. Chicago: Encyclopaedia Britannica, 1979.

SPECIALIZED ENCYCLOPEDIAS

Encyclopedia of American Art. New York: Dutton, 1981.

Encyclopedia of Biological Sciences. 2d ed. Edited by Peter Gray. New York: Van Nostrand Reinhold, 1970.

Encyclopedia of Computer Science and Technology. 14 vols. New York: Dekker, 1980.

Encyclopedia of Education. 10 vols. Edited by Lee C. Deighton et al. New York: Macmillan, 1971.

Encyclopedia of Human Behavior: Psychology, Psychiatry, and Mental Health. 2 vols. Edited by Robert M. Goldenson. New York: Doubleday, 1974.

Encyclopedia of Management. Edited by C. Heyel. New York: Van Nostrand Reinhold, 1982.

Encyclopedia of Philosophy. 8 vols. Edited by P. Edwards. New York: Macmillan, 1967.

Encyclopedia of Physics. 2d ed. Edited by Robert M. Besancon. New York: Van Nostrand Reinhold, 1974.

Encyclopedia of Sociology. Edited by Gayle Johnson. Guilford, Conn.: Dushkin Press, 1974.

Encyclopedia of World Art. 15 vols. New York: McGraw-Hill, 1959–1968.

Encyclopedia of World History: Ancient, Medieval, and Modern, Chronologically Arranged. 5th ed. Compiled and edited by William Leonard Langer. Boston: Houghton Mifflin, 1972.

International Encyclopedia of the Social Sciences. 17 vols. Edited by D. L. Sills. New York: Free Press, 1972.

McGraw-Hill Encyclopedia of Science and Technology. 15 vols. 4th ed. New York: McGraw-Hill, 1977.

McGraw-Hill Encyclopedia of World Drama. 4 vols. New York: McGraw-Hill, 1972.

New College Encyclopedia of Music. Edited by J. A Westrop and F. L. Harrison; revised by C. Wilson. New York: Norton, 1976.

VNR Concise Encyclopedia of Mathematics. Edited by W. Gellert et al. Florence, Ken.: Van Nostrand Reinhold, 1977.

Dictionaries.   Your general reading and specialized encyclopedias more than likely will raise questions about the meaning, usage, etymology, and pronunciation of unfamiliar words and technical terms. Or you may need a more specific definition of a familiar term to use it effectively with a less knowledgeable audience. General and specialized dictionaries can provide you with this range of information.

General dictionaries are published in either abridged or unabridged form. The desk dictionary you use for daily writing is abridged. Although limited in scope and amount of information, the abridged dictionary, because it is revised frequently, is a good source for information on new words. For more comprehensive coverage, however, you will want an unabridged dictionary. The two most generally accepted un-abridged dictionaries are the *Oxford English Dictionary (OED)* and *Webster's Third.*

Oxford English Dictionary. 20 vols. New York: Oxford University Press, 1989.

Webster's Third New International Dictionary of the English Language. Springfield, Mass.: Merriam, 1981.

Specialized dictionaries concentrate on a single subject or discipline. The words they select and the information they include, consequently, are precise, and authoritative. The list below represents the range of specialization available.

SCIENCE AND TECHNOLOGY

Chamber's Dictionary of Science and Technology

Condensed Chemical Dictionary

Dictionary of Inventions and Discoveries

Ocran's Acronyms: A Dictionary of Abbreviations and Acronyms Used in Scientific and Technical Writing

SOCIAL SCIENCE

Dictionary of Behavioral Sciences

Dictionary of Politics

Dictionary of Psychology

HUMANITIES

Dictionary of Comparative Religions

Dictionary of Contemporary American Artists

Funk & Wagnalls' Standard Dictionary of Folklore, Mythology, and Legend

New Grove Dictionary of Music and Musicians

BUSINESS AND ECONOMICS

Dictionary for Accountants

Dictionary of Advertising Terms

Mathematical Dictionary for Economics and Business Administration

McGraw-Hill Dictionary of Modern Economics: A Handbook of Terms and Organizations

Specialized Sources.   Just as each discipline has its own specialized ency-clopedias and dictionaries, so too do many have additional specialized source guides to reference material. These special sources can provide general background information as well as guide you to reference works in the discipline. If you are unfamiliar with research in your chosen discipline, the following list will introduce helpful sources and methods of research.

SCIENCE AND TECHNOLOGY

Handbook of Chemistry and Physics

Materials Handbook

Reference Sources in Science and Technology

Science and Engineering Literature: A Guide to Current Reference Sources

Science and Technology: An Introduction to the Literature

SOCIAL SCIENCE

Almanac of American Politics

Bibliographical Guide to Educational Research

Congressional Quarterly Almanac

Information Sources of Political Sciences

Sources of Information in the Social Sciences

Student Anthropologist's Handbook

Student Sociologist's Handbook

United States Government Manual

HUMANITIES

Art Research Methods and Resources: A Guide to Finding Art Information

Field Guide to the Study of American Literature

New Cambridge Modern History

Philosopher's Guide to Sources

Reader's Guide to the Great Religions

BUSINESS AND ECONOMICS

Business Information Sources

Economics and Foreign Policy: A Guide to Sources

Standard and Poor's Industry Surveys

2. MEETING THOSE INVOLVED

Biographies. Important people populate every field of study. These are the discoverers, inventors, contributors, critics, adversaries, supporters, law makers, philanthropists, and prize winners. More than likely you were introduced to these people in your background reading, or perhaps a well-known person in the field inspired you to pursue your research. Reading specialized information on these people may provide you with greater insight into the issue you are investigating. Listed here are some sources that will assist you in your research.

GENERAL SOURCES

Current Biography

Dictionary of American Biography

McGraw-Hill Encyclopedia of World Biography

Who's Who

Who's Who in America

SCIENCE AND TECHNOLOGY

American Men and Women of Science

Dictionary of Scientific Biography

Who's Who in Science in Europe

HUMANITIES

American Authors 1600–1900: A Biographical Dictionary of American Literature

American Novelists Since WWII

American Poets Since WWII

British Authors Before 1800: A Biographical Dictionary

Contemporary American Composers

Contemporary Authors: A Biographical Guide to Current Authors and Their Works

Directory of American Scholars

World Authors, 1965–1970

3. TAKING A CLOSER LOOK

Indexes, Bibliographies, and Abstracts. Periodical and newspaper *indexes* help you find the most current information on your topic, including public attitudes about an issue or event when it occurred. All indexes categorize their resources by broad subject headings with subheadings within each category for more specific direction. As with other secondary reference sources, indexes are available in both general and specialized form. The abbreviation guide to the periodicals included in each index will show you that general indexes focus more on popular newsstand magazines while specialized indexes cover professional and academic journals. Both types of indexes will be invaluable to your investigation. This abbreviated list shows the range of available indexes.

GENERAL INDEXES

Periodicals: *Magazine Index* (1978–present)

Reader's Guide to Periodical Literature (1901–present)

Newspapers: *Newspaper Index* (*Chicago Tribune, Los Angeles Times, New Orleans Times-Picayune, Washington Post*)

New York Times Index (1913–present)

Wall Street Journal Index

Others: *Book Review Index* (1965–present, all fields)

Vertical File Index (1935–present, pamphlets)

SPECIALIZED INDEXES

Science and Technology

Applied Science and Technology Index

Biological and Agricultural Index

Cumulative Index to Nursing and Allied Health Literature

Engineering Index

General Science Index

Index Medicus

Social Science

Current Index to Journals in Education (1969–present)

Education Index (1929–present)

Index to Legal Periodicals (1908–present)

Public Affairs Information Service (1915–present)

Resources in Education (ERIC) (1975–present)

Social Science Index

Humanities

Art Index (1930–present)

Essay and General Literature Index (1900–1933), *Supplements* (1934–present)

Film Literature Index (1974–present)

Humanities Index (1974–present)

Music Index (1949–present)

Philosopher's Index (1967–present)

Religion Index I: Periodicals (1977–present)

Business and Economics

> *Accountant's Index* (1920–present)
>
> *Business Periodicals Index* (1958–present)
>
> *Personnel Literature* (1969–present)

Statistical Sources

> *American Statistics Index: A Comprehensive Guide and Index to the Statistical Publications of the U.S. Government* (1973–present)
>
> *Statistical Yearbook* (1949–present; international)

In addition to the periodical and newspaper sources that indexes provide, *bibliographies* also include books and a range of other sources, such as interviews. Just as you will prepare a bibliography or reference list for your research, so, too, do the writers of professional articles and encyclopedia entries. Consequently, many of the index sources you read will include useful bibliographies. And several sources exist primarily to help locate bibliographies on various subjects.

General Bibliographies

> *Bibliographic Index* (1938–present)
>
> *World Bibliography of Bibliographies* (1965–present)

Specialized Bibliographies

> *Cambridge Bibliography of English Literature* (1940–1977)
>
> *International Bibliography of Economics* (1952–present)
>
> *MLA* (Modern Language Association) *International Bibliography of Books and Articles on Modern Languages and Literatures* (1963–present)
>
> *Selective Bibliography for the Study of English and American Literature* (1979–present)

Time is often an important factor in your investigation of sources, especially when you have only one semester to complete your work or when you are working on research for several courses. Fortunately, *abstracts,* which are short summaries of larger works, can help you more selectively choose the most relevant sources. Because an abstract identifies the main points of an article or book, you can decide in advance whether your time will be well spent reading the complete work. Abstracts can be located in specialized reference sources.

Science and Technology

> *Biological Abstracts* (1980–present) (previously *Bioresearch Index,* 1967–1979)
>
> *Chemical Abstracts* (1907–present)
>
> *Science Abstracts* (1898–present, physics)

Social Science

America: History and Life (1964–present)

International Political Science Abstracts (1951–present)

Journal of Human Services Abstracts (1965–present)

Sage Public Administration Abstracts (1979–present)

Social Work Research and Abstracts (1977–present)

Sociological Abstracts (1952–present)

Women's Studies Abstracts (1972–present)

Humanities

Abstracts of English Studies (1958–present)

Historical Abstracts (1955–present)

New York Times Film Reviews (1913–1968, with updates)

Year's Work in English Studies (1919–present)

Business and Economics

Economic Titles/Abstracts (1974–present)

Interdisciplinary

Book Review Digest (1905–present)

Editorials on File (1970–present)

Facts on File (1941–present)

Many of the indexes, bibliographies, and abstract references already listed are also available through data-base searching. *Computerized searches* have the advantage of being faster than conventional methods, but they can be expensive as well. You will need to ask the librarian about the availability of data bases, the appropriateness of using them for your particular investigation, and the approximate cost. Some programs you may want to use are listed here.

Science and Technology

Agricola (agriculture)

Biosis Previews (biology, botany)

CA search (chemistry)

Compendix (engineering)

Geoarchive (geology)

Mathfile (mathematics)

Science and Technology (continued)

    NTIS (science and technology)

    SPIN (physics)

Social Science

    ERIC (education)

    NICEM (nonprint educational materials)

    PAIS (political science)

    Psychinfo (psychology)

    Psychological Abstracts

    Social Scisearch

    Sociological Abstracts

Humanities

    Arts and Humanities Citation Index

    MLA Bibliography (1976–present)

    Philosopher's Index

    Historical Abstracts

Business and Economics

    ABI/INFORM

    Econ Abstracts International

    Labor Statistics

    Management Contexts

    Standard and Poor's News

4. LOCATING SOURCES

To find books appropriate to your investigation, follow these basic steps.

1. First, consult your library's catalog system. Generally one of three systems will be used: a card catalog (in drawers), a microform system, or on-line computer access. Although the type of system may vary from one library to another, each system indexes material by subject, author, and title, and each uses call numbers to identify materials on the shelves. To locate books by specific title or author you choose (or enter) the AUTHOR or TITLE catalog to find out if the library owns the books you need.

2. When looking for books on a particular subject, first consult the *Library of Congress Subject Headings* (LCSH) for terms used in the subject catalog. These two large red volumes generally are kept near the library's catalog

access system and on each floor of the library. Figure 1 is an explanation of an LCSH entry.

3. When you have determined which heading to use, return to the library's catalog system and use the *subject* catalog to find books on your subject.

4. When you have found the catalog entry for the book you want, read the entry carefully. It will tell you if the book includes illustrations, maps, portraits, or a bibliography. Figure 2 is an example of an entry. The *last* series of letters and numbers at the bottom of each entry is the CALL NUMBER. This

Figure 1 *How to read an LCSH entry*

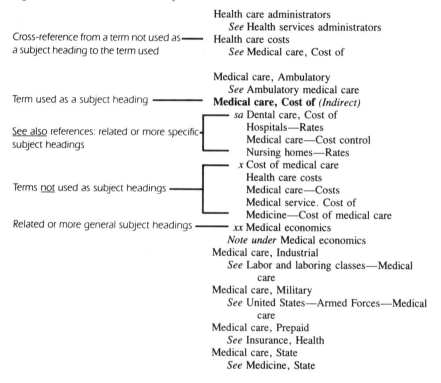

Figure 2 *A catalog entry*

```
HEMINGWAY, ERNEST, 1899-1961
    The sun also rises. --New York:
Charles Scribner's Sons, 1926.
    247 p. ; 22cm.
    ISBN 0-684-15327-0
    B/NA:  v5620866 77081616
```
CALL NUMBER ⟶ `PS 3515 .E37 S8 1926c`

is the number you use to locate the book on the library shelves. Use the library directory to determine on which floor you will find the book.

5. To find reference sources on your subject, consult the SUBJECT section of the catalog system and choose an appropriate FORM subdivision, such as

American Fiction—BIBLIOGRAPHY

Art—DICTIONARIES

Chemistry—INDEXES AND ABSTRACTS

Philosophy—HANDBOOKS, MANUALS

These sources will be found in the reference collection of your library.

To find appropriate articles in periodicals (that is, in magazines, journals, and newspapers), consult one or more indexes or abstracts. Each is arranged by subject or has a subject index. The subject headings will not always match those of the Library of Congress, but they will be similar. *See* and *see also* references will be included. The examples in Figures 3, 4, 5, and 6 will familiarize you with the entries you will find.

To find government publications, you must go beyond the library catalog system, which does not generally list federal publications. They have their own catalog called *Monthly Catalog of United States Publications.* This catalog, which usually is found in the government publications department of your library, works as an index to docu-

Figure 3 *Entry from* General Science Index

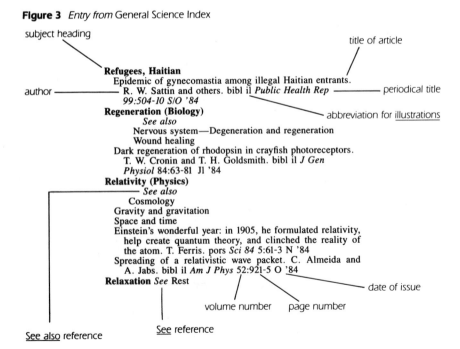

Figure 4 *Entries from* Current Index to Journals in Education

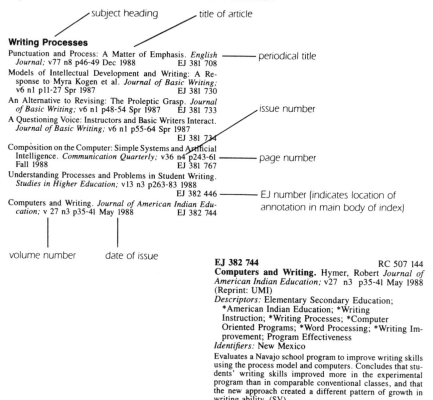

subject heading   title of article

Writing Processes

Punctuation and Process: A Matter of Emphasis. *English Journal;* v77 n8 p46-49 Dec 1988   EJ 381 708 ——— periodical title

Models of Intellectual Development and Writing: A Response to Myra Kogen et al. *Journal of Basic Writing;* v6 n1 p11-27 Spr 1987   EJ 381 730

An Alternative to Revising: The Proleptic Grasp. *Journal of Basic Writing;* v6 n1 p48-54 Spr 1987   EJ 381 733 ——— issue number

A Questioning Voice: Instructors and Basic Writers Interact. *Journal of Basic Writing;* v6 n1 p55-64 Spr 1987   EJ 381 734

Composition on the Computer: Simple Systems and Artificial Intelligence. *Communication Quarterly;* v36 n4 p243-61 Fall 1988   EJ 381 767 ——— page number

Understanding Processes and Problems in Student Writing. *Studies in Higher Education;* v13 n3 p263-83 1988   EJ 382 446 ——— EJ number (indicates location of annotation in main body of index)

Computers and Writing. *Journal of American Indian Education;* v 27 n3 p35-41 May 1988   EJ 382 744

volume number   date of issue

EJ 382 744   RC 507 144
Computers and Writing. Hymer, Robert *Journal of American Indian Education;* v27 n3 p35-41 May 1988 (Reprint: UMI)
Descriptors: Elementary Secondary Education; *American Indian Education; *Writing Instruction; *Writing Processes; *Computer Oriented Programs; *Word Processing; *Writing Improvement; Program Effectiveness
Identifiers: New Mexico
Evaluates a Navajo school program to improve writing skills using the process model and computers. Concludes that students' writing skills improved more in the experimental program than in comparable conventional classes, and that the new approach created a different pattern of growth in writing ability. (SV)

Figure 5 *Entry from* Psychological Abstracts

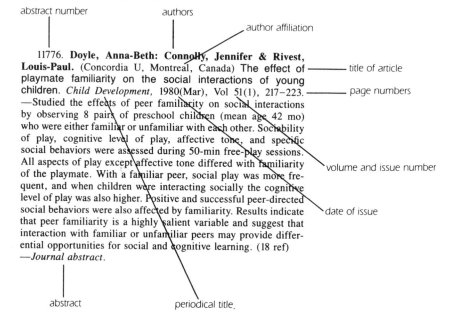

abstract number   authors

author affiliation

11776. **Doyle, Anna-Beth; Connolly, Jennifer & Rivest, Louis-Paul.** (Concordia U, Montreal, Canada) The effect of ——— title of article playmate familiarity on the social interactions of young children. *Child Development,* 1980(Mar), Vol 51(1), 217–223. ——— page numbers
—Studied the effects of peer familiarity on social interactions by observing 8 pairs of preschool children (mean age 42 mo) who were either familiar or unfamiliar with each other. Sociability of play, cognitive level of play, affective tone, and specific social behaviors were assessed during 50-min free-play sessions. All aspects of play except affective tone differed with familiarity ——— volume and issue number of the playmate. With a familiar peer, social play was more frequent, and when children were interacting socially the cognitive level of play was also higher. Positive and successful peer-directed social behaviors were also affected by familiarity. Results indicate ——— date of issue that peer familiarity is a highly salient variable and suggest that interaction with familiar or unfamiliar peers may provide differential opportunities for social and cognitive learning. (18 ref)
—*Journal abstract.*

abstract   periodical title

Figure 6 *Entry from* InfoTrac, *a computerized search system*

Information Access Company   InfoTrac 3.25   1/11/89 at 6:22
WHAT INFORMATION IS AVAILABLE

The following databases may be searched on the system: [See database
selection screen for the databases available in this library.]

INFOTRAC (tm) DATABASE
Contains references to articles from approximately 900 business, technical
and general interest publications. References from the current year plus the
three previous years are included (1984 to present). Plus references from
the last six months of the Wall Street Journal and the last 60 days of the
New York Times. Updated monthly.

INFOTRAC BACKFILE DATABASE
Contains references to articles from approximately 900 business, technical
and general interest publications. (Same title coverage as InfoTrac database
but does not include New York Times and Wall Street Journal.) Covers 1980
through 1983 and is updated annually.

GOVERNMENT PUBLICATIONS INDEX (tm)
An index to the Monthly Catalog of the United States Government Printing
Office. Can be searched by subject, author and issuing agency. Contains
references from 1980 to the present and is updated monthly.

LEGALTRAC (tm) DATABASE
Contains references to articles from approximately 750 legal publications,
including law reviews, bar journals and 7 legal newspapers. Contains
references from 1980 to the present and is updated monthly. [Same
coverage as the Legal Resource Index (tm).]

Information Access Company   InfoTrac 3.25   1/11/89 at 6:21
SAMPLE CITATION:

TAX SHELTERS <---------------------------------------(subject heading)
  see also
    COMMODITY TAX STRADDLES <-------------------(related heading)
    SAFE HARBOR LEASING
-ACCOUNTING <---(subheading)
  Funds that cut your taxes. Changing Times–Nov '85 <--------(reference)
p96(2)
-AGRICULTURE
  BARNS – A Tax Shelter. by A.B. McKie Canadian
Banker–Aug. '83 p16-17
-ANALYSIS

ments such as congressional reports, census materials, military reports, vital statistics, and impact statements on energy and the environment.

The *Monthly Catalog* indexes government documents by author, title, subject, and key word. To use the catalog, first look up your topic in the subject index. Then use the entry number from the subject index to find the place in the catalog section where the document is fully described. The catalog section, which is arranged numerically, gives the full bibliographic information for each item. The government publications librarian will use this number to get the document you request.

5. FINALIZING YOUR STRATEGY

As these resources demonstrate, a basic search strategy moves from material providing general background information to specific documents and opinions on your subject. This systematic approach can help you to answer many of the preliminary questions you have when you begin your investigation.

What are the issues in this subject? Who is involved? What are the effects?

What has been written and documented about this topic?

Which of these sources are available for me to use?

The diagram in Figure 7 illustrates how you can conduct your search in an organized way. As you move from general to specific source information, your preliminary

Figure 7 *A research strategy*

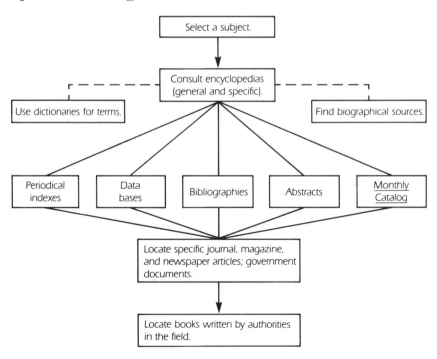

questions will be answered and new questions about the material you find will emerge, giving you a well-directed focus for finding your next source. Of course, some of these sources may not be appropriate to the subject you choose to investigate, but considering the potential use of each one will encourage you to think about the subject from a variety of perspectives and ultimately to narrow your focus. From the sources you do decide to use, you can develop a working bibliography of material from which you can begin writing.

CHOOSING SOURCES

Each argument you pursue and each audience you hope to reach will place different demands on you as a researcher in deciding which sources to use. One way to practice this decision-making skill is to be a more critical reader, to study the way other writers use sources in their writing.

The following selection is an excerpt from Phillip Knightley's book *The First Casualty: From the Crimea to Vietnam: The War Correspondent as Hero, Propagandist, and Myth Maker* (1975). A veteran journalist and special correspondent in several wars, Knightley writes with the authority of professional and personal experience. Possible audiences for the book might include those in the general public interested in how fairly the media report war, journalism students, and Knightley's colleagues and peers who had similar experiences. As you read the selection, consider the notes in the margin commenting on Knightley's choice of sources. (The marginal notes are numbered to correspond to the superscripts in the text. The footnotes, assigned the same numbers, document the sources.)

The First Televised War

PHILLIP KNIGHTLEY

The most intrusive medium in Vietnam was television, and, as the war went on, the hunger of editors for combat footage increased. "Before they were satisfied with a corpse," Richard Lindley, a British television reporter, said. "Then they had to have people dying in action."[1] Michael Herr de-

[1] Uses a direct quote from a reporter whom some of his audience may recognize. The quote was published in a well-

---

[1] *London Sunday Times*, November 26, 1967.

scribed a truck carrying a dying ARVN soldier that stopped near a group of correspondents. The soldier, who was only nineteen or twenty, had been shot in the chest. A television cameraman leaned over the Vietnamese and began filming. The other correspondents watched. "He opened his eyes briefly a few times and looked back at us. The first time he tried to smile . . . then it left him. I'm sure he didn't even see us the last time he looked, but we all knew what it was that he had seen just before that."[2] The Vietnamese had seen the zoom lens of a sixteen-millimeter converted Auricon sound camera capturing his last moments of life on film that, if the flight connections worked and the editors back at the network liked it, would be shown in American living rooms within forty-eight hours.

This little item would not be exceptional. During the Tet offensive, a Vietnamese in a checked shirt appeared on television being walked—that is, dragged—between two soldiers. The soldiers took him over to a man holding a pistol, who held it to the head of the man in the checked shirt and blew his brains out. All of it was seen in full color on television (and later in a memorable series of photographs taken by Eddie Adams of the AP).

Any viewer in the United States who watched regularly the television reporting from Vietnam— and it was from television that 60 per cent of Americans got most of their war news—would agree that he saw scenes of real-life violence, death, and horror on his screen that would have been unthinkable before Vietnam. The risk and intrusion that such filming involved could, perhaps, be justified if it could be shown that television had been particularly effective in revealing the true nature of the war and thus had been able to change people's attitudes to it. Is there any evidence to this effect?

The director of CBS News in Washington, William Small, wrote: "When television covered its 'first war' in Vietnam it showed a terrible truth of war in a manner new to mass audiences. A case can be made, and certainly should be examined, that

2 *Christian Science Monitor,* May 29–June 30, 1970.

---

respected newspaper. The date of publication marks the beginning of active U.S. involvement, and the content of the quote provides background information on the previous view toward media coverage contrasted with the view used in Vietnam.

[2] This quote from a man who may be recognized by some readers provides a more specific example of the media's coverage of the war. The quote was printed in a respected newspaper during a time of heavy fighting in the war. The author implies that the man being quoted is a journalist, but the reader doesn't know for sure. Still, his eyewitness account is convincing.

Question: Does the author need to document that "60 percent of Americans" got their news information on the war from TV?

this was cardinal to the disillusionment of Americans with this war, the cynicism of many young people towards America, and the destruction of Lyndon Johnson's tenure of office."[3] A *Washington Post* reporter, Don Oberdorfer, amply documents, in his book *Tet*, the number of commentators and editors (including those of Time Inc.) who had to re-examine their attitudes after extensive television—and press—coverage brought home to them the bewildering contradictions of a seemingly unending war.

Television's power seems to have impressed British observers even more than American. The director-general of the Royal United Service Institution, Air Vice-Marshal S. W B. Menaul, believes that television had "a lot to answer for [in] the collapse of American morale in relation to the Vietnam war." The then editor of the *Economist*, Alistair Burnet, wrote that the television reporting of Vietnam had made it very difficult for two American administrations to continue that war, "which was going on in American homes," irrespective of the merits or demerits of why the United States was actually involved in Vietnam. Robin Day, the BBC commentator, told a seminar of the Royal United Service Institution that the war on color-television screens in American living rooms had made Americans far more anti-militarist and anti-war than anything else: "One wonders if in the future a democracy which has uninhibited television coverage in every home will ever be able to fight a war, however just. . . . The full brutality of the combat will be there in close up and color, and blood looks very red on the color television screen." And the Director of Defence Operations, Plans and Supplies at the Ministry of Defence, Brigadier F. G. Caldwell, said that the American experience in Vietnam meant that if Britain were to go to war again, "we would have to start saying to ourselves, are we going to let the television cameras loose on the battlefield?"[4]

All this seems very persuasive, and it would

5

6

[3] *Sunday Times*, October 19 and October 10, 1971; *The Times*, July 12, 1971.

[4] J. Lucas, *Dateline Vietnam* (New York: Award Books, 1967), p. 15.

[3] Uses a quote from a person who had the power to decide what was seen on the news to specifically identify the issue. That Small's concern was printed three times during one year in a widely read, respected newspaper emphasizes the concern. Many readers may be familiar with the quote.

Reference to the views of the *Washington Post* reporter further demonstrates the concern the media felt.

[4] Uses a source written near the beginning of the war to demonstrate how the British, our allies, perceived the effects of the war coverage on television. The catalog of quotes further

be difficult to believe that the sight, day after day, of American soldiers and Vietnamese civilians dying in a war that seemed to make no progress could not have had *some* effect on the viewer. Yet a survey conducted for *Newsweek* in 1967 suggested a remarkably different conclusion: that television had encouraged a majority of viewers to *support* the war. When faced with deciding whether television coverage had made them feel more like "backing up the boys in Vietnam" or like opposing the war, 64 per cent of viewers replied that they were moved to support the soldiers and only 26 per cent to oppose the war. A prominent American psychiatrist, Fredric Wertham, said, in the same year, that television had the effect of conditioning its audience to accept war, and a further *Newsweek* enquiry, in 1972, suggested that the public was developing a tolerance of horror in the newscasts from Vietnam—"The only way we can possibly tolerate it is by turning off a part of ourselves instead of the television set."

Edward Jay Epstein's survey of television producers and news editors, for his book *News from Nowhere*, showed that more than two-thirds of those he interviewed felt that television had had little effect in changing public opinion on Vietnam. An opinion commonly expressed was that people saw exactly what they wanted to in a news report and that television only served to reinforce existing views. *The New Yorker*'s television critic, Michael J. Arlen, reported, on several occasions, that viewers had a vague, unhappy feeling that they were not getting "the true picture" of Vietnam from the medium.[5] So if it was true that television did not radically change public opinion about the war, could it have been because of the quality of the coverage?

Television is a comparatively new medium. There were 10,000 sets in the United States in 1941; at the time of Korea there were 10 million, and at the peak of the Vietnam War 100 million. There was some television reporting in Korea, a lot of it daring—an American general had to order the BBC cameraman Cyril Page to get down off the front of a

---

[5] F. Harvey, *Air War Vietnam* (New York: Bantam, 1967), p. 115.

supports the author's negative view of the media's approach and has the effect of intensifying the reader's concern.

This material is in direct contrast to the results of the *Newsweek* polls presented in the next paragraph. As a result of the strong contrast, many of the readers will be perplexed and anxious to better understand the problem.

7

8

[5] Uses one source to quote another source for the purpose of identifying a third possibility: that television coverage of the war did not change opinion. The information is vague and secondhand, presented with little authority. And the poll cited surveyed the opinions of those who produced the news. Perhaps they were not able to measure the effect from where they stood. Also, the date of the source is from the beginning of the war when people

tank to which he had tied himself so as to get a grandstand view of the battle as the tank went into action. But, until Vietnam, no one knew what problems the prolonged day-by-day coverage of a war by television would produce. The first was surprising—a lack of reality. It had been believed that when battle scenes were brought into the living room the reality of war would at last be brought home to a civilian audience. But Arlen was quick to point out, in *The New Yorker,* that by the same process battle scenes are made less real, "diminished in part by the physical size of the television screen, which, for all the industry's advances, still shows one a picture of men three inches tall shooting at other men three inches tall."[6] Sandy Gall of ITN found shooting combat footage difficult and dangerous, and the end result very disappointing. "I think you lose one dimension on television's small screen and things look smaller than life; the sound of battle, for example, never coming across. I am always let down when I eventually see my footage and think, Is that all? The sense of danger never comes across on television and you, the correspondent, always look as though you had an easy time of it."[7]

For many Americans in Vietnam, there 9 emerged a strange side to the war that became directly related to television—the fact that the war seemed so unreal that sometimes it became almost possible to believe that everything was taking place on some giant Hollywood set and all the participants were extras playing a remake of *Back to Bataan.* GIs—and even correspondents—brought up on Second World War movies shown on television, used to seeing Errol Flynn sweeping to victory through the jungles of Burma or Brian Donlevy giving the Japanese hell in the Coral Sea, tended to relate their experiences in Vietnam to the Hollywood version of America at war.[8] Michael Herr, making a

knew little about what was happening. The impact is questionable.

[6] While the quote introduces a possible cause for the effect in question, again it is a very early view and is quoted from another source. The person quoted is an expert TV critic, but what is his experience with war?

[7] Strong use of direct quote from an eyewitness. The quote introduces the element of risk in coverage but again represents a view from early in the war.

[8] Self-explanatory reference to the actor's son as a reporter. Was he for real or playing a role?

---

[6] Harvey, p. 184.

[7] *Washington Post,* February 23, 1966.

[8] The arrival in 1965 of Flynn's son, Sean, as a correspondent tended to confirm this feeling.

dash, with David Greenway of *Time*, from one position at Hué to another, caught himself saying to a Marine a line from a hundred Hollywood war films: "We're going to cut out now. Will you cover us?" One should not be surprised, therefore, to find that GIs sometimes behaved, in the presence of television cameras, as if they were making *Dispatch from Da Nang*. Herr describes soldiers running about during a fight because they knew there was a television crew nearby. "They were actually making war movies in their heads, doing little guts and glory Leatherneck tap dances under fire, getting their pimples shot off for the networks."[9]

So it is not difficult to understand how, when 10 seen on a small screen, in the enveloping and cosy atmosphere of the household, sometime between the afternoon soap-box drama and the late-night war movie, the television version of the war in Vietnam could appear as just another drama, in which the hero is the correspondent and everything will come out all right at the end. Jack Laurence of CBS, an experienced war correspondent, who spent a lot of time in Vietnam, had this possibility brought home to him in Israel during the 1973 conflict. He was in a hotel lobby, and a couple who had just arrived from the United States recognized him and said, "We saw you on television and we knew everything was going to be all right because you were there."[10] There is not much a television correspondent can do about such a situation as that; it seems inherent in the nature of the medium. However, correspondents, or, more fairly, their editors, do have something to answer for in their selection of news in Vietnam.

Years of television news of the war have left 11 viewers with a blur of images consisting mainly of helicopters landing in jungle clearings, soldiers charging into undergrowth, wounded being loaded onto helicopters, artillery and mortar fire, air strikes on distant targets, napalm canisters turning slowly in the sky, and a breathless correspondent poking a

[9]This eyewitness account gives the reader the sense of being there and raises the issue of whether or not the cameras affected the actions of the soldiers. While the source, an interview, yields personal insights, those insights represent only one opinion. Is that enough?'

[10]Although this quote is secondhand, it refers to a period of time much later in the war so it has more impact in explaining the effect of news coverage on the public. It offers a new kind of support and advances the writer's argument.

---

[9]Interview with John Shaw.
[10]Harvey, p. 104.

stick microphone under an army officer's nose and asking, "What's happening up there, Colonel?" (The only honest answer came, in 1972, from a captain on Highway 13. "I wish the hell I knew," he said.) The networks claimed that combat footage was what the public wanted; that concentrating on combat prevented the film's being out of date if it was delayed in transmission; that it was difficult to shoot anything other than combat film when only three or four minutes were available in the average news program for events in Vietnam; and that the illusion of American progress created by combat footage shot from only one side was balanced by what the correspondent had to say.

This is simply not true. To begin with, combat 12 footage fails to convey all aspects of combat. "A cameraman feels so inadequate, being able to record only a minute part of the misery, a minute part of the fighting," said Kurt Volkert, a CBS cameraman. "You have to decide what the most important action is. Is it the woman holding her crying baby? Is it the young girl cringing near her house because of the exploding grenades? Or is it the defiant looking Vietcong with blood on his face just after capture?" [11] When the cameraman's thirty minutes of combat footage are edited down to three minutes—not an unusual editing ratio—the result is a segment of action that bears about as much relation to the reality in Vietnam as a battle scene shot in Hollywood does. In fact, the Hollywood version would probably appear more realistic.

The American viewer who hoped to learn 13 something serious about Vietnam was subjected, instead, to a television course in the techniques of war, and he was not sufficiently exposed either to what the war meant to the people over whose land it was being fought, or to the political complexities of the situation, or even to the considered personal views of reporters who had spent years covering the situation. Yet, even by the networks' own standards, the limited aspects of the war that the viewer

[11] Uses the quote to represent a different point of view, that of the camera operator. The quote provides new information, showing the choices in the conflict and in the editing process. The date of the source strengthens the information, but the title of the source implies that the views expressed in the book may be one-sided. Still, the inexperienced members of the audience are given an authentic quandary to consider.

[11] P. Jones Griffiths, *Vietnam Inc.* (New York: Macmillan, 1971), p. 60.

was permitted to see could produce excellent television. One of the most dramatic pieces of film on the war was shot by a CBS team on Highway 13 late in April 1972. A South Vietnamese mine, intended to stop advancing enemy tanks, had caught a truck loaded with refugees. The film showed deaf children, distressed babies, and a woman weeping over the body of her son. The reporter, Bob Simon, described what had happened and then, with perhaps the best sign-off line from Vietnam, said simply, "There's nothing left to say about this war, nothing at all." "Morley Safer's Vietnam," an hour-long report by the CBS correspondent in Saigon, was Safer's own explicit view, and was hailed by *The New Yorker*'s critic, Michael J. Arlen, as "one of the best pieces of journalism to come out of the Vietnam war in any medium." But film like this was rare.

Competition for combat footage was so intense that it not only forced American television teams to follow each other into what the BBC's correspondent Michael Clayton called "appallingly dangerous situations," but it also made editors reluctant to risk allowing a team the time and the freedom to make its own film of the war. Where were the television equivalents of Martha Gellhorn's series on Vietnamese orphanages and hospitals, or Philip Jones Griffiths' searing book on the nature of the war, *Vietnam Inc.?* True, television was handicapped by its mechanics—a three-man, or even a two-man, team loaded with camera, sound equipment, and film is less mobile and more dependent on military transport, and in a dangerous situation more vulnerable, than a journalist or a photographer. In its presentation, too, television is sometimes handicapped by its commercial associations. The Vietnamese cameraman Vo Suu filmed the brutal shooting of a Vietcong suspect by General Nguyen Ngoc Loan during the Tet offensive. NBC blacked out the screen for three seconds after the dead man hit the ground, so as to provide a buffer before the commercial that followed. (What television *really* wanted was action in which the men died cleanly and not too bloodily. "When they get a film which shows what a mortar does to a man, really shows the flesh torn and the blood flowing, they get squeamish," says Richard Lindley. "They want it to be just so. They want television to be cinema."[12])

American television executives showed too 15 little courage in their approach to Vietnam. They followed each other into paths the army had chosen for them. They saw the war as "an American war in Asia—and that's the only story the American audience is interested in," and they let other, equally important, aspects of Vietnam go uncovered.

_____

[12] Jones Griffiths, p. 62.

[12] This quote, while strong support for the writer's critical view, is presented in parentheses as if it were not important. Maybe the writer is trying to be ironic. The eyewitness account and graphic details certainly leave an impact on the reader. The comment made above on the source's date and title also apply here.

After looking closely at Knightley's use of sources, you can see that his primary criteria for selecting sources were that they be direct quotes, that those quoted be experts with firsthand experience, and that the opinions represent the various positions (correspondent, camera operator, news director) responsible for making the decisions that caused the effect he was criticizing. If the sources he chose effectively conveyed his purpose to his intended audience, then his choices were good ones. But an audience that questioned his use of sources at any point might not accept his point of view on the subject, at least not completely.

Each audience and subject combination may require that you choose sources for different purposes; however, readers generally expect certain qualities of all sources. First, readers expect sources to be informative, to provide specific, precise information that verifies what they know and explains what they need to know. Second, readers expect authoritative sources—that is, they want to hear from those who have experience and expertise, those who are closest to the subject. And third, readers expect sources that are recognized and respected in the field.

Learning what sources are available and locating those sources can be accomplished by using an organized search strategy. Choosing the sources for your writing will include *many* strategies depending on what assumptions your audience holds (see Chapter 6) and how you plan to appeal to the audience (see Chapters 7 and 8). The sources you choose and where you position them will ultimately shape the success of your argument.

EXERCISES: CHOOSING SOURCES

1. Choose one of the subjects listed below or one of your own choice and design a search strategy. Use the list of references presented in the chapter and the diagram in Figure 7 to guide you in making your decisions.

pay equity	polygraph tests
cultural literacy	compact discs
immigration laws	metaphysical conceit
national park protection	dolphin language

2. Analyze the selection of sources in the following essay, "Why Women Aren't Getting to the Top," by Susan Fraker, which appeared in *Fortune* (April 16, 1984). On a sheet of paper, first write the rhetorical context for the essay: subject, audience, purpose, occasion. Next, make three columns across the paper. Label them, from left to right, Description of Source, Writer's Use of the Source, Effect on Audience. After filling out the chart for the essay, write a paragraph assessing the writer's criteria for selecting the sources and the effectiveness of the sources in conveying the writer's purpose to the intended audience.

Why Women Aren't Getting to the Top

SUSAN FRAKER

Ten years have passed since U.S. corporations began hiring more than 1
token numbers of women for jobs at the bottom rung of the management ladder. A decade into their careers, how far up have these women climbed? The answer: not as far as their male counterparts. Despite impressive progress at the entry level and in middle management, women are having trouble breaking into senior management. "There is an invisible ceiling for women at that level," says Janet Jones-Parker, executive director of the Association of Executive Search Consultants Inc. "After eight or ten years, they hit a barrier."

The trouble begins at about the $75,000 to $100,000 salary level, 2
and seems to get worse the higher one looks. Only one company on *Fortune*'s list of the 500 largest U.S. industrial corporations has a woman chief executive. That woman, Katharine Graham of the Washington Post Co. (No. 342), readily admits she got the job because her family owns a controlling share of the corporation.

More surprising, given that women have been on the ladder for 3
ten years, is that none currently seems to have a shot at the top rung. Executive recruiters, asked to identify women who might become presidents or chief executives of *Fortune 500* companies, draw a blank. Even companies that have women in senior management privately concede that these women aren't going to occupy the chairman's office.

Women have only four of the 154 spots this year at the Harvard 4
Business School's Advanced Management Program—a prestigious 13-
week conclave to which companies send executives they are grooming
for the corridors of power. The numbers aren't much better at comparable programs at Stanford and at Dartmouth's Tuck School. But perhaps the most telling admission of trouble comes from men at the top.
"The women aren't making it," confessed the chief executive of a *Fortune 500* company to a consultant. "Can you help us find out why?"

All explanations are controversial to one faction or another in 5
this highly charged debate. At one extreme, many women—and some
men—maintain that women are the victims of blatant sexism. At the
other extreme, many men—and a few women—believe women are
unsuitable for the highest managerial jobs: they lack the necessary assertiveness, they don't know how to get along in this rarefied world, or
they have children and lose interest in—or time for—their careers.
Somewhere in between is a surprisingly large group of men and women
who see "discrimination" as the major problem, but who often can't
define precisely what they mean by the term.

The discrimination they talk about is not the simple-minded sex- 6
ism of dirty jokes and references to "girls." It is not born of hatred, or
indeed of any ill will that the bearer may be conscious of. What they
call discrimination consists simply of treating women differently from
men. The notion dumbfounds some male managers. You mean to say,
they ask, that managerial women don't want to be treated differently
from men in any respect, and that by acting otherwise—as I was raised
to think only decent and gentlemanly—I'm somehow prejudicing
their chances for success? Yes, the women respond.

"Men I talk to would like to see more women in senior manage- 7
ment," says Ann Carol Brown, a consultant to several *Fortune 500*
companies. "But they don't recognize the subtle barriers that stand in
the way." Brown thinks the biggest hurdle is a matter of comfort, not
competence. "At senior management levels, competence is assumed,"
she says. "What you're looking for is someone who fits, someone who
gets along, someone you trust. Now that's subtle stuff. How does a group
of men feel that a woman is going to fit? I think it's very hard."

The experience of an executive at a large Northeastern bank illus- 8
trates how many managerial women see the problem. Promoted to senior vice president several years ago, she was the first woman named
to that position. But she now believes it will be many years before the
bank appoints a woman executive vice president. "The men just don't
feel comfortable," she says. "They make all sorts of excuses—that I'm
not a banker [she worked as a consultant originally], that I don't know
the culture. There's a smoke screen four miles thick. I attribute it to
being a woman." Similarly, 117 to 300 women executives polled re-

cently by UCLA's Graduate School of Management and Korn/Ferry International, an executive search firm, felt that being a woman was the greatest obstacle to their success.

A common concern among women, particularly in law and investment banking, is that the best assignments go to men. "Some departments—like sales and trading or mergers and acquisitions—are considered more macho, hence more prestigious," says a woman at a New York investment bank. "It's nothing explicit. But if women can't get the assignments that allow them to shine, how can they advance?" 9

Women also worry that they don't receive the same kind of constructive criticism that men do. While these women probably overestimate the amount of feedback their male colleagues receive, even some men acknowledge widespread male reluctance to criticize a woman. "There are vast numbers of men who can't do it," says Eugene Jennings, professor of business administration at Michigan State University and a consultant to a dozen large companies. A male banking executive agrees: "A male boss will haul a guy aside and just kick ass if the subordinate performs badly in front of a client. But I heard about a woman here who gets nervous and tends to giggle in front of customers. She's unaware of it and her boss hasn't told her. But behind her back he downgrades her for not being smooth with customers." 10

Sometimes the message that has to be conveyed to a woman manager is much more sensitive. An executive at a large company says he once had to tell a woman that she should either cross her legs or keep her legs together when she sat. The encounter was obviously painful to him. "She listened to me and thanked me and expressed shock at what she was doing," he recalls, with a touch of agony in his voice. "My God, this is something only your mother tells you. I'm a fairly direct person and a great believer in equal opportunity. But it was damn difficult for me to say this to a woman whom I view to be very proper in all other respects." 11

Research by Anne Harlan, a human resource manager at the Federal Aviation Administration, and Carol Weiss, a managing associate of Charles Hamilton Associates, a Boston consulting firm, suggests that the situation doesn't necessarily improve as the number of women in an organization increases. Their study, conducted at the Wellesley College Center for Research on Women and completed in 1982, challenges the theory advanced by some experts that when a corporation attained a "critical mass" of executive women—defined as somewhere between 30% and 35%—job discrimination would vanish naturally as men and women began to take each other for granted. 12

Harlan and Weiss observed the effects of different numbers of women in an organization during a three-year study of 100 men and women managers at two Northeastern retailing corporations. While 13 their sample of companies was not large, after their results were published, other companies said they had similar experiences. Harlan and Weiss found that while overt resistance drops quickly after the first few women become managers, it seems to pick up again as the number of women reaches 15%. In one company they studied, only 6% of the managers were women, compared with 19% in the second company. But more women in the second company complained of discrimination, ranging from sexual harassment to inadequate feedback. Could something other than discrimination—very different corporate cultures, say—have accounted for the result? Harlan and Weiss say no, that the two companies were eminently comparable.

Consultants and executives who think discrimination is the prob- 14 lem tend to believe it persists in part because the government has relaxed its commitment to affirmative action, which they define more narrowly than some advocates do. "We're not talking about quotas or preferential treatment," says Margaret Hennig who, along with Anne Jardim, heads the Simmons College Graduate School of Management. "That's stupid management. We just mean the chance to compete equally." Again, a semantic chasm separates women and men. Women like Hennig and Jardim think of affirmative action as a vigorous effort on the part of companies to ensure that women are treated equally and that sexist prejudices aren't permitted to operate. Men think the term means reverse discrimination, giving women preferential treatment.

Legislation such as the Equal Employment Opportunity Act of 15 1972 prohibits companies from discriminating against women in hiring. The laws worked well—indeed, almost too well. After seven or eight years, says Jennings of Michigan State, the pressure was off and no one pushed hard to see that discrimination was eliminated in selecting people for senior management. Jennings thinks the problem began in the latter days of the Carter Administration, when the economy was lagging and companies worried more about making money than about how their women managers were doing. The Reagan Administration hasn't made equal opportunity a priority either.

What about the belief that women fall behind not because of dis- 16 crimination, but because they are cautious, unaggressive, and differently motivated than men—or less motivated? Even some female executives believe that women derail their careers by choosing staff jobs over high-risk, high-reward line positions. One woman, formerly with a large consumer goods company and now president of a market research firm, urges women to worry less about sexism and more about whether the jobs they take are the right route to the top. "I spent five years thinking the only reason I didn't become a corporate officer at my former company was because of my sex," she says. "I finally had to come to grips with the fact that I overemphasized being a woman and underemphasized what I did for a living. I was in a staff function—the company didn't live and die by what I did."

Men and women alike tend to believe that because women are 17 raised differently they must manage differently. Research to support this belief is hard to come by, though. The women retail managers studied by Harlan and Weiss, while never quarterbacks or catchers, had no trouble playing on management teams. Nor did they perform less well on standardized tests measuring qualities like assertiveness and leadership. "Women don't manage differently," Harlan says flatly.

In a much larger study specifically addressing management 18 styles, psychologists Jay Hall and Susan Donnell of Teleometrics International Inc., a management training company, reached the same conclusion. They matched nearly 2,000 men and women managers according to age, rank in their organization, kind of organization, and the number of people they supervised. The psychologists ran tests to assess everything from managerial philosophies to the ability to get along with people, even quizzing subordinates on their views of the boss. Donnell and Hall concluded, "Male and female managers do not differ in the way they manage the organization's technical and human resources."

Data on how women's expectations—and therefore, arguably, 19 their performance—may differ from men's are more confusing. Stanford Professor Myra Strober studied 150 men and 26 women who graduated from the Stanford Business School in 1974. When she and a colleague, Francine Gordon, polled the MBAs shortly before graduation, they discovered that the women had much lower expectations for their peak earnings. The top salary the women expected during their careers was only 60% of the men's. Four years later the ratio had fallen to 40%.

Did this mean that women were less ambitious or were willing to 20 take lower salaries to get management jobs? Strober doesn't think so. She says a major reason for the women's lower salary expectations was that they took jobs in industries that traditionally pay less, but which, the women thought, offered opportunities for advancement. Almost 20% of the women in her sample went into government, compared with 3% of the men. On the other hand, no women went into investment banking or real estate development, which each employed about 6% of the men. Strober points out, however, that investment banking and big-time real estate were all but closed to women in the early 1970s. "One way people decide what their aspirations are," she says, "is to look around and see what seems realistic. If you look at a field and see no women advancing, you may modify your goals."

Some of what Mary Anne Devanna found in her examination of 21

MBAs contradicts Strober's conclusions. Devanna, research coordinator of the Columbia Business School's Center for Research in Career Development, matched 45 men and 45 women who graduated from the Columbia Business School from 1969 to 1972. Each paired man and woman had similar backgrounds, credentials, and marital status. The starting salaries of the women were 98% of the men's. Using data collected in 1980, Devanna found a big difference in the salaries men and women ultimately achieved, though. In manufacturing, the highest paying sector, women earned $41,818 after ten years vs. $59,733 for the men. Women in finance had salaries of $42,867 vs. $46,786 for the men. The gap in the service industries was smallest: $36,666 vs. $38,600. She then tested four hypotheses in seeking to explain the salary differences: (1) that women are less successful because they are motivated differently than men, (2) that motherhood causes women to divert attention from their careers, (3) that women seek jobs in low-paying industries, and (4) that women seek types of jobs—in human resources, say—that pay less.

Devanna found no major differences between the sexes in the 22 importance they attached to the psychic or monetary rewards of work. "The women did not expect to earn less than the men," she says. Nor did she find that motherhood led women to abandon their careers. Although several women took maternity leaves, all returned to work full time within six months. Finally, Devanna found no big differences in the MBAs' choice of industry or function, either when they took their first jobs or ten years later.

Devanna concluded that discrimination, not level of motivation 23 or choice of job, accounted for the pay differences. Could the problem simply have been performance—that the women didn't manage as well as men? Devanna claims that while she couldn't take this variable into account specifically, she controlled for all the variables that should have made for a difference in performance—from family background to grades in business school.

In their discussions with male executives, researchers like De- 24 vanna hear a recurrent theme—a conviction that women don't take their careers seriously. Even though most female managers were regarded as extremely competent, the men thought they would eventually leave—either to have children or because the tensions of work became too much. Both are legitimate concerns. A woman on the fast track is under intense pressure. Many corporate types believe that she gets much more scrutiny than a man and must work harder to succeed. The pressures increase geometrically if she has small children at home.

Perhaps as a result, thousands of women have careers rather 25 than husbands and children. In the UCLA-Korn/Ferry study of executive women, 52% had never married, were divorced, or were widowed, and 61% had no children. A similar study of male executives done in 1979 found that only 5% of the men had never married or were divorced and even fewer—3%—had no children.

Statistics on how many women bear children and then leave the corporation are incomplete. Catalyst, a nonprofit organization that encourages the participation of women in business, studied 815 two-career families in 1980. It found that 37% of the new mothers in the study returned to work within two months; 68% were back after 4½ months; 87% in eight months. To a company, of course, an eight-month absence is a long time. Moreover, the 10% or so who never come back—most males are convinced the figure is higher—represent a substantial capital investment lost. It would be naive to think that companies don't crank this into their calculation of how much the women who remain are worth.

Motherhood clearly slows the progress of women who decide to take long maternity leaves or who choose to work part time. But even those committed to working full time on their return believe they are sometimes held back—purposely or inadvertently. "Men make too many assumptions that women with children aren't free to take on time-consuming tasks," says Gene Kofke, director of human resources at AT&T. Karen Gonçalves, 34, quit her job as a consultant when she was denied challenging assignments after the birth of her daughter. "I was told clearly that I couldn't expect to move ahead as fast as I had been," she says. Later, when Gonçalves began working at the consulting firm of Arthur D. Little Inc. in Cambridge, Massachusetts, she intentionally avoided discussions of family and children: "I didn't keep a picture of my daughter in the office, and I would travel anywhere, no matter how hard it was for me."

Sometimes pregnancy is more of an issue for the men who witness it than for the women who go through it. Karol Emmerich, 35, now treasurer of Dayton Hudson Corp., was the first high-level woman at the department-store company to become pregnant. "The men didn't really know what to do," she recalls. "They were worried when I wanted to take three months off. But they wanted to encourage me to come back. So they promoted me to treasurer when I was seven months pregnant. Management got a lot of good feedback." Emmerich's experience would please Simmons Dean Anne Jardim, who worries that most organizations aren't doing enough to keep women who want to have children. "It's mind-boggling," she argues. "Either some of the brightest women in this country aren't going to reproduce or the companies are going to write off women in whom they have a tremendous investment."

To the corporation it may seem wasteful to train a woman and then be unable to promote her because she won't move to take the new job. The Catalyst study found that 40% of the men surveyed had moved for their jobs, vs. only 21% of the women. An argument can be made that an immobile executive is worth less to the corporation—and hence may be paid less.

Where women frequently do go is out of the company and into business for themselves. "When the achievements you want aren't forthcoming, it makes going out on your own easier," says a woman who has set up her own consultancy. "I was told I wouldn't make it into senior management at my bank. Maybe I just didn't have it. But the bank never found any woman who did. They were operating under a consent decree and they brought in a lot of women at the vice president level. Every single one of them left." Karen Gonçalves left Arthur D. Little to do part-time teaching and consulting when she was pregnant with her second child. "I didn't think I would get the professional satisfaction I wanted at ADL," she says.

From 1977 to 1980, according to the Small Business Administration, the number of businesses owned by women increased 33%, compared with an 11% increase for men—though admittedly the women's increase started from a much smaller base. While it's not clear from the numbers that women are entering the entrepreneurial ranks in greater numbers than they are joining corporations, some experts think so. "It's ironic," says Strober of Stanford. "The problem of the 1970s was bringing women into the corporation. The problem of the 1980s is keeping them there."

A few companies, convinced that women face special problems and that it's in the corporation's interest to help overcome them, are working hard at solutions. At Penn Mutual Life Insurance Co. in Philadelphia, where nearly half the managers are women, executives conducted a series of off-site seminars on gender issues and sex-role stereotypes. Dayton Hudson provides support (moral and financial) for a program whereby women in the company trade information on issues like personal financial planning and child care.

What women need most, the experts say, are loud, clear, continuing statements of support from senior management. Women have come a long way at Merck, says B. Lawrence Branch, the company's director of equal employment affairs, because Chairman John J. Horan insisted that their progress be watched. Merck has a program that identifies 10% of its women and 10% of minorities as "most promising." The company prepares a written agenda of what it will take for them to move to the next level. Progress upward may mean changing jobs or switching functions, so Merck circulates their credentials throughout the company. "We have a timetable and we track these women carefully," says Branch. Since 1979 almost 40% of the net growth in Merck's managerial staff has been women.

Sensitive to charges of reverse discrimination, Branch explains 34
that Merck has for years singled out the best employees to make sure
they get opportunities to advance. Women, he notes, were consistently
underrepresented in that group. In his view the tracking program simply allows women to get into the competition with fast-track men.
Others might not be so charitable. Any company that undertakes to
do something on behalf of its managerial women leaves itself open to
the charge that it too is discriminating—treating women and men
differently.

What everyone may be able to agree on is that opening corpora- 35
tions to competition in the executive ranks is clearly good for performance and profits. But how can a company do this? It can try to find
productive part-time work for all employees who want to work part
time—even managers. It can structure promotions so that fewer careers are derailed by an absence of a few months or the unwillingness
to relocate. It can make sure that the right information, particularly on
job openings, reaches everyone. Perhaps most importantly, it can reward its managers for developing talent of all sorts and sexes, penalize
them if they don't, and vigilantly supervise the process.

---

3. Choose ten different kinds of entries from the "Harper's Index" (*Harper's Magazine*,
September 1987). For each entry, list where you would go, what sources you would
consult (primary and secondary) to find that information.

Harper's Index

Number of the 142 nominations to the Supreme Court since 1789 that
    were not confirmed : 34

Number of the six Supreme Court nominations made by John Tyler
    that were not confirmed : 5

    Number of the four made by Millard Fillmore : 3

Average age of federal judges appointed by President Reagan : 49

Percentage of Americans who say that parents should not be allowed
    to choose the sex of their child : 69

Number of geep, a cross between a sheep and a goat, that have been
    genetically engineered : 2

Percentage of U.S. hospitals that have applied for patents on inventions
    using human tissues and cells : 50

Average price of an artificial arm (operation included):$25,000

Of an artificial blood vessel:$15,000

Number of Cessna 172s that can be bought for the price of one ground-launched cruise missile:122

Number of states that have paid more in taxes to finance SDI than they have received in SDI contracts:43

Percentage of the National Security Council's staff that were military officers in January 1981:18

Percentage in November 1986:40

Total number of vetoes cast by the United States in the U.N. Security Council:50

Number of those that have been cast since 1980:28

Number of vetoes that have been cast by the Soviet Union since 1980:2

Number of countries that have a lower rate of infant mortality than the United States:16

Soup kitchens in New York City in 1980:30   Today:560

Chances that a bride or fiancée whose picture appeared in the Sunday *New York Times* in June wore pearls:3 in 5

Letters to the editor received each day by *Pravda*:2,000

By the *New York Times*:400

Percentage increase, since 1986, in the number of fashion pages in *Vogue* and *Elle* featuring black models:64

Percentage of public school students in Manhattan who are white:9

Percentage of private school students in Manhattan who are not:14

Number of honorary degrees awarded to Bob Hope:52

Portion of residential telephone numbers in Los Angeles that are unlisted:½

Number of citizen's arrests made in Los Angeles in 1986:4,322

Days in 1986 on which no one was murdered in New York City:8

Number of those days that were Wednesdays:4

Americans killed by sharks since 1983:2

By pit bulls:20

Amount that two Sioux arrows used in the Battle of the Little Big Horn brought at auction:$17,000

Amount the New York Mets spend each season for tape to wrap Gary Carter:$5,000

Number of the 161 players in baseball's Hall of Fame who wore glasses while on the field: 2

Pairs of elastic sock garters George Bush received as gifts in 1986: 34

Percentage of cat owners who say they confide in their cats about important matters: 57

Proposed fine for selling or eating dog meat in Manila: $100

Percentage of the members of the Texas Restaurant Association that serve chicken-fried steak: 90

Paces at which the crunch of a pickle should be audible, according to Pickle Packers International: 10

---

4. The reference section of the library contains many unusual sources that can contribute unexpected discoveries to your investigation. For example, the book *The Encyclopedia of Associations* describes more than 20,000 organizations nationwide, ranging from the Chili Appreciation Society International to the Society for the Eradication of Television and the New York Stock Exchange. Visit the reference shelves and browse among the books until you find one you think is particularly unusual or interesting. When you have familiarized yourself with its contents, write a short essay espousing its merits to the audience most likely to use it or benefit by its contents.

5. Walter Isaacson's essay (*Time*, August 31, 1987) defines how the methods of researching history have changed. Some of the changes he notes, in fact, may have affected how research is done in your chosen discipline. Using the events and changes Isaacson discusses as a beginning point, develop a list of questions for interviewing a librarian and several teachers in your major field. When you have completed the interviews, write a short essay presenting your findings.

History Without Letters

WALTER ISAACSON

Pity the poor historian. The wonders of modern technology have combined with the dynamics of government scandals to make his task next to impossible.   1

    First came the telephone, which replaced the letter as the preferred means of business and social discourse. Letter writing, like   2 keeping faithful diaries, became a lost art. The advent of the tape recorder offered some hope, until Watergate made taping one's own phone for posterity seem both sordid and self-incriminating. Anointing a personal Boswell to hang around the house also turned out to be troublesome, as shown by the ill-conceived rumblings about summoning Edmund Morris, the President's designated biographer, to testify before the Iran-*contra* probers. Not even silicon chips offer much promise anymore. Those electronic messages that national-security staffers zapped to one another's computer screens, which were fortunately recorded in deep memory for future scribes, violated the cardinal rule of modern government: never leave footprints. Electronic memory shredders will, no doubt, be a feature of the next generation of DELETE keys.

As a result, historians may be left with nothing more than cabi- 3 nets filled with butt-covering memos designed more to obscure than illuminate the origins of critical decisions. "It's a real problem," says Morris. "There is more paper now, but its value declines in inverse proportion to its bulk."

One of the great troves for students of 20th century American di- 4 plomacy was left by Henry Stimson, a tireless diarist and letter writer who served a number of stints as Secretary of War and State from 1911 until 1945. Stimson was the man who ordered the dismantling of a government code-breaking outfit, later explaining "Gentlemen do not read other people's mail." This mind-set led to some very frank and revealing letters and diary entries. Historians piecing together the momentous decisions of World War II have the luxury of comparing personal writings in which Stimson and Navy Secretary James Forrestal describe the same sets of events.

Of course, some letters are a bit dry and impersonal, like those of 5 General George Marshall. But others impart an intimate texture to the tide of history. The candid correspondence between Franklin Roosevelt and Winston Churchill, for example, casts vivid light on the minds of these two great men and the depth of the wartime alliance that they were able to forge. Likewise, Eleanor Roosevelt wrote letters every day. "They provide a diary of the movement of her psyche," says Joseph Lash. "Without them, *Eleanor and Franklin* and *Eleanor: The Years Alone* could not have been written."

In a satiric essay called "Igor Stravinsky: The Selected Phone 6 Calls," the humorist Ian Frazier pretends to rummage through old telephone bills for clues to the composer's life. For serious historians, the situation seems less funny. "I know more about the Kennedy assassination than anyone," says William Manchester, author of *The Death of a President*, "but I know more about the Dardanelles in 1915 than I do about the assassination. In 1915, people put everything on paper. Now, it's all done over the telephone." Notes Historian Barbara

Tuchman: "Phone bills won't tell you much, and as a result, contemporary history has less perspective."

The last President to leave a cache of candid correspondence 7 was Harry Truman, who wrote more than 1,200 letters just to his wife. Not only do they reveal his delightful personal style, they provide convincing insights on matters ranging from his dealings with Stalin to his decision to drop the atom bomb. There is even a book filled with letters that Truman wrote in moments of pique, then wisely filed away unmailed. His diaries, though intermittent, are no less revealing. In June 1945, as General Douglas MacArthur was closing in on the islands near Japan, Truman's entries foreshadow the bitter personal battles that lay ahead. He describes the general as "Mr. Prima Donna, Brass Hat Five Star MacArthur" in one entry and adds, "He's worse than the Cabots and the Lodges—they at least talked to one another before they told God what to do."

Robert Caro, now at work on the second volume of his definitive 8 biography of Lyndon Johnson, says the historical record abruptly changes in the early 1940s, when people began to rely on the telephone more than the mail. "Through Johnson's detailed correspondence with his patron Alvin Wirtz and others, you could trace the most intricate deals and such matters as his stormy relationship with Sam Rayburn," says Caro. "Then, at a crucial moment, just when you want to know what someone is thinking, you'll run into a telegram or note saying 'Phone me tonight.' That's when you feel the impact of the telephone right in your gut." In researching L.B.J.'s role in the passage of the 1957 Civil Rights Bill, Caro says he has been reduced to deciphering scrawls at the bottom of telephone-message slips.

Back when the telephone was a relatively new contraption, people 9 often regarded it as too ephemeral for important communications. Averell Harriman and Robert Lovett, two great statesmen who had been Wall Street partners, talked on the phone regularly when they were apart and then would exchange letters the same afternoon, putting to paper what they had said. "As I told you over the telephone this morning . . ." they would typically begin. Back then, of course, the post was more efficient: the letter would usually arrive before the next morning's phone conversation.

Their successors, on the other hand, abandoned letters in favor 10 of obfuscating memos when it came to discussing, say, the Viet Nam War. Some of the most candid records of that period come from times when a few of the old statesmen were called in for counsel and then, as was their wont, exchanged letters about what they had discussed.

Harriman was one of those who believed in having important 11 telephone conversations transcribed for his files. His personal papers describe a classic exchange with Robert Kennedy, who phoned after announcing on television that he was challenging President Johnson for the Democratic nomination. Kennedy: "I'm running for President." Harriman: "Next time tell the children to smile. Ethel looked great. The kids looked bored." Kennedy: "They were." Harriman: "I don't expect to have a press conference soon, but if it does come around, I'm going to support the President."

Franklin Roosevelt was the first to set up a secret taping system 12 in the Oval Office. A microphone was hidden in his desk lamp to record his press conferences, though some private talks got taped as well. In a conversation recorded in October 1940, Roosevelt had this reaction to a telegram written by a Japanese press official: "This country is ready to pull the trigger if the Japs do anything."

John Kennedy likewise used a rudimentary recording system. 13 The tapes from such dramatic conversations as his telephone showdown with Governor Ross Barnett during the Ole Miss desegregation crisis provide historians with raw data that is even more gripping than most old letters. But Richard Nixon spoiled it all by going too far, both in what he said and how he recorded it.

As a result, taping phone conversations came to be regarded as 14 terribly sleazy. At least a dozen states have laws against such secret self-taps, as U.S. Information Agency Director Charles Wick was reminded when he tried to resurrect the practice.

The national penchant for exposing as quickly as possible every- 15 thing done by public officials, which is codified by the Freedom of Information Act, is, on balance, a good thing for democracy. But it is not the best thing for history. It has taught statesmen to be very careful about what they put on paper. "For all its advantages, the FOIA inhibits people from writing," says Robert Donovan, whose noted biographies of Truman depended heavily on letters and frank memos. "Officials shred it all now. A lot of serious history is vanishing."

Future historians will no doubt find different source material. In- 16 stead of rummaging through the Beinecke Library at Yale, they will spend their time in video archives watching old segments of *Nightline* and the MacNeil-Lehrer report. "So much is preserved in audio and visual these days," says Morris, "that it gives you much of a person's life and demeanor." Well, yes, the historians of the next century will be a lot more accurate in their portrayal of how people looked and spoke. But it is naive to believe that the way Caspar Weinberger answers a Ted Koppel question about America's stake in the Persian Gulf could provide the same candid insight that is available in Dean Acheson's letters to his daughter on the same subject during the Iranian crisis 41 years ago.

One solution would be to make it once again respectable—per- 17 haps even mandatory—to tape important discussions and phone conversations for the historical record. The tapes would become the property of the National Archives and could be tightly sealed from all scrutiny for at least two decades, the way that sensitive diplomatic cables were generally treated before the Freedom of Information Act came along. But aside from the legal and practical questions involved, such an idea would face philosophic objections: it could be seen as both an unwarranted invasion of privacy and a dangerous attempt to preserve the privacy of important exchanges.

Then again, preserving such a record may not be worth the vast 18 effort, expense or constraints involved. After all, only history is at stake. But if top officials knew in the back of their minds that future generations were listening in, it might have a salutary effect on the present. Had the judgment of history been hovering over their shoulders, the architects of the Iran-*contra* affair, for example, might have reflected a moment longer on the long-term implications of their actions. Indeed, the dulling of our historical sense could be one reason that the U.S. needs so many special prosecutors these days.

Chapter 5

CRITICAL READING: READING FOR UNDERSTANDING AND RESEARCH

Although you may deliberately create a comfortable, quiet, solitary environment for reading, remember that reading requires conversation, an active dialogue between writer and reader. Writers know they must anticipate and meet the needs of their readers in both content and style. In writing academic and research material, writers rely on facts, the research of others, their own expertise and experience, and the testimony of experts in the field to present new ideas or a new view of previously held beliefs. Writers attribute to their readers a substantial level of intelligence, expecting them to use their spirit of investigation and thirst for learning to question the ideas and resources presented. Consequently, your goal as a reader is to be discriminating and critical before you accept the writer's views.

The first step in investigating your source requires a close analysis of the rhetorical context. From that point you can focus on understanding the content and recording information in a usable form for research. These steps will provide you with a comprehensive foundation for determining the acceptability of the information presented in your sources.

ANALYZING RHETORICAL CONTEXT

Before you begin reading, you can examine several features of your source that will prepare you for understanding and evaluating its content.

TITLE

The *title* is probably the first feature that catches your attention. The title already has indicated that it might be a good source. Now you will examine its potential more closely. Use these questions to preview the significance of the title:

Does the title refer to the subject in broad, generalized terms ("The Benefits of Solar Energy") or does it place the subject in a specific context ("Solar Energy: Cheaper Winters for Detroit")?

Does the writer reveal his or her attitude toward the subject in the title? If so, what words indicate this tone to you?

Does the title arouse any attitudes in you that might affect how you read the article?

What kind of information does the title lead you to believe you will find in the source?

DATE OF PUBLICATION

When a source was published affects the availability of information to the writer. Knowing the date of publication can help you put the writer's viewpoint into perspective: Is the person writing from firsthand experience or is the writer interpreting events of last month, last year, or a century ago? Your needs, of course, will also determine the significance of the publication date. Here are some questions to help you determine that usefulness:

What is the distance of the publication date from the origination of the information presented?

Will this source provide the most current views on the subject?

Will this source offer a historical perspective on the subject?

TYPE OF PUBLICATION

Each publication focuses on meeting the needs of a particular reading audience, but in deciding how to fulfill those needs, each type of publication is subject to the benefits and restrictions of the frequency with which it is published. Knowing how the information is affected by the publishing schedule helps you to know what kind of information to expect. The general descriptions of three main types of publications will assist you in answering two important preview questions:

Does this publication emphasize the immediacy of the information or the quality of both the content and the writer?

How much time and what kind of resources did the writer have available for researching and developing the material?

CONSUMER WEEKLY: These magazines, such as *Time*, *Newsweek*, *U.S. News and World Report*, and *Business Week*, respond to what is currently happening. They generally use staff reporters to write short articles packed with factual rather than interpretive information. The immediacy of the news story is often more important than who reports it. For many crucial issues reporters use the wide variety of resources available to such large publications to write occasional in-depth articles. The general public has easy access to this information.

CONSUMER MONTHLY: *Psychology Today, Fortune, Harper's Magazine, Atlantic Monthly,* and *Esquire* represent the popular magazines included in this classification. Because more time is available for preparation, these publications generally include several in-depth articles written by guest experts, in addition to regular features and columns. The additional planning time allows for a more specific focus and longer articles emphasizing both content and writer. The general public has easy access to this information.

PROFESSIONAL JOURNALS: These publications, accessible only by subscription, present lengthy, well-researched articles that include both factual and interpretive information. Their monthly or quarterly publication schedule gives writers ample time to research and develop their work. In fact, writers may work from several months to a year to make their articles worthy of selection. Most of these journals have an editorial board of experts who select the best of the articles submitted.

BOOKS: The length of the books you will be using in research gives the writer considerable space to develop the subject. Still, the content of a book is often subject to the editorial approval of the publisher; length limitations may be imposed to lower production costs. Because books are often both a scholarly and commercial enterprise, marketing considerations may also impose some restrictions on content. The length of time required to write and print a book may affect the immediacy of the information as well.

AUTHOR

Perhaps the most important concern about the author is the level of credibility he or she establishes. Much of this credibility is established within the article itself, but you can also preview the writer's credentials before reading. In some cases you may actually recognize the author's name; when you don't, look carefully for professional titles, lists of other publications, academic degrees, and information about the author's occupation and experiences or accomplishments that may indicate a level of expertise or attitude toward the subject. Sometimes this information appears in a headnote at the beginning of an article or in a footnote at the bottom of the first page or at the end of the article. In books you can generally find this information inside the front or back cover. You may need to refer to *Current Biography* for more information. When previewing a source for information on the author, ask yourself this question:

What knowledge does the writer bring to the material?

AUDIENCE

Some publications present information for a general reading audience while others focus their material for a more specialized audience, which may itself contain special interest subgroups. Undoubtedly the writer has the audience clearly in mind when developing the material. Recognizing the intended audience will help you to know what kind of information to expect. Ask yourself these questions about the audience before you begin to read:

What knowledge does the writer expect the reader to have already?

What are the reader's expectations in reading this publication? What does the reader *need* to know?

OCCASION

Some people write to fulfill an assignment as a reporter or contributing editor to a publication. Others may want to report their own research, establish a reputation for themselves, or contribute a new point of view. You need to recognize that the occasion for the writing may have some bearing on the writer's commitment or purpose. Before reading the material, ask yourself this question:

What reason did the writer have for publishing this material?

READABILITY

How an article or chapter is presented, or its **readability,** makes it easier to read and can help you anticipate the content. Before reading, scan the material for headings, boldface print, illustrations; also check the length of the article and the average length of paragraphs. Spotting these features can prepare you for the writer's organization and emphasis.

YOUR OWN EXPERIENCE

You bring your own reading experience to whatever you read; this experience operates on two levels. First, consider your experience in reading this type of publication. Are you familiar with the format? Do you understand the documentation the writer uses? Do you understand how to interpret the graphs or charts? Second, consider the experience you have in reading about this subject. Have you already formed opinions that might interfere with your accepting the writer's view? Can you read the material objectively? Ask yourself these questions on both levels before you begin reading.

EXERCISE: RHETORICAL CONTEXT

Each of the following excerpts represents the first page of an article. Where author information was provided for an article it has been included in the excerpt. Using the criteria discussed earlier in this chapter, analyze the rhetorical context for each excerpt. Examine each feature carefully before writing out your analysis.

Student Writers and Word Processing: A Preliminary Evaluation

JEANETTE HARRIS

Rather extravagant, and largely unsubstantiated, claims have recently 1
been made about the potential of word processing to improve student
writing. We are told that word processing not only reduces the number of errors in our students' writing but also encourages them to experiment, increases the amount of revising they do, enables them to
perceive writing as a process, and gives them a sense of audience.[1] In
fact, as a result of our enthusiasm for word processing, our discipline's
initial skepticism about computers has been replaced by an acceptance of their instructional potential that is perhaps too uncritical.

Few existing studies provide useful information about how word 2
processing affects student writing or offer realistic evaluations of its
effects on the process of composing. Rather than investigating a specific feature of writing, many of these studies attempt to determine the
effects of computers on writing in general. Those that do focus on
a specific feature of writing usually deal with revision, but few researchers define what they mean by the term *revision*, using it to encompass all rewriting operations and failing to distinguish among revising, editing, and proofreading. Because editing and proofreading
affect only the surface features of a text, they should be distinguished
from revision, which is more accurately defined as making semantic
and rhetorical changes that affect the content and organization of a
piece of discourse.[2]

In a small pilot study involving six student writers, I investigated 3
the effect of word processing on revising. Using a case study approach,
I attempted to discover whether the use of word processing increases
the number of revisions—significant modifications in content and organization—that a student makes in his or her text.

My subjects were six student writers, volunteers who were se- 4
lected from two classes—an honors freshman English course and an
advanced composition course. In selecting these six subjects, I considered two qualifications: ability to type and prior experience with a
computer. However, the computer. . . .

*Jeanette Harris is Assistant Professor of English and Director of the Writing
Center at Texas Tech University. She has published essays in* Rhetoric Review,
Journal of Basic Writing *and* WPA *(the journal of the Organization of Writing
Program Administrators). She is also coauthor of a forthcoming textbook,*
Contexts: Writing and Reading.
College Composition and Communication, Vol. 36, No. 3, October 1985

Quantum Physics' World: Now You See It, Now You Don't

JAMES TREFIL

*If you have to cope with atomic particles that can read
your mind even when they don't exist, it can be hard
to explain what you do all day.*

Some people have it easy. When their kids ask them what they do 1
at work, they can give a simple, direct answer: "I put out fires" or "I
fix sick people" or "I do arbitrage." As a theoretical physicist, I never
had this luxury. Society has come to expect many things from physicists. It used to be that we only had to discover the basic laws that
govern the world and supply the technical breakthroughs that would
fuel the next Silicon Valley. With these expectations we were fairly
comfortable: they involve the sorts of things we think we know how to
do. What bothers us—and what makes it hard for us to tell our kids
what we're up to—is that in this century we have become, albeit un-
willingly, gurus on philosophical questions such as "What is the nature of Reality?"

We now deal with a whole new class of problems. We ask how 2
the Universe began and what is the ultimate nature of matter. The answers we are coming up with just do not lend themselves to simple
explanations.

In the good old days we could explain Sir Isaac Newton's clock- 3
work Universe by making analogies with things familiar to everyone.
And if the math got a little complicated, that was all right: it gave a
certain panache to the whole enterprise. But those days are gone forever. How is a physicist supposed to find a simple way of explaining
that some of his colleagues think our familiar world is actually embedded in an 11-dimensional Universe? Or that space itself is curved
and expanding? The math is still there; the theories are as coherent as
they ever were. What's missing is the link between those theories and
things that "make sense"—things the average person can picture. This
leads to a situation where it's easy for anyone to ask questions that
can't be answered without recourse to mathematics, such as my all-
time least favorite: "Well, if the Universe is really expanding, what is it
expanding *into*?"

There's no place where this problem is worse than in the theory   4
that underlies things like digital watches and personal computers.
This theory, called quantum mechanics, describes the behavior of
atoms and their constituents. It tells us that the world of the physicist
is not at all like the world we are used to. When physicists get out of
their cars in the morning, have a cup of coffee and sit down in front of
computer terminals, they leave a familiar, cozy environment and enter
a place where things act in strange, virtually inexplicable ways.

Let me give you an example of what I mean. When you run into a   5
wall, you expect to bounce off. If you were an electron, however, our
theories say there is some chance that you would simply appear on
the other side of the wall without leaving a hole behind you. In fact, if
electrons didn't behave this way, your transistor radio wouldn't work.
How do you explain something like *that* to your kids? And what does it
tell you about whether the electron is "real" or not?

Don't get me wrong. I don't think that people—even physicists—   6
go around with these sorts of questions on their minds all the time.
But as one friend put it to me, "It's not so much that I want to know
the answers myself, it's just that I want to know that they're in good
hands." It is this obligation to provide the good hands that in this century has been thrust on me and my colleagues.

Confused Chitchat at Cocktail Parties

Physicists get involved in trying to explain these kinds of things be-   7
cause two of our 20th-century theories—relativity and quantum mechanics—have dealt major blows to accepted ideas about what is real
in the world. The shock of relativity pretty well played itself out in the
1920s, mainly in cocktail party chitchat that confused relativity (a well-
defined theory in physics) with philosophical and moral relativism,
with which it has nothing in common except the name. It now looks
as if quantum mechanics is about to suffer through its own period of
popular misunderstanding, making physicists even more uncomfortable with their role as philosophical arbiters.

Physics has gone from studying familiar things in our everyday   8
lives like tides and baseballs to strange things like atoms and the
particles from which they are made: things we do not (indeed, cannot) ever. . . .

Smithsonian, August 1987

Baltistan

The 20th Century Comes to Shangri-la

GALEN ROWELL
*Photographs by the author and
Barbara Cushman Rowell*

The old man wore the simplest cottons, faded from long use and 1
countless washings. His skin was as parched and brown as the slopes
above his high pasture in Baltistan's Karakoram Range. Only the old
man's eyes, twinkling like diamonds behind thick glasses, hinted that
this was no ordinary farmer.

My friend Shah Jehan introduced me: "Galen Rowell, meet Wazir 2
Ghulam Mahdi. He is one of our land's very few scholars. He has a law
degree and a master's degree in history, both earned in British India,
and he has served in our national assembly. But he prefers the quiet
life of farming."

The old man smiled. "That is so," he said in careful English, "but 3
my education is notable only because Baltistan is such a small and
backward place."

I asked him then why he chose to live here, so far from the cul- 4
tured surroundings of his earlier days. In answer, he swept a hand
around him, at golden shafts of sunlight beaming through the mountain haze, at emerald stalks of young barley sprouting in the fields, at
evening clouds hovering pink in the fading light above distant snow
peaks.

Wazir Ghulam Mahdi is right: His is a land of great beauty. There 5
is a mystical, Shangri-la quality about Baltistan, the lofty and remote
northeastern district of Pakistan that borders on both China and
Indian-held Kashmir (map, page 532). For centuries the Karakorams
and Himalayas so insulated Baltistan that the country became a cultural fossil—a timeless imprint of great civilizations that had touched
there.

"Our language is unwritten and our history and our deeds are 6
passed down from father to son," Wazir Ghulam Mahdi told me. "Dates
are not important to us; few Baltis even know the year of their birth."

Until the late 16th century Baltistan was just another small moun- 7
tain kingdom whose strongest defenses were its high altitude, its cold,
and its vast isolation. Then the legendary Balti hero, Ali Sher Khan, rose

to power and won control over the surrounding kingdoms, from Chitral on the west to Ladakh in the east. He married a Mogul princess from India named Mindok Gyalmo and continued to expand his empire.

"While Ali Sher Khan was off in battle," Wazir Ghulam Mahdi told 8 me, "Queen Mindok imported sculptors, artists, and engineers from Delhi. She laid out magnificent gardens in the royal city of Skardu, built a great aqueduct system to irrigate Skardu Valley, and constructed a road up a steep cliffside to a fort overlooking the city.

"When Ali Sher Khan returned, he told her: 'You have built an 9 aqueduct, and for that you should. . . .

Sharing a private moment with her son, a Balti woman in the village of Askole faces a world of change. Her tradition-bound people, isolated among some of the world's highest mountains, are rapidly being drawn into modern Pakistani culture.

National Geographic, October 1987

READING FOR CONTENT

Being an active reader requires an inquisitive attitude and a great deal of concentrated effort. When you genuinely want to understand what you read, you will find it necessary to *annotate* the selection. Annotation gives you the opportunity to have an active dialogue with the author. This process involves literally marking the text (or a copy if you don't own the original) with the comments and questions that come to mind as you read the material.

The most effective annotation is selective. If you've ever bought a used textbook, you've probably observed two kinds of annotation: one especially colorful with its extensive highlighting and the other confusing with its hieroglyphic abbreviations. Probably neither of these forms has made much sense to you, not because they are highly personalized but because neither records the same distinctions and concerns you have as a reader. When you make your comments clearly and selectively, the material should have greater meaning when you review it.

The sources you read for investigation more than likely will contain more complex ideas and vocabulary than your usual reading material. You will need to mark the terms that are unfamiliar to you. You should also register your response, positive or negative, to the author's ideas. Many of the author's views will remind you of related material you have read, and some may raise questions in your mind about what you already know. Responding to these issues in your own words, instead of merely underlining or abbreviating what has already been said, will help you to remember each point more easily. The following questions will guide you in selecting information to annotate:

What terms or phrases are unfamiliar?

What is the main idea in each section?

How does one point relate to the next point?

How can I express this concept in my own words?

Do I agree with the author's point of view?

What questions would I ask the author?

How does this information relate to what I already know about the subject?

"Life in a Greenhouse" by Stanley N. Wellborn (*U.S. News and World Report*, September 29, 1986) is an example of an annotated reading. Examine the marginal comments to see what questions guided the reader.

Life in a Greenhouse

STANLEY N. WELLBORN

Is the much discussed greenhouse effect the disas- 1
ter of the twenty-first century—a gradual warming
of the earth that threatens life itself? Or is it a political tool for environmentalist doomsayers? For 30
years, scientists have theorized that as harmful
gases accumulate in the atmosphere, the earth's
blanket of air will become a global heat trap, triggering long-term and possibly cataclysmic changes in
climate. Individual studies have tended to confirm *What would the*
the theory, but some scientists have taken sharp ex- *political*
ception to a doomsday scenario, arguing that it *advantage be?*
is being used to generate research funding and to
further the political objectives of environmentalist
groups.

The verdict <u>seems</u> to be in. The evidence for a 2 *tentative*
greenhouse effect, bearing up to scrutiny at a recent

series of international symposiums, suggests that the earth clearly is in the early stages of a long-term warming trend. "All of us who looked at the data came to the inescapable conclusion that the greenhouse effect is for real," says Marvin Geller, chief of the laboratory for atmospheres at the National Aeronautics and Space Administration's Goddard Space Flight Center in Greenbelt, Maryland. "Atmospheric buildup of chemical compounds from human activity will change the earth's climate more over the next 50 years than it has since agriculture began," adds Sandra Postel, author of *Altering the Earth's Chemistry: Assessing the Risks*, a new report from the Worldwatch Institute, an environmentalist group located in Washington, DC.

What kind of human activity? How am I contributing?

At August meetings in Vienna and Geneva, the United Nations-sponsored Advisory Group on Greenhouse Gases warned, "The question is no longer whether, but how, policymakers will cope with a warmer world by the first half of the next century."

> political objectives ?

3 *> political interests*

concern for policy to protect future

The greenhouse effect originates with one of the most abundant elements—carbon. When fossil fuels are burned, compounds such as carbon monoxide and carbon dioxide are emitted. The sun's rays, reflecting off the earth's surface, are trapped as heat by these atmospheric pollutants, just as a covered greenhouse captures solar heat.

4

PROCESS

Since the beginning of the Industrial Revolution in the mid-eighteenth century, roughly 200 billion tons of carbon dioxide have been released into the atmosphere from both industrial and natural processes. Over the past 50 years, other harmful gases—chlorofluorocarbons, nitrous oxide, and methane—have been accumulating as well in the atmosphere.

5

Which industries? What are their > sources? When did environmental policy begin?

The world's oceans and forests normally absorb most of these carbon-based by-products, but geochemists worry that they may be approaching their limit. If so, the greenhouse scenario unfolds. The earth eventually bakes, rich farmlands turn into deserts, forests wither and die. Oceans swollen by melted polar and glacial ice inundate coastal areas.

6

overly dramatic? Not sure the author believes or wants to believe it will go this far

7 Indications of a warming trend are unmistakable. Instruments atop an extinct volcano in Hawaii have monitored the earth's atmosphere for 30 years and show a steady increase in carbon dioxide. Moreover, readings taken on seagoing research vessels confirm that the world's oceans are rising inexorably at the rate of four-tenths of an inch per decade.

Where exactly? Why there? How measured?

8 As critics point out, however, much of the data refuses to mesh. Some temperature trends, for example, seem contradictory. Global air temperatures have risen slightly during the last century, but the tendency has been much more pronounced in the Southern Hemisphere than in the industrial world north of the equator. At the same time, the south polar ice sheet has been expanding, not melting, during the last decade. Finally, sea and land temperatures have generally risen in the Northern Hemisphere over the past century, while temperatures in North America have actually declined slightly since World War II.

opposing view
are the critics scientists or politicians?

Why would they be affected differently
industry
culture

9 Scientists agree that the data don't jibe. They explain that many factors influence the earth's biosphere, and their interaction—the greenhouse effect is one product—is only beginning to be understood. And the biggest unknown of all concerns timing: no one can say for sure when the dire effects of a global warming may be felt. "It would be a foolhardy scientist who would categorically predict those kinds of specifics," says Carl Wunsch, professor of physical oceanography at the Massachusetts Institute of Technology's Center for Physical Oceanography and Meteorology.

*TIMING

10 For now, researchers at the government's National Center for Atmospheric Research in Boulder, Colorado, who use computer models to forecast trends in temperature and sea level, only will go so far as to predict a gradual warming in the Northern Hemisphere, averaging one to two degrees Fahrenheit by the year 2000 and an additional two to four degrees by 2020.

11 While small, such increases could have significant ramifications. By the year 2030, for example, the heat buildup would translate into 20 days a year in which temperatures in Omaha would

POSSIBLE EFFECTS

pass 100 degrees, compared with an average of three days a year now.

Sea levels, which have risen about one foot over the past 100 years, could rise by an additional three feet by the year 2030, according to Environmental Protection Agency projections. Such a rise would bring the seas about 100 feet farther inland along some shorelines of the U.S. Atlantic and Gulf coasts, inundating river-delta cities such as New Orleans or sea-level metropolises such as Miami.

first mention of EPA

hotter and less land

F. Sherwood Rowland, chemistry professor at the University of California at Irvine, warns, "If you have the greenhouse effect going on indefinitely, then you have a temperature rise that will bring about the extinction of human life in 500 to 1,000 years."

PROBLEM WITH TIME
doesn't sound like much of a threat to most Patriotism appeal?

Most scientists feel that the evidence for a greenhouse effect is strong enough to warrant corrective action now. Among the recommendations issued by the United Nations task force: renew the search for safe, clean alternatives to fossil fuels like coal and oil; curb the release of harmful gases from industrial processes; and stop clearing the tropical forests that absorb huge amounts of carbon dioxide.

Recommendation

The U.S. already has banned aerosol products that use fluorocarbons as propellants and has stiffened regulations on coal emissions. But according to a U.N. survey, most developing nations have no such curbs. Scientists say that nothing short of a global campaign to reduce chemical pollutants will work. Such warnings prompt considerable resistance from industries and utilities that would largely bear the cost of scrubbing the atmosphere of greenhouse gases.

local /regional/ national?

What laws are they under now? Are the current laws dated?

The EPA and various officials in the Reagan administration continue to insist that the jury is still out on the greenhouse effect. But a growing number of scientists say that continuing to delay regulatory actions will only mean that future generations will have to contend with a sure environmental time bomb.

How long?

Why not lobby harder?

12

13

14

15

16

EXERCISE: CONTEXT AND CONTENT

Prepare your expectations for reading Richard M. Restak's article (in the Appeal to Logic section in Chapter 7) "The Other Difference Between Boys and Girls" by analyzing its rhetorical context. Next, read the article straight through to familiarize yourself with the content, pausing only to circle terms you are unfamiliar with. When you reread the article, annotate it carefully. Use the questions in the section Reading for Content in this chapter to guide you in reacting to the article *and* formulating questions of your own.

READING FOR RESEARCH

Once you have a firm grasp of the content in a source, you can decide the best way to formalize that understanding to use in your research. Summary and paraphrase are the primary means of reporting to others what you have learned. Both methods allow you to report on a variety of sources in your own words. Both summarized and paraphrased material must be credited to the source. Although writers generally use a combination of the two methods in presenting their research, summary and paraphrase represent information in distinctly different forms. Writers must clearly establish their purpose before choosing one of these techniques.

USING SUMMARY

In a **summary** you use your own words to present a condensed version of the original material. A summary may range in length from a few sentences to several paragraphs, but in each case, whether summarizing a paragraph, an article, a chapter, or a book, the form of your summary will be *brief, comprehensive,* and *objective.*

A summary is comprehensive in that it focuses on the central idea of the work—the underlying meaning, from beginning to end, that all other information in the piece supports. The author's thesis and the topic sentences within paragraphs will help you to state this focus in your own words. In the briefest summary only the central idea is stated; in a longer summary the main points that develop the idea are included.

The summary is objective. Although it is written in your own words, a summary *does not include your own opinion.* Interpreting or evaluating the material, even if you agree with the author, could misrepresent the author's intention. Avoid using any qualifiers—adjectives and adverbs—that judge the material. By focusing on the central idea, you will present the information accurately and fairly. Because it is written in your own words, your summary will blend in voice and style with the rest of your essay.

The summary's purpose in your research often determines its length, but in all cases the summary is brief—significantly shorter than the source. Eliminating repetitions, specific examples, and minor details will allow you to stay focused on the central idea.

In the following article from the *New York Times* (March 1, 1987), James S. Newton surveys music technology from several angles. Read the article twice, the second time underlining main ideas and recording your annotations. Then try to summarize the article in one sentence.

What's New
in Music Technology

JAMES S. NEWTON

Guitars, a few brass instruments, even a violin or two line the counters 1 along the entrance to Alex Musical Instruments on Manhattan's 48th Street. But it is the equipment in the back of the store, which overflows with a dazzling array of electronic keyboards, drum machines, synthesizers and computer software, that provides most of the sales.

Electronic musical technology is driving the music business 2 these days. According to the American Music Conference, a Chicago-based nonprofit group catering to amateur musicians, Americans bought 392,000 digital keyboards in 1983. Two years later, sales of the instruments, which range in price from $800 to $10,000, topped 1.3 million. Over the same period, sales of pianos and other traditional instruments dropped by a third to a half.

Computers are firmly entrenched in the making of modern mu- 3 sic. And that has meant a boon not only for denizens of Silicon Valley, but for software writers as well. "There's a tremendous demand for new software, for new ways of capturing and creating sounds," said Rob Manning, a product specialist at Digidesign, a Palo Alto, Calif., company that sold about $300,000 worth of software packages for making music last year.

To musicians—composers, live performers and recording artists 4 alike—computerization is a mixed blessing. Computers have given them more precise control over the way their recordings sound, have made it easier for them to compose musical scores, and have given them a wider range of sounds and tones to work with. But some musicians complain that the "art" of music has been made subservient to the technology. Others have less esthetic worries; they fear they will be automated out of their jobs.

Officials from the American Federation of Musicians, the national 5 musicians union, note that machines have already replaced studio musicians on many movie soundtracks and in the jingle business. If that continues, some worry, live musicians may give way to computer tracks, and the music may lose much of its character.

That sort of scenario already is showing up in advertisements for 6 equipment. Typical is a pamphlet put out by the Fostex Corporation, a Japanese company that produces musical equipment. It shows a musician in front of an Apple Macintosh computer, surrounded by an artificial drum machine, a reel-to-reel tape recorder and a video monitor. There is not a single "instrument"—or human accompanist—in sight. "As these machines take over jobs once done by studio musicians, we're talking about the loss of a lot of people's livelihood," said John Glasel, president of New York's Local 802 of the American Federation of Musicians.

Whether music lovers will be shortchanged remains to be seen. 7 Jon Appleton, a professor of music at Dartmouth College and co-developer of the first synclavier, one of the earliest and most successful of the computerized instruments, does not think so. "It's not that people are making less music than they used to," he said. "It's just that they're making it in a different way."

A one-sentence summary might look like this:

The popularity of advances in electronic music technology has musicians concerned about whether the artistic control gained is worth the increasing loss of jobs and the potential loss of culture.

Notice how the summary writer has focused on the central cause/effect issues of the article without including any examples or details. The increase in sales of digital equipment and computer software are condensed into the phrase, "The popularity of advances in electronic music technology," in which three paragraphs are represented by eight words. The remaining four paragraphs are reduced to three major points: gain in artistic control, loss of jobs, and loss of culture. Notice, too, the lack of description that could easily convey the summarizer's opinion of the issues. This one-sentence summary, then, successfully fulfills all three requirements: it is comprehensive, objective, and brief.

When writing a longer summary, you can build your statement of the main ideas by writing a one-sentence summary of each paragraph and then combining them in a logical manner. Using this approach with the same article, your summary would have the following sequence:

WHAT'S NEW IN MUSIC TECHNOLOGY:

Paragraph 1: Electronic instruments and computer software sell better than traditional instruments today.

Paragraph 2: Over the past several years sales of electronic musical instruments have increased while sales of traditional instruments have greatly decreased.

Paragraph 3: Demand for computer software in music has benefited both computer companies and software writers.

Paragraph 4: While musicians enjoy the artistic control they have gained through computerization, they are concerned about the effect of computerization on culture and the loss of jobs.

Paragraph 5: Officials from the musicians union are concerned that the growing trend of replacing live musicians with machine-produced soundtracks may eventually change the integrity of music.

Paragraph 6: Advertisements depicting how music can be made without instruments may contribute to the loss of work for musicians.

Paragraph 7: Some feel these changes will make music less fulfilling for those who enjoy music; others disagree.

In combining several paragraph summaries into a final one-paragraph summary, you need to follow the same rules of brevity, completeness, and objectivity. Eliminate any repetitions, minor details, and judgmental words that might have slipped in. For example, paragraphs 1 and 2 contain similar information, and the paragraph 4 summary includes an unnecessary repetition, so this material can be either combined or eliminated. Your final summary may be similar to this one:

> Recent sales figures indicate that electronic music instruments and computer software are more in demand than traditional instruments. While this growth has benefited the music and computer industries, the musicians are concerned that the gain computerization gives them in artistic control does not outweigh the increasing loss of jobs and potential loss of culture. Use of electronic music technology in the movie and advertising industries has replaced many musicians with machines already, a trend, some fear, that could make music less fulfilling to performers and listeners.

EXERCISES: SUMMARIZING I

1. Choose two movies that you have seen recently—one you really enjoyed and one you would not recommend. Write a one-sentence summary for each; carefully avoid expressing any opinions.

2. Figure 1 is a biographical entry on Robert Creeley taken from *The Oxford Compan-*

Figure 1 *A biographical entry*

CREELEY, ROBERT [WHITE] (1926–), Massachusetts-born poet, graduated from Black Mountain College, where he became close to Charles Olson, whose *Selected Writings* he edited (1966), and where he was editor of *The Black Mountain Review* ◆ (1954–57). He subsequently traveled widely and became a faculty member (1963) of the State University of New York at Buffalo. With *Le Fou* (1952) he began publication of numerous brief collections of poetry, selected in *For Love* (1962), marked by terse, laconic treatments of love, presented with great immediacy. Later volumes—*Words* (1967), *Pieces* (1969), *The Finger* (1970), *St. Martin's* (1971), *A Day Book* (1972), *Thirty Things* (1974), *Away* (1976), *Later* (1978), and *Collected Poems* (1982), among others—show him continuing a stripped-down style and diction in presenting the problems of understanding in dealing with personal feelings and relations. He has also written stories, *The Gold Diggers* (1954, enlarged 1965); a quasi-autobiographical novel, *The Island* (1963), about a young American writer living on Majorca; and critical essays, *A Quick Graph* (1970) and *Was That a Real Poem* (1979).

ion to American Literature. The entry itself presents a summary of Creeley's literary career. After reading the entry, summarize it in two to three sentences.

3. After reading and annotating Meg Gerken's essay, from *Women's Sports and Fitness*, write a one-sentence summary. Then, return to the essay, write a one-sentence summary for each paragraph, and compose a longer summary.

Battle of the Sexes

MEG GERKEN

Despite the significant gains made by women in sports over the past 1 few years, the belief persists that they are unable to approach the performance level of men. Even a top athlete like Grete Waitz, the world-record holder in the marathon, has said, "I don't think a woman can run a marathon as fast as a man. Physically men are stronger than we are."

Her statement reflects the widely held view that men are, and always will be, superior in sporting achievement because of inherent biological factors. On the average, so the theory goes, men are stronger, bigger, have more muscle mass and greater cardiovascular capacity than women. Women are weaker, smaller, fatter and have less endurance than men. Moreover, the psychological traits deemed necessary to excel in sports are regarded as masculine. For a woman to be aggressive, competitive or self-assertive is to risk her femininity by being "unnatural." 2

In a paper presented at the International Congress on Women and Sport in Rome, Italy, last summer, Dr. Elizabeth A. E. Ferris of England refutes what she terms the "orthodox view." A medical research officer and former champion springboard diver, Ferris reveals that data used to prove the theory often compares active males to sedentary females. 3

What the studies really suggest, she proposes, is more a difference in lifestyle than physiological function. In fact, recent documentation has pointed to much similarity between highly trained, postpubescent male and female athletes, especially when they are involved in the same event or sport. 4

The evidence is astounding. In weight lifting, for example, Bev Francis of Australia broke a *men's* middleweight world record two years ago. Her feat is all the more remarkable because it was achieved in the bench press, a test of upper body strength. Women in general are weaker in that area than men. 5

However, studies have shown that the lower body is another matter. According to Ferris, females are actually stronger in the legs than males when compared in terms of lean muscle mass. 6

That brings up the question of body composition. Whereas the average female is 25 percent fat, her male counterpart is only 15 percent. Yet one should not equate fatness with being female. Recent reports indicate that women distance runners have relative fat values of less than 10 percent, far lower than the average female or male, and on a par with male distance runners. 7

Ferris also contends that women are indeed suited for such endurance races as the marathon, now—finally—an Olympic event. In the past researchers had concluded that inferior aerobic power made vigorous exercise inadvisable for females. Using maximal oxygen intake to measure endurance capacity, they found female volume to be 70–75 percent of that in the male. But the subjects were untrained young adults, and the difference could easily be attributed to the female's smaller body size after puberty. 8

By contrast, a recent study of a group of female distance run- 9
ners in the U.S. proved that their cardiovascular endurance capacity
matched that of male athletes of the same age and caliber. Still other
evidence implies that active men and women of the same age, not just
highly trained athletes, have similar endurance capacities when volume is expressed relative to body weight.

The myth surrounding heat regulation has been another reason 10
for excluding women from endurance competition. The syllogism
went like this: Men sweat sooner and more heavily than women; per-
spiring is an effective way to cool body temperature; therefore, men
have more efficient heat-regulating systems than women.

But this logical progression fails to take some facts into account. 11
Ferris notes that while exposure to excess heat results in an increased
sweat rate for men, women acclimatize with far less loss of fluid.

In addition, when physically fit subjects exercised under heat- 12
stress conditions, the women expended less energy than the men.
That fact, Ferris observes, may account for why most men finish mara-
thons in a state of near collapse. It also leads to the conclusion that
women seem to be better equipped than men for distance running.

With respect to some endurance events, one can reasonably as- 13
sume·that female performance potential is at least equal to, if not superior to, that of males. This principle already applies in open water
swimming. In 1978 Penny Dean of California churned through the
cold seas of the English Channel in seven hours and 40 minutes,
breaking the old record—held by a man—by almost two hours. Again,
women appear to be better thermoregulators. Ferris believes the female system is more efficient not only in losing heat, but in retaining it
as well.

Interestingly, when one compares men's and women's world 14
records in both running and swimming, the female performances are
improving at a more rapid rate at nearly every distance. In the 800-
meter run, for instance, the percentage difference between the sexes in
1976 was half that in 1948.

The gaps closing the fastest are in the longer events, which women 15
have been competing in for the shortest time. In the marathon, Waitz's
current mark would have won the men's event in every Olympics up to
1952. Swimmer Mary T. Meagher's record clocking in the 200-meter
butterfly would have captured the men's gold as recently as 1968. Such
accomplishments prompt Ferris to predict equality between the sexes
in running and swimming within the next half century.

The physiological element is not the only thing holding back fe- 16
male sporting performance. Ferris also places cycling on the trend to
equality, but she draws a distinction: Women cyclists do not yet have
the incentive of Olympic competition. The sport-governing bodies will

have to open their doors to women athletes all the way before women can reach their ultimate performance levels in all sports. The IOC's recent approval of the women's marathon in the 1984 Games was an encouraging step along the road of progress.

Lingering social biases also create barriers for women athletes. 17 For example, a recent *New York Times* article told of menstrual irregularities in some endurance athletes. Readers could infer incorrectly that loss of periods means permanent infertility and that strenuous exercise thereby jeopardizes femininity.

The article failed to mention that many ballerinas are also amen- 18 orrheic. Since our culture approves of ballet as an activity for women, one hears nothing about its being too strenuous or unfeminine.

Yet another fallacy is that physical activity injures the female re- 19 productive organs. The uterus and ovaries lie well-protected deep within the pelvic cavity. It is the far more vulnerable male organs which run the higher risk of injury during exercise.

Another example of psychosocial factors in operation is that in 20 East Germany, women are encouraged to participate in sports—and the excellent opportunities for training and competition result in high levels of female performance. Few women champions come from France, however, where social prejudice creates psychological barriers to achievement. A low achievement record is inevitable when girls are instructed to shy away from the "male" arena of sport.

When summaries are written well, they can provide a great deal of information in a small space. Condensing material allows writers to cover more ground for their readers. But, because summaries generalize information, a writer who overuses them will leave readers begging for more specific evidence. For this reason, writers need to be selective in using summaries.

What your readers already know and what they need to know will be the best criteria for deciding when to use the summary. For example, summarizing background information or historical perspectives credits your audience with knowing the specifics and identifies a common starting point. And a summary of a new point of view can be an effective introduction to specific supporting evidence. Even a catalog of summaries can be used to indicate that a wealth of material or perhaps several points of view exist for that section of your argument. The rhetorical context of your writing will guide you in determining which of many uses of summary to choose.

Another look at "Life in a Greenhouse," an essay presented earlier in this chapter will show that the writer uses summary for a variety of purposes. Use the paragraph numbers here to locate the summaries within the article, which is found on p. 000. Remember that Wellborn's audience in *U.S. News and World Report* is the educated general public interested in being informed on world and national events and issues. They want serious, informative articles that help them make decisions.

LIFE IN A GREENHOUSE

1. Summarizes conflicting points to identify the main issue

2. Summarizes the present condition

5. Gives historical overview

6. Summarizes geochemists' views
   Summarizes effects

7. Summarizes results of monitoring

8. Summarizes critics' views
   Lists effects in summary rather than specific terms

9. Summarizes scientists' views in broad terms

10. Summarizes predictions

14. Summarizes scientists' recommendations

15. Summarizes further recommendations

16. Summarizes the two opposing views for consideration

Wellborn's article demonstrates how summary can be used at every point in an essay: the introduction, development of views and predictions, conclusion, and recommendations. Notice also the interplay of specific sources, quotes, and details that support those summaries. This list of possible uses for summary will guide you in choosing those appropriate for your purpose and your audience:

- Introduce an issue

- Provide a historical overview

- Identify with the reader's knowledge

- Refer to many sources

- Identify present conditions

- Represent various points of view

- Present predictions and recommendations

- Conclude

EXERCISES: SUMMARIZING II

1. The following article, "Winter Depression: Day for Night" by Jeff Meer, is a summary of a research study for the readers of *Psychology Today* (June 1987). As you read the article, underline the sentences that summarize. On a separate sheet of paper, write out the summaries and explain the purpose each serves for this particular audience.

Winter Depression:
Day for Night

JEFF MEER

For several years scientists have known that some people become se-   1
verely depressed during the winter months, perhaps because of the
decreased availability of natural light. In fact, many of these people
have already been treated successfully with daily exposure to extremely bright artificial lighting. Now recent research suggests that
this treatment may be most effective when done in the morning.

Psychiatrist Alfred J. Lewy and colleagues had eight winter-   2
depressed people and seven others sleep from 10 p.m. to 6 a.m. for
four weeks. After adjusting to this sleep schedule for one week, half
were exposed to two hours of artificial bright light after awakening
each day, while the others were exposed for two hours before going to
bed. A week later, the assignments were reversed, and in the final
week, everyone received bright-light treatment during both the morning and the evening.

Lewy and colleagues report that morning light treatment was   3
most effective in helping the seasonally depressed. In fact, their moods
rose to levels comparable to those reported by individuals without the
disorder. With evening light treatment, individuals remained about as
depressed as they always had been. Combined morning and evening
treatments improved moods somewhat, but not as much as morning
light alone.

Why the greater changes in depression for the morning light   4
group? Evidence points to the effects of a hormone called melatonin,
known to fluctuate with a daily rhythm. When the researchers measured the melatonin production of those in the study, they found that
the winter-depressed people secreted melatonin later in the evening
than did the others. With morning light, their bodies began producing
melatonin earlier in the evening (close to a normal schedule), while
evening light actually further delayed production of the hormone.
Those who got both morning and evening light began producing
melatonin at an intermediate hour.

Lewy is reluctant to say that correction of the timing of melatonin   5
production is the whole, or only, answer to treating winter depression,
since other psychological and biological factors may have a role in its
development. But he is confident that the disorder "appears to be
effectively treated" by the morning light regimen and that the findings

may also help in assessing and treating "other types of sleep and mood disorders, shift work difficulties and jet lag."

---

2. After reading the next essay, by Margaret Mead (from the *New York Times,* May 20, 1965) once, read it again and write a one-sentence summary for each paragraph. Then, write a short essay, directed to your classmates, on a common event that involves anxiety. Incorporate several of your summaries from Mead's article in your essay at strategic points. Be prepared to explain *why* you used the summaries where you chose to.

One Vote for This Age of Anxiety

MARGARET MEAD

When critics wish to repudiate the world in which we live today, one 1 of their familiar ways of doing it is to castigate modern man because anxiety is his chief problem. This, they say, in W. H. Auden's phrase, is the age of anxiety. That is what we have arrived at with all our vaunted progress, our great technological advances, our great wealth— everyone goes about with a burden of anxiety so enormous that, in the end, our stomachs and our arteries and our skins express the tension under which we live. Americans who have lived in Europe come back to comment on our favorite farewell which, instead of the old goodbye (God be with you), is now "Take it easy," each American admonishing the other not to break down from the tension and strain of modern life.

Whenever an age is characterized by a phrase, it is presumably 2 in contrast to other ages. If we are the age of anxiety, what were the other ages? And here the critics and carpers do a very amusing thing. First, they give us lists of the opposites of anxiety: security, trust, self-confidence, self-direction. Then, without much further discussion, they let us assume that other ages, other periods of history, were somehow the ages of trust or confident direction.

The savage who, on his South Sea island, simply sat and let 3 breadfruit fall into his lap, the simple peasant, at one with the fields he ploughed and the beasts he tended, the craftsman busy with his tools and lost in the fulfillment of the instinct of workmanship—these are the counter-images conjured up by descriptions of the strain under which men live today. But no one who lived in those days has returned to testify how paradisiacal they really were.

Certainly if we observe and question the savages or simple peas- 4 ants in the world today, we find something quite different. The untouched savage in the middle of New Guinea isn't anxious; he is seriously and continually *frightened*—of black magic, of enemies with spears who may kill him or his wives and children at any moment, while they stoop to drink from a spring, or climb a palm tree for a coconut. He goes warily, day and night, taut and fearful.

As for the peasant populations of a great part of the world, they 5 aren't so much anxious as hungry. They aren't anxious about whether they will get a salary raise, or which of the three colleges of their choice they will be admitted to, or whether to buy a Ford or Cadillac, or whether the kind of TV set they want is too expensive. They are hungry, cold and, in many parts of the world, they dread that local warfare, bandits, political coups may endanger their homes, their meager livelihoods and their lives. But surely they are not anxious.

For anxiety, as we have come to use it to describe our character- 6 istic state of mind, can be contrasted with the active fear of hunger, loss, violence and death. Anxiety is the appropriate emotion when the immediate personal terror—of a volcano, an arrow, the sorcerer's spell, a stab in the back and other calamities, all directed against one's self—disappears.

This is not to say that there isn't plenty to worry about in our 7 world of today. The explosion of a bomb in the streets of a city whose name no one had ever heard before may set in motion forces which end up by ruining one's carefully planned education in law school, half a world away. But there is still not the personal, immediate, active sense of impending disaster that the savage knows. There is rather the vague anxiety, the sense that the future is unmanageable.

The kind of world that produces anxiety is actually a world of 8 relative safety, a world in which no one feels that he himself is facing sudden death. Possibly sudden death may strike a certain number of unidentified other people—but not him. The anxiety exists as an uneasy state of mind, in which one has a feeling that something unspecified and undeterminable may go wrong. If the world seems to be going well, this produces anxiety—for good times may end. If the world is going badly—it may get worse. Anxiety tends to be without locus; the anxious person doesn't know whether to blame himself or other people. He isn't sure whether it is the current year or the Administration or a change in climate or the atom bomb that is to blame for this undefined sense of unease.

It is clear that we have developed a society which depends on 9 having the *right* amount of anxiety to make it work. Psychiatrists have been heard to say, "He didn't have enough anxiety to get well," indicating that, while we agree that too much anxiety is inimical to mental health, we have come to rely on anxiety to push and prod us into seeing a doctor about a symptom which may indicate cancer, into checking up on that old life-insurance policy which may have out-of-date clauses in it, into having a conference with Billy's teacher even though his report card looks all right.

People who are anxious enough keep their car insurance up, 10 have the brakes checked, don't take a second drink when they have to drive, are careful where they go and with whom they drive on holidays. People who are too anxious either refuse to go into cars at all—and so complicate the ordinary course of life—or drive so tensely and overcautiously that they help cause accidents. People who aren't anxious enough take chance after chance, which increases the terrible death toll of the roads.

On balance, our age of anxiety represents a large advance over 11 savage and peasant cultures. Out of a productive system of technology drawing upon enormous resources, we have created a nation in which anxiety has replaced terror and despair, for all except the severely disturbed. The specter of hunger means something only to those Americans who can identify themselves with the millions of hungry people on other continents. The specter of terror may still be roused in some by a knock at the door in a few parts of the South, or in those who have just escaped from a totalitarian regime or who have kin still behind the Curtains.

But in this twilight world which is neither at peace nor at war, 12 and where there is insurance against certain immediate, downright, personal disasters, for most Americans there remains only anxiety over what may happen, might happen, could happen.

This is the world out of which grows the hope, for the first time 13 in history, of a society where there will be freedom from want and freedom from fear. Our very anxiety is born of our knowledge of what is now possible for each and for all. The number of people who consult psychiatrists today is not, as is sometimes felt, a symptom of increasing mental ill health, but rather the precursor of a world in which the hope of genuine mental health will be open to everyone, a world in which no individual feels that he need be hopelessly brokenhearted, a failure, a menace to others or a traitor to himself.

But if, then, our anxieties are actually signs of hope, why is there 14 such a voice of discontent abroad in the land? I think this comes perhaps because our anxiety exists without an accompanying recognition of the tragedy which will always be inherent in human life, however well we build our world. We may banish hunger, and fear of sorcery, violence or secret police; we may bring up children who have learned to trust life and who have the spontaneity and curiosity necessary to devise ways of making trips to the moon; we cannot—as we have tried to do—banish death itself.

Americans who stem from generations which left their old people 15 behind and never closed their parents' eyelids in death, and who have experienced the additional distance from death provided by two world wars fought far from our shores are today pushing away from them both a recognition of death and a recognition of the tremendous significance—for the future—of the way we live our lives. Acceptance of the inevitability of death, which, when faced, can give dignity to life, and acceptance of our inescapable role in the modern world, might transmute our anxiety about making the right choices, taking the right precautions, and the right risks into the sterner stuff of responsibility, which ennobles the whole face rather than furrowing the forehead with the little anxious wrinkles of worry.

Worry in an empty context means that men die daily little deaths. 16 But good anxiety—not about the things that were left undone long ago, but which return to haunt and harry men's minds, but active, vivid anxiety about what must be done and that quickly—binds men to life with an intense concern.

This is still a world in which too many of the wrong things hap- 17 pen somewhere. But this is a world in which we now have the means to make a great many more of the right things happen everywhere. For Americans, the generalization which a Swedish social scientist made about our attitudes on race relations is true in many other fields: anticipated change which we feel is right and necessary but difficult makes us unduly anxious and apprehensive, but such change, once consummated, brings a glow of relief. We are still a people who—in the literal sense—believe in making good.

USING PARAPHRASE

Like summary, **paraphrase** requires that you present material in your own words. But where *summary* is a condensed form of the original material, *paraphrase* follows the original point by point, resulting in a passage of similar length. This difference in length also means a difference in purpose.

Use summary when you need to generalize and condense into a small space an entire piece of writing.

Use paraphrase when you need to specify and clarify everything included in a short passage within an article or chapter.

The length of your paraphrase, then, may be a sentence or a full paragraph. When you write a paraphrase, following three principles will help you maintain the integrity of the original passage: order, reasoning, and emphasis.

Establishing accurate *order* in your paraphrase shows that you understand the content as the author intended. One way to clarify the ideas of a passage is to outline or list each point as you reread the passage, keeping the sequence in which the information is presented.

How the author views the relationships among the ideas presented demonstrates his or her *reasoning.* To discover these relationships you can begin by locating the transitional words used between ideas. These words generally fall into three categories that classify the direction of an author's thought on a subject. Use the list below to find these words in the passage you are paraphrasing. Then place those words, or a synonym for each, at the beginning of each point on your list. The combination of the direction of the thought and the thought itself should give you a clear idea of the relationship of ideas the author intends.

Same direction: These words signal that an idea will in some way be like the previous one.

and	another	what's more
in addition	first	moreover
also	second	furthermore
similarly	then	indeed
too	finally	in fact
likewise		

Change in direction: These words signal that an idea will be different from or opposite to the previous one.

but	on the other hand
instead	conversely
yet	in contrast
however	unfortunately
nevertheless	nonetheless

Concluding direction: These words signal that the next idea presented will be the result of the previous idea or ideas. The concluding thought signals a cause-and-effect relationship.

therefore	consequently
thus	accordingly
hence	as a result

The author's attitude toward the subject, or the tone of the piece, will indicate the author's intended *emphasis.* Sometimes this emphasis is indicated by the number of examples the author chooses to include. The more examples, the more attention the author is giving to that particular point.

The words the author chooses to describe the ideas also indicate the emphasis. To capture this emphasis in your paraphrase you first need to locate those descriptors (adjectives and adverbs) and the nouns and verbs they describe. Then, to determine the author's tone, arrange these choices on a connotation scale, as shown here. Identifying the connotation level of the author's words will guide your selection of the synonyms to represent the author's emphasis accurately in your own words.

	CONNOTATING APPROVAL	NEUTRAL	CONNOTATING DISAPPROVAL
Author's choice:	ADVOCATE		
Synonym choices:	champion	support	plead
	favor	recommend	justify
	promote	maintain	
Author's choice:		PASSIVE	
Synonym choices:	quiescent	receptive	submissive
		unresisting	indifferent

As the paraphraser, you will need to identify the connotation level of the author's word choice according to context. The word *passive*, for instance, can be used to connote disapproval, but if the author uses it as a neutral term, the synonyms you choose must also be neutral. Punctuation marks, such as parentheses, question marks, and exclamation marks, may also indicate to you the tone of the passage.

Using these principles, you might develop your paraphrase as did Rosalind Coward in this excerpt from the essay "Let's Have a Meal Together," from her book *Female Desires* (1985).

A close scrutiny of the average restaurant shows that even the lay-out seems designed to affirm the symbolism of business man–client relationship, whether it is between the sexes or between companies. The only people who can afford to eat out are either people with expense accounts or those who do so for special occasions. Restaurants always seem to be packed with business men doing deals or row after row of heterosexual couples. Locked in intense dialogue (propositions or arguments) or staring at each other in stony silence, you might get the impression visiting the average restaurant for the first time that no other relationship existed under the sun. (And that this wasn't good news.) This is quite different from other societies, such as the Chinese, where eating out is habitual, and eating with any less than ten people decidedly odd. Restaurants in our society, however, seem to reinforce the impression that special-occasion meals are more often than not symbolic affirmations of relations of power and obligations.

SIGNAL WORDS	POINTS	NEED SYNONYMS
	1. Restaurant lay-out projects a "business man–client relationship"	average lay-out affirm
only	2. Eating out is expensive so only those with expense accounts or those with a special reason do it.	afford special
	3. Restaurants "packed" with business men and rows of heterosexual couples.	always packed
parenthetical expressions	4. Intense dialogue and silent staring give a negative impression of relationships.	intense staring impression under the sun
different	5. Other societies, such as Chinese, eat out often and in large groups.	different societies habitual decidedly odd
however	6. Our restaurants reinforce impression that special-occasion meals usually symbolize relationships of power and obligation.	reinforce symbolic affirmations relations

After analyzing direction signals, exploring possible synonym choices, and experimenting with rephrasing the original points, you will be ready to compose your paraphrase. As the translator of another person's ideas, you want to be sure to make exactly the same point using the same reasoning; nevertheless, your final version should represent your own voice and the sentence structure natural to your own style of writing. A successful paraphrase will blend into your writing.

When your final version of the paraphrase is prepared, you have one last step to complete: the citation. Including the author's name—possibly with an identifying phrase—and the name of the source you used tells the reader clearly and honestly which ideas are yours and which are the views of others. This type of citation is called an **acknowledgement phrase.** How much information you include in your acknowledgement phrase will depend on your audience's familiarity with the source. The following are examples of acknowledgement forms:

Albert Einstein maintains that . . .

According to Barbara Tuchman, historian and Pulitzer Prize winner, Vietnam . . .

Cultural anthropologist Margaret Mead argues that . . .

A more detailed discussion of acknowledging sources appears in Chapter 11.

While your acknowledgement phrase should clearly mark the beginning of your paraphrase, you must also indicate where the source material ends. Note how the paraphrase below acknowledges Rosalind Coward's work and then flows naturally to another source.

> In her examination of how traditional social eating habits affect women, Rosalind Coward, in her book *Female Desires* (1985), notes that even the floor plan of the typical restaurant asserts a "business man–client relationship." Since eating out is reserved for those compensated by their businesses or those doing so for a distinctive reason, restaurants are densely packed by conferencing businessmen or continuous rows of mixed couples, gripped in concentrated discussion or gazing at one another in dazed muteness. Unfortunately, these pairings are so common that the novice observer entering a normal restaurant would believe them to be the only relationships in existence. Thus, whereas other cultural communities, such as the Chinese, view eating out in groups of ten or more as common practice, in contrast, our restaurants strengthen the image that "special-occasion meals" generally indicate the assertion of authority and duty. John Ellis agrees with Coward's view when he states . . .

EXERCISE: PARAPHRASING I

Here are two excerpts from the remainder of Rosalind Coward's essay. Use the suggestions demonstrated earlier to develop a paraphrase for each excerpt.

The criterion by which a Christmas dinner is judged successful is the extent to which it defeats the eater. What is noted is the enormous size of the turkey, the number of mince pies consumed. Even falling into an unconscious stupor acquires a certain glamour, the culmination of the curious pattern of Christmas eating—intensive preparation, high expectations, exchange, indulgence, anti-climax, sleep. Even the food combinations are transgressive. Sweet foods and savoury are combined in ways which are on the whole confined to Christmas meals—jam with meat, fruit and savouries in puddings, and so on.

The alimentary disorders which rack our society may well be the physical expression of the limitations of an ideology which claims that a small family can provide for all our needs. Family festivities can be a real gut-bomb, because along with the food go complex feelings of inadequacy, disappointment and guilt. Expecting too much from too few is a certain recipe for disaster, and all the members of the family are likely to suffer. Because the symbolism suggests that the family can provide everything, family members feel guilt if they express a need for emotional support from outsiders. This need is sometimes experienced as guilt for rejecting the family's love, when it is merely recognizing more extensive social needs that can't always be met in the family.

Paraphrase is one of the best methods of presenting another person's ideas to your reader. First, it demonstrates that you understand the material well enough to express it in your own words. Second, by taking the time to express the idea in an alternate form, you compliment the reader and make the material more comprehensible.

When presenting research, you will use paraphrase to support the points you are making. Offering several voices of authority that agree with your views builds credibility with your audience. And paraphrasing an expert's opinion in one or two concise sentences allows the support of several people to be included in one paragraph.

In this paragraph from *The Cosmic Code: Quantum Physics as the Language of Nature* (1982) physicist Heinz Pagels states that he doesn't know what the universe is. Because he knows that his audience will be surprised at this admission, he supports his statement by paraphrasing and quoting others.

I don't know what the universe is or whether it has a purpose, but like most physicists I have to find some way to think about it. Einstein thought it a mistake to project our human needs onto the universe because, he felt, it is indifferent to those needs. Steven Weinberg agreed: ". . . the more we know about the universe the more it is evident that it is pointless and meaningless." Like Gertrude Stein's rose, the universe is what it is what it is. But what "is" it? The question will not go away.

The acknowledgement phrases in the paragraph show where the writer has used sources for support. Pagels' first source, Einstein, is a familiar and authoritative voice to both scientific and general readers. Consequently, Pagels has no need to include additional identifying information to introduce the paraphrase. Notice that he adjusts the paraphrase to *his* writing style by including the words "he felt." The second source also must be familiar to his audience (perhaps through previous reference in the book), for Pagels uses only the physicist's name to introduce the quote. He also expects the audience to recognize the third source, Gertrude Stein; but even if the reader does not recognize this often-quoted American expatriate writer, the comparison-based paraphrase makes clear why Pagels chose to build on her statement "a rose is a rose is a rose."

Observe also how Pagels orders his sources and uses signal words to connect them (*agreed* and *like*). The content from each source is ordered to lead naturally to Pagels' final question. Variety in style—a straight paraphrase, a quote, a comparative paraphrase—improves readability. This variety will help keep the reader attentive when you combine several sources in one paragraph.

Paraphrase helps you avoid quoting your sources too often and quoting insignificant or ordinary phrases. And it is particularly effective when the original language is intended for a different audience than the one you are addressing. This usually happens when you are using research material written for professional and academic audiences who expect the material to be written in the **jargon** or special language of their field.

The parody of "government" language in "A Bureaucrat's Guide to Chocolate Chip Cookies" from the *Washington Post* (1983) illustrates just how ridiculous specialized language can sound in an inappropriate context.

A Bureaucrat's Guide to Chocolate Chip Cookies

SUSAN E. RUSS

For those government employes and bureaucrats who have problems with standard recipes, here's one that should make the grade—a classic version of the chocolate-chip cookie translated for easy reading.

Total Lead Time: 35 minutes.
Inputs:
    1 cup packed brown sugar
    ½ cup granulated sugar
    ½ cup softened butter
    ½ cup shortening
    2 eggs
    1½ teaspoons vanilla
    2½ cups all-purpose flour
    1 teaspoon baking soda
    ½ teaspoon salt
    12-ounce package semi-sweet chocolate pieces
    1 cup chopped walnuts or pecans

Guidance:

After procurement actions, decontainerize inputs. Perform measurement tasks on a case-by-case basis. In a mixing type bowl, impact heavily on brown sugar, granulated sugar, softened butter and shortening. Coordinate the interface of eggs and vanilla, avoiding an overrun scenario to the best of your skills and abilities.

At this point in time, leverage flour, baking soda and salt into a bowl and aggregate. Equalize with prior mixture and develop intense and continuous liaison among inputs until well-coordinated. Associate key chocolate and nut subsystems and execute stirring operations.

Within this time frame, take action to prepare the heating environment for throughput by manually setting the oven baking unit by hand to a temperature of 375 degrees Fahrenheit (190 degrees Celsius). Drop mixture in an ongoing fashion from a teaspoon implement onto an ungreased cookie sheet at intervals sufficient enough apart to permit total and permanent separation of throughputs to the maximum extent practicable under operating conditions.

Position cookie sheet in a bake situation and surveil for 8 to 10 minutes or until cooking action terminates. Initiate coordination of outputs within the cooling rack function. Containerize, wrap in red tape and disseminate to authorized staff personnel on a timely and expeditious basis.

Output:

Six dozen official government chocolate-chip cookie units.

When paraphrasing a passage written in specialized language, give close attention to your audience's level of knowledge on the topic. While you may not be operating on an expert level yourself, you probably have acquired a familiarity with the terms through your research. Before you begin paraphrasing, make an effort to identify the terms your audience may have difficulty recognizing.

This excerpt is from the pamphlet "Medicines and You" issued by the National Institute of Health. As you read the paragraph, consider which terms will be too specialized for the general reader.

Because of the large individual variations in people's ability to metabolize drugs, giving patients an "average" dose of a lipid-soluble medicine implies that it must be inappropriate for some of them. If your metabolism of this particular medicine is very rapid, the average dose may be insufficient to treat you, and if your metabolism is very slow, the medicine may accumulate to toxic levels in your blood.

More than likely these terms came to your mind: *metabolize, lipid-soluble, metabolism, toxic.* Many readers will recognize these terms, but they may not fully understand their meaning, especially in the context above. For each term you need to find a non-specialized word. Your final paraphrase may be similar to this:

> The National Institute of Health explains that the rate at which your body is able to chemically process fat-dissolvable medicine determines whether an "average" dose will be beneficial, ineffective (too fast) or harmful (too slow).

EXERCISES: PARAPHRASING II

1. For each of the following quotes write a paraphrase of the person's ideas. Present your paraphrase in a complete sentence that includes an acknowledgement phrase.

a. The more people have studied different methods of bringing up children the more they have come to the conclusion that what good mothers and fathers instinctively feel like doing for their babies is the best after all.

BENJAMIN SPOCK
The Common Sense Book of Baby and Child Care (1946)

b. When you reread a classic you do not see more in the book than you did before; you see more in *you* than there was before.

CLIFTON FADIMAN
Any Number Can Play (1957)

c. Good sense is of all things in the world the most equally distributed, for everybody thinks he is so well supplied with it, that even those most difficult to please in all other matters never desire more of it than they already possess.

RENÉ DESCARTES
Le Discours de la Méthode (1637)

d. The management of a balance of power is a permanent undertaking, not an exertion that has a foreseeable end.

HENRY KISSINGER
White House Years (1979)

e. Future shock . . . the shattering stress and disorientation that we induce in individuals by subjecting them to too much change in too short a time.

ALVIN TOFFLER
Future Shock (1970)

f. To know that what is impenetrable to us really exists, manifesting itself as the highest wisdom and the most radiant beauty, which our dull facilities can comprehend only in the most primitive forms—this knowledge, this feeling, is at the center of true religiousness. In this sense, and in this sense only, I belong to the devoutly religious ranks of men.

ALBERT EINSTEIN
What I Believe (1930)

2. Each of the following paragraphs is written in a specialized language; the first is from a textbook by Michael Kamil et al. called *Understanding Research in Reading and Writing* (Allyn & Bacon, 1985) and the second is from *Art Fundamentals: Theory and Practice* (William C. Brown, 1981) by Otto G. Ocvirk et al. Write a paraphrase for each, giving special attention to terms that might be unfamiliar to a general audience.

a. Two types of inferences or generalizations can be made by the researcher: *logical* and *statistical.* Logical generalizations are drawn when the researcher has no direct evidence of the sample's ability to represent the population. Instead, the researcher attempts to use logic or intuition in supporting the generalizability of the evidence collected from the sample. The decision to attempt a logical generalization is usually made on the basis of cost, as it is expensive to examine subjects from all parts of the country. However, logical generalization is most appropriate when the researcher has some reason to believe that there is little variance across subjects in the characteristics or behaviors of interest. If there is a great deal of variance in the population, the researcher runs the risk of selecting a sample that only represents a portion of the population distribution. In cases in which much population variance is expected, it is usually more appropriate to make statistical generalizations.

b. In three-dimensional art, we have the additional dimension of *depth.* Depth results in a greater sense of reality and, as a consequence, increases physical impact. This is true because graphic work is limited to one format plan, always bounded by a geometric shape called the picture plane. The format in three-dimensional work, on the other hand, is the outer contour of any number of views and contains spatial planes.

3. Read the following article from *Psychology Today* (June 1987) and identify those places where the author has paraphrased information. Either underline the paraphrased material or write the paraphrases on a separate sheet of paper.

Motherhood and Science Do Mix

ELIZABETH STARK

A common assumption among scientists has been that women can 1
only succeed in science if they forgo marriage and family. Domestic
and child-rearing responsibilities supposedly prevent them from devoting sufficient time to research and writing in a field in which "publish or perish" is the rule. However, although studies have shown that
women scientists do publish less than their male colleagues do, marriage and family are apparently not to blame.

Sociologists Jonathan R. Cole and Harriet Zuckerman found 2
that single, childless women are no more prolific than their married
counterparts are, even those with children. They asked 73 female scientists about important events in their lives and careers and recorded
the number of papers they had published each year. The scientists
were divided into two categories, "eminent" and "rank-and-file," based
on peer recognition, membership in honorary societies and academic
level. Women in both groups were equally likely to marry and have
children.

Overall, Cole and Zuckerman found that marriage and/or chil- 3
dren did not significantly affect the scientists' productivity. In fact,
among eminent female scientists, married women actually published
more than did their single peers: at least three papers per year on
average for married women without children, almost three per year
for married women with children and about two per year for single
women. Among rank-and-file scientists, single women did publish
more papers than married ones did—nearly two papers per year,
compared with slightly more than one paper per year—but married
women with children published just as often as did married women
without children.

The researchers explain that, in general, rank-and-file scientists 4
publish less than do their more eminent colleagues. And the women
they interviewed tended to blame factors other than marriage and
children for their lower publication rates. One young scientist with a
new baby told the researchers that her child was just another excuse.
Before that it had been "too many graduate students . . . [a] grant reviewing committee . . . [an] editorship. . . ."

Despite their claim that child rearing and marriage made no sig- 5
nificant difference, Cole and Zuckerman admit that women do "pay a
price to remain scientifically productive." Many mothers said they

lacked the flexibility to work late, had little time to become part of an academic circle and almost no time to spend on ". . . movies, social life and things like that."

Perhaps the most significant factor for married women was 6 whether they were married to another scientist, as about four-fifths of the married women were. Women married to scientists published 40 percent more, on average, than women married to nonscientists did. They said that their husbands understood the obligations of science and offered a great deal of support and help, as well as professional advice.

Among the many obstacles married women and mothers face as 7 scientists, one of the biggest, according to Cole and Zuckerman, is convincing their supervisors and peers that family and science can mix. A distinguished biologist now in her 70s told Cole and Zuckerman that when she was young her boss "threw me out of the lab the minute she heard I was going to get married because that was treason against women." Unfortunately, despite changing social attitudes, this view still prevails in many academic circles.

The issue people should be looking into, Cole and Zuckerman 8 say, is why women in general publish less than men do. A variety of explanations have been suggested, including sex discrimination, but, the sociologists claim, it is not marriage and motherhood.

---

4. Each of these quotes from *Bartlett's Familiar Quotations* presents a view of patriotism. After reading and paraphrasing each opinion, write a short essay incorporating at least three paraphrases to support your view of the qualities that constitute patriotism.

> That man is little to be envied whose patriotism would not gain force upon the plain of Marathon, or whose piety would not grow warmer among the ruins of Iona.
>
> SAMUEL JOHNSON
> *Journey to the Western Islands* (1775)

> The unfailing formula for production of morale is patriotism, self-respect, discipline, and self-confidence within a military unit, joined with fair treatment and merited appreciation from without. . . . It will quickly wither and die if soldiers come to believe themselves the victims of indifference or injustice on the part of their government, or of ignorance, personal ambition, or ineptitude on the part of their military leaders.
>
> DOUGLAS MACARTHUR
> Annual Report of the Chief of Staff,
> U.S. Army, June 30, 1933

I realize that patriotism is not enough. I must have no hatred or bitterness towards anyone.

EDITH CAVELL

Last words before her execution
by the Germans, October 12, 1915

Priests are no more necessary to religion than politicians to patriotism.

JOHN HAYNES HOLMES

The Sensible Man's View of Religion (1933)

Protection and patriotism are reciprocal.

JOHN CALDWELL CALHOUN

Speech in the U.S. House of Representatives
December 12, 1811

Patriotism in the female sex is the most disinterested of all virtues. Excluded from honors and from offices, we cannot attach ourselves to the State or Government from having held a place of eminence. Even in the freest countries our property is subject to the control and disposal of our partners, to whom the laws have given a sovereign authority. Deprived of a voice in legislation, obliged to submit to those laws which are imposed upon us, is it not sufficient to make us indifferent to the public welfare? Yet all history and every age exhibit instances of patriotic virtue in the female sex; which considering our situation equals the most heroic of yours.

ABIGAIL ADAMS

Letter to John Adams
June 17, 1782

WRITING SUGGESTIONS

The group of articles that follow looks at ethics in business. Use these articles to serve as a research base for an essay. Use the summary and paraphrase skills you studied in this chapter to develop and integrate support for your views. Refer to Chapter 11 for the correct summary and paraphrase attribution form. Read and annotate each article carefully before deciding what to summarize or paraphrase. You may wish to read additional material. Define your audience carefully for this subject.

Lester C. Thurow, whose article appeared in the *New York Times* June 14, 1987, is dean of the Sloan School of Management at Massachusetts Institute of Technology. Ellen Goodman writes a nationally syndicated column; this column appeared in the *Virginian-Pilot and Ledger-Star* on February 7, 1987. The article on U.S. banks was a

United Press International story in the *Los Angeles Times* July 20, 1987. The interview of Dr. Pellegrino by Karen S. Peterson was in *USA Today* July 15, 1987.

Ethics Doesn't Start
in Business Schools

LESTER C. THUROW

As the new dean of a business school, I am barraged with questions 1
about what I am going to do to improve business ethics. The questions are usually accompanied by a strong undercurrent of accusation
that business schools are responsible for the bad ethics of corporate
America.

The best solution, the accusers suggest, would be to abolish busi- 2
ness schools, but if that is impossible the schools should at least take
responsibility for the mess they have created and clean it up.

These assertions are unfair. Business students come to us from 3
our society. If they haven't been taught ethics by their families, their
clergymen, their elementary and secondary schools, their liberal arts
colleges or engineering schools or the business firms where most of
them have already worked prior to getting a business degree, there is
very little we can do.

Injunctions to "be good" don't sway young men and women in 4
their mid- to late 20's. In the final analysis, what we produce is no
worse than what we get. If some group of potential business people
were more ethical than others, we would be glad to limit our admissions to the more virtuous, but I know of no such applicant pool.

Nor is this a new problem. Aristotle had some rather harsh things 5
to say about the ethics of tradesmen more than 2,000 years ago. They
were to be carefully excluded from what now would be called the
"corridors of power." The financial scandals of the 1920's managed to
occur before business schools were established, and West Germany is
currently uncovering financial crookedness at Volkswagen without the
benefit of having business schools. No business schools dot the Japanese landscape, but Japanese business ethics also seem on occasion
to be something less than desirable.

While such defenses are more than sufficient if one is simply at- 6
tempting to counter silly accusations, they are ultimately inadequate.

The serious collective interest for improving business ethics merits more than a debating response from officials at schools of management.

The key to what must be done is found in the words "collective 7 interest." Ethical questions arise because we live in communities that function according to rules and laws that promote the long-run interests of the community. Ethics is not arbitrary. It is functional, but it functions to allow a group of human beings to successfully live with each other.

A hermit can neither be ethical or unethical. He simply exists. 8 Ethical dilemmas arise when a person's actions may contribute to the common good of the community but at the same time hurt his self-interest. Choosing to sacrifice one's appetites and self-interest is at the heart of ethical action.

The doctrine that one should sacrifice self-interest for the collec- 9 tive good, however, is a message that is seldom preached in America. In our secular religion, the importance of the individual greatly overshadows the importance of the community. The bumper sticker "The Man Who Dies With the Most Toys Wins" depicts the current state of American ethics.

If the only legitimate goal is maximizing personal income, then 10 there are no ethical principles that must be obeyed. Individuals simply face a cost-benefit calculus where there is some probability of being punished if one is caught violating society's ethical principles. A person may obey the law because the costs of getting caught outweigh the benefits of getting away with it, but in doing so he or she is being clever or cautious not ethical.

How can this country restore the belief that social goals and so- 11 cial responsibilities are so important that they override one's personal gratification? Ethics will be restored when most individuals come to the realization that they play for a common team and are willing to sacrifice self-interest for the team. While such a message is regarded as self-evident in sports, it is seen as strangely wrong in economics and business. There only self-interest counts.

Those who do believe that the team sometimes merits priority 12 over the individual have to preach that message at all levels of American society if our ethics is to be improved. Business schools are in a unique position to preach ethics in the field of economics.

To do this, business schools cannot simply add courses in ethics 13 to the curriculum. We have to change what is taught in business classes.

Today's finance classes teach that the sole goal of business man- 14 agers should be to maximize the net worth of shareholders. Managers follow this principle because doing so maximizes his or her personal net worth.

If the only goals of firms and individuals are monetary, however, 15 it is but a short jump to maximizing those monetary variables with means that are illegal or unethical. To create ethical business behavior, we must place higher value on goals other than personal or shareholder net worth.

Business law courses outline what is legal and imply that firms 16 and individuals should go right up to the line between legality and illegality. Ethics does not consist of asking one's lawyer, "Is it legal?" The question "Is it right?" is not the same as "Is it legal?" Yet most Americans act as if it were so.

Sacrificing self-interest for the common good is not going to be 17 advocated by business schools or accepted by our students unless a majority of Americans also support the premise. In the end, business ethics is merely a reflection of American ethics.

Rating the Corporate Conscience

ELLEN GOODMAN

Alice Tepper Marlin is not your ordinary, everyday shopper. When 1 Alice goes to market, she takes along an extra mental list.

While the rest of us stand in front of the laundry detergents or 2 breakfast cereals, trying to decipher unit-pricing and chemical ingredients, she is comparison-shopping the companies. Which of these breakfast cereals has championed minority hiring? Which of these laundry detergents subsidizes day care? Do they do business in South Africa? Do they make weapons? What's their charity record? How do they treat the environment?

If at all possible, she chooses to brush her teeth, wash her hair, 3 clean her clothes and feed her family in a socially responsible fashion. Alice prefers to put her money where her mouth is and (if this metaphor hasn't gone berserk) eat her own political menu. What's more, she's making it easier for other people to do the same.

Alice Marlin is the president of the Council on Economic Priori- 4 ties, a public-research organization that has been studying businesses and their social policies for some time. Along with two colleagues, she has put together a political consumer's guide. It's called *Rating America's Corporate Conscience* and, in a modest way, it does that.

Between paperback covers are thumbnail sketches of 130 major 5 American companies and their everyday products. It is possible using their charts to pick the disposable diaper that doesn't do business in South Africa. It is also possible to choose between cookie companies that do and do not also push cigarettes, and to find a washing machine whose manufacturers do not also make nuclear weapons.

"We were sitting around," remembers Marlin, a former securities 6 analyst who helped create stock portfolios for people concerned about these issues, "thinking that there must be thousands of consumers who want to cast economic votes."

But in the current Pac-Man climate of corporate takeovers, the 7 average consumer might not know, for example, that Chapstick is owned by A. H. Robins, let alone that Robins is the much-sued former maker of the Dalkon Shield. For that matter, they may not know that Pepperidge Farm belongs to Campbell Soup and that Campbell has a good record with women and minorities.

The book they compiled makes this sort of information more ac- 8 cessible, but doesn't always make the judgments easy. "There isn't any company that we consider a saint," admits Marlin, "and even the worst have some redeeming characteristic."

One reader may laud Procter & Gamble's uniquely progressive 9 parental-leave policy for its workers while lamenting its charitable support for conservative think tanks. Another may applaud Philip Morris for its record in minority economic development while criticizing the product it sells to minorities.

"We set it up so that people could use their own judgment," says 10 Marlin. "Some people feel that the South Africa issue is so important, it's all they look at; others want to look at animal testing or weapons or PACs. Not all people would pick the same favorites, but overall we felt there were differences."

CEP doesn't expect that the consumer in search of the best prod- 11 uct at the best price will always give priority to the best-rated company. Nor do they expect that in a blizzard someone will refuse to sleep another night at a Sheraton because ITT has major contracts in nuclear weapons.

"We're not saying that people should throw out everything they 12 bought or if there's a product you love or one that's rated 30 percent less, the social criteria should rule. I don't use it that way myself. It's for consumers who are indifferent at the margin. It's great to know the brand names that are best." Even her children agree. Ever since they discovered that the Hershey Co. was half-owned by a school for orphaned children, Marlin can't pass a candy counter without hearing a plea "to buy them candy for the sake of the poor orphaned children."

The profit margin on a single bar of candy or a package of English 13
muffins may not influence a multinational corporation. The current
password of corporate life is "competitiveness." There is the notion in
some quarters that the most streamlined, hardheaded, no-frills business decisions are the smartest. A social conscience is often considered a frill.

Socially conscious shopping is a heartening way to exercise a 14
franchise. How remarkable, though, if consumers could together create
a new race to be No. 1: No. 1 corporate citizen.

U.S. Banks Defrauded of
Record $1.1 Billion in 1986

FROM UNITED PRESS INTERNATIONAL

The nation's banks lost a record $1.11 billion through fraud and em- 1
bezzlement last year, nearly a third more than they did in 1985, a
weekly newsletter on white-collar crime said Sunday.

The Corporate Crime Reporter said FBI documents it obtained 2
show agents closed 10,416 cases in 1986, 44.9% more than in 1985.
There were 1,957 bank fraud and embezzlement convictions last year.

Of those cases closed in 1986, 72% involved fraud and embezzle- 3
ments by someone who worked in the bank and 39% of all cases involved over $100,000, the FBI documents showed.

The $1.1 billion taken overall is 32% more than the $841.9 billion 4
lost in 1985, the newsletter said. Cases in the FBI's New York field office
led the nation in losses at $369 million, followed by Houston, $196.6
million; Oklahoma City, $81.3 million; Jackson, Miss., $42.4 million; and
Dallas, $37.9 million.

Going into 1987, the Los Angeles field office had the most pend- 5
ing cases with 290. Dallas was next at 189, followed by Houston with
140, Chicago with 118 and New York with 117.

The newsletter said Rep. Douglas Barnard, D-Ga., chairman of 6
the House Subcommittee on Commerce, Consumer and Monetary Affairs, plans hearings in September on insider bank fraud and whether
it relates to financial problems suffered by banks and thrift institutions. A subcommittee report in June said insider abuse "has been a

significant factor" in failures involving California savings and loans since 1984.

Tough Questions—
and Not-So-Easy Answers

KAREN S. PETERSON

Dr. Edmund D. Pellegrino is director of the Joseph and Rose Kennedy Institute of Ethics at Georgetown University, Washington, D.C. He offers his opinions on these ethical questions:

Q. *You are privy to confidential information that your company is* 1 *about to be involved in a takeover that will greatly increase the value of its stock. Do you tell your father, who really needs the money for a family emergency?*

A. The answer is no. It is unethical to take advantage of confidential information like this and equally unethical to assist others to do so, including your father.

Like many questions of ethics, this deals with conflicts among obligations. The task of ethical judgment is to resolve these conflicts in a morally defensible way, placing one obligation ahead of the other.

Q. *You are a journalist. You have found out that the governor's* 2 *daughter is a drug addict. The governor has taken a strong anti-drug stance. What do you do?*

A. Unless the daughter's problem affects public welfare, she is entitled to privacy like any citizen. Freedom of the press is a right, but not one that should always be exercised by prudent and fair persons.

Q. *Your daughter confides to you—her dad—that she is taking* 3 *birth control pills. She does not want her mother to know. But you and your wife have an understanding to tell each other everything. What do you do?*

A. You must keep the confidence. But ideally, you should inform your daughter of your agreement with your wife *before* she confides anything to you. Then she will know whether to confide in you or not.

Q. *You know a fellow worker takes drugs on a job that involves the* 4 *nation's defense. He appears to be doing his job well. Do you report him?*

A. The crucial point is whether his drug use would imperil national security or endanger others. If it does, you must report him out of justice to others. If it doesn't, he is entitled to privacy about his personal habits.

Q. *The FBI is running a security check on a friend whom you know* 5 *to be gay and in the closet. Should you tell the truth if asked about his homosexuality?*

A. Is this question relevant to the job in question? If it is, you must reveal it. If it is not, you must respect your friend's privacy since this kind of information may be misused. If asked directly, you should be honest and refuse to answer if you feel it would endanger your friend. You must also be prepared to take the consequences of your refusal.

Q. *You are a religious telecaster. You raise money from your flock* 6 *without specifying how it will be used. Can you use any of it for yourself?*

A. You must detail how you use money you raise from others in some public way. This is particularly obligatory for a religious telecaster who should be a model of probity. Others have a right to know they are supporting you as well as the cause you represent.

Q. *Your husband is terminally ill and in pain and asks you to help* 7 *him die. Can you help even if that is against the law?*

A. It depends on what your husband means by "help." To kill him intentionally is, in my view, against both law and morality. But to ease pain, provide comfort to a hopelessly ill patient, is morally defensible and may even be obligatory.

Q. *You are a psychiatrist whose patient tells you during therapy* 8 *that he might kill a specific person. What do you do?*

A. As with other questions about confidentiality, the central issue is the possibility of harm to others. If in your professional judgment you think the threat genuine and direct, you must take whatever reasonable measures are available to prevent harm to another person.

Q. *You are a doctor whose patient has died of AIDS. By law you* 9 *must report the death as AIDS, but you know that knowledge will deeply distress his family. What do you do?*

A. You must report the diagnosis as the law requires. But you are not morally bound to volunteer the information to the family, unless doing so prevents harm to others.

For example, the spouse might wish to remarry. If he/she knew, he/she might wish to be tested to avoid infecting a future spouse or children.

If the question is asked directly by the family, the truth should be told, taking care to do so as compassionately as possible.

PART III

Planning

E very semester begins with good intentions. "This semester," you tell yourself, "I'm going to be organized." So
it's off to the bookstore to buy a calendar for keeping track of
what you have to do. The wide selection available forces you
to analyze exactly what your needs are. What kind of information will you be recording—class assignments, social events,
work hours, or all three? Do you need to know the time of day
for this information or just the day of the week? How far ahead
do you need to plan what you are doing—weekly, monthly, or
both? Do you need a place to keep addresses and phone
numbers? What size should the calendar be—wall size, book
bag size, or pocket size? Just when and where do you plan to
use this organizer? Although this may be a lot of questions to
ask before making such a simple purchase, your final decision
will influence how well you meet your goal of being organized.

Similarly, planning an effective argument requires several
levels of decision making: What does your intended audience
believe and value? How do those beliefs differ from yours?
How can you appeal most persuasively to your audience?
What options do you have for strategically arranging your information? Asking the right questions is the first step to a careful analysis. The chapters in Part III will guide you in forming
the necessary questions and analyzing the answers to those
questions.

Chapter 6

ANALYZING AUDIENCE

When you began investigating the subject for your argument, two questions directed your search:

> What do I already know about the subject?

> What do I need to know about the subject?

Before you can decide what information from your investigation to use in constructing your argument, you will need to ask the same questions about your intended audience:

> What do they already know about the subject?

> What do they need to know about the subject?

Answering these questions requires you to make certain *assumptions* about your audience: What do they believe? Why do they believe what they do?

IDENTIFYING ASSUMPTIONS

An **assumption** is a belief that you take for granted to be true. Naturally, when you believe something to be true, you presume most other people share your belief. But do they? And why should they? Have you had similar experiences and influences in your lives? From the time you were a small child, you have been developing assumptions about everything from how the world was created to why people own pets to what constitutes fairness. These assumptions form the belief system from which you make decisions and state opinions. Recognizing what these assumptions are and how you came to accept these beliefs helps you to determine if you should rely on your assumptions in reasoning with other people.

One way to identify your own assumptions and test their reliability is by exploring the path that led to making a particular decision. What beliefs, for instance, led you to pursue a college degree? Are any of those beliefs listed below?

I believe I can successfully complete the courses.

I believe a college degree will enable me to obtain a secure, high-paying, rewarding job.

I believe that better educated people are more respected.

You probably would not have much difficulty finding other college students who share these assumptions, but what about those people who did not attend college or those who have not yet decided to attend? Are your assumptions reliable enough to serve as the foundation for an argument addressed to that audience? What influences and experiences might lead a person to accept the beliefs listed above? An examination of those beliefs would follow a process such as this:

ASSUMPTION: I believe I can successfully complete the courses.

BASIS FOR BELIEF:

- My grades were good in high school.
- My SAT scores were high.
- My parents and teachers said I would do well.

The reasons supporting this belief reflect the standard criteria used in college applications, making the reasoning familiar to a wide range of people.

ASSUMPTION: I believe a college degree will enable me to obtain a secure, high-paying job.

BASIS FOR BELIEF:

- My brother finished college and he is a successful geologist who travels around the world.
- The people with college degrees who work for my father hold management positions.
- When my cousin applied for a job, the personnel director told her she needed a college degree to complement her four years of communications experience with the Navy.
- One look at the classified ads shows that a college degree is required for any professional job with a starting salary over $20,000.

The first three reasons for this belief are based on the experience of relatives. Even though each experience reveals a different dimension of the belief, the experiences are highly individualized and may not be accepted as representative by other people. The last reason has more potential for being accepted as reliable because the information can be easily verified by others. Still, some people might have different ideas about what constitutes a "secure, high-paying, rewarding job."

ASSUMPTION: I believe that better educated people are more respected.

BASIS FOR BELIEF:

- When there is a local or national crisis, news reporters interview experts from universities, national agencies, government, and corporations for their opinions.
- Well-educated people often have titles, such as doctor, senator, district attorney, or CEO.
- People with a better education achieve positions of authority over others.

These reasons illustrate how a faulty assumption is formed. Are experts who are interviewed necessarily respected by people who see or read the interview? Are there other experts who hold opposing opinions? Have people with titles ever been disgraced rather than respected? Do people with authority necessarily use their authority wisely? Are dictators respected?

The reasons reflect what the person making the assumption *wants* to believe, but they are unreliable as a basis for accepting the assumption. The person making the assumption has also failed to consider that people are respected for many different qualities and that respect is shown in many ways.

Identifying and testing your own assumptions, difficult as it may be, is important not only to building your argument but also to analyzing your audience. How you characterize people and their thoughts is formed by your beliefs. Identifying the assumptions you hold toward a certain audience is the beginning point of your analysis of what they already know and what they need to know.

One of the earliest examples of audience analysis comes from the Greek philosopher and rhetorician Aristotle (384–322 B.C.). In the following passages from his *Rhetoric,* Aristotle characterizes the differences between young men and elderly men to demonstrate to his students that an audience's needs affect how information is presented to that audience.[1]

Young men have strong passions, and tend to grafity them indiscriminately. Of the bodily desires, it is the sexual by which they are most swayed and in which they show absence of self-control. They are changeable and fickle in their desires, which are violent while they last, but quickly over: their impulses are keen but not deep-rooted, and are like sick people's attacks of hunger and thirst. They are hot-tempered and quick-tempered, and apt to give way to their anger; bad temper often gets the better of them, for owing to their love of honor they cannot bear being slighted, and are indignant if they imagine themselves unfairly treated. While they love honour, they love victory still more; for youth is eager for superiority over others, and victory is one form of

---

[1] Lane Cooper, ed. and trans., *The Rhetoric of Aristotle* (Englewood Cliffs, N.J.: Prentice-Hall, 1960), pp. 132–133.

this. They love both more than they love money, which indeed they love very little, not having yet learnt what it means to be without it—this is the point of Pittacus' remark about Amphiaraus. They look at the good side rather than the bad, not having yet witnessed many instances of wickedness. They trust others readily, because they have not yet often been cheated. They are sanguine: nature warms their blood as though with excess of wine; and besides that, they have as yet met with few disappointments. Their lives are mainly spent not in memory but in expectation; for expectation refers to the future, memory to the past, and youth has a long future before it and a short past behind it: on the first day of one's life one has nothing at all to remember, and can only look forward. They are easily cheated, owing to the sanguine disposition just mentioned. Their hot tempers and hopeful dispositions make them more courageous than older men are; the hot temper prevents fear, and the hopeful disposition creates confidence; we cannot feel fear so long as we are feeling angry, and any expectation of good makes us confident. They are shy, accepting the rules of society in which they have been trained, and not yet believing in any other standard of honour. They have exalted notions, because they have not yet been humbled by life or learnt its necessary limitations; moreover, their hopeful disposition makes them think themselves equal to great things—and that means having exalted notions. They would always rather do noble deeds than useful ones: their lives are regulated more by moral feeling than by reasoning; and whereas reasoning leads us to choose what is useful, moral goodness leads us to choose what is noble. They are fonder of their friends, intimates, and companions than older men are, because they like spending their days in the company of others, and have not yet come to value either their friends or anything else by their usefulness to themselves. All their mistakes are in the direction of doing things excessively and vehemently. They disobey Chilon's precept by overdoing everything; they love too much and hate too much, and the same with everything else. They think they know everything, and are always quite sure about it; this, in fact, is why they overdo everything. If they do wrong to others, it is because they mean to insult them, not to do them actual harm. They are ready to pity others, because they think every one an honest man, or anyhow better than he is: they judge their neighbour by their own harmless natures, and so cannot think he deserves to be treated in that way. They are fond of fun and therefore witty, wit being well-bred insolence.

ANALYSIS: Because they lack experience, the young have a confident, passionate, and positive outlook. Therefore, the writer can easily motivate them to participate by appealing to their emotional need to achieve.

In his characterization of elderly men, also in the *Rhetoric,* Aristotle views experience as having a dramatically different effect on the audience's needs.[2]

The character of Elderly Men—men who are past their prime—may be said to be formed for the most part of elements that are the contrary of all these. They have lived many years; they have often been taken in, and often made mistakes, and life on the whole is a bad business. The result is that they are sure about nothing and *under-do* everything. They "think," but they never "know"; and because of their hesitation they always add a "possibly" or a "perhaps," putting everything this way and nothing positively. They are cynical; that is, they tend to put the worse construction on everything. Further, their experience makes them distrustful and therefore suspicious of evil. Consequently they neither love warmly nor hate bitterly, but following the hint of Bias they love as though they will some day hate and hate as though they will some day love. They are small-minded, because they have been humbled by life: their desires are set upon nothing more exalted or unusual than what will help them to keep alive. They are not generous, because money is one of the things they must have, and at the same time their experience has taught them how hard it is to get and how easy to lose. They are cowardly, and are always anticipating danger; unlike that of the young, who are warm-blooded, their temperament is chilly; old age has paved the way for cowardice; fear is, in fact, a form of chill. They love life; and all the more when their last day has come, because the object of all desire is something we have not got, and also because we desire more strongly that which we need most urgently. They are too fond of themselves; this is one form that small-mindedness takes. Because of this, they guide their lives too much by considerations of what is useful and too little by what is noble—for the useful is what is good for oneself, and the noble what is good absolutely. They are not shy, but shameless rather; caring less for what is noble than for what is useful, they feel contempt for what people may think of them. They lack confidence in the future; partly through experience—for most things go wrong, or anyhow turn out worse than one expects; and partly because of their cowardice. They live by memory rather than by hope; for what is left to them of life is but little as compared with the long past; and hope is of the future, memory of the past. This, again, is the cause of their loquacity; they are continually talking of the past, because they enjoy remembering it. Their fits of anger are sudden but feeble. Their sensual passions have either altogether gone or have lost their vigour: consequently they do

---

[2]Cooper, 134–135.

not feel their passions much, and their actions are inspired less by what they do feel than by the love of gain. Hence men at this time of life are often supposed to have a self-controlled character; the fact is that their passions have slackened, and they are slaves to the love of gain. They guide their lives by reasoning more than by moral feeling; reasoning being directed to utility and moral feeling to moral goodness. If they wrong others, they mean to injure them, not to insult them. Old men may feel pity, as well as young men, but not for the same reason. Young men feel it out of kindness; old men out of weakness, imagining that anything that befalls any one else might easily happen to them, which, as we saw, is a thought that excites pity. Hence they are querulous, and not disposed to jesting or laughter— the love of laughter being the very opposite of querulousness.

> **ANALYSIS:** Because they have experienced a great deal, the elderly are cautious, distrustful, and unemotional. Therefore, in order to make decisions, they require strong appeals to reason.

An analysis of these two audience groups in today's world might produce very different profiles, but the procedure remains the same. By examining closely the actions and reactions, likes and dislikes of a group of people, you can generalize about their interests and needs. In fact, you use this procedure intuitively each time you survey a newsstand to decide which magazine to buy. The publications you reject do not satisfy your interests and needs; and you make assumptions about how your needs will be met by those you do select. The publishers, then, must make the right assumptions about those needs as they select articles, features, photographs, and even advertisements that satisfy your expectations. Here are some assumptions of different students about the audiences of certain periodicals:

> Readers of the *National Review* are generally well-educated, upper-middle class, and ultraconservative in their political views. Deeply concerned with the decay of Western civilization, they are pessimistic, believing that this is humanity's darkest hour.

> The college-age to middle-age reader of *Essence* is an educated, socially and politically conscious black woman ready to act on issues of importance. She expects to be stirred through information about and affirmation of her identity.

> The young (aged 15–30) audience of *Rolling Stone* is deeply engrossed in rock music in particular and the entertainment industry in general. Members of this group are impressionable and perhaps looking for leaders. Their political naiveté makes them vulnerable to editorial innuendo.

> *Vogue* readers are generally educated females over 21 who have or aspire to membership in the upper class. Their concern with fash-

ion and the latest in social trends may indicate a tendency toward a more liberal point of view. Primarily they are interested in how their appearance measures up to that of others.

Looking carefully at these brief analyses of audience, you see two kinds of assumptions. One assumption is based on objective data (that is, age, socioeconomic class, and education) that can be verified. The other assumptions (for instance, desires and points of vulnerability) are based on subjectively drawn implications. Is an ultraconservative necessarily pessimistic? Are people "deeply engrossed" in rock music necessarily impressionable and politically naive? To the students' credit, they express some of their subjective assumptions tentatively: "*perhaps* looking for leaders" and "*may* indicate a *tendency* toward a more liberal point of view."

To prevent your own subjective assumptions from interfering with the accuracy of your audience analysis, begin by asking questions that will result in an objective index of the audience's general characteristics.

- What is the general range of ages in this audience?
- What is the audience's social and economic status?
- What is the audience's educational experience? High school, undergraduate (2 years, 4 years), graduate, postgraduate?
- What kinds of work experiences typify this audience?
- Does the audience have strong ethnic or regional ties?
- What feature or interest creates the strongest bond for this audience? Gender, marital status, politics, profession, hobby?

ESTABLISHING OPPOSITION

From the general characteristics of your audience, you can begin to make assumptions about the relationship between your audience and the central issue of your argument. What is their basic attitude—do they support your view or oppose it? How strongly? More than likely your audience's attitude toward the issue will fall into one of the following five categories:

Unconditional opposition	Conditional opposition	Undecided or ambivalent	Conditional support	Unconditional support

To place your intended audience on this opinion scale, you need to identify their specific beliefs and values. These assumptions are difficult to identify because your own value system affects how you judge the beliefs of others. However, attempting to identify the values you associate with each of the opinion levels helps you go beyond your own view and see the reasoning that shapes others' ideas. Consider the full range of experiences and influences that could affect people's values. To see how this process works, let's identify beliefs and values surrounding the issue of reinstating the draft.

UNCONDITIONAL OPPOSITION

Are against all war

Believe in "Thou shalt not kill"

Support civil disobedience

Have lost a loved one in a previous war

Have had bad military experience

Believe pen is mightier than the sword

CONDITIONAL OPPOSITION

Believe recent wars haven't accomplished much

Don't want their education interrupted

Are concerned for son, spouse, brother, boyfriend

Think we should take care of social problems in our own country first

UNDECIDED OR AMBIVALENT

Have had no direct military experience

Don't feel threatened, have no personal stake

Have other priorities

Have a wait-and-see attitude

May not be informed

CONDITIONAL SUPPORT

Believe country needs to be prepared

Feel patriotic obligation

Have had some previous direct or indirect positive military experience

Believe draft should be used only if there is an immediate threat

UNCONDITIONAL SUPPORT

Are openly patriotic

Feel that might makes right

Are veterans with positive military experience

Have tradition of military family

Feel threatened by opposing ideologies

By anticipating associations such as these, you can begin to understand why you believe your audience holds a particular opinion. This range of specific assumptions related to your issue can serve as the starting point for analyzing how your beliefs and those of your audience coincide and differ.

BRIDGING AUDIENCE OPPOSITION

Although an argument involves controversy, your purpose as the writer is not to knock out your opponent but rather to reach an understanding. Consequently, recognizing the points of agreement you share with your audience is just as important as identifying your points of departure.

A list of *We believe* statements can show you what your audience already knows and values—the point at which you can begin viewing the issue together. As an example of how this level of analysis works, let's use the possibility of a state lottery as the issue.

WE BELIEVE

The state government should provide good schools and roads.

Taxes should not be raised.

State-endorsed programs should not favor the rich or take advantage of the poor; all people should benefit.

The state has an obligation to protect its people from crime.

Because you and your audience share these beliefs, you are relieved of the obligation of demonstrating their significance. Instead you can use them as a positive perspective with which to bridge your differences. Next, determine your primary differences to see what your audience *needs* to know to understand your view. Here is how the differences on the state lottery issue might be stated:

I BELIEVE	THEY BELIEVE
It will generate millions of dollars in revenue for the state general fund.	The state treasury does not have a deficit.
Everyone in the state benefits from more money for education and roads.	The benefits are inequitable; participating merchants get a 5 percent commission, but there are few winners.
People can always find a way to gamble.	The lottery capitalizes on human weaknesses, especially the hopes of the poor.
Endorsement from law enforcement shows confidence that crime will not increase.	Lotteries encourage organized crime.

While other beliefs may cause differences on this issue, these lists illustrate the distances that can exist between the writer and the audience. Presenting convincing information and emphasizing the beliefs you share can shorten that distance enough to make your audience reconsider the issue from your point of view. For instance, in the first point on the lottery the writer and the audience are not far apart. Both want the state treasury to have enough money to prevent taxes from being raised (shared belief). On the second and the fourth points, however, the opinions diverge further. To shorten this distance, the writer will need to document other states' experiences with lotteries to demonstrate the potential revenue benefits and the lack of an increase in crime. Discussion of these effects can reinforce the shared beliefs. The third point shows the greatest distance because it deals with moral opinion. Still, writer and audience agree that people have weaknesses, so advocating some kind of controls, especially in advertising, might help to bridge the distance.

By fulfilling your audience's needs for information, you strengthen your argument and bring your audience closer to understanding your view of the issue. But to determine what information to select and how to present it, you first need to know your audience well—their general characteristics, the reasoning that informs their assumptions, and the specific beliefs that separate you and bring you together on the issue.

EXERCISES: AUDIENCE ANALYSIS

1. Behind every decision lies an assumption or two that accounts for the choice made. The following situations involve fairly common decisions. After reading each scene, clearly identify the assumption or assumptions behind the decision. State the assumptions in a complete sentence.

a. For the first four weeks of class Rick sat in the second desk in the fourth row. One day when he enters the classroom, someone else is sitting in that seat. Rick stands there frozen, staring at the person in the seat. What assumptions cause him to respond in this way?

b. Diana's 72-year-old grandmother has been widowed for two years. Diana recently bought her a puppy. What assumptions motivated Diana to buy the dog?

c. Erik had five C's and two B's on work in his composition course. He never missed a class, he turned in all his work on time, and he participated regularly in discussions. He was genuinely surprised when he received a C in the course. Why? What assumptions caused this surprise?

d. When the Gordons received an inheritance, they divided the money equally into individual accounts for their three children's education. What assumptions motivated them to do this?

e. Mari told her parents she wanted to find a way to get more regular exercise. For her birthday they gave her a membership to a popular health club in her neighborhood. Mari asked if she could cash in the membership to buy workout equipment for her home. Why? What assumptions led Mari to this decision?

f. When Alex received his first appointment for a job interview, he bought a new suit for the occasion. What assumptions motivated this purchase?

2. Choose three of the magazines listed below. For each write a two-paragraph analysis of the audience. Base the first paragraph on objective assumptions and the second paragraph on subjective assumptions.

Smithsonian	Good Housekeeping	TV Guide
Esquire	Popular Mechanics	Omni
Elle	Changing Times	Ebony
Reader's Digest	National Geographic	Spin
Newsweek	Gentlemen's Quarterly	Byte
Discover	Psychology Today	Forbes

3. Aristotle made many distinctions between young men and elderly men. Choose one of the following pairs and write a fully developed paragraph on each, using the same criteria for analysis and making as many distinctions as you can.

jazz musicians *vs.* rock musicians

new mother or father *vs.* experienced mother or father

a used car *vs.* a previously owned car

a red Ferrari *vs.* a silver Ferrari

4. Using the opinion scale in this chapter, explore a subject of your own interest or from the list below. For each level of opinion list what you assume to be the reasons someone would have that particular view.

a. Building a nuclear plant in your town
b. Censoring rock music lyrics
c. Requiring two years of national service before college
d. Investing in the stock market
e. Requiring a full year of foreign language study for all college graduates

5. Using the subject you selected for exercise 4, develop the beliefs you and your opposing audience hold on the issue by writing out the *We believe, I believe, They believe* lists.

6. Choose an editorial or argumentative article that interests you and that addresses you as part of the intended audience. Follow this procedure:

1. List any information and strong opinions you already have on the issue.
2. List what you expect to find in the article.
3. Read the article.
4. Reread the article, taking notes on how the writer fulfilled your information needs.

Then write an essay evaluating the writer's success in fulfilling your information needs. Consider the choices the writer made in bridging the distance between your views. (Your teacher may request that you turn in your preliminary notes with the essay.)

Chapter 7

DEVELOPING
APPEALS

On any given day you are likely to receive mail inviting you to attend an event, buy a new product, use a service, or donate money to a cause. Each presentation tries its best to convince you that your support (in time, money, vote, patronage, or attendance) will be well worth the effort. And regardless of the nature of the subject—mail order seeds, adopt-a-pet, or nuclear disarmament—the writer will find some way of appealing to you.

Using appeals is part of everyday conversation. If you want someone to take your shift at work so you can attend a concert, you might appeal to the person's sense of friendship. If that doesn't persuade the person, you might offer to work her holiday shift, an appeal to fairness. When you are face-to-face with your audience, using appeals seems fairly easy. A facial expression or gesture from your audience can signal you to intensify your appeal or choose another direction. But in writing your audience is not visible, and your use of appeals depends on how well you have anticipated your audience's needs and reactions and how well you understand the effect of appeals.

Appeals help shorten the distance between you and your audience; they enable you to support your purpose in terms that you and your audience value. Let's say you want the voters in your relatively small town to support a raise in taxes to improve local educational facilities. Unfortunately, 55 percent of the voting constituency consists of retired people on restricted incomes. With no children to benefit directly from this tax increase, they find it difficult to support your view. How, then, can you present the issue in a meaningful way to them? Given their age, they might value a sense of pride in how the town has developed; they might value an endorsement by others their age or by a trusted official; or they might value a sense of their own legacy to the town. Appealing to one or more of these values will bridge the distance in your understanding.

Deciding what appeals to use with your audience involves more than guessing what might work. Once you have analyzed who your audience is and what they believe, you need to know *why* they believe what they do. Consider, for a moment, why you believe the following:

The sun rises in the east and sets in the west.

Your parents will remember your birthday.

The *Mona Lisa* is a masterpiece.

A college education is important to success.

High cholesterol contributes to heart disease.

You can be put in jail if you refuse to pay your taxes.

Scientific proof, laws, the testimony of experts, family loyalty, personal experience—these and many other factors persuade you to believe what you do. These reasons for belief can be categorized into three basic appeals: the appeal to reason (logical appeal), the appeal to the character of the speaker (ethical appeal), and the appeal to emotions (emotional appeal). Each plays a distinct role in reaching your audience with the information you have to present and in persuading them to accept your views.

THE APPEAL TO ETHICS: *ETHOS*

Your sense of ethics—the standards by which you judge something to be good or right—determines to a great extent not only *what* you believe but also *whom* you believe. Often you respect someone's opinion so highly that you accept it without question. If, for instance, the dentist you have been going to for ten years explains that you need a root canal to save your tooth, you trust in that judgment even if you dread the physical and financial pain. Your experience of the dentist's professional service and concern for your well-being gives you reason to believe his or her opinion. But when you don't know the person providing the information, it is difficult to accept what is being said with confidence. This is the problem you have when presenting an argument to an audience that doesn't know you.

Conveying the "goodness" of your character—establishing a high level of credibility through your writing voice, or persona—is the essence of the **ethical appeal.** If the audience doesn't trust the authenticity of your concern or if they have reason to lose respect for your judgment, then they will not believe you or accept what you have to say. The challenge, then, is to represent yourself as reputable.

As students you might feel at a disadvantage in developing the ethical appeal because you haven't had the opportunity to establish a reputation yet. But ethical appeal is not just a matter of reputation; it is a matter of judgment. The voice you use and the information you choose will establish the credibility of your judgment.

"Let's change 'Some of us guys' to 'We the people.'"

CHOOSING A VOICE

You will present most of your argument in an objective voice, using the idea under discussion and its related parts as the subjects of your sentences. And you will need to establish a relationship between yourself and the audience before they will pay attention to what you say. The pronoun you choose to identify yourself will establish that relationship. Before making your decision, consider the following advantages and disadvantages of each.

Using *I*.   When you use *I* in an argument, you draw immediate attention to yourself. Naturally the readers will expect you to make a connection between yourself and them, and yourself and the subject. "Why is what *you* know or think so important?" they will ask. To satisfy this need for credibility you can respond on three levels: your expertise, a personal experience, or your view as a representative member of a group.

Expertise can be established in many ways. Of course, people who have gained fame for their professional accomplishments have no problem establishing credibility *in their field*. But while you would readily accept views on astronaut training from Sally Ride or Neil Armstrong, you might question their opinions on music. Your readers expect from you an honest, significant connection. If you have achieved a high level of proficiency at something or if the length of your service has given you a fair view of the problem, your audience may see you as having a credible level of expertise. In these two settings your expertise would establish an ethical appeal:

From the 312 hours I have spent piloting my father's small cargo plane on the weekends, I can testify to the growing congestion in this area that the study reports.

As a lifeguard at the community center I have been required to renew my CPR certification every year. The growing number of people who attend the class each year and the diversity of their ages lead me to believe that more people are realizing the need to be prepared to help others in emergency situations.

In both cases the writer clearly explains the extent of his or her expertise, which led to the opinion stated. Used in combination with research or testimony of experts in the field, your own expertise can reinforce the credibility of your persona.

Sometimes the *I* of personal experience can bring you closer to an audience, especially one that questions why you are concerned about an issue. But personal experience, which is generally limited and often biased, conveys a tone of informality that can be interpreted as an insignificant digression in your argument. And the last thing you want your audience to say is "So what?" Yet if your personal experience is significant enough to demonstrate the origin of your concern, then using it might be effective.

Some writers begin their argument with a personal experience to establish a friendly tone with their audience and a focus for the problem before they define it. In this way, a personal experience can convey your tone or attitude toward your subject. This is how one student used a personal experience to introduce an issue to the audience:

Finding a parking place in Washington, D.C., can be an all-day task, so when I saw the empty space after only thirty minutes of searching, I got pretty excited. Unfortunately, the One Way sign at the end of the row meant I would have to take the long way around to get to the space. By that time someone else might get the spot. Knowing I wouldn't block traffic, I edged past the sign and eased into the empty parking space. But as I got out of my car, a motorcycle patrol officer pulled up and walked toward me with his ticket book.

"Didn't you see that One Way sign?" he asked.

"Yes," I replied, "but the lane was clear."

"Then you knowingly disobeyed the law," he explained and handed me a $40 ticket for a moving violation. "If you had said you didn't see the sign, I would have given you only a warning."

Somehow this just didn't make sense. If I had lied, I would have saved $40, but by telling the truth, I was penalized. What kind of a system is this? If it's beneficial to perjure yourself on a small scale, I wondered, is it just as beneficial to perjure yourself on a large scale, like pretending you didn't see someone commit a violent crime? When telling the truth makes a person a victim, maybe honesty isn't the best policy.

By using an experience common to the reader's frame of reference, the writer creates a closer bond of knowledge with the reader that, in turn, increases the level of credibility. If the experience were unusual, the reader would be more likely to dismiss it and question the rest of the content.

Readers want to trust the person presenting the information. To accommodate them, your use of *I* must be linked to the subject in some *representative* way. If you are part of a group whose understanding of the issue can help to clarify or emphasize a point, then using *I* as a representative member can be effective. People who write letters to the editor often identify themselves in this way:

> As a mother of three elementary-age children, I understand the need for additional playground supervision.

> As one of the growing number of college students who must work part-time, I realize the necessity for keeping the library open longer on the weekends.

Even though *I* is used in these sentences, it receives little attention buried in the middle of the sentence. Instead, the emphasis is on the identity of the group and on the opinion, keeping the information representative.

Using *I* always shifts the focus from the subject to you, the writer. If you shift too often, your argument will not be objective. Overuse of *I* separates the writer from the reader by placing the authority of the writer *above* the reader. This could be insulting. But small injections at the right points can give the argument a human dimension and increase your ethical appeal.

Using You.   In establishing an ethical appeal you want to convince the audience that you are genuinely interested in their concerns. Using *you* produces that effect. By directly addressing the audience, you immediately gain their attention and show your interest in them. But while using *you* can more closely identify the writer with the audience, overuse of you can create a dictatorial or preachy tone that separates the writer from the reader. Rarely if ever would *you* be used in an academic paper, where the subject of the argument should be the main focus.

Think of using *you* as a way of establishing eye contact with a public audience. The challenge is deciding *when* to directly acknowledge their presence—and that decision depends on the kind of audience you are addressing. A general audience with a diversity of interests will need strong reminders of their involvement, whereas an audience with whom you have personal contact—for instance, a special interest group like Save the Whales—will need fewer reminders.

Imagine yourself standing on a stage in front of an auditorium full of people. This impersonal relationship may require more frequent use of *you* to maintain the audience's attention. First, they will want to know what their relationship is to the argument. The sooner you establish this relationship, the more closely the audience will pay attention to your line of argument. This opening draws the reader into the argument:

> Your use of old newspapers probably has become fairly routine by now: from training puppies and lining bird cages to painting and

packaging presents for mailing. Still, you are bound to find yourself with a substantial surplus at the end of each week . . . and that's exactly what this country needs. Your old newspapers, when recycled, not only save our natural resources but also contribute to our export potential with countries who have limited forests.

By identifying the role of the audience, the writer provides an understanding of the audience's qualities and a reason for them to continue reading.

Using *you* can also increase the readers' involvement by personalizing the information. The closer you bring the audience to the issue, the more attention they will give to thinking about it. The student writing about the need to recycle paper involved the audience in this way:

You might find yourself considering some of these implications the next time you choose a birthday card for someone. Let's say you are in a card shop where you find three cards your sister would really enjoy. How do you decide which one to buy? If the cards are equally attractive, try looking on the back, not for the price but for the recycled paper logo and the statement: No trees were destroyed to produce this card.

With this short scene the writer involves the reader directly in applying the information presented. This directness strengthens the contact between the reader and the subject and increases the credibility of the writer's concern for the readers.

An indirect method of involving the audience is through the *understood you* of **rhetorical questions.** People have a natural instinct for answering questions and wanting them answered. With rhetorical questions you don't have to provide the answer; instead, you *anticipate* the reader's answering mentally in a *predictable* way. Asking "Do we want to risk further increases in illiteracy?" will surely bring an automatic "No" from the reader. Likewise, you can safely predict an audience will answer "Yes" to the rhetorical question, "Will these adversaries willingly join forces to protect our own shores from invasion?" Neither question uses *you* directly, yet each involves the reader in an unspoken dialogue. And, because rhetorical questions require short, predictable answers, you and your audience reach a close point of agreement. Just be sure to frame your rhetorical question in a form that all readers will answer in exactly the same way.

Using We. Another way to directly increase your ethical appeal with the audience is through the shared authority of the pronoun *we*. By combining both *I* and *you*, the pronoun *we* conveys a strong *with*-relationship. While these sentences express virtually the same meaning, notice how each creates a different relationship with the audience:

Freshmen often learn more about their parents in one semester away from home than they did in 18 years living at home.

As a freshman *I* learned more about *my* parents in one semester away from home than *I* did in 18 years living at home.

As a freshman *you* learned more about *your* parents in one semester away from home than *you* did in 18 years living at home.

As freshmen *we* learned more about *our* parents in one semester away from home than *we* did in 18 years living at home.

In the first sentence the writer removes his or her personal voice to focus objectively on the subject. The relationship between reader and writer is indirect; while both stand outside the writing, observing the freshmen and their learning, there is no indication that the writer and reader share a common understanding of the subject.

In contrast, the *I* of the second sentence is highly subjective. And while it may draw the reader closer with its personal voice, it does not include the audience in a direct relationship with the subject. The *you* used in the third sentence also separates the writer from the reader; however, the direct address and personal voice form a close relationship between reader and subject.

Only in the fourth sentence do the writer, the reader, and the subject share a direct and personal relationship.

In effect, using *we* creates a strong ethical appeal through mutual authority. When you are sure that you and your audience have some identical experience related to the point you are making, you can use *we* effectively. When you don't share this background, using *we* can be patronizing or set you above the reader in an official, editorial capacity. Notice how this happens in the following version:

According to the survey data *we* collected, freshmen learn more about their parents in one semester away from home than they did in 18 years living at home.

Clearly the *we* in this version does not include the reader. Instead of a personal, shared authority, this *we* conveys the official judgment of a group that intends this separation.

In many ways, *we* can convey the agreement between writer and reader that the argument hopes to achieve, but if overused or used with an incompatible audience, it could do more to undermine your credibility than establish it.

CHOOSING INFORMATION

Establishing ethical appeal also requires judgment in selecting information to support the points of your argument. The resources that convinced you may be a good place to begin, but your final selection must also satisfy the needs of your audience. If, for instance, your intended readers are undecided on the issue, they may need more background information; if, however, they oppose your viewpoint on a particular condition, you need to provide more convincing information on that point.

The needs-analysis strategies in Chapter 6 will guide you in determining what your audience already knows and what they *need* to know. From that point you can choose from a wide range of resources, including interviews, statistics, graphs, laws, expert testimony, and research studies. An evaluation of these sources follows in the Appeal to Logic section.

As important as your selection of sources is the integrity of your presentation of the information. Senator Joseph Biden discovered when he failed to acknowledge his sources in his speeches during the 1988 presidential campaign that once you lose your credibility, your audience loses all confidence in your ideas. Presenting someone else's ideas as your own constitutes **plagiarism.** Chapter 11 demonstrates how you can avoid plagiarizing by properly acknowledging your sources and providing accurate citations. The integrity you use in choosing a voice, selecting information, and presenting your sources can produce a pervasive ethical appeal in your writing.

EXERCISES: ETHICAL APPEAL

1. What expertise do you have that can contribute to establishing your ethical appeal with a reader? Inventory your expertise by identifying what you know in each of the following categories: personal experience, work experience, educational experience, travel experience, research experience.

2. Write three versions of each statement below. In each version change your choice of pronouns. When you finish writing the different versions, evaluate each for its level of credibility, and identify an appropriate audience for whom the version would establish an ethical appeal. Use the examples in the Using *We* section as a model.

> Once you determine your major, you can be more selective in choosing your elective courses.

> My experience was just the opposite. Even though I didn't know much Spanish, I still enjoyed visiting Barcelona.

> If we really think the current financial aid practices are unfair, then we should voice our opinion more publicly as a group.

3. Choose an editorial from your local newspaper or a weekly news magazine. Underline each place where the writer tries to establish an ethical appeal. Write a one-page analysis of how effectively the writer uses ethical appeal to advocate his or her argument.

THE APPEAL TO LOGIC: *LOGOS*

At the center of all arguments is a strong **appeal to logic**—that is, an appeal to the intellect and reasoning of your audience. Using this appeal you can reconstruct the thought processes that persuaded you to believe in your thesis. When you think about your subject, linking the generalizations and supportive details, you use one or both of two logical reasoning processes: **Induction** and **deduction.** These processes and the quality of the information on which you base your conclusions are the methods that make the logical appeal to your audience. Together, your reasoning process and the verification of the information you present answer the question "Why?" about your subject.

ESTABLISHING LOGIC

Logic is the study of orderly thinking, the sequence and connection of thoughts and ideas as they relate to one another. The basic elements of argument used to produce logical thought are the **premises,** the statements upon which an argument is based; the **conclusion,** the statement or claim being supported; and the **reasoning,** the sequence of thought that connects the premises to the conclusion. These elements form what is known as a **syllogism,** a structure Aristotle designed to test the logic of an argument.

By arranging the sequence of the premises and conclusion of an argument in the form of a syllogism, you can determine what kind of reasoning was used. A **deductive argument,** for example, has a conclusion that follows with *certainty* from its premises.

> **Premises:** All the plums in that bowl are ripe.
> All these plums are from that bowl.
>
> **Conclusion:** *Therefore, all these plums are ripe.*

An **inductive argument,** however, has a conclusion that follows only with some degree of *probability* from its premises.

> **Premises:** All these plums are from that bowl.
> All these plums are ripe.
>
> **Conclusion:** *Therefore, all the plums in that bowl are ripe.*

Putting the premises and conclusion of an argument in the form of a syllogism *does not* establish the logic of the argument, but it does reveal the basic structure of the argument so you can examine the language, sequence, and connections. If the reasoning structure follows a *valid* form and if the premises are *true,* then the conditions for establishing logic will be met. The next two sections will show you how to establish these conditions when using inductive and deductive reasoning.

Induction

Valid Reasoning. When reasoning inductively, you look into or examine evidence about specific, individual cases to discover what generalizations apply to all of those cases. As certain features repeatedly occur in each example, *patterns* emerge from which you form generalizations. A person deciding which presidential candidate to vote for might use the inductive process in this way:

IMPORTANT ISSUES	CANDIDATES WHO SUPPORT THEM
Increase in student financial aid	Adams, Carlyle, Fernandez
Decrease in military spending	Carlyle, Strauss, Thomas
Passage of ERA	Adams, Carlyle, Thomas
Environmental protection	Carlyle, Fernandez, Strauss

Generalization: Carlyle supports the same issues I do.

Conclusion: *Vote for Carlyle.*

In this case, the pattern that emerged convinced the person of the candidate's worthiness. But, is pattern enough evidence on which to develop a reliable conclusion, or has the voter, in this case, made too great an *inductive leap*? Because we can't examine *every* piece of evidence, we must sometimes make an inductive leap to form a conclusion. But people who generalize from too little evidence or from evidence that is biased or poorly chosen are unlikely to make an informed inductive leap when forming their conclusions.

The voter above chooses four issues on which to examine the candidates. Are four issues enough evidence? Are the kinds of issues chosen biased or not representative enough for the decision the person plans to make? Is support for the issues the only type of evidence that needs examination? If you answer "No" to any of these questions, then the voter's conclusion will appear neither logical nor reliable to you. Patterns, then, are insufficient for making reliable generalizations *unless* they are based on a sufficient amount of representative evidence.

In some cases you can observe all the instances in a particular situation. For instance, by interviewing *every* resident on both sides of your street, you can arrive at an accurate assessment of the number of parking spaces needed on your street. But observing every possible example in all situations is rarely possible. How can you question every college junior on the fairness of grading procedures? How could you discover the child care needs of every working mother? For this reason, the results of inductive reasoning can offer only *probable*, not certain truth.

To increase the probability or reliability of your inductive conclusions, your evidence should have both *quantity* and *quality*. Basically, the more times something happens, the more people it happens to, and the more places it happens, the stronger will be a person's belief in the occurrence. If, for instance, you want to represent the view of the 2,500 freshmen on campus, the 25 people in your composition class would be a small sample on which to base generalizations about the whole group; 100 freshmen would increase the probability of your generalizations, but 250 would provide a much higher level of confidence. Likewise, if you were surveying the same group on the issue of increasing the number of parking spaces on campus, your observation should focus on those students who are part of the issue—the commuter students who use on-campus parking. Surveying all of them would be difficult. When you cannot make the observations yourself, you must rely on the testimony of those who have had the opportunity. For instance, you could get statistics on the number of registered cars from the campus public safety office. The section on Assessing Supportive Information in this chapter will demonstrate how to verify the testimony of others.

Inductive Structures. The goal of any inductive argument is to establish that the conclusion is true. Although this cannot be done with absolute certainty, an inductive argument should provide some assurance that the conclusion will be true if the premises are all true. Testing the validity of the reasoning—the quantity and quality of the evidence—is the first step in determining the truth of the\premises. The form or structure of an inductive argument also affects the level of confidence with which a reader can accept the probability of an inductive conclusion. The two most common forms of inductive argument are *arguments based on samples* and *arguments from analogy.*

In inductive arguments based on enumerated samples and statistical surveys, the premises state what happens in *particular* cases (what happens in the sample), and the conclusions state what happens in general. This type of reasoning structure is used frequently in political predictions, quality control studies, and many types of scientific studies. The basic structure of this reasoning follows the form below:

Premise: X percent or number of *observed* A's are B's.

Conclusion: *X percent or number of all A's are B's.*

Used with actual arguments, this structure would be expressed in these ways:

EXAMPLE A

Premise: Of the 2,000 voters polled, 1,500 plan to vote for Mayor Wilson.

Conclusion: *Seventy-five percent of all voters plan to vote for Mayor Wilson.*

EXAMPLE B

Premise: The seatbelts in 98 out of 100 Chevy Blazers examined at the Ohio plant were without defects.

Conclusion: *Ninety-eight percent of the seatbelts in Chevy Blazers produced at the Ohio plant are without defects.*

EXAMPLE C

Premise: More than 95 percent of hyperactives are male.

Conclusion: *Almost all hyperactives are male.*
or
Very few hyperactives are female.

EXAMPLE D

Premise: One hundred percent of all faculty members in the English department donated to the United Way.

Conclusion: *All faculty in the English department donated to the United Way.*

The generalizations that form the conclusions of sample-based inductive arguments may be universal or statistical. *Universal generalizations* state that *all* (100 percent) or *none* (0 percent) of the members of a class have a certain property. Example D uses the universal generalization to apply to one department within a university. *Statistical generalizations* state that some percentage—less than 100 percent, but more than 0 percent—of members of a class have the property. Statistical generalizations may be stated in numerical terms, as in Examples A and B, or in non-numerical terms, as in Example C.

An inductive argument based on statistics also may be expressed in the form of a syllogism. The statistical syllogism conveys the reasoning that what is generally true (or false) is also true (or false) for a particular case.

Premises

What is generally true: Ninety percent of the doctors who practice medicine at Colonial Health Center prescribed nonbuffered aspirin.

A member of the whole: Dr. Burns practices medicine at Colonial Health Center.

Conclusion

What is probably true
for a particular case: *Dr. Burns prescribes nonbuffered aspirin.*

The statistical generalization that forms a first premise may be stated in non-numerical terms also:

Premises

What is generally true: Freshmen at State College almost never own cars.

A member of the whole: Jack is a freshman at State College.

Conclusion

What is true for a
particular case: *Jack does not own a car.*

Statistical syllogisms are exceptions to the generally accepted principle that inductive reasoning goes from the particular to the general. However, as these examples have illustrated, the conclusions of inductive arguments always lack certainty, and, in fact, may be false even though their premises are true. Review the discussion on evaluating statistical samples in Chapter 3 to test the strength of the statistical generalizations you use in inductive premises.

Both of the following statements use reasoning from analogy.

Ellen and Ben stayed at Miller's Bed and Breakfast in the English countryside, and they had a great trip. We should stay there too.

The Twenty-first amendment legalized the manufacture and distribution of alcoholic beverages and put an end to bootlegging and the widespread lawbreaking associated with Prohibition. A similar law should be passed to legalize drugs.

By comparing two similar cases, these statements *infer* that what is true for one must be true for the other. Is this reasoning valid? The answer depends on whether the two cases being compared are essentially alike. In the above examples, how similar to Ellen and Ben are the *we* making the comparison? Do they use the same criteria to define *a great trip*? Are alcoholic beverages and drugs essentially alike? Are they associated with the same kind of lawbreaking? How similar are the 1930s and the 1990s?

An **analogy** is an extended comparison. In an inductive argument this extended comparison between items that are similar in *observed* ways is used to support some further *unobserved* similarity. The structure of this reasoning would have the following relationship between premises and conclusion:

Premises: X has properties A, B, C, etc.
Y has properties A, B, C, etc. and, in addition, property Z

Conclusion: *X has property Z as well.*

A familiar inductive argument from analogy widely accepted by the general public is that used by scientists to predict the effects of drugs and other harmful substances on humans. In their experiments scientists use rats because they have *established* physiological properties similar to those of humans. An argument based on that analogy follows the form of the previous example.

Premises: Humans have physiological properties A, B, and C.
Rats have physiological properties A, B, and C, and when given large doses of saccharine, they develop cancer.

Conclusion: *Humans who ingest large amounts of saccharine will develop cancer.*

To be a convincing form of inductive reasoning, an analogy must have a strong balance of similarity and *relevance*. The person who attempts to convince herself that because she knows how to roller skate she will be able to ice skate might spend more time sitting on the ice than gliding across it. The two sports appear to share many similarities and one main difference—skates with one thin blade instead of four wheels. But that difference, as it turns out, is more relevant than the similarities. The stress on the ankle and the balance required in ice skating make ballet a more valid analogy.

Analogies frequently suppress dissimilarities. When a reader can detect relevant dissimilarities, the analogy loses its power, as in this example:

> In both England and Japan the ownership of guns is severely restricted. Both countries have lower murder and crime rates than does the United States.

Are the people and living conditions in England and Japan similar enough to those in the United States to conclude this effect of gun control? A reader who believes the differences are too great to accept the analogy might use that dissimilarity as a point of relevance in a response such as this:

> Switzerland has a militia system: 600,000 assault rifles each with two magazines of ammunition are sitting at this moment in Swiss homes. Yet Switzerland's murder rate is only 15 percent of ours. In other words, cultural factors are much more important than gun control laws when it comes to eliminating violent crime.

In all analogies there will be some elements that do not correspond, but if the differences are not relevant to the issue of the argument, the strength of the similarities can support the probability of the conclusion.

Inductive reasoning, whether based on sampling, analogy, or another form of particular cases, has the advantage of involving the audience directly in formulating the conclusion *with* the writer. In one sense this sharing can create a strong impact on the audience, but if there are flaws in the evidence—if the quality and quantity are insufficient—confidence in the writer's logic may be questioned at an early point in the argument, thereby decreasing the writer's credibility (ethical appeal) and the probability of the conclusion. More discussion of the incorrect use of logic appears in this chapter under the heading Detecting Common Fallacies.

Deduction

Valid Reasoning. Deductive reasoning and inductive reasoning differ in the structure each uses to arrive at a conclusion, but both are dependent upon the audience's acceptance of the conditions for the reasoning to have an effective logical appeal. As you have seen, inductive reasoning moves from the examination of specific cases to the development of a probable conclusion. But even a probable conclusion cannot be accepted unless the audience first accepts the conditions of the evidence—its quantity and quality. Similarly, the conclusion of deductive reasoning cannot be accepted as true unless the audience accepts the premises on which it is based.

To understand how this condition of acceptance affects deductive reasoning, let's look at the basic structure of a syllogism. *Basic deductive structure is composed of two assertions (or premises) and a conclusion:*

Major premise: All national television networks use commercials to fund their programming.

Minor premise: NBC is a national television network.

Conclusion: *NBC uses commercials to fund its programming.*

This syllogism is considered *valid* or logically consistent because it derives a conclusion as the *inevitable consequence* of two linked premises. No other conclusion is possible. Determining the validity of the deductive reasoning structure is the first level of evaluating its effectiveness as an appeal to logic. While a syllogism can appear in various forms, the basic principles of reasoning follow as this example explains.

Major Premise: (makes a generalization based on the whole)	$\dfrac{\text{All national television networks}}{A}$ $\dfrac{\text{use commercials to fund programming.}}{B}$	All $\underline{A}$ is $\underline{B}$
Minor Premise: (assigns a specific member to the general class)	$\dfrac{\text{NBC}}{C}$ is a $\dfrac{\text{national network.}}{A}$	$\underline{C}$ is $\underline{A}$
Conclusion: (connects the conditions of the two premises; *therefore*)	$\dfrac{\text{NBC}}{C}$ *uses* $\dfrac{\text{commercials to fund programming.}}{B}$	$\underline{C}$ is $\underline{B}$

The three statements in the syllogism relate in different ways through the distribution of terms. When an argument follows this reasoning structure, you can say that it is valid. If an argument does not have a valid reasoning structure, there is no need to evaluate it for the truth of its premises. Look closely at the difference in the reasoning structures in these syllogisms:

Valid Form:

All police detectives wear guns.	All $\underline{A}$ is $\underline{B}$
Sharon is a police detective.	$\underline{C}$ is $\underline{A}$
(*Therefore*) Sharon is wearing a gun.	$\underline{C}$ is $\underline{B}$

Invalid Form:

All police detectives wear guns.	All $\underline{A}$ is $\underline{B}$
Sharon is wearing a gun.	$\underline{C}$ is $\underline{B}$
(*Therefore*) Sharon is a police detective.	$\underline{C}$ is $\underline{A}$

The reasoning process in the second example fails to establish logical consistency—the conclusion is *not* an inevitable consequence of the two premises. Sharon is never established as a member of the general class. The fact that a person (Sharon) is wearing a gun doesn't mean that person is a police detective.

With syllogisms, once you have determined the validity of the deductive reasoning structure, you must verify the *truth of the premises* before you can accept the conclusion. The following syllogism is valid, even though one of its premises is not true:

All modes of transportation have wheels.

A boat is a mode of transportation.

Therefore, a boat has wheels.

While *most* modes of transportation may have wheels and while a boat, such as a hydrofoil, *might* have wheels, the major premise is not *universally* true; therefore the conclusion is unacceptable. The fact that valid reasoning is not necessarily true reasoning means that reasoning is always *conditional;* acceptable conclusions follow from premises *only if* the premises are accepted. In a syllogism the premises must be universally true to be accepted; if the premises are not true, the reasoning behind the premises will not support the conclusion. If the premises of a syllogism are true and the form used to construct the syllogism is valid, we say that the syllogism is *sound.* Is this syllogism both valid *and* true?

All judges are honest.

Hugh Taylor is a judge.

Therefore, Hugh Taylor is honest.

In this case the syllogism is valid because it follows proper structure, but the major premise may not be considered universally true by all people. If the acceptance of a premise is dependent on the individual experience of the reader, then the premise would be considered *probable* rather than universally true. When the major premise is probable, the deductive reasoning structure generally is stated as an enthymeme, an abbreviated form of a syllogism. An **enthymeme** is any combination of a conclusion and a reason connected by the assumed beliefs of the audience. Enthymemes, like syllogisms, derive their conclusions from premises. But, unlike syllogisms, enthymemes derive premises from beliefs that a particular audience is assumed to accept as given. Enthymemes also differ from syllogisms in the way premises are expressed. Enthymemes need only imply all of the statements that a complete syllogism might contain. Here is an example of how an enthymeme is stated:

Mary will not win the triathlon *because* she hasn't practiced.
(Conclusion)   **(Minor premise)**

All people who win triathlons must practice.
(Implied major premise)

To accept the conclusion of this enthymeme as inevitable, the audience must first accept the probability of the implied major premise which provides the reasoning for the stated premise. If the audience believes that practice is necessary to winning, then they will accept the stated reason as true in supporting the conclusion. But if they believe that experience or natural ability is more necessary to winning than practice is, they might reject the stated reason.

You can see from this example that although the enthymeme has its own form, its requirement for achieving logical consistency is similar to that required in the syllogism: both premises (stated and implied) must be accepted by the audience *before* the conclusion can be accepted. And in an argument to which the audience may be strongly opposed, even probability can be difficult to establish in the premises. This problem becomes more complex when the way an enthymeme is stated requires the audience to accept several implied assumptions. As the following example demonstrates, planning your argument in enthymeme form can point out to you these layers of implied assumptions.

Enthymeme: Because the secretary of the interior has announced publicly his support for the state environmental protection bill, it will pass during this session of the legislature.

Implied Major Premise: The support of the federal government on an issue convinces state legislators to vote in support of the issue.

To accept the implied major premise as probable, the audience also would need to accept the assumptions behind the reasoning of the premise:

1. The federal government is a reliable source of expertise on an issue.

2. State legislators are strongly influenced by their federal counterparts.

Determining the implied assumptions behind your reasoning will show you whether you are ready to proceed with your support, or whether you need to explore alternative ways of expressing your enthymeme to reach a higher level of probable acceptance by your audience.

Merely asserting a point of view is not enough to persuade an audience to accept your assertions. Constructing an enthymeme for your argument enables you to use a logical appeal to bridge the distance between what you believe and know and what your audience believes and needs to know. Both the enthymeme and the syllogism help you systematically determine the logical effectiveness of a deductive argument.

Deductive Structures. In deductive reasoning the structure of the syllogism and the enthymeme identify the nature of the argument. The three most common deductive arguments are *categorical, hypothetical,* and *disjunctive.* Each is characterized by the way the major premise is stated, and each follows specific rules for forming valid structures.

The purpose of a **categorical argument** is to reach a logical conclusion on the state of being of a particular member within a general category or class. The *major premise,* whether stated or implied, identifies the general category of people, things, or ideas being studied and a specific attribute generally assumed to characterize that category. This premise is expressed using one of these forms:

A universal affirmative: All alcoholic beverages are depressants.

A universal negative: No unregistered U.S. citizen can vote in a presidential election.

The *minor premise* in a categorical argument introduces a particular member or instance within the general category.

Wine coolers are alcoholic beverages.

Dennis is an unregistered U.S. citizen.

The conclusion that necessarily follows from the premises should establish that what is true of the whole class or category is true of its members:

Major premise: All alcoholic beverages are depressants.
Minor premise: Wine coolers are alcoholic beverages.
    Conclusion: *Wine coolers are depressants.*

Major premise: No unregistered U.S. citizen can vote in a presidential election.
Minor premise: Dennis is an unregistered U.S. citizen.
    Conclusion: *Dennis cannot vote in a presidential election.*

Categorical arguments also can be expressed in an enthymeme form in which one of the premises is implied:

Dennis is still not registered, so he will be unable to vote in the presidential election.

(Implied major premise: No unregistered U.S. citizen can vote in a presidential election.)

The discussion in the beginning of the Deduction section used several categorical syllogisms to test the validity of the reasoning. How the terms are stated and how they are positioned in the premises and conclusion determine the logic of the reasoning. In addition, there are two rules to follow when using negative statements:

1. You cannot draw a conclusion from two negative premises.
2. If one of your premises is negative, then your conclusion must be negative.

A **hypothetical argument** is characterized by a *conditional* major premise stated in an *if/then* clause:

If unemployment decreases, *then* there will be no recession.

In the conditional major premise, the *if* clause is called the *antecedent*. The second clause to which the condition is applied, the *then* clause, is called the *consequent*.

The minor premise *affirms* the antecedent (*if* clause) of the major premise (that is, it agrees to the truth of the antecedent):

If unemployment decreases, then there will be no recession. Unemployment will decrease.

If you affirm the truth of the antecedent with the minor premise, then the consequent necessarily follows, and the conclusion is valid:

If unemployment decreases, then there will be no recession.
Unemployment will decrease.

Therefore, there will be no recession.

If is the key word in signaling a hypothetical argument. Once the argument is identified, the emphasis shifts to affirming the antecedent. In the case above this would mean providing conclusive evidence that unemployment will, in fact, decrease.

A **disjunctive argument** is characterized by a major premise that presents alternative possibilities introduced by *either/or:*

Either a conspiracy existed or President Kennedy was killed by an assassin acting alone.

The alternatives presented in the major premise must be *mutually exclusive* and therefore contradictory. If not, the conclusion will not necessarily follow.

The function of the minor premise is to deny one of the disjuncts or alternatives.

Either a conspiracy existed or President Kennedy was killed by an assassin acting alone.
A conspiracy did not exist.

Therefore, President Kennedy was killed by an assassin acting alone.

or

Either a conspiracy existed or President Kennedy was killed by an assassin acting alone.

President Kennedy was not killed by an assassin acting alone.

Therefore, a conspiracy existed.

When the alternatives in the major premise are mutually exclusive and when the minor premise denies and eliminates one of the alternatives, then the conclusion will be valid.

TESTING LOGIC

The basic elements of logic used in formulating syllogisms and enthymemes correspond closely with the elements in the Toulmin model presented in Chapter 2. This parallel relationship makes the Toulmin model an effective method for testing the basic reasoning that leads you to make a particular claim *and* for assessing the strength of your support. This assessment, in turn, helps you determine what you need to include to reach your audience. Figure 1 shows how closely the basic elements correspond.

Let's use the following context to see how the reasoning or logic of an argument can be outlined for evaluation:

The commuter students of a college are outraged that the administration has decided to spend a great sum of money on placing computers in all dormitory rooms.

The commuter students' argument can be expressed as a syllogism:

Major Premise: If a proposal to expand the college's educational program benefits all students, then money should be appropriated in support of that proposal.

Minor Premise: Placing computers in all dormitory rooms does not benefit all students.

Conclusion: *Therefore, money should not be appropriated to place computers in all dormitory rooms.*

Figure 1 *Syllogisms, enthymemes, and the Toulmin model*

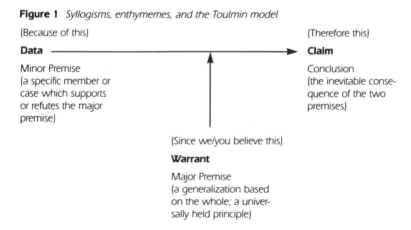

(Because of this)

Data

Minor Premise
(a specific member or
case which supports
or refutes the major
premise)

(Therefore this)

Claim

Conclusion
(the inevitable conse-
quence of the two
premises)

(Since we/you believe this)

Warrant

Major Premise
(a generalization based
on the whole; a univer-
sally held principle)

Figure 2 *Testing an assumption with the Toulmin model*

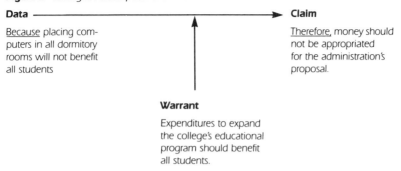

Data ——————————————————————→ **Claim**

Because placing com-
puters in all dormitory
rooms will not benefit
all students

Therefore, money should
not be appropriated
for the administration's
proposal.

Warrant

Expenditures to expand
the college's educational
program should benefit
all students.

As an enthymeme:

> Because placing computers in all dormitory rooms will not benefit all students, money should not be appropriated for the administration's proposal.

Figure 2 shows this as a Toulmin model diagram.

On the surface these three forms appear to illustrate merely a rearrangement of phrases, but the different terms used in the Toulmin model force you to begin asking more specific questions about your major premise as a valid assumption held by your intended audience and the acceptability of your minor premise as evidence for that audience. If the audience for this argument is the student body, can the writer assume they are more concerned with fairness to *all* students than with their own priorities? If the audience is the administration, can the writer assume that the administrators' definition of the term *benefit* is the same? These questions lead to an examination of Toulmin's second-level elements to determine the force or strength of the argument from the audience's point of view. Let's assume that the administrators are the intended audience because they are the people with the power to make the decision. The advantage of the Toulmin model is that it allows you to analyze your argument specifically with respect to your audience. Figure 3 shows how the second level of analysis might look.

By specifying the backing for both the data and the warrant and by testing the warrant for possible reservations, the writer has discovered a rebuttal possibility that could change the force of the claim. If the writer believes that commuter students could be guaranteed priority in access to the computer labs, then he or she will need to re-think the claim if it is based on the warrant as presently stated. If, however, the writer does not believe the administration can enforce the priority guarantee to commuter students, then he or she can assert the claim with greater confidence, knowing that the rebuttal can be refuted in the argument. The writer's decision, of course, would depend on the *specific context* for this argument. The number of computer labs available, the difficulty of getting access to a computer in the lab, and the ability of the administration to control use of the labs are a few of the considerations needed for such a decision.

Figure 3 *Toulmin second-level analysis*

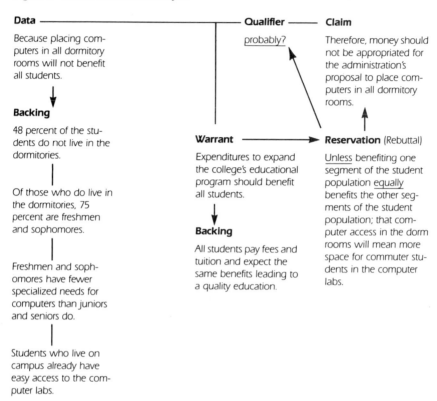

Using the Toulmin model to test your logic *before* you begin drafting your argument is an important step in the planning process.

DETECTING COMMON FALLACIES

Fallacy, or *faulty reasoning,* presents an argument built on false or deceptive relationships between the premises and the conclusion. Sometimes fallacies occur as a result of hasty or lazy thinking, but often they are used intentionally to produce implications the audience is likely to believe without close examination. This persuasive power can be very subtle, making fallacies difficult to detect.

If the common fallacies could be easily classified, they would be easier to detect, but because the ways to error are so numerous and complex, classification becomes difficult. One source of error common to many fallacies, however, is the use of language in ways that obscure correct meaning. In both inductive and deductive reasoning the structure of the reasoning may be valid, but the language in which the premises are stated may create a false or deceptive relationship between the premises and the conclusion. These false relationships can be classified as *fallacies of presumption, fallacies of relevance,* and *fallacies of ambiguity.*

Fallacies of Presumption.   Arguments that contain unfounded or unproven assumptions are guilty of presumption. Since no conclusions can be more reliable than the assumptions on which they are based, the conclusions in such arguments cannot be trusted. The fallacy of presumption occurs when the premises overlook, evade, or distort significant facts.

Hasty Generalization. When an argument assumes that what is true for an isolated or exceptional case is true for a group of people or things, it draws a conclusion based on insufficient evidence. Too often daily decisions are the result of *hasty generalizations* such as these:

> Bob always took me for granted.
> *I'll never date another accounting major.*

> My best friend Sarah took philosophy from Professor Bernard and hated the course.
> *I'll never take a course that he teaches.*

Unrepresentative samples and small sample size—lack of quality and quantity—produce assumptions that result in hasty generalizations. In turn, these hasty generalizations are likely to produce biased and prejudicial reasoning—for instance, that women are more emotional than men, Asian students excel in math, and short people are insecure.

Hasty generalizations also occur when premises overlook facts that are necessary to examining a particular case. For instance, the argument

> Senator Collins has a long voting history of supporting civil rights.
> *Senator Collins will continue to represent us well.*

overlooks the senator's voting record on other, more specific issues related to civil rights and on a wider range of issues. The advertisement in Figure 4 has the same problem. In addition to other faulty lines of reasoning, the ad overlooks the actual safety features that make the car an "intelligent" choice. Dr. Selker's experience in emergency rooms is both a small and an unrepresentative sample on which to base a generalization.

False Cause or Post Hoc. The *false cause* or *post hoc* fallacy relies on the inference that because one event follows another, the first event must be the cause of the second. This results in simplistic reasoning, such as "Since Mayor Jones has been in office, tourism in our city has increased. If Mayor Jones were governor, the tourism of the whole state would increase. Elect Jones for governor." What is missing in this expression of cause-effect relationship are the conditions under which Mayor Jones was able to increase tourism. If no special conditions were present, then perhaps Mayor Jones was the cause of increased tourism. To discover the cause convincingly, the reasoning must systematically trace the sequence of events.

Figure 4 *Hasty generalization*

The Lufthansa airline advertisement in Figure 5 relies on the false cause fallacy to convince readers to believe in the quality of the airline. Can the design of a napkin convince you to fly a plane across the Atlantic Ocean?

Either/Or Fallacy. When an argument states or implies that only two alternatives exist, although other solutions or explanations are available, an *either/or* or *false dilemma* fallacy results. By overlooking related facts or possibilities or intentionally evading those alternatives that might cause doubt about a conclusion, the either/or fallacy over-simplifies a complex problem. This kind of reasoning often results in two extreme alternatives:

Figure 5 *False cause fallacy*

Either we increase our nuclear stockpiles, or we will be too weak to defend ourselves.

If we outlaw guns, only outlaws will have guns.

Either buy American-made products, or admit you are not patriotic.

The words *either/or* and *if/then* help to identify where this faulty reasoning might occur in an argument. However, the false dilemma that this reasoning produces also can be implied, making it more difficult to detect. In the advertisement in Figure 6 Time Inc. uses an implied if/then argument: If children in communities with a high rate of illit-

Figure 6 *False dilemma fallacy*

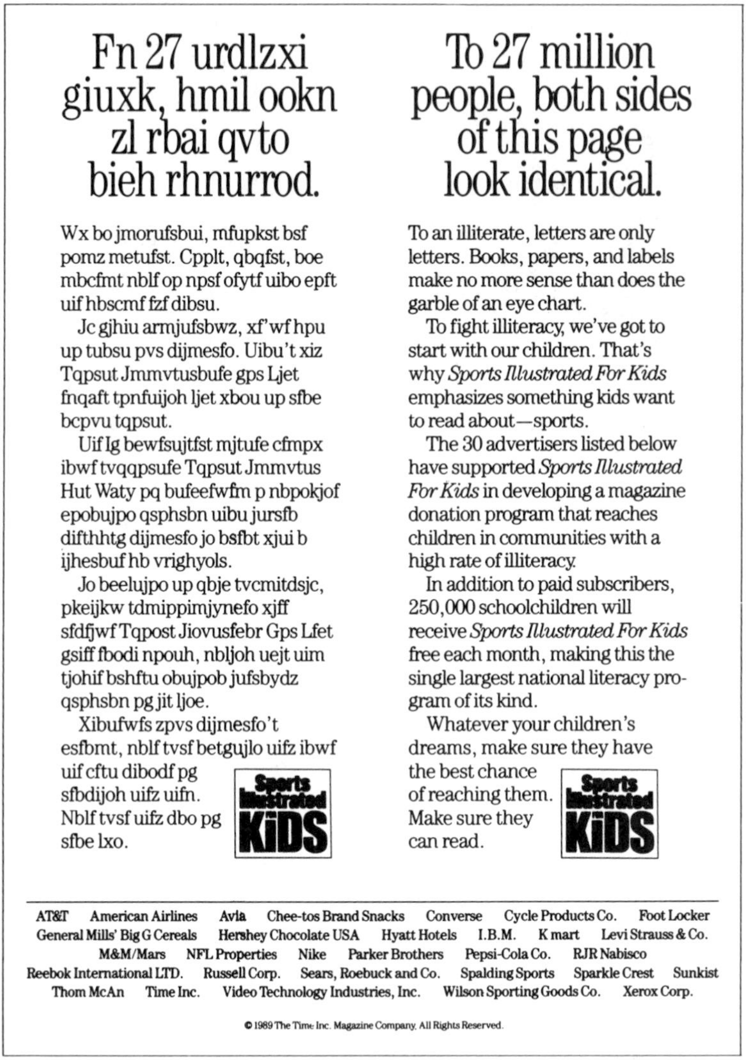

To 27 million people, both sides of this page look identical.

To an illiterate, letters are only letters. Books, papers, and labels make no more sense than does the garble of an eye chart.

To fight illiteracy, we've got to start with our children. That's why *Sports Illustrated For Kids* emphasizes something kids want to read about—sports.

The 30 advertisers listed below have supported *Sports Illustrated For Kids* in developing a magazine donation program that reaches children in communities with a high rate of illiteracy.

In addition to paid subscribers, 250,000 schoolchildren will receive *Sports Illustrated For Kids* free each month, making this the single largest national literacy program of its kind.

Whatever your children's dreams, make sure they have the best chance of reaching them. Make sure they can read.

eracy receive more interesting reading material (*Sports Illustrated for Kids*), then they will be more motivated to read. While this reasoning may be valid, it is not complete in considering the alternatives that can motivate children to read, such as teachers, instructional methods, parental involvement, or the environment in which the reading takes place. If other alternatives exist, either/or and if/then reasoning can be judged to be faulty.

Begging the Question. Begging *the question* as a form of reasoning is circular: It asserts that something is because it is. When an argument restates a premise as the conclu-

Figure 7 *Begging the question fallacy*

sion, it commits the fallacy of begging the question. The assertion "Unsafe generic drugs should be taken off the market for further testing" begs the question "What *is* an *unsafe* generic drug?" The audience can accept the premise that unsafe drugs should not be sold, but the writer has evaded the responsibility of providing proof of their existence. This is like defining a word by using the word: An osteopath is someone who practices osteopathy.

The begging the question fallacy presumes that evidence is not needed to support the premise contained in the conclusion. The Sony Corporation uses this faulty reasoning in the ad in Figure 7. Does Sony provide proof that this product is their best television? Do they, in fact, establish that *any* of their televisions have value? Obviously the company assumes the consumer has faith in the reputation of its products.

The fallacy of begging the question appears in subtler forms as well. When a favorable or unfavorable label is attached to the subject of the premise—for example, in the statement "This *prejudicial* behavior should be censured" or "Such *altruistic* deeds should be applauded"—connotation is substituted for argument. This form of the fallacy is used frequently in highly controversial arguments on issues like abortion. Using the word *baby* rather than *fetus* begs the question of whether or not a fetus is a human being.

False Analogy. Writers who use *false analogies* expect the audience to ignore the differences between the two things being compared. In arguing for euthanasia, the analogy "We put animals who are in irreversible pain out of their misery, so we should do the same for people" expects the audience to ignore the differences between people and animals, between human pain and that felt by animals, between the conditions under which humans are treated for pain and those for animals. When the differences are relevant, the analogy cannot be convincing; it may have emotional appeal but not the logical force needed for its conclusion to be accepted as valid.

Analogies in advertisements often use visual appeals more than logical reasoning. The ad in Figure 8 comparing a Lincoln model car to a Stradivarius violin does just that. Notice that there are no direct comparisons made after the initial identification of the analogy. In this case the analogy distorts the facts.

Slippery Slope. Writers who use the *slippery slope* fallacy predict that taking a first step will lead inevitably to a second, usually undesirable, condition: "Allowing parents to teach their own children at home will mean the death of our public schools." If the writer of this assertion does not provide evidence to support the predicted undesirable condition, then slippery slope reasoning is present.

Slippery slope predictions evade the complexity of an issue by using simplistic cause-effect relationships that are emotionally charged. Asserting that listening to heavy metal music leads to membership in satanic cults might in itself scare parents of young children enough to prevent their opposing the possibility, but for the argument to be logical, it must present systematically the events and conditions that lead from the cause to the effect. Even when evidence is provided, slippery slope reasoning can occur if the complexity of the problem is not addressed. In the AT&T advertisement in Figure 9, the company tries to specify systematically the sequence of cause-effect relationships involved in meeting a writer's needs. Does the ad avoid using slippery slope reasoning? You decide.

Fallacies of Relevance.   Fallacies of relevance are arguments in which the premises introduce some kind of inessential or irrelevant information that distracts or confuses. By doing this, the argument stirs the emotions in an attempt to obscure the real issue.

Figure 8 *False analogy*

Ad Hominem: Fallacy of Personal Attack. Ad hominem arguments, meaning *to the man* or *against the man,* divert attention away from proving the truth of what is asserted by attacking the person who made the assertion. When the personal character of a person is not relevant to the truth or falsehood of the assertion in question, this reasoning is fallacious. For instance, to argue that the company should not accept Ms. Harper's proposal because she has been with the company for only six months or because she is not married to the man she lives with obscures the real issue: What is the quality of the proposal? Will it benefit the company?

The assumption of the ad hominem fallacy is that if an attitude of disapproval toward a person can be evoked, then what he or she asserts will be discredited. Establishing the credibility of a witness's personal character is common practice in a court of law, where people judged relevant to the case are approved as witnesses. But even in

Figure 9 *Slippery slope fallacy*

the courts the ad hominem fallacy sometimes is used to discredit testimony. The most frequent use, however, is found in political campaigning, where rivals often find it easier to engage in mudslinging than to debate issues. This excerpt from *Time* (October 10, 1988) and the poll results that accompany the article describe the effects this type of fallacious reasoning can have.

"Spotlight on the A.C.L.U."

MARGARET CARLSON

Campaign '88 has yielded another nugget of politi- 1
cal wisdom: never join an organization more controversial than the Boy Scouts or the American Automobile Association. Had Michael Dukakis known
that membership in the American Civil Liberties
Union would identify him personally with every
position it has taken—and some it has not—he
might have rethought those $20 annual dues.

The A.C.L.U. has replaced the flag and the 2
Pledge of Allegiance as George Bush's hot-button
"values" issue, quite an achievement for a 68-year-
old association with 250,000 members that was until recently often confused with a large California
school with a good football team. One of Bush's
most effective thrusts in the first debate was his
list of causes the A.C.L.U.—and, by extension, Dukakis—supposedly favors: removing the tax exemption from the Roman Catholic Church, repealing
child-pornography laws, deleting "God" on the cur-
rency and dismantling the movie-ratings system.
Bush fumed, "I don't want my ten-year-old grand-
child to go into an X-rated movie."

Does Dukakis want Bush's ten-year-old grand- 3
child to see *Deep Throat*? Not likely. Nor does
the A.C.L.U., which explains that it is not pro-
pornography but is anti-censorship. Says executive
director Ira Glasser: "Anyone who uses a child in
pornography is violating the law and should be
prosecuted, period." The group has not spent one
cent to dismantle the movie ratings but has merely
met with the judges to find ways to make it less
categorical.

These are distinctions not easily made. The 4
causes that receive the backing of the A.C.L.U.—
which is dedicated to defending the individual
freedoms in the Bill of Rights—often require that
even its supporters hold their noses. The A.C.L.U.
has made enemies left and right in defense of draft-

Is Dukakis' A.C.L.U. membership a real campaign issue?

Real	24%
Phony	65%

Does Dukakis' membership make you more inclined to vote for him?

More	17%
Less	36%

Does Bush's attack on Dukakis make you more inclined to vote for Bush?

More	17%
Less	45%

Asked of the 54% who said they knew what the A.C.L.U. is
TIME Poll taken by Yankelovich Clancy Shulman

card burners during the Viet Nam War, Jehovah's Witnesses who choose not to recite the Pledge of Allegiance, Nazis who wanted to march in Skokie, Ill., and a fair trial for Oliver North. Says William Schneider, a fellow at the American Enterprise Institute: "Being linked to the A.C.L.U. is a problem because it takes up unpopular causes. Presidential candidates prefer popular causes."

Ad Populum: Argument to the People. The *ad populum* fallacy occurs when an argument makes an appeal to biases of an audience as a substitute for evidence. Often emotionally charged language is used to distract the audience from the main issues, leaving the audience vulnerable to accepting assertions without proof. When this fallacy is used in speeches at political rallies—where the audience is already emotionally charged—it is sometimes referred to as *flag waving.*

The ad populum argument presumes that the audience already holds a particular attitude and specific beliefs on the issue. Consequently, the need for evidence is irrelevant. Instead, the arguer chooses to lead the audience to a conclusion by means of passion rather than reason. Feelings, however, do not constitute evidence for the truth of a conclusion.

Red Herring. A common trick used in mystery stories, the *red herring* is a device used to avoid the central issue of an argument by changing the subject or digressing in some way to sidetrack the audience. The term comes from the old hunting practice of dragging a red herring across an animal's trail to confuse the hunting dogs.

The fallacy occurs where the point of diversion begins. If, for example, a social worker were arguing for stricter enforcement of child support payments but spent much of her time discussing how cutbacks in federal spending have affected the nutritional value of school lunch programs, she would be using a red herring fallacy. Although there may be some causal connection between the nutritional needs of children from single-parent homes and stricter enforcement of child support payments, the connection is too far removed to be relevant.

Appeal to Authority. Arguments based on *authority* are valid when they use the views of experts in related fields to establish the truth of a conclusion. However, when authorities are used to establish truths on issues *outside* their fields of expertise, the use of authority is fallacious. The surgeon general of the United States, for example, is considered an authority on health issues, but his position and authority in the federal government does not make him an expert on foreign policy.

An argument based on a fallacious appeal to authority assumes that the audience holds the authority in such high respect that they will not question his or her views. This is especially true when unfamiliar authorities with impressive titles and credentials are used to support written arguments. Readers need to be cautious in accepting the views of these unknown authorities, when even respected authorities in the

Figure 10 *Fallacious appeal to authority*

"You'll get a lifetime of home comfort from Bryant's new 'thinking' gas furnace. I've seen the tests that prove it."
Gen. Chuck Yeager, Test Pilot

Bryant announces a major advance in home comfort: the Plus 90i—the "thinking" gas furnace. It has an electronic brain that constantly monitors and adjusts its performance to deliver a more even level of warmth than you've ever experienced.

Along with greater comfort, you'll enjoy lower energy bills. Because this is the most efficient Bryant furnace ever made. Not only does it use less gas, it also uses 80% less electricity than conventional furnaces.

To make sure you get this outstanding performance and economy year after year, the entire furnace, as well as each individual component, is thoroughly tested. One example is the "cycle-run" test the furnace must complete 10,000 times. And, to express our confidence in the Plus 90i's

dependability, we back the heat exchanger with a lifetime limited warranty.

One talk with your Bryant dealer and we're sure you'll want a "thinking" gas furnace. After all, this is the furnace that convinced Chuck Yeager it's got the right stuff.

For the name of your nearest Bryant dealer, call **1-800-HOT-SALE.**

bryant ®

The right stuff to last.

Gas. America's best energy value.
© 1988 American Gas Association

For comfort you can afford, choose gas—America's favorite way to heat.

same field often disagree. The most obvious use of this fallacy is in advertising. In the Bryant ad in Figure 10 the claims made by Chuck Yeager are far removed from his expertise developed at the National Aeronautic and Space Administration (NASA).

Appeal to Ignorance. The fallacy of *appeal to ignorance* (*argumentum ad ignoratiam*) is an argument that asserts a claim is true because no one can prove that it is wrong. This shifts the burden of proof on the opponent and in doing so makes the argument irrelevant. A person's inability to disprove a conclusion cannot by itself be regarded as proof that the conclusion is true.

For example, people who argue that flying saucers visit the earth on the basis that no one has ever proved that they don't shifts the burden of proof to the opponent. In placing the opponent on the defensive, the arguer hopes to intimidate the opponent into believing the proposed conclusion because he or she cannot prove otherwise. This is an emotional rather than a logical appeal. In logical argument the person proposing the conclusion is responsible for providing the proof.

Faulty Emotional Appeals. *Appeals to emotions* are considered valid when they are used to motivate the audience to act on a logically established conclusion. (The validity of emotional appeals is discussed in the next section of this chapter.) If, however, appeals to emotions are used to divert attention from the issue being argued or to evade the responsibility of providing factual evidence, then they are recognized as fallacious.

The two most common faulty emotional appeals are the appeal to pity and the appeal to fear. Lawyers who argue for their client's innocence based on the number of children who will be left fatherless or motherless divert attention from the crime the person committed. Likewise, advertisements featuring oversized photographs of sad-eyed, poverty-stricken children often evade the responsibility of providing evidence when requesting charitable contributions. Exactly what is done with the money? These appeals to pity evoke emotional response, not logical reasoning, in asking the audience to accept a conclusion.

The appeal to fear, or argument by force, can be even more coercive. For example, lobbyists who remind legislators that they represent thousands of voting constituents and potential campaign donors appeal to the legislators' fears concerning reelection. Similarly, advertisements for products such as smoke alarms or insurance use a fallacious appeal to fear when they portray only the destruction and destitution that can occur. However, if these same ads included evidence proving the likelihood of such disasters taking place and the prevention or restitution that would be provided by the product, then the appeal would be more likely to be valid. Unless the logical appeal of the argument is satisfied, the use of emotional appeal is generally fallacious.

Non Sequitur. A *non sequitur* is an argument whose conclusion fails to follow logically from the given premises. In this sense, all fallacies of relevance and presumption can be classified as non sequiturs because they rely on invalid inferences to form their conclusions.

Fallacies of Ambiguity. When arguments use language in ways that make the meaning of an issue unclear, they commit a fallacy of ambiguity. Unclear meaning shifts the responsibility of interpretation from the writer to the reader, thereby making the reader suspicious of the writer's claim. Clarifying meaning is the writer's responsibility. When the writer accepts that responsibility, potentially ambiguous uses of words and phrases become clever and often inject issues with new life. The beef industry advertisement in Figure 11 illustrates a valid use of ambiguity. The word *grill* in the headline immediately evokes two meanings: (1) a method of cooking and (2) interrogation. The ad clarifies both meanings by answering questions on health that the audience may have and by providing suggestions for cooking beef. In this way the ad neither avoids supporting the main issues nor shifts responsibility to the reader for determining meaning.

Figure 11 *Valid use of ambiguity*

Amphiboly. The fallacy of *amphiboly* is the result of poor sentence structure that produces ambiguous or deceptive meaning. When this occurs, the burden of proof is shifted onto the reader. For example, a sign on an isolated roadhouse in Key West, Florida, reads:

FREE COLD BEER TOMORROW

This loosely structured sentence excludes several essential elements to the claim—who will dispense the beer, where, and on which tomorrow. The structure puts the burden of proof on the reader, who is left in a continuous state of ambiguity by the undesignated date, "tomorrow." Although the effect of the claim may be clever, its intention is to deceive.

Even when a sentence contains the necessary elements for completeness, amphiboly can occur. Consider the following claim:

Eating bears can be dangerous.

The structural ambiguity of the sentence suggests two possible meanings:

Bears, when they are eating, can be dangerous (to people or each other?).

or

Eating bear meat can be dangerous (to the eater).

The fallacy of amphiboly makes the claim unclear: in which of the two possible ways might bears be dangerous?

In the advertisement in Figure 12 the careless use of the pronoun *they're* with no antecedent creates intentional ambiguity when juxtaposed with the picture. The two levels of ambiguity combined put the responsibility on the reader to clarify the claim. Careless use of pronouns is a common source of amphiboly.

Equivocation. A word or phrase is used ambiguously or equivocally in an argument when it shifts meaning in the course of the argument. In the claim below the word *power* appears to have the same meaning both times it is used.

The *power* of her position gives her the *power* to control the problem.

In its first use, *power* appears to mean *authority* or *responsibility;* its second use appears to have the same meaning. Rearranging the possible synonyms in place of the word *power* creates only a slight variation of meaning. But if the sentence read

The power of her position justifies her power in controlling the problem.

the first use would refer to the concept of *authority,* while the second would refer to *ability* in action taken. This difference in meaning would be a point of *equivocation.*

The next example illustrates how the ambiguity created by equivocation can produce a significant difference in tone.

Whatever behavior *violates* the right to privacy *violates* the law.

The first use of *violates* means *intrudes on,* as in disrespect, whereas the second use clearly means *break.* The sentence, then, could read

Whatever behavior intrudes on the right to privacy breaks the law.

When the distinctions in the term's use are identified, the meaning is clearer, but notice the difference in tone in the two versions. *Violates* is a stronger term than *intrudes on,* making the intent of the behavior sound more criminal before it is identified. In this way the ambiguity of equivocation can emotionally alter the readers' acceptance of the

Figure 12 *Amphiboly*

We know why they're here.

The richest coffee in the world.™

claim instead of using logic as its proof. A reader who discovers equivocation will most likely be suspicious of the writer's intentions. The more levels of meaning involved in the use of a word, the greater the potential for producing the fallacy of equivocation.

ASSESSING SUPPORTIVE INFORMATION

Both inductive and deductive reasoning rely on well-chosen information. To accept either form of reasoning as convincing, the audience will require accurate, objective information. This means you, the writer, will need to *verify* your evidence. Verifying the information you present as factual simply means establishing a connection between the statement of fact and the way you came to know it: Did you see or experience it yourself? Did you read about it? Did you learn about it from experts?

As you research information to support your argument, you will, no doubt, come across a wide variety of choices. But when planning your essay, remember that writing is a deliberate act; choose supportive information that will most convincingly bring you and your audience to an understanding on the issue.

In both inductive and de luctive reasoning your concern is with choosing information that will form or explain your premises or generalizations. And behind each of those premises lie your assumptions about your audience's beliefs. So the information you choose must not only support your premises but also lead the audience logically from their assumptions to your conclusions.

You can verify your information in three ways before making choices that will best demonstrate your logical appeal.

Personal Experience.   More than likely, the interest you have in presenting an argument will originate from your personal experience: you are frightened walking from the library to the dorm late at night; several of your credits from a previous school did not transfer; you have been laughed at because of your regional accent. These experiences actually happened to you. They are facts that can be used in support of your argument.

When you present personal experience, emphasizing details related to the argument and minimizing your personal feelings will produce the accuracy and objectivity needed to keep the audience focused on the issue instead of on you. In one sense, personal experience gives your argument a lively, human dimension that says, "This could happen to anyone"; but if the experience is extreme or biased, your audience is unlikely to accept it as probable.

Reference Information.   Over the years you have collected facts unconsciously on a variety of subjects from many sources: the number of career touchdown passes by Dan Marino from *Sports Illustrated;* the history of the Vietnam conflict from the PBS documentary; the number of active volcanoes from the *World Almanac;* the periodic table from your chemistry textbook. Each source you use has a different purpose in mind—some offering well-researched, in-depth reports and others brief, encapsulated updates of news. And the intended audience, of course, determines how you present the information: objectively, with no interpretation; in a scholarly manner, using a specialized language and thorough documentation; or slanted, reaffirming the values of a special-interest group.

No matter how impressive some of these sources may appear, you still need to verify their usefulness in supporting your reasoning if they are to establish a logical appeal for your audience. The following list of questions will guide you in choosing your sources.

1. **Is the source trustworthy for the type of information being presented?**
   How familiar is the name of the publication? To whom? How well researched is the information? How is this research indicated? Why do readers

generally consult this source? (Refer to the description of sources in Chapter 4 if you have questions about the authority and use of the source.)

2. **Is the publication date of the source appropriate to the reasoning of the argument you are presenting?**
Some arguments require the most current information available while others benefit from a historical perspective. Be particularly careful in using books (which take longer to get into print) when attempting to present the most current view; for that purpose a well-respected international newspaper may be your best source.

3. **Is the information representative?**
This question refers to both the quantity and the quality of the examples or subjects (people) used in the source. With statistics, graphs, charts, and other means of comparison representation is a particular problem. Were there enough people or examples surveyed? Were they typical of the whole group? (Chapter 3 will help you explore the question of representation further.)

4. **Are terms clearly defined?**
Professional journals and magazines targeted for highly specialized audiences often use technical jargon. Make sure you understand the terms used before you consider selecting the source and use paraphrase to help your audience understand. Abstract and controversial terms also need clear definitions, especially if they are presented in statistical data. How can you accept a measurement of success or failure, poverty, abuse, or health unless you know precisely how the researcher defines the term?

5. **Is the information complete?**
Answering this question will help you to determine whether any significant information has been omitted. If two books are being compared on how thoroughly each covers the subject, have the respective publication dates been taken into consideration? When the maintenance records of two cars are compared, does the researcher include the type of driving each was used for? In all cases, consider the significant parts of the whole before accepting information as being complete.

6. **Are the examples consistent with your experience and that of your audience?**
New and interesting examples can broaden your views and those of your audience, but *Guinness Book of World Records* data will not do much to increase the probability of your logic.

Expert Testimony. The words of famous historical figures, such as presidents, military leaders, inventors, and pioneers; and quotations from revered documents, such as the Constitution, lend an authoritative appeal to your reasoning. But who are the experts in the field on which you are writing? Are they well established or self-proclaimed experts? The questions below will help you determine whether the person's level of expertise will support your logical appeal.

1. **Is this level of authority needed for the audience to accept the probability of your reasoning?**
   Before selecting authorities in support of your reasoning, you first need to determine whether expert testimony is even needed. When information you use is already accepted by your audience, there is no need to verify it further with expert testimony. To quote Martin Luther King, Jr., merely to prove the existence of a civil rights movement would be insulting to your audience.

2. **Is the person qualified?**
   While some people are considered experts in their field through the competitive awards they have won (Nobel Prize, Olympic medal, Hall of Fame designation), others are assumed to be experts by the title they hold (secretary of education, doctor, chief executive officer, manager, captain). Even when the person's name is familiar to your audience, you should include the credentials you are relying upon to convey authority. And when the person is not familiar to your audience, you will need to *check* the person's credentials: What is the person's educational background? What else has the person published? Is the person's work respected? How long and where has the person been practicing in this field?

3. **Is the person biased?**
   Bias can occur in the expert's selection of examples, sources, and word choice as a result of the person's special interests (politics, religion, funding, or corporate sponsorship for research). In an effort to support his or her own theory, the expert could overlook opposing evidence. Bias might be difficult to determine, but you should at least question the motives of the expert before using the source.

4. **Are the experts in conflict?**
   The nature of argument is controversy, so you can expect to find experts who differ in their opinion. In some cases you will need to present both viewpoints, especially when your audience is aware that both exist. In other cases you may want to give only general acknowledgement to the opposition's ideas. But in either case you will need to be aware of opposing views to verify your own reasoning and maintain the integrity of your presentation.

In Chapter 11 you will find specific guidelines for integrating expert testimony and attributing the credentials of authorities.

EXERCISES: LOGICAL APPEAL

1. Decide whether the argument is deductive or inductive, and defend your judgment.
   a. Debbie has lived in the United States for eight years, but she is ineligible to vote because she is a British citizen.

b. At nearly half of the 30 colleges studied, more than 30 percent of the graduates did not complete three courses in math and science. "Undergraduate exposure to the natural sciences and mathematics is dangerously low," University of Pennsylvania Professor Robert Zemsky concluded. (Knight-Ridder News Service, January 7, 1989)

c. Frank broke his arm and several ribs when the state car he was driving to a conference was hit by a car that ran a red light. The state should pay for Frank's medical bills.

d. The surgeon general has determined that cigarette smoking is dangerous to your health.

e. The right to privacy is one of our constitutional rights, so random testing for drugs should not be permitted.

f. Urine specimens that had been adulterated with drugs were sent with other specimens to be tested at 31 different laboratories. The reports on the test specimens produced 97% accuracy. "After today, inaccuracies should not be used as an argument against drug testing," said Christopher S. Frings, director of the study conducted by the American Association of Clinical Chemistry. (Washington Post News Service, January 11, 1989)

g. All life requires water. There is no water on the planet Venus. Therefore there is no life on that planet.

h. The university catalog states that a person must be a junior to take Marketing 435, so everyone in this course must be at least a junior.

2. Determine whether the argument has a valid structure. Explain what makes each valid or invalid.

a. Geniuses wear glasses.
Allen wears glasses.

Allen is a genius.

b. Barbara received an A on the first calculus test.

If I study with Barbara, I'll get an A in the course.

c. Beagles make good pets.
Sparky is a beagle.

Sparky will make a good pet.

d. Eighty-five percent of the class attended the reunion.

Most of the class attended the reunion.

e. Either we missed them or they took a different train.
We did not miss them.

They took a different train.

f. Only seniors are allowed to park in Lot G.
Janice parked in Lot G.

Janice is a senior.

g. If it doesn't snow, we'll drive to grandmother's.
We didn't drive to grandmother's.

It snowed.

h. All Jesuits are priests.
No women are priests.

No women are Jesuits.

I. Professor Collins teaches biology and he went to Avion University.
Professor Burnett teaches biology, went to Avion University, and fails two-thirds of his 101 class.

Professor Collins will fail two-thirds of his 101 class.

J. All members of Congress are elected officials.
Some elected officials are crooks.

Some members of Congress are crooks.

3. Convert the enthymemes into syllogisms, supplying the missing premise. Then determine if each is valid or not.

a. Capital punishment is wrong because it is murder.

b. Most of Eddie Murphy's movies are comedies, so his new movie is probably a comedy too.

c. Last summer's drought in the Midwest means higher prices for bread and cereal next fall.

d. Because she doesn't receive any financial aid, Sandra must come from an affluent family.

e. Kevin could never be elected class president with that Irish temper of his.

f. If you hear it on "60 Minutes," you can believe it.

g. Dr. Wilson will win the award because he can remember all of his students' names.

h. There is no sense in paying for season tickets to the football games when you can watch most of them on television.

4. What kind of evidence would you need to support the following generalizations?

a. Soccer will soon eclipse baseball in popularity.

b. Raising the drinking age has increased crime.

c. People who graduated from private high schools have a better chance of getting accepted to Ivy League colleges.

d. Skydiving is a dangerous sport.

e. Dr. VanCleef is the best teacher in the psychology department.

f. Cable television is a major cause of growing illiteracy.

5. Decide whether the reasoning in the arguments below is faulty. Explain your answers and identify the fallacy that makes the reasoning faulty.

a. If we discontinued unemployment insurance, everyone would get a job.

b. That Swiss car is your best investment. You know the reputation Swiss watches have.

c. "She was Law Review. *And* she drinks Johnnie Walker." Good taste is always an asset. (Ad for Johnnie Walker, 1988)

d. Wearing a copper bracelet will help your arthritis. No one has proved it won't.

Figure 13 *Timex ad*

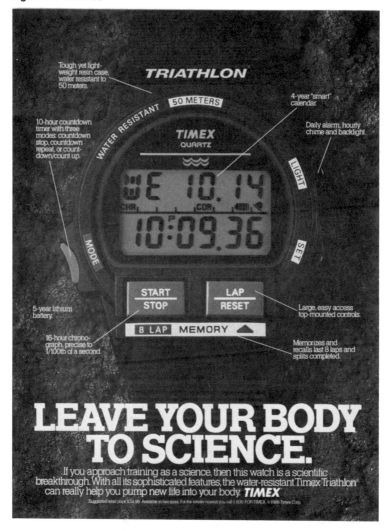

e. Are we going to lower class size in public schools or are we going to watch SAT scores drop further?

f. You can't cure poverty by giving people here and there a job, any more than you can stop cancer by putting a Band-Aid on it.

g. No wonder the senator supports resumption of the draft—she's a woman.

h. If you want to stop people from drinking and driving, either put warning labels on alcoholic beverages or make alcohol illegal.

i. Smoking is dangerous because it harms the human body.

j. Accident records show that 243 men and 112 women were involved in collisions

Figure 14 *Travelers ad*

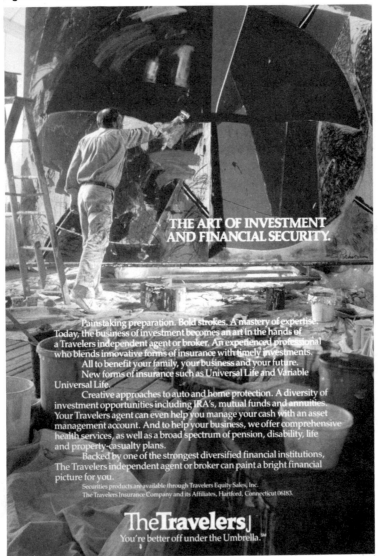

in Suffolk County last year. Women have a better driving record than men do in our county.

k. Once the government outlaws handguns, we'll soon have a police state.

l. All concerned parents will begin their children's education before they are even born.

m. "I wanted to be a rock star, but my father convinced me women worship doctors." Cognac Hennessy. The Spirit of the Civilized Rogue. (Ad in *Esquire,* 1988)

Figure 15 *SunTour ad*

GROUND BREAKING PERFORMANCE.

When you challenge the wilderness, survival often depends on the quality of your equipment. In Mountain Biking, that means dependable, durable, light and flawlessly performing components. Like the SunTour XCD-6000 group: the result of our single-minded insistence on giving you better value by offering components with top-of-the-line reliability and performance without the top-of-the-line price. Example: the XCD-6000 shift lever, designed to allow light and accurate response to sudden changes in terrain. Its AccuShift indexed shifting is assisted by our patented Power Ratchet Mechanism, and its shape and mounting position are ideal for simultaneous braking and shifting. So, when you challenge the wilderness, depend on SunTour XCD-6000.

2 Cranberry Road, Parsippany, N.J. 07054

n. All loyal Americans will vote against this bill.

o. Thomas Edison never finished high school, so why should kids today be forced to?

6. Write a one-page analysis of the reasoning used in each of the ads in Figures 13, 14, and 15. In your analysis consider what audience the ad might have been designed for and how likely they are to accept the reasoning as presented.

7. Many arguments contain both inductive and deductive reasoning. As you read the essay by Richard M. Restak from his book *The Brain: The Last Frontier* (1979), identify which sections are inductive and which are deductive. Next, outline the premises and conclusions of each part. Finally, evaluate the evidence the author uses to reach his conclusions.

The Other Difference
Between Boys and Girls

RICHARD M. RESTAK

Boys think differently from girls. Recent research on brain behavior   1
makes that conclusion inescapable, and it is unrealistic to keep denying it.

I know how offensive that will sound to feminists and others   2
committed to overcoming sexual stereotypes. As the father of three
daughters, I am well aware of the discrimination girls suffer. But social
equality for men and women really depends on recognizing these differences in brain behavior.

At present, schooling and testing discriminate against both boys   3
and girls in different ways, ignoring differences that have been observed by parents and educators for years. Boys suffer in elementary
school classrooms, which are ideally suited to the way girls think. Girls
suffer later on, in crucial ways, taking scholarship tests that are geared
for male performance.

Anyone who has spent time with children in a playground or   4
school setting is aware of differences in the way boys and girls respond
to similar situations. Think of the last time you supervised a birthday
party attended by five-year-olds. It's not usually the girls who pull hair,
throw punches or smear each other with food.

Usually such differences are explained on a cultural basis. Boys   5
are expected to be more aggressive and play rough games, while girls
are presumably encouraged to be gentle, nonassertive and passive.
After several years of exposure to such expectations, the theory goes,
men and women wind up with widely varying behavioral and intellectual repertoires. As a corollary to this, many people believe that if
child-rearing practices could be equalized and sexual stereotypes
eliminated, most of these differences would eventually disappear. As
often happens, however, the true state of affairs is not that simple.

Undoubtedly, many of the differences traditionally believed to 6
exist between the sexes are based on stereotypes. But despite this, evidence from recent brain research indicates that many behavioral differences between men and women are based on differences in brain functioning that are biologically inherent and unlikely to be modified by cultural factors alone.

The first clue to brain differences between the sexes came from 7
observations of male and female infants. From birth, female infants are more sensitive to sounds, particularly to their mother's voice. In a laboratory, if the sound of the mother's voice is displaced to another part of the room, female babies will react while male babies usually seem oblivious to the displacement. Female babies are also more easily startled by loud noises. In fact, their enhanced hearing performance persists throughout life, with females experiencing a fall-off in hearing much later than males.

Tests involving girls old enough to cooperate show increased 8
skin sensitivity, particularly in the fingertips, which have a lower threshold for touch identification. Females are also more proficient at fine motor performance. Rapid tapping movements are carried out quickly and more efficiently by girls than by boys.

In addition, there are differences in what attracts a girl's atten- 9
tion. Generally, females are more attentive to social contexts—faces, speech patterns and subtle vocal cues. By four months of age, a female infant is socially aware enough to distinguish photographs of familiar people, a task rarely performed well by boys of that age. Also at four months, girls will babble to a mother's face, seemingly recognizing her as a person, while boys fail to distinguish between a face and a dangling toy, babbling equally to both.

Female infants also speak sooner, have larger vocabularies and 10
rarely demonstrate speech defects. Stuttering, for instance, occurs almost exclusively among boys.

Girls can also sing in tune at an earlier age. In fact, if we think of 11
the muscles of the throat as muscles of fine control—those in which girls excel—then it should come as no surprise that girls exceed boys in language abilities. This early linguistic bias often prevails throughout life. Girls read sooner, learn foreign languages more easily and, as a result, are more likely to enter occupations involving language mastery.

Boys, in contrast, show an early visual superiority. They are also 12
clumsier, performing poorly at something like arranging a row of beads, but excel at other activities calling on total body coordination. Their attentional mechanisms are also different. A boy will react to an inanimate object as quickly as he will to a person. A male baby will often ignore the mother and babble to a blinking light, fixate on a geometric figure and, at a later point, manipulate it and attempt to take it apart.

A study of nursery preschool children carried by psychologist 13
Diane McGuinness of Stanford University found boys more curious,
especially in regard to exploring their environment. McGuinness'
studies also confirmed that males are better at manipulating three-
dimensional space. When boys and girls are asked to mentally rotate
or fold an object, boys overwhelmingly outperform girls. "I folded it in
my mind" is a typical male response. Girls, when explaining how they
perform the same task, are likely to produce elaborate verbal descriptions which, because they are less appropriate to the task, result in frequent errors.

In an attempt to understand the sex differences in spatial ability, 14
electroencephalogram (EEG) measurements have recently been made
of the accompanying electrical events going on within the brain.

Ordinarily, the two brain hemispheres produce a similar elec- 15
trical background that can be measured by an EEG. When a person is
involved in a mental task—say, subtracting 73 from 102—the hemisphere that is activated will demonstrate a change in its electrical
background. When boys are involved in tasks employing spatial concepts, such as figuring out mentally which of three folded shapes can
be made from a flat, irregular piece of paper, the right hemisphere is
activated consistently. Girls, in contrast, are more likely to activate both
hemispheres, indicating that spatial ability is more widely dispersed
in the female brain.

When it comes to psychological measurements of brain function- 16
ing between the sexes, unmistakable differences emerge. In 11 subtests
of the most widely used test of general intelligence, only two subtests
reveal similar mean scores for males and females. These sex differences
have been substantiated across cultures and are so consistent that the
standard battery of this intelligence test now contains a masculinity-
femininity index.

Further support for sex differences in brain functioning comes 17
from experience with subtests that eventually had to be omitted from
the original test battery. A cube-analysis test, for example, was excluded because, after testing thousands of subjects, a large sex bias appeared to favor males. In all, over 30 tests eventually had to be eliminated because they discriminated in favor of one or the other sex. One
test, involving mentally working oneself through a maze, favored boys
so overwhelmingly that, for a while, some psychologists speculated
that girls were totally lacking in a "spatial factor."

Most thought-provoking of all is a series of findings by Eleanor 18
Maccoby and Carol Nagly Jacklin of Stanford on personality traits and
intellectual achievement. They found that girls whose intellectual
achievement is greatest tend to be unusually active, independent,
competitive and free of fear or anxiety, while intellectually outstanding
boys are often timid, anxious, not overtly aggressive and less active.

In essence, Maccoby and Jacklin's findings suggest that intellec- 19
tual performance is incompatible with our stereotype of femininity in
girls or masculinity in boys.

Research evidence within the last six months indicates that many 20
of these brain sex differences persist over a person's lifetime. In a study
at the University Hospital in Ontario that compared verbal and spatial
abilities of men and women after a stroke, the women did better than
men in key categories tested. After the stroke, women tended to be less
disabled and recovered more quickly.

Research at the National Institute of Mental Health is even un- 21
covering biochemical differences in the brains of men and women.
Women's brains, it seems, are more sensitive to experimentally administered lights and sounds. The investigator in charge of this research,
Dr. Monte Buchsbaum, speculates that the enhanced response of the
female brain depends on the effect of sex hormones on the formation
of a key brain chemical. This increased sensibility to stimuli by the female brain may explain why women more often than men respond to
loss and stress by developing depression.

It's important to remember that we're not talking about one sex 22
being generally superior or inferior to another. Rather, psychobiological
research is turning up important functional differences between male
and female brains. The discoveries might possibly contribute to further resentments and divisions in our society. But must they? Why are
sex differences in brain functioning disturbing to so many people?
And why do women react so vehemently to findings that, if anything,
indicate enhanced capabilities in the female brain?

It seems to me that we can make two responses to these findings 23
on brain-sex differences. First, we can use them to help bring about
true social equity. One way of doing this might be to change such practices as nationwide competitive examinations. If boys, for instance,
truly do excel in right-hemisphere tasks, then tests such as the National Merit Scholarship Examination should be radically redesigned
to assure that both sexes have an equal chance. As things now stand,
the tests are heavily weighted with items that virtually guarantee superior male performance.

Attitude changes are also needed in our approach to "hyperac- 24
tive" or "learning disabled" children. The evidence for sex differences
here is staggering: More than 95 percent of hyperactives are males.
And why should this be surprising in light of the sex differences in
brain function that we've just discussed?

The male brain learns by manipulating its environment, yet the 25
typical student is forced to sit still for long hours in the classroom. The
male brain is primarily visual, while classroom instruction demands
attentive listening. Boys are clumsy in fine hand coordination, yet are
forced at an early age to express themselves in writing. Finally, there is

little opportunity in most schools, other than during recess, for gross motor movements or rapid muscular responses. In essence, the classrooms in most of our nation's primary grades are geared to skills that come naturally to girls but develop very slowly in boys. The results shouldn't be surprising: a "learning disabled" child who is also frequently "hyperactive."

"He can't sit still, can't write legibly, is always trying to take things 26 apart, won't follow instructions, is loud, and, oh yes, terribly clumsy," is a typical teacher description of male hyperactivity. We now have the opportunity, based on emerging evidence of sex differences in brain functioning, to restructure elementary grades so that boys find their initial educational contacts less stressful.

At more advanced levels of instruction, efforts must be made to 27 develop teaching methods that incorporate verbal and linguistic approaches to physics, engineering and architecture (to mention only three fields where women are conspicuously underrepresented and, on competitive aptitude tests, score well below males).

The second alternative is, of course, to do nothing about brain 28 differences and perhaps even deny them altogether. Certainly there is something to be said for this approach too. In the recent past, enhanced social benefit has usually resulted from stressing the similarities between people rather than their differences. We ignore brain-sex differences, however, at the risk of confusing biology with sociology, and wishful thinking with scientific facts.

The question is not, "Are there brain-sex differences?" but rather, 29 "What is going to be our response to these differences?" Psychobiological research is slowly but surely inching toward scientific proof of a premise first articulated by the psychologist David Wechsler more than 20 years ago:

"The findings suggest that women seemingly call upon different 30 resources or different degrees of like abilities in exercising whatever it is we call intelligence. For the moment, one need not be concerned as to which approach is better or 'superior.' But our findings do confirm what poets and novelists have often asserted, and the average layman long believed, namely, that men not only behave, but 'think' differently from women."

THE APPEAL TO EMOTION: *PATHOS*

If a friend walked up to you and said, "I'm really angry at Sam. I want you to be angry at him too," would you automatically get angry at Sam? Of course not. First you would need to know why you should be angry at him. Emotions can be a strong influence on behavior, but they need a reason for being aroused. Consequently, emotion cannot replace reason in an argument, but it can make the argument more desirable.

CONNECTING EMOTIONS TO NEEDS AND VALUES

In argument you present ideas to others for their approval or rejection. Using logical and ethical appeals, you provide reasons for assent or dissent that involve the audience in interpreting for themselves the implication of these ideas. Emotions are the products of these interpretations and subjective judgments. To evoke these emotions through your reasoning, you first need to consider the range of possible emotions that might connect with your ideas.

What emotions people express and how they express them are strongly linked to culture. In our own culture, for instance, a quick review of changes in movie production code since 1930 reveals dramatic changes in what the public interprets as moral or immoral and consequently what evokes feelings of embarrassment, shame, contempt, and respect, among other responses. One of the first indexes of emotions of a particular culture in a particular time period is Aristotle's list of fourteen basic emotions common to public life in ancient Greece.

ARISTOTLE'S LIST OF BASIC EMOTIONS[1]

Anger	Mildness
Love	Enmity (hatred)
Fear	Confidence
Shame	Shamelessness
Benevolence	Pity
Indignation	Envy
Emulation	Contempt

Naturally the changes in mores and experiences since Aristotle's time make for a wider range of emotional expression in twentieth-century America. Philosopher Robert Solomon has assembled a dictionary of the emotions that characterize contemporary culture. The list below includes twenty-two in addition to those on Aristotle's list.

SOLOMON'S LIST OF BASIC EMOTIONS[2]

Angst (anguish, anxiety)	Frustration	Pride
Depression	Gratitude	Regret, remorse
Despair	Guilt	Respect
Dread	Hope	Sadness
Duty	Indifference	Self-respect
Embarrassment	Innocence	Vanity
Faith	Joy	Worship
Friendship		

---

[1] Lane Cooper, ed. and trans., *The Rhetoric of Aristotle, Book II,* (Englewood Cliffs, N.J.: Prentice-Hall, 1960).

[2] Robert C. Solomon, *The Passions* (Garden City, N.Y.: Anchor, 1976) pp. 282–368.

No index of emotions is likely to be complete, for even as it is being compiled changes in culture can be evoking new or different responses. If the changes in a culture are linked to the needs of the people, then these basic needs must be the connection between ideas and the emotional responses they evoke.

Different theories have tried to explain what human needs motivate different kinds of behavior. One commonly used theory developed by psychologist Abraham H. Maslow classifies human needs into a hierarchical arrangement of five systems of needs, with physiological needs at the lowest level and psychological needs at the highest. The central assumption in Maslow's theory is that people will attend to their higher level needs (psychological) only after satisfying their lower level needs (physiological). For example, when people are starving, they are not likely to be concerned with cultivating their reputation.

MASLOW'S HIERARCHY OF NEEDS[3]

Physiological Needs. Biological maintenance: food, water, health, temperature regulation

Safety Needs. Security, protection, predictable, orderly, nonthreatening environments

Social Needs. Love, reciprocal affection, a sense of belongingness, group membership

Esteem Needs. Respect oneself, recognition by others, prestige, achievement

Self-Actualization Needs. Develop one's identity, self-fulfillment, realization of one's potential to its fullest

Reading over these needs, you can see that each level has a potential connection between logical appeal and emotional response. If you were to present an argument advocating a low-cholesterol diet, the logical appeal of your information would be likely to trigger an emotional response for the health need. In the same way, an argument advocating community service would be likely to trigger emotions for belongingness and recognition or self-esteem. When the reasoning in an argument satisfies a human need, a positive emotional response results and consequently a value judgment of the argument's claim.

Exactly what people value is often difficult to determine. The events they attend, products they buy, places they travel, books or magazines they read, level of education they pursue, number of children they have, and a long list of other behaviors help to indicate what people value in satisfying their needs. In an effort to predict these values, the Stanford Research Institute International used Maslow's classification of needs as the basis for their Values and Lifestyle Program (VALS). VALS is a market research analysis that groups Americans by nine types for advertising purposes. These types are based on the group's self-images and aspirations, and the products they use. One of the origi-

---

[3]Abraham H. Maslow, *Motivation and Personality* (New York: Harper & Row, 1954).

nal VALS researchers, Arnold Mitchell, describes the groups in his book *The Nine American Lifestyles* as follows:[4]

NEED-DRIVEN:	11 percent of the population

Survivors, sustainers: those who get by

OUTER-DIRECTEDS:	68 percent

Belongers: traditional, conformist
Emulators: bewildered about how to achieve,
    steady work
Achievers: money-based, want "the right
    stuff," work hard and long

INNER-DIRECTEDS:	19 percent

I-Am-Me's: rebellious
Experientials: wholesome, looking for adven-
    ture or peak experience
Societally Conscious: active in social issues
    and politics

INTEGRATEDS: creative and prosperous	2 percent

These VALS groupings were designed specifically for advertising, not for developing arguments. Still, they can be of some use in providing further insight into people's values and the motivation for their beliefs. To advertisers these groupings serve as the basis for designing appeals for their products. And while all three appeals are used to some extent in advertising, emotional appeal is the most direct: the consumer must be persuaded to act by buying the product—agreement is not enough. But in argument emotional appeal is subtle and indirect, an extension rather than a competitor of reason.

EVOKING EMOTIONS

Creating an emotional appeal requires subtlety and a careful use of words. You can't *tell* someone how to feel; instead, you need to evoke the response. The most effective way to do this is by contemplating an object or scene in an emotionally detached, controlled manner, allowing the audience to respond with their own emotions. What you select to include in the scene will direct their response. The example below was written in 1943 by Ernie Pyle, a Pulitzer Prize-winning journalist in World War II, in his book *Brave Men.* The scene depicts the beach after the Normandy invasion.

> The strong, swirling tides of the Normandy coast line shifted the contours of the sandy beach as they moved in and out. They carried soldiers' bodies out to sea, and later they returned them. They cov-

---

[4]Arnold Mitchell, *The Nine American Lifestyles* (New York: Macmillan, 1983).

ered the corpses of heroes with sand, and then in their whims they uncovered them.

As I plowed out over the wet sand, I walked around what seemed to be a couple of pieces of driftwood sticking out of the sand. But they weren't driftwood. They were a soldier's two feet. He was completely covered except for his feet; the toes of his GI shoes pointed toward the land he had come so far to see, and which he saw so briefly.

Without using emotional language, Pyle successfully creates a highly emotional scene, one that evokes the horror of war on a very personal level.

Direct emotional appeal is not a necessary part of argument, but if there are points in your argument where the audience may have difficulty accepting your reasoning completely, then emotional appeal can be a motivating factor. These points often occur at the beginning or end of an argument. If your audience is strongly opposed to your view of the issue or if they are ambivalent, an emotional appeal at the beginning of the argument can involve them more personally and give them the motivation to read on. In the following excerpt from her book *The Language of Clothes* (1981), Alison Lurie prepares her readers for the analogy on which her entire book is based—clothing as language. Notice how she uses the simplicity of a daily scene to appeal to the reader's self-esteem needs.

For thousands of years human beings have communicated with one another first in the language of dress. Long before I am near enough to talk to you on the street, in a meeting, or at a party, you announce your sex, age and class to me through what you are wearing—and possibly give me important information (or misinformation) as to your occupation, origin, personality, opinions, tastes, sexual desires and current mood. I may not be able to put what I observe into words, but I register the information unconsciously; and you simultaneously do the same for me. By the time we meet and converse we have already spoken to each other in an older and more universal tongue.

Although the language in Lurie's description is general, it directly involves the audience, thus triggering their memory of real experiences and emotional responses. This connection motivates the audience to read further.

The conclusion of an argument is another likely point to use an emotional appeal either to reinforce the audience's acceptance of your claim or to motivate them to act on it. The next excerpt is the concluding paragraph in Joan Didion's essay "Marrying Absurd" from her book *Slouching Towards Bethlehem* (1968). In the essay she voices her opposition to the Las Vegas view of marriage: "Marriage, like craps, is a game to be played when the table seems hot." Didion avoids making any direct commentary and allows the scene to speak for itself. The reader is left comparing his or her view of marriage with those presented in the scene:

I sat next to one such wedding party in a Strip restaurant the last time I was in Las Vegas. The marriage had just taken place; the bride still wore her dress, the mother her corsage. A bored waiter poured a few swallows of pink champagne ("on the house") for everyone but the bride, who was too young to be served. "You'll need something with more kick than that," the bride's father said with heavy jocularity to his new son-in-law; the ritual jokes about the wedding night had a certain Panglossian character, since the bride was clearly several months pregnant. Another round of pink champagne, this time not on the house, and the bride began to cry. "It was just as nice," she sobbed, "as I hoped and dreamed it would be."

When emotional appeals reinforce the logical reasoning of an argument and when they are used to motivate the audience to act on a logically established conclusion, they are considered valid. But if they are used to divert attention from the issue being argued or to evade the responsibility of providing factual evidence, then they are fallacious.

EXERCISES: EMOTIONAL APPEAL

1. Knowing how you satisfy your own needs helps you to anticipate how others satisfy their needs. On a separate sheet of paper list Maslow's hierarchy and under each category identify the activities and relationships that satisfy those needs for you.

2. For each of the following subjects or situations identify your immediate emotional response. You may use the terms on Aristotle or Solomon's list.
- **a.** When the underdog wins
- **b.** When someone famous gets arrested for drug possession
- **c.** Suicide
- **d.** Refusing to lie for a friend
- **e.** Starving children in a Third World country
- **f.** Appearing in traffic court
- **g.** Being late to class
- **h.** Forgetting your mother's birthday
- **i.** An act of terrorism in a foreign country
- **j.** Donating blood

3. Write a one-page profile of yourself using the VALS groupings. Remember that the criteria for the groups are self-image, aspirations, and products used.

4. Write a one-paragraph description of a scene or experience in which you *evoke* one of the emotions listed below or one of your choice. Keep your description emotionally detached and controlled but directed toward evoking the emotion in the reader.

    pity   fear   respect   regret   gratitude

5. Write a 300- to 500-word analysis on how emotional appeal is used in Mike Royko's column from the *Chicago Daily News,* December 10, 1973. Consider what the claim of Royko's argument is and how and where he uses emotional appeal with respect to the claim. Is his use of emotional appeal valid?

A Faceless Man's Plea

MIKE ROYKO

Leroy Bailey just turned 26. He was one of seven kids from a broken 1 family in Connecticut. He had been in the infantry in Vietnam only one month.

Then the rocket tore through the roof of his tent while he was 2 sleeping and exploded in his face.

He was alive when the medics pulled him out. But he was blind. 3 And his face was gone. It's the simplest way to describe it: He no longer had a face.

That was in the spring of 1968. He went to an Army hospital, was 4 discharged and shipped to Hines VA Hospital, west of Chicago.

After three years and much surgery, they told him there was little 5 more they could do for him. He still had no face.

Now Bailey spends most of his life in the basement of his brother's 6 home in La Grange. The brother moved here from the East to be near him while he was hospitalized.

He knits wool hats, which a friend sells for him. He listens to the 7 radio or to a tape player.

Because of his terrible wound, most of the goals and pleasures of 8 men his age will always be denied him.

But there is one thing he would like to be able to do some day. It 9 isn't much, because most of us take it for granted.

He would like to eat solid foods. 10

Since 1968, he has eaten nothing but liquids. He uses a large sy- 11 ringe to squirt liquid foods down his throat.

Last year, through some friends of his brother, Bailey met a doc- 12 tor who specializes in facial surgery.

The doctor, Charles Janda of Oak Brook, said he believed he 13 could reconstruct Bailey's face so that he could eat solid foods.

But it would require a series of at least six separate operations, 14 possibly more.

Bailey eagerly agreed, and the first operation was performed at 15 Mercy Hospital.

Then Dr. Janda and the hospital sent their bills to the Veterans 16 Administration.

They did this because Bailey and his brother were under the im- 17 pression that the VA would pay for any treatment he needed that wasn't available in the VA.

The VA refuses to pay the bills. The reason was explained in a 18 remarkable letter sent to Bailey by a VA official. (The italics are mine.)

"Dear Mr. Bailey: 19

"Reference is made to the enclosed invoice for services given to 20 you for selective plastic surgery done on Sept. 22, 1972.

"It is regretted that payment on the above cannot be approved, 21 *since the treatment was for a condition other than that of your service-connected disability.*

"Outpatient treatment and/or medication may only be autho- 22 rized for the treatment of a disability which has been adjudicated by the Veterans Administration as incurred in or aggravated by military service.

"Any expense involved for this condition must be a personal 23 transaction between you and the doctor."

It is astonishing, I know, but the VA actually told him that he 24 was being treated for something "other than that of your service-connected disability."

I can't even begin to comprehend what they can be talking about. 25 Until he was hit by a rocket, he had teeth. Now he has none. He had eyes. Now he has none. He had a nose. Now he has none. People could look at him. Now most of them turn away.

So how can this surgery be for anything else but his "service- 26 connected disability"?

I read through his medical records. He could have received a 100- 27 per cent disability rating for any of four separate reasons. He could have received an 80-per cent disability rating for another reason, and a 30-per cent rating for still another.

The medical report uses such language as "scars, disfiguring . . . 28 exceptional repugnant deformity . . . entire midface is missing . . . massive facial injury."

Bailey believes that the VA thinks he wants the surgery just to 29 look better, that it is "cosmetic" surgery.

Even if that were so, then why in the hell not? If we can afford 30 $5 million to make the San Clemente property prettier, we can do whatever is humanly possible for this man's face.

But Bailey insists it isn't his appearance that concerns him. He **31** knows it will never be normal.

He explains his feelings in an appeal he filed months ago with **32** the VA:

"The only thing I am asking for is the ability to chew and swallow **33** my food.

"This was the purpose for the whole series of painful and unsuc- **34** cessful operations I underwent in Hines Hospital between the day of my injury on May 6, 1968, and my eventual discharge from the hospital in 1971.

"At the time, I was told the very depressing news that nothing **35** further could be done.

"I will never be able to accept this decision . . ." **36**

In some bureaucrat's file cabinet is Bailey's appeal. It has been **37** there for many months.

Every day that it sits there, Bailey takes his syringe and squirts **38** liquid nourishment down his throat.

If his appeal is turned down, he will spend the rest of his life **39** doing that. Not even once will he be able to sit down and eat at the dinner table with his brother's family, before going back down to the basement to knit hats.

RECOGNIZING APPEALS

The daily bombardment of advertisements you have grown accustomed to uses a wide variety of the three basic appeals. Through these appeals advertisers hope to gain your interest; establish credibility for their product; and persuade you to invest your money, your time, and your loyalty.

APPEALS IN ADVERTISING

The advertisement in Figure 16 appeared in the Jobs in Education section of the Sunday *New York Times*. The product clearly has an intended audience: people hoping to begin their graduate education or test for their professional credentials. The publication indicates an audience that enjoys reading and needs to be informed. What appeals has the advertiser chosen to use for this rhetorical context?

Logical Appeal. Behind the visual depiction of competition the advertiser presents the following reasoning:

> All competitors must practice to win.
> You are a competitor.

(Therefore) *You must practice to win.*

Figure 16 *Appeals in advertising*

More than likely the target audience will accept the major premise: their experiences as participants and spectators probably have shown this to be true. Acceptance of the minor premise, however, depends on the audience's self-image: How many view themselves as competing intellectually with others? How many view the test as a mere formality? It would seem, then, that the minor premise is more likely to be accepted by those who are less confident or perhaps those who are aggressively competitive.

If the audience accepts the first line of reasoning, then they must accept one more level before being persuaded to act on the ad:

Kaplan students score the most.

(If) You are a Kaplan student.

(Therefore) *You will score the most.*

An intelligent audience will want factual support to verify Kaplan's claims before enrolling for such a course. What does it mean to "score the most"? Does this mean making higher scores than anyone else taking the tests—all the tests listed? And what exactly is a Kaplan student? Are Kaplan students all alike or are they different in intellectual and test-taking ability? The advertiser does present one piece of information explicitly as fact: "Fact is, Kaplan preparation has helped over one million students." This information could be verified easily, but what does it actually contribute in support of the major premise? Nothing really. The audience still has no idea who these people are or how high they actually scored.

Ethical Appeal.   The ad hopes to convey an ethical appeal through its concern for the audience and Kaplan's assumed reputation. Notice the use of *you* to get closer and more familiar with the audience: "To do your best," "If you're facing," "Maybe there's a lesson in it for you." Similarly, the use of the possessive in "Our students are able to score the most, year after year" conveys both pride and reputation. It would seem, then, that the advertiser is interested primarily in the students' success; if students score well, then their needs are met and the company's reputation increases. But what does the potential student have to do to obtain this success? How much time and money must the student invest? Once again the ad falls short in providing the specific, detailed information the audience needs to act.

Emotional Appeal.   As with most ads, the advertiser uses a visual image to evoke a strong emotional appeal. Choosing an individual rather than a team sport for the visual, the advertiser hopes to evoke the audience's desire to achieve its personal best. Even the choice of sport—running—helps to eliminate possible gender barriers; both men and women run as professionals and as amateurs. But the strongest statement made through this visual is the aggressiveness of the competition. The participants are heading for a photo finish, using every bit of their strength. The advertiser expects to evoke the desire to have that extra edge needed to win. And having that extra edge appeals to the reader's need for self-esteem and recognition. Of course, if a reader rejects sports or a physical activity as a worthy analogy, this emotional appeal will fail.

APPEALS IN WRITING

In essays, writers are not restricted to one visual image or a few sentences to develop their appeals. Still, all the words and material they choose to include must have a purpose in presenting their argument to their intended audience. For the article "In Search of Public Servants" the writer chose appeals based on the rhetorical context for the article.

SUBJECT: The need for college graduates to become government public servants

AUDIENCE: The readers of the *Christian Science Monitor* in 1988, well-educated professionals concerned with national and international affairs, politically and socially minded people

PURPOSE: To convince the readers of their obligation to make the changes necessary to inspire college graduates to work in public service

OCCASION: Response to a survey on college students' goals conducted by the American Council on Education

AUTHOR: The writer is a member of the audience to whom he writes. His career with the U.S. foreign service and his present position as executive director of the National Commission on Public Service provide him with a level of expertise and a vested interest in having his argument supported by the audience.

In Search of Public Servants

L. BRUCE LAINGEN

"Ask not what your country can do for you; ask what you can do for 1 your country." Eloquent words from an earlier time, words that still speak to us, whatever our political preference, of what constructive patriotism is all about—especially for our young people.

Now, however, we read of statistics that suggest that those in the 2 future generation of leadership see their world differently. According to surveys by the American Council on Education, 83 percent of college freshmen 20 years ago saw "developing a meaningful philosophy of life" as an "essential" or "very important" life goal. But today only 39 percent feel that way, the council finds. And 76 percent put "being very well off financially" as their prime personal goal, almost twice those who did so in a 1970 poll.

Surveys of college students' career choices suggest a similar phi- 3 losophy. Public service in government is well toward the bottom of the list of options. Apparently young people today—however many of them do engage in some kind of public service during their college years— nonetheless see little reason to opt later for careers in government.

The reasons appear to be many. Low salaries relative to those of 4 other professions are a discouragement, especially when so many have such heavy student-loan burdens. Many would-be public servants are turned off by complicated and time-consuming entrance procedures and disillusioned by what they perceive as serious government policy mistakes and ethical shortcomings. Why bother? they wonder.

If the best and brightest of the next generation will not be enter- 5 ing government service at a time when many of the best are leaving at the top, this country faces a problem of large dimensions, and at a time when the demands facing democratic government in an increasingly crowded and complex world surely will grow rather than lessen.

We all have an obligation to act: the public at large, not least 6 the business community, by recognizing that quality in government matters; the Congress, by acting to close the gap between private-sector salaries and those of the public sector; government workers themselves, by demonstrating a commitment to professionalism and integrity.

But the obligation rests most heavily of all on our future political 7 leadership, to give expression to a public philosophy that includes a strong emphasis on public service—true to the best in that American tradition since Thomas Jefferson's admonition: "There is a debt of service due from every man to his country, proportioned to the bounties which nature and fortune have measured to him." That counsel is surely still valid today.

It is political leadership—from the president on down—that sets 8 the tone, the style, and yes, the energy of our national life; our goals, our sense of needed action and direction. But strangely we hear little of that today.

Our young people need to hear that call, to be reminded of the 9 dignity of public service, to be encouraged to see and recognize the excitement of national challenges, those met and the many not yet met.

And surely that excitement is there—felt by the public servants 10 who helped make possible the recent international agreement on the ozone layer, for instance. Or by all those who labored to make reality of the Intermediate-Range Nuclear Forces Treaty with the Soviet Union; or by the present (and future) Nobel Prize winners in medicine at the National Institutes of Health.

Let's not forget the satisfaction felt by those little-recognized mu- 11 nicipal employees in our great cities who work to make our lives easier and safer, or the determined dedication of Drug Enforcement Administration agents who stop illicit drug traffic across our borders, or the excitement of those workers in the Mine Safety and Health Administration in Midland, Texas, who last year brought little Jessica McClure to safety from the darkness of that abandoned well.

Career servants of government, all of them, join with political 12 leadership to get a job done, to make life a little more promising for everyone. They and others at all levels of government merit the public's recognition and the salute of our political leadership if public service is to remain a high calling in this country. There is excitement out there to be shared and much to be done, and the best of our young people should—must—be a part of it.

Laingen writes to his audience as a member with a similar background and with shared interests and concerns. Each appeal he uses shows that he depends on these shared characteristics.

Logical Appeal. The reasoning of the argument is an extension of the historic quotes used in the essay:

Major premise: The future of our country needs the commitment of public servants.

Minor premise: The young generation is the future of our country.

Conclusion: *The young generation needs to become committed public servants.*

The writer assumes in the major premise that the audience recognizes the value of commitment through its own contributions to the welfare of society. Then, by separating the audience from "our young people," the writer identifies the audience as those with experience, those who, once the young generation themselves, will be replaced eventually. For them to accept the minor premise is, if nothing else, a chronological reality. With the two premises accepted, the conclusion naturally follows.

To make sure his audience accepts the problem as a major issue, Laingen cites statistics from a survey of college students' goals in 1988 and compares them to students' goals in 1970. Then he outlines problems with public service today. Details and examples support his logic and contribute to his ethical appeal in demonstrating his knowledge and concern.

Laingen also uses an enthymeme to present his argument for the solution to the problem:

> When community and government leaders present positive, energetic role models of their work, young people will recognize the value and accept the challenge of public service.

With this line of reasoning the writer bases his readers' acceptance on the assumption that they enjoy their work and are capable of transmitting that excitement. To ensure their acceptance, Laingen provides specific examples on how the members of the audience can make their jobs more appealing to young people and reminds them of several recent events that could be used to inspire young people to accept the challenge. Again, these specific examples reinforce the writer's logic.

Ethical Appeal. The writer's use of *we* and *our* closes any distance between him and his audience. His concerns are their concerns; his values, their values; his goals, their goals.

CONCERNS: "our young people," "our political leadership," "our great cities"

VALUES: "words that speak to us," "whatever our political preference," "We have an obligation";

GOALS: "our future political leadership," "the energy of our national life," "our sense of needed action and direction," "Our young people need to hear that call."

Naturally, Laingen's position as executive director of the National Commission on the Public Service, his career with the government, and his experience in captivity during the Iran hostage crisis demonstrate his knowledgeable background and convey a strong sense of credibility. This level of expertise along with his strong identification with the audience and their concerns presents a convincing ethical appeal.

Emotional Appeal. Laingen appeals to his readers' emotions indirectly with the quotations he includes. The first, a familiar statement by John F. Kennedy, transfers the readers back to the time of their own youth, evoking an historical moment of commitment experienced by a whole nation. This same emotional appeal to pride and patriotism is the purpose for the Jefferson quote. Notice how Laingen prefaces the second quote with a description of public service as "true to the best in that American tradition," an appeal to the audience's sense of respect.

For Laingen's audience and purpose his strong use of logical and ethical appeal make the obligation and action he proposes clear and possible. The better you know your audience—what they know and what they value—the more successfully you, too, will be able to present your argument.

EXERCISES: RECOGNIZING APPEALS

1. Why do you believe what you do? Select one of the following topics or one of your own interest, make a list of your main beliefs on the topic, and next to each belief identify the source and corresponding appeal. Here is an example:

TOPIC: Everyone should study a foreign language.

BELIEFS	SOURCE	APPEAL
Helps you to understand your own language	Personal experience studying French and Spanish	ethical
Gives you a competitive edge in getting a job	Descriptions in the classified ads, interviews with employers in different fields	logical (ads and interviews) emotional (self-esteem)
Increases likelihood of travel	My junior year abroad in France	ethical

POSSIBLE TOPICS:

Gaining work experience while attending school

Putting warning labels on alcoholic beverages

Requiring drug testing as part of job interviews

Developing a rating code for rock music

2. For each of the following advertisements in Figures 17, 18, and 19, explain how the logical, ethical, and emotional appeals are used. Consider the rhetorical context for each ad in determining the effectiveness of the appeals.

Figure 17 Time, *1985*

How to fix an American symbol.

A worn-out baseball is easily replaced.
You just go out and buy a new one.
But there's another American symbol
that's going to take all of us to fix.
We can't just go out and buy a new
Statue of Liberty. We have to fix
the one we have. Please help
by sending $20...more,
if you can afford it... to:
The Statue of Liberty/
Ellis Island Foundation,
P.O.Box 1992, Dept. E
New York, NY 10008.

Ross Roy Advertising, Detroit

3. Choose one of the following rhetorical contexts or outline one of your own. Write a short essay analyzing the rhetorical context and suggesting how the three appeals could be used to achieve the intended purpose for the specified audience.

> **SUBJECT:** Illiteracy
> **AUDIENCE:** Unknown authority (state governor)
> **PURPOSE:** To convince him or her that growing illiteracy is an economic threat to the state

Figure 19 Mountain & City Biking, *1989*

SOME PEOPLE THINK ALL IT TAKES TO GET AHEAD IS A LITTLE NAME-DROPPING...

THEY'RE RIGHT!

shimano

Drop one name and get yourself three!

More than ever, mountain bike makers and riders are dropping the "other brand" and riding ahead with the high-performance XCE mountain bike component group from SunTour, Dia-Compe and SR Sakae.

3x the off-road performance.

The new XCE component group is from not one, but three bicycle component specialists. That means no compromise or weakness in any area of the group. You get high-performance design and workmanship that comes from a team of independent specialists working together.

SunTour and SR Sakae drive you to new levels of performance.

Right at your fingertips in the XCE shift lever, safe from mud and grit, is the primary trigger mechanism of SunTour's AccuShift Index System™. With the quick action of the floating slant trapezoid rear derailleur along the 6 or 7 speed delta-cut freewheel, your XCE drivetrain kicks into gear cleanly and securely every time. And the XCE quick-release, double-sealed alloy hubs are smooth and tough.

The XCE rubber-sealed bottom bracket and triple crankset feature SR Sakae's Enhanced OvalTech Design™ — round outer/oval middle and inner chainrings beautifully mounted with Sakae's Flush-Surface™ design. Plus, Accurad™ — the extreme pressure forging system that guarantees you unequalled strength, rigidity and finish.

Dia-Compe stops you at any level.

The XCE brakeset is pure Dia-Compe — steel-tech gray composite canti-front and canti-rear for great looking strength and rigidity. Plus, the exclusive Balanced Response System™ — the original, total integration of brake, spring-assisted return lever and zinc cable/moly-sulfite casing for full brake modulation and maximum fine-tuning.

The trail is more secure on XCE.

Visit your local shop today or call 1 **800-835-2246 ext. 147,** and discover which high-performance mountain bikes ride with XCE. After all, selecting a bike with SunTour, Dia-Compe and SR Sakae is more than just dropping a name... **it's like getting three times the bike.**

SUNTOUR   DIA-COMPE   SR SAKAE

SUBJECT: Arms reduction
AUDIENCE: Political science teacher
PURPOSE: To demonstrate the ineffectiveness of treaties as a means of reducing arms

SUBJECT: Music lessons
AUDIENCE: General public (parents)
PURPOSE: To persuade parents to provide music lessons for their children during the elementary grades

SUBJECT: Staying informed on current events
AUDIENCE: General age group (college students)
PURPOSE: To convince students to read a daily newspaper

WRITING SUGGESTION

Ellen Goodman is a syndicated columnist who writes for members of the general public who read the editorial page of the newspaper. Write an analysis of her column published March 10, 1988 in the *Boston Globe,* demonstrating how the appeals are successful or unsuccessful in convincing the audience to accept her argument.

From Voters
to Passive Viewers

ELLEN GOODMAN

I am sitting on a podium next to Barney Rosenzweig when the genial 1
producer of "Cagney and Lacey" refers to his television audience as a
"constituency of 30 million viewers." The discussion moves on, but my
mind sticks on that phrase. A "constituency of viewers"?

My dictionary defines a "constituency" as a body of voters. By all 2
accounts it is a political word. But the producer has used it deliberately in describing his campaign for entertainment victories. People,
he says, vote with their fingers every week.

I might have expected Hollywood to fuse such terms. Viewers 3
and voters. Consumers and constituents. But sitting here, I was reminded of the other way we've become part of the role confusion. To
the television moguls, we may be constituents. But in the political
world, we have become viewers.

This is not the first presidential race to be played out on the tele- 4
vision screen. By now, we have accepted the campaign as performance. We have become sophisticated about 30-second bites. We
know that candidates fly from market to market instead of city to city.
We've seen presidents sold like products; we know what goes on the
political screen.

But there is a more subtle impact of television on our political behavior. Not television as a series of images on a screen but television watching as an activity, THE dominant political activity. We have become better viewers than voters.

The only thing that television itself asks is that people watch. There is something intrinsically passive about this. Eyeball participation seems to me quite different from the whole-bodied politics that a democracy is supposed to demand of its people. It may be as different as the word "audience" is from the word "citizen."

I won't indulge too deeply in television-bashing. The up-close and personal politics of this era is not intrinsically worse than the grand old gestures of hall orators. There is no greater civic virtue in attending a rally than in watching one. More people see a candidate than at any time in our history.

But television has produced a couch-potato constituency. Sitting in front of the set, we expect to be amused, entertained, informed, inactive. Everything comes to us in the same one-way human channel: news and entertainment, political debates and sitcoms. Watching television we expect to be, rather than to do. The set permits no entry from home.

In some curious way, the most experienced political viewer becomes expert at one thing: television criticism. We become better equipped to criticize performance than policies. It is, after all, easier. Having done this for years, we are no longer even embarrassed at criticizing the star quality of a candidate. This has become our job as members of the audience/electorate.

In 1984, I remember Tom Brokaw's post-debate analysis vividly. He announced that a candidate had scored with two uses of humor. With that scorecard in hand, the anchorman became the critic, closing the political circle. Then it was notable. Now it is routine. We are comfortable watching, comfortable criticizing. We sink into our role as easily as we sink into the couch. It's hard to get up again.

I cannot prove that the rise of politics-as-television is responsible for the decrease of actual real, live voters. But how many viewer-voters have learned from television that they can reject politics because the program is boring? How many think they've done enough when they voted with their fingers?

In front of the television set, citizens are transformed into an audience. We can only, passively, receive the messages. Or we can turn off.

Chapter 8

USING APPEALS

Fortunately, there is no magic formula for using appeals in your argument. Each writer has an individual voice and each audience has specific needs. These conditions give you a wide range of choices in planning your content. But where do you begin?

Argumentation requires that the logical and ethical appeals provide the foundation for understanding between you and your audience—the audience needs the proof and the confidence to accept your view. But the balance and positioning of those appeals—and the extent to which you use emotional appeal—are determined by the *distance* between you and your audience. The size of that distance and the difference in reasoning that creates the distance will direct your choices of appeals to build a relationship with your audience.

As Chapter 6 pointed out, your opposition generally falls into one of three levels: undecided or ambivalent, conditionally opposed, or unconditionally opposed. The distance at each level poses a different problem for the writer in choosing how to arrange his or her ideas.

UNDECIDED OR AMBIVALENT AUDIENCE

An audience at this level is not demonstrating *any* level of opposition. In fact, the main problem is that the audience has not yet discovered a connection to the issue. Consequently, the writer's first choice is to determine which appeal will best establish the need for the audience to be concerned about the issue.

You can assume that the undecided audience needs more information about the issue before making a decision. Using the logical appeal early in the essay to provide the background material necessary for understanding the issue will prepare this audience for the reasoning that shapes your opinion.

Another basic need of this audience is trust in you as the "knowledge giver." Why do you want them to be involved? Is your concern genuine? Is your information fair and representative? Who else believes as you do? For this audience you will need an explicit and convincing use of the ethical appeal throughout the essay.

Often the writer's purpose in presenting an argument to an undecided audience is merely to get the audience involved in the issue and lead them to the point of making a decision. Notice how Ed Henry uses this strategy for arranging his appeals in the following article from *Changing Times* (March 1988).

Air Bags vs. Seat Belts

Why You Should Care

ED HENRY

Next time you buy a car you could be faced with a choice between air 1 bags and automatic seat belts. Does it make a difference which you choose? Yes it does, to both your safety and your pocketbook.

Under current federal regulations, 25% of all 1988 cars must be 2 equipped with some sort of passive restraint—an air bag or automatic seat belt—to protect the front-seat passengers in a crash. Next fall the number will jump to 40%, and by 1990 every new car sold in the U.S. will be required to have automatic protection in the front seat. To encourage the installation of air bags, the National Highway Traffic Safety Administration (NHTSA) is permitting cars that are equipped with driver's-side air bags to have manual front-passenger belts until 1994, when all cars must have full front automatic protection. Only front-center seats are exempt from the federal regulation.

There are four main types of passive restraints. The first, a motor- 3 ized shoulder belt that rides a track above the driver's and passenger's doors, moves into place when the door is closed. An accompanying lap belt must be hooked up manually. Such belts are standard equipment on some Chrysler, Ford and Toyota cars.

A second type of passive belt—found on General Motors and 4 Honda cars—is connected at three points, two of which are on the door and the other at your hip. The belt moves aside when the doors are opened and swings into place when they're closed. With this sys-

Make/Model	Driver Air Bags	Belts	
		Motorized	Nonmotorized
Acura Legend LS	●		
Alfa Romeo Spider Veloce		●	
Alfa Romeo Spider Quadrifoglio		●	
Austin Rover Sterling		■	
Buick LeSabre			●
Buick Regal fwd			●
Buick Skylark			●
BMW six series	●		
BMW seven series	●		
Chevrolet Beretta			●
Chrysler Conquest		●	
Chrysler Fifth Avenue[†]	●		
Chrysler LeBaron Coupe[*]			●
Dodge Daytona[*]			●
Dodge Diplomat[†]	●		
Dodge Shadow[†]		●	
Eagle Premier bucket seats[†]		●	
Ford Escort		●	
Ford Tempo	■	●	
Honda Accord 2dr			●
Honda Prelude			●
Hyundai Excel GL 4dr			■
Hyundai Excel GLS 4dr			■
Isuzu Impulse		●	
Jaguar XJ-S		●	
Jaguar XJ-SC		●	
Mazda 626		●	
Medallion (imported for Eagle)[††]		●	
Mercedes-Benz (all models)	●		
Mercury Topaz	■	●	
Mitsubishi Precis 4dr hatch			■
Mitsubishi Starion		●	
Nissan Maxima		●	
Oldsmobile Calais			●
Oldsmobile Cutlass Supreme fwd			●
Oldsmobile Delta 88	■		●

tem you don't have to connect a lap belt by hand. As with all of the passive seat-belt systems there's an emergency release.

Another type, a two-point belt attached to the doors of some 5 Chryslers, Peugeots and Volkswagens, also swings into place when the door is closed. The strap goes from a seat fastener at the hip, across the body and shoulder, to the door. There are no lap belts for Volkswagen's restraints. Instead, knee bolsters on the dash and other padding help keep you in place during a crash.

Make/Model	Driver Air Bags	Belts	
		Motorized	Nonmotorized
Peugeot 505 GLS			●
Peugeot 505 STI 4dr			●
Plymouth Gran Fury†	●		
Plymouth Sundance†		●	
Pontiac Bonneville			●
Pontiac Grand Am			●
Pontiac Grand Prix fwd			●
Porsche 944**	■		
Porsche 944S**	●		
Porsche 944 Turbo**	●		
Saab 9000 Turbo†	■		
Saab 900S 3dr#		●	
Subaru GL fwd (sedans and wagons with auto. trans.)		●	
Subaru GL-10 fwd (sedans and wagons with auto. trans.)		●	
Subaru XT Coupe		●	
Subaru XT6		●	
Toyota Camry		●	
Toyota Cressida		●	
Volkswagen Golf GL			●
Volkswagen Jetta GL			●
Volvo 740 GLE	■		
Volvo 740 Turbo (sedans and wagons)	●		
Volvo 760 (sedans and wagons)	●		
Volvo 780	●		
Yugo GVS			●
Yugo GVLS			●

*Late-production models will switch to air bags. †Applies to late-production models only.
**Passenger-side air bags standard with driver air bag. ††In 1989 models, available spring 1988.
#All late-production Saab 900 three-door models except SPG will have motorized belts as standard equipment. fwd front-wheel drive
● standard. ■ option

Source: Insurance Institute for Highway Safety

The fourth option, the air bag, is designed to be used with a seat belt; an unbelted driver would move too much in a crash for the bag to be effective. Sensors in the front of a car react to a crash of about 12 miles per hour into a fixed object or 25 miles per hour or more into another car, deploying a bag that inflates from the hub of the steering wheel. Several Porsche models have passenger-side bags as well.

A few years ago most car companies opposed air bags. Only Mercedes-Benz bucked the trend, followed recently by Ford. Now others are rushing to join in. Air bags are being installed in Chrysler,

General Motors and Japanese cars, with more to follow in the next few years. The air bag's trouble-free record—there have been no recent cases of accidental deployment—has quieted companies' fears of lawsuits. A federal credit for cars with air bags that allows makers extra time to plan for the 1994 deadline has sweetened the pot.

Safety Versus Cost

There's no question that air bags are safer than automatic seat 8
belts when they're used with three-point lap and shoulder belts. Seat belts tend to stretch during a crash and provide limited protection against head and face injuries in high-speed crashes.

Government studies show that the combination of a three-point 9
belt and an air bag reduces fatalities by as much as 55%. Those same studies demonstrate that air bags even without use of seat belts would save a significant number of lives. But they also show that the number of lives saved using automatic belts alone is hard to predict because people can choose not to use them.

Of equal importance is the kind of protection you get from air 10
bags. "What the air bag offers that no belt system can is optimum protection for your face, head and brain in serious crashes," says Brian O'Neill, president of the Insurance Institute for Highway Safety.

But until their costs come down, air bags represent something of 11
a mixed blessing to car buyers. Whether you purchase them as an option or as standard equipment, they add $500 to $1,000 to the price of a car. (Production levels of more than a million a year by 1990 are expected to lower the price to an estimated $300 apiece.) If a bag is deployed in an accident, it can cost up to $2,000 to restore the system to a workable condition. Says Earl Kautz, a ratings specialist for GEICO: "While the bag and components might cost $800, actual cost might be $1,800 because of the labor involved."

Those costs aren't expected to affect your collision rates appre- 12
ciably. But you can expect better discounts for personal injury protection and possibly better rates for bodily injury protection.

The cost of medical-payment coverage also drops as much as 13
40% for cars with passive restraints, depending on the insurer. GEICO and American Family Mutual offer 30% discounts for all passive restraints; Hartford Fire offers 30% for full front passive-restraint protection and 20% for driver's-side-only protection. Allstate gives a 30% discount for full front air bags but none for automatic belts. Prudential gives 30% for air bags and 20% for automatic belts. Nationwide gives a 25% discount for driver's-side air bags, 40% for full front air bags and 10% for two automatic seat belts.

The discounts don't make much of a dent in the cost of the 14 bag, however. A Cleveland family with a Ford Topaz that insures with GEICO, for example, would pay $16.50 for mandatory personal injury protection as part of an overall $641.30 liability, fire, theft and comprehensive policy. With an air bag, the cost for medical coverage drops 30%, or $4.90. In another area, such as Baltimore, the same discount would be worth more because the personal injury protection rates are about seven times as expensive as in Cleveland.

Because the discounts aren't that significant, you spend much 15 less in the long run on a car with automatic seat belts than you would on a car with an air bag. But you also give up a measure of safety. That's no easy choice. Check the table . . . ; it will steer you through the passive-restraint devices of all major manufacturers.

The rhetorical context for this argument demonstrates the importance of matching your strategy to the subject and audience. *Changing Times* has a readership comprised primarily of white-collar professionals whose earning power makes them careful consumers—people who want to be well informed before making a decision. These readers are the classic undecided audience.

The use of air bags and automatic seat belts is reaching the stage where car buyers will need to make new decisions. In the opening paragraph the writer uses this occasion of consumers' being faced with a choice to connect the audience with the subject. And, recognizing that the audience will want to know what that choice is, he identifies the two main concerns—safety and money—both practical, logical issues with emotionally based needs.

The writer's strategy for arranging ideas responds to the basic needs of this audience. After introducing the subject, the issue, and the connection with the audience through the informal use of *you,* he uses logical appeal to provide updated information on federal regulations (paragraph 2), definitions and descriptions of the available options (paragraphs 3–6), and an explanation of the practices currently in use (paragraph 7). The audience will use all this information in forming an opinion. Notice that the first section contains no opinion on the issue from the writer, whereas the following section, Safety Versus Cost, presents the writer's interpretation of the available research—his line of reasoning. Paragraphs 8–10 focus on safety and paragraphs 11–14 cover cost. Why did the writer present safety before cost? Probably because the audience would be concerned first with safety—a physiological, basic need (refer to Maslow's hierarchy of needs, Chapter 7).

Notice that the writer chooses not to impose a particular opinion on the audience in the conclusion. Instead, he summarizes the two choices, each in one sentence, and agrees with what he predicts the reader is thinking at this point: "That's no easy choice." By leaving the choice open and referring the audience to the chart to further consider the options, the writer fulfills his purpose of leading the audience to the point of making an informed decision on the issue.

You will notice that the writer chooses not to use a direct emotional appeal. Why? Surely he could include descriptions of accidents and statistics on the number of children who have lost their lives in car accidents to get the audience involved. But is that what his audience needs? Because both safety and cost already evoke emotional concerns in the audience, there is no need to include that appeal. Instead, the writer chooses to appeal to the readers' intelligence.

CONDITIONALLY OPPOSED AUDIENCE

An audience that already is sufficiently aware of the issue to be opposed creates a different set of choices for the writer. The first step is to identify the *condition* that separates the reader from the writer's position. *This* is what the readers need to understand in a new way; this is the writer's challenge.

When writing to this audience, you need to determine *why* they reject your point of view. Do they not respect the people who hold that opinion (ethical appeal)? Do they need more information (logical appeal)? Is their reasoning valid (logical appeal)? Have they not considered all the possible consequences of their reasoning (logical and emotional appeal)? Knowing precisely why the readers oppose your viewpoint defines the appeals you need to use when you present your position.

Readers who have already formed an opinion on an issue expect you to recognize that opinion. They don't want to be insulted or told that they are wrong. One way to satisfy these needs is to begin your essay at a point at which you can both agree. After all, you have both established a connection to the issue. Whatever appeal motivates that shared connection can shape your introduction.

Next, recognizing that you and your readers have different views, you will need to explore those differences in a way that will bring you and your audience to a closer understanding. The appeals you use will depend on the kinds of differences that separate you; but, in any case, you will want to minimize those differences as much as possible. And once you reach the point of presenting your position, you will want to show the logic of your reasoning clearly to prevent confusion or doubt.

Finally, before you complete your presentation, you will want to convince your readers of your credibility and concern for their acceptance. This may take a combination of ethical and emotional appeal because you want them to have enough confidence in your argument to change their position.

Observe how Frank Trippett identifies a shared view of conditions with his audience before asserting his argument in the following essay from *Time* (1983).

A Red Light for Scofflaws

FRANK TRIPPETT

Law-and-order is the longest-running and probably the bestloved po- 1
litical issue in U.S. history. Yet it is painfully apparent that millions of
Americans who would never think of themselves as lawbreakers, let
alone criminals, are taking increasing liberties with the legal codes
that are designed to protect and nourish their society. Indeed, there
are moments today—amid outlaw litter, tax cheating, illicit noise, and
motorized anarchy—when it seems as though the scofflaw represents
the wave of the future. Harvard sociologist David Riesman suspects
that a majority of Americans have blithely taken to committing supposedly minor derelictions as a matter of course. Already, Riesman
says, the ethic of U.S. society is in danger of becoming this: "You're a
fool if you obey the rules."

Nothing could be more obvious than the evidence supporting 2
Riesman. Scofflaws abound in amazing variety. The graffiti-prone turn
public surfaces into visual rubbish. Bicyclists often ride as though two-
wheeled vehicles are exempt from all traffic laws. Litterbugs convert
their communities into trash dumps. Widespread flurries of ordinances
have failed to clear public places of high-decibel portable radios, just
as earlier laws failed to wipe out the beer-soaked hooliganism that
plagues many parks. Tobacco addicts remain hopelessly blind to signs
that say NO SMOKING. Respectably dressed pot smokers no longer
bother to duck out of public sight to pass around a joint. The flagrant
use of cocaine is a festering scandal in middle- and upper-class life.
And then there are (hello, Everybody!) the jaywalkers.

The dangers of scofflawry vary wildly. The person who illegally 3
spits on the sidewalk remains disgusting, but clearly poses less risk to
others than the company that illegally buries hazardous chemical
waste in an unauthorized location. The fare beater on the subway
presents less threat to life than the landlord who ignores fire safety
statutes. The most immediately and measurably dangerous scofflawry,
however, also happens to be the most visible. The culprit is the American driver, whose lawless activities today add up to a colossal public
nuisance. The hazards range from routine double parking that jams
city streets to the drunk driving that kills some 25,000 people and injures at least 650,000 others yearly. Illegal speeding on open highways?
New surveys show that on some interstate highways 83 percent of all
drivers are currently ignoring the federal 55 m.p.h. speed limit.

The most flagrant scofflaw of them all is the red-light runner. The 4
flouting of stop signals has got so bad in Boston that residents tell an

anecdote about a cabby who insists that red lights are "just for decoration." The power of the stoplight to control traffic seems to be waning everywhere. In Los Angeles, red-light running has become perhaps the city's most common traffic violation. In New York City, going through an intersection is like Russian roulette. Admits Police Commissioner Robert J. McGuire: "Today it's a 50-50 toss-up as to whether people will stop for a red light." Meanwhile, his own police largely ignore the lawbreaking.

Red-light running has always been ranked as a minor wrong, and 5 so it may be in individual instances. When the violation becomes habitual, widespread, and incessant, however, a great deal more than a traffic management problem is involved. The flouting of basic rules of the road leaves deep dents in the social mood. Innocent drivers and pedestrians pay a repetitive price in frustration, inconvenience, and outrage, not to mention a justified sense of mortal peril. The significance of red-light running is magnified by its high visibility. If hypocrisy is the tribute that vice pays to virtue, then furtiveness is the true outlaw's salute to the force of law-and-order. The red-light runner, however, shows no respect whatever for the social rules, and society cannot help being harmed by any repetitive and brazen display of contempt for the fundamentals of order.

The scofflaw spirit is pervasive. It is not really surprising when 6 schools find, as some do, that children frequently enter not knowing some of the basic rules of living together. For all their differences, today's scofflaws are of a piece as a symptom of elementary social demoralization—the loss by individuals of the capacity to govern their own behavior in the interest of others.

The prospect of the collapse of public manners is not merely a 7 matter of etiquette. Society's first concern will remain major crime, but a foretaste of the seriousness of incivility is suggested by what has been happening in Houston. Drivers on Houston freeways have been showing an increasing tendency to replace the rules of the road with violent outbreaks. Items from the Houston police department's new statistical category—freeway traffic violence: (1) Driver flashes high-beam lights at car that cut in front of him, whose occupants then hurl a beer can at his windshield, kick out his tail lights, slug him eight stitches' worth. (2) Dump-truck driver annoyed by delay batters trunk of stalled car ahead and its driver with steel bolt. (3) Hurrying driver of 18-wheel truck deliberately rear-ends car whose driver was trying to stay within 55 m.p.h. limit. The Houston Freeway Syndrome has fortunately not spread everywhere. But the question is: Will it?

Americans are used to thinking that law-and-order is threatened 8 mainly by stereotypical violent crime. When the foundations of U.S. law have actually been shaken, however, it has always been because ordinary law-abiding citizens took to skirting the law. Major instance:

Prohibition. Recalls Donald Barr Chidsey in *On and Off the Wagon:* "Lawbreaking proved to be not painful, not even uncomfortable, but, in a mild and perfectly safe way, exhilarating." People wiped out Prohibition at last not only because of the alcohol issue but because scofflawry was seriously undermining the authority and legitimacy of government. Ironically, today's scofflaw spirit, whatever its undetermined origins, is being encouraged unwittingly by government at many levels. The failure of police to enforce certain laws is only the surface of the problem; they take their mandate from the officials and constituents they serve. Worse, most state legislatures have helped subvert popular compliance with the federal 55 m.p.h. law, some of them by enacting puny fines that trivialize transgressions. On a higher level, the Administration in Washington has dramatized its wish to nullify civil rights laws simply by opposing instead of supporting certain court-ordered desegregation rulings. With considerable justification, environmental groups, in the words of *Wilderness* magazine, accuse the Administration of "destroying environmental laws by failing to enforce them, or by enforcing them in ways that deliberately encourage noncompliance." Translation: scofflawry at the top.

The most disquieting thing about the scofflaw spirit is its extreme 9 infectiousness. Only a terminally foolish society would sit still and allow it to spread indefinitely.

In the introduction to this article in *Time* (January 24, 1983) Frank Trippett clearly identifies the subject (law and order); his position ("it seems as though the scofflaw represents the wave of the future"); and the issue (Americans "are taking increasing liberties with the legal codes"), which includes the readers' connection to the issue. As readers of *Time*, the audience expects to be informed about current events that affect society, but they don't expect to be part of the problem. The author has avoided any direct blame by using the general term *Americans.* Even his identification of scofflaws in paragraph 2 evades reproach by naming the *doer* by the *deed:* "the graffiti-prone," "litterbugs," "tobacco addicts," "respectably dressed pot smokers." Not until his last example—the least criminal action—does the writer implicate the readers *and* himself as lawbreakers who contribute to the problem. The informality of the parenthetical expression "hello, Everybody!" to identify the lawbreaking jaywalkers involves the reader in a nonthreatening way. But at the same time it distinguishes the *condition* that separates the writer from the readers: the extent or level of danger the crime represents. The writer's challenge, then, is to convince the readers that even the smallest infraction of the law has meaningful consequences.

Trippett builds the logic of his argument inductively with examples of traffic violations (paragraphs 3–7) ranging from double parking, drunk driving, and speeding to running red lights. Why does he focus so much on red-light running, and why does he discuss it last? Like jaywalking, running red lights is an infraction most readers have experienced; they can understand the frustration it causes and its potential for danger. But Trippett takes the readers beyond what they already know to the point of his argument:

> **The red-light runner, however, shows no respect whatever for the social rules, and society cannot help being harmed by any repetitious and brazen display of contempt for the fundamentals of order.**

The line of reasoning then shifts to deductive as the writer supports the above generalization, which evolved from his inductive investigation, with a representative view of the effects on Houston drivers. The historical comparison and incidents of noncompliance at different governmental levels further develop and strengthen Trippett's thesis, both leading to the thought-provoking final appeal—the audience's need for a sense of well-being.

With logical appeal as the main force of this argument, the writer allows the conditions of the issue to evolve naturally to an understandable conclusion. And while he chooses not to be involved directly, the writer aligns himself with the audience as an American—part of a society at risk. This mutual concern produces an indirect but convincing ethical appeal.

UNCONDITIONALLY OPPOSED AUDIENCE

With this audience you face the challenge of a mental confrontation: your opinion versus theirs. And often these opinions evoke strong emotion. A comparison of your points of disagreement will help you narrow your focus, control the force of your emotions, and choose a strategy for your appeals. The R. J. Reynolds Tobacco Company demonstrates this point-by-point comparison in one of their ads (see Figure 1).

Obviously this advertisement is designed to produce an ethical appeal. What better way than to demonstrate that the company understands both points of view? An unconditionally opposed audience will expect the same respect from you. They will expect you to know what the issues are and why people favor or reject them *before* you present your objections. The appeal you choose to begin your essay should convey your understanding of both sides of the issue.

The R. J. Reynolds ad also demonstrates how two opposing points of view can merge into one shared concern. This is what you are searching for: a level of mutual understanding. The question is, Which point in your argument will best lead your audience to that understanding? That point will direct your choice of appeals. Do you have new research or evidence for them to consider (logical appeal)? Do you offer experience or expertise with which they are unfamiliar (ethical appeal)? Are you defining your terms differently (logical appeal)? Are there new consequences that threaten the opposition's well-being (emotional appeal)?

The ad in Figure 2 shows how R. J. Reynolds used the strategy of focusing on one main point in the argument that would lead to a mutual understanding on the issue with the audience.

Figure 1 *Comparison of points of disagreement*

A message from those who don't to those who do.

We're uncomfortable.

To us, the smoke from your cigarettes can be anything from a minor nuisance to a real annoyance.

We're frustrated.

Even though we've chosen not to smoke, we're exposed to second-hand smoke anyway.

We feel a little powerless.

Because you can invade our privacy without even trying. Often without noticing.

And sometimes when we speak up and let you know how we feel, you react as though *we* were the bad guys.

We're not fanatics. We're not out to deprive you of something you enjoy. We don't want to be your enemies.

We just wish you'd be more considerate and responsible about how, when, and where you smoke.

We know you've got rights and feelings. We just want you to respect our rights and feelings, as well.

A message from those who do to those who don't.

We're on the spot.

Smoking is something we consider to be a very personal choice, yet it's become a very public issue.

We're confused.

Smoking is something that gives us enjoyment, but it gives you offense.

We feel singled out.

We're doing something perfectly legal, yet we're often segregated, discriminated against, even legislated against.

Total strangers feel free to abuse us verbally in public without warning.

We're not criminals. We don't mean to bother or offend you. And we don't like confrontations with you.

We're just doing something we enjoy, and trying to understand your concerns.

We know you've got rights and feelings. We just want you to respect our rights and feelings, as well.

Brought to you in the interest of common courtesy by

R.J. Reynolds Tobacco Company

Even though this ad is not as fully developed as your argument will be, it follows the strategy needed to achieve a similar purpose—to convince the audience that the writer's is a worthy point of view. To accomplish this, the advertiser identifies immediately with the opponents' opinion by using a familiar line of dialogue. This one line evokes an emotional appeal in readers that responds, "I agree." The statements that follow demonstrate the advertiser's understanding of the issue from both points of view, producing a logical appeal and an ethical appeal; the writer is well informed and concerned. By line 5 the writer identifies the main point of the argument: social harmony. Thus, the first half of the ad uses all three appeals to identify with the audience, review the issues of the controversy, and identify the main point of the argument.

Figure 2 *Focus on mutual understanding*

The most inflammatory question of our time.

"Hey, would you put out that cigarette?"
Just seven little words. But in today's over-heated climate of opinion, they can make sparks fly.

For with all the rhetoric about "second-hand smoke," many non-smokers are beginning to feel not just bothered but threatened by cigarettes.

And with all the talk about anti-smoking legislation, many smokers are beginning to feel threatened by non-smokers.

This is not exactly a recipe for social harmony. In fact, it's practically a guarantee of further discord.

Since we have discussed scientific aspects of the "passive smoking" controversy in previous messages, we'd like to focus here on the social questions.

Will more confrontation or more segregation produce less abrasion? Do we solve anything by creating yet another way to divide our society? Shouldn't all of us be wary of inviting government to involve itself further in our private lives?

At R.J. Reynolds, we see an alternative.

We think we should start not by raising barriers, but by lowering our voices. We think smokers and non-smokers can work out their differences together, in a spirit of tolerance and fairness and respect for each other's rights and feelings. We think common courtesy can succeed where coercion is bound to fail.

And maybe, after we have learned peaceful coexistence by talking to each other civilly and sensibly, we can apply the same approach to our many other problems.

Because, after all, this is hardly the most inflammatory question of our time.

Brought to you in the interest of common courtesy by

R.J. Reynolds Tobacco Company

© 1985 R. J. REYNOLDS TOBACCO CO

The second half of the ad presents the advertiser's point of view. Notice how the use of *we* cleverly shifts in each of the remaining paragraphs. In paragraph 5 "we'd like to focus" refers to the company, while in paragraph 6 the "we solve," "our society," "us," and "our private lives" refer to society in general—the merging of the writer and the audience. This shift in the meaning of *we* continues in the next three paragraphs in hopes of strengthening the company's ethical appeal.

By the end of the ad the writer has used logical appeal (constitutional rights), emotional appeal (tolerance, fairness, and respect; courtesy and success), and ethical appeal (*we* are concerned) to persuade readers to consider a seldom addressed part of the issue: the process of solving problems. Using this focus and arrangement, the writer avoids direct confrontation with the readers' opposing views and relies on their desire for social harmony to reach agreement. Thus the advertiser has succeeded in reaching a mutual understanding with the audience on the point of social harmony, but whether this agreement will affect their opinion on the smoking issue is highly debatable.

Unconditionally opposed readers are not likely to change their opinion easily. Their logical and emotional commitment to their view is reflected in their actions as well as their thoughts. This strong commitment can produce a stubbornness that creates problems with tone for the writer. When you think about many of the face-to-face arguments you have witnessed, you quickly realize that shouting louder or using more insults doesn't change minds. The same holds true for presenting a written argument. Because the audience is already skeptical of your point of view, the tone you use needs to convey your trustworthiness and that of your material. Attempts to be too assertive or overly sentimental more than likely will undermine the audience's confidence in you and your message. The more reasonable your tone, the more willing your audience will be to listen to your views. (For more help in planning an argument for this audience, read the section on Rogerian argument in Chapter 9.)

While each of the three categories of opposition requires that specific needs be met by your choice of appeals, all three audiences also have common needs.

1. Readers need to have the problem clearly identified.
2. Readers need to understand their connection to the problem.
3. Readers need to know the reasoning that informs an opinion.
4. Readers need to have confidence in the writer.

Meeting these needs with your choice of appeals can mean many different arrangement strategies, as the reading selections in this chapter have demonstrated. Some of the most common strategies are these:

A. The closest point of agreement with your audience

to

The point of view that separates you from your audience

B. The information most familiar to your audience

to

The information least familiar to your audience

C. The most common everyday sources of information

to

The most authoritative sources of information

D. The history or background of the problem

to

The thesis or conclusion of the writer

E. A chronology of the writer's discovery of the problem

to

The writer's thesis or conclusion

F. The physiological needs of the audience

to

The intellectual needs of the audience

to

The psychological needs of the audience

Applying these strategies to the rhetorical context for your argument can help you discover which arrangement will most effectively reach your audience and lead them from the beginning to the end of your argument. Don't be surprised if you need to try several strategies or combine a few before deciding on a plan that works best for you and your audience.

Figure 3 *Essay plan*

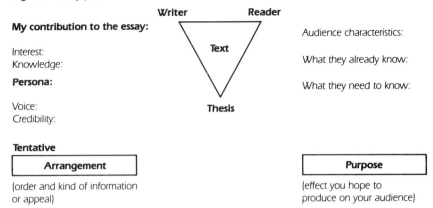

My contribution to the essay:

Interest:
Knowledge:

Persona:

Voice:
Credibility:

Audience characteristics:

What they already know:

What they need to know:

Tentative

Arrangement

(order and kind of information
or appeal)

Purpose

(effect you hope to
produce on your audience)

Once you do choose a strategy for arranging your appeals, you might find that preparing a tentative essay plan can guide you when you begin composing. The essay plan in Figure 3 includes the features of the rhetorical context to be analyzed and the arrangement you choose to achieve your purpose.

EXERCISES: USING APPEALS

1. For each of the issues listed after the example, identify a specific audience representative of each distance level of opposition: undecided, conditionally opposed, and unconditionally opposed.

> *Example:* X-rated cable television stations broadcasting in your local community
>
> **Undecided:** Lawyers, city council members
>
> **Conditionally Opposed:** Parents with children under 17
>
> **Unconditionally Opposed:** Religious groups
>
> **ISSUES:** 1. Censoring rock music albums
>
> 2. Allowing women to enter the priesthood
>
> 3. Requiring computer literacy programs in high school
>
> 4. Raising the driver's license age to 18
>
> 5. Paying a copyright fee for blank videocassettes

2. The logical, ethical, and emotional appeals can be used to present any issue. For each issue listed after the example, identify *two* sources or means of presenting *each appeal* in relation to the issue.

> *Example:* Increasing historical preservation projects:

LOGICAL APPEAL

1. Examples of famous sites that have been preserved
2. Statistics showing increase in tourism revenue from visits to historical sites

ETHICAL APPEAL

1. Personal visit to the art deco district and architectural tours of several cities
2. Use of *we* to merge writer and reader as *society*, as beneficiaries

EMOTIONAL APPEAL

1. Pride
2. Legacy to future generations

ISSUES: 1. The need for regular exercise
2. The development of birth control pills for men
3. Restricting the sale of foreign imports in the U.S.
4. Subject of your choice

3. Using one of the rhetorical contexts outlined after the example or one of your own design, explore the arrangement possibilities using *at least three* of strategies A–F presented earlier in this chapter.

Example: Rhetorical Context

Issue: Increasing the use of carpooling lanes on the expressway
Audience: College student commuters
Purpose: To convince them of the educational value of carpooling

a. *Chronology of my discovery of the problem*

A typical frustrating drive to and from campus, including problems with parking
Freshman year commuting alone, effects on work and morale
Sophomore year commuting alone, effects on work, morale, and car maintenance
Junior year of carpooling, change in effects on work and morale
Anticipation of effects culminating at end of senior year
Thesis/Conclusion

b. *The most common everyday sources of information*

Survey and testimony of commuter students' views
Personal experience of commuting alone and carpooling

The most authoritative sources of information

Testimony of business people and future employers who carpool daily
Testimony of insurance company officials (lower rates?)
Testimony of Environmental Protection Agency officials (effect of fewer cars on the road on protecting the environment)

c. *The closest point of agreement with my audience*

Need to express independence
Work schedule problems
Need to have choices

The point that separates me from my audience

Informed use of choices, changing life-style, making a commitment to studying
and to the environment

RHETORICAL CONTEXT CHOICES:

A. ISSUE: Use of herbal medicine
   AUDIENCE: General public who use conventional medicine
   PURPOSE: To convince the public that herbal medicine offers a healthier
   alternative to conventional medicine

B. ISSUE: Volunteering to work with community programs
   AUDIENCE: General age group, local college students
   PURPOSE: To convince them that volunteer community service should
   be a required part of the curriculum

C. ISSUE: Drug testing on job interviews
   AUDIENCE: Employers
   PURPOSE: To convince them that drug testing should not be used un-
   less reasonable cause is established

D. Design your own rhetorical context

WRITING SUGGESTION

Write an argumentative essay using one of the plans you generated for the rhetorical
context you selected in exercise 3.

PART IV

Composing

B y its very nature, composing is where your discoveries, investigations, and analysis come together. But determining how everything comes together requires more discovery and experimentation before the argument takes its final shape.

Shaping begins with the writing of your first draft, the point where your decision making assumes a different set of priorities. In the earlier stages of building your argument you worked from the inside, discovering a personal association with an idea, to the outside, finding support and an audience for that idea. In the composing stage the direction reverses as you take all that you know about your subject and audience and design a manageable internal path for your material that will lead the readers to a new understanding. After experimenting with the overall shape of your reasoning from the first paragraph to the last, your next priority is the shape of your language: Are your words chosen carefully enough to produce the effect you intend on the reader? Are your sources documented accurately to ensure your credibility?

Composing takes a willingness to make new discoveries and a great deal of time to act on those discoveries—to "re-see" the issue in yet another new way, to re-investigate sources, to re-analyze, to re-plan, to re-word until the shape of the argument's written form conveys your thoughts precisely as you experience them. As the English author and critic Samuel Johnson reminded us:

> What is written without effort is generally read
> without pleasure.

Chapter 9

SHAPING YOUR ARGUMENT

Composing your ideas, research, experience, and opinions into a coherent shape requires several decisions. The exploration you did with arranging appeals at the planning stage provides a tentative outline—the possibility of *how* to compose your argument. But composing is more than following an outline. Composing means shaping your thoughts at each point so that the *why* of your argument clearly reaches your readers.

The infinite number of writer-audience-subject combinations makes it virtually impossible to use a single structure to shape an argument. There are approaches, however, whose principles will guide you in deciding which shape is most effective for your context. In some cases these approaches will provide just the shape you need, but the primary direction they offer is a way to test the thinking that informs your argument.

CLASSICAL STRUCTURE

From the history of argument as used in public debate or in courts of law evolved a formal structure organized by the *functions* of the various parts of a discourse. This structure helped citizens who had to represent themselves in the courts of ancient Greece and Rome to move from the emotional level of "I want this land" to the rational level of "This is why I should be granted this land." This principle of emphasizing the objective or logical over the subjective or emotional remains the center of argumentation today, as do many features of the classical structure. The basic formal structure includes five parts, each with a corresponding function.

The **introduction** has two primary functions: (1) to present the object or thesis of the argument, and (2) to prepare the reader to receive the argument and accept the subject as worthy.

The **statement of fact** informs or reminds the readers of the facts and past events that need to be known about the subject before considering the argument.

In the **confirmation** the writer presents the main argument and proof to substantiate the thesis. This is the central and longest part of the discourse.

The **refutation** anticipates and answers any objections the readers have to the thesis of the argument.

The **conclusion** brings a meaningful end to the discourse.

The functions of each part of the formal structure remain important to reaching an audience with your argument: no matter what the occasion or who the audience, you still must state your case and prove it. But while the classical arrangement just listed might fit the needs of some deductive arguments the *sequence* of the parts will need adjusting for each particular context. In fact, you will probably discover unique ways of merging the sections to achieve your purpose. The merging and repositioning of this backbone structure shape your argument. And the shaping conveys the substance and meaning.

Here are some strategies and methods classical rhetoricians and modern writers use to adapt the formal structure to their needs. In each case the adjustments reflect a conscientious attention to what the audience already knows and what it needs to know.

INTRODUCTION

Introductions are generally just long enough to connect the readers to the subject. Gaining their attention and establishing the worthiness of your subject can be done in several ways.

Using a Question. If you want to involve your readers immediately in the discourse, beginning with a well-designed question is an effective means of starting a dialogue. A question stimulates the need for an answer; it propels your audience forward to discover your answer and encourages them to be inquisitive about the subject. In her article "Demise of a Daily: Why It Matters" in the *Christian Science Monitor* (February 25, 1988), Eugenie Dickerson uses two questions framed to represent what she assumes is the audience's attitude toward the subject. This close identification with readers encourages them to read further to discover the answers.

> So what if another newspaper goes out of business? What does it matter as long as it wasn't the paper I read?

Using a Quotation. The punctuation of quotations signals the readers that something significant is being said. A well-chosen quotation not only gains immediate attention, it also sets the tone for the argument. A statement from a well-known authority in support of your view contributes to the credibility of your opinion and gains the respect of your readers. Likewise, a quotation representing the opposing viewpoint can be used to evoke the audience's understanding of the need for refutation.

In the introduction to his article "In Search of Public Servants," reprinted in Chapter 7, L. Bruce Laingen uses a familiar quote from John F. Kennedy's inaugural address to introduce the focus of his issue while setting a tone of mutual understanding and respect with his audience.

> "Ask not what your country can do for you; ask what you can do for your country." Eloquent words from an earlier time, words that still speak to us, whatever our political preference, of what constructive patriotism is all about—especially for our young people.

Laingen uses the quotation to make a significant connection with the readers and the subject, a connection that starts them thinking about the issue in a specific way. If you choose to use a quotation, make certain that it establishes that connection.

Using an Anecdote.   Anecdotes come in several forms, including personal experience, current event, hypothetical scenario, and case study. Each has the advantage of illustrating your issue in action. And, as a narrative form with a beginning, a middle, and an end, an anecdote includes the cause-and-effect relationships necessary to your thesis. Writers often use anecdotes to involve readers on an emotional level, to arouse their concern for the issue.

In his essay "A Holocaust of Words" (*Time*, May 2, 1988), Lance Morrow recounts an event and its aftermath to evoke a concern and a viewpoint he wants the reader to use throughout the essay.

A Holocaust of Words

LANCE MORROW

The library in Leningrad burned for a night and a day. By the time the   1
fire was out at the National Academy of Sciences, 400,000 books had been incinerated. An additional 3.6 million had been damaged by water. In the weeks since the fire, workmen have been shoveling blackened remains of books into trash bins and hanging the sodden survivors on lines to dry in front of enormous electric fans.

The mind cracks a little in contemplating a holocaust of words.   2
No one died in the fire. And yet whenever books burn, one is haunted by a sense of mourning. For books are not inanimate objects, not really, and the death of books, especially by fire, especially in such numbers, has the power of a kind of tragedy. Books are life-forms, children of the mind. Words (in the beginning was the Word) have about them some of the mystery of creation.

Russians have always loved their books profoundly. Literature   3 has sometimes sustained the Russians when almost everything else was gone. During the siege of Leningrad, the city's population, frozen and starving down to the verge of cannibalism, drew strength by listening to a team of poets as they read on the radio from the works of Pushkin and other writers. "Never before nor ever in the future," said a survivor, "will people listen to poetry as did Leningrad in that winter—hungry, swollen and hardly living." Today Russians will fill a stadium to hear a poetry reading.

There is of course some irony in the Russian passion for books. 4 Knowing the power of written words, Russian authority has for centuries accorded books the brutal compliment of suppression. It has slain books by other means than fire. Book publishing first flourished in Russia under Catherine the Great, and yet it was she who used local police, corrupt and ignorant, to enforce the country's first censorship regulations. Czar Nicholas I conducted a sort of terrorism against certain books and writers. He functioned as personal censor for Pushkin and banished Dostoyevsky to Siberia. Revolution only encouraged the Russian candle-snuffers. Lenin said, "Ideas are much more fatal things than guns," a founder's *nihil obstat* that culminated in the years of poet destruction (Osip Mandelstam, Marina Tsvetaeva) and book murder under Stalin.

For generations of Russians, books have been surrounded by ex- 5 altation and tragedy. In a prison camp in the Gulag during the 1960s, the poet and essayist Andrei Sinyavsky hid hand-copied pages of the *Book of Revelations* in the calf of his boot. He wrote, "What is the most precious, the most exciting smell waiting for you in the house when you return to it after half a dozen years or so? The smell of roses, you think? No, mouldering books."

Vladimir Nabokov carried his love of Russian into exile: "Beyond 6 the seas where I have lost a sceptre,/ I hear the neighing of my dappled nouns./ Soft participles coming down the steps,/ Treading on leaves, trailing their rustling gowns . . ."

Americans don't take books that seriously anymore. Perhaps 7 Russians don't either; their popular culture has begun to succumb to television. In America one rarely encounters the mystical book worship. Everything in the West today seems infinitely replicable, by computer, microfilm, somehow, so that if a book chances to burn up, there must be thousands more where that came from. If anything, there seem to be entirely too many words and numbers in circulation, too many sinister records of everything crammed into the microchips of FBI, IRS, police departments. Too many books altogether, perhaps. The glut of books subverts a reverence for them. Bookstore tables groan under the piles of remaindered volumes. In the U.S. more than 50,000 new titles are published every year. Forests cry out in despair that they are being scythed so that the works of Jackie Collins might live.

It was the Dominican zealot Girolamo Savonarola who presided 8
over the Bonfire of the Vanities during Carnival in Florence in 1497.
Thousands of the Florentine children who were Savonarola's followers
went through the city collecting what they deemed to be lewd books,
as well as pictures, lutes, playing cards, mirrors and other vanities, and
piled them in the great Piazza della Signoria of Florence. The pyramid
of offending objects rose 60 feet high, and went up in flames. One year
later Savonarola had a political quarrel with Pope Alexander VI, was
excommunicated, tried and hanged. His body was burned at the stake.
Savonarola went up in smoke.

The Leningrad library fire was a natural disaster. Deliberate book 9
burning seems not only criminal but evil. Why? Is it worse to destroy
a book by burning it than to throw it into the trash compactor? Or
to shred it? Not in effect. But somehow the irrevocable reduction of
words to smoke and, poof!, into nonentity haunts the imagination. In
Hitler's bonfires in 1933, the works of Kafka, Freud, Einstein, Zola and
Proust were incinerated—their smoke a prefiguration of the terrible
clouds that came from the Nazi chimneys later.

Anyone who loves books knows how hard it is to throw even one 10
of them away, even one that is silly or stupid or vicious and full of lies.
How much more criminal, how much more a sin against consciousness, to burn a book. A question then: What if one were to gather from
the corners of the earth all the existing copies of *Mein Kampf* and
make a bonfire of them? Would that be an act of virtue? Or of evil?

Sometimes it seems that the right books never get burnt. But the 11
world has its quota of idiotic and vicious people just as it has its supplies of books that are vicious, trashy and witless. Books can eventually
be as mortal as people—the acids in the paper eat them, the bindings
decay and at last they crumble in one's hands. But their ambition anyway is to outlast the flesh. Books have a kind of enshrining counterlife.
One can live with the thought of one's own death. It is the thought of
the death of words and books that is terrifying. For that is the deeper
extinction.

One problem with using anecdotes is their length. The longer the anecdote, the more
willing your audience must be to wait for the significant point. Another problem is familiarity with the subject. If the audience already has firsthand experience with the subject, then an anecdote is not needed to illustrate the problem.

Using a Thesis Statement. When you begin with your thesis statement,
you assume that the audience is already interested in the subject. These readers are
seeking information on the subject and want to know as soon as possible what you
plan to present. In the introduction to his article "Let's Go to the Videotape, Tolstoy"

(March 6, 1988), Anatole Broyard, an editor of the *New York Times Book Review,* assumes a personal relationship with readers in opening with his thesis.

> After watching the Super Bowl on television, I realized that what modern fiction needs is instant replay. Instant replay is more than a video technique: it's an epiphany, the moment of truth caught, held and made accessible. Until the 20th century, people had only one look, but art is so ambiguous now that the single look won't do. The single look is what Willem de Kooning called "a slipping glimpse." Even Baudelaire said, "I have seen everything twice," but we don't know how he did it.

When your readers already know a great deal about the subject and when you are certain that your opinion provides an ethical appeal to your readers, you can effectively begin your argument with your thesis. If your audience is not familiar with the subject, such a beginning can be too abrupt.

STATEMENT OF FACT

The statement of fact can often be successfully merged with the introduction. This is especially true when your audience is already familiar with the subject and needs only to be reminded of the facts. A combination of your thesis and a brief review of the circumstances that led to the controversy being discussed can accomplish the functions of both parts of discourse.

This introductory paragraph from "The Myth of a Post-Industrial Recovery" (May 17, 1987), was written for the readers of *The New York Times* business section, an audience quite knowledgeable about the trends and policies that affect our economy. The writers, Stephen S. Cohen and John Zysman, rely on that knowledge in the historical references they review before stating their thesis.

> In the 1960's, when Americans still looked to the future with unbounded optimism, analysts such as Daniel Bell and, later on, popularizers such as Alvin Toffler, confidently predicted an imminent and historic transition from a dirty and dank industrial era to a lean, clean information age—the post-industrial economy. Today, that vision has become the accepted wisdom that guides policy. But it is guiding policy the wrong way.

Other audiences who are equally knowledgeable about a subject might need an expanded review of the facts or a summary of the history of the idea. When you plan on using several theories as the basis for your argument or when the development of the issue needs to be viewed from a new angle, you can expand this section to meet the needs of your purpose.

Pulitzer Prize-winning historian and biographer Arthur M. Schlesinger, Jr., uses this approach in his article "The Challenge of Change," from the *New York Times Magazine* (July 27, 1986). Given the author's credentials, you expect him to present a historical overview, but on careful examination you can see that he has selected events that dramatize the way he expects the readers to view change in relation to his thesis in paragraph 7.

The Challenge of Change

ARTHUR M. SCHLESINGER, JR.

The last three centuries have seen dazzling revolutions in scientific theory and dazzling advances in the translation of theory into technology. This cumulative increase in the rate of change has been the decisive factor in the making of the modern world. The world has moved faster than ever before, and until recently it has moved fastest of all in the United States.

The American Revolution and the Industrial Revolution began at about the same time. From the start, Americans have rejoiced in unremitting technological change. Innovation was unrestrained by custom or tradition or timidity. "I simply experiment," said Ralph Waldo Emerson, the quintessential American, "an endless seeker with no Past at my back." It is hardly surprising that the first historian to emphasize the accelerating velocity of history should have been an American. "The world did not double or treble its movement between 1800 and 1900," Henry Adams wrote in 1909, "but, measured by any standard known to science—by horsepower, calories, volts, mass in any shape—the tension and vibration and volume and so-called progression of society were fully a thousand times greater in 1900 than in 1800." Acceleration left man and mind far behind. Adams's own education, the best an American could get in the 19th century, was, he concluded in the early 20th century, a total waste; the Harvard freshman he was in 1854 probably stood nearer to the thought of the year 1 than to that of the year 1904. "The law of acceleration," Adams said, "definite and constant as any law of mechanics, cannot be supposed to relax its energy to suit the convenience of man."

Adams's appeal to scientific law was both romantic and ironic. His notion that history could be reduced to mathematical physics was a delusion, or perhaps an elaborate joke. Still, as metaphor, his point is powerful. William James, who patiently explained to Adams why the second law of thermodynamics did not apply to history, agreed that humanity had experienced only the most preliminary impact of science and technology. "Think how many absolutely new scientific conceptions have arisen in our own generation," he wrote, "how many new problems have been formulated that were never thought of before, and then cast an eye upon the brevity of science's career. . . . Is it credible that such a mushroom knowledge, such a growth overnight as this *can* represent more than the minutest glimpse of what the universe will really prove to be when adequately understood? No! our science is a drop, our ignorance a sea."

Humans have lived on earth for possibly 800 lifetimes, most of 4 which they spent in caves. "Some five or six score people," James said, "if each . . . could speak for his own generation, would carry us away to the black unknown of the human species, to days without a document or monument to tell their tale." Movable type appeared only eight lifetimes ago, industrialization in the last three lifetimes. The static societies that consumed most of human history perceived no great difference between present and past. Society subsisted on the existing stock of wisdom for a long time. The functional need for new ideas was limited. Tradition was sacred and controlling.

The last two lifetimes have seen more scientific and technologi- 5 cal achievement than the first 798 put together. The shift to a swiftly changing society has not greatly affected the surfaces of daily living. The New York of the 1980's resembles the New York of the 1930's more than the New York of the 1930's resembles the New York of the 1880's. But the shift has profoundly altered inner perceptions and expectations. It has placed traditional roles and institutions under severe and incomprehensible strain. It has cast off reference points and rituals that had stabilized and sanctified life for generations. It has left the experience of elders useless to the tribulations of the young. Children, knowing how different their own lives will be, no longer look to parents as models and authorities; rather, parents now learn from their children.

The pace of change grows ever faster. A boy who saw the Wright 6 brothers fly for a few seconds at Kitty Hawk in 1903 could have watched Apollo 11 land on the moon in 1969. The first rockets were launched in the 1920's; today, astronauts roam outer space. The first electronic computer was built in 1946; today, the world rushes from the mechanical into the electronic age. The double helix was first unveiled in 1953; today, biotechnology threatens to remake mankind. The first atomic bomb fell in 1945; today, the world shudders under the threat of nuclear obliteration.

The acceleration of change compels us to perceive life as motion, 7 not as order; the universe not as complete, but as unfinished. For people of buoyant courage, like William James, the prospect was exhilarating. Henry Adams saw change as irreversible, but contemplated the future with foreboding. Others, in the midst of flounder and flux, strive to resurrect the old ways.

The hunger for stability is entirely natural. Change is scary; un-   8
charted change, demoralizing. If the law of acceleration is not to spin
the world out of control, society must cherish its lifelines into the past.
That is why, even in this age of whirl, so much of the old abides. People
instinctively defend the self against disruption. "In this matter of belief," said James, "we are all extreme conservatives." When new facts
finally drive out old opinions, we take care to graft the new perception
on the ancient stock with "a minimum of jolt, a maximum of continuity." Everyone becomes his own Landmarks Preservation Commission.
We seek with T. S. Eliot the still point in the turning world.

Traditions endure, from which, consciously or not, we draw sus-   9
tenance. It is not fashionable these days for historians to talk about
"national character." But of course persisting traits, values, folkways,
create a palpable national identity. The reader of Alexis de Tocqueville
is constantly astonished to recognize the lineaments of modern America in his great work, though Tocqueville visited a predominantly agricultural nation of 13 million people a century and a half ago. Even
J. Hector St. John de Crèvecoeur still astonishes by the contemporane-
ity of his 18th-century answer to his own famous question: "What then
is the American, this new man?"

"*He* is an American, who, leaving behind him all his ancient 10
prejudices and manners, receives new ones from the new mode of life
he has embraced, the new government he obeys, and the new rank he
holds. . . . Here individuals of all nations are melted into a new race of
men, whose labours and posterity will one day cause great changes in
the world. Americans are the western pilgrims, who are carrying with
them that great mass of arts, sciences, vigour, and industry which began long since in the east; they will finish the great circle. . . . The
American is a new man, who acts upon new principles; he must therefore entertain new ideas, and form new opinions."

The law of acceleration hurtles us into the inscrutable future. But 11
it cannot wipe clean the slate of the past. History haunts even generations who refuse to learn history. Rhythms, patterns, continuities, drift
out of time long forgotten to mold the present and to color the shape
of things to come. Science and technology revolutionize our lives, but
memory, tradition and myth frame our response. Expelled from individual consciousness by the rush of change, history finds its revenge
by stamping the collective unconscious with habits, values, expectations, dreams. The dialectic between past and future will continue to
form our lives.

These reflections are not presented in any confidence that his- 12
tory is the cure for all that ails us. Still, the past helps explain where we
are today and how we got there. Knowledge of what Americans have
been through in earlier times will do us no harm as we grope through

the darkness of our own days. During the Soviet blockade of Berlin in 1948, when forebodings of a third World War swept Washington, a young assistant secretary exclaimed to Secretary of State George C. Marshall at a panicky staff meeting, "How in the world can you remain so calm during this appalling crisis?" Marshall replied, calmly, "I've seen worse."

Americans have indeed seen worse. History, by putting crisis in perspective, supplies the antidote to every generation's illusion that its own problems are uniquely oppressive. Troubles impending always seem worse than troubles surmounted, but this does not prove that they really are. Nuclear weapons excepted, the problems of the 1980's are modest compared to the problems that confronted George Washington's generation in achieving independence and fashioning a free state, or to the problems that confronted Abraham Lincoln's generation in bringing the Republic through the glare of civil war, or to the problems that confronted Franklin Roosevelt's generation in surviving the worst depression and winning the greatest war in American history. "So hot? my little Sir," said Emerson, warning us not to mistake the sound of a popgun for the crack of doom. 13

Nuclear weapons, however, are the fatal exception. They introduce a qualitatively new factor into the historical process. For the first time in the life of humanity, the crack of doom becomes a realistic possibility. So history embraces discontinuity as well as continuity. Knowledge of the past should inoculate against hysteria but should not instill complacency. History walks on a knife edge. 14

No one knew the risks of history better than Henry Adams. Humanity, Adams well understood, had been subjected to a succession of technological shocks, each of which by itself would have taken decades to digest and control. Every shock increased the velocity of history. The nuclear shock threatens the end of history. "Man has mounted science and is now run away with," Adams wrote to his brother on 11 April 1862, a few days after the Battle of Shiloh, while the Monitor and the Merrimack were maneuvering around Newport News. "I firmly believe that before many centuries more, science will be the master of man. The engines he will have invented will be beyond his strength to control. Some day science shall have the existence of mankind in its power, and the human race commit suicide by blowing up the world." 15

To decide how long your statement of fact section needs to be and whether to merge it with your introduction, you will need a clear sense of what your audience already knows about the subject and how they view the issue in relation to your thesis. The more relevant the information, the more concern you will establish in the reader.

CONFIRMATION AND REFUTATION

You have even greater flexibility in positioning the *confirmation* and *refutation* parts of your discourse. The strategy you choose will depend on the opposition level of your audience. If the audience is undecided, you might choose to follow the formal structure by presenting your case first, followed by a refutation of the objections you anticipate in your readers and opponents. This strategy is used frequently to present the solution to the problem before the readers can identify their objections.

Mark Kleiman, a research fellow at Harvard University in 1985 when he wrote the article "Grant Bachelor's Degrees by Examination," uses this strategy in addressing his proposal to the readers of the *Wall Street Journal* (September 6, 1985). He knows that his readers are well educated and more than likely will have objections to his proposal. But because they do *not* know his arguments *for* the proposal, he presents those arguments first, then answers the objections he anticipates.

Grant Bachelor's Degrees by Examination

MARK KLEIMAN

Colleges and universities offer their undergraduate students two distinct commodities: an education (or rather the opportunity for one) and a degree. The offer is what antitrust lawyers call a "tie sale": They won't sell you the diplomas unless you buy the whole package.

As fall approaches and parents dig into their pockets (or apply to their banks) for the $15,000 a year it now costs to send a child to a "prestige" institution such as the one where I work, it's time to ask why the education-and-degree package shouldn't be unbundled. If a student can achieve on his own, and demonstrate to the faculty, knowledge and competence higher than, say, the median of a school's graduating class, why shouldn't he be able to buy a certificate testifying as much?

Such a certificate—a B.A. by examination—would qualify its holder for employment, or for graduate or professional study, without costing him four years of forgone earnings plus the cash price of a small house.

Rather than thinking of this proposal as unbundling credential-granting from education, one might prefer to consider it as substituting a performance standard for a technical-specification standard in the award of degrees.

There are three arguments for such a proposal. 5

First, it would save resources. 6

Second, it would make a valuable credential available to some 7 who cannot now afford it, thus contributing to social mobility. (In addition to those earning their first degrees in this way, B.A.-by-exam programs at high-prestige schools might attract students who feel, often correctly, that their obscure sheepskins are holding them back.)

Third, and more speculatively, it might free high-powered but un- 8 conventional high-school graduates to pursue a self-education more useful to them than any pre-packaged education, without shutting themselves out of jobs and advanced-degree programs.

There are two obvious objections. Those who took their B.A.s by 9 examination might miss out on the opportunities college provides for social interaction and other forms of personal and intellectual development. It might also be said that, since no examination could capture the richness of an undergraduate education, B.A.s by exam would have incentives to become, and would in fact be, narrower and shallower than their eight-semester-in-residence counterparts.

The first objection is probably true but not conclusive. Some who 10 would choose the exam route over the regular undergraduate course would probably be wise not to buy the nonacademic attributes of college for four years' income plus $60,000; others will not, in fact, choose the more expensive option, even if it is the only one offered.

To the second objection there are two solutions: high standards 11 and resource-intensive examinations. A process lasting a month and costing $3,000 to administer and score, testing both general knowledge and competence in a major field, and involving written, oral and practical components and the preparation of a thesis or the equivalent should suffice to evaluate breadth and depth at least as well as the current system does. The interests of the group running an examinator program would run parallel with those of the rest of the institution in keeping standards high, and the social and moral pressure to award degrees in borderline cases ought to be much less for exam students than for ordinary undergraduates. By setting standards for examination B.A.s above the median of the eight-semester graduates, an institution could ensure that the exam program raised the average educational level of its degree-holders.

The price to candidates could reflect fully loaded cost plus a sub- 12 stantial contribution to overhead and still look like a bargain. To deal with the unwillingness of potential candidates to gamble several thousand dollars on their chances of success, it might make sense to administer a fairly cheap ($200) screening test and give anyone who passed a money-back guarantee on the more thorough (and expensive) degree exam. The failure rate could be built into the price, or some insurance company might be willing to administer the screening test and sell failure insurance.

The proposal should not be confused with college credit for "life 13 experience," "urban semesters" or other moves to substitute the pragmatic for the scholarly in undergraduate education. The point is to tie the degree more rather than less tightly to specific academic competence, to certify the result—an educated person—rather than the process leading to that result.

If this idea required a consensus in order to be tried out, it would 14 never stand a chance. Fortunately, no such consensus is needed. All it takes is one undeniably first-rate institution willing to break the credential cartel.

If the audience is clearly opposed from the outset, you can consider using two strategies. First, by acknowledging the opposing viewpoint *before* presenting your argument, you can attempt to clear the air and find a common ground for acceptance of your own views. However, if the opposing arguments are particularly strong, you could be more effective by delaying your refutation, or using the second strategy: order the points of your argument by the objections you anticipate your audience will have. In this way, you merge the two sections in an attempt to reach a reasonable understanding. This strategy seeks to keep the reader with the writer at each point of development.

The newspaper column that follows, "Why Women Are Paid Less Than Men," has been reprinted many times since it first appeared in the *New York Times* in March 1981. Its author, Lester C. Thurow, a professor of economics, argues his thesis by merging the confirmation with the refutation. As you read, keep a list of each cause he discusses and refutes before he presents his main argument in paragraphs 13–17.

Why Women Are Paid Less Than Men

LESTER C. THUROW

In the 40 years from 1939 to 1979 white women who work full time 1 have with monotonous regularity made slightly less than 60 percent as much as white men. Why?

Over the same time period, minorities have made substantial 2 progress in catching up with whites, with minority women making even more progress than minority men.

Black men now earn 72 percent as much as white men (up 16 per- 3 centage points since the mid-1950's) but black women earn 92 percent as much as white women. Hispanic men make 71 percent of what their white counterparts do, but Hispanic women make 82 percent as much as white women. As a result of their faster progress, fully employed black women make 75 percent as much as fully employed black men while Hispanic women earn 68 percent as much as Hispanic men.

This faster progress may, however, end when minority women fi- 4 nally catch up with white women. In the bible of the New Right, George Gilder's "Wealth and Poverty," the 60 percent is just one of Mother Nature's constants like the speed of light or the force of gravity.

Men are programmed to provide for their families economically 5 while women are programmed to provide for their families emotionally and physically. As a result men put more effort into their jobs than women. The net result is a difference in work intensity that leads to that 40 percent gap in earnings. But there is no discrimination against women—only the biological facts of life.

The problem with this assertion is just that. It is an assertion 6 with no evidence for it other than the fact that white women have made 60 percent as much as men for a long period of time.

"Discrimination against women" is an easy answer but it also has 7 its problems as an adequate explanation. Why is discrimination against women not declining under the same social forces that are leading to a lessening of discrimination against minorities? In recent years women have made more use of the enforcement provisions of the Equal Employment Opportunities Commission and the courts than minorities. Why do the laws that prohibit discrimination against women and minorities work for minorities but not for women?

When men discriminate against women, they run into a prob- 8 lem. To discriminate against women is to discriminate against your own wife and to lower your own family income. To prevent women from working is to force men to work more.

When whites discriminate against blacks, they can at least think 9 that they are raising their own incomes. When men discriminate against women they have to know that they are lowering their own family income and increasing their own work effort.

While discrimination undoubtedly explains part of the male- 10 female earnings differential, one has to believe that men are monumentally stupid or irrational to explain all of the earnings gap in terms of discrimination. There must be something else going on.

Back in 1939 it was possible to attribute the earnings gap to large 11 differences in educational attainments. But the educational gap between men and women has been eliminated since World War II. It is no longer possible to use education as an explanation for the lower earnings of women.

Some observers have argued that women earn less money since 12 they are less reliable workers who are more apt to leave the labor force. But it is difficult to maintain this position since women are less apt to quit one job to take another and as a result they tend to work as long, or longer, for any one employer. From any employer's perspective they are more reliable, not less reliable, than men.

Part of the answer is visible if you look at the lifetime earnings 13 profile of 25-year-olds would become economically successful. At age 25 it is difficult to tell who will be economically successful and your predictions are apt to be highly inaccurate.

But suppose that you were asked to predict which men in a 14 group of 35-year-olds would become economically successful. If you are successful at age 35, you are very likely to remain successful for the rest of your life. If you have not become economically successful by age 35, you are very unlikely to do so later.

The decade between 25 and 35 is when men either succeed or 15 fail. It is the decade when lawyers become partners in the good firms, when business managers make it onto the "fast track," when academics get tenure at good universities, and when blue collar workers find the job opportunities that will lead to training opportunities and the skills that will generate high earnings.

If there is any one decade when it pays to work hard and to be 16 consistently in the labor force, it is the decade between 25 and 35. For those who succeed, earnings will rise rapidly. For those who fail, earnings will remain flat for the rest of their lives.

But the decade between 25 and 35 is precisely the decade when 17 women are most apt to leave the labor force or become part-time workers to have children. When they do, the current system of promotion and skill acquisition will extract an enormous lifetime price. This leaves essentially two avenues for equalizing male and female earnings.

Families where women who wish to have successful careers, 18 compete with men, and achieve the same earnings should alter their family plans and have their children either before 25 or after 35. Or society can attempt to alter the existing promotion and skill acquisition system so that there is a longer time period in which both men and women can attempt to successfully enter the labor force.

Without some combination of these two factors, a substantial 19 fraction of the male-female earnings differentials are apt to persist for the next 40 years, even if discrimination against women is eliminated.

Thurow orders his combined confirmation and refutation so that he moves from those points his audience knows the most about and believes most strongly in to those it has considered less. He is then able to lead the audience to a more logical understanding of his thesis.

The sequence of the points in your confirmation and refutation depends a great deal on the subject and the audience. You may choose a shape inherent to the subject itself: its chronology, process, or cause-and-effect structure. Or you may want to emphasize the readers' relationship to the subject: progressing from what is most familiar to what is least familiar, or from the point you agree on to your own point of departure. Or you may want to shape your points according to appeals: ethical, logical, or emotional. The complete Toulmin diagram of your argument can help guide you in choosing the most effective strategy (you can review the Toulmin model in Chapters 2 and 7). By examining closely any reservation for the warrant, you can determine the most effective way to arrange your data for reaching your audience.

Whichever shaping strategy you choose, the most important principle guiding your decision should be that of achieving a **climactic order**—one that convinces your audience of your point of view. To accomplish this you will want to arrange your points so that they lead to your strongest argument.

CONCLUSION

Naturally, the choices you make in shaping the main part of your argument will affect the strategy you use for shaping the conclusion. The most common purpose of the conclusion is summarizing the main points of the argument. In lengthy, highly technical, or scientific arguments, writers sometimes preface their summary remarks with "in conclusion" or "in summary"; however, these phrases are not necessary, and in shorter or less formal arguments those phrases can interrupt the flow of thought and abruptly change the tone. If you do choose to summarize or restate your main points, you should do so because the summary has some value to your readers. The two most common reasons for summarizing are amplification and extenuation. With **amplification** you emphasize and enlarge the importance of the main points of your argument. This process leads to a consideration of the ultimate advantages of accepting the view you advocate and possibly to a recommendation for a course of action.

In her speech to the incoming students of Douglass College on September 6, 1977, poet Adrienne Rich hoped to persuade the women students to "claim an education." In the conclusion reprinted here, Rich used the process of amplification to summarize her main points and recommend the action the students should take.

> I have said that the contract on the student's part involves that you demand to be taken seriously so that you can also go on taking yourself seriously. This means seeking out criticism, recognizing that the most affirming thing anyone can do for you is demand that you push yourself further, show you the range of what you *can* do. It means rejecting attitudes of "take-it-easy," "why-be-so-serious," "why-worry-you'll-probably-get-married-anyway." It means assum-

ing your share of responsibility for what happens in the classroom, because that affects the quality of your daily life here. It means that the student sees herself engaged *with* her teachers in an active, ongoing struggle for a real education. But for her to do this, her teachers must be committed to the belief that women's minds and experience are intrinsically valuable and indispensable to any civilization worthy the name; that there is no more exhilarating and intellectually fertile place in the academic world today than a women's college—*if* both students and teachers in large enough numbers are trying to fulfill this contract. The contract is really a pledge of mutual seriousness about women, about language, ideas, methods, and values. It is our shared commitment toward a world in which the inborn potentialities of so many women's minds will no longer be wasted, raveled-away, paralyzed, or denied.

Extenuation produces the opposite effect from that of amplification: it *reduces the significance of the opposition's points.* Using this strategy, you can reaffirm and highlight, either implicitly or explicitly, the reasonableness of your argument. The influential cultural and political commentator H. L. Mencken used extenuation to shape his conclusion in this passage from "Why Nobody Loves a Politician" (*Liberty Magazine,* 1934). Notice how effectively Mencken compared and contrasted the abilities of the general population with those of politicians to summarize *and* reemphasize his main point.

The schema may sound crazy at first sight; but if we are content to choose men at random and against their will to go into a jury box and decide the gravest matters of life and death, then why shouldn't we be willing to trust the same men with other matters? If they are fit to execute the laws, then why aren't they fit to make them? That making laws requires any special knowledge is surely not a fact, for it is done today mainly by amateurs, and the professionals intermingled with them are more often than not incompetent or dishonest. The only real difference between the amateurs in a jury box and those in a legislature is that the former have no private interest in the case before them.

I offer my plan to the Brain Trust.[1] If it is adopted before Congress meets in January the professors will have a much easier time than they now seem likely to have.

Conclusions also can be shaped by an emotional or ethical appeal. In fact, the two appeals can be merged effectively. Your choice will depend on the nature of the material that precedes the conclusion and the transition between the two, as well as on the final impact you want to have on the reader.

A classic use of the ethical appeal in the conclusion appears in Jonathan Swift's

---

[1] A popular name for Franklin D. Roosevelt's policy advisers selected from universities.

"A Modest Proposal," written in 1729 (this essay appears in full in the Classic Arguments section of Part V). The essay, a satirical attack on inhumanity, advocates the eating of Ireland's children to solve its problems of hunger and overpopulation. To assure his audience that his interest is for the public good and not his own personal gain, Swift concludes with the following direct ethical appeal:

> I profess in the sincerity of my heart, that I have not the least personal interest in endeavouring to promote this necessary work, having no other motive than the publick good of my country, by advancing our trade, providing for infants, relieving the poor, and giving some pleasure to the rich. I have no children by which I can propose to get a single penny; the youngest being nine years old and my wife past child-bearing.

Ethical appeal is often used in the conclusion to reaffirm the writer's beliefs in relation to the opposing view. When the writer's professional credentials are already established with the audience, this strategy can effectively summarize and finalize the issue. Neil Postman, professor at New York University and author of numerous books and articles on education, uses this approach to conclude a section in his book *Teaching as a Conserving Activity* (1979):

> I trust that the reader is not misled by what I have been saying. As I see it, nothing in any of the above leads to the conclusion that I favor a classroom that is authoritarian or coldhearted, or dominated by a teacher insensitive to students and how they learn. I merely want to affirm the importance of the classroom as a special place, aloof from the biases of the media, a place in which the uses of the intellect are given prominence in a setting of elevated language, civilized manners, and respect for social symbols.

In some cases the writer might choose to use a quote from a respected person or document to strengthen his or her ethical appeal. This strategy can also evoke an emotional response from the audience, depending on the source selected. Paul M. Levitt, a professor of English at the University of Colorado at Boulder, selects a familiar verse from the Bible to begin the conclusion of his opinion essay, "Why Are Students Unprepared for College?' That's the Way Our Society Wants Them to Be" (May 4, 1988). Although Levitt shares a close identification and mutual level of credibility with his readers—the university professors and administrators who subscribe to the *Chronicle of Higher Education*—he chooses to strengthen his credibility with a quote. However, the subjective choice he makes could possibly alienate some of his readers—the opposite of the effect he desires. You be the judge!

> The Bible says: "When I was a child, I spake as a child, I understood as a child, I thought as a child: but when I became a man, I put away childish things." The time, I submit, has come for colleges to take that bit of biblical wisdom to heart, and stop admitting students who are unprepared for the rigors of higher education. Only then will the American public grow up.

Some writers, like syndicated columnist George Will, have established reputations as writers, but their particular expertise is not necessarily in the subject on which they choose to base their argument. In his column entitled "The Barbarity of Boxing" (*Washington Post*, November 21, 1982), this is the case with George Will. His issue is the barbarity of sports, but he has chosen boxing as the example to support his argument. Because George Will has no credibility as a boxer, he must find some way to impress readers with the brutality of boxing and persuade them to change their taste in sports. Will describes a specific incident in hope of evoking an emotional response in his readers.

> Richard Hoffer of the *Los Angeles Times* remembers the death of Johnny Owen, a young 118-pound bantamweight who died before he had fulfilled his modest ambition of buying a hardware store back home in Wales. Hoffer remembers that "Owen was put in a coma by a single punch, carried out of the Olympic (arena) under a hail of beer cups, some of which were filled with urine."
>
> The law cannot prudently move far in advance of mass taste, so boxing cannot be outlawed. But in a world in which many barbarities are unavoidable, perhaps it is not too much to hope that some of the optional sorts will be outgrown.

Although the reasonableness of an argument is based on its logical appeal, the subjects of arguments are often emotional. When this is the case, using an emotional appeal in the conclusion is a natural extension of the argument. But an emotional appeal used with an emotion-based subject runs the risk of being too sentimental. When you choose to conclude your argument with an emotional appeal, your purpose should be to inspire the audience to take action *after* convincing them of the logic of your reasoning.

In his article "Family Matters, of the Heart" (*New York Times*, May 10, 1978), Anatole Broyard, a book editor for the *New York Times*, uses his persona as a father to advocate the need for parents to break their children's hearts before someone else hurts them. The subject is indeed an emotional one, one that could easily become sentimental if presented with too much emotional appeal, especially in the conclusion. To avoid the sentimentality, Broyard portrays himself preparing to act, a scene he hopes will provoke the same action in his readers.

> Still, no matter how painstakingly I plan it, I'm not looking forward to the thing, to the moment of breaking when I can feel their hearts squirm, like a bird or fish in my hands, the flutter and wriggle, the suck and slather, the gradual subsiding. I steel myself by recalling my own misadventures, how I had to muddle through life as a disadvantaged person because my parents were too old-fashioned to understand the need. Because they never thought to break it, I've got what you might call athlete's heart and I'll die of it one of these days.
>
> There isn't much time. My son is 13 and my daughter is 11. Soon it will be too late. I lie in bed at night, listening to my own heart beat, and consider ways and means.

Conclusions can have a variety of forms, but they do have two qualities in common: they are relatively brief and they create an impact on the readers' thinking. As the saying goes, "You never get a second chance to make a first impression"; the more carefully you choose the shape of your conclusion, the more significant and effective the impact will be.

THE ROGERIAN ARGUMENT

People seldom enjoy being told that they have done something wrong or made a poor decision. Criticism makes people defensive, and, when people are busy defending themselves, they have difficulty learning from the opposition. This defensiveness creates a barrier in communication, even in written argument. Psychologist Carl Rogers believes there is a *nonthreatening* means of presenting an argument that encourages an exchange of opinion and leads to a productive understanding between opponents.[2]

To shape your argument in a nonthreatening way, Rogers recommends that you establish an atmosphere of trust. Demonstrating that you understand the opposition's point of view and using neutral, unbiased language are the keys to reducing the threat that so often surfaces in arguments about highly controversial and sensitive issues. When the principal concern of the argument is understanding rather than attacking, then the audience should be less defensive of their opinions and more willing to listen to yours.

The **Rogerian argument** follows specific guidelines to achieve this common ground of trust and understanding:

1. An opening statement that briefly and objectively defines the issue
2. An objective, neutral analysis of the opposing view, one that demonstrates your understanding of why the opposition holds the opinions they do
3. An objective, neutral analysis of your position, one that carefully avoids evaluating your judgment as superior
4. An analysis of the goals and values shared by the two positions
5. A resolution that accommodates the interests of both views as much as possible[3]

Composing a Rogerian argument requires a great deal of control and open-mindedness. The writer must be more concerned with convincing the reader to "listen" than with "winning" the argument. The procedure discussed in Chapter 6 for analyzing your audience—the I Believe, They Believe, We Believe charts—will help you discover the possibilities for using the Rogerian approach. When you and your audience dis-

---

[2] Carl Rogers, *On Becoming a Person* (Boston: Houghton Mifflin, 1961).

[3] Rogers, p. 333.

agree because your differences are rooted in deeply felt personal and emotional values, the nonthreatening Rogerian strategy might offer the most effective means for shaping your argument.

In Rachel Richardson Smith's essay "Abortion, Right and Wrong," which appeared in the My Turn column of *Newsweek* (March 25, 1985), she carefully controls her emotions as she presents both sides of the issue from her personal vantage point as a mother, a writer, and a student of theology. In paragraphs 9 and 10 her language becomes emotional and threatening, but the remainder of the essay is under control. In fact, notice how she effectively focuses on goals and concerns shared with the audience through her use of *we* beginning in paragraph 13.

Abortion, Right and Wrong

RACHEL RICHARDSON SMITH

I cannot bring myself to say I am in favor of abortion. I don't want any- 1
one to have one. I want people to use contraceptives and for those contraceptives to be foolproof. I want people to be responsible for their actions; mature in their decisions. I want children to be loved, wanted, well cared for.

I cannot bring myself to say I am against choice. I want women 2
who are young, poor, single or all three to be able to direct the course of their lives. I want women who have had all the children they want or can afford or their bodies can withstand to be able to decide their future. I want women who are in bad marriages or destructive relationships to avoid being trapped by pregnancy.

So in these days when thousands rally in opposition to legalized 3
abortion, when facilities providing abortions are bombed, when the president speaks glowingly of the growing momentum behind the anti-abortion movement, I find myself increasingly alienated from the pro-life groups.

At the same time, I am overwhelmed with mail from pro-choice 4
groups. They, too, are mobilizing their forces, growing articulate in support of their cause, and they want my support. I am not sure I can give it.

I find myself in the awkward position of being both anti-abortion 5
and pro-choice. Neither group seems to be completely right—or wrong.

It is not that I think abortion is wrong for me but acceptable for some-one else. The question is far more complex than that.

Part of my problem is that what I think and how I feel about this 6 issue are two entirely different matters. I know that unwanted children are often neglected, even abandoned. I know that many of those seek-ing abortions are children themselves. I know that making abortion il-legal will not stop all women from having them.

I also know from experience the crisis an unplanned pregnancy 7 can cause. Yet I have felt the joy of giving birth, the delight that comes from feeling a baby's skin against my own. I know how hard it is to parent a child and how deeply satisfying it can be. My children some-times provoke me and cause me endless frustration, but I can still look at them with tenderness and wonder at the miracle of it all. The les-sons of my own experience produce conflicting emotions. Theory col-lides with reality.

It concerns me that both groups present themselves in absolutes. 8 They are committed and they want me to commit. They do not recog-nize the gray area where I seem to be languishing. Each group has the right answer—the only answer.

Yet I am uncomfortable in either camp. I have nothing in com- 9 mon with the pro-lifers. I am horrified by their scare tactics, their pic-tures of well-formed fetuses tossed in a metal pan, their cruel slogans. I cannot condone their flagrant misuse of Scripture and unforgiving spirit. There is a meanness about their position that causes them to pass judgment on the lives of women in a way I could never do.

The pro-life groups, with their fundamentalist religious attitudes, 10 have a fear and an abhorrence of sex, especially premarital sex. In their view abortion only compounds the sexual sin. What I find incompre-hensible is that even as they are opposed to abortion they are also op-posed to alternative solutions. They are squeamish about sex educa-tion in the schools. They don't want teens to have contraceptives without parental consent. They offer little aid or sympathy to unwed mothers. They are the vigilant guardians of a narrow morality.

I wonder how abortion got to be the greatest of all sins? What 11 about poverty, ignorance, hunger, weaponry?

The only thing the anti-abortion groups seem to have right is that 12 abortion is indeed the taking of human life. I simply cannot escape this one glaring fact. Call it what you will—fertilized egg, embryo, fetus. What we have here is human life. If it were just a mass of tissue there would be no debate. So I agree that abortion ends a life. But the anti-abortionists are wrong to call it murder.

The sad truth is that homicide is not always against the law. Our 13 society does not categorically recognize the sanctity of human life. There are a number of legal and apparently socially acceptable ways to take human life. "Justifiable" homicide includes the death penalty, war, killing in self-defense. It seems to me that as a society we need to come to grips with our own ambiguity concerning the value of human life. If we are to value and protect unborn life so stringently, why do we not also value and protect life already born?

Why can't we see abortion for the human tragedy it is? No woman 14 plans for her life to turn out that way. Even the most effective contraceptives are no guarantee against pregnancy. Loneliness, ignorance, immaturity can lead to decisions (or lack of decisions) that may result in untimely pregnancy. People make mistakes.

What many people seem to misunderstand is that no woman 15 wants to have an abortion. Circumstances demand it; women do it. No woman reacts to abortion with joy. Relief, yes. But also ambivalence, grief, despair, guilt.

The pro-choice groups do not seem to acknowledge that abor- 16 tion is not a perfect answer. What goes unsaid is that when a woman has an abortion she loses more than an unwanted pregnancy. Often she loses her self-respect. No woman can forget a pregnancy no matter how it ends.

Why can we not view abortion as one of those anguished deci- 17 sions in which human beings struggle to do the best they can in trying circumstances? Why is abortion viewed so coldly and factually on the one hand and so judgmentally on the other? Why is it not akin to the same painful experience families must sometimes make to allow a loved one to die?

I wonder how we can begin to change the context in which we 18 think about abortion. How can we begin to think about it redemptively? What is it in the trauma of loss of life—be it loved or unloved, born or unborn—from which we can learn? There is much I have yet to resolve. Even as I refuse to pass judgment on other women's lives, I weep for the children who might have been. I suspect I am not alone.

MONROE'S MOTIVATED SEQUENCE

Monroe's motivated sequence, like the original classical structure, has its roots in the oral tradition. Alan Monroe, a professor of speech, developed the motivated sequence based on the psychology of persuasion.[4] This organizational structure is particularly effective when your argument includes a proposal on which you expect your readers to act.

Monroe's motivated sequence has five sections:

---

[4]Alan Monroe, *Principles of Speech Communication,* 6th ed. (Chicago: Scott, Foresman, 1969).

ATTENTION: Gain the reader's attention using any of the methods discussed at the beginning of this chapter—a question, quotation, anecdote, startling fact, or any other means of relating the importance of the topic to the intended audience.

NEED: Make the audience feel the need for change. Show there is a serious problem with the existing situation, using strong supporting material—examples, testimony, statistics—that relate directly to the audience's values or vital concerns. The strength of your logic and the authenticity of your concern should psychologically prime the audience for the solution.

SATISFACTION: Having aroused a sense of need, you satisfy it by providing a solution to the problem. Present a detailed plan to give the audience a clear understanding of it.

VISUALIZATION: Once your proposed plan is presented, you intensify desire for it by visualizing its benefits. Use vivid imagery to demonstrate how the readers will profit from your policy. Make them see specifically how much better conditions will be once your plan is adopted.

ACTION: After convincing the audience that your plan is beneficial, you are ready to call for action. Say exactly what they can do and how—give addresses and tell where to go to join and how to contact those in charge. Then conclude with a stirring appeal that reinforces their commitment to act.

Unlike the Rogerian argument, which is designed to neutralize a strongly opposed audience or a controversial issue, the Monroe motivated sequence assumes neutrality on the part of the audience. The audience needs to know that the problem is significant, that a remedy is proposed, *and* that they have the ability to make the proposed solution work.

Here is how this sequence could be used to organize a claim of policy argument based on the "bottle bill" introduced in the U.S. Congress by Senator Mark Hatfield of Oregon.

ATTENTION: Formulate a question asking what simple action could result in the benefits Senator Hatfield outlines in his bill proposal: reduce litter, create more jobs, save energy, reduce the amount of space needed for garbage disposal, and save consumers money. Then answer the questions by introducing the topic.

A nationwide bottle bill requiring a deposit of at least 5 cents on all disposable cans and throwaway bottles could make all of this possible.

NEED: Evidence can focus on problems of excess litter and garbage (remember the garbage barge no one wanted?), wasted natural resources (particularly the oil used to make disposable plastic products), and the needless cost to consumers created by the beverage companies' use of disposable cans and throwaway bottles.

SATISFACTION: Present each point of Hatfield's proposed bottle bill, explaining how each problem identified in the Need section would be improved.

VISUALIZATION: Detail the benefits of the policy by illustrating how similar bills have worked at the state level in Oregon, Vermont, Michigan, Maine, Connecticut, and Iowa.

ACTION: Outline the direct action that can be taken for national results, such as signing petitions locally and sending them to state representatives in Congress, letter-writing campaigns, and contacting state agencies for assistance.

EXERCISES: SHAPING ARGUMENTS

1. Both of the following arguments were written for the same audience, readers of the *New York Times* business section (March 20, 1988). The writers, Patricia Taylor and James C. Sanders, advocate opposing views on the same subject. While both articles follow a formal structure in presenting their argument, each puts the elements in a different configuration. Outline each article by describing the choices the writer made for each part of the discourse (introduction, statement of fact, confirmation, refutation, conclusion). Then write a paragraph explaining which argument you find more convincing and why.

It's Time to Put Warnings on Alcohol

PATRICIA TAYLOR

Spuds MacKenzie is tending goal. It's the last shot of the game, and Spuds makes an incredible save. The skillful maneuver by Anheuser-Busch's mascot is part of an Olympian effort to convince Americans that drinking is harmless and all-American. But during the next Olympiad, the ads may have a new twist. The bottle of Bud hoisted by the Spudettes may carry a message about the risks of alcohol. 1

Since 1977, when the Food and Drug Administration commissioner, Donald Kennedy, first recommended warning labels on alcoholic beverages, more than one million people have died from alcohol-related problems, one-fourth due to drinking and driving. The costs have been equally staggering—over one trillion dollars. 2

Congress is now considering a bill that would require health warning labels on all alcoholic beverages, much as cigarettes are now 3 labeled. Drinkers would be alerted to the risks of alcohol, just as consumers of bubble bath, over-the-counter drugs, and other products are told about the health risks of those products.

While industry opponents deride the usefulness of warning labels, the United States Public Health Service says, "Studies which have examined the impact of health warning labels in 'real world' situations have concluded that the labels did have an impact on consumer behavior." 4

Five different proposed labels would cover proven risks related to alcoholic beverages, ranging from birth defects to auto crashes. In 1981 the Surgeon General of the United States first advised women who are pregnant or considering pregnancy not to drink. Last year the National Institute on Alcohol Abuse and Alcoholism concluded that alcohol is the leading cause of mental retardation caused by known teratogenic agents (those that produce birth defects). 5

Alcohol is still involved in more than 50 percent of traffic fatalities. For those between the ages of 16 and 24, alcohol-related traffic deaths are the No. 1 killer. Warning labels would reinforce programs to reduce drinking and driving. 6

Another label, this one warning that alcohol is a potentially addictive drug, would dispel any notion that some alcoholic beverages are as harmless as soft drinks. New "cooler" products barely taste of alcohol but contain more than beer. In many states, you can walk into your local grocery store and purchase alcoholic beverages off the fruit juice shelf with names that give no hint that the product contains alcohol. 7

And on beer labels there isn't a single word to indicate that the contents are alcoholic. Many beer drinkers, especially teen-agers, think a can of beer is "safer" than a rum and Coke, even though the two contain equal amounts of alcohol. 8

Other labels would inform consumers about alcohol's contribution to liver disease, hypertension and cancer, and about the risk of drinking while taking prescription and over-the-counter drugs. 9

Alcoholic beverage producers certainly don't want consumers to associate drinking with mental retardation, alcoholism, cirrhosis of the liver, and death on the highways. So instead of informing drinkers about health and safety risks, they bombard us with $2 billion worth of slick promotional campaigns annually. According to Neil Postman, professor of media ecology at New York University, and his colleagues, children see more than 100,000 beer commercials on television before they are old enough to legally drink and drive. The ads do more than sell particular brands; they sell the assumption that drinking is not just safe, but essential to a happy, successful life. 10

Some companies do sponsor occasional ads to remind us to drink "moderately." Unfortunately, those ads are designed more to 11 undercut prevention-oriented legislative initiatives than to educate drinkers about health risks. The fact is, the $70 billion-a-year booze industry simply can't afford moderate drinking. Its best customers are heavy drinkers, who account for half of all sales. If those drinkers drank less, sales—and profits—would plummet.

Industry officials often argue that warnings on their products 12 would ultimately lead to warnings on everything from eggs to underwear. It's a cute argument, but it just doesn't wash. Only two products—alcohol and tobacco—are potentially addictive and sold legally directly to consumers despite their destructive impact on our nation's health.

With some luck, Congress will see through the anti-warning propaganda and respond to their constituents' concerns about alcohol. 13

Of course, health warnings alone won't eliminate alcohol problems. We really need a comprehensive strategy that would include expanded educational programs, mass media campaigns to neutralize industry's huge ad campaigns, and sharply higher Federal alcohol excise taxes. But passage of the pending bill with its clear, concise label notices, is an important place to start. 14

We Need Role Models, Not Labels

JAMES C. SANDERS

Warning labels on alcoholic beverages could shape up as the "Why 1 not" issue of 1988. And that would be a shame.

No one really knows what warning labels will accomplish. And if 2 you cut through all the rhetoric, it's apparent that no one expects them to accomplish much of anything. But why not?

There are several good answers, and they can be summed up in 3 two sentences. First, warning labels won't have the beneficial effects their advocates claim. And second, they could hamper efforts to provide legitimate and useful education about safe drinking. The battle against alcohol abuse is too important to be entrusted to the "it can't hurt and it might help" mentality that is moving warning labels up on some legislative agendas.

Because when all is said and done, warning labels can hurt.   4

Cultures that successfully encourage responsible alcohol con-   5
sumption do so by providing credible role models for safe drinking—
not by condemning all drinking as bad. Our Government should emphasize the differences between moderate and abusive consumption
rather than obscuring them through the use of warning labels.

Warning labels won't foster safe drinking among the general pop-   6
ulation. And there's even less chance that they will have a beneficial
effect on abusers. Alcohol has been a part of society for well over 5,000
years. No one can argue that alcohol abusers drink because they do
not know abuse can be bad for them.

More important, almost everyone agrees that serious, chronic   7
abuse requires in-depth intervention. When Congress considered
warning labels on alcoholic beverages in 1979, Dr. Jack H. Mendelson,
director of the Alcohol and Drug Research Center at Harvard, testified
that such labels could cause "immeasurable harm."

"The warning label approach would be a regressive step in that it   8
would emphasize the primary importance of individual 'willpower' to
abstain," Dr. Mendelson said. In other words, it could make the barrier between abusers and the help they need higher than is already
the case.

Can warning labels help educate underage drinkers? That's not   9
very likely either. Most counselors who work with adolescents agree
that a vital factor in helping teen-agers deal with subjects like drinking
is honesty. One-sided, black-and-white arguments will be dismissed as
adult scare tactics—particularly since they ignore the fact that two-
thirds of adults drink.

In fact, warning labels are likely to make alcoholic beverages even   10
more of an alluring "forbidden fruit" for adolescents than they already
are. A few words on the side of a beverage container won't convince
teen-agers who are already risking trouble with the law to put off
drinking until they are 21. It is a lot more likely that such a label will
act as a challenge, taunting adolescents to prove they can handle drinking no matter what the older generation says.

It makes no sense to brand all drinking as undesirable when the   11
American Journal of Public Health reports—as it did earlier this year—
that women who drink moderately are about one-third less likely to be
hospitalized than lifelong abstainers. And moderate male drinkers are
about 25 percent less likely to be hospitalized than people who have
never taken a drink.

Researchers concluded that while some causes of hospitaliza-   12
tion are clearly increased among abusive drinkers, "the overall acute
care hospitalization experience of moderate drinkers appears to be
favorable." If we're after legitimate education, we can't ignore this half
of the story.

Massachusetts State Representative Suzanna Bump, who has 13
sponsored a warning label bill in that state, recently told the Associated Press that warning labels on alcoholic beverages "would contribute to public health education, much like warnings that already appear on cigarettes." But from a public policy perspective, there's a major difference between tobacco and alcohol. Before the imposition of warning labels on cigarettes, the Government decided that smoking in any amount could be hazardous. In sharp contrast, respected researchers have compiled considerable evidence that moderate consumers may benefit from their drinking.

No one within the alcoholic beverage industry would argue 14
against productive efforts to promote safe drinking practices in our society. In fact, our industry supports hundreds of programs around the country.

But the warning label advocates have completely failed to make 15
their case. "Why not?" is never a good reason to do anything. Ours is a free and open society. One in which most people would just as soon be left alone by government unless there is a good probability that government intervention will provide a benefit.

In the case of alcoholic beverage warning labels, that justification 16
simply doesn't exist. "Why not?" just isn't good enough.

---

2. Write a brief analysis of the argument in "Let's Stop Punishing the Homeless—and
Ourselves" (*Christian Science Monitor,* March 10, 1988), showing how it demonstrates
the principles of the Rogerian model. At the end of your analysis, explain why you believe this approach to the issue is or is not effective.

Let's Stop Punishing the Homeless—and Ourselves

TOM SIMMONS

Sometimes court decisions stand as monuments of wisdom, but more 1
often they reveal subtle flaws or problems in the culture at large. So it
happened in a recent federal court decision in Florida.

The case revolves around financier Victor Posner, a multimillion- 2
aire who pleaded no contest last September to 10 counts of tax eva-

sion. He could have been sentenced to 40 years in prison. Instead, Judge Eugene Spellman sentenced Mr. Posner to five years of helping the homeless. Posner will have to spend 20 hours a week for the next five years, as well as at least $3 million, to aid society's castoffs in south Florida.

It's an admirably innovative decision, but there is a problem here. 3 Ironically, it's the idea of punishment.

Posner is being "punished" by being required to help the helpless. This is not the fault of Judge Spellman, nor of the criminal-justice system. But in punishing Posner by making him help the least fortunate Americans, the court is also telling us something about our priorities, our values.

Too often we think of helping the homeless or needy as a form of 4 punishment, or at least a kind of penance. Given the choice, we would like them to go away. We move to the other side of the street when we see a derelict passed out on the sidewalk. And we cut housing, welfare, and legal benefits for the homeless and indigent, hoping that somehow the problem is not as severe as it seems and that the "bottom out-of-sighters," as Paul Fussell calls them, will quietly fade away.

Instead the opposite happens: We institutionalize indigency. 5 Lacking sufficient resources and vision, we punish the poor, and ourselves, by making desperate piecemeal attempts at solving the problem—a run-down shelter here, a soup kitchen there, a handful of job-training programs. In these conditions the homeless do not escape their tragedy, but become more deeply mired in it.

For our part, we stand by, too often feeling impotent. Safe in our 6 homes and jobs, we punish ourselves, condemning ourselves to the prison of unresolved feelings. The problem is too big for us; therefore we must turn away, or look on against our wills.

But the problem is not too big for us. The solutions to home- 7 lessness are not forms of punishment. Solutions exist already in our humanity; they rest implicitly in our instinct to help those who need help. It is no accident of sentimentality that stories about homelessness touch us deeply. We want to help. But how can we, when the resources in our own communities seem stretched to the limit and no coherent policy on homelessness exists?

A shift in the wind can bring comfort to an arid desert. The 8 Reagan administration recently announced its own shift in the wind—135,500 new units of government-subsidized housing for the poor. It's a welcome step forward, but it's a very small step.

What's needed at the federal level is something on the order of a 9 national task force on the homeless. Well funded and well staffed—with a budget pegged at perhaps 2 percent of the defense budget—this program would explore the dimensions of homelessness and indigency in the United States and promote imaginative responses to the problem in specific communities. Such a program would provide much-needed vision and action, based on a sense of our shared humanity with those in need.

To continue viewing the poor and homeless as a form of punish- 10 ment, a weight around our neck, is to hobble our own ability to respond. Yet the possible responses, coordinated at a national level, would do us all proud.

Working with state and city governments, this national task force 11 could create innovative financing arrangements for housing for the homeless, drawing on a combination of federal, local, and private funding. The homeless themselves could be employed as apprentice carpenters, plumbers, electricians. Such experiments have already been tried successfully on a small scale in several cities. College students could receive credit for working with the homeless, tutoring them, helping them with child care, even serving as paralegal assistants when they have grievances that they cannot resolve on their own.

For their part, the homeless and indigent might begin to see a 12 glimmer of hope in this vast social system that we who are well off call home. They might begin to see that work has its rewards; that dreams can sometimes become reality; that planning for the future is not an exercise in futility. In short, they might begin to become a contributing part of our social structure, rather than a fanned flame of discontent and misery.

This task will not be easy, for we are not in the business of social 13 engineering: We cannot simply tell the poor and the homeless how to live. We must work with them, and listen to them, as well as offering them help.

But above all, we must stop equating aid to the homeless with 14 self-punishment. It is time to stop feeling guilty, time to stop wringing our hands and turning away.

It is time to feed the hungry, and heal the heart. We can, of 15 course, do this as individuals; but the scale of the problem itself contributes to our sense of being overwhelmed.

Because feeling overwhelmed is part of the way we punish our- 16 selves, we must join forces, and build, with the homeless, a vision of hope.

---

3. Choose one of the issues below or one of your own interest. Using the Monroe motivated sequence, outline a claim of policy argument to a clearly defined audience. In your outline, include the specific points of evidence you plan to focus on in both the Need and Satisfaction sections. Then write the argumentative essay.

   a. Should the electoral college be abolished?

   b. Should there be a permanent site for the Olympic Games?

c. Is there a need to provide day-care centers at places of employment?

d. What steps should be taken to control child abuse?

e. Should genetic research be more strictly controlled?

f. Should students be required to pay a university activity fee if they do not attend those activities?

WRITING SUGGESTION

Choose one of the following quotations on which to design an argument, or choose a subject of your own interest. Present your design in essay form, beginning with a description of the rhetorical context and focusing on the choices you would make and the effects you intend to produce. "Elevator Mentality," the student essay that follows, should be helpful in demonstrating how this decision-making process can develop.

As you get older it is harder to have heroes, but it is sort of necessary.

ERNEST HEMINGWAY

The mind is not sex-typed.

MARGARET MEAD

There is a great deal of difference in believing something still, and believing it again.

W. H. AUDEN

Authority without wisdom is like a heavy axe without an edge, fitter to bruise than polish.

ANNE BRADSTREET

Wherever they burn books, they will also, in the end, burn people.

HEINRICH HEINE

Loyalty to petrified opinion never yet broke a chain or freed a human soul.

MARK TWAIN

ELEVATOR MENTALITY

Sheila Powell

Elevators are strange places—especially crowded ones. Everyone is   1
crammed in close with folks we've never met, so the object becomes not
to touch anyone. And no one talks either. The only thing you might
hear is an occasional "Out, please," or "Oh, I'm sorry" as somebody
clumsily steps on someone else's toe. No one looks at anyone; in fact, no

one looks anywhere but up, watching those numbers go up and down, on and off. Strange. People who are about the same height and who speak the same language are suddenly as silent as a roomful of nuns in prayer. It's almost as if there's an official sign that reads:

NO TALKING, NO SMILING, NO TOUCHING AND
NO EYE CONTACT ALLOWED WITHOUT WRITTEN CONSENT
OF THE MANAGEMENT. NO EXCEPTIONS!!

An elevator is a microcosm of our country today: an impersonal   2
institution where anonymity, isolation, and independence are the uniform of the day. A basic quality of our healthy social lives is being diluted, distorted, and demeaned by the "elevator mentality." We are way out of balance in the area of involvement. And one area that especially needs our attention is voter registration and participation.

Because this essay is being written to the general national public, I   3
would use this introduction to lead into the topic of decline in voter turnout. I think this audience is like me when they hear this topic. They immediately see our forefathers standing nearby shaking their fingers accusingly and saying, "Shame, shame, you're not using your constitutional rights." And they immediately tune it out. So, I could use this introduction as a surprise to get their attention in an unexpected way by using this common experience everyone has probably shared. Then, I could inductively lead to the topic by gaining their trust that I do indeed know what kinds of experiences people have. Using the analogy as a vocabulary intensifier will amplify the dimly felt idea of voter turnout into a vivid picture. Perhaps, every time they ride an elevator, they will think of voting or registering to vote. Maybe I will gain a listening audience by approaching them in this manner. I hope to gain credibility with a tone that is knowledgeable and concerned, placing myself on the same level as my reader. This is why I chose to use "we" and "our" pronouns.

But most importantly, I think this essay needs a refreshing point of 4
view and unexpected points. For this reason, I would use a sort of comparison/contrast format using analogies to bind it all together.

A recently published report by Ralph Larkin, a sociologist, on the 5
crisis facing suburban youth, underscores several aspects of this new
malaise of the spirit. Many children of American affluence are depicted
as passively accepting a way of life they view as empty and meaningless.
Exit: Involvement and motivation. Enter: Indifference, noncommitment,
and disengagement. No hassles . . . no conflicts . . . no accountability.
Just watch the numbers and look at nobody.

I would bring in the preceding paragraph to further establish credi- 6
bility with an expert's testimony who also sees apathy attacking our
country. I would then turn back to the elevator analogy to reinforce the
topic of the "elevator mentality affecting voter turnout." I do this in
order to raise the vague idea to a great visibility, to vivify my argument.
I would choose not to use arguments about our constitutional right to
vote and other stock details often used as sentimental attack in this
kind of an essay.

In organizing this paper, I would develop a rhythmic momentum to 7
intensify the paragraphs rising in order of importance. This climactic
order is also useful with the paragraphs and sentences to build sus-
pense by delaying closure and the key idea until the end. For instance, I
might begin a paragraph about regaining our freedom in this way:

There is something we all want to be, need to be, and ought to be, 8
but only a few really are. A very small percentage of us in America can
honestly and boldly declare, "I am _____." Even though we think it is
good and we say it is right, even though we love its benefits and we
defend its value, even though it is available for us to enjoy (parallel
structure), we risk losing it. What is it? Freedom.

I would then tie this idea back into the main topic. 9

The only escape from indifference is to think of freedom as our most cherished resource. We need to work hard at regaining this invaluable antique that has been cast aside, forgotten like a dust-covered treasure. All of us want to be free, need to be free, ought to be free.

Then I would discuss ways in which our freedom can be stolen by our apathy and lack of participation at the polls. Again, I would not let this become a sentimental attack by using unsupported emotional assertions and stock, predictable detail, by evoking standard images, or by stacking tender detail. I could start off by saying, "I still get a chill down my spine when I hear the national anthem playing at the Olympics or when I remember standing at ramrod attention while reciting the Pledge of Allegiance in elementary school." But I won't make this a predictable emotional attack. Instead, I might bring in another illustration like:

The life cycle of a silkworm from egg to worm to moth includes the stage at which the worm spins about itself a remarkable cocoon. This little sack is composed of 400 to 800 yards of silk fiber which seals it from the inside as it awaits metamorphosis. At the completion of the cycle, the adult moth will break the cocoon, tearing apart the fine silk cords that bind it, and fly free. But the silkworm farmer does not allow most worms to become adults. At a key point in the cycle, he steams the cocoons to keep the moths inside from maturing. If he didn't do this, they would go free, leaving a trail of broken threads which are useless to the exploiters. (I chose the word "exploiters" because it fits the analogy I plan on using.) If they were allowed to mature and escape, the reproductive moth would lay about 350 eggs. But they are not allowed to do so. . . .

Then, in order to conclude this essay, I would provide a kind of shock effect to leave the reader with the need to act on what I have said. And I would use mixed images to go back to both analogies to reinforce both of the main ideas.

Could it be that many immature, caged Americans—like you or   14
me—are being kept from maturing because our political "captors" cannot fulfill selfish purposes with free people who vote to make their
choices known? Besides, a room full of moths is certainly a bigger challenge than a box full of worms.

Stop the elevator. Let's get off.   15

Chapter 10

CONTROLLING LANGUAGE

> A writer's problem does not change. . . . It is always how to write truly and having found what is true, to project it in such a way that it becomes a part of the experience of the person who reads it.
>
> ERNEST HEMINGWAY

In words the writer and the reader literally meet on the page. They are the smallest unit of meaning in your argument, yet the most powerful. They are the voice of your thoughts and the heart of your ability to create a convincing experience for the reader. Your decision is *how* and *when* to choose them.

As Hemingway recommends, the time to choose your words carefully is when you have found something "true" to write, something you believe in. After you have written enough drafts to determine the most effective shape for what you truly want to present, you can consciously choose the words that best represent that truth.

The *how* of choosing words involves the same principles on which argument is based: clarity and motivation. When you select the words that most clearly describe the issue and most accurately state the logic of your reasoning, the reader can experience the truth or probable truth of the argument. In turn, the clarity and accuracy of your expression strengthens your *ethos*, thus motivating the audience to accept and act on your reasoning.

ESTABLISHING CLARITY

BALANCING ABSTRACT AND CONCRETE LANGUAGE

Abstractions express the ideas, qualities, values, and conditions on which the conclusions of your argument are based. *Dignity, accountability, failure, honor, nihilism, poetic justice,* and *freedom* characterize the kinds of abstract terms likely to appear

throughout an argument. They represent important intellectual concerns to you and your reader, concerns worth defending. And perhaps the best way to explain and defend an abstract term is with the concrete details and incidences that persuaded you to draw your conclusion. Concrete language, then, comprises the specifics that led you to believe what you do.

Abstract and concrete words can be placed on a continuum of language use. In his book *Language in Thought and Action* the semanticist S. I. Hayakawa labels this continuum "the ladder of abstraction."[1] This concept demonstrates how the form of a word moves from its most concrete level to its least concrete or abstract level. A ladder of abstraction looks like this:

Most Abstract

ARTIST

Writer

Novelist

Modern novelist

Modern British novelist

VIRGINIA WOOLF

Most Concrete

Building a ladder of abstraction for the abstract ideas that underlie your argument gives you a full range of choices from which to select concrete details. From the levels you generate, you can then choose the specific word that will best clarify the abstract term for your audience. In some instances you may want to combine more than one level of concrete details to create a fuller effect. For example, an audience not familiar with Virginia Woolf would benefit more by the combination, "As an artist, the modern British novelist Virginia Woolf," than from the single reference, "As an artist, Virginia Woolf."

When reading the following excerpt from a *New York Times* article (February 7, 1988), notice how many levels of concrete specification the writer uses to clarify the abstract point of his discussion: "Olympic realism has replaced Olympic idealism."

---

[1] S. I. Hayakawa, *Language in Thought and Action*, 4th ed. (New York: Harcourt Brace Jovanovich, 1978).

Olympics Take a First Step on the Road to Reality

DAVE ANDERSON

When the Olympic athletes from 57 nations parade Saturday during 1
the opening ceremony of the 15th Winter Games, one of the Canadian
team members will be Andy Moog, the same Andy Moog who was an
established goaltender for the Edmonton Oilers of the National Hockey
League. And more than any other athlete in Calgary, he will be taking
the first step to Olympic reality.

Just as the International Olympic Committee now markets the 2
Games as big business, it now allows its athletes to market themselves
as big business. Olympic realism has replaced Olympic idealism.

"This is a move that simply legalizes what's already gone on for 3
quite a while in many sports," Richard W. Pound, a Montreal attorney
and a member of the I.O.C.'s executive board, has said. "No more will
athletes or officials have to close their eyes, hold their noses and sign a
form that requires them to lie about the truth of their lives and careers."

When the I.O.C. turned pro in 1985 by selling its Olympic-rings 4
logo to worldwide corporations, in conscience it had to allow its athletes to sell their skills.

By the 21st century, virtually every Olympic sport will probably 5
be open to whatever competitors wish to enter. Not to amateurs or
pros, but simply to competitors. Andy Moog is the first of these Olympic competitors.

The concrete language Anderson uses to describe Andy Moog would form this ladder
of abstraction:

Most Abstract

COMPETITOR

Olympic competitor

Professional competitor

Professional hockey player for the NHL

Edmonton Oilers player

ANDY MOOG

Most Concrete

In these few paragraphs the writer manages to include *every* detail on the abstraction ladder. Why? Even though his audience is interested in sports and probably familiar with Andy Moog's experience, the concrete language gives them a clearer understanding of the reasoning behind the change in the rules for Olympic participation.

The clarity that results from the use of concrete language and specific details strengthens your argument in three important ways: (1) it illustrates the logic of your reasoning; (2) it develops your *ethos* ("The writer really knows this subject well!"); and (3) it brings the reader closer to the subject, thus evoking an emotional response. How can you determine when to use concrete language? How can you avoid overcrowding the argument with unnecessary details? The best place to begin is the basic framework of your reasoning. From this point you can determine which abstract terms will need further clarification.

Let's say the basic claim of your argument is the following:

People who do volunteer civic service when they are young become patriotic adults.

The main focus of the claim is on the cause-effect relationship between *civic service* and *patriotic*. Both terms will be familiar to most audiences, but the connection between the two is definitely abstract. You need to clarify what patriotism is and how the qualities of patriotism are a part of civic service. Maybe as a child you helped your parents hand out campaign materials or voter registration information, an activity that formed your political conscience early in life and contributed to your steady voting record. The concrete details need to be directed to clarifying the abstract terms of your claim. When your reasoning is clear, your use of abstract and concrete language is balanced.

AVOIDING CLICHÉS AND EUPHEMISMS

Two forms of language that can interfere with your clarity are clichés and euphemisms. **Clichés** are expressions that have been so overused that they have lost their impact. Some you are likely to hear in everyday conversation are *last but not least, back to square one, few and far between, bored to tears,* and *a shot in the arm.* Even though some clichés do use specific language, they all are predictable. And when what you write is predictable, your reader doesn't have to think about what you're saying. The whole effect of your point is lost. (These problems are the subject of George Orwell's essay, "Politics in the English Language," included in the Classic Arguments section in this book.)

Euphemisms also lack directness. A **euphemism** is a word with a pleasant association substituted for a word with unpleasant or offensive associations; in other words, a euphemism is a nice way of expressing an uncomfortable or offensive condition or idea. In some social situations using a euphemism is considered the polite thing to do, as in using *perspire* for *sweat* or *passed away* for *died.* Too often euphemisms are used to upgrade facts or blur details. Calling a used car a *pre-owned car* or referring to wiretapping as *electronic surveillance* is the kind of pretense that a reader can easily see through.

PROMOTING FAIRNESS

Historically, language use has discriminated against women by using masculine pronouns to refer to men and women, by using the word *man* to identify professions (for instance, in *mailman* or *businessman*) and as a generic term for *people*, and by reinforcing negative stereotypes and attitudes through derogatory connotations (Mr. Smith and his wife). Today this use of **sexist language** is offensive to most people, especially an educated reading audience. And sexist language, like clichés and euphemisms, hinders the directness, honesty, and fairness needed for clear reasoning.

USING NONSEXIST LANGUAGE

Fortunately, there are several ways to eliminate sexist language from your writing. Here are some examples of alternatives to inappropriate language to guide you.

INAPPROPRIATE	ALTERNATIVES
1. We hope the winner will make **his** speech short.	We hope **you** will make **your** speech short. *or* We hope the **winners** will make **their** speeches short.
2. An adolescent is often pressured by **his** peers.	**Adolescents** are often pressured by **their** peers.
3. In the interest of **mankind**	In the interest of **humanity**
4. The average **man** uses **his** time wisely at work.	The average **person** uses time wisely at work.
5. Contact your **congressman**.	Contact your **congressional representative**.
6. work**man** policе**man** mail**man** chair**man**	worker police officer mail (letter) carrier chair, chairperson
7. Dear **Sir** or **Gentlemen**	Dear (Name) Dear (functional title)
8. **man** and wife	**husband** and wife
9. Mr. Howard and his wife Karen	Joe and Karen Howard Karen and Joe Howard
10. President Reagan and Mrs. Thatcher	President Reagan and Prime Minister Thatcher Reagan and Thatcher
11. **lady** mayor **male** nurse steward**ess** wait**ress**	mayor nurse flight attendant waiter or server
12. **feminine** intuition **masculine** drive	intuition drive

AVOIDING JARGON

Most professions use a specialized language in writing formally to one another within the profession. When two nuclear physicists write or speak to one other, a highly specialized language may be needed. But in most cases, so-called specialized language is nothing more than jargon—a pretentious, evasive, and often incomprehensible use of language designed to intimidate readers and conceal meaning.

In its most common, everyday use, jargon merely reflects the dullness and laziness of the writer who doesn't know enough or care enough to concretely detail what "the bottom line" is or what "red tape" is delaying a process. Others, thinking they will be considered intelligent, try to impress their readers with important-sounding terms. The following excerpt from the May 6, 1968, issue of *Newsweek* demonstrates how meaningless this use of jargon really is.

How to Win at Wordmanship

After years of hacking through etymological thickets at the U.S. Public Health Service, a 63-year-old official named Philip Broughton hit upon a sure-fire method for converting frustration into fulfillment (jargonwise). Euphemistically called the Systematic Buzz Phrase Projector, Broughton's system employs a lexicon of 30 carefully chosen "buzzwords":

COLUMN 1	COLUMN 2	COLUMN 3
0. integrated	0. management	0. options
1. total	1. organizational	1. flexibility
2. systematized	2. monitored	2. capability
3. parallel	3. reciprocal	3. mobility
4. functional	4. digital	4. programing
5. responsive	5. logistical	5. concept
6. optional	6. transitional	6. time-phase
7. synchronized	7. incremental	7. projection
8. compatible	8. third-generation	8. hardware
9. balanced	9. policy	9. contingency

The procedure is simple. Think of any three-digit number, then select the corresponding buzzword from each column. For instance, number 257 produces "systematized logistical projection," a phrase that can be dropped into virtually any report with that ring of decisive, knowledgeable authority. "No one will have the remotest idea of what you're talking about," says Broughton, "but the important thing is that they're not about to admit it."

Too often jargon is used intentionally to confuse readers and conceal meaning. In fact, this use of jargon has become so prevalent that the National Council of Teachers of English (NCTE) has named it *doublespeak* (a combination of "doublethink" and "newspeak," from George Orwell's novel *1984*) to warn readers of its deception. Every year NCTE tries to keep the public aware of the most flagrant use of this deceptive jargon by giving the Doublespeak Award to its most dishonorable users. Government officials are usually the recipients. Here are some examples of award-winning doublespeak:

inoperative statement	lie
terminate with extreme prejudice	kill
liberate, pacify	invade
therapeutic misadventure	malpractice
downsizing personnel	firing employees
advanced downward adjustments	budget cuts
philosophically disillusioned	scared
terminal episode	death
ballistically induced aperture in the subcutaneous environment	bullet hole

The next time you find yourself adding an *-ize* or *-wise* to the end of a concrete word, or relying on phrases such as *at this point in time* and *in today's modern society,* or using a thesaurus to replace every fifth word, stop and rethink exactly what it is you are trying to say and who your audience is. Jargon jeopardizes both your logical and ethical appeal.

ESTABLISHING MOTIVATION

EXPRESSING CONNOTATION

The emotion of argument is never neutral. Regardless of the issue, you advocate approval or disapproval through the connotation of the words you choose. The **connotation** is the emotional implication of a word or phrase, all the associations activated by the values, beliefs, and feelings you and your audience hold. Before you choose a word at a critical point, consider the range of connotative responses it may trigger. Would you refer to someone's comment as *a lie, an untruth,* or *a fib*? If you wanted to minimize the effect, you would choose *untruth* or *fib.* But if you wanted to register your disapproval, you would choose *lie.* Here are some other examples:

NEUTRAL	APPROVAL	DISAPPROVAL
alone	unaccompanied	isolated
antique	heirloom	junk
work	employment	labor
underweight	slim	skinny
obey	assent	submit

Even with these common terms it is hard to reach consensus. Determining the range of connotative responses an audience might have becomes increasingly more difficult as the audience becomes more general and the topic more sentimental. The writer of the following essay, "A Love That Transcends Sadness," which appeared in *Parade* magazine in 1981, has both problems: (1) The readers of *Parade,* a Sunday magazine supplement carried by newspapers nationwide, are diverse in interests, experiences, and age; and (2) the topic of cemeteries generally evokes strong feelings, some merely negative and others queasy or ghoulish. How does Willie Morris solve these problems with the choices he makes in language? What differences in connotation are conveyed by the synonyms he uses for *cemeteries*?

A Love That Transcends Sadness

WILLIE MORRIS

Not too long ago, in a small Southern town where I live, I was invited   1
by friends to go with them and their children to the cemetery to help
choose their burial plot. My friends are in the heartiest prime of life

and do not anticipate departing the Lord's earth immediately, and hence, far from being funereal, our search had an adventurous mood to it, like picking out a Christmas tree. It was that hour before twilight, and the marvelous old graveyard with its cedars and magnolias and flowering glades sang with the Mississippi springtime. The honeysuckled air was an affirmation of the tugs and tremors of living. My companions had spent all their lives in the town, and the names on even the oldest stones were as familiar to them as the people they saw everyday. "Location," the man of the family said, laughing. "As the real-estate magnates say, we want *location*."

At last they found a plot in the most venerable section which was 2 to their liking, having spurned a shady spot which I had recommended under a giant oak. I know the caretaker would soon have to come to this place of their choice with a long, thin steel rod, shoving it into the ground every few inches to see if it struck forgotten coffins. If not, this plot was theirs. Our quest had been a tentative success, and we retired elsewhere to celebrate.

Their humor coincided with mine, for I am no stranger to grave- 3 yards. With rare exceptions, ever since my childhood, they have suffused me not with foreboding but with a sense of belonging and, as I grow older, with a curious, ineffable tenderness. My dog Pete and I go out into the cemeteries, not only to escape the telephone, and those living beings who place more demands on us than the dead ever would, but to feel a continuity with the flow of the generations. "Living," William Faulkner wrote, "is a process of getting ready to be dead for a long time."

I have never been lonely in a cemetery. They are perfect places to 4 observe the slow changing of the seasons, and to absorb human history—the tragedies and anguishes, the violences and treacheries, and always the guilts and sorrows of vanished people. In a preternatural quiet, one can almost hear the palpable, long-ago voices.

I like especially the small-town cemeteries of America where the 5 children come for picnics and games, as we did when I was growing up—wandering among the stones on our own, with no adults about, to regard the mystery and inevitability of death, on its terms and ours. I remember we would watch the funerals from afar in a hushed awe, and I believe that was when I became obsessed not with death itself but with the singular community of death and life together—and life's secrets, life's fears, life's surprises. Later, in high school, as I waited on a hill to play the echo to taps on my trumpet for the Korean War dead, the tableau below with its shining black hearse and the coffin enshrouded with the flag and the gathering mourners was like a folk drama, with the earth as its stage.

The great urban cemeteries of New York City always filled me 6 with horror, the mile after mile of crowded tombstones which no one ever seemed to visit, as if one could *find* anyone in there even if he wished to. Likewise, the suburban cemeteries of this generation with their carefully manicured lawns and bronze plaques embedded in the ground, all imbued with affluence and artifice, are much too remote for me. My favorites have always been in the old, established places where people honor the long dead and the new graves are in proximity with the most ancient. The churchyard cemeteries of England haunted me with the eternal rhythms of time. In one of these, years ago as a student at Oxford, I found this inscription:

> Here lies Johnny Kongapod,
> Have mercy on him, gracious God,
> As he would on You if he was God,
> And You were Johnny Kongapod

Equally magnetic were the graveyards of eastern Long Island, 7 with their patina of the past touched ever so mellowly with the present. The cemetery of Wainscott, Long Island, only a few hundred yards from the Atlantic Ocean, surrounded the schoolhouse. I would watch the children playing at recess among the graves. Later I discovered a man and his wife juxtaposed under identical stones. On the wife's tomb was "Rest in Peace." On the man's at the same level, was "No Comment." I admired the audacity of that.

But it is the graveyards of Mississippi which are the most moving 8 for me, having to do, I believe, with my belonging here. They spring from the earth itself, and beckon me time and again. The crumbling stones of my people evoke in me the terrible enigmas of living. In a small Civil War cemetery which I came across recently, the markers stretching away in a misty haze, it occurred to me that most of these boys had never even had a girl friend. I have found a remote graveyard in the hills with photographs on many of the stones, some nearly one hundred years old, the women in bonnets and Sunday dresses, the men in overalls—"the short and simple annals of the poor." I am drawn here to the tiny grave of a little girl. Her name was Fairy Jumper, and she lived from April 14, 1914 to Jan. 16, 1919. There is a miniature lamb at the top of the stone, and the words: "A fairer bud of promise never bloomed." There are no other Jumpers around her, and there she is, my Fairy, in a far corner of that country burial ground, so forlorn and alone that it is difficult to bear. It was in this cemetery on a bleak February noon that I caught sight of four men digging a grave in the hard, unyielding soil. After a time they gave up. After they left, a man drove toward me in a battered truck. He wanted to know if some fellows had been working on the grave. Yes, I said, but they went away. "Well, I can't finish all by myself." Wordlessly, I helped him dig.

One lonesome, windswept afternoon my dog and I were sitting at 9 the crest of a hill in the town cemetery. Down below us, the acres of empty land were covered with wildflowers. A new road was going in down there, the caretaker had told me; the area was large enough to accommodate the next three generations. "With the economy so bad," I had asked him, "how can you be *expanding*?" He had replied: "It comes in spurts. Not a one last week. Five put down the week before. It's a pretty steady business."

Sitting there now in the dappled sunshine, a middle-aged man 10 and his middle-aged dog, gazing across at the untenanted terrain awaiting its dead, I thought of how each generation lives with its own exclusive solicitudes—the passions, the defeats, the victories, the sacrifices, the names and dates and the faces belong to each generation in its own passing, for much of everything except the most unforgettable is soon forgotten. And yet: though much is taken, much abides. I thought then of human beings, on this cinder of a planet out at the edge of the universe, not knowing where we came from, why we are here, or where we might go after death—and yet we still laugh, and cry, and feel, and love.

"All that we can know about those we have loved and lost," 11 Thornton Wilder wrote, "is that they would wish us to remember them with a more intensified realization of their reality. What is essential does not die but clarifies. The highest tribute to the dead is not grief but gratitude."

Morris knows that he cannot completely eliminate his readers' predictable images of cemeteries in one essay, nor can he risk insulting his readers by avoiding these images. Apparently he decided on an if-you-can't-beat-'em-join-'em approach. Notice how he uses the more macabre term *graveyard* interchangeably with the more neutral *cemetery*; phrases such as "burial ground" and "untenanted terrain awaiting its dead" further broaden the range of responses. This blending acknowledges the readers' predisposition while presenting a new viewpoint. Morris follows the same strategy in using terms of death: "departing the Lord's earth immediately," "the flow of generations," "dead," "vanished people," "the next three generations," "steady business," "its own passing," and "much is taken."

Morris hopes to convince his audience that a cemetery is a place of belongingness, a place where families, generations, and history reside. To achieve this he emphasizes positive, life-giving images and close relationships. The opening paragraph is filled with concrete images that set a positive tone: "adventurous mood," "like picking out a Christmas tree," "cedars and magnolias and flowering glades sang," "the honeysuckled air," and "as familiar to them as people they saw everyday." The opening paragraph also establishes the association between companionship and the cemetery. First, his friends "invite" him to join them on their "quest." Their adventure gives them reason to "celebrate." Then there are the recurring images of children (including the author) playing in the cemeteries and the author and his dog visiting cemeteries for quiet reflection on several occasions over time. That continuity reaches its full force in the conclusion, where the author, sitting in the "dappled sunshine" joins the reader directly through his use of the pronoun *we.*

Good use of **diction,** the careful choice of individual words and phrases to express just the right shade of meaning, will keep your readers emotionally involved in your writing. Each association you are able to evoke forms a connection with what the reader already knows and believes, and with each connection the reader is further motivated to see things as you do.

Connotation can also strengthen the reader's understanding of your logic. When you use *metaphor,* you develop your reader's understanding of the *unfamiliar* by showing its similarity to something that *is* familiar. Metaphor can be created using many kinds of figurative language. What each form has in common is a comparison, implied or directly stated, that generates new meaning by connecting the reader with the subject in an *unexpected* way. Here are some of the most commonly used forms:

METAPHOR: an implied comparison th1t equates two things or qualities without an explicit connecting word.

My geology exam was a nightmare.
Henry's sister, the sergeant at arms of the family, called a halt to our argument.

SIMILE: a direct comparison using the connecting words *like* or *as.*

She raced toward me like a train without brakes.
With intuition as keen as a bloodhound's, Sam chose the fastest moving line at the bank.

ALLUSION: a comparison to a well-known historical, literary, mythological, or contemporary figure or event.

James turned out to be the Judas of the group.
Driving across the country in Ellen's van would be like booking passage on the *Titanic.*

PERSONIFICATION: giving human qualities to inanimate or nonhuman objects.

The tree branches kissed our shoulders as we walked through the grove.
The new foreign trade policy strutted across the Senate floor hoping for attention.

HYPERBOLE: an elaborate exaggeration, often intended to be humorous or ironic.

His knowledge on the subject would fill the Grand Canyon.
I would climb to the top of Mount Everest for that job.

METONYMY: the representation of an object, an institution, or concept by something associated with it.

All the big brass attended the dedication of the ship.
The latest Oval Office report started fresh battles on the Hill.

Strategically placed metaphors generate the intellectual connections the readers need to arrive at the same conclusions you have. Introducing your argument with a metaphor can allow the audience to read the entire essay with new understanding. And concluding the argument with a metaphor can clarify the logic of your entire argument. In Paul Johnson's essay on the need for popularizing history ("Popular Pastimes, Unpopular Books: The Past as Unstudied Prologue," *Los Angeles Times,* July 19, 1987), he concludes with a metaphor that aptly reinforces his claim:

> In the age of the mass electorate, easily swayed and manipulated by the media, it has never been more important for historians of all kinds to accept their public responsibility by helping to regraft the writing of history onto the tree of literature, and by making the past real and living in the consciousness of ordinary people. History is the great lamp of humanity: It should be held high and boldly and cast its beams so that all of us, the lowly and the mighty alike, can see our way forward.

Metaphors can also serve as a structure for an entire essay or a major portion of an essay. When they do, they are called *extended metaphors.* The concentrated focus of an extended metaphor creates many connections that can lead your reader to a deeper understanding. The problem lies in finding a metaphor that can be sustained vividly. If you have to force the connections, the metaphor loses its effect. But when you are able to extend a metaphor far enough to address the main points of your argument, the audience will be more convincingly informed and motivated to accept your view.

In "A View from the Upper Deck" from his 1971 book *The Summer Game,* Roger Angell uses an extended metaphor to persuade his audience to view baseball in a new way—as a game that defeats time both literally and figuratively. To do this he compares baseball to physics, from the vantage point of the upper deck of the stadium.

A View from
the Upper Deck

ROGER ANGELL

Always, it seems, there is something more to be discovered about this 1
game. Sit quietly in the upper stand and look at the field. Half close
your eyes against the sun, so that the players recede a little, and watch
the movements of baseball. The pitcher, immobile on the mound,

holds the inert white ball, his little lump of physics. Now, with abrupt gestures, he gives it enormous speed and direction, converting it suddenly into a line, a moving line. The batter, wielding a plane, attempts to intercept the line and acutely alter it, but he fails; the ball, a line again, is redrawn to the pitcher, in the center of this square, the diamond. Again the pitcher studies his task—the projection of his next line through the smallest possible segment of an invisible seven-sided solid (the strike zone has depth as well as height and width) sixty feet and six inches away; again the batter considers his even more difficult proposition, which is to reverse this imminent white speck, to redirect its energy not in a soft parabola or a series of diminishing squiggles but into a beautiful and dangerous new force, of perfect straightness and immense distance. In time, these and other lines are drawn on the field; the batter and the fielders are also transformed into fluidity, moving and converging, and we see now that all movement in baseball is a convergence toward fixed points—the pitched ball toward the plate, the thrown ball toward the right angles of the bases, the batted ball toward the as yet undrawn but already visible point of congruence with either the ground or a glove. Simultaneously, the fielders hasten toward that same point of meeting with the ball, and both the base-runner and the ball, now redirected, toward their encounter at the base. From our perch, we can sometimes see three or four or more such geometries appearing at the same instant on the green board below us, and, mathematicians that we are, can sense their solution even before they are fully drawn. It is neat, it is pretty, it is satisfying. Scientists speak of the profoundly moving aesthetic beauty of mathematics, and perhaps the baseball field is one of the few places where the rest of us can glimpse this mystery.

The last dimension is time. Within the ballpark, time moves differently, marked by no clock except the events of the game. This is the unique, unchangeable feature of baseball, and perhaps explains why this sport, for all the enormous changes it has undergone in the past decade or two, remains somehow rustic, unviolent, and introspective. Baseball's time is seamless and invisible, a bubble within which players move at exactly the same pace and rhythms as all their predecessors. This is the way the game was played in our youth and in our fathers' youth, and even back then—back in the country days—there must have been the same feeling that time could be stopped. Since baseball time is measured only in outs, all you have to do is succeed utterly; keep hitting, keep the rally alive, and you have defeated time. You remain forever young. Sitting in the stands, we sense this, if only dimly. The players below us—Mays, DiMaggio, Ruth, Snodgrass—swim and blur in memory, the ball floats over to Terry Turner, and the end of this game may never come.

Angell chooses an unexpected metaphor for his audience of avid baseball spectators. Do they understand physics? Maybe not, but Angell does not use the technical language of physics to make his comparison. Instead he uses major physics principles to reinforce an appreciation of baseball and to give new dimension to its enduring qualities. And that, of course, is his point.

All types of figurative language have the power to be persuasive and informative; they can also be fun and clever. But, if overused, metaphor can wear down your reader; too indirect or unfamiliar, it can confuse. The best strategy is to anchor your use of connotation at the main points of your argument, where the strongest impact will be.

PROJECTING TONE

Tone is the writer's attitude toward subject and audience. Much like the tone of your speaking voice, your tone as a writer can range from angry and indignant to amused or passionate. If you have chosen an issue for your argument that genuinely interests you, then you are bound to have strong feelings of approval or disapproval toward that issue. But because logic, not emotion, lies at the center of argument, you need to control and direct your tone to project a balance between knowledge and emotion. Your audience also influences the tone you use. What tone will get a hostile audience to listen? What tone will move an undecided audience to make up its mind? What tone will get an ambivalent audience interested enough to be concerned? For any of these audience levels the tone you choose needs to project a reliable, trustworthy image.

Reliability can be projected through several voices: personal, impersonal, humorous, and ironic. The reader can judge the reliability of the tone of voice by the choices the writer makes in diction and syntax and by the writer's ability to maintain the tone.

Personal Tone. A comfortable informality characterizes the personal tone. The writer keeps a respectful distance from the reader but feels free to use the personal pronouns *I, you,* and *we.* The writer views the reader as a person with mutual concerns, so high-powered connotation is rarely necessary. Still, assuming that the audience wants to be informed, the writer balances abstract ideas with concrete details, sometimes using contractions to take the academic edge off of definitions of terms or reports from research. Sentence structure is chosen to maintain clarity and interest through variety.

You can observe these characteristics in this excerpt from Jeffrey Pasley's essay "The Idiocy of Rural Life" from the *New Republic,* December 8, 1986. In addition, he includes an informal reference to a television program.

> But what about the benefits of good-old-fashioned-lemonade values and the supportive friendliness of a rural community? Though hard data is difficult to come by, many small towns appear to suffer from teenage pregnancy, alcoholism, and other social maladies at rates that are higher than average. One New England study showed relatively high suicide rates among farmers during a period antedating the farm crisis. And rural communities haven't always stood by

their financially troubled members. Sociologist Paul Lasley's Iowa Farm and Rural Life Poll reported that a majority of Iowa farmers felt they received little or no support from their churches, neighbors, schools, or local voluntary organizations. At a "town meeting" with Representative Tim Penny, Democrat of Minnesota, in New Market, Minnesota, I heard farmers ridicule the idea of slightly higher property taxes to improve the area's meager school system practically in the same breath that they demanded higher subsidies for themselves. These things never happened on "The Waltons."

Impersonal Tone.   Formality and distance characterize the impersonal tone. The sophisticated vocabulary and dense sentence structure convey the seriousness of the topic and the well-educated background of the intended audience. Generally this tone is reserved for scholarly writing. There is an abundance of abstract terms and few personal pronouns are used other than *they* and *it*. When *I* is used, it generally refers to the writer as researcher or as part of the scholarly community. Essays written in an impersonal, formal tone, such as the excerpt from Sissela Bok's "The Need for Secrecy" (from her 1982 book *Secrets: On the Ethics of Concealment and Revelation*), require more effort and more knowledge from the reader.

Secrecy is as indispensable to human beings as fire, and as greatly feared. Both enhance and protect life, yet both can stifle, lay waste, spread out of all control. Both may be used to guard intimacy or to invade it, to nurture or to consume. And each can be turned against itself; barriers of secrecy are set up to guard against secret plots and surreptitious prying, just as fire is used to fight fire.

We must keep in mind this conflicted, ambivalent experience of secrecy as we study it in its many guises, and seek standards for dealing with it. But because secrecy is so often negatively defined and viewed as primarily immature, guilty, conspiratorial, or downright pathological, I shall first discuss the need for the protection it affords.

Humorous Tone.   What's funny to one person isn't necessarily funny to another. The first challenge of creating a humorous tone is finding an appropriate subject. In many ways the humorous tone resembles the personal tone in vocabulary, sentence structure, and distance from the audience—all are at comfortable levels with the audience. Sometimes the humorous tone is more informal, using dialogue, slang, and contractions. But the most noticeable difference is the emphasis on connotation, particularly figures of speech. As this selection from "The Plot Against People" (*New York Times*, 1968) by the Pulitzer Prize-winning author Russell Baker illustrates, personification is an effective way to project a humorous tone.

Inanimate objects are classified scientifically into three major categories—those that break down, those that get lost, and those that don't work.

The goal of all inanimate objects is to resist man and ultimately to defeat him, and the three major classifications are based on the method each object uses to achieve its purpose. As a general rule, any object capable of breaking down at the moment when it is most needed will do so. The automobile is typical of the category.

With the cunning peculiar to its breed, the automobile never breaks down while entering a filling station which has a large staff of idle mechanics. It waits until it reaches a downtown intersection in the middle of the rush hour, or until it is fully loaded with family and luggage on the Ohio Turnpike. Thus it creates maximum inconvenience, frustration, and irritability, thereby reducing its owner's lifespan.

Ironic Tone. When people use irony in their speech, it is generally easy to detect in the tone of the voice. But in written form, irony and ironic tone are more difficult to detect. Because ironic tone is based on the incongruity of asserting approval when disapproval is actually intended (or the reverse), the writer relies on the audience's sophistication or insight. Ironic tone is characterized by indirectness and often a grim humor. Vocabulary and sentence structure are similar to those used for informal tone, except when the irony is designed for particular audiences. Writers try not to use an ironic tone conspicuously. They expect their audience to enjoy the challenge. Henry Fairlie presents that challenge in his essay "The Idiocy of Urban Life" from the *New Republic* (January 1987). From the opening paragraphs you can see the beginning of the ironic line of thought he plans to develop.

Between about 3 a.m. and 6 a.m. the life of the city is civil. Occasionally the lone footsteps of someone walking to or from work echo along the sidewalk. All work that has to be done at those hours is useful—in bakeries, for example. Even the newspaper presses stop turning forests into lies. Now and then a car comes out of the silence and cruises easily through the blinking traffic lights. The natural inhabitants of the city come out from damp basements and cellars. With their pink ears and paws, sleek, well-groomed, their whiskers combed, rats are true city dwellers. Urban life, during the hours when they reign, is urbane.

These rats are social creatures, as you can tell if you look out on the city street during an insomniac night. But after 6 a.m., the two-legged, daytime creatures of the city begin to stir; and it is they, not the rats, who bring the rat race. You might think that human beings congregate in large cities because they are gregarious. The opposite is true. Urban life today is aggressively individualistic and atomized. Cities are not social places.

The lunacy of modern city life lies first in the fact that most city dwellers who can do so try to live outside the city boundaries. So the two-legged creatures have created suburbs, exurbs, and finally rururbs (rurbs to some). Disdaining rural life, they try to create simulations of it. No effort is spared to let city dwellers imagine they are living anywhere but in a city: patches of grass in the more modest suburbs, broader spreads in the richer ones further out; prim new trees planted along the streets; at the foot of the larger back yards, a pretense to bosky woodlands. Black & Decker thrives partly on this basic do-it-yourself rural impulse in urban life; and with the declining demand for the great brutes of farm tractors, John Deere has turned to the undignified business of making dinky toy tractors for the suburbanites to ride like Roman charioteers as they mow their lawns.

EXERCISES: CONTROLLING LANGUAGE

1. For each of the abstract words below list three concrete details that would clarify the concept.

pride	democracy
subsidy	alienation
seniority	obligation

2. Design a ladder of abstraction that includes at least four rungs to use with each term below. Place each term where you think it belongs on the ladder and fill in the remaining levels.

music   jogging shoes   triathlon
The Great Gatsby   transportation

3. Rewrite the following sentences, making the italicized terms more concrete.
   a. *In the evening,* Joe attends *class* to *broaden his horizons.*
   b. *The flowers* they sent *improved her outlook.*
   c. *The college administrator* suggested *the conflict* be resolved soon or *the event* would be canceled.
   d. This *new technology* makes *my job so much easier.*
   e. Unless the dropout rate is *substantially lowered,* our nation faces *social and economic disaster.*

4. Explain the meaning of these clichés and replace each with a concrete synonym or a fresh expression.

bite the bullet	the straw that broke the camel's back
down to the wire	shot in the arm
snow job	burning the midnight oil
take your medicine	white elephant
touch base with	cool as a cucumber

5. Revise these sentences to eliminate sexist language or sexist implications.

a. The average student feels cheated when he sells his books at the end of the year and gets less than one-fourth of what he paid for them.

b. The booster club treated the varsity athletes and their girlfriends to an end-of-the-year banquet.

c. Writers become so involved in their work that they neglect their wives and children.

d. Myra's friends suggested that a lady lawyer could get her a better settlement.

e. Mothers should label their children's camp clothes with name tags.

f. Men who plan to become astronauts need to stay in excellent physical and mental health.

6. Find a magazine that specializes in one of your professional or hobby interests (for instance, computers, photography, sailing, or tropical fish) and select a passage that you understand but that would be difficult reading for people unfamiliar with the field. Copy the passage and then paraphrase it so that nonspecialists can understand it.

7. William Safire, a twice-weekly columnist for the *New York Times,* is well known for his strong opinions on language use and current issues. This column is rich with connotative language, brimming with abstract terms and concrete details, and definitive in tone. To analyze Safire's control of language, begin by outlining the major points of his argument in "Curbing Lie Detectors" (*New York Times,* February 29, 1988). Then, under each major point, list how he uses language to clarify and motivate. Arranging the language uses by category will focus on Safire's methods. When you have finished analyzing the data, summarize your findings in 250 words.

Curbing Lie Detectors

WILLIAM SAFIRE

Two million times a year, American citizens—people who have done   1
nothing more criminal than to apply for a job—are subjected to the
humiliation of being hooked up to a polygraph machine.

This inaccurate and fear-inspiring device, the modern equivalent   2
of the hot lights and truncheons of the "third degree," measures only
nervousness. But operators of "lie detectors" presume to make or break
careers by pronouncing pseudoscientific decisions about truthfulness.

Federal courts do not accept the opinion of the Sweat Merchants   3
in evidence, but a growing number of employers with little regard for
individual freedom have been using this abomination frequently to

scare off unwanted job applicants or to intimidate employees who may have "something to hide." (We all should have something to hide.)

Three months ago, when last we visited the need to outlaw the 4 polygraph, the House had passed a tough bill by Pat Williams of Montana prohibiting any private employer, except security firms and drug companies, from using polygraphs for any reason.

The ball was in the Senate's court. Ted Kennedy, chairman of the 5 Labor Committee, looked to the committee's ranking Republican, Orrin Hatch, to hammer out a compromise that would (a) protect the privacy of individual workers, and (b) satisfy the specific investigatory needs of managers in curbing losses they claim to be $40 billion a year. Hatch, a principled conservative who had seen a trusted aide nearly ruined by a runaway Sweat Merchant, assured us that he would be "a libertarian in this matter."

Hatch and Kennedy came up with a bill that won the support 6 of major trade associations previously opposed to any polygraph limitation. In their legislation, polygraphs could not be used in pre-employment testing, nor would random testing of employees be permitted. Those two limitations alone would reduce "this dirty business" by 75 percent right away.

However, under this bipartisan proposal, the employer could call 7 in the Sweat Merchants when investigating a specific incident of theft, embezzlement or sabotage—provided he files a police report and an insurance claim, proving that he is not fishing. No questions allowed on sex, politics or union activity; all questions must be furnished the worker before the test begins; no firing based on test results unsupported by other evidence.

This was the bill reported out of the Senate committee in De- 8 cember, accompanied by a Kennedy blast at "inaccurate instruments of intimidation." (That was the senator's subtle acknowledgment of support on this issue to a usually hostile columnist who in an earlier incarnation had once zapped him as a "nattering nabob of negativism.")

I'm not altogether happy with the Hatch compromise, which 9 seems to make legitimate a nefarious invasion of privacy, but it's a half-loaf that libertarians can live with, muttering.

Now comes the latest battle for President Reagan's soul. The ad- 10 ministration has not yet informed the Senate of its position before the floor vote scheduled this week. Sources at Justice tell me that the new secretary of labor, Ann McLaughlin, would like the president to support the bill to curtail polygraphs, but Attorney General Meese opposes.

I reached Ed Meese at home this weekend and recalled the time 11 he assured me (at a party for Bill Casey) that "You've got me wrong, I'm no nut on polygraphs." Why has the attorney general suddenly become a nut on polygraphs?

"I think polygraphs have a place in the screening of applicants 12 for particularly sensitive types of work," Ed Meese replied, "provided there are adequate safeguards to be sure that the polygraph process itself is valid." He would defer to the states to regulate and license operators.

But that misses the point: The best operators will often fail be- 13 cause honest people do get nervous and liars can be trained to beat the system. Let's hope that Justice reconsiders, or that the president sides with his secretary of labor. If the administration double-crosses Orrin Hatch and blocks this year's chance for sensible restraints, the battle next year will be winner-take-all.

In that case, the Nosy Parkers will be driven to the wall. No more 14 faceless trade associations fronting for employers who engage in mental rape; instead, individual banks, factories, truckers and department stores may be spotlighted, boycotted and picketed. And no longer will protection be limited to private employees: throughout our government, the tens of thousands of workers now under the threat of mental rape will also be freed from fear.

WRITING SUGGESTIONS

1. This editorial cartoon by Conrad (*Los Angeles Times,* August 10, 1987) includes numerous details (some more concrete than others) that contribute to the artist's unstated claim. Interpret that claim and state it in your own words. Then, write the editorial col-

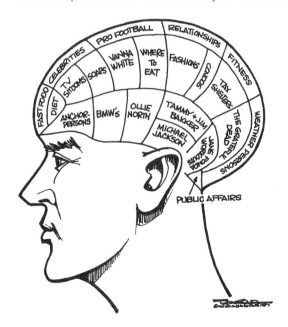

umn that would appear under the cartoon. Choose a tone appropriate to your claim and the general educated public (those interested in having an opinion). Use your best editorial voice.

2. Many ads deal with personal subjects that often make people uncomfortable, such as body odor, bad breath, hemorrhoids, constipation, diarrhea, feminine hygiene, birth control, and measures for preventing the sexual transmission of disease. Choose an ad on one of these subjects, and write a 400- to 600-word analysis of the ad that (1) demonstrates your control of language, and (2) evaluates the advertiser's use of language for sensitivity, clarity, and motivation (abstract terms and concrete details, jargon and sexist language, connotation and metaphor, tone) in reaching the intended audience.

Chapter 11

DOCUMENTING SOURCES

Argument involves many layers of choice—choices of issue and audience, arrangement and sources, and appeals and language. Even the **documentation**, the full acknowledgment of your sources, involves choices: What do I need to document? What style of documentation do I use? How do I integrate this documentation and still maintain my own writing voice? These decisions should be the guiding principles in one of the final *substantive* revisions of your work. In this revision you reread your writing solely to determine how well your use of sources (1) develops and supports your logical appeal, and (2) contributes to your ethical appeal. Once you are satisfied with the substance of your sources, you begin the meticulous process of checking the accuracy of your documentation. *With accuracy there are no choices, only right and wrong.* Accuracy requires two attributes of the writer: (1) the *integrity* to follow the principles of scholarship, and (2) the *initiative* to check the documentation format used to present *each* source.

Most student writers have the integrity to want their work to be as accurate as possible. When you have chosen to develop an argument because you have a genuine personal interest (not just an assignment due), you want what you say to be correct in every respect. Initiative, however, is a real problem for many students, especially those who wait until the last minute to revise their work. Too often these writers rely on their "memory" in documenting sources. To them, looking up the correct punctuation to use when incorporating a quote or deciding whether or not to document a summary statement are impositions on their time. Unfortunately, this reliance on their inexperienced memory makes them vulnerable to plagiarism.

Plagiarism is the unacknowledged use of another writer's words and ideas. There is absolutely no situation in which plagiarism is accepted—not in any form of language, written or spoken; not in music, art, or dance; not in business, law, or technology. Copyrights and patents protect original ideas, and in performance, accurate documentation protects your right to use those ideas.

In argument, the audience expects the writer to be a knowledgeable source of information. Using documentation demonstrates the extent of your knowledge, builds the reader's trust in your opinions, and increases your ethical appeal. Accurate documentation of sources is the backbone of your logical and ethical appeal.

WHAT DO I NEED TO DOCUMENT?

Information that is easily accessible to the reader, such as the date of an influential person's birth or death, the date of an event, or commonly accepted information (for instance, the effect of alcoholism on health or the laws of gravity) does not need documentation. But, when the information is exclusively the idea or outcome of someone else's work, you must use documentation. The material you need to document appears either as a *paraphrase*, a *summary*, or a *direct quotation* in your writing.

PARAPHRASE

When you restate an author's ideas in your own words, you are using paraphrase. Most of the references you document will be in this form; paraphrase is more concise than quotation *and* it has the advantage of being written in your own voice. If you need to review how to write a paraphrase, see Chapter 5.

Paraphrase can be expressed either with or without the author's name in the sentence. When the author's name is not part of the sentence, it must be part of the documentation. Observe the variety of positions for the author's name in these examples, which illustrate Modern Language Association (MLA) documentation style.

> Morris Freedman, an English professor at the University of Maryland, believes that learning and winning are common to both academics and sports (43).

> Title IX gave women more opportunities to compete, but past cultural influences still controlled women's motivation to participate in sports professionally (Neal 25).

> Money spent on women athletes in college rose to 16.4 percent in 1980, up from 2 percent in 1972 (deVarona 2).

Note that the *end punctuation follows* the parenthetical citation.

In the first example the paraphrase includes an acknowledgment of the source of the information. The writer probably chose to include the person with the idea not because Freedman is a well-known expert but because it is unusual for an academic professor to express support for the athletic program. Had the writer positioned Freedman's name in the documentation parentheses, the reader would not have had the full impact of his opinion. Remember, if the name of the source is included in the paraphrase itself, then only the page number where the information is located needs to be documented in parentheses.

In the second paraphrase the writer chose not to include the name of the source in the sentence. For this reason *both* the author's name and the page number on which the information appeared need to be given in parentheses. Perhaps the writer chose not to include the author's name directly because she had been introduced with her credentials earlier. Readers have the right to know who your sources of information are, which is why the author's name *must* be included in some part of the paraphrase.

The third example, though similar to the second, raises an important point: you should give the source of any figures you cite. Many readers are suspicious of statistics and the way some agencies or organizations arrive at their figures. Whenever you include figures in a paraphrase, specify as much verification for them as possible.

SUMMARY

Summaries are particularly helpful when you need to compare different authors' views on an issue or present the main points of a long study. Although summaries are written in your own words, because they require accurate representation of an author's original thoughts—with no distortion of meaning or emphasis—you must credit the source for your reader. Then the reader who needs a more detailed explanation can refer easily to the original source by using your documentation. If you need to review how to write a summary, see Chapter 5.

The following example shows how a student summarizes in one sentence what the author, Gary D. Gaddy, originally presented in a full paragraph in his article, "The Power of the Religious Media," published in the June 1984 issue of *Review of Religious Research*.

SUMMARY

There has not been much research into why people actually prefer to tune into prime-time religion, but a recent study by Gary D. Gaddy points out that the viewing audience largely consists of those who already agree with the broadcasters and wish to reinforce their opinions and interests (290).

ORIGINAL

Regardless of the psychological mechanism or mechanisms which underlie the process, selection does take place. It may be partly a simple preference for a particular program style without regard to religious content. It has been found, for example, that religious media users are more likely to prefer educational and instructional programs in general (Robinson, 1964). In some cases it may be a need for affective, rather than intellectual reinforcement. Or it could be simply a result of the community of interest between the audience members and the broadcaster they view because the broadcaster talks about things they're interested in, or alternatively, they don't view because they're not interested. The net consequence is the same in every instance—the audience of religious broadcasts is a relatively homogenous group, with values, beliefs, and even behaviors that are to a large degree congruent with those of the religious broadcasters.

Because the student cites in her summary the author's name, only the page number on which the original paragraph can be found is needed in parentheses to complete the documentation. As with paraphrase, both the author and source must be identified.

When the view you summarize represents the conclusion reached by several different authors, list those authors and their source identification in the same parentheses. The following example from Gaddy's research uses the American Psychological Association (APA) style discussed in more detail later in this chapter.

In particular, previous research clearly demonstrates that the religious are more likely to use religious broadcasts (e.g., Parker, Barry and Smythe, 1955; Casmir, 1959; Dennis, 1961; Robinson, 1964; Ringe, 1969; Solt, 1971; Johnstone, 1971–72; Gaddy, 1980, 1981; Buddenbaum, 1981).

Note that the parenthetical documentation *precedes* the period used as end punctuation.

QUOTATIONS

Using someone's *exact* words, either in complete or partial form, requires documentation. These examples demonstrate the most common variations in methods of using quotations.

As a result of the study, Paternoster formed the following conclusion: "South Carolina prosecutors are influenced by the race of the victim. They are significantly more likely to seek the death penalty when victims are white" (455).

Racial disparity is lessened in "more serious, multiple felony homicides" (Paternoster 450).

In an older book dealing with graphology, Allport and Vernon noted that among American psychologists the attitudes toward graphology were "skepticism and distrust" (185).

As Senator Ted Stevens of Alaska states, "People who sell secrets vital to our security jeopardize the lives of millions. They deserve a public execution" (as quoted in "Should U.S. Execute" 40).

Leon F. Bouvier, a senior research associate at the Population Reference Bureau in Washington, D.C., expands on the dilemma of inequalities, saying:

> What is more natural than to expect the destitute masses of the underprivileged regions to swarm across international and continental boundaries into the better regions? . . . One wonders how long the inequities of growth between major regions can continue without an explosion that will somehow quickly restore the imbalance. (27)

Note that the end punctuation *follows* the parenthetical citation except in the last example, where a longer, indented quote uses no quotation marks and the parenthetical citation appears *after* the period. This is the only instance in which the period *precedes* the documentation.

The first two examples use quotes from the same person in different ways. Documentation for quotations follows the same principles used for paraphrase and summary: the source of the quote must be stated either in an acknowledgement phrase or in the documentation in parentheses. The first example uses a complete quote and includes the name of the source, so only the page number where the quote appears is needed in the documentation parentheses. The partial quote used in the second example also clearly documents the source and the location of the quote; however, putting both in the parentheses emphasizes the words in the quote more than the person who said them.

At first glance the third and fourth examples look like duplications of the first two uses of quotation. In format they are the same; they follow the correct principles of acknowledgement. But a closer look reveals that the third example does not attribute the quote to a specific person, making the effect somewhat weaker than a *direct* quote. And the fourth example is actually a *reported* quote. The readers must trust the magazine reporters that they heard the senator correctly and that the quote is not reported out of context.

The last example illustrates a form of quotation that should be reserved for special points in your argument that will benefit most from expert testimony. If two of these lengthy quotations appeared on one page, there would be little room left for the writer's own words. The last section of this chapter will deal with how to balance the use of quotations and paraphrase in your writing.

WHAT FORMAT DO I USE?

There are several ways to document your research findings, but all of them have the same purpose: to make the source of the findings clear to the reader—clear enough to locate and read the material independently. Documentation styles differ mainly in small details of capitalization, punctuation, spacing, and positioning. You need to recognize these differences and use the style you select *consistently* for your reader's benefit.

Documentation styles are developed by professional organizations for reporting and exchanging ideas and research in a uniform manner. The documentation style used in the paraphrase and quotation examples is the MLA style, a form developed by the Modern Language Association. This style is commonly used by writers in the humanities (English, history, philosophy, and foreign languages), but it is also accepted by many other disciplines.

Another commonly used style is called the APA style, recommended in the *Publication Manual of the American Psychological Association* and used by writers in the social sciences, biology, earth sciences, and business. Some of the sciences, however, have designed their own systems of notation, such as those recommended by the American Chemical Society and the *CBE Style Manual* of the Council of Biological Editors.

Your choice of documentation style depends either on your subject or on the preference of the person, publication, or organization you are writing for. Knowing the conventions of both MLA and APA style will prepare you to document accurately any paper you write and to interpret the documentation of professional articles and books you read.

INTERNAL DOCUMENTATION

The documentation of sources you use *within* your text is a form referred to as notes. A *note* identifies the specific location within a source where the specific piece of information being presented appeared. This procedure verifies your information and creates a stronger connection between your reader and the ideas you are advocating. The principal kinds of notes are *footnotes, endnotes,* and *parentheses notes.*

Footnotes and Endnotes. Footnotes and endnotes look alike, but you place them in different parts of your paper. As the names imply, footnotes appear at the *foot* of the page they appear on, while endnotes appear at the *end* of the paper. The text to which the note refers would look like this:

> While the rate of growth in the underdeveloped countries has been steadily increasing, the rate of growth in the developed countries has slowed down.[1]

The note at the bottom of the page or at the end of the paper would use this form:

> [1] Paul Harrison, *Inside the Third World* (Harmondsworth, England: Penguin Books, 1985) 217.

In most cases endnotes and parentheses notes have replaced footnotes, which require considerable planning to allow the necessary space at the bottom of the page. But even with endnotes the system seems unnecessarily complicated and redundant. Both endnotes and footnotes repeat the information available in the list of references required at the end of all papers involving research. The only new information added is the page number. Parentheses notes simplify the procedure.

Parentheses Notes. Parentheses notes provide *immediate* source information, using the most *specific* information the reader needs to locate and consult the bibliography of references. The physical and social sciences have used this method for a long time, and since 1984 the MLA has recommended it as the preferred style for their publications. Because of this widespread acceptance, this chapter will use parentheses notes only.

Parentheses notes in the MLA style focus on the author and page number location of the source. Those used in the APA style include author, date, and occasionally page number.

MLA STYLE

While the rate of growth in the underdeveloped countries has been steadily increasing, the rate of growth in the developed countries has slowed down (Harrison 217).

APA STYLE

While the rate of growth in the underdeveloped countries has been steadily increasing, the rate of growth in the developed countries has slowed down (Harrison, 1985, p. 217).

The chart on the next page demonstrates the small differences in the two styles as used with different types of sources.

When providing documentation, keep in mind that the purpose is to acknowledge your sources clearly, briefly, consistently, and with as little interruption to your flow of words as possible. The more practice you have in using documentation the easier it will become. To be fully prepared for writing research papers while in college and professional articles after graduation, invest in a copy of the *MLA Handbook for Writers of Research Papers* (1988) or the *Publication Manual of the American Psychological Association* (1983). Both should be available in your campus bookstore.

Content or Explanatory Notes.   Occasionally you may need to explain or amplify information further for the reader, but at the same time you don't want to divert attention from the thought you are developing. When you are certain that the information will be interesting to your reader (further sources, explanation of procedures used, unusual details or statistics), you may use an explanatory note.

If you are using parenthetical documentation rather than endnotes or footnotes, you can type superscript numbers to designate explanatory notes.

The Romantic Movement, important though it is to literary studies and, indeed, to any understanding of the development of European and American culture, has until recently been given little consideration as a force in nineteenth-century rhetoric.[3]

Then, either at the bottom of the page or at the end of your essay under the heading Notes, write your note using this form:

3. James Berlin has done much to spur investigation of romantic influences on rhetoric, most obviously in his *Writing Instruction in Nineteenth-Century American Colleges* (1985).

OCCASION FOR DOCUMENTATION	MLA STYLE	APA STYLE
Reference to the whole work	The focus of the Clarke-Stewart study was children's leadership abilities.	The focus of the Clarke-Stewart (1982) study was children's leadership abilities.
Reference to author in text	Clarke-Stewart found day care children more likely to be leaders (76).	Clarke-Stewart (1982) found day care children more likely to be leaders. *or* . . . to be leaders (p. 76). *When quotes are included, the page number reference *must* be used.
Works with no author	("Getting the Best" 70).	("Getting the Best," 1985). ("Getting the Best," 1985, p. 70).
Works with two or more authors		
First appearance	(Colangelo, Rosenthal, and Dettmann 694).	(Colangelo, Rosenthal, and Dettmann, 1984).
Future appearances	(Colangelo, et al. 694).	(Colangelo et al., 1984).
Two or more works by the same author	(Farrington, *Aristotle* 17). (Farrington, *The Philosophy* 24).	(Farrington, 1969) (Farrington, 1964). *If both works have the same publication date, use this form: (Farrington, 1969a). (Farrington, 1969b).
One source cited in another		
Acceptable	(Stanek 52).	(Stanek, 1981, p. 52).
More precise	(as quoted in Stanek 52).	(as quoted in Stanek, 1981, p. 52).
(Whenever possible use the original or primary source.)		

Works cited in explanatory notes are generally included in the bibliography or list of references consulted at the end of the paper.

If you are using the numbering system for endnotes, use an asterisk (*) to designate an explanatory note. When using this system, you must place the explanatory note at the bottom of the page. A second note on the same page would need two asterisks (**).

Explanatory notes should be used sparingly. They divert the reader's attention from the text, so they should be used only when they make an important contribution.

EXTERNAL DOCUMENTATION

At the end of your writing—and after the explanatory note section if you include one— you will list the references you used to compose your work. This list is called *Bibliography*, *Works Cited*, or *Works Consulted*. A bibliography, sometimes called *Works Consulted*, is an alphabetical list of all the sources you consulted and cited in your research; a works cited list, also alphabetically arranged, is a list limited to the sources you cited in your paper. In APA style this section is called *References*. These examples of each style will give you an overview of their differences.

MLA STYLE

Works Cited

Ainslie, Ricardo C. *The Child and the Day Care Setting.* New York: Praeger, 1984.

Alexander, Lenora Cole. *Time of Changes: 1983 Handbook on Women Workers.* Washington: GPO, 1983.

Clarke-Stewart, Alison. *Daycare.* Cambridge, Mass.: Harvard UP, 1982.

Colangelo, Nicholas, David M. Rosenthal, and David F. Dettmann. "Maternal Employment and Job Satisfaction and Their Relationship to Children's Perceptions and Behaviors." *Sex Roles* 10 (1984): 693–702.

"Getting the Best Child Care—Other Than Mom." *U.S. News & World Report* 21 Oct. 1985: 70–71.

Kaercher, Dan. "Finding the Best Day Care for Your Child." *Better Homes and Gardens* June 1984: 25+.

APA STYLE

References

Acosta, V. R., & Carpenter, J. C. (1985). Women in athletics: A status report. *Journal of Physical Education and Recreational Dance, 56,* 30–34.

deVarona, D. (1984, March 18). Women's fight for sports equality begins again. *New York Times,* sec. E, p. 2.

Stanek, C. (1981). *The complete guide to women's college athletics.* Chicago: Contemporary Books.

Swift, E. M. (1986, February 17). Books or blades, there's no doubting Thomas. *Sports Illustrated,* pp. 22–24.

Women's equality day (1984, August 26). *Washington Post,* sec. C, p. 6.

As you can see, the MLA and APA styles have several differences in format. Whichever style you choose, you need to follow punctuation and capitalization conventions *exactly* when presenting your sources. The two styles do share certain characteristics of bibliographies.

- Present the sources in alphabetical order, alphabetized by the first word in each entry.

- Begin each entry with the author's last name. If no author is listed, begin the entry with the first word of the title of the source. When *a, an,* or *the* is the first word, use the next word to determine alphabetical order.

- Begin the first line of each entry at the left margin. The second and all other lines of the entry are indented (five spaces for MLA and three spaces for APA). This allows readers to locate individual sources easily.

- End each entry with a period.

- Include author, title, and publication information, including date, for all entries.

The following section presents models of bibliographic format for both documentation styles. Sources from a wide variety of categories are included, but the list is not comprehensive. If you have further questions about how to write an entry, ask your teacher or consult one of the style manuals.

BASIC BIBLIOGRAPHIC FORMS

These are the most common forms for compiling your list of Works Cited or References when you write an essay or research paper using MLA or APA parenthetical documentation. For further assistance, consult the *MLA Handbook,* Fourth Edition or the *Publication Manual of the American Psychological Association,* Third Edition.

Book by a Single Author

MLA   Laird, Charlton. *The Miracle of Language.* Greenwich, CT: Fawcett, 1953.

APA   Laird, C. (1953). *The miracle of language.* Greenwich, CT: Fawcett.

Book by Two or More Authors

MLA   Winsor, Frederick, and Marian Parry. *The Space Child's Mother Goose.* New York: Simon, 1958.

APA   Winsor, F., & Parry, M. (1958). *The space child's mother goose.* New York: Simon & Schuster.

Essay or Chapter from an Edited Collection

MLA   Harris, Wilson. "Tradition and the West Indian Novel." *Modern Black Novelists.* Ed. M. G. Cooke. Englewood Cliffs: Prentice, 1971. 30–43.

APA   Harris, W. (1971). Tradition and the West Indian novel. In M. G. Cooke (Ed.), *Modern black novelists* (pp. 30–43). Englewood Cliffs, NJ: Prentice-Hall.

Corporate Authorship

MLA   National Commission on Excellence in Education. *A Nation at Risk: The Imperative for Educational Reform.* Washington: GPO, 1983.

APA   National Commission on Excellence in Education. (1983). *A nation at risk: The imperative for educational reform.* Washington, DC: U.S. Government Printing Office.

    Note: In both styles, GPO may be used to abbreviate Government Printing Office.

One Volume in a Multivolume Work

MLA   May, Ernest R. *The Progressive Era.* New York: Time, 1964. Vol. 9 of *The Life History of the United States.* 12 vols.

APA   May, E. R. (1964). *The life history of the United States: Vol. 9. The progressive era.* New York: Time Incorporated.

Journal Article: One Author

MLA   Fontaine, Sheryl. "The Unfinished Story of the Interpretive Community." *Rhetoric Review* 7 (1988): 86–95.

APA   Fontaine, S. (1988). The unfinished story of the interpretive community. *Rhetoric Review, 7,* 86–95.

Journal Article: Two Authors

MLA   Johnson, Mildred I., and Karen S. Sterkel. "Computer Text Analysis." *National Forum* 65 (1985): 36–40.

APA   Johnson, M. I., & Sterkel, K. S. (1985). Computer text analysis. *National Forum, 65,* 36–40.

Article in a Monthly Periodical

MLA   Gagnon, Paul. "Why Study History?" *Atlantic Monthly* Nov. 1988: 43+.

APA   Gagnon, P. (1988, November). Why study history? *Atlantic Monthly,* pp. 43, 53–55, 57.

Article in a Weekly Periodical

MLA   Rosenblatt, Roger. "Do You Feel the Death of Strangers?" *Time* 17 Dec. 1984: 100.

APA   Rosenblatt, R. (1984, December 17). Do you feel the death of strangers? *Time,* p. 100.

Article in a Newspaper

MLA   Shanker, Albert. "Why Are We So Far Behind?" *New York Times* 23 Apr. 1989, late ed.: E7.

APA   Shanker, A. (1989, April 23). Why are we so far behind? *New York Times,* sec. E, p. 7.

Lecture

MLA   Boggs, Jean Sutherland. "Degas." Chrysler Museum Lecture Series. Norfolk, 12 May 1989.

APA   Boggs, J. S. (1989, May 12). Degas. Lecture presented at the Chrysler Museum, Norfolk, VA.

Interview

MLA   Steinem, Gloria. Personal interview. 28 June 1989.

APA   (indexes published interviews only)

HOW DO I INTEGRATE DOCUMENTED INFORMATION?

From the planning of your argument you know that different audience-subject-purpose combinations require different kinds of documented support. And the authority of your knowledge and experience will play an important role in determining how much additional documented support you need. But once you have decided what sources you need and where you need them in the development of your argument, you need to choose a form for the information: should it be paraphrase, summary, or quotation?

Generally you will paraphrase and summarize more often than you will quote. Why? Because the more you quote what others have to say, the less your reader will think *you* have to say on the issue. Too many voices in your paper can become confusing. But at the same time you don't want paraphrase and summary to control your paper either. These techniques can provide effective background information to support your main points. But a series of paraphrases or summaries will condense too much information into too brief a space for your reader to absorb.

The *readability* of your paper is important to your reader's understanding. Let your own words be the dominant force of your argument, and use your own judgment and these guidelines to decide when to incorporate summary, paraphrase, and quotation.

- When a source provides significant factual information and you can say it more clearly and more concisely in your own words, use paraphrase.
- When the source material contains digressions that are not related to the points in your paper or that can be rendered more concisely, use summary.
- When the source is an expert whose *exact* words will support the credibility of your claim, use a quotation.
- When the source or something the source said is your subject, use quotation.
- When the source's words express a significant point in an exceptional way, use quotation.

This draft of a paragraph from a student's argument on the inequities that exist in college women's competitive athletic programs demonstrates the problems with readability that occur when you let your sources dominate your writing.

The Title IX rule was the start of many new factors leading to advances in women's athletics. Due to this rule, "in 1966—67 about 16,000 women participated in intercollegiate athletics and a decade later the number had grown to over 64,000" (Acosta 30). Another factor that arose because of Title IX was a variety of sports for women (Acosta 30). A federal law was also passed requiring schools and colleges to spend more on women's athletic programs ("Women's Equality" 22). Because of this law, more than 10,000 scholarships for women in college are available and the budget spent on women athletes has risen to 16.4 percent in 1980, up from 2 percent in 1972 (deVarona 2). Along with these advances from Title IX came the development of women's leagues. The most important association for women's advancement was the Association for Intercollegiate Athletics for Women (AIAW) which allowed for the advancements made along with Title IX (Acosta 30). Women were finally being noticed for their athletic ability and their need to compete: "Because it satisfies our human need to use our human abilities, to experience ourselves as significant, creative, and therefore, personalized beings in an impersonal world" (Neal 53).

This student's problems with incorporating source material are common to inexperienced writers. As the writer strains to make connections between sources, the writing becomes difficult to read and understand. Let's look at each sentence that is documented. The first, a quote, does need to be documented to verify the figures, but because it has none of the criteria for using a quote, it should be restated as a paraphrase. The second, a paraphrase from the same source, could easily be combined with the first into one notation. The third, a paraphrase, does not need to be documented. Laws are part of the public record and can be considered common knowledge. The next paraphrase, citing deVarona as a source, is correctly incorporated, but the paraphrase on the formation of the AIAW is not needed. Again, the formation of a public organization can be considered common knowledge. The last sentence provides a worthwhile quote but the authoritative force behind the quote is missing. Who said it? Neal? If so, who is she? He?

This paragraph needs to be revised and written in the writer's voice, conveying a smooth flow of thought that develops the focus of the paragraph clearly. Here is the student's revision:

Title IX led to a greater variety of sports for college women and greater intercollegiate participation, marked by an increase from 16,000 in 1966–67 to over 64,000 in the late 1970s (Acosta 30). To support this noticeable growth, the government passed a law requiring schools and colleges to spend more money on women's athletic programs. As a result more than 10,000 scholarships for women in college are available and the budget spent on women athletes has risen to 16.4 percent in 1980, up from 2 percent in 1972 (deVarona 2). Meanwhile, further support developed with the formation of the Association for Intercollegiate Athletics for Women (AIAW). With these advancements women were finally given the opportunity to express the need to compete that Coach Patsy Neal feels is a part of everyone: "It satisfies our human need to use our human abilities, to experience ourselves as significant, creative, and therefore, personalized beings in an impersonal world" (53).

This version is considerably more coherent and unified in focus. The writer's voice, now more consistent, speaks directly to the reader while the documented sources emerge only when needed as support. This is the kind of balance you want to achieve with your sources.

Clear readability is also a product of *accuracy,* your ability to apply the appropriate rules of punctuation when incorporating your quotations. Although sometimes complicated, punctuation will help you to maintain your own voice by clarifying for your reader which passages are your own. Before submitting your essay for evaluation or publication, read it at least once just to check these rules for punctuating quotations.

INTRODUCING QUOTATIONS

Use a comma or a colon to introduce a quotation that can stand alone grammatically. Use a comma for short quotations and a colon for a long quotation.

> Susanne Langer responded, "The vulgarization of art is the surest symptom of ethnic decline" (310).

> On the marble fireplace in the mathematics building at Princeton University is carved, in the original German, what Hoffmann calls Einstein's scientific credo: "God is subtle, but he is not malicious" (94).

A comma is preferred when the introduction to the quotation is *not* a complete sentence.

A colon is preferred when the introduction to the quotation *is* a complete sentence.

Use a comma to separate an introductory quote from the attribution phrase, unless the quotation ends in a question mark or exclamation point.

"Power is the great aphrodisiac," cautioned Henry Kissinger.

"What does a woman want?" asked Freud.

When the acknowledgement phrase is inserted within a quotation, begin and end it with commas.

"Power," cautioned Henry Kissinger, "is the great aphrodisiac."

Use no punctuation at all when you incorporate a partial or full quotation into your own sentence.

John Locke believed that "wherever law ends, tyranny begins."

When the word *that* precedes a quotation in your sentence, *do not use a comma.*

Capitalize the first word of a quotation when you use it as an independent sentence, but *not* when you incorporate it into your own sentence.

Jacques Barzun has his own prescription for learning about this country: "Whoever wants to know the heart and mind of America had better learn baseball."

If you believe as Jacques Barzun does that "whoever wants to know the heart and mind of America had better learn baseball," then you'll coach this team.

Remember that when parenthetical documentation is used the parentheses *precedes* the final end punctuation.

ENDING QUOTATIONS

Place all commas and periods inside a closing quotation mark, except when parenthetical notation is included.

"A culture is no better than its woods," remarked W. H. Auden.

W. H. Auden remarked that "a culture is no better than its woods."

W. H. Auden remarked that "a culture is no better than its woods" (271).

Place all colons, semicolons, and dashes *outside* a closing quotation mark.

"I think, therefore I am": Descartes' philosophy continues to influence us.

Churchill promised his country his "blood, toil, tears and sweat"; what do our leaders promise today?

Place question marks and exclamation points *inside* the closing quotation marks when they belong to the quotation, but *outside* if they do not.

> If you wonder why you study writing, remember what E. M. Forster said: "How can I know what I think till I see what I say?"

> Who said, "Some books are undeservedly forgotten; none are undeservedly remembered"?

ALTERING QUOTATIONS

Do not use quotation marks with a long quote that you indent. (Quotations more than two sentences long or more than four lines long are indented.)

> Machiavelli gave absolute instructions for leadership:

>> A prince should therefore have no other aim or thought, nor take up any other thing for his study, but war and its organization and discipline, for that is the only art that is necessary to one who commands. (Ch. XIV)

Note that this is the only instance in which the period at the end of the sentence precedes the parenthetical documentation.
Use slashes (/) to divide quoted lines of poetry.

> Commenting on marriage, Marianne Moore writes: "I wonder what Adam and Eve / think of it by this time."

Use brackets [ ] when you add your own words to a quote to make its meaning clear.

> The words of Thomas Jefferson offer us a philosophy for detente: "We must therefore . . . hold them [the British] as we hold the rest of mankind, enemies in war, in peace friends."

(Brackets clarify pronoun reference.)

> Chaucer tells us, "Hard is the herte [heart] that loveth nought / In May."

(Brackets clarify foreign or obsolete words.)

> According to Sartre, "We do not do what we want and yet we are *responsible* [emphasis added] for what we are."

(Brackets clarify the emphasis you want indicated.)

> Teaching can be frustrating to the point that Mark Twain once described: "I'll learn [*sic*] him or kill him."

(Brackets clarify that you know there is an error, usually grammatical, in the quotation. The word *sic* is Latin for *thus*.)

Henley's poem "Invictus" reminds us that with self-determination we can be "the master[s] of [our] fate."

(Brackets clarify changes you make in a quote to render it grammatically correct for *your* sentence.)

Use three ellipsis points or spaced periods (. . .) with a space before and after each point to indicate you have left out part of a quoted passage.

Susan B. Anthony inspires us to take action when she reminds us that "cautious, careful people . . . never can bring about reform."

Follow-through is important, Justice Oliver Wendell Holmes tells us: "The riders in a race do not stop short when they reach the goal. . . ."

(When you omit material at the end of a quoted sentence, place the period at the end as you normally would next to the last word. Then add three ellipsis points. Use this same procedure when you omit a sentence or more in the middle of a quote.)

In *The Feminine Mystique,* Betty Friedan advises women on what to do after college:

Girls must be encouraged to go on, to make a life plan. It has been shown that girls with this kind of commitment are less eager to rush into early marriage. . . . Most of them marry, of course, but on a much more mature basis.

EXERCISES: DOCUMENTING SOURCES

1. Practice writing and documenting paraphrase, summary, and direct quotations using the two selections that follow. The first is "Carey Edwards, 25" from Studs Terkel's book *American Dreams: Lost and Found,* published in New York by Ballantine Books in 1980. The second is "Useful Unemployment and Its Professional Enemies" from Ivan Illich's book *Toward a History of Needs,* published in New York by Random House in 1977.

Compose and document four paraphrases, one summary of a paragraph, and four sentences that include direct quotations. Identify whether you are using MLA or APA style. The numbers printed on the pages of the selections are the page numbers from the original sources.

Carey Edwards, 25

Bearded, skinny, freckled, red-headed.

My mother came from a poor family. When she was growin' up, she always wanted to be an actress. She took tap-dancing lessons. We all did a little bit of show business. My older brother was on the cover of *Liberty* magazine. It was during the war, had something to do with being bandaged up. Ansel Adams took pictures of him and my sister. I became a model when I was three. Modeling clothes and stuff for catalogs, billboards, and magazines. A freckle-faced little red-headed kid.

He shows me a photograph of himself at ten. He bears a startling resemblance to Wesley Barry, the All-American country-boy hero of silent films.

I did about a hundred TV commercials. My younger brother and I were the "Look, Mom, no cavities" kids. We each did three Crest commercials. They showed 'em a lot and were much quoted. (Laughs.) Of course, they don't do that any more. Now they say: "Look, I only got one or two cavities." The announcer comes in and says: "Even Colgate or whatever cannot guarantee you'll get only two cavities per checkup."

My brother and I were flown to New York, along with my mother, to do a Crest commercial live. Just this one-minute commercial. They interviewed us. I had three cavities at the time. I told the director that. He said: "Just go ahead and say you don't have any." In other words, lie to these millions of people who were watching and believing everything you say. I did what he said, and it really left a deep impression with me, about the power of the media and how it's abused.

I had to do it because it was my job. I didn't feel quite right about it. It's different when they give you a script and you're playing a part, a character, but they were interviewing me. They were saying: Here's Carey Edwards.

They were interviewing us with our mother. They asked her: "Do you always use Crest?" "Yes." Even though sometimes we used Colgate or Ipana. The whole thing rubbed me the wrong way.

I didn't want to get out of the business. It was a very enjoyable way to grow up. I remember the TV shows better than the commercials. I did a lot of westerns. I was very good at learning my lines. I was on *The Virginian* three times, once in a major role.

When I was twelve, I decided to get out of it. I wanted to be a normal teenager. Growing up as a child actor has certain disadvantages. We went on interviews after school, four, sometimes five times a week. We were in an adult world. We were workers. At first, I liked it very much. I got a lot of attention. It was like being a grownup. We had to go up to these producers and directors by ourselves and convince them we were right for the part. We'd introduce ourselves, shake hands, selling ourselves . . .

They were interviewing other freckle-faced red-headed kids. They'd ask me what I had done, credits and stuff like that. They'd rarely ask what your interests were. I'd have to read a script, which I was pretty good at. It all seemed perfectly normal and natural to me, because I'd started so young. I didn't have any inhibitions.

Television affected my life not only just by being on it but by watching. It was like an electronic parent. I spent a lot of time with it, and I learned a lot from it. You pick up things about what's going on in the world. It helped me get involved in what I'm doing. My brother and I used to sit around making up new lyrics to TV commercials, the jingles and all that. It was a fairly new medium, and I grew up with it. It came like right after the Milton Berle era. Being born and raised in Hollywood, it was all around us anyway.

I could still get back into show business if I really wanted to. If I had the chance to do the types Dustin Hoffman does—but I did not enjoy doing TV commercials. When I was eighteen, I went to a meeting of the Screen Actors Guild, I gave a short talk in favor of truth in advertising. The president pounded his gavel. He didn't like what I was saying. Since then, I've seen him on Bank of America commercials. (Laughs.)

I guess I'm still looking for the American Dream. To me, it's people having control over their lives. I feel like I have a hell of a lot of control over my own life, but I know that's not true for a lot of people. The real dream to me—I don't know whether it's a fantasy—is the attitude you see in the movies of the thirties and forties. Where people don't even have to lock their doors, you know all the neighbors and the milkman, friendly. That's not the way it is in the seventies at all. Maybe the image I have is just a Hollywood image and is not real after all.

We observed the photograph once more: Carey Edwards at ten: freckles.

I was on the Hennessey show with Jackie Cooper. (Wistfully, softly) After the show was over, he bought me an ice cream cone for each hand. A chocolate one and a vanilla one. He raised me up on his shoulders, and the crew all gave me three cheers. He'd been a child star himself, so I guess he knew how it felt. It was a small triumph.

Oh, I've had my moments of glory. (Laughs.)

Useful Unemployment and Its Professional Enemies

There is a further distinction between professional power and that of other occupations: professional power springs from a different source. A guild, a union, or a gang forces respect for its interest and rights by a strike, blackmail, or overt violence. In contrast, a profession, like a priesthood, holds power by concession from an elite whose interests it props up. As a priesthood offers the way to salvation in the train of an anointed king, so a profession interprets, protects, and supplies a special this-wordly interest to the constituency of modern rulers. Professional power is a specialized form of the privilege to prescribe what is right for others and what they therefore need. It is the source of prestige and control within the industrial state. This kind of professional power could, of course, come into existence only in societies where elite membership itself is legitimated, if not acquired, by professional status: a society where governing elites are attributed a unique kind of objectivity in defining the moral status of a lack. It fits like a glove the age in which even access to parliament, the house of commons, is in fact limited to those who have acquired the title of master by accumulating knowledge stock in some college, Professional autonomy and license in defining the needs of society are the logical forms that oligarchy takes in a political culture that has replaced the means test by knowledge-stock certificates issued by schools. The professions' power over the work their members do is thus distinct in both scope and origin.

---

2. Compile a bibliography in MLA style using the following sources.

    a. A book written by R. Charles Johnson and published by Nolo Press of Occidental, California. The book was written in 1984 and published in 1985. The title is *Draft Registration and the Law.*

    b. A newspaper article printed in the *Miami Herald* on April 28, 1985. It appeared in section D on page 11. Mark Potok wrote the article entitled "Historic Lesson Lost in Many Classrooms."

    c. Published in Michigan by the Dean-Hicks Company in 1967, this book, *Drafted or Deferred: Practices Past and Present,* was written by Albert A. Blum.

    d. A phone interview that took place on April 16 and 17, 1987, with Sergeant Gerald Elliott, a Vietnam veteran.

    e. "The Refuseniks," an article written by Samuel H. Stoloff, appeared in the *Nation* on September 11, 1982. The article was on page 197 and continued on other pages throughout the magazine.

    f. Bernard Edelman is the editor of the book *Dear America: Letters Home from Vietnam,* published in 1985. W. W. Norton & Co., a publisher located in New York, published the book. In 1988 there was an HBO special based on the book.

    g. A special edition of *Time,* published on April 15, 1985, commemorated the tenth anniversary of our withdrawal from Vietnam. "Vietnam Ten Years Later" spans pages 16–61. The section called "A Bloody Rite of Passage" by Lance Morrow is the section cited in the paper. It appeared on pages 20–31.

    h. Vincent P. Barabba wrote a two-volume set of books called *Historical Statistics of the U.S.: Colonial Times–1970.* The set is published in Washington, D.C., by the U.S. Department of Commerce, Bureau of Census. It was published in 1975. The writer used volume 2 for the paper.

3. Compose sentences that incorporate quotations according to the following directions:

    a. Use the following quote by Louis Pasteur in a sentence that begins with an acknowledgement phrase.

        In the fields of observation, chance favors only the mind that is prepared.

    b. When you quote the following, indicate to the reader that the profession Phyllis McGinley refers to is housewife.

We who belong to that Profession hold the fate of the world in our hands.

c. Use the following quote by George Santayana in a sentence with an acknowledgement phrase inserted within it.

Those who cannot remember the past are condemned to repeat it.

d. Use the following quote by René Descartes in a sentence that ends with an acknowledgement phrase.

It is not enough to have a good mind. The main thing is to use it well.

e. Use the following lines of poetry by Anne Sexton in a sentence.

I say Live, Live, because of the sun,
The dream, the excitable gift.

f. Use the following quote by P. T. Barnum in a sentence that asks a question. End the sentence with the quote.

There's a sucker born every minute.

WRITING SUGGESTION

1. Many informative magazines on the newsstand don't allow their writers to include formal documentation or bibliographies in their articles. Instead, writers must incorporate their sources inconspicuously for their general public audience. Read "The Growing Danger from Gene-Spliced Hormones" by Thomas Murray (a professor of ethics and public policy at the University of Texas Medical School in Galveston) from *Discover,* February 1987. Make a list of all the sources the writer uses that would normally be documented. Include as much bibliographic information as you can find and identify how the writer has used the source in the article—as paraphrase, summary, or quotation. When you finish, write a 250- to 300-word evaluation on the effectiveness of these sources in supporting the writer's purpose.

The Growing Danger from Gene-Spliced Hormones

THOMAS MURRAY

My son Peter is twelve, and lately the cuffs of his pants have been 1
racing up his ankles—a sure sign that growth hormone is coursing
through his body. He's on about the same growth schedule I was. By
my fourteenth birthday I was already just shy of six feet, and hopeful
of four or five inches more. I thought that would be enough to give me
a shot at playing basketball in college. Alas, I'd reached my limit. Lacking any notable physical talents, I had to rely on guile; if you can't
shoot over the guy, get him looking one way and then scurry past on
the other side. (As we used to say, "Fake left, go right.") Recent happen-
ings in genetic engineering make me wonder if something similar, albeit unintentional, is going on there: Is our attention being directed
one way while what's important is slipping by on the other side?

At least since 1980, worries about using recombinant DNA tech- 2
nology to alter "human nature" have focused on gene therapy—the
direct and intentional alteration of genetic material to treat disease.
On June 20 of that year the general secretaries of three national organizations, for Protestants, Jews, and Catholics, wrote the President to
warn: "History has shown us that there will always be those who believe it appropriate to 'correct' our mental and social structures by genetic means, so as to fit their vision of humanity. This becomes more
dangerous when the basic tools to do so are finally at hand. Those
who would play God will be tempted as never before."

Nothing garners attention as quickly as a nice little scandal; 3
within a month of the letter, Dr. Martin Cline of UCLA provided one by
experimenting on two patients with beta-zero thalassemia, a genetic
condition that causes severe anemia. Cline removed some of their
bone marrow, treated it with recombinant DNA containing normal hemoglobin genes, then reinserted it into the bone (after making room
by killing some of the remaining marrow cells with radiation). The
hope was that the treated cells would multiply and produce normal
hemoglobin.

They didn't. Worse, Cline didn't have the approval of the UCLA 4
committee that oversees research with human subjects. When the affair became public, the National Institutes of Health (NIH) stripped
Cline of $162,000 in grant money and demanded strict supervision of
his research. For those suspicious of human gene therapy, the case
was proof that scientists couldn't be trusted to regulate themselves.

Since then, such work has proceeded very cautiously. A presi- 5
dential commission gave its tentative blessing to gene therapy with
somatic cells—those that don't pass the altered genes on to future
generations. The NIH's watchdog recombinant DNA advisory committee set up a "human gene therapy subcommittee," which has suggested "points to consider" for doctors who propose to tinker with
genes. Among them: whether the benefits of the treatment outweigh
the risks, how to choose patients fairly, and how to publicize the results of the research. Thanks to the brouhaha over gene therapy, no
great threats to humanity are likely to slip by in the near future—at
least not on that side.

But there's another side to genetic engineering that has the power 6
to alter us physically and socially. Rather than directly altering our
genes, it can modify our bodies by supplementing the natural supply
of important regulatory hormones with genetically engineered ones.
A prime example is biosynthetically manufactured human growth
hormone—hGH. Except for one additional amino acid—methionine
(which appears to have no effect on its action)—biosynthetic hGH is
identical to the hormone that promotes normal growth.

Produced in the pituitary gland, hGH plays a key role in deter- 7
mining how tall we'll become. So-called pituitary dwarfs usually lack
an adequate supply of bioactive hGH. To treat them, for more than
twenty years we've been harvesting pituitaries from human cadavers,
each of which yields a minute quantity of hGH. Until recently the supply was barely adequate. In 1979 genetic engineers cloned the gene
carrying instructions for making hGH, inserted it into a microorga-
nism, and coaxed the bug to produce the human hormone. Just in
time, it appears, because some hGH recovered from human pituitaries
seems to have been contaminated with the slow virus that causes
Creutzfeldt-Jakob disease (CJD), a degenerative infection of the brain.
In April 1985 the Food and Drug Administration (FDA) halted the sale
of natural growth hormone, and shortly thereafter approved Genentech's biosynthetic version. Since no human tissue is used in producing it, there's no danger of contamination with the CJD virus. Also,
we're no longer limited by the scarcity of cadaver pituitaries, and other
uses for hGH can be explored.

Biotechnology came to the rescue of kids deficient in growth hor- 8
mone. But if hGH injections can make extremely short children a bit
taller, what can it do for those who aren't dwarfs, but just shorter than
average? What about the youngster who would have been only of average height? And what about the basketball player for whom a couple of
inches more might mean the difference between the schoolyard and
the NBA? In short (no pun intended), why not use hGH to give your
child the advantages that come with being tall?

Years ago, at an FDA hearing, I speculated that once biosynthetic 9 hGH was approved, people would want to use it for all sorts of non-therapeutic purposes. One member of the FDA committee told me that several parents had already asked her if they could get the drug for their kids, who weren't hGH-deficient. All, she recalled, were physicians. Rebecca Kirkland, who does clinical trials of biosynthetic hGH at the Baylor College of Medicine, recently said she's had inquiries from five parents wanting to get hGH for their normal children.

Why would parents want to go to such expense (treatment with 10 biosynthetic hGH costs roughly $10,000 a year), cause their children pain (the shots hurt a bit), and risk unknown long-term side effects? Quite simply, because it's advantageous to be tall—within limits. A modest body of scientific evidence supports the commonsense observation that taller people often get the nod over their shorter counterparts, because they're perceived as more intelligent, good-looking, likable, extroverted, and attractive. Being very much taller than average is a mixed blessing. To be sure. But being a few inches above average seems to help.

A survey at the University of Pittsburgh in 1968 found that start- 11 ing salaries for graduates varied with height: roughly $300 an inch up to six feet two inches. In a study of men whose heights had been recorded twenty-five years earlier, a graduate student at Washington University in St. Louis demonstrated a "height bonus" of approximately $400 per inch.

When a researcher at Eastern Michigan University presented two 12 hypothetical job candidates to recruiters, one eight inches taller than the other, 72 per cent preferred the taller one, 27 per cent said there was no difference, and only one chose the shorter applicant. And much has been made of the fact that the taller candidate for President usually wins. Only two presidents—Madison and Benjamin Harrison—were shorter than the average American male of their eras.

If some parents want to give their child the edge that height 13 seems to confer, what's wrong with that? If it's O.K. to spend $2,500 on orthodontics, to buy your kid private tennis and music lessons, or to spend $10,000 a year and up for prep school and private college, what's a few thousand bucks more to buy a couple of inches? The kid could turn out to be a klutz at tennis, have a tin ear, and major in Michelob, but taller is taller.

In this century, we make a strong presumption in favor of liberty. 14 Before we interfere with the right of parents to bring up their children as they judge best, we demand strong reasons for doing so. Can we find them in the case of hGH?

Let me ask a skeptical question: What's the disease for which hu- 15 man growth hormone is the cure? Philosophers have a difficult time agreeing on the definition of disease, but most would recognize a physiological deficiency in hGH as a genuine disease, and hGH injections as a reasonable treatment. There are some kids, though, who aren't measurably deficient in hGH but who are very short. Their shortness can be the consequence of any one of numerous medical problems, or they may fall into the category of "familial short stature"—that is, short like mom or pop. Either way, can their shortness ever be a disability? A disability is a condition that interferes with the tasks of daily living. If people are so short that they qualify for the elevator riddle,* their shortness may well be a disability. Disabilities usually justify medical intervention. But what if a person isn't suffering from a disease, and isn't so short that the lack of height becomes a disability? What if it's merely a disadvantage?

Even if hGH turns out to be physiologically harmless—some experts have warned of possible effects on glucose regulation, as well as an increased risk of atherosclerosis and high blood pressure—there may be psychological consequences to treating children with the hormone. The unmistakable message given to a child is that shortness is a grave enough problem to justify the considerable expense, inconvenience, and discomfort of hGH treatment. It's likely to increase the child's self-consciousness about height. And since children rarely grow as much with the hormone as they or their parents hope, disappointment is likely. 16

A study of hGH-deficient children and their families found that the most psychologically mature kids weren't those who grew the most but those whom parents and other adults had treated appropriately for their age rather than their size. Kids who were encouraged to pursue interests where their height wasn't a disadvantage were much happier with themselves. 17

People differ in so many ways: in intelligence, charm, quickness of hand and foot, facility with words, wit, etc. But when we put children through hGH treatments, we focus almost entirely on their height (where they don't "measure up") and ignore their other talents and abilities. Understandably, short kids receiving hGH may come to feel that they're inadequate and inferior. 18

All other things being equal, taller basketball players are more effective than shorter ones. Height is an advantage in basketball and some other sports. In almost all other realms of human endeavor, though, height bears no relationship to the ability to do a job well. But in a culture that regularly imputes desirable characteristics to tall people and undesirable ones to short ones, shortness is surely a disadvantage. (Even our language is laden with "heightisms": we look up to people we admire, look down on those we don't.) 19

---

*Why did the man always take the elevator to the sixth floor, then walk up four more flights to his apartment? Because he could only reach the button for the sixth floor.

Like other "isms," such as racism and sexism, heightism involves 20
making unwarranted judgments about people based on irrelevant criteria. Does anyone believe the solution to racism is to find a drug that
lightens black skin? The mind boggles at the possible biotechnological
remedies for sexism. And yet those who want to give their kids hGH
are proposing just this sort of technological end-run around heightism.

If we choose to allow hGH to be used for non-disease, non- 21
disabling shortness, then we must make a choice. Either we let those
who can afford it buy it for their children, or we make it available at
public expense to all children whose parents want it.

Suppose we let it be sold. The children of rich parents will have 22
one more leg up, so to speak, on their peers. You could ask, what's one
more advantage in light of all the others available to people with means?
But the prospect of two classes—one tall and monied, the other short
and poor—is ugly and disquieting. It would allow injustice to be piled
upon injustice.

Suppose we take the other route and provide hGH to anyone 23
who wants it. If all parents (short and tall alike) rushed out to get hGH
shots for their kids, the average height of the entire population might
increase. But in all likelihood the distribution of height in the population wouldn't change much, if at all. There would still be the taller and
the shorter, and since we're doing nothing to diminish heightism, discrimination against the shorter would continue. Some people would
benefit, of course—for example, the stockholders in Genentech (which
holds a patent for making biosynthetic hGH) and those who produce
fabrics (since everyone will be wearing bigger sizes). Meanwhile, at
considerable social expense, kids would get their three shots a week
with a little pain and, we hope, minimal side effects.

Inevitably, a few eager parents would want to regain the edge for 24
their kids and try to get bigger doses of hGH, like those athletes who
take increasing amounts of anabolic steroids in the hope of obtaining
an advantage over their rivals. In both cases, individuals pursue their
own interests, only to make everyone worse off.

Whether hGH is available just to those who can pay for it or to 25
everyone, the results would be unfortunate. In one instance, we use
biotechnology to reinforce the advantages of wealth; in the other, we
incur enormous expense and unknown risks without making anyone
better off. The wisest course is to restrict hGH to cases of disease and
disability.

Although hGH may be the first biosynthetic hormone to tempt us 26
to improve on human nature, it won't be the last. Imagine what we
might do with a hormone that prompted damaged nerves to regener-
ate. Someone would wonder whether it would also stimulate growth
in the brain. And soon we'd be trying to enlarge our brains, however,
misguided that might be, scientifically or morally.

It also occurs to me that simply by writing this article I may spur 27 some parents to seek out growth hormone for their child of normal height. I fervently hope not. But the temptation posed by hGH, and by other fruits of biotechnology as yet unripened, will be great. And it will require all our collective common sense to use them wisely.

---

2. Advertisements can often lure you to the product but are unable to sell you on the product or service because they don't include convincing documentation. Choose an ad for a product or service that interests you but has failed to persuade you to make a purchase. Write a 300- to 500-word essay analyzing the problems with logical and ethical appeal in the ad and propose how the ad's claims could be documented to make you take action.

3. You have probably experienced loneliness to some degree at some time during your life. Write a page responding to the topic of loneliness. Then read the article by Martha Lear from the *New York Times Magazine* (December 20, 1987). After reading the article, revise your draft, incorporating accurately documented paraphrases and summaries (and quotations, if appropriate) from the article. Exchange your paper with a classmate and read each other's work, paying close attention to balance in the writer's voice, documentation form, and accuracy in punctuation, especially for quotations. The response sheets in Chapter 12 will guide you in making your comments.

The Pain of Loneliness

MARTHA LEAR

The loneliness was terrible, she said.

1

They had called themselves the troika: three elderly widows who had gone to the movies together, shopped and dined together, talked often on the telephone, and now one had died, another lay dying and the third was feeling so lonely. And she couldn't understand it, for it wasn't as though she were alone. She had three good children, grandchildren, a devoted younger brother, plenty of kin, and though certainly it was sad to lose one's friends, why should she feel so *lonely*?

We are just now learning that loneliness, that most intimate and least congenial of companions—not Alienated-in-America loneliness, but the real stuff—follows in our developmental footsteps, keeping a growth chart of its own. Elderly people, like this widow who was interviewed for a study on loneliness; teen-agers, young adults—we all get lonely for strikingly different reasons at different stages of life.

2

At the University of Iowa, recent work with students has shown that these reasons change fast. What typically makes college freshmen lonely is not homesickness; it is a lack of friends. But for seniors, just three or four years older, the issue is no longer friendships; it is romantic bonding. Are you seeing someone special? Are you living with anyone?—these are the questions that best predict loneliness among older students.

3

All this makes sense developmentally. The sociologist Robert S. Weiss, of the University of Massachusetts, who some years ago set out the first theory of loneliness and remains the don in the field, thinks there may be an "attachment latency" in late adolescence: "At 17, 18, kids feel ambivalent about relinquishing parental attachment and seem not to want to get too committed in new intimate relationships. It's a kind of cautiousness, a self-protectiveness. They seem to know instinctively that these relationships are not going to last."

4

But what makes no sense to anyone are findings on the elderly. It is one of our cultural givens that old age is the loneliest time of all. But in a yet-unpublished study, Iowa researchers, Daniel W. Russell and Carolyn E. Cutrona, both psychologists, using the same test they used with students, have found that elderly people were *less* lonely by every measure; and that lack of friends, not lack of kin, was the main cause

5

of their loneliness. In a study with Dr. Robert Wallace, a physician, they have found, too, that loneliness among the elderly was a better predictor of mortality than blood pressure, and one of the best predictors of admission to nursing homes.

"It's not that family relations are unimportant to older people," Dr. Russell says. "They turn to family for assistance. But they can have *lots* of family to assist them, and still feel terribly lonely if they don't have friends. Why? We all wonder. Why aren't they lonelier? We don't know. They may have adjusted to lacking certain relationships, but no one knows, really." 6

It may be a developmental form of beating the rap, a mixed blessing. Dr. Weiss, who some years ago set out the first generally accepted theory of loneliness and remains pre-eminent in the field, says: "My guess is that *everything* is becoming less pressing and less responsive as people age. It happens with sexuality, despite those upbeat outlooks that we keep hearing now. And I think it also happens with the need for emotional attachment." 7

The findings on loneliness and mortality become urgent in light of a new study at the Ohio State University College of Medicine, which confirms a precise and dramatic connection between loneliness and physiological function. (A *linkage*, this is called; it's a hot word now among behavioral scientists, who love these linkages because they rebut a traditional clinical resistance, persisting even today, to the idea that feelings have physiological consequences.) 8

We seem always to have known, in a common-sensical, folkloric sort of way, that loneliness can make you sick. *Dying of loneliness*, we say. And not long ago, widely publicized epidemiological studies of men recently separated or divorced and testing high for loneliness, showed that they did have more illness than married men. But the specific linkages were guesswork. 9

Now, the Ohio State study demonstrates that such men, at least in the first year of divorce or separation, have different immunological profiles than those of married men. Their immune systems do not function as well, leaving them more vulnerable to a whole range of infectious diseases. If loneliness were found to take the same toll in old age, when immune function is diminished anyway, it would appear that one can indeed, without poetics, die of loneliness. 10

The research was done by Dr. Janice K. Kiecolt-Glaser, a clinical psychologist, and Dr. Ronald Glaser, an immunologist. The findings confirm those that emerged from their earlier study of divorced and separated women, but with a tantalizing difference: the women do better. They, too, show lower immune-system function than their married counterparts, and get sick more often—but not as often as the 11

QUANTIFYING THE EMOTION

Answer never, rarely, sometimes or often.

How often do you feel unhappy doing so many things alone?

How often do you feel you have nobody to talk to?

How often do you feel you cannot tolerate being so alone?

How often do you feel as if nobody really understands you?

How often do you find yourself waiting for people to call or write?

How often do you feel completely alone?

How often do you feel you are unable to reach out and communicate with those around you?

How often do you feel starved for company?

How often do you feel it is difficult for you to make friends?

How often do you feel shut out and excluded by others?

Score 1 point for never, 2 for rarely, 3 for sometimes and 4 for often. A total of 30 or above on these questions, deliberately made repetitious to detect intensity, is seen as an important risk factor in mental health and appears to have physical-health consequences as well.

Source: U.C.L.A. Loneliness Scale; 10-question version

men. (Though they admit more readily to loneliness. In other tests that ask explicitly "Are you lonely?" women score higher than men. In tests that avoid the L-word, they score the same. "It appears," says Iowa's Dr. Russell, "that men just don't want to say they feel lonely.")

From all possible explanations, Dr. Kiecolt-Glaser plucks a fact of   12 contemporary life: "Across our samples, and across all the current literature on divorce, you find that two-thirds of the initiators are women. It makes sense that the ones who are saying 'I want out' would experience less loneliness, with less effect on the immune system."

Beyond the loneliness of circumstance, which is bad enough (so   13 bad, in fact, that people often describe it as being "painful beyond description" and cannot, when it's over, in any way recall how it felt), and beyond the loneliness of season, which for many people is an annual malaise that hangs on like a germ from Thanksgiving through New Year's, is the persistent, pervasive loneliness that is dictated from within. There is the lonely personality.

The social psychologist Warren H. Jones, of the University of   14 Tulsa, has studied subjects who go through long stretches of life feeling lonely. He placed them in social situations, such as cocktail parties, where they behaved ostensibly quite the same as everyone else. But they asked fewer questions. They talked more about themselves. Most tellingly, later they were far more critical of the social performance of others ("unfriendly, cold") and of their own social performance than the others were of them.

It is not mere shyness, Jones says. Loneliness-prone personali- 15 ties consistently show a lack of empathy and an avoidance of intimacy: "They say that they are lonely because they lack social opportunities. But the question that keeps gnawing at me is, is this lack *real*? Or does it reflect their own negativism?

"Therapy—almost any kind—will help such people somewhat. 16 But at the end of it, they'll still be lonelier than other people. I'm sure it begins in the prototype relationship we all have. If that one doesn't go well, if it nurtures suspicion and distrust, subsequent relationships won't go well either."

Current research generally confirms Robert Weiss's theory of 17 loneliness. It comes, he suggests, in two bitter flavors: the loneliness of emotional isolation, which means the lack of an intimate emotional at- tachment, most typically a spouse; and the loneliness of social isola- tion, which means the lack of friends, community, social networks. The lack of either can cause feelings of the most desperate, desolate loneliness.

This model helps to explain why people who lack one-on-one re- 18 lationships can feel wretchedly lonely amid good friends; and why happily married people can feel miserably alone when they move to strange communities. But the mechanism that makes such feelings palpable—the muscular tension, the pulmonary agitation, the visceral wrench—is still a mystery.

Recently contemplating this mystery, Dr. Weiss exhorted sociolo- 19 gists and biologists to look to the chemistry of loneliness: "How else except by finding some triggering mechanism can we explain how the perception of emotional isolation is followed by a dull ache in one's chest, a sense of wanting to cry or having cried, a need to search, and a high level of physiological mobilization? . . . My question would be, 'How does it work?' And I can't imagine the answer being in terms other than neurochemical."

Perhaps, then, the cure as well. A linkage, a loneliness pill; how 20 our pharmacopeia grows.

Chapter 12

WRITING THE ARGUMENTATIVE RESEARCH PAPER

Why is the research paper the common denominator that links all your course work? First, through writing, your teachers can evaluate how well you think: Can you express yourself clearly and logically? Can you develop and support your ideas coherently enough to inform or convince others? Can you synthesize information well enough to generate new ideas? Your writing reveals these levels of thinking through your command of language. Second, research depends on a wide knowledge of sources, the curiosity to pursue an idea, and the initiative to direct your own learning. Combining the two rationales, then, it becomes obvious that teachers in all disciplines require research papers to determine whether you are a rigorous thinker and an autonomous learner with the ability to contribute meaningful ideas to the university community and eventually to your profession and society.

As an application of your learning, writing the research paper requires you to use the processes presented in this text for conceiving and developing arguments into a meaningful whole—a presentation of your thinking designed to influence the thinking of others. In the discovery stage (Chapters 1 and 2) you used invention strategies to choose an arguable topic with meaningful connections to a discourse community. This led you to the investigative stage (Chapters 3, 4, and 5), where you explored and gathered sources and ideas related to your topic. From your investigations you identified your beliefs and the claim you hoped to convey in your argument. In the planning stage (Chapters 6, 7, and 8) you began shaping your claim with strategies of appeal to fulfill what your audience needs to know. And, in the composing stage (Chapters 9, 10, and 11) you chose how to control the entire essay—arrangement, documentation, and language—to achieve your intended purpose.

To write a successful research paper you will need to use this entire process. This chapter will guide you in *formalizing* your research at the investigative stage, your arrangement at the planning stage, and the readability of your final presentation at the composing stage.

FORMALIZING YOUR INVESTIGATION

When you begin investigating sources to learn more about the issue of your argument, your *research clusters* (Chapter 3) direct you to sources for interviewing, observing, and surveying while your *library research strategy* (Chapter 4) directs you to print sources. After gathering this array of sources, you can formalize your research investigation by preparing bibliography cards and note cards. These procedures keep your research well organized, accessible, and on target.

PREPARING BIBLIOGRAPHY CARDS

All the sources you consult in preparing your paper constitute your bibliography. The larger the research project, the longer and more diverse your bibliography will be, and the more organized you will need to be. Whether the project is large or small, bibliography cards can make the research process easier, as well as more organized from beginning to end.

Bibliography cards are three-by-five-inch index cards with a different source notated on each. When notating the source, write down complete and accurate bibliographic information. If you can't remember the exact form or punctuation when writing out the card in the library, be sure to check the form when you get home and revise the card *immediately* for future reference (see Chapter 11 for correct bibliographic format). If you have trouble with the form, at least make sure you write down the following basic information:

BOOKS	ARTICLES
1. Author or editor	1. Author
2. Title	2. Title
3. Publication date	3. Publication date
4. Publisher	4. Name of the periodical
5. Place of publication	5. Page numbers
	6. Volume number

A bibliography card for a book would look like the one in Figure 1. Notice that the student has included the call number so she can locate the book easily. (The call number is *not* included in the bibliography.) A bibliography card for an article would look like that in Figure 2.

The students who wrote these bibliography cards remembered another important feature of the format: correct indentation. When writing out the entry, remember to indent beginning with the *second* line. This will be an important detail at the end of your research when you use the cards to type your final bibliography.

But how do you decide which sources to notate on cards? At the beginning of any research project your focus will be broadly defined, but your research cluster will provide key terms you can use to select sources for a *working bibliography*, or preliminary list of materials you think will be most promising. Starting with your library's on-

Figure 1 *Bibliography card for a book*

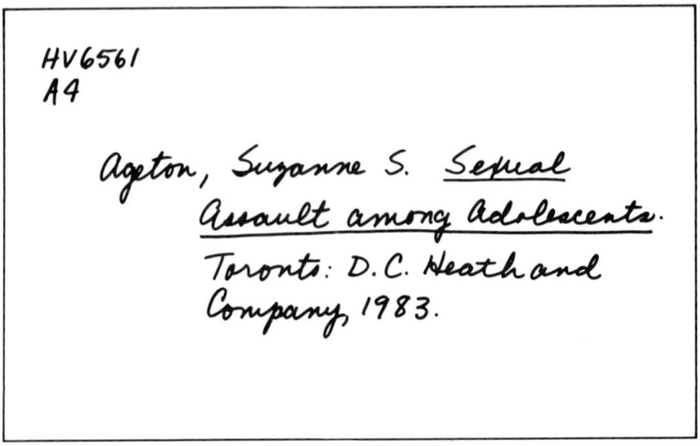

> HV6561
> A4
>
> Agton, Suzanne S. *Sexual*
>   *Assault among Adolescents.*
>   Toronto: D.C. Heath and
>   Company, 1983.

Figure 2 *Bibliography card for an article*

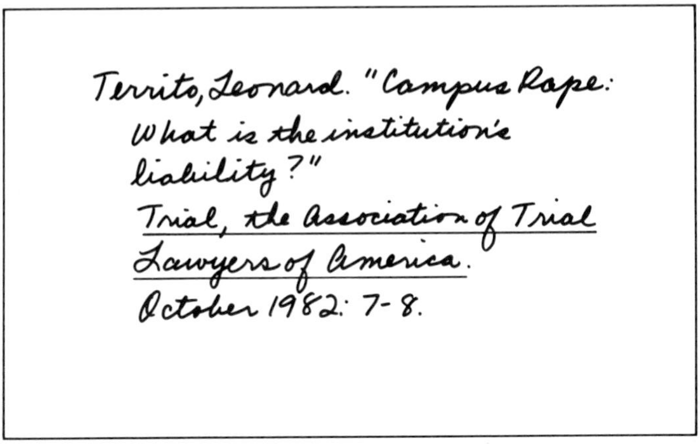

> Territo, Leonard. "Campus Rape:
> What is the institution's
> liability?"
> *Trial, the Association of Trial*
> *Lawyers of America.*
> October 1982: 7-8.

line catalogue of holdings, COMCAT or card catalog for books, the reference collection, an INFOTRAC printout or *The Reader's Guide* for general articles, and a specialized index for scholarly articles, select those sources that relate directly to your key terms and that seem to offer the most comprehensive, current information. This type of source is likely to cite significant historical developments, laws, and research studies. And the more scholarly the book or article, the more likely it is to include a bibliography of additional relevant resources, a time-saving feature for the reseacher.

Notate each of these sources on a separate index card *before* locating it in the library. Your next concern is whether or not the sources are available. Categorize your index cards by type of source—as books, articles, and reference works. If you begin with books, arrange the cards by call number so you can find the books efficiently. If the book is on the shelf, look over the table of contents and the index to get an idea of the extent of its coverage of your subject. If it looks useful, check it out; it could be gone when you return. After you locate an article in a recent periodical and on examination decide that it looks promising, photocopy it *immediately*. Then you will always have it available for note taking. Some articles in magazines and most in newspapers take longer to examine because they are on microfilm. Try skimming the article carefully, and if it looks worthwhile, photocopy it. While going through this preliminary process, you can make brief notations on the *back* of the card indicating why it *is* or *isn't useful*.

As you examine these initial sources, eliminating some that are repetitive, leads to other sources will emerge. When they do, record them on bibliography cards and examine them. Expect your working bibliography to change frequently. You will be automatically revising it as you evaluate your sources and narrow the shape of your focus. When you feel you have enough material to begin taking notes on your sources, put aside the cards of those sources you have rejected. If you do not come across more sources during your note taking, all you need do when it's time to type your bibliography is alphabetize the cards of the sources you cited from and type!

TAKING NOTES

Reading your sources should confirm what you already know about the issue, what you need to know to develop the logic of your claim, and what your audience needs to know to be convinced of your view. These are the criteria you should use in taking notes on your sources.

Note taking needs to be highly *selective* to (1) make the best use of your time, (2) consolidate the focus of your ideas, and (3) avoid plagiarism. The best method of satisfying all three needs is using four-by-six-inch index cards to write your notes on. Because note cards have a small surface space, it is difficult to copy long passages from your sources. Consequently, you are more likely to paraphrase the information to fit on the card. By paraphrasing and summarizing more often, you will consolidate your understanding of the material more quickly. Your paper will also reflect *your* voice rather than a collage of voices (see Chapters 5 and 11 for a review of summary and paraphrase). When you do select quotes, they should be short and significant. To avoid quoting too much, keep the cards with quotations in a separate pile; the size of the pile will show you how much you are relying on others' voices.

Like the procedure used for bibliography cards, note card procedure *formalizes* your note taking, giving it organization and purpose that you can see. Each card should contain *only one idea*, expressed in the form of summary, paraphrase, quotation, or personal comment. This will allow you the flexibility to organize information as the paper develops. Each card should also have *the name of the source* in one top corner and *a subject heading* in the other corner. The *page number* the information appeared on should be placed either in the corner with the name of the source or just below the notation. Use ink (pencil can smear), write clearly, write on only one side of the card if possible, and *be sure to include quotation marks with all quotes*.

Note cards are not meant to be perfect specimens of enlightened understanding and synthesis that can be automatically incorporated into your final paper. In effect they are drafts of your own thoughts as they develop—some messy and incomplete, others brilliant. But by imposing an organized procedure from the beginning of your note

Figure 3 *Paraphrase note card*

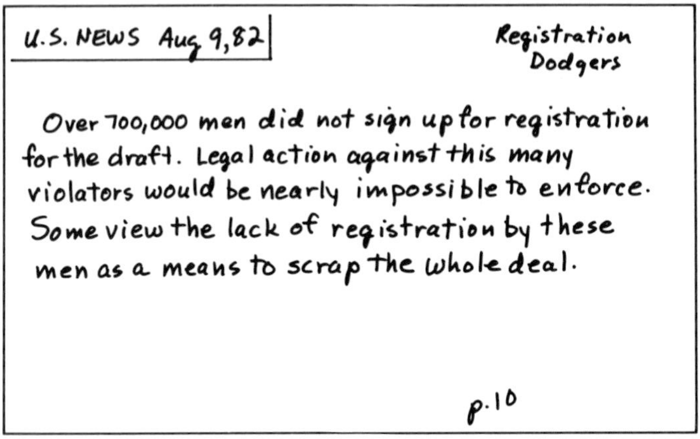

```
U.S. NEWS  Aug 9,82               Registration
                                    Dodgers

   Over 700,000 men did not sign up for registration
for the draft. Legal action against this many
violators would be nearly impossible to enforce.
Some view the lack of registration by these
men as a means to scrap the whole deal.




                            p.10
```

Figure 4 *Quotation note card*

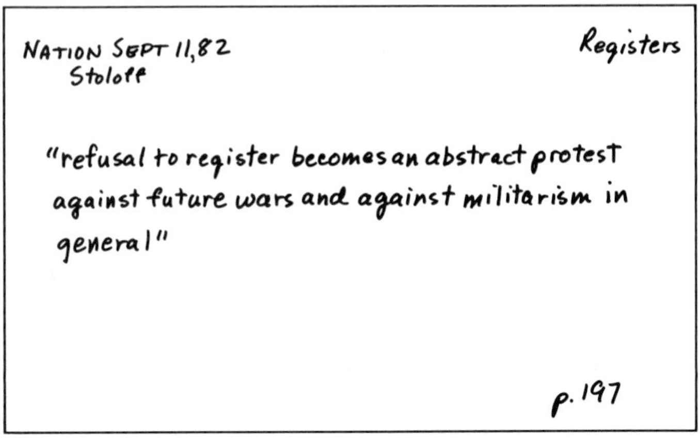

```
NATION SEPT 11,82                    Registers
   Stoloff


   "refusal to register becomes an abstract protest
against future wars and against militarism in
general"




                            p.197
```

taking, you will be more critical of what you read, more selective in what you write, and more aware of how information does or doesn't fit together. If the information doesn't fit, be prepared to search for more resources and to revise your own claim if the evidence persuades you to do so.

Figures 3 through 9 are examples of note cards from a student's research. Each serves as a record of the student's developing thoughts on the issue of the draft.

Figure 3 shows a paraphrase note card. The student's expression is not yet refined, but she has identified the relationships she will need to incorporate the information well.

In Figure 4, the quotation note card, the student has remembered to enclose the quote in quotation marks; the quote is brief yet significant for her purpose.

Notice that the information on the paraphrase note card with quoted term, Fig-

Figure 5 *Paraphrase note card with quoted term*

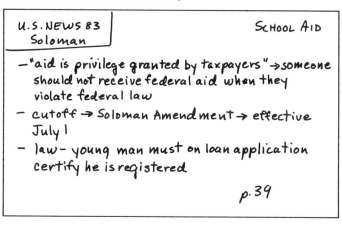

```
NATION SEPT 11, 82                          Registers
     Stoloff

Stoloff believes that the "scare" tactics for nonregisters
just shows that the fact that the arguments
serves that proves that there is a strong
national feeling against military intervention. —
even from men too young to recall Vietnam.



                                    p. 197
```

Figure 6 *Mixed information for summary note card*

```
U.S. NEWS 83                           SCHOOL AID
   Soloman

 —"aid is privilege granted by taxpayers"→someone
   should not receive federal aid when they
   violate federal law
 — cutoff → Soloman Amendment → effective
   July 1
 — law— young man must on loan application
   certify he is registered
                              p. 39
```

ure 5, is from the same source and appeared on the same page as the information on the note card in Figure 4, yet the student has written a separate card.

The student begins the note in Figure 6, the mixed information with summary note card, with information for summarizing and includes the background information on the law referred to in the summary.

The background history note card is shown in Figure 7. In many cases historical information is considered common knowledge. But if you are not familiar with that background, you may need to take notes.

The law reference note card is shown in Figure 8. Laws are part of the public record accessible to your readers, but if you don't know the exact terms of the law, you may need to write them down.

As the statistical reference note card in Figure 9 shows, when you want to re-

Figure 7 *Background history note card*

K. Lasson   History

From Rev – WWI → there was not really any long-
standing armed services. Volunteers were
secured when needed. After the need was gone
they were dismissed and the standing army
broke apart. Men at these times were
more than willing to volunteer.

                                          p.13

Figure 8 *Law reference note card*

CR)   Law

       order
    1) Volunteers
    2) Age twenty selection group
    3) Age twenty one
    4) Age twenty two – twenty 5
    5) Age 26 - 34
    6) Age 19 and 18½

                                     p. 56-57

Figure 9 *Statistical reference note card*

Johnston   Vietnam Statistics

            TABLE P. 14

                 CLASSIFICATION STATUS
                 OF SELECTIVE SERVICE
                 REGISTRANTS

produce a chart or graph that would be particularly useful to your readers, there is no need to copy it on the note card. Instead, just make a reference on the card and keep a photocopy of the chart in a folder (see the Typing Text and Handling Additional Material section of this chapter for suggestions on presenting charts).

FORMALIZING YOUR PLANNING

Once you have finished taking notes on your sources, you begin deciding how those source notes can contribute to the development of your paper. Your audience analysis (see Chapter 6) and preliminary planning on using the three appeals to reach your audience (see Chapter 8) give you a way to begin organizing your note cards. To formalize this process, you can use two procedures: the précis and the outline.

WRITING A PRÉCIS

A **précis** is a concise summary of essential points that can provide a useful bridge between your note taking and the outline of your presentation. While there is no one form to follow, using these guidelines will enable you to formalize the relationship of your purpose, your available support, and your claim:

1. Identify the issue as you see it.
2. State your claim.
3. Specify how you plan to support your claim.

The examples of précis that follow use these guidelines, but they differ in the ways they describe their support. One identifies kinds of sources available and the other specifies topic areas. While a list limited to the kinds of sources for support gives only a broad indication of the writer's plans, it does reveal variety in his sources. Relying on only one kind of source could limit your view (see the evaluation of sources in Chapters 4 and 7). The précis of the other writer indicates that she is ready to begin formalizing her outline.

Précis

FOR THE LOVE OF MONEY

There is an alarming number of people in our society who are willing to do anything for money. American citizens are performing the roles of spies for foreign nations by passing classified information to foreign agents in exchange for money. Money is the reason behind a vast majority of the reported espionage cases in the United States and must be curtailed through greatly increased penalties. Through the use of case studies, periodicals, and books written on espionage, I hope to persuade people of the need to increase penalties for crimes involving espionage.

Outline

I. Introduction (problem with espionage)

II. Why do people do it?

III. What do they get from it?

IV. What are the effects of it?

V. What are the penalties for it?

VI. Conclusion

Précis

A MOTHER'S PLACE ISN'T IN THE HOME

Today more and more mothers are returning to work when their infants are as young as four months old. Although there are some people who still hold the traditional belief that a mother's place is in the home, some researchers have found that mothers may work without interfering with the emotional and intellectual development of their children and that day care may even enhance development.

The purpose of this research paper is to convince mothers who feel that they *must* stay at home with their babies that day care is a smart alternative for mothers and that day care does enhance cognitive and social development. I plan to demonstrate this by showing statistics of how many mothers are working, the type of day care that children of working mothers are in, and how development of children in day care differs from that of the child at home.

I. WORKING MOTHERS

    A. Statistics

    B. Case Studies

II. CRITICAL PERIODS

    A. Periods of attachment

    B. Periods of stress

    C. Quality time vs. quantity time

III. DAY CARE

    A. Different types

    B. Different choices

IV. CHILDREN'S DEVELOPMENT

    A. Physically

    B. Intellectually

    C. Socially

ORGANIZING THE OUTLINE

Many teachers require that an outline be included with the final research paper. If this is the case, you will probably draft your paper from a *working outline* and revise the final copy to reflect any changes you made. But even if it isn't required, an outline is an effective means of formalizing your thoughts and support in a meaningful pattern of development, the sequence you want your audience to follow in understanding your view of the issue.

Outlines can follow a variety of formats but they all have two main features: they identify the *main topics* of the paper, and they indicate the *logic* of the sequence (for a review of logic and argument development see Chapters 7 and 9). Our two examples of outlines use different formats, but you can see in both a logical sequence of main ideas based on the writer's purpose. The one quality the formats share that is important to all outlines is *parallel consistency:* one uses a series of questions and the other a list of nouns grouped by main topic and subtopic. Other alternatives include phrases and complete sentences. An outline can take many forms, but the form chosen should remain internally consistent.

Whatever form you decide to use, your outline will alert you to weaknesses in your thinking or your support before you begin drafting your paper. When you have chosen your main topics, ask yourself, "Is this the clearest sequence for my audience to use in viewing this issue? Will they see why I believe what I do?" Then arrange your note cards for each section of your outline to evaluate the quantity and quality of your available sources. Code each note card with the number or letter of the outline section where you plan to use it.

Here are some examples of other outline formats.

Formal Structure   (using numerals and letters)

I. Introduction
   A. Description of landscape architecture
   B. Growth of profession
   C. THESIS: Landscape architecture is an environmental and social necessity.

II. Common Beliefs about Landscape Architecture
   A. Aesthetic beautification
   B. Land use

III. Why Landscape Architects Are Needed
   A. Preservation and protection
      1. Design
         a. Artistic skills
         b. Scientific skills
      2. Management
   B. Energy conservation
      1. Laws
      2. Case studies
         a. Florida International University study
         b. Stone and Associates' study
            (1) Hot, humid region
            (2) Functional composition

IV. Conclusion

Formal Structure   (using decimals)

1.0 Reviewing your entire draft
   1.1 Format
   1.2 Heading and subheadings
      1.2.1 Typography
      1.2.2 Position
      1.2.3 Numbering
      1.2.4 Phrasing
   1.3 Visual aids
      1.3.1 Numbering
      1.3.2 Captions and labels
      1.3.3 Placement
   1.4 Paragraphs

Formal Structure   (using decimals) (*continued*)

2.0 Editing sentences
    2.1 Sentence structure
        2.1.1 Subject, verb, and object
        2.1.2 Subject-verb agreement

Mixed Structure   (with consistent parallelism with main topics)

1. Précis
2. Introduction
    a. why deforestation is a problem
    b. why we need to become involved
3. Tropical forests
    a. what they are
    b. where they are
4. Function of tropical forests
    a. watershed protection
    b. food
    c. building materials
    d. fuel
    e. medicines
    f. industrial products
    g. home to species
5. Tropical deforestation
    a. how fast it's occurring
    b. where it's occurring
6. Causes of deforestation
    a. clearing of land for agricultural purposes
    b. logging
    c. construction projects
    d. fuelwood gathering
    e. resettlement projects
    f. inadequate management, protection, and reforestation
7. Local effects of deforestation
    a. loss of soil fertility
    b. fuel scarcity
    c. flooding
    d. decrease in rainfall
8. Global effects of deforestation
    a. greenhouse effect
    b. ozone depletion
    c. species loss
9. Conclusion

FORMALIZING YOUR PRESENTATION

By the time you actually sit down to compose your paper, you should know the direction you will take. Still, because writing allows you to discover what you think, new thoughts are very likely to come to mind while you are composing.

These new thoughts could be important to your paper, but don't stop to evaluate them during the first draft. Composing an effective research paper usually takes several drafts to *formalize* your writing for the final presentation. Allow several days *at least* for composing the paper and ample time for reading it with a fresh, critical eye for detail.

Formalizing your presentation requires a systematic procedure that helps you focus at each composing level. While the composing process is not the same for everyone, certain stages and concerns are fundamental to producing the final presentation.

DRAFTING

Preliminary Draft

FOCUS: Striving for content flow and voice

The best way to start your first draft is to clear your writing area of all source material and notes so you won't be tempted to stop your flow of words. Keep your working outline nearby so you can check where to go next if you begin to have writer's block in a section of your paper. If you can't think of a way to express yourself at a particular point, describe in parentheses what you want to do. If a particular source for your idea comes to mind, simply make a note of it and go on. By writing as much as you can from the beginning to the end of the paper you will establish your own writing voice—not the voice of your sources—and a flow of content that shows you how familiar you are with the ideas. This is one suggestion for making your own connections with the material in the first draft.

Second Draft

FOCUS: Incorporating sources

The second time you write your draft, keep your outline and note cards handy for reference. As you read the first draft, keep your focus on support for your ideas. Make a notation at each point where you think a source would be helpful. Then begin composing your second draft. This time, double space your work (to prepare for the next revision level) and add the material from the source notations you made.

REVISION

Revising for Logical Consistency

FOCUS: Effect of sequence

Reread your second draft and on a separate sheet of paper write down the main topic of each paragraph. Check these topics against the outline you worked out earlier. Has the sequence changed? If so, is it better? Are all the topics you included in your draft relevant? Will the reader be able to follow the sequence clearly? Use the space between the lines to make any changes you need. If you need to change an entire sequence, write out another double-spaced draft. At this point, get a second reader for your draft, someone willing to give you an honest opinion on how clearly you have developed the sequence of your argument. Ask your reader to complete the Reading for Content sheet on p. 448. This and the other peer response sheets in this chapter will guide others in responding to your writing and you in reacting to theirs.

Revising for Control of Language

FOCUS: Clarity and motivation

After making any changes in sequence that your trusted reader has suggested, reread your draft, paying close attention to your use of language (see Chapter 10). Have you provided enough concrete details to explain the abstract terms you include? Is your writing free of jargon, clichés, and sexist language? Is your tone clear and consistent? Are your sentences too complex for your reader to follow or too simple to make the necessary connections? How will the reader characterize you—as fair, unfair, emotional, angry? After changing any language you think interferes with your purpose, have someone else read your paper and mark any language that isn't clear. Ask the reader to use the Reading for Style sheet on p. 449.

Revising for Documentation

FOCUS: Accuracy

The models in Chapter 11 will guide you in checking the accuracy of your documentation. Be consistent in the style you use, whether MLA or APA. Look carefully at quotations to make sure quotation marks and punctuation are correctly positioned. Check for acknowledgment phrasing in paraphrases or inclusion of the author's name in the end parentheses. Have someone read your paper and underline any undocumented sentence that does not seem to be expressed in your own words. If there is any question, check your sources to make sure you haven't plagiarized unintentionally. Use the Reading for Documentation sheet on p. 450 to organize your reader's response.

EDITING

FOCUS: Mechanics and grammar

The final stage of composing focuses on the refinements of usage and mechanics: spelling, subject-verb agreement, punctuation, parallel structure, pronoun agreement, and sentence structure. Read and correct any errors you find, but be sure to have someone else read your paper for typographical errors after it is typed. You probably won't find any because you don't want them to be there.

READING FOR CONTENT

WRITER _____

RESPONDER _____

1. State the writer's claim and the premises on which it is based. Comment on the validity of this reasoning, and make any suggestions for revising the reasoning that would make it clearer to the reader.

2. What assumptions is the writer making about the audience's relationship to the issue being argued? Should the writer make these assumptions about the audience's knowledge and experience? Explain your answer.

3. Comment on the quantity and quality of the evidence the writer has selected to support the claim. Make suggestions for adding or deleting information, keeping in mind the appropriateness of the material for the audience's needs.

4. Describe the arrangement of the information. Where does it begin and where does it lead? Using broad categories, outline the arrangement on the back of this sheet. Then make suggestions for rearrangement, if needed.

5. Has the writer achieved credibility through his or her persona? Describe how. If necessary, make suggestions that would increase the writer's *ethos*.

6. What do you feel is the strongest feature of the paper?

7. What do you feel is the weakest feature of the paper?

8. If you were the intended audience, how would you respond to the paper?

READING FOR STYLE

WRITER _____

RESPONDER _____

1. What effect does the title have on the intended audience?

2. Has the reader designed the piece for high readability? Explain.

3. How does the introduction engage the intended reader's interest?

4. Describe how the writer has paced the content for the reader.

5. Describe how the writer has paced the language for the reader. Consider the use of tension in diction and sentence structure.

6. List some uses of language you find particularly engaging.

7. Comment on the effectiveness of the writer's choice of persona and tone.

READING FOR DOCUMENTATION

WRITER _____

RESPONDER _____

1. Has the writer documented all quotations? Read through the paper, stopping wherever quotation marks are used. Note below any pages where parenthetical citation or endnote numbering is needed or needs to be revised in some way.

2. Has the writer documented all paraphrased material? If there are sections that do not seem to be in the writer's own voice, note the page and section below. If paraphrases are documented, check the accuracy of the form.

3. How well has the writer used acknowledgement phrases to introduce sources? Note places where this material is awkwardly expressed or where the credentials of the authority are not established well.

4. Does the writer need more documented sources to support his or her claim? Explain where and why more sources are needed. What kind of sources would you suggest?

5. Has the writer used too many sources? Is the flow of the information interrupted too often? Where?

6. How accurate are the external documentation sections (works cited, bibliography, references, endnotes)? Read each entry carefully, checking it against the style format the writer chose.

7. Comment on how the writer's use of documentation affects his or her *ethos.*

PREPARING THE FINAL COPY

FOCUS: Completeness

Depending on your teacher's requirements, your final presentation will include some or all of these elements:

Title page

Abstract or précis

Outline

Text of paper

Appendix

Content or explanatory notes (if parenthetical documentation is used)

Endnotes (if parenthetical documentation is not used)

Works Cited or References

Blank sheet of paper for instructor's comments

An **abstract** or brief summary is often placed at the beginning of the paper to allow readers to survey the contents. Just as the abstracts you read during your investigation helped you select your sources, so too will your abstract guide readers in determining their interest in your research. Abstracts are generally required in APA-style papers.

Two kinds of abstracts serve different purposes. The *descriptive abstract* describes what the purpose of the paper is and explains how the purpose is achieved. This is generally a short summary, 75 to 100 words long, similar in content to the précis. The sample MLA style paper at the end of this chapter includes a descriptive abstract that is labeled a précis. The *informative abstract* tells what a paper *says,* summarizing the basic content and structure of the paper. The informative abstract is generally longer than the descriptive abstract, ranging from 100 to 150 words. The sample APA-style paper at the end of this chapter includes an informative abstract.

Typing Text and Handling Additional Material. If you do include a *title page,* center the title in the middle of the page. Do not underline your title or put it in quotation marks. Capitalize the first word, the last word, and any word after a colon; also capitalize all other words except articles, conjunctions, and prepositions.

An inch below the title center the word "By," and two spaces below that center your name. An inch below your name center and type double spaced the course number, your instructor's name, and the date (see the example at the top of the next page). Do not number the title page.

The Prime-Time Preacher:

Brother Love or Brother $$$?

By

Howard Murtry

English 111

Dr. W. Sanderson

April 6, 19___

    Leave one-inch *margins* on all sides of the text, including the top and bottom. *Double space* the entire text, notes, works cited, outline, and all long quotations. Indent paragraphs five spaces and long quotations ten spaces (long quotations are approximately fifty words or four to five lines). If the title appears on the first page of the text, quadruple space between the title and the beginning of the first paragraph. Quadruple space also after Works Cited, centered one inch from the top, on the last page.

    Place the *page number* in the upper righthand corner one-half inch from the top of the page and one inch from the right. Do not use punctuation with page numbers. If you don't have a title page, number all pages and place your name before each number beginning with page 2. If you use a title page and an outline, number the pages of the outline with small Roman numerals, starting with page ii (the title page is counted as page i but is not numbered).

    Occasionally you may find *tables, graphs, charts, maps,* or *illustrations* useful. If you plan to use them as an additional reference only, place them in an appendix at the end of the paper. But if they are important to your text, place them as closely as possible to the section of the paper that refers to them. Tables present information listed in columns. They are labeled *Tables,* assigned Arabic numerals, captioned in sequence to identify purpose, and double spaced. Place the source of the information below the table unless you compiled the information yourself.

    Illustrations, graphs, maps, charts, and photographs are labeled *Figures,* often abbreviated "Fig.," given an Arabic numeral, and identified by a title. This information and the name of the source appear below the figure. An example is given in Figure 10. Remember that somewhere in the text of your paper, there must be a reference to each table or figure.

Figure 10 *An example of a figure*

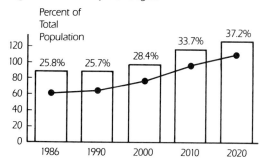

Figure 4: 50 and Over, a Growing Force
Note: Line shows projection to the year 2020 of the number of people in the U.S. 50 years and older, starting with an estimate for July, 1986, in millions. Bars show the percent of the population 50 and older.
Source: U.S. Census Bureau, <u>New York Times,</u> February 7, 1988.

When presenting research in some disciplines, you may be required to use *headings* to indicate the organization of your paper. Papers in the humanities usually do not use headings, but disciplines requiring the APA style use five different levels of headings. Each of these levels has a distinct positioning and typing form.

LEVEL I
(centered uppercase)

Level 2
(centered upper- and lowercase)

<u>Level 3</u>
(centered, underlined, upper- and lowercase)

<u>Level 4</u> (flush left, underlined, upper- and lowercase)

    <u>Level 5.</u> (indented, underlined, paragraph opening ending with a period, lowercase except for first letter)

An example using all five levels is given on the next page.

SOUTH AMERICAN TROPICAL DEFORESTATION

External Validation

Effects

Local Evidence

Loss of soil fertility.

With the exception of masters' theses and doctoral dissertations, most APA research presentations require only two or three levels of headings. For two levels the APA recommends using Level 2 and Level 4 headings; for three levels use Level 2, Level 4, and Level 5 headings. The sample APA-style essay on pages 468–485 uses two levels of headings.

If you are required to use headings, remember that headings must be visually and grammatically parallel, as in outlines, and any information in the heading must be repeated somewhere in the text that follows, usually in the first sentence after the heading.

As an extra margin of safety, be sure to make a photocopy of your paper before turning it in to your teacher. If you are using a word processor, always remember to save your paper periodically (after every 15 minutes of typing), and be sure to SAVE the paper before you proceed to PRINT it.

A sample argumentative research paper in MLA style follows (pages 455–467). A sample argumentative research paper in APA style follows the MLA paper on pages 468–485.

When a Woman's Place Is in the Home

By

Leslie Nelson

ENGL 111

Dr. K. Bell

April 8, 1990

RHETORICAL CONTEXT

SUBJECT: Homemaker protection

AUDIENCE: Unmarried or newly married women

PURPOSE: To persuade them to insulate their
rights in a marriage before trouble
begins

Précis

All too often a woman enters into a marriage certain it will "last forever," and after years of caring for her husband and their home, finds herself abandoned with virtually no resources to fall back on. Through careful planning and active participation in household matters, though, homemakers can insulate themselves from the ravages of divorce. With the aid of interviews and statistics obtained through current periodicals and books, I will attempt to convince potential and new homemakers of the very real possibility of divorce and the need for protecting themselves against it.

The information included in this précis parallels the information in a descriptive abstract.

OUTLINE

I. Introduction

    A. Example of homemaker who has been devastated by divorce

    B. Research support

II. Origination of no-fault laws

    A. Traditional laws

        1. Grounds for divorce

        2. Punishment and reward

        3. Courtroom battles

    B. No-fault laws

        1. Grounds for divorce

        2. Property division

III. Women and poverty

    A. Inequalities in "equal" distribution

        1. Inequalities created by marriage

        2. Inequalities created by society

    B. Equitable distribution as a replacement for alimony

        1. The value of marital property

        2. The amount awarded to women

IV. The reality of divorce

    A. Divorce rates

    B. Precautions for married women

V. Conclusion

    A. Necessary precautions

    B. Positive events

When a Woman's Place is in the Home

Sandra and Lenny were married 25 years when Lenny decided to leave his wife for a younger woman. At the time of the divorce, Lenny was earning a six-figure salary; however, Sandra had no income because she had spent those 25 years as a wife and mother. Except for the family home, all of their assets were in Lenny's name. Thus, when the judge decided on the terms of the settlement, Sandra received only one-half the value of the house and $100 a week in maintenance. Lenny, the spouse who had been responsible for the demise of their marriage, was not required to even *contribute* to Sandra's legal fees which totaled a whopping $65,000! What was the reasoning behind such a settlement? Sandra had this comment:

> The judge had the gall to tell me that in mid-life both my ex-husband and I were starting new lives and new careers. He forgot to mention that [my husband] is working with 30 years of business experience and $600,000 of capital he got out of my father's company. My "new career," on the other hand, will barely keep me above the poverty level. (Hewlett 4)

While this example may appear to be out of the ordinary, it is not. Due to the divorce revolution

1   *Opens with an anec-dote to illustrate issue. Uses questions as bridge to quote.*

2   *Quote expresses emotional impact of the issue in someone else's words.*

     Quotes of more than four lines are indented. Parenthetical notation after end punctuation.

3   *Places examples within a class. Introduces credentials of researcher as expert witness.*

inspired by California's no-fault laws, countless women have found themselves in similar, or worse, situations. Dr. Lenore J. Weitzman, a sociologist and associate professor at Harvard University, conducted research on the no-fault laws. During interviews with judges, lawyers, and divorced persons she kept hearing disturbing stories about older homemakers who had been cut off with only a few years of alimony and no chance of decent employment: "At first," said Dr. Weitzman, "I thought these heartbreaking stories were the exceptions, but after years of research I had to admit they were the rule" (Hunt 160).

Direct quote from expert to verify conflict.

Before the 1970's no-fault divorces were unheard of. In order for someone to get a divorce under the traditional laws, they had to prove that their spouse had victimized them in some way. For example, adultery, desertion, and physical or mental cruelty were considered sufficient grounds for divorce. Marital breakdown was not (Weitzman 7). After the offense was determined and the guilty party identified, property was divided on a punishment and reward system. The "guilty" husband was punished by being required to pay alimony and perhaps forfeit a good deal of the marital property to his ex-wife. If the woman, on the other hand, was found to be the culprit, she would not be entitled to financial support from her ex-husband (Weitzman 14).

4

Summarizes divorce law before no-fault in terms of grounds and basic settlement procedure.

Because their financial well-being often hinged 5
on the outcome of the divorce proceedings, men and
women took great pains to prove their spouse's
guilt. "Couples often reacted excessively, so that
many divorce struggles left both parties even more
deeply wounded than they need have been" (Hunt
160). Thus, when California enacted the first laws to
allow divorce on the basis of "irreconcilable differences," it was considered a major breakthrough for
those individuals "trapped" in bad marriages (Weitzman 15). The no-fault divorces became so popular
that eventually every state, except for South Dakota,
adopted some version of the law. In fact, "marital
breakdown" is the only basis for divorce in 14 states
(Weitzman 41).

Because guilt is not a factor in no-fault proceed- 6
ings, the division of marital property is thrust into
an entirely new context. Eight western and south-
western states subscribe to community property
laws. "All property . . . ," says Linda Ferguson, a Los
Angeles attorney, "must be split 50—50 between the
couple" (Gupta 48). In the past, the remaining states
practiced common law property rules which meant
that property was awarded to whichever spouse
held the title. Forty of these states eventually replaced the common law property rules with equitable distribution laws which, according to attorney
Patricia J. Powers, consider all property that is ob-

tained while the couple is married as belonging to both parties. Before the final settlement, though, the earning potential of both partners is considered so that, in theory, homemakers are awarded a larger percentage of the marital assets (Gupta 48).

Unfortunately, theory is a long way from reality   7
and, in reality, no-fault divorces and their "humane" property settlements have often hurt the very people they were designed to protect. A 1986 White House report on the American family stated: "Divorce reform was supposed to be a panacea for women trapped in bad marriages. It has trapped many of them in poverty" (Hewlett 4). The standard of living for the average woman drops 73% after divorce while her ex-husband's actually rises 42% (Weitzman xii). What can account for such an overwhelming difference? Dr. Weitzman believes one reason is a "legal   Basis of no-fault divorce
system [that] treats men and women 'equally' at di-   in paraphrase, summary,
                                                                 and quotation
vorce [and] ignores the very real economic in-   combined.
equalities that marriage creates" (xi). By this, she is referring to the community property laws which op-
erate under the assumption that a 50–50 split is equal; however, when a woman spends her adult life as a homemaker, she excludes herself from the workforce and limits her employment opportunities. Therefore, the ex-husband of a homemaker has a much greater earning capacity.

As Dr. Weitzman points out, the legal system   8

"also ignores the economic inequalities between men and women in the larger society" (xi). When the newly divorced woman enters the workforce in search of a job, she discovers what all women face—59 cents to every dollar earned by a man (Riley 11). Thus, when society and marriage have already tipped the financial scales in favor of men, a divorce settlement that divides property in half is hardly equal.

Another reason that divorced women face such a bleak economic future is that fewer women receive alimony and those that do, get it for a much shorter period of time than in the past. Under traditional divorce laws, 62% of all alimony awards lasted until the woman remarried or died, compared to 32% under the present system (Hunt 160). Alimony awards are gradually being replaced by equitable distribution laws which are *supposed* to award marital assets according to each party's earning potential. Putting this supposition aside for a moment, consider what political scientist Herbert Jacob has found: "The major asset of most marriages is the income stream—earning power of the chief wage-earner—and that is not touched by divorce law" (Hunt 160–161). The average couple, according to a 1984 New Jersey Supreme Court task force, has only $4000 worth of assets that are "touchable" (Hewlett

9   *Uses direct and indirect quotations to explain application of no-fault laws to property settlement.*

5). Now, consider what Chicago lawyer Vernon Rine-

hart says when discussing equitable distribution:

> As a rule, women continue to get shortchanged
>
> during the process. One study estimates that
>
> females receive about one-third of the total
>
> family assets . . . after divorce. (Gupta 48)

How is the homemaker, with virtually no job experi-

ence and little or no monthly support from her ex-

husband, supposed to survive on one-third of $4000,

or $1333.33? She barely does.

This is not the end of a sad story. When most

young women get married, the last thing they want

to think about is their "perfect marriage" coming to

an end; but, the stark, ugly reality is that many of

these relationships *do* end. In a one year period end-

ing April 1984 there were 1.17 million divorces in

the United States. If current trends continue, one-

half of all newly married couples will end up di-

vorced (Kidder 26). Just how many of these women

wind up in financial ruin may depend upon their

willingness to face the possibility of divorce before it

occurs. "To acknowledge that divorce is *possible*

does not mean you expect your marriage to fail"

(Hunt 161). It just makes good sense to face facts.

Does this mean that a woman who plans to be a

homemaker should abandon that idea in order to

protect herself from economic oblivion? Certainly

Marginal annotations:

Addresses the audience directly.

10   Indents quote more for readability and empha-sis than because of length.

Responds to quote.

11   Identifies connection between audience and issue.

Uses question to keep dialogue with audience.

not. It does mean, however, that she needs to take certain precautions just in case she does wind up as a divorce statistic. Fern Susan Garber, a lawyer in New York City, recommends three simple steps be taken by all married women:

1. *They should establish their own line of credit and open up their own bank account.* If the only credit and bank accounts a woman has access to are jointly held with her husband, he can close them at any time without her permission or knowledge. Thus, if the couple separates, the woman may be left without any financial resources at a time when she really needs them.

   12   Includes recommendations for preventing problem.

2. *A woman should make certain that at least some property is in her name or in both her and her husband's name.* While states that subscribe to equitable distribution consider all marital property as jointly held, all states do not classify property this way. Some states award property to the spouse that holds the title.

   13

3. *Women should be aware of all financial transactions.* They should be familiar with their husband's yearly income, where the family banks, the contents of their stock portfolio, etc. This information will be needed to determine the amount of child support and maintenance awards. If it is not readily available, the wife's

   14

attorney will have to collect the data which will take much more . . . time and money. (162–163)

Another precautionary measure recommended by divorce lawyers is that women insist on a pre- nuptial contract. In order for the contract to be con- sidered valid both the husband and wife should have legal counsel to aid in drafting the agreement. Typi- cally, a prenuptial contract specifies the terms for property division including just what assets are considered marital property, the conditions under which alimony would be awarded, and the provision that the custodial parent retain the right to the fam- ily home (Hunt 161–162).

15

Recommendations con- tinue, using paraphrase.

All of this careful attention to the possibility that one may find herself the victim of divorce some- how dampens the excitement of a new marriage. Un- fortunately, because of the unfair treatment women have received under the newer property laws, such precautions have become necessary. On the plus side, though, certain steps have been taken to even out the inequity. For example, due to the Child Sup- port Enforcement Amendment of 1984, most states are now toughening up on parents who fail to meet child support payments. Also, many states are re- forming their existing divorce laws in order to better protect women and children. Another major breakthrough occurred in July 1987 when the state of Wisconsin began withholding support payments

16

Identifies well with pos- sible effect of informa- tion on audience.

from the paychecks of non-custodial parents
(Hewlett 5).

Perhaps one of the most exciting examples is
the story of Loretta O'Brien. In 1985 the New York
court of appeals ruled that she was entitled to a
share of her ex-husband's medical license because
she had supported both of them while he was in
medical school. Loretta's share came to $188,000
(Hunt 161).

17   Cites incident that conveys hope for more equity in settlements. Logical and emotional appeal.

These are but a few positive incidents amidst a
vast number of negative ones. Therefore, as encouraging as these victories may be, they by no means
diminish the need for taking the precautions mentioned earlier. If it helps, think of them as a sort of
life insurance: "Taking precautions against the *possibility* of a marriage's ending because of divorce is
no less sensible than . . . ensuring a wife will be
cared for should her husband die" (Hunt 161).

18

Ends with quote that has logic and emotional appeal.

Works Cited

Garber, Fern Susan. "A Lawyer Tells Women What
They Should Know about Divorce." *Good Housekeeping* July 1987: 64+.

Gupta, Udayan. "The Economics of Divorce." *Black
Enterprise* April 1984: 47–50.

Hewlett, Sylvia Ann. "When a Husband Walks Out."
Parade 7 June 1987: 4–5.

Hunt, Morton. "What the New Divorce Laws Are
Doing to Women." *Good Housekeeping* July 1987:
64+.

Kidder, Rushworth M. "Marriage in America: Cross
Currents of Change." *Christian Science Monitor*
25 November 1985: 26–27.

Riley, Maria. "Economic Justice for Women: Challenging Those Myths Keeping Women Dependent." *Engaged* January 1984: 9–11.

Weitzman, Lenore J. *The Divorce Revolution*. New
York: Free Press, 1985.

A Prescription for Teaching Writing

By

Sheila Cooper Powell

English 327

Professor Reynolds

April 18, 1990

Short title (running head) repeated on each page. Use small roman numerals in unpublished papers for pages preliminary to the text.

RHETORICAL CONTEXT

Occasion: Class assignment to compose an original piece of writing following A.P.A. guidelines, designed for my needs and interests as I define my responsibility as a prospective English teacher.

Purpose: To convince the audience that we as English teachers should practice what we teach—if we teach writing, we should continually make those skills our habit.

Thesis: We must become familiar with the writing process in theory *and in practice* so that we are able to model the writing process before our students.

Audience: This paper is directed toward college students who will become English teachers. Often we subconsciously plan a scheme of revenge to be carried out on our students. We think, "Ah ha, no more papers for me to write—I can just make all my students suffer as I did." As English teachers, we should avoid this attitude about what we teach and practice writing regularly. We are misled if we think we can teach a behavior without continually performing that behavior. This audience usually reads papers of this nature where the syntactic development and level of diction is sophisticated. Some informality achieved by using familiar, real and humorous illustrations that rivet mental handles to abstract concepts might help me be argumentative yet winsomely persuasive by removing some of the sharper edges. I will also strive to attain readability by formatting my writing for eye-appeal.

Abstract

Writing is probably the only art being taught in our schools by teachers who do not regularly practice what they teach. We are neglecting the more effective teaching method of showing and not just telling. Because students in a classroom often become reflections of the behavior modeled by their teacher, we have the responsibility to teach writing by participating in writing with our students. Clearly, teachers who have knowledge of the writing process as well as experience in the writing process and who share their own composing process while teaching their students to write will become more effective English teachers.

An abstract is a brief summary of the main points of a paper. It should indicate the central thesis, the main support, and the conclusions reached. Double space and type in block form flush with the left margin.

A Prescription For Teaching Writing

On the first text page, the title is centered and the introduction is not labeled.

They saunter, strut, slither or plod into the classrooms, each one sending a different signal:

1

I'm not interested.

I'm not going to learn.

I dare you to teach me.

Please teach me; I want to learn.

Students in a classroom can become reflections of their teachers' behavior and mirror their actions to an emphatic degree. The results can be creative or destructive. As teachers win admiration and influence students by the patterns of their lives, they become a kind of carbon paper that transfers behavior by the rubbing of one life against another.

Writer introduces the context for the problem and the thesis.

To the extent that teachers are respected by their students, they influence them.

2

Shortened paragraph form for emphasis and readability.

To the extent that teachers influence their students, they teach them.

3

As prospective English teachers, how will we approach the teaching of writing? It must become obvious that we cannot become peddler teachers standing in front of a captive classroom marketing our wares on platters of persuasion as we dupe our students into buying knowledge with a process which we neither experience nor practice. No, we

4

Writer establishes a direct *we*-relationship with the audience. Notice the writer's effective use of metaphor.

must first become familiar with the writing process
in theory <u>and in practice</u> so that we are able to
model writing behavior before our students.

In APA style underline
words for which special
emphasis is given.

The Writing Process

In APA style first-level
heading is centered.

According to George Hillocks, Jr. (1986), 1963   5
was the year Braddock, Lloyd-Jones, and Schoer
posed the question: "What is involved in the act of
writing?" (p. xvi). That question was the focus of
<u>Research in Written Composition</u> (1963) which be-
gan to effect the changes in teaching writing that
are still evolving today. The essential change shifted
our focus from the written product itself to what the
student does to produce that product. What this behavior does—the act of writing—is known as the
writing process.

Publication date is
placed in parentheses
next to author's name.
Writer uses sources to
establish a historical
point of reference.

The writing process is the core of all writing. It   6
is all that happens from the time the writer's creative spark is ignited until the product is actually
completed. Generally, researchers agree that the
writing process includes three phases (Alloway
1979; Britton 1975; Carroll 1979; Emig 1967, 1979;
Hillocks 1986; King 1979):

When citing two or
more authors in the
same parentheses, give
them in alphabetical
order and separate the
entries with semicolons.

    a. prewriting

    b. composing

    c. revising

A fourth and final but often neglected phase, publishing, must be included—especially when we begin to teach writing.

Prewriting

In APA style second-level heading is flush left and underlined.

Jot-listing, brainstorming, mapping, thinking, reading, imitating, and a variety of other activities all constitute prewriting. Hillocks (1986) found that many researchers define prewriting as "the period of time between the moment the assignment is received and the time the writing begins" (p. 2). This is a decision-making phase. Hillocks (1986) believes the research suggests "what happens in the prewriting period is more important than the length of time involved" (p. 3). While that may be true, it would seem that the average three to five minutes (p. 3) given to prewriting in the classroom cannot be enough time to accomplish what Gauntlett (1978) calls "a procedure for stimulating thinking" (p. 29). He says,

> Prewriting involves sensing, imagining, feeling, talking, and writing. It can also include drawing, dancing, dramatizing, or sculpturing. (p. 29)

As teachers we need to encourage and stimulate thinking to begin writing in whichever ways work with our very different students.

7

Indented quotes do not use quotation marks. The page number reference in parentheses comes *after* the end punctuation. Although this quote is less than forty words, it does take four lines, and indenting it emphasizes important distinctions.

Composing

This is the stage generating a concrete message which begins to communicate the writer's ideas stimulated in the prewriting phase. Perl (1979, p. 331) says composing is a discovery:

> Composing always involves some measure of both construction and discovery. Constructing simultaneously affords discovery. Writers know more fully what they mean only after having written it.

The composing or writing phase is the time to exercise the exacting discipline of squeezing thoughts down through the fingertips, reducing elusive, shadowy ideas to concrete expressions on paper. Composing is best accomplished without concern for mechanics or usage which, according to Kirby and Liner (1981) and other researchers, will be checked for errors as revision occurs. It is important to compose without the fear of making a mistake as Ponsot and Deen (1982) observed:

> A class profits from a pleasant atmosphere—if the pleasure be not idle—since writers work better when they watch not one another out of fear. (p. 139)

This is not the time for us to be overexpecting teachers who constantly correct, berate or cajole—the

The margin notes:

8   The quote is introduced by the author's name, date of source, and page number; therefore, no page reference is needed after the quote.

9   The writer synthesizes three sources to define this stage of the writing process.

message which oozes from our frowns and glares. Like children who wobble and fall as they learn to ride a bike, beginning writers experience shaky imperfection as they learn the composing process. We will sap their motivation and enjoyment if our demands and expectations cause fear by giving the distinct impression that no matter how hard they try, it won't be good enough. At this stage let's keep in mind four words:

The writer uses a simile to further clarify the meaning and evoke an emotional response in the reader.

Acceptance

Tolerance

Acknowledgement

Encouragement

And let them write.

Revising

While prewriting and composing allow students more freedom for individuality, revision becomes more complex and structured. Students need to be shown that most writing requires revision.[1] But it is not a naturally occurring process to inexperienced writers (Bracewell, Scardamalia, and Bereiter 1979).

The superscript number refers to a content note at the end of the paper.

Hayes and Flower (1980) make a distinction in the revision process between editing and reviewing. Editing seems to be "triggered automatically and

may occur in brief episodes interrupting other processes"; reviewing is a decision "to devote a period of
time to systematic examination and improvement of
the text" (p. 18).

In actuality, the writing process as Hayes and   12
Flower (1980) define it is recursive in nature—the
various phases interact and interrupt each other.
They found that:

1. Prewriting is occasionally interrupted by editing.

2. Composing is often interrupted by more prewriting and editing.

3. Revision is often interrupted by prewriting and
   composing. (p. 18)

So the revision phase consisting of at least two sub-
processes occurs to some extent throughout the
writing process. This is what Hayes and Flower
called editing.

Reviewing, on the other hand, is devoting time   13
to systematic review and improvement of the text
(p. 18). This seems to be the act of seeing again, of
structuring according to the given topic or thesis; of
polishing by checking for usage, mechanics, spelling
or grammar errors and adding, deleting or
changing.

Calkins (1981) and Graves (1981) show that   14
revising must be learned. Hillocks (1986) reports
that this research was put into practice by Cohen

and Scardamalia (no date) who taught a group of sixth graders questioning techniques to use as they evaluated their peers' writing. Through these frequent practice techniques, the criteria taught for revision became internalized in these students and they were able to use this revision process very well with their own writing. The researchers then reported "significant gains in the quality of revisions made and in the frequency of revisions, especially in 'idea' revisions" (Hillock 1986, p. 160).

The Writing Teacher

Tucked away in our classrooms will be many young people whose eyes are on us, whose ears are tuned in. But will we know where we are going?   15

A story is often told about Thomas Henry Huxley, devoted disciple of Darwin, famous biologist, teacher, and author, self-avowed humanist, traveling lecturer.   16

In Dublin, Ireland, toward the end of the nineteenth century, Huxley was in a hurry the morning after a lecture to catch a train to the next city. He jumped in one of Dublin's famous horse-drawn taxis and settled back to rest during the ride. He assumed the hotel doorman had told the driver the destination so the only command he barked as he got in was "Hurry—I'm almost late. Drive fast!" The horses galloped across Dublin at a vigorous pace. Before   17   The writer introduces an anecdote used as an analogy.

long Huxley glanced out the window and realized they were going west—the wrong direction. Leaning forward the scholar shouted, "Do you know where you are going?" Without looking back, the driver yelled, "No, your honor. But I am driving very fast."

And so it is in the classroom as we try to teach writing. If we lose our way, even if we are running very fast, we will not accomplish three worthwhile writing goals.

18   The writer connects the anecdote to the research problem.

Our Students

Our students have the capabilities and the resources to draft pieces of writing which convey their messages. All students have something worthwhile to say, but with that right, they have the responsibility to qualify their statements according to the proof they have.

19

We can encourage our students to write what they think by becoming not pedantic lecturers but facilitators who engage them in writing. Then writing becomes for our students what Kirby and Liner (1981) say "it should have been all along—a high level human activity, at once challenging and satisfying, and very exciting. And for many of them it will be a lifelong pursuit" (p. 227). These writers insist that "[our] job, first and last, is to help [our] students *grow* as writers" (p. 230).

20

Brackets indicate that the writer has changed the pronoun within the quote to maintain consistency in her direct *we*-relationship with the audience.

Ourselves

We teach by our actions. By being late to class,   21
we teach the unimportance of punctuality. By being
discriminative, we teach inequality. And by demanding that our students prewrite, compose, and revise
without demanding the same from ourselves, we
teach that writing is a meaningless exercise ending
outside of the classroom.

Ponsot and Deen in <u>Beat Not the Poor Desk</u>   22
(1982) continually assert that ". . . we too write, as
always what we ask students to write in class . . ."
(p. 15). They have noticed in their classrooms that
students who feel as though they are being watched
produce stilted, self-conscious writing (pp. 163,
164).

> Underline book titles with solid lines; in APA style underline even the spaces between words in a title.

Are we being trained to be only demanding ob-   23
servers and not participants? Covino, Johnson and
Feehan (1980) surveyed forty-five English departments throughout the United States and Canada asking college faculty what courses future writing
teachers should take. Edward Kearns (1985) of the
University of Northern Colorado noted their recommendations did not include a writing course. "The
underlying assumption of both the survey and the
respondents seems clear—one can teach writing
without taking a course in writing" (p. 28). Let's
take the initiative to practice writing for ourselves.

Writing is a behavior demanded of us all. This is 24
the anvil on which Kearns (1985) hammers the
need for teachers to practice what they teach and
teach what they do. He reminds us that:

> Ours is the only art required of all citizens and
> our largest task appears to be to inform them
> it _is_ an art. . . . But perhaps the only risk fac-
> ing us is the one we ourselves must take when
> we sit down with pen or typewriter and begin,
> "Once upon a time. . . ." (p. 33)

Again Kirby and Liner (1981) insist that we 25
write with our students.

> The main point about teaching writing . . . is
> that [we] teach young writers by example, not
> by precept. . . . [We] have to be willing to take
> the same risks [we] ask kids to take, to be as
> vulnerable with [our] writing as [we] want
> them to be, to be open about [our] struggles,
> [our] successes, [our] failures and near-
> misses—[our] writing process—as [we] en-
> courage them to be. (p. 226)

Our Publishing

For writing to become worthwhile, it must have 27
an audience. Writing is meant to be read. As Kirby
(1981) describes the connection, "the writer, the
writing, and the reader are linked in a cooperative

The writer uses a metaphor to strengthen her point.

Ellipsis points or spaced periods are used to indicate part of a quoted passage has been left out. When the omitted material appears at the end of a sentence, the first period closes the sentence and the three ellipsis points indicate the omitted material.

relationship that inevitably changes each of them"
(p. 132). Kirby believes that we must encourage our
students, as well as ourselves, to go public with our
writing to "broaden audience intuition and build motivation" (p. 139).

Publishing (going public) needs to be an experi-   28
ence we as writers model to our students. It is the
natural end to the work of writing since all writing
needs an audience. It is important to our own growth
as writers as well as to our students' growth for
these reasons:

The writer introduces an enumerated list of points. The parallel openings give emphasis to the term publishing.

1. Publishing gives the writer an audience, and the
   writing task becomes a real effort at communication—not just writing to please the teacher.
2. Publishing is the only reason for the writing to
   be important enough for the hard work of
   [revision].
3. Publishing involves the ego, which is the strongest incentive for the . . . writer to keep writing.
4. Publishing is fun. (Liner 1981, p. 215)

This end to the writing process is too often ne-   29
glected and we need to encourage our students to
join us in this exciting venture.[2]

To be sure, this is not all that is involved in the   30
effective teaching of writing. But since we are prospective English teachers, we need to begin considering how we will teach to inspire and motivate our

students to become fluent, life-long writers. Those of us who become master teachers will punctuate our teaching with vulnerability and personal growth as we share our own writing with our students and invite them to participate with us in the writing process. Our writing is like a relay which must be practiced around the track day after day. It is not a sprint, but a marathon. There are no fifty-yard dash courses in becoming a good writer. But, as we write and publish with our students, we outdistance those who stumble with slow-starts and sloppy hand-offs. Relays are won or lost at that critical moment when a young hand reaches back and gropes for the baton. Let's keep our hand-offs crisp and sharp by being teachers who know and experience the writing process, by being teachers who write.

The writer introduces a concluding metaphor to summarize her main points.

Content Notes

1. At least two studies (Hansen 1978; Bracewell, Bereiter, and Scardamalia, 1979) conclude that revision is not profitable to the writing process. Perhaps it is because children cannot separate themselves from their writing enough to be able to criticize it; perhaps it is because they do not know what questions to ask which will lead to idea or content revision and not merely revision correcting mechanical errors.

Content notes give information not essential to the paper but helpful to the reader.

2. Tom Liner (1981) gives many ideas for publishing opportunities in Chapter 16 of *Inside Out.*
These include:

    a.   reading student and teacher writing aloud

    b.   making copies to give to everyone in class

    c.   making booklets of student writing

    d.   making room, hall, bulletin board displays

    e.   making transparencies of well-written
       passages

    f.   being published in the school literary
       magazine, newspaper, or yearbook

    g.   being published in the local newspaper

    h.   competing in national and state contests

    i.   submitting to commercial magazines

References

Alloway, E., Carroll, J., Emig, J., King, B., Marcotri-
giano, I., Smith, J., & Spicer, W. (1979). The New
Jersey Writing Project. (ERIC No. ED 178 943)

Bracewell, R. J., Bereiter, C., & Scardamalia, M.
(1979). A test of two myths about revision. Paper,
Annual Meeting of American Educational Research Association.

Britton, J. N. (1978). The composing processes and
the functions of writing. Research on Composing:
Points of Departure. Cooper, C. R., Odell, L. (Ed.).
London: Macmillan Education Ltd.

Calkins, L. M. (1981). Case study of a nine year old
writer. In A Case Study Observing The Development of Primary Children's Composing, Spelling,
and Motor Behaviors During The Writing Process,
Final Report. Graves, D. H. (ED.), pp. 239–62.
Durham, NH: University of New Hampshire.
(ERIC No. ED 218 653)

Covino, W. A., Johnson, N., & Feehan, M. (1980).
Graduate education in rhetoric: Attitudes and implications. College English, 42, 390–398.

Emig, J. (1967). On teaching composition: Some hypotheses as definitions. Research in the Teaching
of English, 1, 127–35.

Gauntlett, J. F. (1978). Project WRITE and its effects
on the writing of high school students. 38, Dis-
sertation Abstracts International: 7189-A.

Graves, D. H. (1981). Break the welfare cycle: Let
writers choose their topics. In A Case Study Observing the Development of Primary Children's
Composing, Spelling, and Motor Behaviors During
the Writing Process, Final Report. Graves, D. H.
(Ed.), pp. 338–94. Durham, NH: University of
New Hampshire. (ERIC No. ED 218 653)

Hayes, J. R., & Flower, L. S. (1980). Identifying the
organization of writing processes. In Cognitive
Processes In Writing. Gregg, L. W., & Steinberg,
E. R. (Ed.). Hillsdale, NJ: Lawrence Erlbaum
Associates.

Usually, only works cited in the text are listed as references. Give last name first, followed by initials.

Titles appear in lower case except for the first word in the title and the first word following a colon.

Hillocks, George Jr. (1986). Research on written
    composition: New directions for teaching. Urbana,
    IL: National Conference on Research in English
    and ERIC.
Kearns, E. A. (1985). Practicing what we teach in
    writing. English Journal, 74, 6, 28–33.
Kirby, D., & Liner, T. (1981). Inside out: Develop-
    mental strategies for teaching writing. Montclair,
    NJ: Boynton/Cook Publishers.
Perl, S. (1979). The composing processes of un-
    skilled college writers. Research in the Teaching
    of English, 13, 317–36.
Ponsot, M., & Deen, R. (1982). Beat not the poor
    desk. Montclair, NJ: Boynton/Cook Publishers.

PART V

Evaluating Arguments

DEBATES

Inspired by the oratory of the ancient Greeks, contemporary debates attempt to establish the truth of a proposition by matching two sides—*pro* and *con*. The paired readings that follow demonstrate how an examination of the assumptions, premises, and evidence on which an argument is based can lead to opposite conclusions. Each pair of readings was written to reach the same audience, and in many cases the articles appeared side by side in the same publication. As an evaluator, then, you can use your understanding of context and appeal strategy to determine which of the two examinations better persuades the intended audience to accept its claim. And from this evaluation you can discover new directions for your own arguments.

AFFIRMATIVE ACTION

Two Views of Affirmative Action

For two decades now, the principles and practices of affirmative action have been hotly contested in every branch and at every level of government. In what follows, William Bradford Reynolds, Assistant Attorney General for Civil Rights in the U.S. Department of Justice, and Richard Wasserstrom, Professor of Philosophy at the University of California at Santa Cruz, present opposing views on how far and on what basis programs of preferential treatment for blacks, women, and ethnic minorities can be justified. Their debate is drawn from papers they presented at a conference on "The Moral Foundations of Civil Rights Policy," held at the University of Maryland on October 18–20, 1984, sponsored by the Center for Philosophy and Public Policy.

WILLIAM BRADFORD REYNOLDS

I.

Two predominant competing values drive the debate on affirmative   1 action in our society today: the value of equal opportunity and the value of equal results. Typically—to the understandable confusion of almost everyone—"affirmative action" is the term used to refer to both of these contrasting values. There is, however, a world of difference between "affirmative action" as a measure for ensuring equality of opportunity and "affirmative action" as a tool for achieving equality of results.

In the former instance, affirmative steps are taken so that all indi-   2 viduals (whatever their race, color, sex, or national origin) will be given the chance to compete with all others on equal terms; each is to be

---

The Origins of Affirmative Action

If the court finds that the respondent has intentionally engaged in or is intentionally engaging in an unlawful employment practice . . . the court may enjoin the respondent from engaging in such unlawful employment practice, and order such *affirmative action* as may be appropriate, which may include, but is not limited to, reinstatement or hiring of employees, with or without back pay . . . or any other equitable relief as the court deems appropriate.

Section 706(g), Title VII,
Civil Rights Act of 1964

The contractor will not discriminate [and] . . . will take *affirmative action* to ensure that applicants are employed, and that employees are treated during employment, without regard to their race, color, religion, sex or national origin.

Section 212, Executive Order 11246, 1965,
as amended by Executive Order 11375, 1968

---

given his or her place at the starting line without advantage or disadvantage. In the latter, the promise of affirmative action is that those who participate will arrive at the finish line in prearranged places—places allocated by race or sex.

Unfortunately the promise of equal results is a false one. We can 3 never assure equal results in a world in which individuals differ greatly in motivation and ability; nor is such a promise either morally or constitutionally acceptable. This was, in fact, well understood at the time that the concept of "affirmative action" was first introduced as a remedial technique in the civil rights arena. In its original formulation, that concept embraced only non-preferential affirmative efforts, in the nature of training programs and enhanced recruitment activities, aimed at opening wide the doors of opportunity to all Americans who cared to enter. No one was to be afforded a preference, or special treatment, because of group membership; rather, all were to be treated equally as individuals based on personal ability and worth.

This administration's commitment is to this "original and un- 4 defiled meaning"—as Morris Abram, Vice Chairman of the Civil Rights Commission, calls it—of "affirmative action." Where unlawful discrimination exists, we see that it is brought to an abrupt and uncompromising halt; we ensure that every identifiable victim of the wrongdoing receives "make whole" relief; and we require affirmative steps such as training programs and enhanced recruitment efforts to force open the doors of opportunity that have too long remained closed to far too many.

The criticism, of course, is that we do not go far enough. The re- 5 medial use of goals and timetables, quotas, or other such numerical devices to achieve a particular balance in the work force has been accepted by the lower federal courts as an available instrument of relief, and it is argued that such an approach should not be abandoned.

Our first response is a strictly legal one; it rests on the Supreme 6 Court's recent decision in *Firefighters Local Union* v. *Stotts*. At issue in *Stotts* was a district court injunction ordering that certain white firefighters with greater seniority be laid off before blacks with less seniority in order to preserve a certain percentage of black representation in the fire department's work force. The Supreme Court held that this order was improper because "there was no finding that any of the blacks protected from layoff had been a victim of discrimination." It ruled that federal courts are without *any* authority under Title VII of the Civil Rights Act to order a remedy that goes beyond enjoining the unlawful conduct and awarding "make whole" relief for actual victims of the discrimination. Quotas are by definition victim-blind: they embrace without distinction nonvictims as well as victims of unlawful discrimination and accord preferential treatment to both. Accordingly, whether such formulas are employed for hiring, promotion, layoffs, or otherwise, they must fail under any reading of the statute's remedial provision.

There are equally strong policy reasons for coming to this con- 7 clusion. The remedial use of preferences has been justified by the courts primarily on the theory that they are necessary to cure "the effects of past discrimination" and thus, in the words of Justice Blackmun, to "get beyond racism." This reasoning is twice flawed.

First, it is premised on the proposition that any racial imbalance 8 in the employer's work force is explainable only as a lingering effect of past racial discrimination. Yet equating "underrepresentation" of certain groups with discrimination against those groups ignores the fact that occupation selection in a free society is determined by a host of factors, principally individual interest, industry, and ability. It simply is not the case that applicants for any given job come proportionally qualified by race, gender, and ethnic origin in accordance with U.S. population statistics. Nor do the career interests of individuals break down proportionally among racial or gender groups.

Second, and more important, there is nothing *remedial*—let 9 alone *equitable*—about a court order that *requires* the hiring, promotion, or retention of a person who has not suffered discrimination solely because that person is a member of the same racial or gender group as other persons who were victimized by the discriminatory employment practices. The rights protected under Title VII belong to individuals, not to groups, as was affirmed in *Stotts*. As indicated, remedying a violation of Title VII requires that the individual victimized by the unlawful discrimination be restored to his or her "rightful place." It should go without saying that a person who is *not* victimized by the employer's discriminatory practices has no claim to a "rightful place" in the employer's work force. According preferential treatment to nonvictims in no way remedies the injury suffered by the actual victims.

Moreover, racial quotas and other forms of preferential treatment 10 unjustifiably infringe on the legitimate employment interests and expectations of third parties, such as incumbent employees, who are free of any involvement in the employer's wrongdoing. To be sure, awarding retroactive seniority and other forms of "rightful place" relief to individual victims of discrimination has some of these same consequences. However, legitimate claims of identifiable victims warrant the imposition of a remedy that places some burden on those innocent employees whose "places" in the work force are the product of unlawful discrimination. Restoring the victim of discrimination to the position he or she would have otherwise occupied merely requires incumbent employees to surrender some of the largesse discriminatorily conferred upon them. *But* an incumbent employee should not be called upon as well to sacrifice or otherwise compromise legitimate employment interests in order to accommodate persons *never wronged* by the employer's unlawful conduct.

Proponents of class-based preferences note that the effort to 11 identify and make whole all victims of the employer's discriminatory practices will never be 100 percent successful. While no one can dispute this unfortunate point, race- and gender-conscious preferences simply do not answer this problem. The injury suffered by a discriminatee who cannot be located is in no way ameliorated by conferring preferential treatment on other, randomly selected members of his or her race or sex.

Proponents of judicially imposed numerical preferences also ar- 12 gue that these are necessary to ensure that the employer does not return to his or her discriminatory ways. But far from *preventing* future discrimination, imposition of such remedial devices *guarantees* future discrimination. Only the color or gender of the ox being gored is changed.

The inescapable consequence of *Stotts* is to move government at 13 the federal, state, and local levels noticeably closer to the overriding objective of providing all citizens with a truly equal opportunity to compete on merit for the benefits that our society has to offer. The use of race or sex in an effort to restructure society along lines that better represent someone's preconceived notions of how our limited educational and economic resources should be allocated among the many groups in our pluralistic society necessarily forecloses opportunities to those having the misfortune—solely by reason of gender or skin color—to be members of a group whose allotment has already been filled. Those so denied, such as the more senior white Memphis firefighters laid off to achieve a more perfect racial balance in the fire department, are discriminated against every bit as much as the black Memphis firefighters originally excluded from employment. In our zeal to eradicate discrimination from society, we must be ever vigilant not to allow considerations of race or sex to intrude upon the decisional processes of government. The simple fact remains that, in the words of Judge Rehnquist, wherever it occurs, and however explained, "no discrimination based on race [or sex] is benign . . . no action disadvantaging a person because of color [or gender] is affirmative."

RICHARD WASSERSTROM

II.

I take programs of preferential treatment to be ones that make relevant 1 the race or sex of individuals in the sense that the fact that an applicant for admission, a job, or a promotion is nonwhite or female constitutes a relevant, although not a decisive, reason for preferring such an applicant over one who is white or male. Here I will consider only programs concerned with racial preferences, but I take what I have to say to be applicable to comparable programs where members of other ethnic or minority groups, or women, are concerned.

The positive case for such programs begins with the following 2 claim, namely, that we are still living in a society in which a person's race is a socially significant and important category. To be black is to be at a disadvantage in terms of most of the measures of success or satisfaction—be they economic, vocational, political, or social. If this claim about the existing social reality of race is correct, then two further claims seem plausible. The first is that there is in place what can correctly be described as a system of racial oppression. It is one both in virtue of the systemic nature of the unequal and maldistributed array of social benefits, opportunities, and burdens, and in virtue of the *way* things are linked together so as to constitute an interlocking, mutually reinforcing system of social benefits, burdens, ideology, and the like, which, when tied to race as they are, make it a system of racial disadvantage and oppression. Second, even if the intentions and motivations of those occupying positions of relative power and opportunity are wholly benign and proper, it is likely that the system will perpetuate itself unless blacks come to occupy substantially more positions of power and authority within the major social institutions.

The case for programs of preferential treatment can thus be seen 3 to rest upon the claim that they do succeed in introducing more blacks into these kinds of vocations, careers, and institutional positions than would have otherwise been present. The programs have worked and do work to produce, for example, black judges, lawyers, and business executives where few if any existed before. And changes of this sort in the racial composition of these institutions have mutually reinforcing consequences that play an important role in dismantling the existing system of racial disadvantage.

The main ground of principled opposition to such programs has 4 to do with the charge that they are themselves substantially unjust. The first argument commonly raised against these programs is this: if it was wrong to take race into account when blacks were the objects of racial policies of exclusion, then it is wrong to take race into account when the objects of the policies differ only in their race. Intellectual consistency requires that what was a good reason then be a good reason now.

The right way to answer this objection is, I think, to agree that the 5 practices of racial exclusion that were an integral part of the fabric of our culture, and which are still to some degree a part of it, were and are pernicious. Yet, one can grant this and also believe that the kinds of racial preferences and quotas that are a part of contemporary preferential treatment programs are commendable and right. There is no inconsistency involved in holding both views. A fundamental feature of programs that discriminated against blacks was that these programs were a part of a larger social universe in which power, authority, and goods were concentrated in the hands of white individuals. The complex system of racial oppression and superiority that was constituted by these institutions and the ideology that accompanied them severely and unjustifiably restricted the autonomy and happiness of members of the less favored category.

Whatever may be wrong with today's programs of preferential 6 treatment, the evil, if any, is simply not the same. Blacks do not constitute the dominant social group. Programs that give a preference to blacks do not add to an already comparatively overabundant supply of resources and opportunities at the disposal of members of the dominant racial group in the way in which exclusionary practices of the past added to the already overabundant supply of resources and opportunities at the disposal of whites.

A related objection that fares no better has to do with the identi- 7 fication of what exactly was wrong with the system of racial discrimination in the South, or with what is wrong with any system of racial discrimination. One very common way to think about the essential wrongness of racial discrimination is to see it as consisting in the use of an irrelevant characteristic, namely race, to allocate social benefits and burdens.

I am far from certain that that is the central flaw at all. Consider, 8 for instance, the most hideous of the practices, human slavery. The primary thing that was wrong with that institution was not that the particular individuals who were assigned the place of slaves were assigned there arbitrarily in virtue of an irrelevant characteristic, i.e., their race. Rather, the fundamental thing that was wrong with slavery was the practice itself—the fact that some human beings were able to own other human beings. And a comparable criticism can be made of many of the other practices and institutions that comprised the system of racial discrimination even after human slavery was abolished. The fundamental wrongness in taking race into account in the way these practices did has to do, perhaps, with arbitrariness, but it is the special arbitrariness attendant upon using race in the constitution and maintenance of a system of oppression so as to make that system a system of racial oppression. Whatever may be true of contemporary programs of preferential treatment, they can hardly be construed as consigning whites to the kind of oppressive status systematically bestowed upon blacks by the dominant social institutions.

A third very common objection is that the category of race is too 9 broad in scope for programs designed to promote equality of opportunity and of political and social status. The relevant characteristic, instead, is disadvantaged socio-economic status. This objection, too, rests on a mistaken conception of the social realities. While socio-economic status unquestionably affects in deep and pervasive ways the kinds of lives persons are able to fashion and live, in our society it is not the sole, or even the primary, locus of systemic oppression. Blackness is as much a primary locus of oppression as is socio-economic status. Socio-economic status is an indirect, imperfect, and overly broad category by which to deal with the phenomenon of *racial* disadvantage, in precisely the same way in which race is an indirect, imperfect, and overly broad category to take on the phenomenon of *socio-economic* disadvantage.

A final objection concerns the claim that these programs are 10 wrong because they take race into account rather than the only thing that does and should matter, namely, an individual's qualifications. And qualifications, it is further claimed, have nothing whatsoever to do with race.

First, it is important to establish what the argument is for basing 11 selections solely on qualifications. One argument is that the most qualified persons should always be selected for a position because the tasks connected with that position will then be done in the most efficient manner. Now, there is nothing wrong in principle with appealing to the good results that will be produced by selecting applicants solely on the basis of their qualifications. But it may be impermissible for opponents of preferential treatment programs to use *this* argument, if it was an analogous appeal to the good results likely to be produced by programs of preferential treatment that they thought was wrong in the first place with justifying these programs in this way.

But there is still the argument that the most qualified deserve to 12 be selected because they are the most qualified. If they do, then to refuse to select them is to treat them unjustly. I am skeptical, however, that a connection of the right sort can be made out between being the most qualified in this sense and deserving to be selected. The problem is that being the best at something does not, by itself, seem readily convertible into a claim about what someone thereby genuinely deserves, given the difficulty of connecting the mere possession of abilities with things that the possessor can claim any credit or responsibility for, and given the alternative plausibility of claims of desert founded upon attributes such as effort or need.

In sum, therefore, preferential treatment programs are presump- 13 tively justifiable in so far as they work to dismantle the system of racial oppression that is still in place, and their justifiability is rendered more secure once it is seen that they are not unjust either in themselves or as constitutive elements of any larger system of racial oppression.

Report from the Center for Philosophy
and Public Policy, University of Maryland,
Winter 1985

DEBATE: AFFIRMATIVE ACTION

CONTEXT

1. Given the title of the conference, its location, and the sponsoring agency, what different groups of people would you expect to be in attendance? What purpose would these groups be likely to share in listening to this debate?

2. Both Reynolds and Wasserstrom initially presented their arguments orally, yet both were aware that their presentations would be published in written form as well. Which argument do you think had a greater impact as an oral presentation? What features of the presentation indicate this strength?

3. Identify the general knowledge and attitudes toward affirmative action you believe the audience had on this occasion.

STRATEGY

1. Based on the titles or professional positions of Reynolds and Wasserstrom, decide which writer has more credibility for the intended purpose and audience. Do you consider them equally credible? Explain the rationale for your decision. In what other ways does each writer establish an ethical appeal?

2. Both writers agree that affirmative action is justified but disagree on how the program should be practiced, particularly with respect to quotas. State each writer's claim and the premises on which each conclusion is based.

3. In both arguments the writers clearly identify assumptions they believe their audience shares before refuting the assumptions that raise objections to their respective points of view. What further assumptions, either stated or implied, do the writers rely on to persuade the audience to accept their refutations?

4. Arguing for the "moral" foundations of affirmative action evokes emotional responses from the audience. Do either of the writers heighten the emotional appeal with word choice, and if so, how? Consider, for example, Reynolds's repetitive use of "affirmative action" compared with Wasserstrom's use of "preferential treatment." Look carefully at qualifying terms and those in quotation marks and italics.

5. The context for this debate—the well-defined purpose, the educated audience, and the authoritative writers—has a direct bearing on the resources each writer selected to support his claim. Identify those resources and evaluate their effectiveness in supporting the writer's claim and reaching the intended audience. You might want to diagram each argument using the Toulmin model (Chapter 2) to analyze how well these relationships were established.

EXTENDING THE ARGUMENT

1. Reynolds cautions his audience not to equate *underrepresentation* of certain groups in a profession with *discrimination*. "Occupation selection in a free society," he says, "is determined by a host of factors, principally individual interest, industry, and ability." Extend this point of Reynolds' argument by advocating the need to retain free choice of occupation or by refuting his claim by proving that underrepresentation is the result of discrimination. Direct your argument to Reynolds or the general public, whichever is more appropriate.

2. Wasserstrom states that he is "skeptical" that being the most qualified at something makes a person the most deserving. Effort and need, he says, are plausible alternatives to the "mere possession of abilities." As a person striving to become competitively qualified for a profession, defend one of the two views in this debate. Direct your argument to a future employer in a specific field or to students in the same major as you.

3. Both writers convey a concern for achieving a racially balanced society. What does *racially balanced* mean to you? Is it desirable? Possible? How can it be achieved or why can't it be achieved? Write an argument to the U.S. Department of Justice or another appropriate audience advocating your view on this subject.

RELATED SUBJECTS

eugenics	comparable worth
genetic engineering	the "glass ceiling"
utopia	the "mommy track"

RELATED READINGS IN THIS TEXT

"Why Women Aren't Getting to the Top"	Chapter 4
"Why Women Are Paid Less than Men"	Chapter 9
Discrimination: What Progress Have We Made?	Issues section

Random Tests
Abuse Dignity

ALLEN L. SACK
*Chair of the Honors Program at the University of
New Haven*

Nothing better illustrates the low regard that the National Collegiate 1
Athletic Association has often had for the rights of student-athletes
than its random drug-testing policy. There are a number of alternatives for addressing the problem of substance abuse. Unfortunately,
the N.C.A.A. chooses an approach that protects the public-relations
image of its member institutions but shows little or no concern for the
dignity and privacy of the vast majority of hard-working young athletes
who are drug-free.

Random drug testing treats all athletes like suspected criminals 2
when there is no probable cause for doing so, and it expects them to
surrender rights docilely that are the cornerstone of American democracy. Most disturbing is the fact that this policy was approved without
even the slightest consultation with the athletes themselves.

The actual procedure for gathering urine samples from ran- 3
domly selected athletes is precisely spelled out in N.C.A.A. documents.
Immediately following participation in a championship event, student-
athletes are selected for drug testing, and are instructed to report to a
urine-collection station within one hour. At the collection station,
what the N.C.A.A. calls a "urine validator" monitors the furnishing of
the specimen.

Judge Conrad L. Rushing of the Superior Court of California de- 4
scribes the process graphically. "Under the N.C.A.A. program last year,
Jennifer Hill was accompanied to a doorless bathroom stall by the
monitor, who stood a few feet away and watched while Hill removed
her shorts and undergarments . . . and urinated into a beaker."

Why should an athlete who has exhibited no behavior that would 5
give rise to suspicion of illegal activity have to submit to this sort of
humiliation, inconvenience and violation of privacy? Why should athletes who only an hour before may have participated in the greatest

athletic event of their careers have to agree to be herded like cattle into a urine-collection station and to be treated like common criminals?

One way to justify the extreme diminution of Fourth Amendment 6 rights implicit in a search without probable cause is to argue that random drug testing of college athletes is crucial to public safety. Few people oppose the kinds of general searches that are carried out at airports while passengers are preparing to board planes. The fact that it is impossible to tell from the outside whether a person is carrying a weapon and the fact that weapons carried illegally onto a plane could take the lives of hundreds of passengers seem like fairly strong justifications for performing searches without reasonable suspicion of a particular individual. In a similar vein, there may be compelling reasons for performing random drug tests on airline pilots and nuclear power operators.

The case for testing college athletes without probable cause 7 seems far less compelling. It is difficult to argue that athletes hold positions of responsibility analogous to those of pilots or air-traffic controllers. There is little doubt that athletes serve as role models for millions of young people. But no one can seriously believe that isolated instances of drug use by college athletes have been a major cause of the rampant substance abuse that plagues this nation. Tragic incidents such as the death of Len Bias of Maryland of a drug overdose can have a devastating effect on a university's public image, but a concern with preventing bad publicity does not justify an assault on the Bill of Rights. Subjecting all athletes to random testing when other less intrusive methods for fighting substance abuse exist seems like the kind of policy the framers of the United States Constitution would have opposed.

It is not my intention here to cover the many complex constitu- 8 tional issues surrounding random drug testing. My argument is simple. The vast, vast majority of college athletes are good, decent, dedicated and drug-free. If the N.C.A.A. had respected these athletes as students and as sensitive human beings, random drug testing would have been instituted only as a last resort, and even then, only after encouraging athletes to consider the constitutional issues involved.

Efforts to fight substance abuse in college sports must be con- 9 cerned with more than keeping athletes drug-free in the short-term. The goal should be to help athletes understand the role that drugs play in our society and to prepare them to fight drug abuse throughout their lives. The N.C.A.A. should take the hundreds of thousands of dollars that are going into random drug testing and undertake a massive program in drug education. Drug education should be an integral part of every athletic department curriculum, and should consist of far more than a couple of talks by prominent athletes.

Drug education should extend to coaches and others who work 10 closely with athletes. Coaches should be taught the symptoms of substance abuse so that they can refer athletes for counseling and treatment. They should also be able (in conjunction with a team physician and the athletic director) to insist that an athlete submit to a drug test if there is some observance of suspicious activity. Athletes who abuse drugs should be subject to strict disciplinary action. Repeat offenders should lose athletic eligibility.

Drug education and drug testing based on probable cause will 11 probably not be as effective in deterring short-term substance abuse as having random drug-testing programs at every university in the country. It should be noted however that a democratic society has to be concerned with more than deterrence. There is no doubt in my mind that certain types of crime could be substantially reduced if the police could ignore large segments of the Constitution. The case of Nazi Germany offers considerable proof that searching people's property and their persons without probable cause can be an effective deterrent. But the price that is exacted is a wholesale assault on human dignity and personal freedom. Such measures have little place in a democracy, and they clearly cannot be justified in college sport.

New York Times, May 29, 1988

N.C.A.A. Plan Is Deterrent

JAMES C. PUFFER
*Chair of the N.C.A.A. competitive safeguards committee,
which handles health and safety issues for intercollegiate
athletics, and head physician for the United States Summer
Olympic team. Dr. Puffer practices in the Division of Family
Medicine at the U.C.L.A. Medical Center.*

The untimely deaths of Len Bias and Don Rogers two years ago fo- 1 cused our attention on the tragic role that substance abuse plays in the lives of performing athletes. The tremendous pressures placed upon them to perform to expectations that are often unrealistic have created circumstances in which athletes frequently turn to drug use either to escape from these pressures or to enhance performance. In fact, the widespread use of performance-enhancing drugs has perhaps become the single most important threat to the integrity of amateur and professional sport.

The use of drugs to enhance performance is not a recent phe- 2
nomenon. The writings of Homer documented ingestion of mush-
rooms by Greek athletes in the third century B.C. during the ancient
Olympic Games. In the 19th century there were reports of widespread
use of caffeine, alcohol, nitroglycerin, ethyl ether and opium by European athletes.

However, it was not until the death of Kurt Enemar Jensen, a 3
Danish cyclist, at the 1960 Summer Olympic Games in Rome that considerable attention was focused on this mounting problem. Jensen
and two of his teammates had taken amphetamines in an attempt to
improve their performance in the 100-kilometer team cycling trials
and this helped contribute to Jensen's death. These events motivated
the International Olympic Committee to begin to question the integrity of games in which athletes were using artificial substances in an
effort to enhance performance.

The rest is well known. The International Olympic Committee 4
instituted drug testing in the 1968 Olympics in both Grenoble and
Mexico City and has tested for drugs since that time. For a time, drug
testing remained a phenomenon that was predominantly limited to
international events such as the Olympic Games and world championships. However, in the past several years drug testing has become
widespread and is used by both the National Collegiate Athletic Association and numerous member institutions in an attempt to stem the
increasing use of drugs by athletes.

The N.C.A.A. has just reported that 1.3 percent of the 1,589 ath- 5
letes who were tested at championship events last fall tested positive
for banned substances. This was a slight increase over the 1 percent of
the 3,360 who tested positive in the 1986–87 academic year. Given the
seemingly small number of positive tests, why would any organization
or institution wish to invest the tremendous amount of financial and
human resources necessary to conduct an exemplary drug testing
program? In order to understand the reasoning, it is essential to understand the notion that drug testing is an adjunctive tool that is used to
deter drug use. The low number of positive samples speaks to the
positive effect that testing has had.

Is drug testing indeed a deterrent to drug use? It would appear 6
that it is. Reports from certified laboratories at which drug testing is
performed indicate that when testing is voluntary and nonpunitive, as
many as 50 percent of the samples may be positive. The institution of
mandatory drug testing at N.C.A.A. championship events two years
ago has had a profound effect on significantly reducing the use of in-
jectable anabolic steroids by college athletes. This is based on the fact
that a recent N.C.A.A. survey indicated that approximately 8 percent of
college athletes admitted to using steroids. The performance of athletes in certain weight events in last year's N.C.A.A. track and field

championships were far below those from the previous year, further testimony that drug testing can have a dramatic effect on the final results.

Many argue that while testing is an effective deterrent in the use 7 of certain types of drugs, it nevertheless violates the personal rights of individual athletes as well as presumes guilt. It is important to note that six court cases have been brought against either the N.C.A.A. or its member institutions in the past year and a half in an attempt to resolve this issue. The cases have yet to resolve the issue satisfactorily.

While the preliminary results from one hearing would indicate 8 that, in fact, drug testing may violate some of the personal rights of athletes in the state of California, others have determined that drug testing may not be an unreasonable condition of participation in intercollegiate athletics. If one appreciates the notion that drug testing is, in fact, a deterrent to drug use, and its sole purpose is to prevent athletes from using banned substances altogether, one can certainly dismiss the notion of presumptive guilt; it is the explicit intent of drug testing programs to find no positive samples if indeed the program is successful.

Finally, some comment must be made about the attitudes of the 9 athletes who undergo drug testing. Numerous surveys on college campuses that conduct their own testing programs have shown that the overwhelming majority of athletes favor drug testing. They think that it guarantees the opportunity to participate in a drug-free environment and provides a valuable crutch that allows them to say no to drugs. This fact has been repeatedly demonstrated by the decreasing use of drugs by college athletes as documented by drug testing at these institutions since the inception of their programs.

Even though testing is far from totally eradicating drug use by 10 college athletes, when used in conjunction with a sound drug education program, it serves as the best method for deterring drug use. Until better means become available, drug testing remains our best option in guaranteeing the safety and well-being of athletes who participate in sport.

New York Times, May 29, 1988

DEBATE: DRUG TESTING IN COLLEGE SPORTS

CONTEXT

1. The *New York Times* has earned an international reputation for its in-depth news coverage and high standards for writing. Its international, national, and local readership consists of well-educated people who enjoy reading. Describe the readers' main purpose in reading this periodical and more specifically their expectations in reading the sports section.

2. People interested in reading about sports are likely to have already formed opinions on the drug testing issue for college athletes. Identify the beliefs the audience is likely to have on this issue *before* reading the articles. Which claim will they be more likely to support and why?

3. Neither argument appears to be responding to a particular occasion or event but rather to the principles of drug testing as they relate in general to college athletes. How is the lack of a specific occasion, such as the Olympics drug scandal that followed that summer, likely to affect the readers' level of involvement and concern?

STRATEGY

1. Using Puffer and Sack's professional positions as a guide, decide which writer has more credibility for the intended purpose and audience and explain your rationale. In what other ways does each writer establish an ethical appeal?

2. State each writer's claim and the premises on which each conclusion is based. Viewing the two arguments in this syllogistic form, are both *valid* and *sound*? Explain how the warrants implicit in the major premise make each argument favorable or conditional for the intended audience.

3. The writers begin their arguments with very different approaches. Describe the difference in these approaches. Explain which one you find more effective for the intended purpose and audience.

4. The two writers use a similar arrangement for positioning their confirmation and refutation. Examine the evidence used in each of these sections to determine which type of data more convincingly supports the reasoning of the argument. Explain your choice.

5. Allen Sack clearly uses a more emotional appeal in his argument. Identify Sack's explicit use of emotional appeal and predict the effect it will have on the audience's acceptance of his claim.

EXTENDING THE ARGUMENT

1. Both arguments specify the importance of drug education programs for deterring drug use. Based on your own experience with such programs, the suggestions proposed by Sack, and any additional information you are able to find, argue for or against drug education programs as an effective deterrent. Direct your argument to educators, coaches, the N.C.A.A., or the secretary of education.

2. Allen Sack states that "there may be more compelling reasons for performing random drug tests on airline pilots and nuclear power operators." Construct an argument directed to an unknown authority audience, such as the Drug Enforcement Agency (DEA), evaluating which professions should be tested for drugs.

3. The nation's concern about the drug abuse problem has led college administrators to consider testing *all* students as a standard part of the admission process. In fact, Reverend Jerry Falwell, Chancellor of Liberty University in Lynchburg, Virginia, requires all entering students to undergo drug testing before being admitted. Liberty is a private university. Should public, state-supported institutions implement the same procedure? Compose an argument directed to college admissions officers or college students defending or refuting this procedure.

RELATED SUBJECTS

Fourth Amendment rights
alternative methods of deterrence
effects of N.C.A.A. sanctions on institutions

RELATED READINGS IN THIS TEXT

"Everyday Drugs"   Chapter 2
"A Red Light for Scofflaws"   Chapter 8

NATIONAL SERVICE CORPS

Many College Officials Oppose Plan That Would Require National Service as a Prerequisite for Federal Student Aid

ROBIN WILSON
Staff writer for The Chronicle of Higher Education

As college officials learn more about a Congressional plan to require at 1 least one year of national service as a prerequisite for receiving federal student aid, the reviews are coming back with near unanimity: Bad idea.

College presidents use such phrases as "indentured servitude," 2 "devastation," and "death blow" to describe the effects of the plan both on students and on the current financial-aid system.

Among the most common complaints are that the program would 3 discourage poor students from enrolling in college, that wealthy students could enroll without serving, and that the plan would not insure that students could receive enough money to attend the college of their choice.

The legislation, introduced by Sen. Sam Nunn, Democrat of Georgia and chairman of the Senate Armed Services Committee, has been embraced by other influential Democrats and is gaining momentum on Capitol Hill. 4

Under the plan, the present array of federal grant and loan programs for students would be phased out. 5

Critics Cite Concerns

Students would receive federal aid to attend college only by performing work in their communities for one or two years or by serving in the military for two years. 6

Those who took part in this "Citizens Corps" would be paid $100 a week during the time they served and then would receive up to $24,000 to pay for a college education or job training, or for a down payment on a home. 7

Students who needed more money to pay for college after serving would be eligible for government-backed loans. 8

College officials cite the following problems with the plan: 9

- Many poor and minority-group students, who already face numerous barriers to enrolling in college, could not afford to work for the $100 a week they would receive while serving and would therefore be unable to participate in the program. College officials say the government should make it easier for such students to enroll. They also complain that the plan favors wealthier students—who, because they could pay for college without help from the government, would not have to participate.
- Wealthy students who did participate would receive the same amount of aid to attend college as poor students. Now, aid is distributed to students based on their financial need, and the wealthiest students are ineligible.
- Some students—particularly those from poor families—would still have to borrow large amounts after they served if they wanted to attend high-priced private institutions.
- Because anyone could participate in a service program, regardless of financial need, the Citizens Corps could end up costing the government much more than the $8 billion that is now spent on federal student aid each year. Aides to Mr. Nunn estimate that the plan would cost $13 billion a year, but Arthur M. Hauptman, an expert on student-aid issues, says the proposal could cost the gov-

ernment as much as $50 billion a year, depending on how many students participated.

- Students' learning would be disrupted if they took a year or two off to serve between high school and college. Most college officials say that continuity is important in education and that, if high-school students did not go directly on to higher education, some might lose interest in education.

- State and local organizations would be responsible for finding community-service work for volunteers; so far, few such organizations exist. Mr. Nunn says people involved in the Citizens Corps would work in hospitals, nursing homes, and shelters for the homeless. But critics fear that if the programs were not run properly, volunteers could end up doing menial work, such as collecting garbage in parks and along highway embankments.

Nunn Expected to Visit Colleges

Aides to Mr. Nunn say the Senator is willing to make changes in his 10 plan to accommodate some of the concerns of college officials, and he is expected to visit college presidents in Georgia soon to discuss the proposal.

They say he is just as concerned as are education officials about 11 access to college for poor students. But he does not believe that the present system of federal aid serves needy students well. Many such students must borrow large amounts to pay for college and some find the debts difficult to repay.

The aides say the Senator also strongly believes that young people 12 who benefit from federal aid should be willing to repay their country by serving.

"The Citizens Corps is based on a very simple but profound prin- 13 ciple: that those who take from the common good should give something back," Mr. Nunn said in a statement when he introduced the legislation.

A few college officials agree with the Senator. 14

"This would force young people to do something for someone 15 else besides themselves," says Abbott A. Brayton, vice-president and dean of faculty at Davis and Elkins College. "For many of them, their goal in life is to make it on the New York Stock Exchange and buy a B.M.W." (Mr. Brayton served in the military after high school.)

Although many college presidents say that encouraging students 16 to serve their communities is a good idea, most oppose any plan to tie aid to service.

Indeed, the idea has stirred strong feelings. 17

"What you're doing is punishing the poor for being poor," says 18 Joseph S. Murphy, chancellor of the City University of New York system. "This is indentured servitude, which was practiced in Senator Nunn's state in the 19th century, so it is based on his own cultural experience."

Called Opportunity, Not Penalty

Asked to respond, Mr. Nunn issued a statement that did not mention 19 Mr. Murphy's comments about Georgia.

He did say: "I don't think it's penalizing anyone to give them one- 20 year job experience and to pay them, albeit a subsistence wage, during that time, and then to give them a $10,000 educational voucher which does not have to be repaid. I don't consider that a penalty, I consider it an opportunity."

But many college officials say that Mr. Nunn's proposal would 21 turn back the clock on efforts to open the doors of colleges and universities to all students, regardless of their financial means. Federal financial-aid programs, such as Pell Grants and College Work Study, were established in the 1960's and 1970's precisely so that students from low-income families could attend college.

"We fought so long and so hard for access for minorities and low- 22 income students to higher education," says Jerry McTier, director of student aid at Georgia State University. "I want to be darn sure that this doesn't limit the numbers of people we can help."

Some college officials fear that needy students would simply 23 forgo college if they had to work one or two years at subsistence-level wages before they could receive federal student aid.

"Many students at urban universities like mine are raising fami- 24 lies and working," says David W. Adamany, president of Wayne State University. For most of those students, he says, working for $100 a week for up to two years before college "probably would not be feasible."

Worries at Private Colleges

Under Mr. Nunn's plan, people 26 years of age and older would be eli- 25 gible for college loans without having to serve. Aides to the Senator say he did not want to require single parents, for example, to serve.

Mr. Adamany says that many Wayne State students who are 26 younger than 26 have the same financial problems and family obligations as older students and would have difficulty serving.

College presidents are also worried about other aspects of Mr. 27 Nunn's proposal that they say could harm colleges themselves. For example, some say, the more expensive private colleges could lose students under Mr. Nunn's plan because people would not earn enough money to pay more than $6,000 a year. The annual cost at some private institutions is more than $18,000, including room and board.

'Devastation' in the First Year

In addition, college officials are worried about what would happen in 28
the first year a community-service plan took effect, when students were
serving in their communities or in the military rather than enrolling in
college. The absence of hundreds of thousands of students would
drain many institutions of revenue they need to continue operating.

"This would be devastating to us," says Adib A. Shakir, president 29
of Tougaloo College, a historically black institution where most of the
780 students receive some federal aid. Mr. Shakir says institutions such
as Tougaloo, which does not have a large endowment and depends
heavily on funds from students, might have to close if Mr. Nunn's plan
were instituted.

Some of those who support the Nunn proposal say that college 30
officials should stop criticizing it and suggest ways of improving it.

"There have been some pot-shots from the sidelines and people 31
who want to dismiss this concept out of hand," says Joseph Duffey,
chancellor of the University of Massachusetts at Amherst and one of
the few college presidents who have endorsed Mr. Nunn's plan. Mr.
Duffey says he will lobby for support from his colleagues.

"Educationally, socially, the time has come when this concept 32
should be considered," he says. "The higher-education community
has to sit down and help work things out."

Chronicle of Higher Education,
February 15, 1989

But Some Student Leaders Approve of the Idea of Public Service

ROBIN WILSON

While many college presidents oppose a new proposal to tie federal 1
aid to students' service in the community or in the military, conversations with student leaders found that some of them think the idea
makes a lot of sense.

"I see a lot of financial-aid recipients who don't deserve aid, and 2 a lot of students who need it but can't get it," says Susan Monahan, news editor of the *Observer*, the student newspaper at Central Washington University.

"This way, students wouldn't get a free ride," she says.   3

The plan to require students to serve before they could receive 4 federal aid is being backed by powerful Democrats in Congress, including Sen. Sam Nunn of Georgia.

Under the plan, the current federal student-aid programs would 5 be eliminated, and people could receive aid to attend college only if they served for up to two years in the military or in volunteer organizations in their communities.

Most students queried were unaware of the plan, although some 6 campus newspapers have printed articles outlining its main points.

Students who are informed about its specifics say the proposal 7 sounds attractive, and many say they would have participated if such a program had been in place before they enrolled in their colleges and universities.

David R. Mark, editor of the *Massachusetts Daily Collegian*—the 8 student newspaper at the University of Massachusetts at Amherst—says the program would solve students' money problems and improve cities' services and their environments.

"There are a lot of students who can't get into colleges because of 9 money and, at the same time, there are a lot of communities going to waste," he says. For example, Mr. Mark says buidings for welfare recipients in many cities are in poor shape, and volunteers could either improve them or help build new ones.

Other students say they would have welcomed the opportunity 10 to earn more money for college. David F. Chapman, a junior and president of the Interfraternity Council at Auburn University, says he was accepted to other, more expensive institutions but could not afford to attend.

"An extra $24,000 certainly would have helped," he says.   11

Some Concerns About the Plan

The students do have some worries about the plan.   12

Some share the concern of college presidents that only needy 13 people would be forced to serve because they would need federal aid to attend college.

"This is linking the disadvantaged and the poor to some kind of 14 draft, whether it is to clean up parks or to train in the military," says Jim Smith, president of the United Council, a group that lobbies Wisconsin legislators on behalf of college students. "I think higher education is financed by the country for betterment down the road. Forcing people to serve to get aid, I just think that's wrong."

Other students worry that participants in the service program 15 would be assigned to community-service work that did not involve a high level of skill.

"If there was a student interested in engineering and they said to 16 him, 'O.K. we're going to send you into New York City to restructure a home for the homeless,' that would be good," says Mr. Mark, "But if they made you mow the grass, it wouldn't be that useful."

Service During College

Some students say it might be more valuable for students to serve dur- 17 ing college, rather than before they enrolled. "Do you really want to say, 'Get it over with in two years and then you've done your service?'" asks Bridget C. Kenny, a senior at the University of Chicago. "If you got into a program that would continue throughout your four years, it would instill the idea that volunteerism isn't something you want to do at one point and then not have to do later."

Still other students say they would not have wanted to live with 18 their parents for two years after high school so that they could work in their communities. People who participated in the community-service program would earn only $100 a week, and many would probably choose to continue living at home.

"This is out of line with the mind-set of a lot of students," says 19 Tracy E. Maple, editor of the *Purdue Exponent*, Purdue University's student newspaper. "I couldn't wait to go to college and get away from home."

Chronicle of Higher Education,
February 15, 1989

DEBATE: NATIONAL SERVICE CORPS

CONTEXT

1. The *Chronicle of Higher Education* is a weekly newspaper with a large national circulation. The periodical includes sections on research, publications, business and philanthropy, international issues, athletics, computers, government and politics, grants, and academic job listings. Describe the range of readership for this publication, the purpose for reading, and the assumptions the readers are likely to hold on the present state of financial aid for students.

2 The writer, Robin Wilson, is a regular staff reporter for the *Chronicle* who was assigned to cover the issue of national service from different points of view. What does the fact that she has a byline in this publication convey about her level of authority as a writer? What would you assume her expertise on the topic to be?

3. Describe what you believe the writer's commitment to the reader should be for this context.

STRATEGY

1. The writer chose to present the opposition to national service *before* the assenting view. Explain why you think she made this choice and how this arrangement strategy affects the audience.

2. State the claim of each argument in the form of an enthymeme. Then test the reasoning of each by diagramming the argument using the Toulmin model. After reviewing the warrants, identify the main issues that separate the college administrators' view from that of the student leaders.

3. Wilson uses primarily quotes from her sources to develop the arguments for both points of view. For each side list the sources she quotes in the exact sequence in which they appear. How would you characterize the authority of these sources? How well does the writer's choice of sources contribute to her ethical appeal?

4. Read the introductory and concluding paragraph in each argument. Why do you believe the writer chose to end each argument with a quote supporting the opposite point of view? What effect is this likely to have on the audience?

5. In what ways is the emotional appeal a natural part of both arguments? Does the writer heighten the emotional appeal with word choice, arrangement of information, or choice of sources? If so, explain how.

EXTENDING THE ARGUMENT

1. College officials and student leaders represent only two of many points of view directly involved in the issue of national service. Reconstruct the argument for or against national service for one of the following audiences: parents, a social agency, or 17- to 20-year-olds from poor families.

2. Franklin D. Roosevelt's Work Projects Administration (WPA) program in the 1930s, John F. Kennedy's Peace Corps and VISTA initiatives in the 1960s, the community service required of conscientious objectors in the Vietnam draft, and the community service penalties readily used as punishment for drunk drivers serve as precedents for the national service issue. Write an argument in which you use these programs and any others you can identify to predict the success or failure of Senator Nunn's proposal.

3. Neither argument links the proposal for national service to a cause for the failure or inadequacy of the present financial aid system. Research the problem with the present system to develop an argument demonstrating how the national service corps will or will not eliminate previous problems.

RELATED SUBJECTS

altruism   the works of Edward Bellamy
volunteerism   philosopher William James'
social contract theory   1910 essay "The Moral
the works of Ayn Rand   Equivalent of War"

RELATED READINGS IN THIS TEXT

WOMEN IN THE MILITARY: COMBAT

Three Myths About Women and Combat

WILLIAM PROXMIRE

The following "Myths of the Day" were read into the Congressional Record by Senator William Proxmire, Democrat from Wisconsin, on March 21, 24, and 25, 1986.

Myth of the Day: Women Should Be Barred from Combat

Mr. President, the myth of the day is that our armed services' combat 1 exclusion policies enhance our national security. In reality, barring women from combat has resulted in complex and arbitrary restrictions that limit our military flexibility.

At the present time, each branch of the military has elaborate de- 2 terminations for which specific assignments have high combat probability. These designations often change depending on the world situation so that in the Navy, for example, all assignments of women to ships in the 6th and 7th Fleets must be approved by the fleet commander. The fleet commander must review each case and use available intelligence resources to determine the likelihood of combat. Such time-consuming judgement calls may be manageable during peacetime, but they would be impossible in the crush of a war situation.

This became abundantly clear during the invasion of Grenada. 3 A group of female military police deploying from Fort Bragg was sent back to the barracks three times before being allowed to deploy. Once in Grenada, they were recalled, and then, 3 days later, they were once again sent back to Grenada. That kind of confusion would only be magnified in a larger maneuver.

Women soldiers make up roughly 10 percent of our Armed Forces 4 and are well integrated throughout. To keep tabs on all of them and try to restrict them from forward battle positions would not only be difficult, it would limit our flexibility and deprive the front-line of skilled female specialists.

This was underscored by Defense Secretary Weinberger in 1983 5 when he remarked to President Reagan that "what we've done is to say that until there is an actual imminence of war, (women) will be grease monkeys if they want to and things like that. But when it comes to actual combat, they will be substituted. It just makes it a little more difficult."

Not only would substituting women make things a little more 6 difficult, it would be downright impossible. In fact, after Defense Secretary Weinberger's comment, Lawrence Korb, Assistant Secretary of Defense for Manpower, told reporters that men could not realistically be substituted for women in units preparing for combat. "Under many circumstances you just don't have that much warning. Women are an integral part of units," he said.

This was reinforced during the invasion of Grenada. A source in 7 the Military Airlift command said that female pilots, flight engineers and loadmasters were included in the Grenada crews because "to have excluded an aircraft simply because there was a woman on board would have lessened our response and reduced our effectiveness."

What's more, the combat exclusion policy is not burdensome 8 only in times of war. It limits our flexibility now—each day that is in effect. After terrorist attacks on several U.S. Embassies, the U.S. Marines decided that using female marines as Embassy guards is "inconsistent with national policy." Consequently, women were removed from guard posts despite the fact that their performance was said to be excellent. Can we afford to exclude competent female soldiers from every assignment that may be dangerous? These women are soldiers, after all.

They knew the dangers involved when they chose the military as a career.

The fact is that we cannot afford to encumber our military com- 9 manders with combat restrictions that affect a large fraction of their troops. We must open up our combat billets to all qualified soldiers in order to maximize our flexibility. The Pentagon proposed repealing the combat exclusion policies in 1979. Today women make up an even larger percentage of our Armed Forces and the need to lift the combat restrictions is that much greater. It is a matter of national security.

Myth of the Day:
Female Soldiers Can Be Protected

Mr. President, the myth of the day is that barring female soldiers from 10 combat somehow protects them. The fact is that it results in a situation in which women can be shot at but cannot shoot. It is time to drop the combat exclusion policy and stop tying the hands of our women soldiers.

First of all, the range and effectiveness of modern weapons have 11 made previous combat/noncombat distinctions obsolete. Women have served in a temporary additional duty capacity off the coast of Lebanon, and now serve at various munitions storage sites, including such dangerous assignments as the Peacekeeper and Minuteman launch sites. They also serve at important command and control positions like the EC-130E Airborne Battlefield Command and control Center.

These are not frontline assignments, but they would obviously be 12 dangerous targets in the event of a war. A recent Congressional Research Service brief stated that:

> Women are now serving in positions where they will certainly become casualties in substantial numbers in any future war.

It is generally agreed that, were there to be a war, women would 13 die in proportion to their numbers. Women now make up 10 percent of our Armed Forces and are well-integrated throughout them. Their numbers are too big and their skills are too important to try to insulate them from danger. The women do not want to be insulated, and we need them too much to try to contain them at low-risk positions.

Why is it then that the combat exclusion policy still exists? Con- 14 trary to popular belief, it is not out of some sentimental desire to spare women from harm. The actual reason is that defense policymakers fear a public backlash against any female casualties in a war. The American public must be made aware that some heroines will lose their lives along with the heroes. Women in the military is no longer a theoretical issue. It is a reality now, and one which our present policies should reflect. That means eliminating the combat exclusion policy.

Our women are capable soldiers. They have proven their compe- 15 tence over the years. The Air Force has listed women officers as capable of accomplishing 100 percent of their job description skills. The Army, 96 percent. The Department of Defense described the increase in the number of female soldiers as a "significant improvement." And Secretary of Defense Caspar Weinberger, in a 1983 memo, directed that combat exclusion rules be interpreted to allow as many possible career opportunities for women to be kept open. All this points to the fact that women have been tested in the field and have proven their ability.

What is more, women soldiers want to be able to volunteer for 16 combat positions. Most think they should be required to serve in combat billets. Since we have allowed these women to risk their lives in becoming part of the All Volunteer Force, perhaps we should also let them volunteer for combat. We cannot just use women to bolster the numbers of our AVF while keeping them in the sitting duck positions. That is not the best way to protect our women or our Nation.

Myth of the Day: The Combat Exclusion Policy Enhances National Security

Mr. President, the myth of the day is that the combat exclusion policy 17 enhances national security. I have spoken several times here on the importance of opening up combat assignments to women in the military. The first consideration in any issue of military personnel must always be national security, and indeed, that is my primary concern. The combat exclusion policies deprive our forward battle areas of available personnel resources and limit our flexibility.

In the two decades since women have been able to serve in the 18 military in substantial numbers, they have proven that they are capable soldiers. What is more, a greater portion of female soldiers have high school diplomas, and women pose fewer disciplinary problems. They are a valuable resource and one that we should utilize to the fullest.

I am not saying that every position should be open to every sol- 19 dier. Of course no soldier should be assigned to a position for which he or she is not qualified. There are some legitimate concerns about the upper body strength of most women, for example. Jobs which require heavy lifting should not be open to anyone who could not complete the required tasks. Gender-neutral physical requirements would address this concern without arbitrarily excluding qualified candidates.

In the Marine Corps, it has been certified that female enlisted [20] personnel are capable of completing 86 percent of Marine job skills, yet, because of the law prohibiting women from combat missions, only 18 percent of total positions are open to them. There is too wide a discrepancy between the abilities of female Marines and their utilization. We are wasting our personnel resources. Can it be in the interest of national security to exclude qualified soldiers from combat positions?

Another way that the combat exclusion policy inhibits the na- [21] tional defense is by lowering morale among an important 10 percent of our troops. Women have become a crucial part of our Armed Forces. The Air Force projects that female applicants will soon make up 18.6 percent of all their enlisted accessions. It is important that those women feel that they are a valued part of our armed services and that they be rewarded with ample opportunities for advancement. We owe them that. The women in the military serve our country faithfully, and, despite the combat exclusion policy, many women risk their lives each day at dangerous posts like the MX and Minuteman launchsites. They must not be treated like second-class soldiers.

The Navy determined that due to the combat exclusion policy [22] there would not be a sufficient number of leadership positions in the future to accommodate the number of women entering the lower ranks. Consequently, they have introduced a new specialists' career path for nonwarfare personnel in the general unrestricted line classification. This alternate career path emphasizes specialty development through repeat tours in a particular field. This will enhance the career opportunities for women in specialized and high technology areas so that in the future women will be able to rise even to the rank of admiral without a warfare specialty.

I have some reservations about this alternate career path. While I [23] commend the Navy's efforts to open advancement opportunities for women, I question whether this will be helpful to women in the military or whether it will hurt them in the long run. What value is there in being a high-ranking military officer with no warfare capacity? Will these women be as highly respected as their male peers? One young male soldier told me that he does not think it is fair for women to be able to advance to the top without sharing the same risks as men.

Dividing the military with alternate career paths is just another [24] example of how the combat exclusion policy places elaborate and cumbersome qualifications on how we can use our military personnel. It is only right that women who devote their lives to the defense of our Nation should have adequate advancement opportunities, but the result will be a situation in which there are career Navy admirals who are not allowed to get near combat.

The bottom line is that combat is the defining role of the military, [25] and until women can be trained in the warfare specialties their status will be that of a protected subclass. This can only lessen the esteem from their male counterparts and hurt their morale. Using qualified female soldiers wherever they are competent to serve will be good not only for the morale of women in the military but for the cohesion and flexiblity of our Armed Forces in general. In short, it will enhance our national security. Should that not be our primary concern?

Minerva, Winter 1986

Moral Considerations
for Combat Assignment

LINDA M. EWING

The views expressed in this article are those of Major Linda M. Ewing, United States Army, and do not reflect the official policy or position of the Department of the Army, Department of Defense, or the U.S. Government.

When the United States goes to war, the priority mission of its military—to overcome the enemy—is supported by the civilian community. Victory is a common goal. With the reestablishment of peace, common goals cease. Societal expectations for the military change. Defense (which was the priority during war) remains an essential concern for the military, but becomes a subordinate interest of peacetime society. Society instead becomes absorbed in social issues and social change. Correspondingly, the expectation for the military from society is that the military act as an agent of change.

Conflict arises in the peacetime military not in resistance to its role as agent of social change, but rather in resistance to any reordering of priorities away from security and defense. Tension between the military and civilian society is a traditional feature of American life. However this falls out, the primary concern for the peacetime military leadership must be to filter out social changes that are detrimental to mission accomplishment during war. Regardless of where security and defense appear on society's list of priorities during peace, the potential for defense as a wartime priority must remain primary for the military.

The intentional assignment of women as combat soldiers is an 3 issue of social change that ought to be examined against a background of war as a potential and priority mission for the military force. Facts intended to influence the current debate do not approach analysis via the essential character of society from which the military derives its charter. The essential character of American society transcends political conditions. As such, the concept which ought to be central to the issue of women in combat is the particular American interpretation of justice in both its legal and moral context. Justice permeates all aspects of American life and is the conceptual basis by which all social issues are evaluated.

Fairness is a common bond in economic, social and legal realms 4 of American society. While the order and degree of influence can be argued, the point that justice as fairness permeates all legal and moral judgements in American society cannot be questioned.

The Claim for Sameness

Despite the absence of any precedent for social issues to be evaluated 5 by sameness rather than fairness, advocates for women in combat roles persist in advancing demands for sameness simultaneously with demands for fairness. This dichotomy has confused and confounded the issue. Certainly everyone desires the same accessibility to the system of fairness. However, this is a very different demand than requesting an evaluation by sameness. To make the latter claim is to ask society to restructure its basis for determining legal, social, and economic questions. Further, to advance claims simultaneously is to ask that all questions be reevaluated and the traditional American idea of justice be scrapped for a new model. If society appears to be lethargic in demanding an end to the combat exclusion policy for the Army, it could be that this challenges current societal perceptions about what constitutes legal and moral justice.

From a viewpoint of sameness, the argument for women's assign- 6 ment to combat roles can be simply stated and resolved: If men go to combat arms branches, women go to combat arms branches. The reason this simple logic has not been followed by simple action is that society does not make social determinations this way. If the question of intentionally committing women to combat is subjected to an evaluation by fairness, the decision is not so simple, the action not so swift.

Justice as Fairness

Today, there are a variety of definitions for justice. Some are purely 7 legal, some are moral, others are philosophical and theoretical. All, however, share a particularization of the idea of equality which Americans not only associate with but demand for any justice consideration. This is justice as fairness. There has never been any suggestion or intention in American society for equality to mean "same." For Americans, to treat all people the same without regard for circumstance and condition is unjust legally and morally. There is no precedent in American society to replace fairness with sameness as a judgement principle for any issue to include deciding whether women ought to be assigned to the combat arms branches.

In the American legal system, any condition or circumstance be- 8 yond the control of the individual is mitigation. Mitigation affects assessing degrees of responsibility and punishment. An action that is premeditated is judged differently than an action that is accidental. Equality before the law is fairness before the law.

Similarly in matters of economics, society recognizes that all 9 people do not have the same ability to maintain the same standard of living. Society allows differences to be mitigating conditions that allow a graduated tax collection system as well as a variable system for distribution of funds. While there can be much debate over the method by which the fairness formula is calculated for the collection and distribution of resources, there is little debate that the elderly, the infirm, and the needy in general ought to be maintained by society in a condition of human dignity. To do otherwise is unfair; it is unjust.

Claims for equal rights, correspondingly, are claims for "fair 10 rights." A group seeks recognition that they have been treated unjustly in terms of society's norm of fairness. Society accepts its position as the mitigating condition which caused the injustice and grants advantage to the group as compensation. This is justice as fairness at work. It would not be allowed under an evaluation by sameness.

The Application of Fairness

A lot of time and money has been spent studying whether women are 11 able to function effectively in combat roles. Studies have been conducted on physical, emotional, and communal abilities.[1] To compensate for physical differences, it has been proposed that equipment redesign can resolve problems of effective utilization.[2] However, all attempts to study the internal military organization ignore the simple truth that armies rarely fight themselves. The neglected consideration is the enemy. To conclude that because women and men can effectively function together within a unit they can effectively function against any enemy requires a quantum leap in logic that is not supportable. The enemy is a mitigating circumstance and as with all mitigation, the nature of the enemy is a variable. As it changes, so does the need for evaluation.

Much of the empirical data as well as the myth about women's 12 ability to perform in combat comes from the Israeli experience. Participation has been overstated and the actual experience is not so different from that of American women. When called to fight because the need was present, American women have performed a combat role. The Israeli government ordered women out of direct and intentional combat assignment in 1950.[3] Women continue to be combat trained, which is not the issue. Anyone, by virtue of military association is designated as a combatant and may coincidentally be in a combat role. American women were present in all theaters during World War II for example. Some were taken prisoner at the fall of Bataan, others were torpedoed off the coast of North Africa and some, because of the fact of their presence, died.[4]

Justification for the 1950 decision by the Israeli government was 13 based on a principle of fairness which is generally shared in Western culture with modification. Captured Arab troops stated that they would fight to the death rather than suffer dishonor by surrendering to women. Subsequent reports state that when women were coincidentally faced with combat in 1967, they suffered disproportionate losses again because of the enemy's refusal to surrender to women even though they knew that the women were better trained and equipped, making defeat inevitable.[5]

To place men and women in the same situation, but to expose 14 women to greater risk violates the conceptual basis of justice. It is simply unfair to the women and to the force of which they are a part. In addition, such action violates the wider realm of Western morality expressed in the Just War tradition of proportionality. Proportionality is an attempt to prevent limitless wars of annihilation by declaring through international and customary laws of warfare that the violence employed in war must be proportionate to the goals of war. Despite bravado to the contrary, war is an act of conservation as well as destruction. No modern army has succeeded by fighting a war of annihilation. Rather, war is fought to a position where peace can be negotiated. To intentionally commit a force to a battle in which it is known that the enemy's cultural position prevents the possibility of negotiation and instead will probably lead to fighting beyond reasonableness causing excessive loss on both sides violates what little logic can be applied to war and must be unconditionally declared an immoral premise.

A Moral Conclusion

Unless the United States declares war on its allies, the most probable 15
adversaries are those who do not share American ideology. While differences ought not to affect internal policy, they should impact on the
development of policy to deal with those outside the Western cultural
umbrella. Successfully defending Western ideology and American heritage, after all, insures the right to have internal policy to formulate.
Legal and moral norms cannot be changed arbitrarily. These are considerations that are far more important than the results of all the
physical, emotional and related studies that have plagued the utilization question for women in today's military.

Notes

1. Among the most complete studies are those done by the U.S. Military Academy since
   the admission of women. These studies are entitled the "Athena Project," I–IV.
2. This suggestion was made by Judith H. Stiehin in her article "Women and the Combat
   Exemption," *Parameters*, V. 19 No. 2, June 1980, p. 53.
3. J. David Truby, *Women at War, A Deadly Species* (Paladin Press, NY, 1977), p. 25.
4. Mattie E. Treadwell, *The Women's Army Corps*, Part 2 of *United States Army in World
   War II: Special Studies*, viii. (Washington: Department of the Army, 1954). This volume
   presents a history of women's involvement in U.S. conflicts through W.W. II.
5. Truby, p. 26.

Minerva, Winter 1986

DEBATE: WOMEN IN THE MILITARY

CONTEXT

1. *Minerva* is a journal devoted to the subject of women in the military. Its audience is
composed of both military personnel and nonmilitary readers. Do you expect the readers to be clearly divided in their beliefs about women in the military or do you think
divisions exist within each group depending on the issue? Identify your assumptions
about this audience's beliefs and explain on what basis you make those assumptions.

2. Senator Proxmire prepared his argument to be delivered orally to his colleagues in
the Senate. At the same time he knew his remarks would become part of the written
Congressional Record available for public use. Do you think his argument is equally
strong in its oral and written form? Explain what specific features of his argument lead
you to your decision.

3. Major Ewing prepared her argument specifically for publication in *Minerva*. Would
you say she has designed her argument more for the military or nonmilitary reader or
both? What features support your decision?

STRATEGY

1. The writers choose different strategies for introducing their claims. Describe these differences and analyze their effectiveness for the intended purpose and audience.

2. Both writers state that combat defines a person's role in the military by virtue of that person's membership in the armed forces. Explain how the writers use this concept to support their reasoning in opposing arguments. Which use do you find more convincing and why?

3. The values readers associate with terms strongly influence the audience's acceptance of an argument. Proxmire bases his argument on the terms *flexibility, protection,* and *security.* Ewing bases hers on the definition of *fairness, sameness,* and *equality* as they relate to *justice.* The writers' method of defining terms conveys their attitude toward the audience they are addressing. Describe the definition methods each writer uses and explain how these methods reveal the writer's attitude toward the audience.

4. Identify at what point each writer positions the refutation. Explain why you think this positioning is or is not effective.

5. Both writers have earned professional positions that lend credibility to their arguments. Comment on the strength of these writers' professional credibility with respect to the combat issue, and explain how they more fully develop their respective ethical appeals through their choices of evidence.

EXTENDING THE ARGUMENT

1. Proxmire and Ewing both distinguish between views of the military during times of war and times of peace. Construct an argument directed to the general public defending the need for these differences in perception or the need to eliminate the differences.

2. In her discussion of the need to consider the enemy's cultural differences in fighting a war, Ewing states that the excessive loss of life that might result on both sides "violates what little logic can be applied to war." Present an argument to a college-age audience defending or refuting the logic of war.

3. Proficiency with weaponry, knowledge of military strategy, mutual respect of colleagues, and upper body strength are all cited as necessary conditions for combat. Are there additional qualities necessary for combat that make women capable or incapable of combat duty? Direct your argument to a female audience.

RELATED SUBJECTS

gender equity	the Amazons of Greek mythology
the role of women in U.S. wars	women astronauts

RELATED READINGS IN THIS TEXT

"Battle of the Sexes"	Chapter 5
"The Other Difference Between Boys and Girls"	Chapter 7
Vietnam: Lessons Learned	Issues section

ISSUES

Every issue has multiple perspectives from which controversy arises. The people directly involved, the observers, the law-making and law-enforcing agencies relied upon, and ultimately the society that enjoys the benefits and bears the burdens of the results—these perspectives provide insights into the nature of a problem.

The readings in this section offer a range of views on several issues. Understanding the points of view from which others argue will help you predict and refute objections to the viewpoints you develop for your own arguments.

AIDS: PUBLIC HEALTH VERSUS CIVIL RIGHTS

College Student Attitudes Toward AIDS Carriers and Knowledge of the Disease

LAWRENCE R. KRUPKA, PH.D.
Professor of Natural Science, Department of Natural Science

ARTHUR M. VENER, PH.D.
Professor of Social Science, Department of Social Science Michigan State University

Introduction

Purpose

In a previous study, we reported our findings regarding the level of 1
biomedical knowledge that college students possessed dealing with

the etiology, epidemiology, transmission, symptomatology, and treatment of Acquired Immune Deficiency Syndrome—AIDS (Vener and Krupka, 1988). The purpose of this paper is threefold: (1) To measure attitudes toward AIDS carriers in various university situations, (2) to ascertain the relative importance that students place on issues centered around public health versus individual rights with regard to AIDS carriers and (3) to determine whether an association exists between attitudes toward AIDS carriers and the level of knowledge that students possess regarding this disease.

Background Information

In a relatively short period of time, the acronym AIDS has become a 2 well known component of American life. The disease was first described in 1981. It is caused by a retrovirus known as human immunodeficiency virus (HIV-1) which attacks an individual's immune system and ultimately destroys the ability to ward off disease. As of April 11, 1988, The Centers for Disease Control reported that 59,287 individuals in the U.S. had acquired AIDS and over half, 33,060, have died (Centers for Disease Control, 1988). Ninety-two percent of the individuals diagnosed as having AIDS in 1981 are no longer alive. The dread of this disease is associated with its high mortality and is exacerbated by the stigma linked with certain high risk behaviors such as homosexual anal intercourse and the sharing of needles among IV drug users. Sixty-four percent of all AIDS cases in the U.S. have been attributed to homosexual or bisexual men without a history of IV drug use, 7% to homosexual males with a history of IV drug use, and 18% to heterosexual IV drug users (Centers for Disease Control, 1988). This amounts to 89% of the total cases reported.

Estimates of the number of individuals already infected with the 3 virus vary. However, the most commonly cited number is 1.5 million. This means that one in 30 American males between the ages of 20 and 50 are infected with HIV-1 (Public Health Service, 1987). On a worldwide basis, as many as 10 million people may be infected (Piot, 1988). Projections made by the Public Health Service indicate that, in the U.S., 270,000 cases of AIDS and 179,000 deaths will have occurred by the end of 1991. New AIDS cases acquired by heterosexuals without a history of IV drug use is expected to more than double, reaching 9% of the total cases by this latter year. Pediatric cases are expected to increase by a factor of ten (Coolfont Report, 1986).

In short, AIDS represents a real threat to human existence. The 4 major goal of the services and institutions of public health is to reduce the amount of disease and premature death in the population as a whole (Last, 1987). It is inevitable that this public health goal will come into conflict, on occasion, with the ideals of maintaining human dignity and individual rights guaranteed by the constitution. Such difficulty is telescoped by the AIDS epidemic. For example, in the domain of surveillance for HIV-1 infection, public health needs require systematic testing of high risk individuals. To be effective, information must be shared with a number of local, state, and federal agencies. Under these circumstances, it may be impossible to always uphold an individual's right to privacy and confidentiality. Further, the identification of AIDS patients or carriers of the virus may result in discriminatory practices by employers, health care providers, landlords, and life or health insurers. Another problematic area is the case of recalcitrants, persons who have the AIDS virus and who knowingly continue to expose others to the disease despite official notice to cease such activity. Does the state have the right to commit such individuals to an appropriate institutional facility in order to isolate them?

AIDS has generated a second epidemic—an epidemic of fear, ignorance, and misunderstanding, referred to by some as AFRAIDS: Acute Fear Regarding AIDS. The fear is multi-dimensional. Individuals are anxious about the possibility of becoming infected with the virus, while those who are already infected fear potential discrimination and are concerned about the poor prospect of living and dying with dignity. The disease has and will continue to challenge our social and political institutions. A pluralistic society is founded upon the competition of different interest groups. In order for these groups to exist in the first place and pursue their interests, a minimal amount of tolerance must exist (Quist, 1986). Previous research has demonstrated that increased knowledge of AIDS among high risk groups has decreased the incidence of infection (Fineberg, 1988). Similarly, we believe that an increase in the scientific knowledge of the disease will also encourage greater public tolerance of those who have become infected with the HIV-1 virus.

Methodology

The Sample

The sample consisted of 1,175 college students attending Michigan State University, a midwest educational institution with an enrollment of approximately 42,000. Respondents were randomly selected from required freshmen and sophomore core classes in the social and natural sciences in November of 1987. The sample contained approximately equal numbers of men and women (men = 582; women = 593).

The Instrument

The instrument consisted of True-False and multiple choice questions which were divided into two sections. The first section elicited information regarding the respondents' biomedical knowledge of AIDS.

Findings from the 35 items in this section of the instrument have been more fully reported elsewhere (Vener and Krupka, 1988). Correct scores ranged from 13 to 33, with the average being 24.77. No significant differences in mean scores were found between the genders. In order to facilitate data analysis, the knowledge test questions were divided into three levels of difficulty: high, moderate, and low. Individuals were placed into the high knowledge category if their scores were at least one standard deviation above the mean, while those individuals scoring at least one standard deviation below the mean were categorized as possessing low knowledge. Operationally, respondents answering 28 or more of the 35 knowledge items correctly were considered to have high knowledge, those with scores between 22 to 27, medium knowledge, and those with scores of 21 or less, low knowledge.

The second section of the survey instrument elicited the respondents' attitudes regarding their willingness to interact with individuals infected with the AIDS virus in various university situations. Other questions in this section measured the relative importance that students place on issues centered around public health and individual rights with regard to carriers of the AIDS virus. On the average, students were able to complete the survey instrument within a period of 20 minutes. Anonymity was assured by not requesting that the names of respondents be placed on the answer sheets. The responses of nine individuals, representing less than 1% of the original sample of 1,184, were discarded because of incomplete answers to questions. 8

Findings

Attitudes and Knowledge

Table 1 demonstrates that students tend to be less willing to associate with AIDS virus carriers in situations of high intimacy. Ninety-one percent of the respondents were unwilling to date an AIDS carrier, and 33% would not wish to be in the same classroom with such individuals. Table 1 also shows that, in general, a positive relationship exists between the willingness to associate with HIV-1 carriers and the level of AIDS knowledge. For example, whereas only 25% of the low knowledge respondents were willing to share the same swimming pool, as many as 51% of high knowledge individuals were willing to do so. Likewise, approximately one out of every two low knowledge students were not willing to be in the same classroom as an AIDS carrier, and in contrast, only about one out of four of the high knowledge respondents were so predisposed. In examining the various situations illustrated in Table 1 on a vertical basis, individuals with high knowledge show a greater range of disinclination to associate with AIDS carriers (high, 92.4%; low 28.4%) than individuals who possess low knowl- 9

TABLE 1. *Disinclination to Associate with AIDS Carriers in Various Situations by Knowledge in Percents*

Situation	AIDS Knowledge			
	High (n = 211)	Medium (n = 802)	Low (n = 162)	Total (n = 1175)
1. Dating	92.4	90.5	89.5 n.s.	90.7
2. Sharing a dorm room	80.6	88.0	93.2 ***	87.4
3. Sharing a bathroom	64.0	78.2	85.2 ***	76.6
4. Using the same swimming pool	48.8	55.0	74.7 ***	56.6
5. Living in the same dormitory	26.1	37.0	42.6 **	35.8
6. Being in the same classroom	28.4	30.4	52.5 ***	33.1

Chi-Square Statistical Differences: $**p < .01$
$***p < .001$
n.s. not significant

edge (high, 89.5%; low 52.5%). The only situation which did not show a statistically significant relationship between knowledge and the disinclination to associate with HIV-1 virus carriers was that of dating. Regardless of the level of knowledge, respondents were extremely reluctant to date such individuals.

Public Health Versus Individual Rights

Table 2 shows students' opinions regarding various social policy state- 10 ments dealing with AIDS carriers. There is an apparent wide range of agreement-disagreement with regard to the eight policy statements. For example, about 88% of the students felt that health care providers should take an AIDS blood test, while only 15% believed that AIDS carriers should be isolated from the rest of the population. In half of the social policy statements, 60% or more of the students favored public health goals over individual rights, and in the other half, 42% or less placed greater emphasis on individual rights. In general, Table 2 also shows that agreement-disagreement with social policy statements is associated with levels of AIDS knowledge. The largest difference was observed in the responses to the statement that food handlers be required to take an AIDS blood test. Almost 78% of the respondents with low knowledge agreed with this statement while only about 50% of those with high knowledge did so. Again, almost half of the students with low knowledge indicated that AIDS test results should be made public and only about 25% of high knowledge individuals also agreed with this policy. A statistically significant association was not in evidence between levels of knowledge and responses to the policy item regarding the jailing of AIDS carriers who insist on having sex with others. Approximately the same percentage of students (slightly over 70%) were in agreement with this statement, despite differences in levels of knowledge.

TABLE 2. *Students Agreeing with Various Social Policy Statements Regarding AIDS Carriers by Knowledge in Percents*

| Situation | **AIDS Knowledge** | | | |
	High (n = 211)	Medium (n = 802)	Low (n = 162)	Total (n = 1175)
1. Health care professionals should be required to take an AIDS blood test.	81.5	88.2	93.8**	87.6
2. AIDS carriers who insist on having sex with a number of people should be jailed.	70.6	73.2	71.6 n.s.	72.5
3. Foreign visitors should be banned from the U.S. if they carry the AIDS virus.	59.7	65.6	74.1*	65.7
4. Food handlers should be required to take an AIDS blood test.	50.2	59.4	77.7**	60.3
5. It is more important to identify an AIDS carrier than to protect personal privacy.	34.6	41.3	55.5***	42.0
6. All individuals in the U.S. should be required to take an AIDS blood test.	31.8	36.9	47.5**	37.4
7. AIDS test results should be made public.	25.6	32.3	47.5***	33.2
8. AIDS carriers should be isolated.	10.0	15.7	19.1*	15.1

Chi-Square Statistical Differences: *p < .05
**p < .01
***p < .001
n.s. not significant

Discussion

Recent polls indicate that Americans believe that AIDS, rather than [11] cancer, is the most serious threat to their health (Gallup Poll, 1987; Segal, 1987). These polls also show that young people are particularly fearful of the disease. Developmentally, they are at the stage of life where dating and sexual intimacy frequently occur. This fear of acquiring AIDS is apparently linked to an attitudinal complex leading to the stigmatization of the AIDS carrier. This is demonstrated by the 91% of our respondents who would not date such a person, the 87% who would not be willing to share a dorm room with them, and the 77% who would also not be willing to share a bathroom. As was anticipated, the findings indicate that stigmatization increases in situations which call for greater intimacy in the interactive process. We can appreciate the sentiment of the 92% of high knowledge respondents who were disinclined to date an AIDS carrier, since this situation involves a high degree of intimacy, especially when sexual activity is involved. On the other hand, using the same swimming pool represents a clear-cut example of casual contact. High knowledge respondents knew that this type of association represented no known risk of infection (Vener and Krupka, 1988). Despite this, almost 50% of them were unwilling to use the same swimming pool as AIDS carriers.

The respondents' attitudinal orientations suggest social policy [12] dilemmas for policy makers. Whose rights shall prevail? Should AIDS carriers have the right of privacy wherein confidentiality is maintained by officials? Should they also have the right of equal access to university facilities? On the other hand, do students have a right to know whether they are sharing living quarters with AIDS carriers? Recall that 87% of those we surveyed were unwilling to share dorm rooms with such infected persons. Intimate relationships are formed within the context of residence hall life, and this could possibly place some students at risk.

A majority of the respondents believed that health care profes- [13] sionals and food handlers should be required to take an AIDS blood test. Again, this response pattern was probably driven by the secondary epidemic of fear. According to current scientific thinking, there is practically no possibility of getting AIDS from such health care professionals as physicians and nurses or from food handlers. Fear of becoming exposed to the disease drove as many as 15% of the respondents to want to isolate AIDS carriers from the rest of the population. On the other hand, fear of acquiring the disease may not be the only factor involved in why two out of every three students would refuse foreign AIDS carriers entrance into the United States. Experts have maintained that the disease originated in Africa (Curran et al., 1985) and the infection prevalence rate in some countries of this continent are among the highest in the world (Francis and Chin, 1987; Fauci, 1988). Therefore, racism as well as the distrust of aliens may also be involved in this rejection of foreign AIDS carriers.

Overall, the findings also show that students tend to be more willing to favor individual rights over public health goals when they have more objective knowledge of the disease. The only policy issue which did not show such a relationship was the notion that AIDS carriers who continue to have sex with others should be jailed. Undergraduates at any level of knowledge (high, medium, and low) knew that AIDS could be transmitted by sexual activity (Vener and Krupka, 1988). In ascertaining the respondents' qualitative reactions to the survey instrument, we discerned a high degree of moral indignation toward AIDS carriers who knowingly continue to have sex with others without informing these others of their health status. Many students felt this was tantamount to murder in the first degree, and therefore strong action should be taken against such perpetrators in order to protect the innocent. A number of students also revealed a distrust of official pronouncements regarding the degree of risk which a typical American actually faces. On the one hand, they are told that HIV-1 is not spread by insects, being coughed or sneezed upon, or by casual contact, while simultaneously, they learn that the virus has been found in human saliva and tears. Furthermore, although educational messages urge precaution with regard to sexual activity, authorities are uncertain as to whether or not conditions in the U.S. will support a widespread epidemic within the heterosexual population (Fineberg, 1988). The promulgation of uncertainty has been exacerbated by the recent publication of *Crisis: Heterosexual Behavior in the Age of AIDS* (Masters, Johnson, and Kolodny, 1988) in which these reputable scientists imply that public health officials and the scientific community have deliberately concealed the real extent of infection among heterosexuals. We suggest, in conclusion, that knowledge will assuage the stigmatization of AIDS carriers to a greater degree when more scientific consensus prevails and when the messages from officials become less ambivalent.

College Student Journal, Fall 1988

References

Centers for Disease Control. (1988). *Aids Weekly Surveillance Report*—April 11, 1988. U.S. AIDS Program. Centers for Disease Control. Atlanta. 5 pages.

Coolfont Report. (1986). "A public health service plan for prevention and control of AIDS and the AIDS virus." *Public Health Report*, 101:341–348.

Curran, J. W., Morgan, W. M., Hardy, A. M., et al. (1985). "The epidemiology of AIDS: Current status and future prospects." *Science*, 229:1352–1357.

Fauci, A. S. (1988). "The human immunodeficiency virus: Infectivity and mechanisms of pathogenesis." *Science,* 239:617–622.

Fineberg, H. V. (1988). "Education to prevent AIDS: Prospects and obstacles." *Science,* 239:592–596.

Francis, D. P., and Chin, J. (1987). "The prevention of acquired immunodeficiency syndrome in the United States." *Journal of the American Medical Association,* 257:1357–1366.

Gallup Poll, (1987). *The New York Times,* 29 November 1987, p. 26.

Last, J. L. (1987). *Public Health and Human Ecology.* Norwalk, Connecticut: Appleton and Lange.

Masters, W. H., Johnson, V. E., and Kolodny, R. C. (1988). *Crisis: Heterosexual Behavior in the Age of AIDS.* New York, New York: Grove Press.

Piot, P., Plummer, F. A., Mhalu, F. S., et al. (1988). "AIDS: An international perspective." *Science,* 239:573–579.

Public Health Service. (1987). *AIDS: A Public Health Challenge, Volume 1: Assessing the Problem.* U.S. Department of Health and Human Services. Washington, D.C.

Quist, N. (1986). "AIDS and public policy." *AIDS and Public Policy Journal,* 1:1–2.

Segal, M. (1987). "AIDS education." *FDA Consumer,* 27:26–30.

Vener, A. M., and Krupka, L. R. (1988). "AIDS Knowledge: the media and the biology teacher." *The American Biology Teacher,* 50: In Press.

Moral Anemia

TRB
FROM WASHINGTON
MICHAEL KINSLEY
Editor of New Republic

The cheapest moral high around is giving blood. It takes about 20   1
minutes, is just barely painful enough to seem serious, and leaves you
feeling smug all day.

Over the years the United States has moved to a voluntary system   2
of blood donation, which depends almost completely on that moral
high as an inducement. For the past decade it has been official government
policy to discourage commercial blood banks, which pay people

to open their veins "Cash blood," which was about a third of the total supply in the 1960s and 11 percent in 1971, is down to two percent today. Even "blood credit" and "replacement" arrangements, where each donation counts toward your own future need or past use, are disappearing in favor of a total reliance on community spirit. Eight million people give blood each year—about ten percent of the eligible pool.

This is a rare example of a work of social philosophy having an 3 immediate practical impact. *The Gift Relationship* by Richard Titmuss was published in 1971. Titmuss, a British philosopher, compared the British system of voluntary blood donation with the American semi-commercial arrangement. He concluded that the voluntary system was not just morally superior, but more practical as well. His strongest evidence was that America's commercial blood supply caused four times as many cases of hepatitis among recipients as Britain's voluntary blood pool. He argued that offering money for blood attracts poorer, sicker donors and induces them to lie about their health. Meanwhile, the profit motive induces the commercial blood bank itself to cut corners in quality control.

Titmuss, now deceased, was a product of his time. He saw blood 4 as a metaphor for the corruptions of capitalism. In our time, naturally, market-oriented scholars have been chipping away at his thesis. My moral high is fraudulent, they would argue. By giving blood I'm denying someone the chance to earn $50 who needs the cash more than I need the frisson. The Red Cross, they say, is just a stodgy blood cartel. The best guarantee of efficiency and quality in blood, as in any other commodity, would be a competitive free market.

Now this interesting debate is being made obsolete by the rapid 5 spread of a third system of blood collection, without benefit of philosophy. This is so-called "autologous" blood, which means putting aside your own blood for your own use. On November 7 the American Medical Association officially endorsed autologous blood and encouraged doctors to encourage their patients to try it. "For the patient," said the AMA, "autologous blood eliminates the risk of alloimmunization or infectious disease from a transfusion." The immediate cause of concern, of course, is AIDS.

As a practical matter, it is hard to think of many things less worth 6 worrying about than catching AIDS from a blood transfusion. Since March 1985, all blood has been tested for AIDS antibodies. The test isn't foolproof, since the antibodies don't develop until a few months after a person is infected. But in 12 million units of blood since testing began, there is only one known case of a recipient catching AIDS. Authoritative estimates of the risk of getting AIDS in a blood transfusion range from one in 250,000 to one in a million.

To put this risk in some perspective, you have a one in 40 million 7 chance of dying in an accident for every mile you drive your car. If it's five miles each way to the hospital and you make four round-trips to store up blood in advance of an operation, your chance of being killed on the road starts to approach your chance of getting AIDS if you don't bother. Of course AIDS can be transmitted to your loved ones, so maybe the risk is worth it. But you take the same risk every day to go to a movie or the supermarket, and you do so without a second thought.

So why is the medical establishment encouraging autologous 8 blood? In part to increase the total blood supply. In part because there are other dangers from donated blood, primarily hepatitis. Although no one is in a panic about it, your chance of dying from hepatitis in a blood transfusion is about four in 10,000—25 to 100 times your chance of getting AIDS from a transfusion. Actually, your chance of catching fatal hepatitis from the blood supply is about as great as your chance of catching AIDS would be if there were no AIDS test. But the hepatitis risk has been there all along, and no one was pushing autologous blood very hard until just now. In part, then, the medical establishment is pandering to our society's chronic inability to think rationally about tiny risks of disastrous outcomes.

The larger risk in all this is the erosion of the voluntary system. 9 The Red Cross is fighting a probably losing battle against the growth of so-called "directed donations," in which friends and relatives collect blood for a specific recipient. Doctors argue that this blood is no safer than the common pool, and possibly less safe since donors may be under special pressure to hide sexual and drug habits. An even more insidious development is the re-emergence of commercial blood banks—not to buy blood, but to charge you a fee for taking your blood and freezing it. Doctors protest in vain that when blood is needed, it is likely to be either in an emergency, with no time to get the frozen supply, or in elective surgery, with plenty of time to store up fresh blood beforehand. But reason is taking a backseat.

The spread of autologous and directed blood is a characteristic 10 development of the Reagan era—a narrowing of the sense of community from society as a whole to one's own friends, family, and good self. Economically, it's a different kind of step backward. If commercial blood is a metaphor for efficient capitalism, and voluntary blood is a metaphor for benign socialism, autologous blood is a metaphor for pre-capitalist self-sufficiency, the world where every family grew its own food and made its own clothes. This was not a world worth envying. Philosophers agree: exchange—whether the capitalist bargain or the socialist gift—makes for greater prosperity and happiness.

New Republic, December 1, 1986

Safety vs. Civil Rights

Police Procedures for Suspects with AIDS Stir Controversy

MARK ROBICHAUX
Staff reporter for The Wall Street Journal

Earlier this summer in White Plains, N.Y., Westchester County Court 1
officers refused to escort Arthur Brodie to the courtroom for a hearing
because they didn't want to touch him. Mr. Brodie, charged with drug
possession, was rumored to have acquired immune deficiency syndrome, or AIDS.

In response, Judge Nicholas Colabella convened the hearing on 2
the steps of the county jail. "I couldn't make the court officers bring him
in the courtroom," he says. But the officers' fears proved unfounded:
Voluntary tests later showed Mr. Brodie didn't have the disease.

Mr. Brodie, who received five years' probation after pleading 3
guilty, now refuses to speak with reporters. His wife, Michelle, calls his
ordeal "horrendous," adding: "It was a rumor (the police) didn't even
confirm. It hurt him."

Law-enforcement agencies across the nation are grappling with 4
the problems posed by criminal suspects who may have AIDS. Civil-
rights activists acknowledge that some departments—primarily those
educated in the facts of AIDS transmission—have followed safe, sensitive policies. But they also contend that in a number of cases officers
have overreacted, and have even violated the rights of citizens, out of
fear for their own lives.

"Real Problems"

"We don't know how this whole AIDS thing will unfold," says Robert 5
Levy, a lawyer with the New York Civil Liberties Union. "But we can see
the beginning of some real problems."

Recently, the National Institute of Justice, a research branch of 6
the U.S. Justice Department, published an 80-page report on the issue.
It asserts that no police officer has ever contracted the disease in the
line of duty and that "there is absolutely no evidence of transmission
through casual contact." Moreover, it concludes, "fear and concern
may adversely affect the level and quality of service delivered by a law-
enforcement agency."

But many officers remain unconvinced. "When all these stories 7
come out about AIDS, whom do you believe?" asks Lt. Dan Cooke of
the Los Angeles Police Department. "All we hear is 'in all probability.'
Don't give me the odds of catching it. Give me something specific."

Police say their fears are justified because they often confront 8
dangerous, potentially infected criminals. About 17% of the estimated
40,000 people in the U.S. with AIDS are intravenous drug abusers. It is
this group—prone to instability and violence—that worries police
the most.

"We're not squeamish people; we face death every day," says Phil 9
Caruso, president of the New York Patrolman's Benevolent Association
and a policeman for more than 20 years. "But I would rather have an
enraged gunman shoot me down than die from AIDS."

The AIDS issue is so delicate that those directly involved in inci- 10
dents are generally reluctant to be interviewed about their experiences. However, police and AIDS organizations agree that difficult
situations have become increasingly common.

"I have two officers right now who don't know if they have AIDS 11
or not," says Jack O'Brien, chairman of health and welfare at the Philadelphia Fraternal Order of Police. In separate incidents, the two officers were pricked with hypodermic needles during body searches of
drug suspects. Both suspects, tested voluntarily, showed positive for
AIDS. (According to the NIJ report, AIDS testing of suspects without
their consent is expressly forbidden in several states, including California and Wisconsin, and subject to a wide range of legal and adminis-
trative obstacles in many other jurisdictions.)

"The officers will have to be tested periodically for a year," says 12
Mr. O'Brien. "They're in limbo. In the meantime, what will they tell
their wives? There are incidents like this all over."

Such concerns have led many police departments to adopt spe- 13
cial precautionary measures. In Baltimore, for example, police officials
set aside $50,000 this year for protection against suspects with AIDS.
Each officer now receives a kit that includes rubber gloves, plastic goggles, disposable boots, cardiopulmonary-resuscitation masks, information manuals and a tube for hypodermic needles.

In Albany, N.Y., police and fire departments went as far as to 14
maintain lists of local AIDS sufferers for several months—a policy that
outraged such groups as the National Association for the Advancement of Colored People, the New York Civil Liberties Union and the
Lambda Legal Defense Fund, a national homosexual rights organization. Those groups sent a six-page letter of protest to Albany's mayor
stating that "the maintenance of such lists violates the legal and constitutional rights of those who are monitored or listed."

Sgt. Robert Wolfgang of the Albany police says the department, 15
which he explains drew up the lists so that officers could be fore-

warned to use caution in dealing with AIDS sufferers, recently abandoned them because it couldn't maintain their accuracy. He adds that "there was no harm intended with keeping them."

Perhaps the most publicized police action occurred June 1 at the 16 Third International Conference on AIDS in Washington, D.C. Police donned bright yellow gloves to arrest 64 people, many of them stricken with AIDS, who were protesting President Reagan's AIDS policies.

"It sent the wrong message out to the country," says Lenny Giteck, 17 editor of the Advocate, a national gay magazine. "The message from wearing dishwashing gloves is that you can catch AIDS just by touching a person. That's simply not true."

Washington police defend the use of the gloves as a reasonable 18 precaution.

Promoting AIDS Education

Medical professionals say education could alleviate much of the prob- 19 lem. Indeed, it has proved effective in San Francisco, where the gay community and the police department say that acrimony between them has fallen sharply as a result of educational efforts by both groups.

The department's approach was illustrated during an incident 20 last Halloween. As patrol officer Dan Linehan stood at the booking counter with a suspect who had admitted to being an AIDS carrier, the suspect spit in his face.

Officer Linehan only tightened his grip on the suspect's arm. 21 "I never really thought about catching anything," he says. "It was just a matter of knowing that you can't catch it through saliva (a conclusion of the federal Centers for Disease Control cited in the NIJ report). The perception is more potent than the reality."

Wall Street Journal, September 18, 1987

Doctors Fear AIDS, Too

MATT CLARK
Staff writer for Newsweek

Many Americans were shocked when Dr. W. Dudley Johnson, one of 1 the pioneers of coronary bypass surgery, said that he would not do complex operations on anyone who tests positive for AIDS. Doesn't the

Dentists Begin to Take Precautions

Dentists may be the most reluctant health professionals to treat people with AIDS. The New York City Commission on Human Rights is currently investigating 25 complaints of discrimination brought against the city's dentists and dental clinics. AIDS specialist Dr. Greg Shipman of the Howard Brown Memorial Clinic in Chicago says he can name only two dentists there who treat anyone with the disease. "The dental profession has buried its head," he says.

But the 4,000 dentists attending the annual meeting of the Academy of General Dentistry in Seattle last week began to face up to the problem. Acknowledging that the profession will have to treat more AIDS patients, the group adopted a resolution asking all dentists to use special precautions against infectious diseases, including AIDS. These measures include wearing masks, gloves and goggles. The action was spurred, in part, by the realization that, while a dentist stands a far greater chance of catching hepatitis than he does of contracting AIDS in his practice, AIDS patients do pose special problems. They can carry unusual organisms, like the fungus candida, in their mouths. And the AIDS virus breaks down immunity generally, so that a routine cleaning, which stirs up the ordinarily harmless bacteria living in a patient's mouth, can cause other infections.

Beside the real dangers of AIDS, officials of the AGD were worried by a report from infection-control expert Dr. James Cottone of San Antonio indicating that only 25 to 33 percent of dentists now take protective precautions when treating their patients. In this connection, AGD president Edward Barrett noted that the profession has not traditionally been well trained in "barrier" techniques to protect themselves from infection. But at many dental schools students are now being taught to use gloves and masks. And in Boston, says Dr. Stephen Sonis, a specialist in infectious disease at Brigham and Women's Hospital, the attitude of most dentists is to "treat everyone as if they're infectious, even if the patient is a little old lady."

tradition of the healer going all the way back to the time of Hippocrates require a physician to tend the victims of contagious disease—even at the risk of his own life? Doctors haven't had to face such a question lately. Vaccines and antibiotics now control the transmission of nearly all the dreaded killers—smallpox, cholera, typhus—and doctors had come to assume that both they and their patients were fully protected against infectious diseases. That is, until AIDS came along.

Right now incurable, untreatable and certainly not preventable, AIDS looks like a throwback to the plagues of the Dark Ages. As such it taxes to the limit the compassion and selflessness that are supposed to distinguish the health professions from all other callings. Medical workers were especially troubled last spring by a report from the Federal Centers for Disease Control that three hospital employees had become infected with the AIDS virus, apparently because they were exposed to contaminated blood. Possibly driven by such revelations, a substantial minority of doctors seem to be avoiding AIDS patients. 2

As it is to most people, the risk that any physician or health worker will contract AIDS is surpassingly small. The few doctors who have actually contracted the disease came from the ranks of persons whose behavior puts them at high risk, including male homosexuals, intravenous drug users and victims of accidental needle sticks. A key question, though, is how much contact with the blood and body fluids of AIDS victims constitutes high-risk behavior. One surgeon contended in response to a survey taken by Surgical Practice News that he had tested AIDS positive but was neither homosexual nor an i.v. drug abuser. This is precisely what worries surgeons like Milwaukee's Johnson. "Today I cleaned a dozen specks of blood off my glasses," he said recently. "How many specks of blood can get in your eye before you're infected? Nobody knows." More than 90 percent of surgeons answering the poll agreed with Johnson's practice of turning away prospective patients whose blood tests positive for the presence of AIDS antibodies. Although the number of surgeons responding was quite small, the percentage translates into 800 surgeons who probably would not treat anyone exposed to the virus. 3

U.S. Surgeon General C. Everett Koop disagrees. Speaking as someone who spent 33 distinguished years as surgeon in chief at Children's Hospital of Philadelphia, Koop says: "I would feel obligated to treat patients with AIDS." (Like many another surgeon, Koop picked up jaundice years ago when he inadvertently stuck himself with a needle.) But in truth, neither the ancient Hippocratic oath nor the modern code of medical ethics *requires* a doctor to treat a patient if he doesn't want to. The American Medical Association's guidelines permit a physician to refuse to take a case, especially if the doctor thinks he isn't qualified to provide adequate care. And the bizarre disorders that AIDS victims 4 get—like the rare cancer called Kaposi's sarcoma and the extremely tricky and dangerous *Pneumocystis carinii* pneumonia—may require the attention of the most highly trained specialist. But in turning down a patient for any reason, a doctor takes on another responsibility: "To simply refuse treatment without referring the patient [to a colleague] is not appropriate," says Dr. Nancy Dickey of Richmond, Texas, a member of the AMA's Council on Ethics and Judicial Affairs.

Dumping Patients

No one knows how many doctors won't treat AIDS victims, or those 5 infected with the virus. A gay support group in Michigan claims to receive at least one such complaint each month. "We have doctors who dump patients, who tell patients they never want to see them again," says Scott Walton of Detroit's Wellness Networks, Inc. Rod Miller, a 38-year-old Washington, D.C. man, contends a Delaware surgeon refused to sew up his injured foot because the doctor suspected he kept company with gays. In Los Angeles, a patient who showed a positive result to an AIDS antibody test was curtly told by his doctor, "You wait to die."

Clearly, ingrained fears and bias will become increasingly impor- 6 tant as the epidemic inexorably spreads from epicenters like New York and San Francisco to communities less experienced with the disease. To assess the attitudes of physicians in medium-size cities, University of Mississippi psychologists Jeffrey A. Kelley and Janet S. St. Lawrence sent a cleverly contrived questionnaire to 500 doctors in Memphis, Columbus and Phoenix. Each was presented with a vignette of a hypothetical patient named Mark, described as an affable, college-educated computer-company employee. But some of the stories said Mark suffered from leukemia, while others described his condition as AIDS. And some suggested that Mark had a male lover. In response to questions about their feelings toward the patient, the doctors displayed decided prejudice against the Mark who had AIDS, blaming him for his plight.

Another study, also reported in this month's American Journal of 7 Public Health, suggests that homophobic attitudes can interfere with a doctor's competence to treat AIDS patients. Dr. Charles E. Lewis of the University of California, Los Angeles, surveyed 1,000 of the state's GP's and internists and learned that most lacked essential knowledge about AIDS. Only 16 to 20 percent knew the symptoms well enough to make a diagnosis, and only 35 percent said they routinely asked about a patient's sex life during a physical exam. The study also showed that a doctor's ignorance about the clinical aspects of AIDS was strongly linked to decidedly negative attitudes toward those at high risk. "When they confront a disease whose modes of transmission they think are evil, sinful or immoral they don't behave or speak rationally," Lewis says.

Sex and Drugs

As AIDS continues to make its unrelenting advance, better education 8 of doctors will be crucial. Few of today's practicing physicians were taught how to deal with AIDS in medical school. Nor were they made sufficiently aware of the social factors—including the varieties of human sexuality and the pervasive use of drugs—that provide the stage on which the AIDS virus makes its deadly appearance. In essence, doctors face the challenge all Americans confront with the deadly epidemic. "You can't segregate AIDS, you can't isolate it," says University of South Florida immunologist Dr. Dennis Ledford. "This is a new era."

Newsweek, August 3, 1987

AIDS and the Workplace

Business Fights the Epidemic

WILLIS B. GOLDBECK
President of the Washington Business Group on Health

Over the next 20 years, AIDS will have a substantial impact on all as- 1 pects of employment. This is true regardless of whether one predicts an optimistic scenario, in which the disease does not spread significantly beyond the currently known high-risk populations, or takes the pessimistic view that the heterosexual population will experience a rapid spread of the disease.

Employers certainly are concerned, but, contrary to popular 2 opinion, most employers will not change their employee-benefit packages in response to this new disease. And they will be right not to do so. On a per-case basis, the United States has more than enough precedent—from the cost of caring for patients with Alzheimer's disease to the expense of medical care for heart attacks—to deal with the level of expenditure required for AIDS patients without taking extraordinary or discriminatory measures.

Employers who provide group health insurance are—and will be—treating AIDS like any other illness. New workers will be subject to traditional preexisting-condition exclusions if they have been diagnosed as having AIDS.

Much less clear is the case when a worker has a positive HIV-antibody test but does not have the disease. As long as a substantial proportion of those who test positive do not get the disease and the tests continue to have significant false-positive problems (especially when used on low-risk populations), employers will not equate a positive test with a preexisting condition.

AIDS is providing a major disincentive for small and new employers to start offering health insurance, an especially significant problem in light of the 37 million uninsured Americans and the growing political pressure to mandate coverage as a condition of employment. The commercial insurance industry has called for the government to establish so-called risk pools so the industry can declare not only all who have AIDS but also those who test antibody-positive to be uninsurable. If such measures were to become law, then the self-insured major employers (nearly all of the nation's major businesses) would have to also turn to the government. Thus, ironically, the very effort to get government to protect the commercial insurance industry may cause the United States to establish a national health insurance system.

Political pressure to do so would escalate dramatically, as every other high-cost disease and injury group would demand the same government insurance protection as that provided to AIDS patients. The emergence of AIDS is just the latest and most dramatic demonstration of the inadequacy of a commercial insurance product designed in the 1940s being asked to serve a social insurance objective of the 1990s.

New Health-Benefit Strategies

Inevitably, headlines will focus on the few employers who place a lifetime cap on medical expenses for AIDS. But such isolated incidents do not suggest a trend. On the contrary, AIDS is proving the wisdom of two of the latest developments in employee health benefit design: case management and comprehensive Employee Assistance Program counseling.

Case management is the system of benefits through which an employee's needs can be met without the normal insurance policy restrictions. Custodial services, home care, respite care for family care givers, home alterations, assistance with the purchase of special drugs (AZT, in the case of AIDS), and the use of non-physician providers and community volunteer groups are examples of the kinds of nontraditional benefits that can be made available through case management.

Employee Assistance Program counseling is especially valuable 9 because it provides a natural and totally confidential setting in which to address the depression that, quite logically, accompanies the receipt of a positive antibody test, a diagnosis of AIDS, or the pending loss of a family member or colleague. The EAP is also a good resource for those workers who are anxious about working with someone who has AIDS.

Finally, AIDS is proving how valuable it was for employers and 10 the government to begin investing in hospice care a few years ago. Economic and training resources for hospices will have to be expanded to meet the demand represented by terminally ill AIDS patients, but there will still be major savings compared with the extended use of inappropriate acute care. Hospice care represents the nexus of humanity, dignity, and responsible cost management.

Corporate Culture

AIDS will have less impact on employee medical benefits than on the 11 production and distribution of goods and services. Companies may discriminate against people with AIDS for fear that the public will abandon a product (meat, drugs) or service (fast-food store, private ambulance service, a hospital or clinic) if people with AIDS work there. (The same public that behaves irrationally about children with AIDS in school cannot be expected to do otherwise as consumers.)

AIDS will also change certain aspects of workplace culture. The 12 degree to which these changes are viewed as significant will vary according to one's values. The Washington Business Group on Health predicts leading companies will:

- Routinely distribute condoms in rest rooms.
- Involve dependents, including pre-teens, in employer-provided health-education and sex-education programs.
- Form new alliances with public-health departments and community groups.
- Become much more tolerant of homosexuality and bisexuality, as AIDS makes it evident that no level or category of employment is exclusively heterosexual.

One of the positive results of the AIDS crisis has been the emergence 13 of major employers, from Akron to San Francisco, working with community groups to provide a support system that can be a model for the management of many other illnesses. The savings achieved in

San Francisco, with the strong and very public participation of leaders from Bank of America, Levi Strauss, and many other recognized employers, are the result of creating an integrated employer-home-hospital-community illness-management system that is as humane as it is cost effective.

Education

Education is not only the best defense against AIDS—it is currently 14 the only defense. An internal educational program at the worksite, supported by top management, will increasingly be the method used to help reduce employees' fears about working with someone who has AIDS and the most-effective means of preventing the disease from spreading.

AIDS education in the workplace is designed to serve several pur- 15 poses, including teaching employees and staff about AIDS and how to prevent transmission by the use of safer sex practices; improving employee morale and creating an atmosphere of support for terminally ill employees; and assuring employees and their families that AIDS cannot be transmitted through casual workplace contact.

Any education program needs to encompass the medical, legal, 16 and psychological dimensions of AIDS. Management needs to be educated as much as the rest of the employees. AIDS educational programs are not simply something that can be addressed on a one-time basis, but rather require frequent repetition, standards of accountability, and evaluation.

Firms that have publicly acknowledged major AIDS efforts in- 17 clude Honeywell, Kimberly-Clark, Westinghouse, and Goodyear. In the near future, associations, community organizations, and local governments will be providing the same services for small businesses.

Employer Leadership

Through all the confusion about AIDS, all the information and all the 18 contradictions, a few conclusions are emerging. Despite remarkable progress, science will not provide humanity with a shield from itself. In the case of AIDS, for the known future, employers and employees will have only common sense and educational skills to rely on.

There are and will be cases of extreme discrimination and mis- 19 treatment by a minority of employers. Unfortunately, it will be these cases that not only attract the media attention but also define the legislative and regulatory response of government.

AIDS is, after all, just a disease. But the issues surrounding this 20 disease are deeply rooted in America's traditional discomfort with the subject of sex, especially homosexuality; an increasing fear and anger at the many costs of drug abuse; and a classically American passion for quick-fix solutions and guarantees of safety.

When issues like AIDS arrive, the very individualism that helps 21 make the United States vital and successful clashes painfully with the unity that is so clearly needed. The healthy tension that always exists between public health and civil liberties is strained and threatens to shatter when confronted with AIDS. Ultimately, a resolution of that tension must be found in each worker and employer as expressed through the many roles they play in their homes and communities.

Employers already have direct economic, productivity, and com- 22 munity reasons to be part of the fight against AIDS. Across the country, attention to these issues will grow as more evidence of the efficacy of employer leadership accumulates.

The Futurist, March–April 1988

Why Mandatory Screening for AIDS Is a Very Bad Idea

KENNETH R. HOWE
*Professor in the School of Education at the University of
Colorado, Boulder, and formerly of the Medical Humanities
Program at Michigan State University*

The initial hysteria about AIDS has diminished somewhat, as the means 1 of transmission have become better understood and as the risk of contracting the disease has become associated with well-defined populations, such as male homosexuals, intravenous drug users, and hemophiliacs. At the same time, however, another threat from AIDS has grown—the prospect of the widespread use of mandatory screening, motivated by desires to protect the public health and the private interests of insurance companies and employers.

Five bills were introduced in Michigan legislative committees— 2 one would permit screening by insurance companies and one would mandate screening as a condition of receiving a marriage license. In New York City, calls have been made for mandatory screening of teachers, health care workers, and barbers. The American Council of Life Insurance and the Health Insurance Corporation of America have assembled a task force on how to respond to the impact of AIDS on the insurance industry, working on the assumption that outlays might be in the billions. In October 1985 the military instituted a program to screen all recruits and active duty personnel. Recruits who test positive are rejected. Active duty personnel who test positive are restricted in duty; those who confess to homosexuality or drug use are discharged. Finally, in mid-1986 a LaRouche-backed initiative, "Proposition 64," calling for mass screening of the general population, garnered enough signatures to appear on the ballot in California.

If screening could identify all and only individuals who would   3 develop AIDS or could transmit the AIDS virus, it would remain to be shown that (probably coercive) mandatory screening to detect all cases could be justified. This question can in general be avoided, however, by focusing on the fact that AIDS screening is riddled with error, which has important consequences. On the one hand, error results in falsely identifying individuals as having AIDS or being carriers (false positives), prompting anxiety about AIDS when the danger is not real and creating the potential for extending the undesirable consequences already suffered by AIDS patients to a larger segment of the population. On the other hand, error also results in falsely classifying individuals as not having AIDS or not being carriers (false negatives), creating a false sense of security and possibly contributing to the spread of the disease. In the context of screening donated blood, false positive donations are mistakenly discarded whereas false negatives contaminate the blood supply.

Although ethicists[1] and medical researchers[2] have . . . raised the   4 problem of error in AIDS screening, ethical and technical considerations have not been combined to the extent that they should be. Not surprisingly, ethicists focus on the problem of balancing the rights of individuals against other private and public goods, whereas individuals schooled in the statistical properties of laboratory tests confine themselves to more-or-less ethically neutral technical reports. By showing how technical difficulties should stop mandatory screening from ever getting off the ground, some of the more troubling outcomes of diagnosed AIDS (encroachments on privacy, threats of quarantine, unwarranted exclusions from school or work, and so forth) can be avoided on a larger scale.

Statistical Properties of AIDS Screening Tests

Three tests, the enzyme-linked immunoabsorbent assay (ELISA), the   5 Western blot, and the immunofluorescence assay (IFA), are currently used to detect antibodies associated with the AIDS virus. (The importance of the fact that the tests are not designed to screen for the virus itself, let alone the disease, will be discussed later.) The precise nature of these tests aside, what is important for present purposes is how they perform in terms of five statistical properties: precision, accuracy, sensitivity, specificity, and predictive value.

Precision

The precision of a test is the degree to which it gives consistent or replicable results. Sources of imprecision include things such as procedures, materials, equipment, and individual laboratory technicians' interpretations. Precision may be measured by running a given test repeatedly and then calculating the variability of results—the lower the variability, the greater the precision. 6

Though always to be taken into consideration, imprecision seems not to present any especially severe problems for AIDS testing. Unclear results, which are fairly common, can usually be handled by simply rerunning the test in question. ELISA tests which are initially positive are routinely run a second time by the Red Cross. 7

Accuracy

Whereas test precision pertains to the consistency of results, accuracy pertains to what test results mean, [that is], what a test detects. Tests can be precise but consistently measure the wrong thing; and this is where AIDS screening becomes problematic. "AIDS screening" is actually a misnomer because none of the three tests detects either the AIDS virus or AIDS; they detect antibodies associated with the virus. The presence of the antibodies is taken to be a highly reliable indicator of the presence of the virus, which, in turn, is taken to be a highly reliable indicator of infectiousness. Extending this chain of inferences to AIDS itself is much more tenuous: Only an estimated 10 percent of individuals infected with the AIDS virus will ever develop the disease.[3] Thus, if the tests in question were otherwise error-free, a (true) positive test would entail only a 10 percent chance that AIDS would eventually be manifested. 8

Sensitivity and Specificity

The sensitivity of a test is the degree to which it yields positive results when the property of interest is present; the specificity of a test is the degree to which a test yields negative results when the property of interest is absent. More formally, the sensitivity of a test relative to a property, A, is the probability of a positive result *given* A; the specificity of a test relative to A is the probability of a negative result *given* not-A. 9

In general, the sensitivity and specificity of a given test are inversely related, depending on what test value serves as the cut point between positive and negative results. A certain set of values is unavoidably shared by the class of interest and its complement, due to both biologic variation and imprecision. With the ELISA test, for in- 10 stance, as the cut point value is decreased, a greater percentage of positives are yielded. As a result, the test becomes more sensitive because it will label as positive samples that have the antibodies for the AIDS virus within the overlapping area of values. At the same time, however, the test becomes less specific because it will also label as positive samples within the area of overlap that fail to have the antibody, reducing the test's ability to correctly identify negatives.

Given this relationship between sensitivity and specificity, a 11 choice has to be made regarding whether it is more important to emphasize sensitivity (and accept an increase in false positives) or specificity (and accept an increase in false negatives). The ELISA test (the most frequent first-used test) tilts toward specificity. On the other hand, and although the claims have been disputed,[4] a recent relatively large sample study[5] indicates that the ELISA test is also highly sensitive. According to the study, the three licensed tests [ELISA, Western blot, and IFA] have respective sensitivities and specificities of 93.4 percent and 99.8 percent, 99.6 percent and 99.2 percent, and 98.9 percent and 99.6 percent. The evidence suggests that, relative to laboratory tests in general, the ELISA has very good sensitivity and specificity.

Predictive Value

Sensitivities and specificities are established by knowing or assuming 12 that the property tested for is present or not present. For instance, to say that the ELISA is 95 percent sensitive is to say that 95 percent of tests will be positive *given* that each individual tested has the antibody for the AIDS virus; to say it is 99 percent specific is to say that 99 percent of tests will be negative *given* that no individuals tested have the antibody for the AIDS virus. It is exceedingly important to recognize that the assumption (or knowledge) about the presence or absence of AIDS antibody in connection with sensitivity and specificity does not apply in either the screening or diagnostic context. Indeed, the status of the individual tested is precisely what needs to be determined.

This leads to the concept of predictive value, in which the rela- 13 tionship between what is assumed or known and what is to be determined is just the reverse of what it is for the concepts of sensitivity and specificity. The predictive value of a positive test is the probability that the property is present *given* a positive test; the predictive value of a negative test is the probability that the property is not present *given* a negative test. As a consequence of Bayes' Theorem, predictive values can be determined given the following information: The sensitivity and specificity of the test in question and the prevalence of the property of interest in the population tested ([or], in the case of the AIDS virus, the proportion of the population that has the antibody).

Predictive values are frequently confused with sensitivities and 14 specificities, and this is a serious mistake. Prevalence is an extremely important component of predictive value and can overwhelm high sensitivity or specificity. The problem may be illustrated by imagining a fisherman who fishes a local bay for heavenly fish, which are numerous in the bay and very large. The fisherman has developed a highly "sensitive" and "specific" net by constructing it in such a way that it will capture almost all of the heavenly fish and allow almost all of the smaller and not very numerous junk fish to pass through the mesh. His net does not work perfectly because it sometimes gets tangled and because there is an overlap in size between unusually small heavenly fish and unusually large junk fish. Suppose one day this fisherman ventures out into the ocean where there are very few heavenly fish and very many junk fish. Although from among the fish that enter his net he will still capture the same high percentage of heavenly fish and the same low percentage of junk fish, he will capture a high percentage of very few heavenly fish and a low percentage of very many junk fish. Overall, and much to his dismay, he will net a much larger proportion of junk fish to heavenly fish than he had in the bay.

Precisely the same problem that the fisherman encountered by 15 venturing out of his bay arises when the ELISA test, with its touted sensitivity and specificity, is applied to a group in which the prevalence of the AIDS antibody is low. For example, the Michigan Department of Public Health estimates that the prevalence of the AIDS virus in the population that excludes high-risk groups is .00001. Assume the ELISA is 98 percent sensitive and 99.5 percent specific and is used on this population. Under these assumptions, the ELISA has only 1 in 100,000 chances to be correctly positive, whereas it has 99,999 in 100,000 chances to go wrong—the result is that a whopping 99.8 percent of positives will be falsely positive.

The proportion of false positives can be substantially reduced by 16 using the Western blot, the IFA, or both to confirm the results from the ELISA. (The ELISA–Western blot sequence is by far the most common procedure.) But just how much of a reduction can be obtained is uncertain because no "gold standard" exists that would permit the three tests to be independently validated.

With this brief overview of technical issues in hand, the ad- 17 visability of AIDS screening with respect to its two general defenses, protecting the public health and protecting private interests, may now be evaluated.

Screening to Protect the Public Health

AIDS screening to protect the public health involves different consid- 18 erations, depending on whether the population to be tested is high risk ([that is], has a high prevalence of the AIDS virus) or is low risk ([that is], has a low prevalence of the AIDS virus).

In the case of high-risk individuals, such as homosexual males 19
and intravenous drug users, the predictive value of positive results will
be much better than it is for the general population because of the
relatively high prevalence of AIDS infections within these populations.
(It should be observed that the predictive value of negative results will
be adversely affected, [that is], high prevalence entails more false negatives.) Even so, a serious question arises regarding screening unwilling
individuals. No one (I hope) would advocate hunting down such individuals and dragging them into testing facilities. If the aim is to protect
these individuals' health, prevention through education about the
practices that increase risk is likely to be the most effective strategy.
Because no effective treatment for AIDS exists, testing individuals so
that they might be cured and become noninfectious does not apply,
and, for the same reason, the practice of contact tracing, associated
with treatable infectious diseases, will not have its usual justification.
Finally, it is unlikely that testing information would be of much value
to the individuals themselves. Homosexual males, for instance, have a
10 percent chance of being infected prior to any testing, and the risk
increases (statistically and in fact) in proportion to the number of sexual contacts. Knowledge about this risk should be sufficient (and apparently has been[6]) to motivate individuals who are so disposed to take
necessary precautions. Moreover, the same advice would be given—
avoid risky practices—no matter what the results of testing.

To examine the issue of AIDS screening for low-risk populations, 20
consider the Michigan proposal to require screening as a condition of
being granted a marriage license. Unlike the special problem posed by
groups such as male homosexuals and drug users, applicants for marriage licenses constitute a captive population that is already required
to undergo various medical tests.

As the risk (prevalence) of AIDS decreases for a group, so does the 21
trustworthiness of positive test results. For example, if the ELISA is assumed to be 98 percent sensitive and 99.5 percent specific, it alone is
used, and if the prevalence is assumed to be .0025 (the estimated
prevalence for Michigan of combining low- and high-risk populations),
then 70 percent of positive results will be false positives; if the ELISA
alone is used and the low-risk prevalence of .00001 is assumed (a reasonable assumption for the marrying population), then 99.8 percent of
positive results will be false positives. Since the percentage of false
positives is unacceptable no matter which assumption is made about
prevalence, confirmation by the Western blot is indicated.

Assume that the Western blot is conditionally independent of the 22
ELISA ([that is], its errors are different from the ELISA's), its sensitivity
is 90 percent, and its specificity is 99.9 percent (these are optimistic
assumptions). Assume also that 140,000 individuals (the approximate

number who marry each year in Michigan) are screened using the ELISA, that all positive ELISA results are confirmed with the Western blot, and that the prevalence is .0025 (the result of combining the high- and low-risk groups in Michigan). Given these assumptions, the expected result would be: 309 true positives, 1 false positive, 41 false negatives, and 139,649 true negatives. This looks like a dramatic improvement over the ELISA alone. However, it is reasonable to assume that the prevalence in the marrying population is likely to be much closer to that of the low-risk population (.00001). When this prevalence is assumed, the following results obtain: 1 true positive, 1 false positive, 139,998 true negatives, and 0 false negatives.

On the assumption they are at low risk, screening marriage li- 23 cense applicants is folly; at $10 per ELISA (what the American Red Cross of Michigan pays) and $65–100 per Western blot,[7] it would cost from $1.45 to $1.47 million to identify one individual at only a 10 percent risk of developing AIDS and at some unknown but lesser risk for passing it on to his or her spouse and offspring.

Assume, for the sake of argument, that Michigan's marrying popu- 24 lation's risk is that of the combined high- and low-risk groups. This makes the question harder, but screening would still appear unjustified. First, it would cost from $1.47 to $1.5 million (using the above prices for the ELISA and the Western blot). Counseling individuals who initially test positive on the ELISA, at $50 each, would add an additional $50,000. It would seem that the overall public health could be more greatly improved by allocating resources in other ways. Furthermore, mandatory screening, by its nature, is ethically problematic, and the defenses that may sometimes justify it do not apply to AIDS screening. Because the individuals identified could not themselves be helped or rendered noninfectious, the public health argument would have to be that testing individuals about to be married and informing them of positive results could help halt the spread of AIDS by preventing the birth of infected babies. But, unless coercive measures were used to prevent procreation, the desired result would obtain only if infected individuals voluntarily decided not to marry or not to have children. Thus, AIDS screening for marriage licenses more closely resembles genetic screening than, say, screening for venereal diseases. Mandatory genetic screening is eschewed on the grounds that it involves too much uncertainty and poses too great a threat to privacy and autonomy relative to its expected benefit; mandatory screening for AIDS faces the same difficulty. The question is not whether it might have *some* beneficial effects, but whether, on balance, the beneficial effects outweigh the harmful ones.

It will be useful to compare the example of mandatory screening 25 for marriage licenses with mandatory screening of donated blood.

Both involve general populations, and the fact that screening donated blood is generally believed to be justifiable may be taken as an obvious counterexample to the arguments so far advanced against mandatory screening of general populations.

In purely utilitarian terms, screening donated blood seems little 26 more justified than screening as a condition of being granted a marriage license. Transfusion-related AIDS, though documented, is rare, even prior to the implementation of blood screening. Thus, one could plausibly argue that the costs associated with ELISA screening, in dollars and in the fear and possible breaches of confidentiality for individuals who test positive, far outweigh the benefits to the public health. This argument, I believe, deserves to be taken seriously, especially in light of the facts that some false negatives will inevitably slip through the screen (the blood supply cannot be rendered *completely safe*) and that over 90 percent of positives will be false positives (nine out of ten pints of blood that are discarded will be mistakes). On the other hand, there are at least three considerations that render screening donated blood considerably more defensible than screening for marriage licenses.

These considerations involve the individuals to be tested, the in- 27 dividuals who handle donated blood, and the attitudes of the public at large. First, individuals have a much greater claim against government and other authorities regarding noninterference in marriage and child-bearing than regarding the practice of donating blood. Opting out of donating blood to avoid screening has a much less profound effect on individuals' lives than opting out of getting married to avoid screening. Second, Red Cross workers and public health authorities, understandably, do not want to be vehicles for the transmission of the AIDS virus. Although rare, infection with AIDS via contaminated blood does occur. Unlike the case of mandatory screening for marriage, in which certain behaviors on the part of others are required to spread the infection, contaminated blood directly puts those who collect, distribute, and infuse it in the uncomfortable position of spreading the AIDS virus. Finally, given the persistence of tremendous public fears and misunderstandings, screening seems required to instill public confidence in the safety of the blood supply. No similar benefits would follow from intruding on individuals' marriage plans.

Screening to Protect Private Interests

Unlike screening to protect the public health, screening to protect pri- 28 vate interests is motivated from private self-interest. Employers and insurers fear they will be required to absorb exorbitant costs in connection with AIDS victims, and there are signs they are beginning to assert their purported right to screen for AIDS in order to protect themselves against the projected costs.[8]

Because the motivation is self-interest, employers and insurers [29] are likely to want to use the ELISA alone as a marker for high risk. At first sight, it may appear that this is similar to rating or excluding smokers, pilots, scuba divers, and so forth. However, because the false positives exceed the true positives by a significant margin, the *actual* source of risk, the AIDS virus, is unlikely to be present even given positive test results. This sort of high-risk rating for AIDS is like giving a nonsmoker whose parents smoke a high-risk rating because an individual's smoking habits are associated with his or her parents' smoking habits. Such rating schemes are clearly inequitable, and insurers and employers should not, in the name of their private interests, be allowed to affront justice in any way they see fit. To avoid this intolerable degree of injustice, then, employers and insurers would have to be required to perform confirmatory testing.

Again, the outcome of AIDS screening depends on the tests used [30] and the prevalence of the AIDS virus in the population tested. As it turns out, in some situations AIDS screening may not even serve private financial interests. Consider the issue of health insurance. (Similar considerations apply to life insurance underwriters and to employers who must pay insurance premiums and accommodate lost work time.)

Screening 140,000 low-risk individuals with the ELISA alone (and [31] making all the other assumptions associated with the parallel example in connection with screening for marriage licenses in Michigan) would cost at least $1.4 million and would detect at most one case of incipient AIDS. Using the Western blot as [a] confirmatory [measure] would increase the costs of screening by $46,000 to $70,000. Since the cost of treating one case of AIDS ranges from $25,000 to $140,000,[9] it would cost a health insurer considerably more to conduct a screening program than to pay for the expected medical costs associated with foregoing such a program.

If the prevalence is assumed to be that which results from combining the low-risk and high-risk Michigan populations, then the ELISA [32] screening costs will remain the same at $1.4 million, and an additional $68,000 to $104,000 in costs would be incurred if ELISA positives were confirmed by the Western blot. From $100,000 to $560,000 would also be added, the expected treatment costs for the four AIDS cases that would result from 41 false negatives. The total cost of screening 140,000 individuals using the ELISA–Western blot sequence, where the prevalence equals .0025, would be $1.67 to $2.06 million. Without such a screening program, 309 infections would be expected, of which 10 percent, or 31, could be expected to develop into full-blown cases of AIDS.

The cost of treating 31 AIDS patients ranges from $775,000 to $4.3 million.

As these scenarios suggest, whether it would be in the financial 33 interests of health insurers to conduct AIDS screening turns importantly on the population tested and the costs of treating AIDS patients, and precise figures would be required to make this judgment in individual cases. But even when private interests can reap financial benefits from mandatory AIDS screening, the practice remains unjustified. The ultimate results would only be higher overall costs and cost shifting. Unless AIDS patients are abandoned, the money for their care will have to come from somewhere. Because AIDS screening could not be used to detect AIDS at some early, treatable stage, and thus reduce health care costs, its only use would be to exclude those at risk from private insurance or employment. This simply shifts the burden from the private to the public sector, and generates the additional, sizable cost of screening (which, no doubt, would be absorbed by policyholders). It is perfectly legitimate for government to override private interests when such interests clearly conflict with equity and the public welfare. Protection of the environment, the work place, and civil rights, as well as unisex life insurance benefits, . . . presumes that private interests are not to be left totally immune from government interference. Finally, regarding the fair treatment of insurance companies themselves, a ban on AIDS screening puts no insurance company at a competitive disadvantage, since all companies would be prevented from obtaining the information needed to exclude or rate individuals who tested positive for the AIDS antibody.[10]

Conclusion

Mandatory AIDS screening is a very bad idea. From a technical per- 34 spective, it is a wholly ineffective and inefficient means of protecting the public health.[11] From a more purely ethical perspective, it unnecessarily threatens the privacy and autonomy of high- and low-risk individuals alike and, because of the uses to which it would be put by private interests, offends any well-developed conception of justice.[12]

Notes

1. See Carol Levine and Ronald Bayer, "Screening Blood: Public Health and Medical Uncertainty," *The Hastings Center Report* (August 1985), pp. 8–11; and Ronald Bayer and Gerald Oppenheimer, "AIDS in the Work Place: The Ethical Ramifications," *Business and Health* (January 1986), pp. 30–34.

2. See the discussions by Michael J. Barry, Albert G. Mulley, and Daniel E. Singer; C. E. Miller; Steven Kleinman; and Stanley H. Weiss and James J. Goedert in "Letters," *Journal of the American Medical Association* 253(23) (June 1985), pp. 3395–97.
3. Estimates of the percentage of individuals infected with the AIDS virus who will develop AIDS or AIDS-related conditions (ARC) range from 1–2 percent to over 35 percent. The higher estimates are typically based on studies of the subset of male homosexuals consisting of highly promiscuous individuals. A number of confounding variables are associated with this subset—a large number of exposures due to a large number of sexual partners; a generally high rate of infection, especially with the Hepatitis B virus; and the use of "poppers"—that compromise their immune systems and probably render them more likely to develop AIDS and ARC if they are infected with the virus. Ten percent is estimated by Leibowitch (as reported by Lieberson) to be the upper limit of individuals infected with the virus that will ever show symptoms of any kind, when the entire population of infected individuals (versus a peculiar subset of male homosexuals) is the basis of the estimate. See Jonathan Lieberson, "The Reality of AIDS," *The New York Review of Books* (January 16, 1986), pp. 43–48; and Jean L. Mark, *Science* (January 31, 1986), pp. 450–51.
4. See "Letters," *op. cit.*
5. John C. Petricciani, "Licensed Tests for Antibody to Human T-Lymphotropic Virus Type III," *Annals of Internal Medicine* 103 (1985), pp. 726–29.
6. The effort to educate at-risk individuals in San Francisco appears to have been effective in reducing risky behavior. See Lieberson, *op. cit.*
7. See Ronald Bayer and Gerald Oppenheimer, "AIDS in the Work Place: The Ethical Ramifications."
8. See The American Council of Life Insurance, "The Acquired Immunodeficiency Syndrome and HTLV-III Antibody Testing," in *Taking Sides: Clashing Views on Controversial Bioethical Issues* (2nd ed.), edited by Carol Levine (Guilford, Conn.: Dushkin Publishing Group, 1987), pp. 316–21.
9. These figures are based on an estimate of the Centers for Disease Control, and costs are likely to be toward the low end of this range. The average cost of treating an AIDS patient at San Francisco General, which has the greatest experience, is $25,000 to $32,000. See Katie Leishman, "San Francisco: A Crisis in Public Health," *The Atlantic Monthly* (October 1985), pp. 18–40.
10. M. Scherzer, "The Public Interest in Maintaining Insurance Coverage for AIDS," in Carol Levine, *op. cit.*, pp. 322–26.
11. The advent of new and better tests, if they are forthcoming, will not render mass screening much more reasonable, for there isn't much room for technical advance. The ELISA and Western blot have good statistical properties themselves (especially when used in combination). The low prevalence of the AIDS virus in the general population is what renders screening so error-prone, and recent findings indicate that infection with the AIDS virus remains largely confined to identified high-risk populations and that the rate of increase of infections is declining within these populations. See James R. Carlson *et al.*, "AIDS Serology Testing in Low- and High-Risk Groups," *Journal of the American Medical Association* 253(23) (June 21, 1985), pp. 3405–08; and Merle A. Sande, "Transmission of AIDS," *New England Journal of Medicine* 314(6) (February 6, 1986), pp. 380–82.
12. I would like to thank Carol Hayes of the Michigan Department of Public Health for her assistance, and my colleagues in the Medical Humanities Program, Tom Tomlinson and Len Fleck, for their helpful comments.

From Christine Pierce and Donald VanDeVeer,
eds., *AIDS: Ethics and Public Policy*
(Belmont, Calif.: Wadsworth, 1988)

ISSUE: AIDS

PERSPECTIVES

1. Many of the authors advocate education as the best defense against AIDS. Identify the premises on which this conclusion is based and explain why you are or are not persuaded to accept that conclusion.

2. The *Newsweek* article compares the AIDS epidemic to the Black Death plague of the Middle Ages. What point is the writer trying to clarify by using this analogy? Why is this analogy effective or ineffective?

3. The article on college student attitudes on AIDS describes the sample populations used in the formal research. Using the necessary conditions for surveys discussed in Chapter 3, explain why you consider the data in this article to be acceptable or unacceptable.

4. Mark Robichaux describes incidents involving the police and alleged AIDS carriers and cites a variety of opinions. Examine carefully the arrangement of these resources and explain how the arrangement leads you to accept or reject the final statement: "The perception is more potent than the reality."

5. In "Moral Anemia" the writer uses economic metaphors to trace our recent history of blood donation. Explain how these metaphors support the writer's claim and describe why you think they will or will not be convincing for the intended audience.

6. According to several of the articles, the medical field is not of one mind on all AIDS-related issues. In "Moral Anemia," for example, the writer uses the opinion of doctors to refute the American Medical Association (AMA) endorsement of autologous blood. Clark shows disagreement between surgeons and the U.S. surgeon general in his *Newsweek* article. In each of these two articles which medical source are you more likely to believe and why?

7. Goldbeck and Howe present very different views of employers' attitudes toward AIDS. Considering the authority of the writers and the credibility of the evidence presented, which view do you find more convincing? Be specific in describing the reasons for your decision.

8. Explain the logic behind Howe's claim that ethical and technical considerations need to be combined to deal with the problem of AIDS screening.

ARGUMENTS FOR INVESTIGATION

The Hippocratic Oath: Ethical Discrimination?	AIDS Education Through Advertising
	The Public's Right to Be Tested
AIDS Education Should Begin in the Home	Colleges Need an AIDS Policy
AIDS Testing: America's Love for the Quick Fix	

DISCRIMINATION: WHAT PROGRESS HAVE WE MADE?

Quietly Keeping Them Out

The Dark Side of Immigration Reform

ALFREDO J. ESTRADA
A lawyer in Washington, D.C.

[These annotations are keyed to the form on the following page.—Ed.]

①

The United States is a nation of immigrants, and of immigration poli-cies—policies designed to facilitate the orderly entry of people into the country, but also to keep them out. Last November, President Reagan signed into law the Immigration Reform and Control Act of 1986, the most comprehensive reform of immigration law in over twenty years. The cornerstone of the new law is the legalization program. It allows illegal aliens who entered the country prior to January 1, 1982—perhaps as many as 4 million—to apply for amnesty, the first step on the road to full citizenship. But there is another, darker side to this reform. It will make it much tougher for those illegal aliens who do not qualify to remain here, while discouraging others from crossing the border.

②

The INS charges a fee of $185 for each application. For children under eighteen, the fee is reduced to $50. Families— husband, wife, children under eighteen—may pay a group fee of $420. Applicants must also pay for required medical examinations, which can cost as much as $75 each, and for any legal fees incurred. Will the costs discourage illegal aliens from applying for amnesty? Many illegal aliens make their living as migrant farm workers. An average migrant farm worker makes about $5,000 a year.

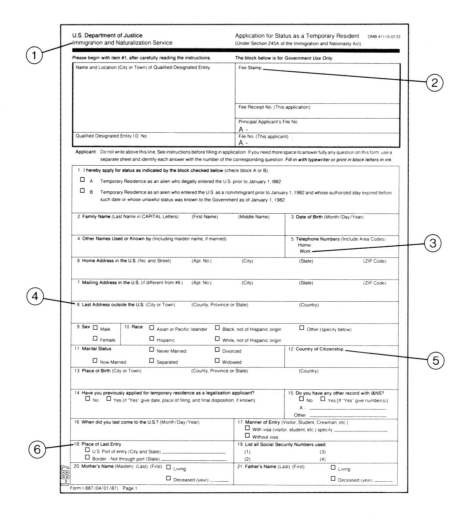

① **U.S. Department of Justice**
Immigration and Naturalization Service

Application for Status as a Temporary Resident   OMB #1115-0133
(Under Section 245A of the Immigration and Nationality Act)

Please begin with item #1, after carefully reading the instructions.

Name and Location (City or Town) of Qualified Designated Entity	The block below is for *Government Use Only.*
	Fee Stamp ②
	Fee Receipt No. (This application)
	Principal Applicant's File No A -
Qualified Designated Entity I.D. No.	File No. (This applicant) A -

Applicant: Do not write above this line. See instructions before filling in application. If you need more space to answer fully any question on this form, use a separate sheet and identify each answer with the number of the corresponding question. *Fill in with typewriter or print in block letters in ink.*

1. I hereby apply for status as indicated by the block checked below (check block A or B).

☐ A   Temporary Residence as an alien who illegally entered the U.S. prior to January 1, 1982.

☐ B   Temporary Residence as an alien who entered the U.S. as a nonimmigrant prior to January 1, 1982 and whose authorized stay expired before such date or whose unlawful status was known to the Government as of January 1, 1982.

2 Family Name (Last Name in CAPITAL Letters) (First Name) (Middle Name)	3. Date of Birth (Month/Day/Year)

| 4 Other Names Used or Known by (Including maiden name, if married) | 5. Telephone Numbers (Include Area Codes)
Home:
Work ③ |

6. Home Address in the U.S. (No. and Street)   (Apt. No.)   (City)   (State)   (ZIP Code)

④ 7. Mailing Address in the U.S. (if different from #6.)   (Apt. No.)   (City)   (State)   (ZIP Code)

8. Last Address outside the U.S. (City or Town)   (County, Province or State)   (Country)

9. Sex ☐ Male ☐ Female	10. Race ☐ Asian or Pacific Islander ☐ Black, not of Hispanic origin ☐ Other (specify below) ☐ Hispanic ☐ White, not of Hispanic origin

| 11. Marital Status ☐ Never Married ☐ Divorced
☐ Now Married ☐ Separated ☐ Widowed | 12. Country of Citizenship ⑤ |

13. Place of Birth (City or Town)   (County, Province or State)   (Country)

| 14. Have you previously applied for temporary residence as a legalization applicant?
☐ No ☐ Yes (if "Yes" give date, place of filing, and final disposition, if known) | 15. Do you have any other record with I&NS?
☐ No ☐ Yes (if "Yes" give number(s))
A -
Other |

| 16. When did you last come to the U.S.? (Month/Day/Year) | 17. Manner of Entry (Visitor, Student, Crewman, etc.)
☐ With visa (visitor, student, etc.) specify
☐ Without visa |

⑥ | 18. Place of Last Entry
☐ U.S. Port of entry (City and State)
☐ Border - Not through port (State) | 19. List all Social Security Numbers used.
(1) (3)
(2) (4) |

| 20. Mother's Name (Maiden) (Last) (First) ☐ Living
☐ Deceased (year) | 21. Father's Name (Last) (First) ☐ Living
☐ Deceased (year) |

Form I-687 (04/01/87) Page 1

③

The new immigration laws impose stiff fines and criminal penalties on employers who knowingly hire or continue to employ illegal aliens. All employers are affected, but the big farms that hire large numbers of illegal aliens at harvest time stand to be hurt most. Worried about this, Congress has set aside a category for "special agricultural workers"—they face less stringent requirements for legalization. So far, however, the exception has done little but sow confusion. The rules are complicated, and many migrant workers believe they will be deported, and lose their chance to become U.S. residents, if they are caught in the country this year. As a result, they are staying away, and already, in June, Oregon's strawberry crop was rotting in the fields for lack of workers.

④

The United States began to restrict immigration on the basis of national origin in 1882, when the Chinese Exclusion Acts banned Chinese laborers. Now it is the Mexicans, Salvadorans, and those from Caribbean islands who are the "problem." The arguments about curbing Hispanic immigration are the familiar ones that have been applied to other groups in the past: they'll take away jobs, crowd cities, strain services, change things.

⑤

Last year, as a result of the worldwide collapse of oil prices, the Mexican economy shrank 5 percent, and underemployment reached 50 percent. Things are worse in El Salvador: along with underemployment above 50 percent, there is the ongoing civil war. So what happens when these countries lose emigration to the United States as a "safety valve" for those without decent jobs, and lose too the benefit of millions of dollars sent back every year? What happens when we send millions of *aliens* back? Moreover, what happens here, in the U.S., if employers begin to see every Hispanic as a possible illegal alien, as trouble? If these problems are not addressed by the Administration, then immigration reform may stand in need of further reform.

⑥

Aliens entering the country illegally have traditionally been hunted down by officers of the Immigration and Naturalization Service. Now the INS has a new and ill-suited role—to implement the legalization program. The INS has taken a very restrictive view of the new law. For example, the law requires that an alien must have "resided continuously" in the United States since January 1, 1982, in order to qualify for amnesty. Immigration law has usually approached the matter of continuous residence on a case-by-case basis, placing great emphasis on the alien's intent to remain here. The INS has interpreted "resided continuously" to mean that any single absence of more than forty-five days, or a cumulative absence of more than 180 days, will disqualify the applicant. This is a problem for many illegal aliens, who frequently criss-cross the border to be with their families, especially at Christmas and other holidays.

Harper's Magazine, August 1987

Storming the Last
Male Bastion

RICHARD LACAYO
Associate editor for Time

There are about as many women on the membership lists of some of 1
the nation's exclusive private clubs as there are in the lineup of the Los
Angeles Rams. Not that life at such all male places is that strenuous;
how much muscle does it take to pick up a lunch check? Yet amid the
antique rugs and deep leather chairs, the clubs do furnish a setting for
the exertions of professional life: back slapping, ego massage and one
"contact" sport—making business connections. In short, though they
offer relaxation, the clubs are places of business too. Meal tabs and annual dues that can run into the thousands of dollars are often picked
up by a member's employer as a business expense.

For that reason the men-only policy of many clubs has been not 2
just a slight to women but a professional liability. Some women guests
have experienced real humiliations too, being shunted inside through
kitchens or hustled around to the back door. So it was a gratifying day
for them last week when the U.S. Supreme Court in effect held the
front door open. The court unanimously upheld a New York City law
that bans such discrimination at many private clubs. Boston, Buffalo,
Chicago, Los Angeles, San Francisco and Washington have already
passed similar laws. More such ordinances are now expected. Says
Donna Lenhoff of the Women's Legal Defense Fund: "The last bastion
of white male power will be forced to throw in the towel."

The decision was not a surprise. In a 1984 case involving the Jay- 3
cees and in a 1987 ruling involving the Rotary International, the Justices
unanimously decided that states could use laws that ban discrimination in public accommodations to compel some private organizations
to admit women. Similarly, the New York ordinance was written to apply to private clubs that are in some respects public. To be affected,
they must have more than 400 members and regularly serve meals and
obtain revenues from nonmembers "for the furtherance of trade or
business." Four of the city's most prestigious men's clubs meet those
criteria.

Though the law forbids discrimination on the basis of race, reli- 4
gion and national origin, among other things, gender was the main
issue. Women were the only group that most clubs would confess to
barring. The ordinance had been challenged in court by the New York

State Club Association, which claimed that it violated the right of free association. Not so, said Justice Byron White, writing for the court. "It may well be that a considerable amount of private or intimate association occurs in such a setting . . . but that fact alone does not afford the entity as a whole any constitutional immunity to practice discrimination." White did indicate, however, that individual clubs could still challenge the law by attempting to prove, for example, that they were formed primarily for religious purposes or to further particular ideas.

Though few Americans are directly affected, the ruling had a potent symbolic value. The men's club is a prime emblem of male bonding, a tree house with more comfortable seating. Men's club members tend to be highly visible figures in the community, the business world, even on the bench; in the past few months, Justices Anthony Kennedy and Harry Blackmun resigned from private clubs that bar women.   5

Washington's Cosmos Club, where Blackmun once belonged, voted to admit women just days before the court handed down its ruling. Many other clubs have opted to do likewise rather than face municipal action that can include embarrassing public inquiries into their admissions policies. Boston's 450-member St. Botolph Club recently admitted Katherine Fanning, editor of the *Christian Science Monitor*, and not a moment too soon. Just a day after last week's ruling, Boston officials warned three other clubs that they face the loss of food and liquor licenses if their membership policies are unchanged by the end of July.   6

Other places have been attempting to have it both ways. In Los Angeles the 3,000-member Jonathan Club (initiation fee: $10,000) is being sued by the city because, though it admits women members, it keeps one dining room for men only. At some clubs the opposition to women has been dwindling with the increase in younger members accustomed to treating women as working colleagues. "It's the entrenched guys who resent the intrusion on their old turf," suggests Alan Baker, a 25-year member of the New York Athletic Club. But even some older men, mindful of their career-conscious daughters, have been having second thoughts. Says Cosmos Club President Tedson Meyers: "If you listen closely, you could hear them saying in the silences, 'I wonder if I'm doing the right thing by her.'"   7

While clubs affected by the ruling begin to grapple with the unfamiliar business of admitting women, a number of other male bastions not directly affected are bracing for the next round of challenges. The top targets: exclusionary country clubs and golf courses. The famed Burning Tree Club in Bethesda, Md., for instance, does not allow women to set foot on its greens as either members or guests. For the record, Justice Sandra Day O'Connor is an avid golfer.   8

Time, July 4, 1988

Defending the Poor

A Harder Task

GEORGE M. ANDERSON, S.J.
St. Aloysius Church, Washington, D.C.

Ever since the Supreme Court ruled that indigent defendants are en- 1
titled to free counsel, there has been an assumption that the poor are
being adequately represented in criminal courts. But now, a quarter of
a century later, legal advocacy groups, as well as many public defenders and private attorneys, are concluding that the promise of Gideon v.
Wainwright has not always been fulfilled.

Among the advocacy groups that have been most outspoken in 2
voicing this belief is the National Legal Aid and Defender Association
(N.L.A.D.A.), a nonprofit organization that focuses on legal issues affecting the poor. Indeed, Mardi Crawford, an N.L.A.D.A. attorney who formerly practiced appellate criminal law in Michigan, asserted during
an interview in Washington, D.C., that indigent defense is in a state of
crisis. "Because of the prevailing tough-on-crime stance, the courts are
jammed," she said. "One result is that lawyers for the poor tend to be
loaded with more cases than they can handle."

In the opinion of Ms. Crawford and others, the problem of too 3
many cases for too few attorneys stems from insufficient funding. "Jurisdictions frequently tighten their purse strings when it comes to
providing more money for indigent defense," she said, "either because
of a basic prejudice against accused persons, or because they are financially strapped."

What complicates the matter of funding is that, although the Su- 4
preme Court's 1963 ruling calls for free counsel for poor defendants
like Clarence Gideon (the Florida man whose trial without counsel led
to the ruling), each jurisdiction can determine for itself not only how
much money is to be provided, but also how it is to be allocated. Thus,
in some areas funds come from the state; in others, from county or city
sources. Telephone conversations with public defenders around the
country revealed that the varying ways in which indigent defense is
approached and the wide disparities in levels of funding can result in
a level of service incommensurate with the concept of equal justice
for all.

Low pay is one of the reasons dedicated lawyers often move on 5
in frustration after a few years of work with the poor, not only in Ken-

tucky, but elsewhere too. "Some are lost to the prosecutor's office," Mr. Isaacs said, "because the pay is better."

Prosecutors are ordinarily paid higher salaries than their coun- 6 terparts who defend the indigent accused. In addition, they have free access to a wide range of investigatory services that are not always available to public defenders and court-appointed attorneys. Both Mr. Isaacs in Kentucky and Mr. Keefe in Nebraska, as well as Ms. Crawford in Washington, D.C., stressed the importance of these services. The lack of them can alter the outcome of a trial, a circumstance that places poor defendants at yet another disadvantage. "When there is a need for investigators to track down witnesses, or for hiring hand-writing experts and psychiatrists to testify, prosecutors have only to ask," Ms. Crawford said. "But when the defense seeks the same kinds of services, the courts may be reluctant to provide them because of the extra cost."

Mr. Keefe used the analogy of an equation: "Money is pumped 7 into the prosecution side, but not into the defense side, so justice is definitely weighted toward the former." In Mr. Keefe's opinion, the im-balance of the equation has its roots in the prevailing punitive attitude, which, over the past dozen years, has manifested itself in the adoption by many states of mandatory and determinate sentencing statutes that have resulted in more people going to prison for longer periods. "The punitive mood plays a significant part in the present situation," he said, "because it prevents indigent defense from being regarded as important."

A considerable number of the appeals cases for which Mr. Colwart 8 is responsible relate to the death penalty, and it is in this area that in-digent defendants are most at risk in terms of adequate representa-tion: Their lives are literally at stake. The risk is all the greater because in establishing the right of indigent defendants to free counsel in Gideon v. Wainwright, the Supreme Court made no provision for rep-resentation at the post-conviction level of the death penalty process. In other words, a person accused of a capital offense is only entitled to counsel at the trial and first appeals level. Once he or she is on death row, most states supply no funds for further representation; such funding must be provided through special branches of public de-fender offices or by volunteer attorneys.

One of the leading figures in the effort to assure representation at 9 the post-conviction stage is Esther Lardent, director of the American Bar Association's Post Conviction Death Penalty Representation Proj-ect. In a conversation at her Washington, D.C., office, she spoke of the project's focus on recruiting qualified volunteer attorneys from large firms around the country. "What is striking," she said, "is that we occa-sionally get offers of help from attorneys who are pro death penalty but who are so dismayed by the lack of assured counsel for people on death row that they say: "Will you take me anyway?"

The American Bar Association has no official stand for or against 10 the death penalty, and as an organization might even be said to typify the mainstream of the legal profession. And yet its advocacy of better legal representation for the poor, especially those on death row, suggests that others besides public defender groups perceive inequities with respect to defending the poor. "Indigent defense in general is ghettoized," Ms. Lardent said. "So what we have tried to do through the project, besides recruiting volunteer lawyers, is to work against the ghettoization by educating both the bar and the bench, especially now that the numbers on death row have risen above 2,000."

Ironically, the acute need for legal counsel at the post-conviction 11 stage would be reduced if better representation had been provided at the trial level. Ms. Lardent explained why: "Sometimes it is only at this final stage before execution that errors at the trial level are uncovered, errors like prosecutorial misconduct and suppression of evidence that might have affected the outcome in the defendant's favor." She spoke of a man once on Florida's death row who was only 12 hours from execution. "His name was Shabaka. He is free because a volunteer attorney in the 11th Circuit Court of Appeals discovered evidence that led to questions that finally resulted in the state's determining that there was no case."

Because of ceilings in some states on what can be spent for legal 12 representation at the trial stage, judges have a difficult time finding competent attorneys willing to provide the initial defense. Ms. Crawford at N.L.A.D.A. remarked that ceilings of this sort put pressure on attorneys either not to exert themselves fully on behalf of their clients, or else to risk financial ruin with regard to their own practices on account of the time required for capital cases. "In addition," she said, "good attorneys sometimes simply burn out because of the emotional stress."

Ms. Crawford, Ms. Lardent and others believe that solutions to 13 the need for adequate representation lie not in establishing an ever-larger pool of volunteer attorneys, but in bringing about changes in the system that would ensure justice for all indigent defendants, from those with lesser charges to those accused of capital offenses. "There is a starkness about indigent defense as a whole," Ms. Lardent said. "At present, the amount spent on it comes to only 3 percent of the total funding provided for the administration of justice in the United States."

With the current punitive mood that prevails throughout the 14 country, significant increases in the resources available for indigent defense are hardly to be expected in the near future. It is therefore likely that a number of jurisdictions will continue to be characterized by a crazy quilt of legal services of such varying quality that many accused women and men will remain underserved. At the same time, however, through groups like Ms. Lardent's and Ms. Crawford's that operate on a national basis, important steps are being taken to press for the fulfillment of the promise of Gideon v. Wainwright.

America, January 14, 1989

Myth of White Supremacy
Is Segregation's Legacy

LES PAYNE
Syndicated columnist

As a practitioner of segregated schooling *de facto*, the North has overtaken the South in this violation of the spirit, if not the letter, of the Supreme Court ruling in the 1954 Brown case. 1

A group of University of Chicago researchers has found that nearly two-thirds of the nation's black students attend predominantly nonwhite schools. Relying on data from the U.S. Education Department, the study revealed that the North—led by Michigan, New York and Illinois—has the most racially segregated public-education systems. 2

The study defined schools with 90% to 100% minority enrollment as "intensely segregated." Topping that class were Illinois with 69% of its black students enrolled in "intensely segregated" schools, New York with 56.7% and Michigan with 56.3%. Other Northern states like New Jersey and Pennsylvania surpassed such Southern bastions as Alabama, Georgia and even Mississippi. 3

Does a desegregated education system make a difference? 4

Some black parents argue that school segregation stifles their children's education. Others say not necessarily. Segregation and the bigotry that spawns it do not yield easily to reason. 5

One thing is certain: School segregation is quite destructive, and blacks are its chief victims. The separate and unequal school—controlled by white authorities—is no accident, but rather a piece of bigotry built to American specifications. Educationally, the Republic has found that it can best deprive black students by isolating them from tender white youths. Segregated schools get less-motivated teachers, inferior books and equipment and proportionately less money for remedying the results of these dire conditions.

The primary, most lasting wounds that such segregation imparts 7 to its victims are not educational but psychological. As Martin Luther King Jr. once said, what used to be known as the Southern reality "gives the segregator a false sense of superiority, and leaves the segregated with a false sense of inferiority."

It was a lesson that I came to understand years after growing up 8 on the black side of the railroad tracks in Tuscaloosa, Ala. I grew up picking its cotton, hoeing its corn, drinking its separate-but-equal water, attending its segregated schools. The dominant society of that day preached that God himself had anointed whites as his superior creatures and placed them in their separate Eden. Under this grand design, each of the anointed was two parts Red Grange to three parts Aristotle. Ku Klux Klan Imperial Wizard Robert Shelton was the equal of Charlemagne. Highly regarded were the likes of Bear Bryant, Gov. James E. (Big Jim) Folsom and all the other red-neck good ol' boys.

Segregated schooling did not permit us to compete with whites 9 and thus to test their alleged superiority. And our parents worried themselves into their graves trying to knock over the Gibraltar that was segregation. They told us that we were just as good as whites. But every aspect of the cruel and terrifying Southern reality contradicted this.

Desegregated education, after the 1954 Brown vs. Board of Edu- 10 cation Supreme Court decision, was deemed the solution to these disparities. And Dr. King was more responsible than anyone else for setting desegregation in motion.

These larger issues, I admit, never occurred to me as a child- 11 victim of segregation. I grew up with two older brothers in circumstances decidedly poor. Learning to read at age 3, I taught my brother, two years my senior. After a week in the first grade I was promoted to the second with an offer, at age 6, to begin school in the third grade. My parents declined, figuring that it would hinder my social adjustment.

Throughout my eight years in a segregated school environment I 12 was near the top of my class, going nowhere, for the Southern reality had taken the reward out of black education. Our college graduates could not realistically aspire to careers offered white high-school dropouts. At 12, having moved to Connecticut, I attended desegregated Hartford Public High School. Here, black students had also been denied the rewards of education—a reality that, for the most part, continues this very hour.

In Hartford I was near the top of my class, still going nowhere, 13 but I was shedding the notion that whites get to the top because they were somehow more intelligent, or more competent, or even better prepared.

The major difference, and the chief benefit, that I found in a 14
desegregated school was that exposure to white students in well-
equipped schools, in due course, cured many blacks of those racial
inferiorities and uncertainties cultivated by what is actually the American reality.

A desegregated school environment will not necessarily improve 15
black achievement. Different prescriptions, like restoring rewards for
black education, must be written for this malady.

A truly desegregated school system, whether in Michigan or Mis- 16
sissippi, poses a serious threat to the myth of white supremacy. And it
is this myth, at bottom, that must be blasted apart if this Republic is
ever to make full, positive use of all its vast resources in human talent
and skills.

Los Angeles Times, August 3, 1987

A "Superminority" Tops Out

JOHN SCHWARTZ, GEORGE RAINE, and KATE ROBINS
Staff writers for Newsweek

Henry S. Tang bitterly remembers the day a corporate recruiter took 1
him aside and said: "I'm really doing you a favor." No, he wasn't going
to give him a job. Instead, he told Tang to give up on his company—
"We prefer to hire American nationals." Tang stumbled into a phone
booth and sat there stunned, choking back tears. It would not be the
last time. Five more companies that rejected Tang for executive-track
jobs hinted that race was a factor. Twenty years later, the Shearson
Lehman Brothers senior vice president won't reveal the companies
that shunned him. "They are all my clients now," he says with a satisfied smile.

The "favor" of telling Tang to look elsewhere would invite a law- 2
suit today. Asians now feel discrimination's sting in more subtle ways.
While employers readily snap up young Asians, promotions into upper
management are rare. In the past, Asians who felt exploited rarely even
complained. That's changing. Some, like Nelvin Gee, sue. The former
General Motors engineer is demanding $4 million after the company
passed him over for a fast-track fellowship. (According to court documents, a GM interviewer judged Gee to be more committed to himself

than to the corporation.) Professionals aren't the only protesters: more than 100 Vietnamese Circle K convenience-store clerks in Houston took their fight against alleged anti-Vietnamese layoffs to the Equal Employment Opportunity Commission.

"Hit a Wall"

It seems Americans have always felt some enmity toward Asians. The latest reasons: the U.S. trade deficit with Japan and Asians' relentless work habits. Though Asian-Americans certainly have not suffered the same magnitude of workplace discrimination as blacks, a 1986 report by the Commission on Civil Rights concluded: "Anti-Asian activity in the form of violence, vandalism, harassment and intimidation continues to occur across the nation." As their presence increases— doubling to 10 million by the end of the century—Asians fear a flood of college-age youths will face increasing discrimination when they reach the work force. Boston lawyer Harry Yee says he hears Asian college kids say, "We're Yuppies now; we just don't have BMW's yet." Yee warns, "These students don't know. When they finish school they're going to hit a wall." 3

Asians say the wall is racism. Once hired, Asian workers complain, they soon "top out," reaching the point beyond which their bosses will not promote them. Asians made up 4.3 percent of professionals and technicians but just 1.4 percent of officials and managers in 1985, according to the EEOC. "Discrimination has to be part of the explanation," says Robert Oxnam, president of The Asia Society in New York. 4

Many of the Asians' problems actually stem from their image as a "superminority." To a large extent the stereotype rings true: the Confucian heritage of discipline, family, hard work and education can be seen from Korean groceries to Wall Street. But that image has a downside: a reputation for quiet achievement can be interpreted as passivity. Bosses frequently cite language deficiencies when denying promotions, but workers suspect that stereotyping is at the bottom of more than a few cases. Says Arthur Hu, an MIT graduate who studies Asian-American demographics: "They're seen as weaker, less capable of handling people. You know, real men aren't engineers or geeks with glasses playing the violin." Betty Vetter, executive director of the Commission on Professionals in Science and Technology, dismisses such talk with a rhetorical question about the Japanese: "If they don't make good managers, how in the world did they get so far ahead of us?" 5

Asians often accept at least partial blame for their troubles. "If you don't make it," explains Ronald Chin, president of the Asian Management and Business Association, "it's basically your fault." Common 6 job mistakes include focusing solely on narrow tasks instead of getting broad experience. Socially, Asians too often confine themselves to an Asian subculture and shun chitchat. "We don't play enough golf," jokes Marisa Chuang, a Detroit mental-health administrator.

When Asians do feel wronged, cultural conditioning pressures them to avoid confrontation. Many Asians face adversity with what the Japanese call *gambare:* simply doing one's best. Many would rather switch than fight, moving to another company or launching their own—though some would chafe under any boss's yoke. One entrepreneur, Moon H. Yuen, realized after 27 years at engineering giant Bechtel that he was unlikely to rise above the rank of chief electrical engineer. So he launched YEI Engineers Inc. Over the past 10 years his company has occasionally outbid his old employer for power-generation projects. Now, turning the other cheek is going out of style, says Yoshio Fujiwara, who helped Toyota and General Motors create their joint effort in Fremont, Calif., when he was a city councilman. Says Fujiwara: "The coming generation will be more prone to fight back when they are slapped." 7

The fighting has already begun. Some Asians even sue—a sure sign of Americanization. Most work grievances used to involve enforcing minimum-wage laws; now more than half of the 125 discrimination complaints heard each year at San Francisco's Chinese for Affirmative Action, a Chinatown community organization, come from white-collar workers. In New York, Lourdes Avelino, a Filipino, was a manager of equal-employment opportunity at RKO. "If they had told me I had to dye my hair blond, I would have," she says. She found she made $10,000 less than white managers despite good work evaluations. She said she was fired for complaining; her suit has not yet come to trial. RKO counters that it has no set manager's salary. 8

Many Asians find a less expensive path than the courts: making themselves more attractive to American business. In part this means going beyond narrow technical training. Asian students now pursue professions ranging from finance to fine arts. Filmmaker Peter Wang, who plays an executive who stalks out of his office after being passed over for a promotion in his "A Great Wall," urges parents to nurture creativity: "Leave these kids alone . . . let them dream." Young Asians are also getting better at fitting in. Soo Kounne, 26, started as a secretary at Chemical Bank in New York and quickly jumped to assistant manager. She doesn't limit her circle of friends to Asians and says she has never encountered discrimination. Like every immigrant group, Asians may pay a price for mainstream success. Each new generation risks becoming, as Asians say, "bananas," yellow on the outside and white on the inside. Kounne says it is possible to have success *and* a heritage: "I call myself Korean, but I'm still Korean-American." 9

Companies, too, try to right past wrongs. Thousands of AT&T em- 10
ployees have attended workshops that boost Asian workers' office
skills and engage managers and workers in group discussion. Companies don't do it out of charity. With Asian nations becoming ever
more powerful in the global economy, the language skills and cultural
backgrounds of Asians are resources too important to leave untapped.
For U.S. firms, it may provide the competitive edge they need.

Newsweek, May 11, 1987

Predisposition
and Prejudice

RICK WEISS
Writer for Science News

Ellen spent four years completing her PhD in industrial and 1
chemical engineering. Now, wincing as a company doctor drew a
few drops of blood for her preemployment physical, she could
hardly contain her excitement about the job she'd been offered at
one of the country's foremost metallurgical research institutes.

Two days later the phone call came. You are perfectly 2
healthy, the young doctor said. But tests have revealed you harbor a gene that can result in decreased levels of a blood enzyme,
glucose-6-phosphate dehydrogenase. Without the enzyme's protection, you have a slightly increased risk of developing a red
blood cell disease if you come into contact with certain chemicals in our laboratory.

I'm sorry, he said. The job has been offered to someone else. 3

When Frank married at age 31 he decided to take out a life insur- 4
ance policy. A swimmer and avid racquetball player with no previous hospitalizations, he felt certain his low premiums would be
a worthy investment for his family.

Weeks later, after a routine physical exam, he was shocked 5
by the insurance company's response. Sophisticated DNA testing

had revealed in Frank's tissues a single missing copy of a so-called RB anti-oncogene and minor variations in two other genes. Computer analys·s showed the molecular misprints more than tripled his risk of getting small-cell lung cancer by age 55. His application was rejected.

These notes from the future illustrate a potential dark side of bio-medicine's present. 6

Scientists rightly point to the recent revolution in molecular biol- 7 ogy and genetics as heralding a new age in medical science. In particular, ongoing efforts to create a map of the entire human genome—the DNA blueprint of heritable traits contained in every cell—promises an ever-growing range of diagnostic and therapeutic benefits.

Biochemical cartographers have already located more than 400 8 genetic "markers," or signposts of genetic diseases, on all 46 human chromosomes. They have mapped, for example, the exact or approximate locations of genes responsible for muscular dystrophy, Huntington's disease, some psychiatric disorders and a variety of cancers.

But as scientists home in on the molecular fine print of that cor- 9 poreal contract called the human genome—and as they learn to interpret the typographical errors that can predestine an individual's medical fate—legal scholars and bioethicists express concern about the possibilities for abuse of this technology. With the newfound ability to reveal an individual's molecular secrets come significant new possibilities for discrimination.

"There are two very broad questions: who decides whether or not 10 you'll get a test and what happens to that information," says Thomas H. Murray, director of the Center for Biomedical Ethics at Case Western Reserve University in Cleveland. "Clearly there are going to be these tests. The question is how are we going to use them and what social limits we're going to put on them."

While the case histories above are hypothetical, the tests them- 11 selves already exist. And while such testing among companies is not yet well established, neither are regulations governing their use. Eventually, experts say, as researchers confirm the detailed molecular bases of physical and mental health, policy makers will have to confront an apparent discrepancy between the reality of genetic variability and the democratic ideal that all citizens are "created equal."

The issue cuts through existing social mores and legal prece- 12 dents, encompassing a body of information the framers of constitutional and early statutory protections could never have envisioned—information that in many respects represents the most personal and intimate details of a person's being.

"Each new [genetic] test is going to have slightly different factual 13 circumstances surrounding it, and each new test is going to raise slightly different ethical questions," says Murray. These questions, which relate to the overall balance between an individual's rights and those of an employer or insurer, are not new. But as scientists refine their understanding of the more than 3,000 diseases known to have genetic components, these questions "are going to come at us much faster," Murray says.

The manner in which society answers these questions, he and 14 others say, will rival in significance the earlier, more straightforward legal and ethical challenges in the civil rights and worker's rights arenas.

It's easy to draw parallels between the specters of genetic and 15 racial discrimination. Indeed, some of the earliest documented cases of potentially discriminatory genetic screening relate to sickle cell anemia, an inherited blood disease that affects blacks almost exclusively.

This potentially fatal disease results from a single gene defect 16 that causes a deformation of oxygen-carrying red blood cells. It became the object of widespread screening in the United States in the early 1970s, partly in response to demands by the black community for better health care.

Almost immediately, however, observers recognized in the pro- 17 grams a double-edged sword, with evidence that some employers might be using test results to discriminate against blacks. Even "carriers" of the disease—whose chromosomes contain only one of two possible genes for the disease and who generally show no ill effects—were sometimes denied jobs as airline pilots, deferred from some branches of the armed forces and saddled with higher insurance premiums.

Several states have since passed laws against the misuse of sickle 18 cell screening. But those early cases put minorities on notice that genetic testing has more than therapeutic possibilities. And now, with the genes for other diseases and medical predispositions coming into focus, every individual becomes, in a sense, a minority member with particular odds of suffering a particular medical fate.

The U.S. Constitution protects citizens from government-inflicted 19 discrimination based on immutable characteristics such as race. And to the extent the Supreme Court has ruled on the issue, federal discrimination on the basis of one's genome would appear equally precluded.

"If it's the government that wants the information for whatever 20 reason, there are all sorts of constitutional issues that arise," says Mark Rothstein, director of the Health Law Institute at the University of Houston. "The government would seemingly have to make a strong showing to gain access to one's genetic profile because it invades the individual's bodily integrity and privacy."

However, notes Lori B. Andrews of the American Bar Foundation 21 in Chicago, "the Constitution protects people from the federal government and in some cases from the states, but it doesn't apply to private companies unless there is a specific statute dealing with the issue." And while Congress has extended some Constitutional protections into the private sector, the protections against private-entity genetic discrimination remain poorly defined.

"There may be a variety of reasons why an employer may want 22 some of this information, and the legal issues are very unsettled as to whether the employer could make participation [in genetic screening] a valid condition of employment," Rothstein says.

A 1982 survey by the Congressional Office of Technology Assess- 23 ment (OTA) found that only six of 366 responding companies used genetic tests on applicants or employees. Those companies tested for genetic susceptibility to environmental or occupational hazards associated with the workplace. But another 55 companies stated they might begin genetic testing within the next five years. A 1988 OTA report, "Biology, Medicine and the Bill of Rights," says "little is known about whether the incidence of genetic screening has increased in the last five years." But other sources suggest such a trend is a near-certainty in coming years.

"Employers are obviously worried about health insurance and 24 health care costs," says Lawrence Miike, a project director at OTA. "My guess is that a lot of employers, if they had no restraints on them, would obviously want to do some kind of testing for increased probability for disease."

In *Medical Genetics: A Legal Frontier* (American Bar Foundation, 25 1987), Andrews cites studies indicating that industrial physicians sometimes reject job applicants with mild diseases that have no effect on job performance. "Employment discrimination against people with potential health problems has been widespread and is likely to further increase" with the advent of better genetic tests, she writes. "The availability of genetic diagnostic technologies now raises questions about whether laws should be passed protecting people against genetic discrimination by private entities."

She concedes genetic tests may someday prove a legitimate 26 means of screening out some workers with health-endangering sensitivities to particular workplace conditions. However, she warns, today's genetic profiles do little to assure an employer that the best person has been hired—especially when, given our incomplete understanding of genetics, job applicants at even higher risk may well be hired simply because their particular genetic weaknesses have not yet been mapped.

Andrews and others also express concern that employers may 27 simply screen out all but the most genetically hardy applicants rather than cleaning up an otherwise unhealthy workplace. Gene mapping "could challenge or overturn a lot of our traditional legal notions about the role of such things as occupational health and safety laws," Andrews told SCIENCE NEWS. Those laws today set safety limits to protect even the most vulnerable employees.

Rothstein notes another interesting and as-yet-unlitigated twist, 28 as employers—while free to hire the most capable applicant—cannot discriminate against the handicapped. "It remains to be seen whether an individual who is currently healthy and asymptomatic but has an atypical genetic trait might not be covered under the definition of handicapped under state or federal law," he says.

Employers are not the only private entities with the potential to 29 discriminate against unusually sequenced genomes. Insurance companies, too, have a substantial financial stake in knowing an individual's propensity for illness or early death.

Already, some insurers are under fire for requiring AIDS-antibody 30 tests as part of their underwriting procedure. While AIDS testing falls short of screening one's genetic profile, it differs from standard blood tests in revealing only an individual's exposure to a virus that *years later* may cause disease.

Some states—led by California—have made it illegal for insur- 31 ance companies to require AIDS tests. So some insurance companies now require specialized white blood cell counts that provide indirect evidence of AIDS infection. "This gives a clue as to what's going to happen in the area of genetics and how hard it is to prohibit the acquiring of information," Rothstein says. "Maybe you can ban the *use* of genetic information, but it's hard to prohibit people from *getting* information."

Deeply embedded within the issue of genetic discrimination lies 32 the fundamental question of confidentiality. "Who should be allowed to know about my genetic profile? That is the significant question," says bioethicist Murray.

There are plenty of reasons why individuals may not want their 33 genetic profiles revealed to an insurer, Rothstein says. "Insurers have a long history of excluding people for all sorts of medical reasons," he says. And today, "if you don't have health insurance, you don't have access to quality health care."

For the insurance industry, however, access to genetic records 34 may become critical to its survival. This will be especially true if, as some predict, genetic testing becomes simplified enough to allow individuals to test themselves at home.

The prospect of individuals performing genetic analyses on them- 35 selves—and not having to reveal the results to a potential insurer—frightens underwriters. The home diagnostics market in the United States already boasts more than 60 do-it-yourself kits, including those that detect pregnancy and some that can provide indirect evidence of colon cancer. Home testing for more specific markers of disease would boost to new heights the insurance industry's arch enemy: "adverse selection."

Adverse selection refers to the probability that people privately 36 aware of a medical problem are more likely to seek medical insurance. The phenomenon concerns insurers because it can result in their insuring too many high-risk individuals, thus throwing off the statistical tables upon which they base their charges.

Luckily for insurers, "there are currently few home diagnostic 37 tests that prospective insurance applicants could use to determine whether they should obtain insurance in anticipation of having to seek medical care," says the OTA.

With the balance of interests thus laid out—individuals con- 38 cerned about confidentiality and discrimination, and insurers and employers concerned about adverse selection and fiscal liability—it will fall upon legislators and the courts to codify the proper use of genetic information. But one thing is certain, most scientists say: Fear of rampant genetic discrimination should not halt current gene-mapping efforts.

"I think to be an ostrich and stick our head in the sand—which is 39 kind of what we've tended to do in the past—would be a really unfortunate way to approach this problem," says Leroy Hood, a leading developer of gene-sequencing technology at the California Institute of Technology in Pasadena. "What science does is give society opportunities. What we have to do is look at these opportunities and then set up the constraints and the rules that will allow society to benefit in appropriate ways."

In *Medical Genetics*, Andrews agrees. "The law's role in regulat- 40 ing uses of the knowledge gleaned from genetics has more than just medical and economic impact. The legal scheme created to handle genetics will also create the blueprint for a particular type of society."

At one extreme, she elaborates in an interview, "we could take an 41 approach that would take us back to feudal times where you're born into your occupation and that type of thing." Or, she suggests, "we could take a more 'individual rights' approach where people could use this information individually to make better decisions about things like where they should live and work."

Science News, January 21, 1989

ISSUE: DISCRIMINATION

PERSPECTIVES

1. Les Payne begins his article by referring to the *spirit* and the *letter* of the law. What distinction is he making and how does he make it in his argument? What evidence of the discrepancy between *spirit* and *letter* do you find in the other discrimination issues represented in the articles in this section of readings?

2. According to the *Newsweek* report, Asian Americans are finding ways to break the cycle of discrimination. Identify these methods and evaluate their potential effectiveness in eliminating future discrimination in promotions at the upper management level.

3. Lacayo states that the Supreme Court's 1988 antidiscrimination ruling that allows women membership in private male-dominated clubs directly affects few Americans. If these clubs are important in making business contacts, why would few Americans be affected? In what ways might discrimination continue in these clubs despite the Supreme Court ruling?

4. In George Anderson's article on defending the poor, American Bar Association representative Esther Lardent claims that "indigent defense in general is *ghettoized*." Explain how Lardent intends to convey discrimination by using this term and its connotations.

5. Most of the articles in this section demonstrate that although the Supreme Court has in its decisions attempted to discourage discrimination, the means for implementing or monitoring its rulings are not always clear. Why, for instance, after thirty-five years, does school desegregation still exist? Who should be responsible for enforcing these laws? Use one or several of the issues in this readings section to explain your answers.

6. Estrada, Schwartz, and Weiss, in particular, report events that appear to show movement away from discrimination. Are they sincere attempts or timely measures that benefit the company more than the person or minority involved? How does the writer's tone influence your explanation?

7. In "Predisposition and Prejudice," Weiss points out the importance of the role the bioethicist plays in procedures for establishing rights. Describe the role of an ethicist in determining antidiscrimination policy.

ARGUMENTS FOR INVESTIGATION

Confidentiality in Testing

Regulating Discrimination in the Private Sector

Although We Are a Nation of Immigrants, English Should Be the Official
    Language

The Mommy Track: A New Method of Discrimination

American Indians: The Forgotten Citizen

Assimilation Should Not Require Cultural Annihilation

A Cult of Ignorance

ISAAC ASIMOV
A professor of biochemistry at Boston University School of Medicine and author of more than 200 books, most of them on various scientific subjects for the general public

It's hard to quarrel with that ancient justification of the free press: 1 "America's right to know." It seems almost cruel to ask, ingenuously, "America's right to know what, please? Science? Mathematics? Economics? Foreign languages?"

None of those things, of course. In fact, one might well suppose 2 that the popular feeling is that Americans are a lot better off without any of that tripe.

There is a cult of ignorance in the United States, and there always 3 has been. The strain of anti-intellectualism has been a constant thread winding its way through our political and cultural life, nurtured by the false notion that democracy means that "my ignorance is just as good as your knowledge."

Politicians have routinely striven to speak the language of Shake- 4 speare and Milton as ungrammatically as possible in order to avoid offending their audiences by appearing to have gone to school. Thus, Adlai Stevenson, who incautiously allowed intelligence and learning and wit to peep out of his speeches, found the American people flocking to a Presidential candidate who invented a version of the English language that was all his own and that has been the despair of satirists ever since.

George Wallace, in his speeches, had, as one of his prime targets, 5 the "pointy-headed professor," and with what a roar of approval that phrase was always greeted by his pointy-headed audience.

Buzzwords

Now we have a new slogan on the part of the obscurantists: "Don't 6 trust the experts!" Ten years ago, it was "Don't trust anyone over 30." But the shouters of that slogan found that the inevitable alchemy of the calendar converted them to the untrustworthiness of the over-30, and, apparently, they determined never to make that mistake again. "Don't trust the experts!" is absolutely safe. Nothing, neither the passing of time nor exposure to information, will convert these shouters to experts in any subject that might conceivably be useful.

We have a new buzzword, too, for anyone who admires compe- 7 tence, knowledge, learning and skill, and who wishes to spread it around. People like that are called "elitists." That's the funniest buzzword ever invented because people who are not members of the intellectual elite don't know what an "elitist" is, or how to pronounce the word. As soon as someone shouts "elitist" it becomes clear that he or she is a closet elitist who is feeling guilty about having gone to school.

All right, then, forget my ingenuous question. America's right to 8 know does not include knowledge of elitist subjects. America's right to know involves something we might express vaguely as "what's going on." America has the right to know "what's going on" in the courts, in Congress, in the White House, in industrial councils, in the regulatory agencies, in labor unions—in the seats of the mighty, generally.

Very good, I'm for that, too. But how are you going to let people 9 know all that?

Grant us a free press, and a corps of independent and fearless 10 investigative reporters, comes the cry, and we can be sure that the people will know.

Yes, *provided they can read!*   11

As it happens, reading is one of those elitist subjects I have been 12 talking about, and the American public, by and large, in their distrust of experts and in their contempt for pointy-headed professors, can't read and don't read.

To be sure, the average American can sign his name more or less 13 legibly, and can make out the sports headlines—but how many non-elitist Americans can, without undue difficulty, read as many as a thousand consecutive words of small print, some of which may be trisyllabic?

Moreover, the situation is growing worse. Reading scores in the 14 schools decline steadily. The highway signs, which used to represent elementary misreading lessons ("Go Slo," "Xroad") are steadily being replaced by little pictures to make them internationally legible and incidentally to help those who know how to drive a car but, not being pointy-headed professors, can't read.

Again, in television commercials, there are frequent printed mes- 15 sages. Well, keep your eyes on them and you'll find out that no advertiser ever believes that anyone but an occasional elitist can read that print. To ensure that more than this mandarin minority gets the message, every word of it is spoken outloud by the announcer.

Honest Effort

If that is so, then how have Americans got the right to know? Grant 16
that there are certain publications that make an honest effort to tell
the public what they should know, but ask yourselves how many actually read them.

There are 200 million Americans who have inhabited school- 17
rooms at some time in their lives and who will admit that they know
how to read (provided you promise not to use their names and shame
them before their neighbors), but most decent periodicals believe they
are doing amazingly well if they have circulations of half a million. It
may be that only 1 percent—or less—of Americans make a stab at exercising their right to know. And if they try to do anything on that basis
they are quite likely to be accused of being elitists.

I contend that the slogan "America's right to know" is a mean- 18
ingless one when we have an ignorant population, and that the function of a free press is virtually zero when hardly anyone can read.

What shall we do about it? 19

We might begin by asking ourselves whether ignorance is so 20
wonderful after all, and whether it makes sense to denounce "elitism."

I believe that every human being with a physically normal brain 21
can learn a great deal and can be surprisingly intellectual. I believe
that what we badly need is social approval of learning and social rewards for learning.

We can *all* be members of the intellectual elite and then, and 22
only then, will a phrase like "America's right to know" and indeed, any
true concept of democracy, have any meaning.

Newsweek, January 21, 1980

Two Kinds of Illiteracy

WILLIAM RASPBERRY
Syndicated columnist

You cannot begin to understand E. D. Hirsch (*Cultural Literacy: What* 1
Every American Needs to Know) unless you first understand that there
are two kinds of illiteracy.

Some illiterates, including many who have been to school, simply 2
cannot read. That is, they cannot translate symbols on paper into

words. They cannot decipher bus route signs, simple instructions, application forms, or letters from friends.

Others—"functional illiterates," as they are called—do reasonably well at calling words but understand too little of what they have read. They may be able to recognize every word in, say, a newspaper article and still have little notion of what the article conveys. 3

They fail, in Hirsch's phrase, in "cultural literacy." That is, they know so little of what ordinary readers are presumed to know that they are unable to glean much meaning from what they read. Take this lead from a recent Associated Press story: 4

"'The stock market retreated for the second straight session today in selling ascribed to concern over a weak dollar and rising interest rates." 5

The words, with the possible exception of "ascribed," are well within the grasp of an ordinary fourth-grade student. But what fourth grader would understand what the reporter was talking about? He might know vaguely what a stock market is, but what is a market "session"? What does it mean to say that the market "retreated"? What was being sold. What is a "weak dollar"? 6

Those who would attack "illiteracy"—perhaps calling for greater use of phonics—often have in mind the first variety, although the second may be far more common. Virginia Gov. Gerald L. Baliles, for instance, recently announced a major effort to help the "450,000 adult Virginians who cannot read, write or compute beyond the eighth-grade level." 7

But surely a reasonably bright eighth grader is sufficiently adept at word-calling to handle the vocabulary of most newspaper articles or employment forms. The problem, Hirsch would insist, is they lack the background information necessary to give meaning to the words and phrases. 8

In short: "Literacy is more than a skill. . . . We know instinctively that to understand what somebody is saying, we must understand more than the surface meanings of words; we have to understand the context as well. To grasp the words on a page, we have to know a lot of information that isn't set down on the page." 9

That insight, in my view, explains why inner-city youngsters, who often read at or near national norms in the first three grades, tend to fall farther and farther behind their national peers as they progress through the elementary grades. It isn't that their word-attack skills decline, or that their teachers fail to teach them "comprehension skills." The problem is that they lack too much of the knowledge the authors assume they possess. 10

That brings us to the most controversial part of Hirsch's book. Acting on his notion that the difference between cultural literacy and cultural illiteracy is "a limited body of knowledge" that can be cata- 11

loged, the University of Virginia professor ends his book with a long list
of words, names and phrases: from Abraham and Isaac, agribusiness,
and albatross around one's neck, Appomattox, through devaluation,
detente and Don Quixote to Yellow Peril, xenophobia, zero-sum game
and Zionism.

There will be—already have been—great arguments over what 12
the list includes or omits. But his point is sound: There are things that
literate Americans know, or, at any rate, know about. A tiny fraction of
educated Americans have read *Mein Kampf;* but most of them at least
have a pretty good idea of what it is.

Is the list—and author's assumptions regarding what literate 13
Americans ought to know—too "white"? Orlando Patterson, the black
Harvard historian-sociologist, takes the question straight-on.

"The people who run society at the macro-level must be literate 14
in this culture. For this reason, it is dangerous to overemphasize the
problems of basic literacy or the relevancy of literacy to specific tasks,
and more constructive to emphasize that blacks will be condemned in
perpetuity to oversimplified, low-level tasks and will never gain their
rightful place in controlling the levers of power unless they also acquire literacy in this wider cultural sense."

A friend of mine puts it more simply. "If you don't know any- 15
thing, it's hard to learn anything else."

Washington Post, September 5, 1987

The Human Cost
of an Illiterate Society

JONATHAN KOZOL
*Jonathan Kozol has taught in the Boston area public schools
as well as at Yale University and the University of Massachusetts
at Amherst. A well-known critic of American schools for the
past two decades, Kozol's ideas on educational reform form
the basis for many of his books, including the award-winning*
Death at an Early Age *(1967),* Children of the Revolution
(1978), On Being a Teacher *(1981), and* Illiterate America
(1985) from which the following selection is excerpted.

PRECAUTIONS. READ BEFORE USING.   1
Poison: Contains sodium hydroxide (caustic soda-lye).

Corrosive: Causes severe eye and skin damage, may cause blindness.

Harmful or fatal if swallowed.

If swallowed, give large quantities of milk or water.

Do not induce vomiting.

Important: Keep water out of can at all times to prevent contents from violently erupting . . .

Warning on a can of Drano

We are speaking here no longer of the dangers faced by passengers on 2 Eastern Airlines or the dollar costs incurred by U.S. corporations and taxpayers. We are speaking now of human suffering and of the ethical dilemmas that are faced by a society that looks upon such suffering with qualified concern but does not take those actions which its wealth and ingenuity would seemingly demand.

Questions of literacy, in Socrates' belief, must at length be judged 3 as matters of morality. Socrates could not have had in mind the moral compromise peculiar to a nation like our own. Some of our Founding Fathers did, however, have this question in their minds. One of the wisest of those Founding Fathers (one who may not have been most compassionate but surely was more prescient than some of his peers) recognized the special dangers that illiteracy would pose to basic equity in the political construction that he helped to shape.

"A people who mean to be their own governors," James Madison 4 wrote, "must arm themselves with the power knowledge gives. A popular government without popular information or the means of acquiring it, is but a prologue to a farce or a tragedy, or perhaps both."

Tragedy looms larger than farce in the United States today. Illit- 5 erate citizens seldom vote. Those who do are forced to cast a vote of questionable worth. They cannot make informed decisions based on serious print information. Sometimes they can be alerted to their interests by aggressive voter education. More frequently, they vote for a face, a smile, or a style, not for a mind or character or body of beliefs.

The number of illiterate adults exceeds by 16 million the entire 6 vote cast for the winner in the 1980 presidential contest. If even one third of all illiterates could vote, and read enough and do sufficient math to vote in their self-interest, Ronald Reagan would not likely have been chosen president. There is, of course, no way to know for sure. We do know this: Democracy is a mendacious term when used by those who are prepared to countenance the forced exclusion of one third of our electorate. So long as 60 million people are denied significant participation, the government is neither of, nor for, nor by, the people. It is a government, at best, of those two thirds whose wealth, skin color, or parental privilege allows them opportunity to profit from the provocation and instruction of the written word.

The undermining of democracy in the United States is one "ex- 7 pense" that sensitive Americans can easily deplore because it repre- sents a contradiction that endangers citizens of all political positions. The human price is not so obvious at first.

Since I first immersed myself within this work I have often had 8 the following dream: I find that I am in a railroad station or a large department store within a city that is utterly unknown to me and where I cannot understand the printed words. None of the signs or symbols is familiar. Everything looks strange: like mirror writing of some kind. Gradually I understand that I am in the Soviet Union. All the letters on the walls around me are Cyrillic. I look for my pocket dictionary but I find that it has been mislaid. Where have I left it? Then I recall that I forgot to bring it with me when I packed my bags in Boston. I struggle to remember the name of my hotel. I try to ask some- body for directions. One person stops and look at me in a peculiar way. I lose the nerve to ask. At last I reach into my wallet for an ID card. The card is missing. Have I lost it? Then I remember that my card was con- fiscated for some reason, many years before. Around this point, I wake up in a panic.

This panic is not so different from the misery that millions of 9 adult illiterates experience each day within the course of their routine existence in the U.S.A.

Illiterates cannot read the menu in a restaurant. 10

They cannot read the cost of items on the menu in the *window* of 11 the restaurant before they enter.

Illiterates cannot read the letters that their children bring home 12 from their teachers. They cannot study school department circulars that tell them of the courses that their children must be taking if they hope to pass the SAT exams. They cannot help with homework. They cannot write a letter to the teacher. They are afraid to visit in the class- room. They do not want to humiliate their child or themselves.

Illiterates cannot read instructions on a bottle of prescription 13 medicine. They cannot find out when a medicine is past the year of safe consumption; nor can they read of allergenic risks, warnings to diabetics, or the potential sedative effect of certain kinds of non- prescription pills. They cannot observe preventive health care admo- nitions. They cannot read about "the seven warning signs of cancer" or the indications of blood-sugar fluctuations or the risks of eating cer- tain foods that aggravate the likelihood of cardiac arrest.

Illiterates live, in more than literal ways, an uninsured existence. 14 They cannot understand the written details on a health insurance form. They cannot read the waivers that they sign preceding surgical procedures. Several women I have known in Boston have entered a slum hospital with the intention of obtaining a tubal ligation and have emerged a few days later after having been subjected to a hysterectomy. Unaware of their rights, incognizant of jargon, intimidated by the unfamiliar air of fear and atmosphere of ether that so many of us find oppressive in the confines even of the most attractive and expensive medical facilities, they have signed their names to documents they could not read and which nobody, in the hectic situation that prevails so often in those overcrowded hospitals that serve the urban poor, had even bothered to explain.

Childbirth might seem to be the last inalienable right of any female citizen within a civilized society. Illiterate mothers, as we shall see, already have been cheated of the power to protect their progeny against the likelihood of demolition in deficient public schools and, as a result, against the verbal servitude within which they themselves exist. Surgical denial of the right to bear that child in the first place represents an ultimate denial, an unspeakable metaphor, a final darkness that denies even the twilight gleamings of our own humanity. What greater violation of our biological, our biblical, our spiritual humanity could possibly exist than that which takes place nightly, perhaps hourly these days, within such overburdened and benighted institutions as the Boston City Hospital? Illiteracy has many costs; few are so irreversible as this. 15

Even the roof above one's head, the gas or other fuel for heating 16 that protects the residents of northern city slums against the threat of illness in the winter months become uncertain guarantees. Illiterates cannot read the lease that they must sign to live in an apartment which, too often, they cannot afford. They cannot manage check accounts and therefore seldom pay for anything by mail. Hours and entire days of difficult travel (and the cost of bus or other public transit) must be added to the real cost of whatever they consume. Loss of interest on the check accounts they do not have, and could not manage if they did, must be regarded as another of the excess costs paid by the citizen who is excluded from the common instruments of commerce in a numerate society.

"I couldn't understand the bills," a woman in Washington, D.C., 17 reports, "and then I couldn't write the checks to pay them. We signed things we didn't know what they were."

Illiterates cannot read the notices that they receive from welfare 18 offices or from the IRS. They must depend on word-of-mouth instruction from the welfare worker—or from other persons whom they have good reason to mistrust. They do not know what rights they have, what deadlines and requirements they face, what options they might choose to exercise. They are half-citizens. Their rights exist in print but not in fact.

Illiterates cannot look up numbers in a telephone directory. Even 19
if they can find the names of friends, few possess the sorting skills to
make use of the yellow pages; categories are bewildering and trade
names are beyond decoding capabilities for millions of nonreaders.
Even the emergency numbers listed on the first page of the phone
book—"Ambulance," "Police," and "Fire"—are too frequently beyond
the recognition of nonreaders.

Many illiterates cannot read the admonition on a pack of ciga- 20
rettes. Neither the Surgeon General's warning nor its reproduction on
the package can alert them to the risks. Although most people learn by
wood of mouth that smoking is related to a number of grave physical
disorders, they do not get the chance to read the detailed stories
which can document this danger with the vividness that turns concern into determination to resist. They can see the handsome cowboy
or the slim Virginia lady lighting up a filter cigarette; they cannot heed
the words that tell them that this product is (not "may be") dangerous
to their health. Sixty million men and women are condemned to be
the unalerted, high-risk candidates for cancer.

Illiterates do not buy "no-name" products in the supermarkets. 21
They must depend on photographs or the familiar logos that are
printed on the packages of brand-name groceries. The poorest people,
therefore, are denied the benefits of the least costly products.

Illiterates depend almost entirely upon label recognition. Many 22
labels, however, are not easy to distinguish. Dozens of different kinds
of Campbell's soup appear identical to the nonreader. The purchaser
who cannot read and does not dare to ask for help, out of the fear of
being stigmatized (a fear which is unfortunately realistic), frequently
comes home with something which she never wanted and her family
never tasted.

Illiterates cannot read instructions on a pack of frozen food. 23
Packages sometimes provide an illustration to explain the cooking
preparations; but illustrations are of little help to someone who must
"boil water, drop the food—*within* its plastic wrapper—in the boiling
water, wait for it to simmer, instantly remove."

Even when labels are seemingly clear, they may be easily mis- 24
taken. A woman in Detroit brought home a gallon of Crisco for her
children's dinner. She thought that she had bought the chicken that
was pictured on the label. She had enough Crisco now to last a year—
but no more money to go back and buy the food for dinner.

Recipes provided on the packages of certain staples sometimes 25
tempt a semiliterate person to prepare a meal her children have not
tasted. The longing to vary the uniform and often starchy content of
low-budget meals provided to the family that relies on food stamps
commonly leads to ruinous results. Scarce funds have been wasted
and the food must be thrown out. The same applies to distribution of

food-surplus produce in emergency conditions. Government induce-ments to poor people to "explore the ways" by which to make a tasty meal from tasteless noodles, surplus cheese, and powdered milk are useless to nonreaders. Intended as benevolent advice, such recom-mendations mock reality and foster deeper feelings of resentment and of inability to cope. (Those, on the other hand, who cautiously refrain from "innovative" recipes in preparation of their children's meals must suffer the opprobrium of "laziness," "lack of imagination . . .")

Illiterates cannot travel freely. When they attempt to do so, they 26 encounter risks that few of us can dream of. They cannot read traffic signs and, while they often learn to recognize and to decipher sym-bols, they cannot manage street names which they haven't seen be-fore. The same is true for bus and subway stops. While ingenuity can sometimes help a man or woman to discern directions from familiar landmarks, buildings, cemeteries, churches, and the like, most illiter-ates are virtually immobilized. They seldom wander past the streets and neighborhoods they know. Geographical paralysis becomes a bitter metaphor for their entire existence. They are immobilized in al-most every sense we can imagine. They can't move up. They can't move out. They cannot see beyond. Illiterates may take an oral test for drivers' permits in most sections of America. It is a questionable con-cession. Where will they go? How will they get there? How will they get home? Could it be that some of us might like it better if they stayed where they belong?

Travel is only one of many instances of circumscribed existence. 27 Choice, in almost all its facets, is diminished in the life of an illiterate adult. Even the printed TV schedule, which provides most people with the luxury of preselection, does not belong within the arsenal of options in illiterate existence. One consequence is that the viewer watches only what appears at moments when he happens to have time to turn the switch. Another consequence, a lot more common, is that the TV set remains in operation night and day. Whatever the program offered at the hour when he walks into the room will be the nutriment that he accepts and swallows. Thus, to passivity, is added frequency—indeed, almost uninterrupted continuity. Freedom to select is no more possible here than in the choice of home or surgery or food.

"You don't choose," said one illiterate woman. "You take your 28 wishes from somebody else." Whether in perusal of a menu, selection of highways, purchase of groceries, or determination of affordable en-joyment, illiterate Americans must trust somebody else: a friend, a relative, a stranger on the street, a grocery clerk, a TV copywriter.

"All of our mail we get, it's hard for her to read. Settin' down and 29 writing a letter, she can't do it. Like if we get a bill . . . we take it over to my sister-in-law. . . . My sister-in-law reads it."

Billing agencies harass poor people for the payment of the bills 30 for purchases that might have taken place six months before. Utility companies offer an agreement for a staggered payment schedule on a bill past due. "You have to trust them," one man said. Precisely for this reason, you end up by trusting no one and suspecting everyone of possible deceit. A submerged sense of distrust becomes the corollary to a constant need to trust. "They are cheating me . . . I have been tricked . . . I do not know. . . ."

Not knowing: This is a familiar theme. Not knowing the right 31 word for the right thing at the right time is one form of subjugation. Not knowing the world that lies concealed behind those words is a more terrifying feeling. The longitude and latitude of one's existence are beyond all easy apprehension. Even the hard, cold stars within the firmament above one's head begin to mock the possibilities for self-location. Where am I? Where did I come from? Where will I go?

"I've lost a lot of jobs," one man explains. "Today, even if you're a 32 janitor, there's still reading and writing. . . . They leave a note saying, 'Go to room so-and-so . . .' You can't do it. You can't read it. You don't know."

"The hardest thing about it is that I've been places where I didn't 33 know where I was. You don't know where you are. . . . You're lost."

"Like I said: I have two kids. What do I do if one of my kids starts 34 choking? I go running to the phone . . . I can't look up the hospital phone number. That's if we're at home. Out on the street, I can't read the sign. I get to a pay phone. 'Okay, tell us where you are. We'll send an ambulance.' I look at the street sign. Right there, I can't tell you what it says. I'd have to spell it out, letter for letter. By that time, one of my kids would be dead. . . . These are the kinds of fears you go with, every single day. . . ."

"Reading directions, I suffer with. I work with chemicals. . . . 35 That's scary to begin with. . . ."

"You sit down. They throw the menu in front of you. Where do 36 you go from there? Nine times out of ten you say, 'Go ahead. Pick out something for the both of us.' I've eaten some weird things, let me tell you!"

Menus. Chemicals. A child choking while his mother searches for 37 a word she does not know to find assistance that will come too late. Another mother speaks about the inability to help her kids to read: "I can't read to them. Of course that's leaving them out of something they should have. Oh, it matters. You *believe* it matters! I ordered all these books. The kids belong to a book club. Donny wanted me to read a book to him. I told Donny: 'I can't read.' He said: 'Mommy, you sit down. I'll read it to you.' I tried it one day, reading from the pictures. Donny looked at me. He said, 'Mommy, that's not right.' He's only five. He knew I couldn't read. . . ."

A landlord tells a woman that her lease allows him to evict her if 38 her baby cries and causes inconvenience to her neighbors. The consequence of challenging his words conveys a danger which appears, unlikely as it seems, even more alarming than the danger of eviction. Once she admits that she can't read, in the desire to maneuver for the time in which to call a friend, she will have defined herself in terms of an explicit impotence that she cannot endure. Capitulation in this case is preferable to self-humiliation. Resisting the definition of oneself in terms of what one cannot do, what others take for granted, represents a need so great that other imperatives (even one so urgent as the need to keep one's home in winter's cold) evaporate and fall away in face of fear. Even the loss of home and shelter, in this case, is not so terrifying as the loss of self.

"I come out of school. I was sixteen. They had their meetings. 39 The directors meet. They said that I was wasting their school paper. I was wasting pencils. . . ."

Another illiterate, looking back, believes she was not worthy of 40 her teacher's time. She believes that it was wrong of her to take up space within her school. She believes that it was right to leave in order that somebody more deserving could receive her place.

Children choke. Their mother chokes another way: on more than 41 chicken bones.

People eat what others order, know what others tell them, struggle 42 not to see themselves as they believe the world perceives them. A man in California speaks about his own loss of identity, of self-location, definition:

"I stood at the bottom of the ramp. My car had broke down on 43 the freeway. There was a phone. I asked for the police. They was nice. They said to tell them where I was. I looked up at the signs. There was one that I had seen before. I read it to them: ONE WAY STREET. They thought it was a joke. I told them I couldn't read. There was other signs above the ramp. They told me to try. I looked around for somebody to help. All the cars was going by real fast. I couldn't make them understand that I was lost. The cop was nice. He told me: 'Try once more.' I did my best. I couldn't read. I only knew the sign above my head. The cop was trying to be nice. He knew that I was trapped. 'I can't send out a car to you if you can't tell me where you are.' I felt afraid. I nearly cried. I'm forty-eight years old. I only said: 'I'm on a one-way street. . . .'"

Perhaps we might slow down a moment here and look at the re- 44 alities described above. This is the nation that we live in. This is a society that most of us did not create but which our President and other leaders have been willing to sustain by virtue of malign neglect. Do we possess the character and courage to address a problem which so many nations, poorer than our own, have found it natural to correct?

The answers to these questions represent a reasonable test of our 45
belief in the democracy to which we have been asked in public school
to swear allegiance.

Illiterate America (New York:
Anchor Doubleday, 1985)

Scientific Literacy

A Conceptual and Empirical Review

JON D. MILLER
*A teacher and director of the Public Opinion Laboratory at
Northern Illinois University, Miller specializes in studies of
public attitudes toward science and technology. His books
include* Citizenship in an Age of Science *(1980) and* The
American People and Science Policy *(1983).*

In a democratic society, the level of scientific literacy in the population 1
has important implications for science policy decisions. As this essay
will show, the level of scientific literacy in the United States is deplor-
ably low; thus any measures we can take to raise this level, to foster
informed and intelligent participation in science policy issues, will
improve the quality of both our science and technology and our political life.

The development of scientific literacy by a broader public did not 2
become the subject of systematic study until the 1930s, when John
Dewey, in a paper entitled "The Supreme Intellectual Obligation," declared that

> the responsibility of science cannot be fulfilled by methods that
> are chiefly concerned with self-perpetuation of specialized sci-
> ence to the neglect of influencing the much larger number to
> adopt into the very make-up of their minds those attitudes of
> openmindedness, intellectual integrity, observation, and interest
> in testing their opinions and beliefs, that are characteristic of the
> scientific attitude.[1]

Following Dewey's charge, a number of science educators began 3
to think about the formal definition and measurement of the scientific

attitude. Ira C. Davis, for one, believed that the individual who possesses this attitude will "show a willingness to change his opinion on the basis of new evidence; . . . search for the whole truth without prejudice; . . . have a concept of cause and effect relationships; . . . make a habit of basing judgment on fact; and . . . have the ability to distinguish between fact and theory."[2] Victor H. Noll and A. G. Hoff came up with similar definitions, and they began the task of developing items for use in testing.[3] Virtually all of the empirical work done before the Second World War had as its focus the development of a scientific attitude.

With the postwar growth of standardized testing, a number of   4
science educators and test developers began to focus on the level of comprehension of basic scientific constructs and terms. A growing number of studies, epitomized by the standardized tests of the Educational Testing Service (ETS) and the College Board, attempted to chart the level of cognitive scientific knowledge among various groups in the population.

Beginning in the mid-sixties, the National Assessment of Educa-   5
tional Progress (NAEP) started to collect data from national random samples of precollegiate students concerning, among other categories, their level of scientific knowledge. These studies were the first to measure systematically both the understanding of the norms, or processes, of science and the cognitive content of the major disciplines. These two dimensions together—an understanding of the norms of science and knowledge of major scientific constructs—constitute the traditional meaning of scientific literacy as applied to broader populations. But if scientific literacy is to become truly relevant to our contemporary situation, one additional dimension must be added: awareness of the impact of science and technology on society and the policy choices that must inevitably emerge.

About fifteen years ago, concern about the public's knowledge of   6
various scientific or technological public policy issues began to surface. Environmental groups, for example, found that some minimal level of scientific knowledge was necessary if individuals were to understand debates about pollution of the environment. In addition, the increasing number of state referenda on issues such as nuclear power and laetrile were generating apprehension in the scientific community about the public's ability to understand the issues and to make an informed judgment. These concerns echo those of the fifties, when groups opposed to fluoridation of water were able to win referenda on this issue, primarily because the majority of those voting were not scientifically literate. Not able to comprehend the arguments about fluoridation, many voters appeared to prefer not to drink something whose potential effects they did not understand.

In summarizing the case for a broader public understanding of public policy issues—what Benjamin Shen has recently characterized as "civic science literacy"[4]—Robert Morison wrote: 7

> Science can no longer be content to present itself as an activity independent of the rest of society, governed by its own rules and directed by the inner dynamics of its own processes. Too many of these processes have effects which, though beneficial in many respects, often strike the average man as a threat to his autonomy. Too often science seems to be thrusting society as a whole in directions in which it does not fully understand and which it certainly has not chosen.
>
> The scientific community must redouble its efforts to present science—in the classroom, in the public press, and through education-extension activities of various kinds—as a fully understandable process, "justifiable to man," and controllable by him.[5]

Cognitive Science Knowledge

As the use of standardized testing expanded during the fifties and sixties, a number of tests were developed to measure a student's knowledge of basic scientific constructs.[6] A majority were used by teachers and school systems to evaluate individual students, to determine admission or placement, or for related academic counseling purposes. While some test score summaries have been published by the ETS and other national testing services, these reports reflect the scores of only those students who plan to attend college or who for some other reason have elected to take the test; and it is this self-selected nature of the student populations involved that continues to raise substantial problems for interpretation and analysis. (The NAEP studies cited previously are noteworthy in that they are the only national data collection program in which the bias of self-selection inherent in voluntary testing programs has been eliminated.) 8

The only national data set that provides scores of cognitive science knowledge for broad and randomly selected populations is the National Assessment, which for over a decade has periodically collected cognitive science knowledge data from national samples of nine-, thirteen-, and seventeen-year-olds. In some years, a national sample of young adults twenty-six through thirty-five was also used to assess the continuing impact of formal study. 9

On the basis of three assessments between 1969 and 1977, NAEP found declining science achievement scores for all age groups and almost all socioeconomic subgroups. Female students, black students, 10 students whose parents did not complete high school, and students who live in large central cities were all substantially below the national average in science achievement.[7]

Attitudes Toward Organized Science

The first national study that included a meaningful set of measures of 11 attitudes toward organized science and knowledge about it was a 1957 science news survey conducted by the Survey Research Center at the University of Michigan for the National Association of Science Writers. Although the purpose of the survey was to study the public's interest in science news and its information consumption patterns, the interview schedule also included measures of general attitudes toward organized science and knowledge of it, as well as some issues that were then current.[8]

The survey found that only a minority of the public was strongly 12 interested in scientific issues and that the level of public knowledge about science was relatively low. It found, too, that the public tended to hold high expectations for the future achievements of science and technology, but were aware of the two-edged nature of the scientific enterprise. Stephen Withey summarized the public mood: "On the surface the natives are quiet, supportive, and appreciative but there is some questioning, some alert watching, and considerable mistrust. The public will wait and see; they have no reason to do anything else, and many have no other place to turn."[9]

Beginning in 1972, the National Science Board initiated a biennial 13 survey of public attitudes toward science and technology,[10] which found that the public retained a high level of appreciation and expectation amid signs of an increasing wariness. Yet, there was no evidence to indicate the development of a strong antiscience sentiment.

In subsequent surveys in 1979 and 1981, the focus changed to a 14 more structured approach, in an attempt to identify the segment of the population interested in, and knowledgeable about, science policy matters, and to examine the attitudes of this "attentive public."[11] The results showed that about 20 percent of American adults followed scientific matters regularly and that their attitude toward organized science was more favorable as a rule than that of the general population groups previously measured.

The attitudes of young adults toward organized science was even 15 more positive. In a 1978 national survey of high-school and college students, researchers identified the developmental roots of adult attentiveness to science matters, and determined that the attitudes of these young adults were generally positive and supportive of science.[12] Like older Americans surveyed, however, substantial segments of these young adults were not very interested in, and had little information about, scientific and technological matters. Approximately 90 percent of the high-school students who did not plan to attend college failed to meet minimal criteria for interest in scientific issues or for cognitive knowledge of basic scientific constructs. There is no reason to believe that the next generation will be antiscientific; more likely, it will continue to hold the same attitudes—corrected for the rising levels of educational achievement of the new generation—as do adults today.

.   .   .

Political Specialization

No individual today, no matter how good his or her intentions, can 16 hope to acquire and maintain a mastery of more than a few political issues at one time. Thus the modern citizen who chooses to follow political affairs opts for political specialization—that is, selects out of the myriad issues those few in which he or she is willing to invest the time and other resources necessary to become and remain informed.

The need for specialization springs from a combination of two 17 basic forces. First, participation in the political process is but one of the many demands on the time of contemporary men and women. That many adults choose to devote a smaller share of their time to political affairs, in favor of more attractive, perhaps more personally satisfying alternatives, can be seen in the steady decline of public participation in the political system over the last four decades. Even presidential elections, which command the highest levels of public concern and participation, attract barely half the eligible adults in the United States.

Second, the specialized information required to be knowledge- 18 able about almost any given political issue is increasing rapidly. Issues involving science fall into this category, as do most of the issues on the national political agenda. For example, an area like economic policy— often referred to as the pocketbook issue—has become increasingly complex and is beyond the ken of a substantial majority of American adults. If only 31 percent of the adult population professed to have a clear understanding of a term like GNP,[13] how many citizens, then, might be expected to comprehend the current debate over "supply-side economics" or the fate of the dollar in international monetary markets?

Both forces have worked to narrow the political horizon of most 19 American adults. Unlike "single-issue" politics, where the interest of the participant revolves totally around one strongly felt political position, political specialization is a rational and gradual narrowing of the

Figure 1 *A stratified model of science and technology policy formulation*

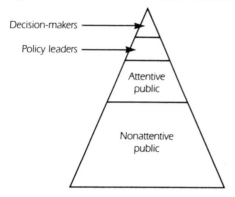

number of topics on which an individual can hope to remain adequately informed. Even then, they are not nearly as well informed about an issue as their interest would imply.

How does this specialization process affect the more general political system? Three decades ago, Gabriel Almond described the process as it applied to public attitudes toward foreign policy and public participation in its formulation. In his original work, he illustrated, in stratified pyramidal form, the types of public participation in the political process that were likely to occur under conditions of issue specialization (Figure 1).[14] At the pinnacle are those who have the power to make binding policy decisions, a group that would include a mix of executive, legislative, and judicial officers. In the case of science policy, the officers would be primarily at the federal level.

Nongovernmental policy leaders, often referred to as elites in political science, comprise the second level. This group interacts regularly with the decision-makers, and from time to time, as noted by James Rosenau and others, there is some flow of elites into decision-making posts, and of decision-makers into the leadership group.[15] When there is a high level of concurrence between the decision-makers and the leadership group, policy is made, and normally there is no wider public participation in the policy process. The policy leadership group may itself divide on some issues. In this case, appeals may be made to the attentive public—the third level—to join in the policy process and to try to influence decision-makers by contacting them directly and by persuasion. The attentive public is composed of individuals interested in a particular policy area and willing to become and remain knowledgeable about the issue. In 1979 the attentive public for science policy included about 27 million adults, or about 18 percent of the adult population.[16]

Although the processes for mobilizing the attentive public for sci- 22
ence policy are only now being studied, the flow of appeals from leaders to the attentive public apparently takes place through professional
organizations, specialized journals and magazines, and employment-
related institutions. The flow of concerns from the attentive public to
the decision-makers, on the other hand, undoubtedly goes through
the traditional avenues of letter writing and telephone and personal
contacts.

The attentive public also becomes involved when there is a high 23
degree of consensus among the leadership group but a lack of concurrence by some or all of the decision-makers. In this case, the leadership groups work to mobilize the attentive public to contact the
decision-makers and to argue directly for the preferred policy. The recent discussions of federal funding for science illustrate this case.

At the bottom of the pyramid is the general, or nonattentive, pub- 24
lic. For the most part, these individuals have little interest in science
policy and a low level of knowledge about organized science. Two very
important points must be understood about this group, however. First,
should the general population become sufficiently unhappy about the
policies that the decision-makers, leaders, and the attentive public
have fostered in any area, it can exercise a political veto. The public's
role in ending the wars in Korea and Vietnam illustrate how powerful
this option can be. It is this very ability of the general population to
intervene and veto that sustains the democratic nature of the policy
formulation process.

Second, it is important not to equate nonattentiveness to science 25
policy with ignorance or lack of intellectual activity. We are all nonattentive to a vast number of issues. Many of the nonattentive public
may be well educated, interested in other issues and knowledgeable
about them, and politically active. According to the data from the 1979
NSF survey, about half of the adult population in the United States at
the time of the survey were attentive to one or more political issues.[17]

Scientific Literacy and the Formulation
of Science Policy

Given this stratified decision-making process, the low level of scien- 26
tific literacy raises two important problems. First, among the 80 percent of the population not attentive to science policy, the level of scientific literacy is extraordinarily low—in the 2 to 3 percent range. In
the context of the political specialization process, we would not expect a very high rate of scientific literacy in the nonattentive public,
and few voters would be expected to make their choices primarily on

the basis of scientific or technological issues. Yet in recent years, an increasing number of referenda have concerned issues related to science or technology—nuclear power, laetrile, recombinant DNA facilities, fluoridation—and it is apparent that a substantial majority of the general electorate will not be able to make informed judgments on these issues.

Second, approximately 70 percent of the attentive public for science policy did *not* meet the minimal criteria for scientific literacy. This is a surprising result, but not an inexplicable one. Almost half of the adult population had a minimal facility with basic scientific terms, and 40 percent had at least a minimal level of issue information. Many of these individuals may have had a high level of interest in one or more science-related issues and may have followed them through popular magazines such as *Science 83, Smithsonian, National Geographic, Discover,* or *Omni,* without understanding the scientific processes involved. They would perhaps have more difficulty comprehending articles in *Science, Scientific American,* or in professional or disciplinary journals, but can undoubtedly write very clear letters to their congressmen and senators. They would appear to be dependent upon science journalists to "interpret" the scientific debate on most issues.

As more appeals are made to the attentive public to pressure directly for public policy outcomes, the importance of this group will grow. Yet, the situation is a fragile one. Given the large numbers in this group who are dependent on "translators," the personality or philosophical perspective of the translator may become as important—if not more so—than the substance of the scientific arguments.

There are compelling cultural, economic, and political arguments for a major effort to expand scientific literacy in both the general and attentive publics. In my opinion, the most effective place to start is in the elementary and secondary schools. . . . Beyond improved science education at this level, I would urge that high priority be placed on the expansion of scientific literacy among the attentive public for science policy, both in terms of increasing their overall numbers and in augmenting their basic level of literacy. What makes political specialization possible is just this basic level of literacy in any given issue area. There is an interested audience searching for more sophisticated information than is normally available in the news media. The extraordinary growth of semisophisticated science magazines like *Discover, Omni,* and *Science 83,* for example, represents in large part the desire for more and better information among the attentive public for science policy.

From Dewey to Morison, the scientific community has been urged to communicate more effectively and openly with the public,

27

28

29

30

especially the informed public—and scientists and engineers are responding by showing a new level of willingness to explain their problems and aspirations to interested lay audiences. But if this communication is to continue and expand so that the science policy process can function effectively, there must be an audience capable of understanding both the substance of the arguments and the basic processes of science. We can accomplish this by addressing, without delay, the educational needs of the attentive public for science policy.

Notes

1. John Dewey, "The Supreme Intellectual Obligation," *Science Education* 18 (1934): 1–4.
2. Ira C. Davis, "The Measurement of Scientific Attitudes," *Science Education* 19 (1935): 117–22.
3. A. G. Hoff, "A Test for Scientific Attitude," *School Science and Mathematics* 36 (1936): 763–70; Victor H. Noll, "Measuring the Scientific Attitude," *Journal of Abnormal and Social Psychology* 30 (1935): 145–54.
4. Benjamin Shen, "Scientific Literacy and the Public Understanding of Science," in *Communication of Scientific Information,* edited by S. Day (Basel: Karger, 1975).
5. Robert S. Morison, "Science and Social Attitudes," *Science* 165 (1969): 150–56.
6. Oscar K. Buros, *The Sixth Mental Measurements Yearbook* (Highland Park, New Jersey: Gryphon Press, 1965).
7. National Assessment of Educational Progress, *Three National Assessments of Science: 1969–1977,* Science Report No. 08-S-00 (Denver: Educational Commission of the States, 1978a); and *Science Achievement in the Schools,* No. 08-S-01 (Denver: Educational Commission of the States, 1978b).
8. Robert C. Davis, *The Public Impact of Science in the Mass Media,* Survey Research Center, Monograph No. 25, University of Michigan, Ann Arbor, 1958; and Stephen B. Withey, "Public Opinion about Science and the Scientists," *Public Opinion Quarterly* 23 (1959): 382–88.
9. Withey, Ibid.
10. National Science Board, *Science Indicators 1972; Science Indicators 1974; Science Indicators 1976;* and *Science Indicators 1980* (Washington, D.C.: Government Printing Office, 1973, 1975, 1977, 1981).
11. Jon D. Miller, *The American People and Science Policy* (New York: Pergamon, 1983); Jon D. Miller, Kenneth Prewitt, and Robert Pearson, *The Attitudes of the U.S. Public toward Science and Technology,* a final report to the National Science Foundation, 1980.
12. Jon D. Miller, Robert W. Suchner, and Alan V. Voelker, *Citizenship in an Age of Science* (New York: Pergamon, 1980).
13. Miller et al., *The Attitudes of the U.S. Public toward Science and Technology.*
14. Gabriel Almond, *The American People and Foreign Policy* (New York: Harcourt Brace, 1950).
15. James Rosenau, *Citizenship Between Elections* (New York: Free Press, 1974).
16. Miller, *The American People and Science Policy;* Miller et al., *The Attitudes of the U.S. Public toward Science and Technology.*
17. Miller et al., *The Attitudes of the U.S. Public toward Science and Technology.*

Daedalus, Spring 1983

Corporations Take Aim at the High Cost of Worker Illiteracy

KERRY ELIZABETH KNOBELSDORFF
Staff writer for the Christian Science Monitor

When Calvin Miles started working at a New York cable TV company, 1
he was unable to read or write. No one knew, he says, because he was
going to school at the time, and he could read a map, which was an
important part of the job.

But reading names or notices was a different story. 2

"One lady had left a note on the door telling me she would be in 3
the backyard, and to come around and find her," he says. "I didn't
know what it said, so I just left." When the woman called to find out
what happened, Mr. Miles told her the cable man must not have seen
the note.

"Sixty percent of the people at the company probably couldn't
read and were just bluffing it," Miles adds.

About 13 percent of American adults live like Miles used to, 4
hiding from their employers, co-workers, and friends day after day the
fact that they can't read or write. Like Miles, almost half of these adults
live in central United States cities, a US Department of Education study
reports.

Corporate America does not seem to know which way to turn. 5
For one thing, technology has wiped out a lot of low-scale jobs, the
kind that someone with little or no education can handle, and created
many more middle- and upper-level service positions, says Lawrence
Mikulecky, a professor of education at Indiana University.

"We're losing those jobs to technology and overseas production 6
very fast. . . . At some point there aren't going to be many of those left,"
says Tony Carnivale, chief economist at the American Society for Training and Development, in Alexandria, Va.

The Hudson Institute's recent Workforce 2000 report says that in 7
1990, for the first time in history, more than 50 percent of the jobs
being created will demand post-secondary training.

"Very few new jobs will be created for those who cannot read, 8
follow directions, and use mathematics," the report continues. "Ironically, the demographic trends in the work force, coupled with the
higher skill requirements of the economy, will lead to both higher and

lower unemployment: more joblessness among the least-skilled and less among the most educationally advantaged."

In other words, the fastest-growing group of new workers appears to be the least literate, with the worst access to education: "Nonwhites, women, and immigrants will make up more than five-sixths of the net additions to the work force between now and the year 2000, though they make up only about half of it today," the report says. 9

A phenomenal high school dropout rate is also pushing more than half the teen-age population out into the work force with minimal reading and writing abilities, little analytical practice, almost no understanding of how to operate a computer, and no vocational training. 10

Even a college diploma—received by just a fifth of young Americans—does not guarantee a high level of literacy. According to a survey in 1986 by the Educational Testing Service in Princeton, N.J., 40 percent of those tested could not calculate the amount of change they should have received from a lunch, nor could 60 percent read a long-distance bus schedule. 11

Finding qualified people has become a challenge for the first time since World War II. "We're on something of a collision course," says Dr. Carnivale, who has been studying the problem for three years. "America's unemployment rate is headed for 5 percent, and industry will have to hire from populations we've traditionally ignored." This, he says, is the best part of the problem. "People will be scarce, so these groups—minorities, women, the handicapped, and even immigrants—will finally be valued economically." 12

But doing that will take time and a lot of money, Carnivale says. 13

One state has begun. Rhode Island just initiated a program, named Workforce 2000 after the Hudson Report, to do something about the problems outlined in the report. A council appointed by the governor will attempt to raise $3 million to $4 million a year to "learn to utilize the underemployed in the state," says executive director Henry Woodbridge. 14

But Carnivale and others expect American corporations to dodge the issue and continue pulling workers from traditional labor pools, until those pools dry up. 15

Many companies already spend large amounts upgrading their employees. IBM says it spent about $700 million last year for on-the-job, though not remedial, instruction. "Every workday, 10,000 workers leave their regular jobs to attend some kind of training," says spokesman Edward Stobbey. 16

Xerox spent $220 million on training, and Texas Instruments says it schools each employee 10 days a year. 17

Several sources say US companies spend a total of about $30 bil- 18 lion a year on formal training, though there are many that provide no such assistance.

For these, and all employers, teaching employees how to read 19 and write is an expensive and often exasperating task. "You can't teach new skills to those who don't even have the basics," says Frank Barnett, assistant director of the US Department of Education's Adult Literacy Initiative.

Primary training in addition to retraining programs can run up a 20 bill as high as $225 billion a year, says the Institute for the Study of Adult Literacy at Pennsylvania State University. The cost of not helping these people, however, for employers "is increased errors, lower productivity, and lost potential of employees," says James Wall, at Pratt & Whitney Aircraft Group, in Connecticut. Mr. Wall is reinstating a much-needed employee high-school equivalency program that was disconnected several years ago after it "put itself out of business."

Author Jonathan Kozol estimates in his book "Illiterate America" 21 that US corporations alone may forfeit $20 billion a year in lost profits, lower productivity, reduced international competitiveness, job immobility, and increased remedial training.

Companies that depend on more entry-level workers, recogniz- 22 ing the need to cultivate employees, have begun footing the bill for city literacy programs, or offering in-house courses to train illiterate workers or those who lack job-specific skills. General Motors Corporation, IBM, and United Technologies support job training centers that prepare people for basic positions.

Major firms like Chemical Bank, City Bank, the New York Times, 23 and J. C. Penney are opening their cafeterias after hours to literacy workshops, like New York's Literacy Volunteers. "They provide us with volunteers, fund raising, and technical assistance, and they print our newsletter," says director Eli Zal, "and we get over $200,000 a year from over 85 companies, more than we do from federal, state, and local governments."

Other companies, like American Telephone & Telegraph, work 24 with a large percentage of employees for whom English is a second language. "A dialect or pronunciation problem can lead to a misunderstanding that can lose your company thousands of dollars," says Burke Stinson at AT&T.

Some companies try to simplify their entry-level jobs, usually by 25 mechanizing them. But this "dumbing down," as some educators call it, "means you can only hold onto a few people at the low level, and the next step is one they'll never ever pass," says Dr. Mikulecky at Indiana University.

Many uneducated workers are afraid to try to move up, lest their 26 illiteracy be discovered and they lose their jobs, says Mr. Wall at Pratt & Whitney. Often, if they can't catch on quickly and keep up with everyone else, "they either quit or end up getting fired, and then they lose confidence in themselves," says Gerald Ogren, plant manager at Outboard Marine Corporation, in Lincoln, Neb.

"We're neglecting the noncollege-bound by not giving them op- 27 tions. . . . The curriculum isn't relevant to half the kids, because it's made up by college graduates who still think vocational and technical education is for problem kids," Mr. Ogren says. "The kids who do come in here with vocational training have a grasp of the fundamentals that we can really nurture."

Christian Science Monitor, March 10, 1988

ISSUE: ILLITERACY

PERSPECTIVES

1. Asimov and Miller argue that literacy is a democratic responsibility. Explain how each writer defines literacy with respect to democracy, and tell why you believe the general public will or will not accept these definitions.

2. William Raspberry supports E. D. Hirsch's claim (in Hirsch's book *Cultural Literacy: What Every American Needs to Know*) that people are functionally illiterate when they lack cultural literacy. Examine Raspberry's evidence in support of this claim. How does this evidence lead you to accept or reject the reasoning that underlies the claim?

3. Kozol confronts the reader with a staggering list of the results of illiteracy. Examine the sequence in which these results are presented and explain the sequence's support of Kozol's claim that illiteracy is a moral problem.

4. Without providing background information, Kozol makes references to Socrates, the Founding Fathers, James Madison, and the 1980 presidential election. Considering Kozol's use of these references to build his argument, identify the assumptions he makes about his readers.

5. Knobelsdorff focuses her argument on the present and future economic costs of illiteracy. Identify the cause-and-effect relationships of this problem and explain the implications the writer hopes to convey.

6. Unlike the other articles, which were written for a general public audience, Miller's article was written for an academic audience of professors. Discuss the difference in the evidence and tone Miller uses.

7. Looking at the audience for which each article was written, determine which article has the strongest logical appeal, which the strongest ethical appeal, and which the strongest emotional appeal. Defend your selection for each category.

LAWS: THE ETHICS OF FREEDOM AND PROTECTION

Physicians Ponder Role as the Agent of Death

BARBARA DOW
Writer for American Medical News

Illinois may become the fourth state in the country to execute a prisoner by lethal injection, raising once again the ethical dilemma of the physician's role in ending—rather than preserving—life. 1

Charles Walker, the 47-year-old confessed killer of a Mascoutah, Ill., couple, terminated all his appeals after the state Supreme Court upheld his sentence in 1985 and has asked that he be allowed to die. Walker is the first Illinois convict to face execution by injection since the procedure replaced the electric chair in 1983. 2

Although officials at the Illinois Dept. of Corrections have not yet decided what role physicians will play in the execution, many MDs consider the mere concept of lethal injections a misuse of biomedical knowledge and skill. 3

"It ties a medical procedure to capital punishment, and the two should in no way be linked," said Nancy Dickey, MD, chairwoman of the Council of Ethical and Judicial Affairs of the American Medical Association. 4

Since 1980, physicians have had the formal backing of AMA policy over the issue. It states that although an individual's opinion concerning capital punishment is a moral decision, "a physician as a member 5 of a profession dedicated to preserving life when there is hope of doing so should not participate in a legally authorized execution."

The AMA policy sanctions the physician's role in executions as one of determining death only, "as currently provided for by law in any situation." 6

Death pronouncements, reasoned the authors of the policy, have traditionally not been considered participation in executions and therefore are acceptable procedures in which physicians can participate, Dr. Dickey said. 7

The AMA policy came on the heels of increased activity in states to replace their modes of execution with lethal injection. 8

After the U.S. Supreme Court's decision in 1976 to uphold the constitutionality of capital punishment codes, proponents of death by lethal injection asserted that it was a less painful and a more humane way of killing someone. 9

Because of that point, they reasoned that jurors would be more likely to impose the death penalty and courts would be less likely to strike down lethal injection statutes as cruel and unusual punishment. 10

Capital punishment opponents and physicians, however, immediately objected to any attempts to disguise the execution method as a medical procedure and thus encourage juries to apply the death penalty more extensively. 11

Oklahoma and Texas were the first states to adopt lethal injection as a means of execution in 1977. 12

Twenty-five prisoners have been executed in Texas since 1982. Oklahoma's first prisoner, scheduled to be executed last month, was granted an indefinite stay of execution by the 10th District Court of Appeals hours before the execution was to take place. Three prisoners from North Carolina and one from Nevada have been executed by lethal injection since 1984. 13

An initial uproar in the Oklahoma and Texas medical communities, after lethal injection statutes in those states were adopted, forced lawmakers to abandon language that required a physician to administer the lethal dosage of barbiturates and paralytic agents. Currently, none of the 16 states that provide for death by lethal injection requires an MD to administer the fatal combination of drugs. 14

Following the precedent set by those states, the Illinois statute passed in 1983 calls for a medically trained person such as a medical technician to insert the intravenous catheter that supplies the lethal dosage. It notes that the execution must be conducted in the presence of two physicians, one of whom must pronounce death. 15

The procedure also states that a complete physical exam must be conducted before the execution date and that the drugs and dosages may be altered and administered in quantities determined by a "qualified health care person." 16

Although the Illinois law does not specifically state that a physi- 17
cian must administer the drug, many opponents, including physicians, argue that the mere presence of an MD at an execution gives the
impression of moral sanction by the profession.

"Participation [by physicians] in an execution in any manner 18
would be an unethical practice," said Alfred Kiessel, MD, chairman of
the board of the Illinois State Medical Society, adding that "participation" could range from ordering and prescribing the barbiturates to
monitoring a prisoner during the course of the execution.

As medical director of the Texas prisons during the country's 19
first execution by lethal injection in 1983, Ralph Gray, MD, was severely
criticized by the medical community for monitoring convicted mur-
derer Charlie Brooks' heartbeat during the procedure and later pronouncing him dead.

Officials also revealed that the drugs used in the execution came 20
from a pharmacy under his control and that the medical technicians
who administered the lethal chemicals were members of his staff.

Dr. Gray's critics made it clear that they did not think physicians 21
should be even peripherally involved in capital punishment.

"Hopefully physicians will have nothing to do with the [Illinois 22
execution] procedures," said Ronald Shansky, MD, medical director of
the Illinois Dept. of Corrections. An MD's presence would not be necessary, because a coroner could pronounce death, he said.

"Murdering someone is not a medical procedure," Dr. Shansky 23
said. "I was trained in medical school to protect the health and welfare
of humans. I was not trained to be a butcher."

So far, 108 men are on "Death Row" in Illinois prisons and are in 24
various stages of the complicated and lengthy appeals process.

In June a downstate Illinois judge set a Sept. 15 date for Walker's 25
execution, following the prisoner's request to terminate his appeals.

The Illinois Supreme Court vacated the execution date and sched- 26
uled a hearing instead to determine his mental competency.

Walker was sentenced to death in 1984 after pleading guilty to 27
the robbery and execution-style murder of a 25-year-old downstate
woman and her 21-year-old fiance.

If Walker eventually gets his way, he could be executed as early as 28
November or December, said officials at the State Appellate Defender's
Office.

But physicians at the Stateville correctional facilities in Joliet, 29
where the execution will be carried out, say they have no intention of
being present at the execution when it finally comes to pass.

"Executions don't fall into my job qualifications," said Jeff Styno- 30
wick, MD. "This is a difficult enough place to work in already."

Dr. Stynowick said he thought that corrections officials would 31
need to bring in medical technicians from elsewhere, noting that it

would be "absurd" to expect any of the three Stateville MDs to be involved.

Corrections officials had no comment concerning the profes- 32 sionals who would perform executions.

Even the AMA's position that an MD can be present to pro- 33 nounce the prisoner dead has drawn criticism.

"What happens when the physician finds that the prisoner is not 34 dead?" asked Howard Zonana, MD, chairman of the American Psychiatric Policy and the Law. "He is then put in a position to order that the execution continue."

If the continuous intravenous injection ends only when the 35 monitoring physician pronounces the prisoner dead, "the physician then becomes the instrument, the order to stop the lethal action," wrote Ward Casscells, MD, and William Curran in a Jan. 24, 1980, issue of *The New England Journal of Medicine*.

Lethal injection is a "more obvious application of biomedical 36 knowledge and skills than any other method of execution," Dr. Casscells and Curran wrote.

"Physician or other medical participation in carrying out a death 37 sentence by intentional, careful, skillful injection of a medically prepared substance into the veins of the prisoner seems to us to constitute a grievous expansion of medical condonation of and participation in capital punishment."

But the solution to whether a physician should participate in le- 38 thal injections is not simple. Without an MD's intervention, a prisoner may suffer more by having the procedure carried out by less competent people.

Executions to date have forced physicians to make such deci- 39 sions between their professional goals to preserve life and their desire to minimize suffering.

Dr. Gray, for example, said he was tempted to take over after 40 three non-physician employees repeatedly missed the veins in Charlie Brooks' arms, splattering blood all over the gurney that held his body. Venous cutdowns have been required in similar cases to reach the healthy veins in the arms of habitual intravenous drug users.

In another incident, the "fast-acting" lethal chemicals that are 41 supposed to cause death within 30 seconds took closer to 15 minutes to kill Texas prisoner James Autry, during which time he repeatedly complained of pain.

One physician suggested afterwards that the catheter may have 42 become clogged, prolonging Autry's death. Officials have since discovered that improperly prescribed drug dosages can make the chemicals mix together too soon, causing the solution to thicken and flow at a slower rate, which prolongs a prisoner's death.

Physicians also have noted that skill is required in determining 43 the correct dosage of chemicals to be used in executing a prisoner with a history of drug and alcohol abuse, according to publications by Amnesty International. Greater dosages of chemicals may be needed in such cases.

Because of those factors, physicians must be ready to intervene 44 when technicians have difficulty with catheterizations or drug dosages, a situation that challenges their moral and ethical position, noted Dr. Casscells and Curran. "The physician should not excape moral responsibility by ordering a subordinate to do what he or she may not properly do directly."

Anticipating that nurses would be substituted for physicians 45 who refuse to participate in lethal injections, the American Nursing Assn.'s Committee on Ethics adopted its own policy in 1983. It states that nurses' participation either directly or indirectly in legally authorized executions would be a breach of the nursing code of professional ethics.

Participation in state-sanctioned executions also is disallowed by 46 the AMA policy, which stresses that pharmacists, nurses, technicians, and other members of the healing professions are dedicated to the preservation of life, said Dr. Dickey.

The Hippocratic Oath itself provides the foundation for the AMA's 47 position: "I will use treatment to help the sick according to my ability and judgment, but never with a view to injury and wrongdoing. Neither will I administer a poison to anyone when asked to do so nor will I suggest such a course."

American Medical News, September 4, 1987

The Colorization of Films Insults Artists and Society

WOODY ALLEN
Writer, actor, and director of more than 16 films

In the world of potent self-annihilation, famine and AIDS, terrorists 1 and dishonest public servants and quack evangelists and contras and Sandinistas and cancer, does it really matter if some kid snaps on his TV and happens to see "The Maltese Falcon" in color? Especially if he can simply dial the color out and choose to view it in its original black and white?

I think it does make a difference and the ramifications of what's called colorization are not wonderful to contemplate. Simply put, the owners of thousands of classic American black and white films believe that there would be a larger public for the movies, and consequently more money, if they were reissued in color. Since they have computers that can change such masterpieces as "Citizen Kane" and "City Lights" and "It's A Wonderful Life" into color, it has become a serious problem for anyone who cares about these movies and has feelings about our image of ourselves as a culture. 2

I won't comment about the quality of the color. It's not good, but probably it will get better. Right now it's like elevator music. It has no soul. All faces are rendered with the same deadening pleasance. The choices of what colors people should be wearing or what colors rooms should be (all crucial artistic decisions in making a film) are left to caprices and speculations by computer technicians who are not qualified to make those choices. 3

Probably false, but not worth debating here, is the claim that young people won't watch black and white. I would think they would, judging from the amount of stylish music videos and MTV ads that are done in black and white, undoubtedly after market research. The fact that audiences of all ages have been watching Charlie Chaplin, Humphrey Bogart, Jimmy Stewart, Fred Astaire—in fact, all the stars and films of the so-called Golden Age of Hollywood—in black and white for decades with no diminution of joy also makes me wonder about these high claims for color. Another point the coloroids make is that one can always view the original if one prefers. The truth is, however, that in practical terms, what will happen is that the color versions will be aired while token copies of the original black and white will lie around preserved in a vault, unpromoted and unseen. 4

Another aspect of the problem that one should mention (although it is not the crucial ground on which I will make my stand) is that American films are a landmark heritage that do our nation proud all over the world, and should be seen as they were intended to be. 5

One would wince at defacing great buildings or paintings, and, in the case of movies, what began as a popular entertainment has, like jazz music, developed into a serious art form. Now, someone might ask: "Is an old Abbott and Costello movie art? Should it be viewed in the same way as 'Citizen Kane'?" The answer is that it should be protected, because all movies are entitled to their personal integrity and, after all, who knows what future generations will regard as art works of our epoch? 6

Yet another question: "Why were directors not up in arms about 7 cutting films for television or breaking them up for commercials, insulting them with any number of technical alterations to accommodate the television format?" The answer is that directors always hated these assaults on their work but were powerless to stop them. As in life, one lives with the first few wounds, because to do battle is an overwhelmingly time-consuming and pessimistic prospect.

Still, when the assaults come too often, there is a revolution. The 8
outrage of seeing one's work transformed into color is so dramatically appalling, so "obvious"—as against stopping sporadically for commercials—that this time all the directors, writers and actors chose to fight.

But let me get to the real heart of the matter and to why I think 9
the issue is not merely one that affronts the parties directly involved but has a larger meaning. What's at stake is a moral issue and how our culture chooses to define itself. No one should be able to alter an artist's work in any way whatsoever, for any reason, without the artist's consent. It's really as simple as that.

John Huston has made it clear that he doesn't want "The Maltese 10
Falcon" seen in color. This is his right as an artist and certainly must be his choice alone. Nor would I want to see my film "Manhattan" in color. Not if it would bring in 10 times the revenue. Not if all the audiences in the world begged or demanded to see it that way.

I believe the people who are coloring movies have contempt for 11
the audience by claiming, in effect, that viewers are too stupid and too insensitive to appreciate black and white photography—that they must be given, like infants or monkeys, bright colors to keep them amused.

They have contempt for the artist, caring little for the moral right 12
these directors have over their own creations.

And, finally, they have contempt for society because they help 13
define it as one that chooses to milk every last dollar out of its artists' work, even if it means mutilating the work and humiliating the culture's creative talent.

This is how we are viewed around the world and how we will be 14
viewed by future generations. Most civilized governments abroad, realizing that their society is at least as much shaped and identified by its artists as by its businessmen, have laws to protect such things from happening. In our society, merchants are willing to degrade anything or anyone so long as it brings in a financial profit.

Allowing the colorization of films is a good example of our coun- 15
try's regard for its artists, and why I think the issue of moral rights requires legislative help and protection.

The recent Federal copyright decision says that if a human being 16
uses a certain minimum amount of creativity in coloring a black and white film, the new color version is a separate work that can be copyrighted. In short, if a man colors "Citizen Kane," it becomes a new

movie that can be copyrighted. This must be changed. How? By making sure that Representative Richard A. Gephardt's film integrity bill is passed. It would legalize the moral rights of film artists and, in the process, make colorization without consent illegal.

It is, after all, a very short step to removing the score from "Gone 17 With the Wind" and replacing it with a rock score under the mistaken notion that it will render it more enjoyable to young people.

New York Times, June 28, 1987

Demise of a Daily

Why It Matters

EUGENIE DICKERSON
Free-lance writer residing in Bellevue, Washington

So what if another newspaper goes out of business? What does it matter 1 *as long as it wasn't the paper I read?*

During the past 70 years hundreds of American newspapers have 2 died, bequeathing their readerships to surviving competitors. The major cause of death has been the loss of advertising income, along with government "help," poor management, television news, and public apathy.

As recently as 1974, Chicago had four major dailies; now there 3 are two. Where the public saw four knowledgeable and thoughtful opinions, only two remain.

Yet Chicago fares better than most American cities. All but a few 4 limp along without even two actively competing newspapers. In 1954 there were 88 cities with at least two independent dailies.

Independent newspapers shine as the jewels of American cul- 5 ture. After 1690, when the first one was published, the number of independent papers in the 13 Colonies grew to 37 in 1776. By 1789, the year of the adoption of the United States Constitution, there were over a hundred.

On a visit to Massachusetts La Rochefoucauld wrote, "All these 6 people busy themselves much with politics, and from the landlord down to the housemaid they all read two newspapers a day."

In 1789 there was one independent newspaper publishing daily 7 for every 39,000 people. Today, there is only one daily for every 138,000 people.

And chains like Gannett and Knight-Ridder have bought most of 8 the dailies. Those papers survive under their old names, but surrender a measure of editorial policy to the chains.

In turn, the directorates of the 25 largest newspaper companies 9 are interlocked by most of their members with institutions the papers cover.

The Newspaper Preservation Act of 1970 entered the federal 10 government into the problem. In dozens of two-paper communities where one of the dailies claimed to be in danger of financial failure, the Justice Department exempted partial mergers from antitrust laws.

In some of these partial mergers, buyers had come forward for 11 the red-ink papers, saying they would be able to run the same presses at a profit. Their offers and competition itself were rejected.

Under the new law, production, business, advertising, and cir- 12 culation functions of two dailies combine. These joint operating agreements state that news and editorial departments are to remain separate. But can an audience really expect the same director to produce different interpretations of one drama?

The hometown gazette is less and less a local product. Not only 13 are national news, columns, features, and comic strips syndicated, but even editorials can be bought from national syndicates.

Americans who prefer to shop for their news electronically find 14 the market sewn up by a handful of national networks.

But what's wrong with mergers? After all, larger organizations 15 *make better, more economical use of facilities and personnel, don't they?*

Competition sharpens quality and cuts cost. The American auto 16 industry declined as the large number of major manufacturers whittled down to three. Now foreign competition is spurring the domestic industry to improvements and efficiency.

Consider the possibility of every newspaper in the country being 17 owned by three major organizations.

Consolidation drives up prices in the long run, for one thing. In 18 Seattle, for example, advertising rates jumped after the two independent dailies, the Times and the Post-Intelligencer, obtained a partial monopoly under a joint operating agreement.

The many small, independent restaurants and clothing manu- 19 facturers keep competition keen in those industries. Prices would soar and quality dive if all restaurants were enfranchised by a few huge corporations or all retail clothing were produced by a few central factories.

Most Americans have heard how expensive and shoddy the retail 20 clothing is in the Soviet Union. A monopolized clothing industry would be the same here. So would a monopolized newspaper industry.

Smaller businesses respond more to their customers. The larger a 21
newspaper, the less reason it has to cover readers' concerns adequately.

Let us not forget the one organization richer and stronger than 22
any of the newspapers and by nature desirous of ever-increasing
power: government. It is the federal government that approves joint
operating agreements, undoubtedly with an ax to grind.

Government would be most happy if there were fewer news- 23
papers. Remaining newspapers would be more dependent on government news releases and interviews, thus pressured toward an approv-
ing editorial stance on every government action.

But does it really matter if a couple of essays on the editorial page 24
of a large newspaper present a narrowed perspective compared with
the editorials of several smaller, more independent papers?

The most serious drawback to the newspaper consolidation 25
trend is the compromise of viewpoints. On the editorial page of a
newspaper, the reader used to find a clear opinion on some of the important problems of the day.

As newspapers combined, sales aimed at larger, disparate reader- 26
ships. The order of the day has become generally agreeable editorials,
as inoffensive and unenlightening as politicians' campaign speeches.

Yet the editorial page isn't the only instrument of editorial policy. 27
The slant, weight, and color of all parts of the newspaper reflect editorial policy, though less directly.

Slant is the difference between the headline "Union Succumbs to 28
Overwhelming Pressure" and another headline on the same labor dispute from a different angle, "Company Routs Union."

Weight is the difference between printing the labor-dispute story 29
on the front page and printing it at the bottom of Page 8. The newspaper could publish a long, detailed article or a short onceover.

Variations and follow-ups could keep an issue hot day after day. 30
The paper might also choose not to publish the information at all, diminishing its importance to zero.

Color is interesting vocabulary, vivid character, and grace of style. 31
The publisher's pet topics get the most colorful writers.

Why shouldn't newspapers just print the straight facts throughout 32
the paper? Shouldn't we abolish opinion, slant, weight, and color, and
choose news strictly according to its value to the public?

Experience teaches that logical and good individuals may arrive 33
at different conclusions about what is of public value. Opinion will be
there whether we like it or not.

It is this honest diversity of thought that breeds cultural develop- 34
ment. Out of one naturally occurs the other. That competing newspapers differ in thinking indicates a healthy society.

John Milton said that differences of opinion are an integral part 35 of the desire to learn. Intelligence isn't something grown during the school years that remains static throughout life; rather, intelligence fades if it isn't challenged by independent opinions. We need the voices of independent newspapers to encourage the intelligence of the adult population—the electorate.

A variety of opinions should be considered exciting, not threat- 36 ening. Mark Twain said that differences of opinion are what make horse races.

What can Americans do to support a varied press? 37

Lawmakers should review the Newspaper Preservation Act for 38 possible repeal, because publishers might sharpen their business skills if they weren't assured of a free lunch.

Journalists can harness their literary skills to tease the public to 39 appreciate the advantages of learning several opinions. Writers might also replace their greed for the salary and prestige of larger papers with the pride of working for smaller, bolder organizations.

To do their part, advertisers might allocate more of their budgets 40 to smaller newspapers. Businesses now tend to spend dispropor- tionate funds on larger-circulation papers. Advertisers need to stand firmer against threats of reprisal from larger papers for splitting their budgets among competitors.

Public awareness is essential. If Americans will discourage gov- 41 ernment interference, support competing newspapers, send letters to the editors, follow the advertising, and discuss recent news with fam- ily, friends, and associates, our free press will surely thrive.

Christian Science Monitor, February 25, 1988

Air Travelers Must Be Told of Risks

RICHARD COHEN
Columnist for the Washington Post

On Dec. 5, the government received a tip that a bomb would be placed 1 on a Pan Am flight from Frankfurt to the United States. On Dec. 7, the Federal Aviation Administration warned airports, carriers and Ameri- can embassies abroad about the terrorist threat. On Dec. 8, I boarded a Pan Am flight from Frankfurt to New York.

After every airline disaster, we hear about the "almosts." These 2
are the people who "almost" boarded the plane, who got delayed in
traffic, who got bumped at the last moment, who lost their passport or,
for some other reason, failed to make the doomed flight. I am not one
of those.

I raise a different issue: Should I have been informed of the 3
heightened peril? I wonder why embassy employees in Moscow were
told of the terrorist threat in a bulletin board notice ("Post leaves to the
discretion of the individual traveler on altering personal travel. . . .")—
why, in short, they had information that was denied me. I wonder because I consider my life to be as valuable as theirs.

And I make the same claim for the 258 people on Pan Am Flight 4
103. Some of them were people of note—a high U.N. official, for instance, and someone from the Justice Department. But we are not in
the business of playing airborne triage: deciding whose life is worth
saving and whose is not. If State Department personnel were told to
use their own "discretion" when traveling back to the States, so should
have everyone else.

It's easy to bash the State Department, but three U.S. diplomats 5
were on Pan Am 103. Ironically, they must have breathed a sigh of relief
when their plane took off. At last, they were safe.

For failing to inform the public of the terrorist threat, the govern- 6
ment has explanations aplenty. It says that such tips are routine—
maybe as many as one a day. But if that was the case, why was this one
posted in Moscow for the benefit of American diplomats?

It seems this particular tip was being treated with more se- 7
riousness than usual.

The government also says—and President-elect Bush affirms— 8
that publicizing such tips would cripple the U.S. airline industry. They
have a point. It is the United States, not, say, Switzerland, that is a terrorist target. Knowing of a terrorist threat and given the choice between flying Pan Am (or TWA) and Swissair, who would not choose
Swissair? I would. For one thing, the food is better.

And what about our anti-terrorist effort? By publicizing tips, the 9
government not only alerts the public but the terrorists as well. They
might abandon an operation they might otherwise be caught attempting—and, in the process, search out the informant.

Pan Am, the U.S. government and the German government say 10
that security was tightened at Frankfurt. Not that I could see. This
particular traveler breezed through security. My carry-on bags were
X-rayed, but not searched. As for the luggage I checked, at no time before the flight did I have to identify my bags. This is one way to ensure
that no one checks a bag and then fails to take the plane.

So I sit here, happy to be visiting my parents for the holidays and 11
celebrating my father's 80th birthday. As a journalist, I recognize the

dilemmas that face the government and the airlines. Given the silly bravado of my profession, I might have flown Pan Am from Frankfurt to New York anyway. But the choice would have been mine.

The passengers on Pan Am Flight 103 were given no such choice. 12 They were not told of the tip, that security had been heightened, that U.S. Embassy employees in Moscow were given information that they did not have. The conclusion is inescapable: Some lives were valued over others. The functioning, even the profitability, of the airlines was placed over human life.

The government, no matter what its motives, is guilty of arro- 13 gance—and maybe negligence too. The questions it has to deal with are difficult beyond comprehension. But the most difficult question of all now comes from the loved ones of those who died in Pan Am 103: Why weren't the passengers told?

Washington Post, December 28, 1988

Smoking and Responsibility

CARL T. ROWAN
Syndicated columnist

Even though I detest tobacco smoke, I found myself cheering Tuesday 1 when the tobacco industry won a big one in the 1st Circuit Court of Appeals in Boston.

What the court said, in simple terms, is that the heirs of a man 2 who smoked heavily for 23 years and died of cancer cannot get $3 million from Liggett & Myers Tobacco Co. on grounds that the company did not give the deceased man adequate warning about the dangers of smoking cigarettes.

My regret is that the court backed the tobacco industry on a le- 3 galism rather than take the common-sense approach to justice by saying, "Anyone who has smoked as many as three or four packs of cigarettes a day for 23 years, and did not know he was imperiling his life, had to be hiding under a tobacco plant." Who smokes, abuses drugs, runs up his cholesterol level, or his weight, without doctors giving ample warning at some time over two decades?

What the appeals court said to the heirs of Joseph C. Palmer of 4 Newton, Mass., who died of cancer seven years ago, is that the federally mandated warnings on cigarette packages are ample and that no matter what state officials want, the federal warnings are overriding and protect tobacco companies from product-liability litigation of the sort before the court.

What I want the judges to say is that there are areas of life in which individuals must accept responsibility for their own behavior. Manufacturers ought to pay dearly if they make a toy that blows up in a child's face, an automobile that races out of control when put in reverse, or a nightgown that erupts in flames while the wearer is merely standing in front of a fireplace.

But there must be common-sense limits to this business of making someone else liable for any individual's recklessness—or stupidity. The courts ought to make this clear, and in doing so rein in the vast army of lawyers who see "product liability" in just about every personal tragedy.

I have written before that it is ludicrous to think the host of a cocktail party of, say, 100 people can be held liable for an automobile accident involving one guest who may have had a drink too many at the party, or a few too many before arriving at the party. Owners of bars and restaurants cannot reasonably be expected to know when the alcohol blood level of a guest has passed the point where the state says that person is "driving under the influence" of beer, booze or wine.

I have this weakness for M&Ms candy. There's nothing on the wrapper that says that if I let them melt in my mouth until my sweet tooth is satiated, my other teeth may fall out. But out there somewhere is a lawyer who would haul any decayed molars into court and say that the manufacturer of those little chocolate gems owes me a few million bucks.

There must be a thousand lawyers salivating at the prospect of suing condom manufacturers on the grounds that their client got AIDS practicing unsafe sex only because the condom was defective.

In this society of speedy and all-encompassing communications, everyone of reasonable intelligence knows that smoking cigarettes, abusing drugs, drinking excessive amounts of booze and perhaps even eating 14 eggs and seven steaks a week can be hazardous to health. I find it revoltingly unjust that anyone who flouts the warnings should be able to go into court and ask for a fortune from whichever manufacturer made the product that the victim used in outlandish excess.

Washington Post, 1987

The Wiretapping Law Needs Some Renovation

LINDA GREENHOUSE
Writer for the New York Times

Laws, like technology, can grow obsolete. That is particularly true of 1
laws that deal with technology. It is only 18 years since Congress
passed the statute that prohibits tapping a telephone without a search
warrant. But that law protects an ever-shrinking portion of a communications universe that has grown to include electronic mail, cellular
telephones and other devices unknown to its drafters in 1968.

Now Congress is moving to narrow that gap with a bill that 2
cleared a House of Representatives subcommittee last month and may
reach the floor within the next few weeks. The progress of the measure
is the result of an unusual coalition of civil liberties and industry interests, both of whom see much to gain from protecting new kinds of
communication.

The 1968 wiretap law, which the Electronic Communication Pri- 3
vacy Act of 1986 would amend, protects "aural" communications transmitted by wire and capable of being understood by the human ear,
but technology that falls outside that definition is either clearly un-
protected or in a legal limbo.

Electronic mail—that is, messages sent between computers 4
within a company or from one computer to another over a commercial
network—is actually more vulnerable to official or competitive snoop-
ing than the old-fashioned telephone system. While telephone companies keep records of the numbers their subscribers dial, they do
not record the conversations. But electronic mail services routinely
keep "back-up" copies of all messages as protection against computer
problems.

Cellular telephones, which are used primarily in cars and oper- 5
ate by radio signal, are also more vulnerable than ordinary phones that
rely on wires. Conversations involving them can be plucked out of the
air with scanning devices available for about $600.

Both of the new technologies are growing rapidly. There are 6
350,000 cellular telephones in use, and the number of messages sent
by electronic mail, now in the hundreds of millions annually, is expected to reach the billions within a few years.

If Congress does not act, the courts will eventually sort out on a 7 case-by-case basis the level of protection these new devices will receive. Representative Robert W. Kastenmeier, the chairman of the Subcommittee on Courts, Civil Liberties and the Administration of Justice, which voted unanimously in favor of the new measure two weeks ago, says Congress has to choose between making policy and abdicating that role to the judicial and executive branches. Mr. Kastenmeier, a Wisconsin Democrat who has been at the forefront of this issue for years, sponsored the bill now under consideration.

Its sponsors in the Senate, where hearings were held late last 8 year, are Senators Patrick J. Leahy, Democrat of Vermont, and Charles McC. Mathias Jr., Republican of Maryland.

Under the bill, law enforcement officials would need warrants 9 demonstrating probable cause to believe that a search would reveal evidence of a crime before they could intercept electronic mail less than six months old. Most users of such services keep messages only a few months. The bill makes it somewhat easier to obtain older messages, requiring a subpoena or court order based on reason to believe that information "relevant to legitimate law enforcement purposes" would be found.

The bill clarifies the wiretap act to specify that cellular tele- 10 phones are to be treated like their traditional counterparts, with warrants required to intercept conversations. But the measure would not protect cordless telephones, on the theory that users are aware of how easily those conversations can be picked up by radio and do not expect privacy.

The Justice Department originally opposed the bill, which ini- 11 tially included limits on tracking devices and other surveillance technology that Federal authorities use regularly. Since those sections were dropped, the department has supported the measure.

It is also backed by manufacturers and trade associations. For 12 them, privacy is a pocketbook issue, a question of competitive position. They are afraid that potential customers, with many options to choose from, may shy from new technologies that offer less protection than older ones. For the American Civil Liberties Union, a major force behind the bill, the commitment is philosophical rather than economic. "This is a very good bill," said Jerry Berman, the head of the union's Privacy Technology Project, who worked to bring the business groups together. "It demonstrates that you can put together a privacy coalition and make it work."

New York Times, May 17, 1987

ISSUE: LAWS

PERSPECTIVES

1. In explaining the AMA policy on the role of physicians in legal executions, Barbara Dow distinguishes between a *moral decision* on an issue and the *ethics* of a profession. The writers of several of the readings in this section also use *morals* and *ethics* as distinct terms. Explain the difference between the two concepts as presented in two of the articles.

2. Often a law that protects the rights of one group of people may restrict the freedom of another group. Illustrate how this dilemma is the basis for argument in at least three of the issues presented in this section.

3. While all laws ultimately are expressions of our culture, Dickerson and Allen use our cultural development and global image as a basis for their arguments. Explain their reasoning and evaluate its effectiveness in appealing to the intended audiences.

4. These articles on laws represent several different stages of the law-making process: initiating (Cohen), implementing (Rowan), updating (Dow and Greenhouse), and repealing (Dickerson and Allen). From these examples, explain what the main purpose would be for constructing an argument at each stage and consequently what appeal would be most effective to emphasize.

5. Both Cohen and Dickerson argue for our freedom of choice; in both cases having that choice depends on our access to information. Reconstruct the reasoning these writers use to convince their readers that they are not receiving the information they need to exercise freedom of choice.

6. Explain how each of the arguments in the readings implicitly or explicitly demonstrate the need for individual responsibility to ensure the freedom and protection of our laws.

7. Several of the writers use analogies to clarify points in their arguments: Allen compares colorization to elevator music, Rowan compares his obsession with M&Ms to smoking, Dickerson compares the consolidation of daily newspapers to the decline of the car industry. What effect are these analogies likely to have on the readers? Will they have the intended result?

ARGUMENTS FOR INVESTIGATION

Community Service as Punishment: A Practice That Needs Repeal

There Ought to Be a Law (you choose an issue)

Taking Away Drivers' Licenses May Lower High-School Dropout Rates But Won't Make People More Literate

Protect Patriotism: Repeal Flag Burning

VIETNAM: LESSONS LEARNED

Lessons from a Lost War

GEORGE J. CHURCH
Senior writer for Time

. . . The most bedeviling of all the dilemmas raised by Viet Nam concerns the issue of public support. On the surface it might seem to be no issue at all: just about everybody agrees that Viet Nam proved the futility of trying to fight a war without a strong base of popular support. But just how strong exactly? Rostow argues that the only U.S. war fought with tremendous public backing was World War II.[1] He points out that World War I "brought riots and splits," the War of 1812 was "vastly divisive" and even during the War of Independence one-third of the population was pro-revolution, one-third pro-British and one-third "out to lunch." Rostow proposes a 60-25-15 split as about the best that can be expected now in support of a controversial policy: a bipartisan 60% in favor, 25% against and 15% out to lunch.

A strong current of opinion holds that Lyndon Johnson guaranteed a disastrously low level of support by getting into a long, bloody war without ever admitting (perhaps even to himself) the extent of the commitment he was making. Colonel Summers, who considers Viet Nam a just war that the U.S. could and should have won, insists that any similar conflict in the future ought to be "legitimized" by a formal, congressional declaration of war.[2] Says Summers: "All of America's previous wars were fought in the heat of passion. Viet Nam was fought in cold blood, and that was intolerable to the American people. In an immediate crisis the tendency of the American people is to rally around the flag. But God help you if it goes beyond that and you haven't built a base of support."

> "In the final analysis it is their war. . . . We can help them
> . . . but they have to win it, the people of Viet Nam."
>
> *Kennedy, 1963*
>
> "We are not about to send American boys 10,000 miles away
> to do what Asian boys ought to be doing for themselves."
>
> *Johnson, 1964*
>
> "Hell no, we won't go!"
>
> *Antiwar chant, 1965*
>
> "I'm not going to be the first president who loses a war."
>
> *Richard Nixon, 1969*
>
> "Peace is at hand."
>
> *Henry Kissinger, 1972*

At the other extreme, former Secretary of State Dean Rusk de- 3
fends to this day the Johnson Administration's effort "to do in cold
blood at home what we were asking men to do in hot blood out in the
field." Rusk points out that the war began with impressive public and
congressional support. It was only in early 1968, says Rusk, that "many
at the grass-roots level came to the opinion that if we didn't give them
some idea when this war would come to an end, we might as well
chuck it." The decisive factor probably was the defection of middle-
class youths and their parents, a highly articulate segment that saw an
endless war as a personal threat—though in fact the burden of the
draft fell most heavily on low-income youths.

Paradoxically, though, Johnson might well have been able to win 4
public support for a bigger war than he was willing to fight. As late as
February 1968, at the height of the Tet offensive, one poll found 53%
favoring stronger U.S. military action, even at the risk of a clash with
the Soviet Union or China, vs. only 24% opting to wind down the war.
Rusk insists that the Administration was right not to capitalize on this
sentiment. Says he: "We made a deliberate decision not to whip up
war fever in this country. We did not have parades and movie stars selling war bonds, as we did in World War II. We thought that in a nuclear
world it is dangerous for a country to become too angry too quickly.
That is something people will have to think about in the future."

It certainly is. Viet Nam veterans argue passionately that Ameri- 5
cans must never again be sent out to die in a war that "the politicians
will not let them win." And by win they clearly mean something like a
World War II–style triumph ending with unconditional surrender.
One lesson of Viet Nam, observes George Christian, who was L.B.J.'s
press secretary, is that "it is very tough for Americans to stick in long
situations. We are always looking for a quick fix." But nuclear missiles

make the unconditional-surrender kind of war an anachronism. Viet Nam raised, and left unsolved for the next conflict, the question posed by Lincoln Bloomfield, an M.I.T. professor of political science who once served on Jimmy Carter's National Security Council: "How is it that you can 'win' so that when you leave two years later you do not lose the country to those forces who have committed themselves to victory at any cost?"

It is a question that cannot be suppressed much longer. Ameri- 6 cans have a deep ambiguity toward military power: they like to feel strong, but often shy away from actually using that strength. There is a growing recognition, however, that shunning all battles less easily winnable than Grenada would mean abandoning America's role as a world power, and that, in turn, is no way to assure the nation's survival as a free society. Americans, observes Secretary of State [George P.] Schultz, "will always be reluctant to use force. It is the mark of our decency." But, he adds, "a great power cannot free itself so easily from the burden of choice. It must bear responsibility for the consequences of its inaction as well as for the consequences of its action."

Time, April 15, 1985

Editor's Notes

1. Rostow, Lyndon Johnson's national security adviser.
2. Col. Harry G. Summers, Jr., author of *On Strategy: A Critical Analysis of the Vietnam War,* from which an excerpt appears in this section of readings.

The Stab-in-the-Back Legend and the Vietnam War

JEFFREY P. KIMBALL
Jeffrey Kimball teaches U.S. military, diplomatic, and peace history at Miami University. He has published articles in numerous scholarly journals, contributed to the Encyclopedia of Southern History *and* Great Events in American History, *and serves as associate editor of the journal* Diplomatic History.

Originating during the Vietnam War in the debate over U.S. policy and 1 strategy, the stab-in-the-back theme developed into a full-fledged explanation for American defeat after the war ended and as another, related debate unfolded over the causes of failure and the future of policy. The existence of the legend—which condemns the antiwar movement, civilian strategists, Democratic presidents, Congress, leftists, liberals, and the press for snatching defeat from the jaws of victory—has not gone unnoticed. Several observers have made passing reference to an approximate similarity between the response of some Americans to defeat in that war and the response of some Germans to defeat in World War I—the best-known manifestation of the legend.[1]

A nearly pure form of the theory is represented in the writings 2 and statements of Richard Nixon, Ronald Reagan, William Westmoreland, U.S. Grant Sharp, the John Birch Society, writers for *National Review*, and Accuracy in Media—to name some of the most conspicuous examples. All have a tenacious commitment to the containment doctrine, though some more than others; and all blame the press, the antiwar movement, leftists, liberals, Democratic presidents, Congress, and civilian strategy intellectuals for the defeat in Vietnam. As they see it, the war can best be understood as a war of aggression instigated by world communism, with the "nation" of North Vietnam as the instrument of the aggression against the "nation" of South Vietnam. They agree that the war aim of effecting the independence of the Republic of Vietnam was correct, but some question whether it was the right war in the right place at the right time.[2] All agree that, once committed, the United States should have pursued it to a victorious conclusion, though Nixon has some reservations on this score.

Almost exclusively emphasizing military force over other factors, 3 these stab-in-the-back advocates claim that the war could have been won if the correct strategy had been followed and if certain of the civilian strategists had stood by South Vietnamese allies and allowed the U.S. military to fight the kind of war they were most experienced with. This would have involved calling up reserves and using more force, especially bombing the North more heavily and sooner; mining Haiphong Harbor; destroying bridges to China; removing target restrictions in general; attacking "sanctuaries"; and invading the North and stopping "infiltration" from that area. Presidents, and especially the Democratic ones, they argue, pursued incorrect strategies and were overly concerned with politics, the achievement of domestic programs, the threat of Chinese and Soviet intervention, and world opinion.

Furthermore, they maintain, if the will of the American people 4 had not been undermined by antiwar activists, students, professors, movie stars, and the press (notably during the Tet offensive), and if Congress had not had its share of critics and also lost its nerve after 1973, there would not have been the confusion that characterized civilian leadership. Nor would the morale of the armed forces have been lowered. Home-front criticism and turmoil had a particularly adverse effect on the army's efficiency and, in addition, encouraged the enemy to persevere. Losing the war was a terrible blow to the United States, and the Vietnam syndrome now threatens its great-power credibility.

Staunchest Proponents: Reagan, Westmoreland

While sharing a general perspective, the specific arguments and claims 5 of the stab-in-the-back pleaders differ in emphasis and on minor details. Reagan and Westmoreland, for example, are probably among the purest and staunchest proponents of the thesis. The president's criticism of so-called back-stabbers has a long pedigree, dating to the Vietnam War era, when he alternately and contradictorily referred to antiwar demonstrators as "Communists," "cowardly little Fascist bands," and instruments of an "international conspiracy"; he also criticized the Johnson administration for sending "its young men to fight and die in a war the government is afraid to let them win."

In the postwar period before his selection Reagan repeated ear- 6 lier themes, maintaining that more B-52 bombings could have prevented defeat, accusing Congress of acting irresponsibly and of having "blood on its hands" for failing to support a stronger military effort and for tying President Nixon's hands with the War Powers Act, and blaming the "liberal press" for undermining the will of the people to support "wars of the Vietnam type . . . in the defense of freedom and our own country."[3]

. . . General Westmoreland, who believes that "our Achilles' heel 7 is our resolve"[4] and that the enemy won "the war politically in Washington," blames a "no-win policy" on partisan politicians who accommodated "a misguided minority opposition . . . masterfully manipulated by Hanoi and Moscow."[5] The former commander of Military Assistance Command Vietnam is probably most critical of two groups: "vocal antiwar elements" for rebuking the military, encouraging the enemy, and weakening congressional resolve; and the media for the impact of its "no-holds-barred," misleading, and defeatest reporting upon "timid" Washington officials and the public. He also indicts the Johnson administration, civilian strategists, diplomats, intellectuals, reformers, and Congress for faulty strategies, weak wills, and expedient policies, all of which had the effect of prolonging and losing the war.[6] In the end, "our erstwhile honorable country betrayed and deserted the Republic of Vietnam. . . . It was a shabby performance by America, a blemish on our history and a possible blight on our future. Our credibility has been damaged."[7] . . .

Dissenters from the Theory

Strategy

In general, the claim of stab-in-the-back theorists that victory was pos- 8 sible amounts to speculation founded upon hypothetical strategic scenarios, with "victory" understood to mean a military one. In particular, it is by no means certain that invasions of North Vietnam, Laos, and Cambodia, or the cutting of supply routes to the South, or heavier bombing of the North much earlier than 1972 would have "won" the war for the United States—even if those steps had been feasible.[8]

The establishment of a military cordon across the South/North 9 Vietnamese border would have required the sending of many more American troops, besides resulting in an expansion of the war. An invasion of North Vietnam would have meant more American troops, a widened war, and (as all the U.S. presidents feared) the possible intervention of the Soviet Union and China. Had it been logistically possible, the earlier and heavier bombing of North Vietnam might also have brought on Soviet or Chinese intervention. And even if not, destruction through heavier bombing would still have left the United States with the problem of "pacifying" the country.

As it happened, wartime bombing seems at best to have enabled 10 the United States to stalemate the war and postpone the end. The bombings of 1972 did not produce victorious results, and their consequences could be interpreted to demonstrate that, despite the enormous expenditure of American armaments, the other side was shaken but undaunted, with its political influence in the South Vietnamese countryside enlarged. The heavy bombing of the North, while physically destructive, was politically counterproductive.[9] Hawk and dove critics alike, moreover, pointed out not only that bombing was cost-ineffective but also that a greater escalation of it or of troop strength was logistically infeasible and undesirable in relation to their perceptions of America's global commitments.[10]

It is rather ludicrous to argue in any event that the military strat- 11 egy pursued was one of gradualism, a concept that makes sense only in terms of American superpower potential. The dropping of several times the tonnage of bombs used in World War II, the introduction of 530,000 American troops in three years, the employment of tens of thousands of other "free world" troops, the creation of a large South Vietnamese army, and the employment of massive firepower and chemical weapons did not add up to a strategy of mere *gradualism*. The term fails to capture the reality and immensity of the American way of "capital-intensive" war.[11] Many critics argue that greater destruction would have caused an even greater erosion of the moral and political standing of the United States in the eyes of the world and its own people, a not inconsequential price to pay for hypothetical victory.

From a different but related perspective, the war was lost because [12] the U.S. officials who waged it had not even learned the lessons of failed strategic bombing campaigns in previous wars and failed interventions in past revolutions; they did not understand its political, social, nationalistic, cultural, and revolutionary nature. By placing an excessive reliance on military methods and power, they revealed the strategic bankruptcy of "Americanizing" the war. Even before Americanization, their counter-insurgency approach was half-hearted, poorly coordinated, misguided, and overly military.[12]

Civilian Interference

With respect to the charge of *excessive* civilian interference, General [13] Kinnard maintains

> There was not *enough* civilian participation in terms of asking the big questions about what we were really doing in Vietnam. In part, this was a matter of personality. . . . In part, it was also the "big war" mentality—let the military run it—in what was a very political affair indeed. Most of all, it was a lack of communication between civilians and military.

Moreover, the "can do" military ethos inhibited practical assessments [13] of what was possible and what was not.[13] It would be simplistic to argue that the U.S. military command alone was responsible for the American failure in Vietnam, but it is nevertheless true that there were serious deficiencies in leadership, management, manpower policy, morale, tactics, and strategy attributable to the military command.[14]

The Press

The press did influence public opinion, but it was often the servant of [14] the state, especially in the war's early stages, when it generally supported cold war visions and Third World interventions. Although both the print and broadcast media did write about and televise scenes of the carnage, the media told of and broadcast far fewer of the horrors than actually occurred. Editors of national organizations, moreover, often censored stories from the battle zone.

Throughout the conflict, the government tried to manipulate [15] and pressure the press to hew to the administration line. During the Johnson years, for example, the administration persuaded "front" groups of distinguished citizens to profess support for the war.[15] During the Nixon watch, then Vice President Spiro Agnew verbally flayed the media. For its part, the press was far from monolithic; many, if not most, local newspapers and television stations, for example, editorialized in favor of the war.[16] Eventually—at least by 1968—the press had to come to grips with and report some of the tragic realities of the war.[17]

Even if the press distorted the war coverage—and this is subjec- 16 tive—it is another thing to say that such reportage undermined the people's support of the war, and that the weakening of public support caused American leaders to pursue a no-win policy. Some analysts argue that dinnertime television-news coverage inured American viewers to the bloodshed, numbing them into acquiescence.[18] In any case, the people have a right to decide to fight wars or not and to know what is being done in their name.

Antiwar Protest

Both the nature and degree of influence of the antiwar movement on 17 the prosecution of the war are difficult issues to assess. Analyses of its impact range from the view that the movement was counterproductive, having the effect of increasing popular support for the war,[19] to the stab-in-the-back notion that it encouraged and was even inspired by the enemy, undermining the will and ability of the American people and government to wage and win the war.

The claim that the movement was counterproductive is most 18 probably overstated, fails to take the complexity of the issues into account, begs empirical proof, and contradicts common sense, anecdotal evidence, personal experience, and the testimony of the war wagers. At the other extreme, the charge of foreign manipulation is groundless. Despite vigorous and sustained efforts, the government itself was never able to demonstrate that the antiwar opposition was inspired or controlled by international Communists or anyone else.[20] On the issue of whether antiwar activity encouraged the enemy, one scholar, generally unsympathetic to the antiwar movement, suggests that while it probably encouraged the Vietnamese, "the crucial consideration . . . is not whether the war protest was encouraging to the Communists but whether that encouragement was important to their ability to continue their war effort."[21] He and others deny its importance and point instead to the psychological commitment of the Vietnamese to the nationalistic struggle, their willingness to endure heavy losses, and the greater interest of the Democratic Republic of Vietnam and the National Liberation Front in South Vietnamese politics rather than American politics. Other causes of American failure include the difficult terrain, flawed strategy, and the limits of military force in revolutionary wars.[22]

Scholars sympathetic with the antiwar movement maintain that 19 it and other "rebellions" of the era had a "direct veto power" over the ability of the government to escalate the war.[23] Although they thereby provide grist for the mill of the stab-in-the-back accusers, these scholars argue from the point of view that antiwar protest—and protest in general—reflected the problems of American society and the general unpopularity of a senseless and immoral war in Southeast Asia: the war was but a symptom of the contradictions of U.S. government policies, and protest the cure. To some, the protesters deserve credit for saving American and Vietnamese lives and for stopping the war and should not cower and recant in the face of right-wing criticism.[24] Other analysts, however, regret the influence of the "romantic" elements in the movement.[25] The antiwar opposition was a home-front, overwhelmingly nonviolent "guerrilla army"; it achieved no decisive victories but nevertheless ate away at the government's position, gradually wearing it down.

Yet other sympathetic scholars hedge their assessment. Charles 20 DeBenedetti concludes:

> [The] antiwar opposition performed two vital functions. First, it produced awareness of an alternative America that stripped away through dissent and resistance the rational, moral, and political legitimacy of Washington's war in Indochina. Second, it provided . . . a respectable haven for those many Americans who shifted against the war in the late winter of 1968. . . .[26] The dissidents did not stop the war. But they made it stoppable.[27]

From this perspective, the antiwar movement was a slap-in-the-face of the government, not a stab-in-the-back of the armed forces or the nation.

Although the true impact of the antiwar movement on policy is 21 far from certain,[28] it seems safe to say that the argument of the stab-in-the-back purveyors is seriously wanting. Its perspective on the role of the opposition is flawed from the outset, for it fails to appreciate the war itself as the driving force of domestic reactions. The history of the period reveals that the war gave rise to antiwar protest, which grew as the war widened. Even though the heterogeneous antiwar "movement" originated with a few core peace groups, they were of diverse origins and followed different agendas. As the war escalated, their attention focused increasingly on it, and the opposition in general grew. The movement evolved with fits and starts to encompass many different elements, united in opposition to the war but at odds on solutions and tactics. The opposition included pre–Vietnam-era peace activists; religious, secular, liberal, and radical pacifists; civil rights activists; the old and new Left; church groups; disaffected cold war and antimilitarist liberals; students; intellectuals; the politically conscious counterculture; politicians; portions of labor and business; soldiers; and, eventually, the nonactivist majority of the American people. Viewed developmentally, it was fundamentally the nature of the struggle and the failure of the war itself that produced disaffection. Although it exerted a powerful influence on popular and elite opinion, the peace movement alone did not give rise to weariness with America's longest war but was itself a symptom of it.

Notes

1. See Richard Dean Burns and Milton Leitenberg, eds., *The Wars in Vietnam, Cambodia and Laos, 1945–1982: A Bibliographic Guide* (Santa Barbara, Calif.: ABC-Clio Information Services, 1984), p. 141; Marvin E. Gettleman et al., eds., *Vietnam and America: A Documented History* (New York: Grove Press, 1985), p. xv; George C. Herring, "American Strategy in Vietnam: The Postwar Debate," *Military Affairs* 46, 2 (April 1982): n. 8; Guenter Lewy, *America in Vietnam* (New York: Oxford University Press, 1978), p. vi; Evan Thomas, "West Point Makes a Comeback," *Time*, 4 November 1985, p. 32.
2. William C. Westmoreland, "Vietnam in Perspective," *Military Review* 59 (January 1979): p. 35, and "The Handling of the Vietnam Episode Was a Shameful National Blunder," (Louisville) *Courier-Journal*, 26 March 1978, pp. D-1, D-3; Richard M. Nixon, *The Real War* (New York: Warner Books, 1980), pp. 100–102.
3. Quoted in Ronnie Dugger, *On Reagan: The Man and His Presidency* (New York: McGraw-Hill, 1983), pp. 240, 244, 343–349, 512–514.
4. Quoted in Robert Pisor, *The End of the Line: The Siege of Khe Sanh* (New York: Ballantine, 1983), p. 50.
5. Quoted in Walter LaFeber, "The Last War, the Next War, and the New Revisionists," *Democracy* 1, 1 (January 1981): p. 93.
6. William C. Westmoreland, *A Soldier Reports* (Garden City, N.Y.: Doubleday, 1976), pp. 357–358, 410; "If We'd Kept Pressure On, We'd Have Won It," *USA Today*, 18 April 1985, p. 11A; Westmoreland, "Vietnam in Perspective," pp. 34–42; Westmoreland, "Handling of the Vietnam Episode," pp. D-1, D-3.
7. Westmoreland, "Vietnam in Perspective," p. 34.
8. See James Clay Thompson, *Rolling Thunder: Understanding Policy and Program Failure* (Chapel Hill: University of North Carolina Press, 1980); "The Air War in North Vietnam, 1965–1968," chap. 1 of *Senator Gravel Edition, Pentagon Papers*, vol. 4 (Boston: Beacon Press, 1971); and see esp. "The JASON Summer Study Reports," ibid., pp. 115–124; Raphael Littauer and Norman Uphoff, eds., Air War Study Group, Cornell University, *The Air War in Indochina*, rev. ed. (Boston: Beacon Press, 1972), pp. 35–36ff.
9. Guenter Lewy, "Some Political-Military Lessons of the Vietnam War," *Parameters* 14, 1 (Spring 1984): p. 13; Dorothy C. Donnelly, "A Settlement of Sorts: Henry Kissinger's Negotiations and America's Extrication from Vietnam," *Peace and Change* 9, 2/3 (Summer 1983): pp. 55–79; Truong Nhu Tang, *A Vietcong Memoir* (New York: Harcourt Brace Jovanovich, 1985), pp. 165–175, 205–209.
10. Jerry Sanders, *Peddlers of Crisis: The Committee on the Present Danger and the Politics of Containment* (Boston: South End Press, 1983), p. 141.
11. See Bernard Brodie, "Vietnam: Why We Failed," chap. 5, *War and Politics* (New York: Macmillan, 1973), pp. 187–190; Littauer and Uphoff, eds., *The Air War in Indochina*; Pisor, *End of the Line*, passim; Fred Branfman, "Beyond the Pentagon Papers: The Pathology of Power," *Senator Gravel Edition, Pentagon Papers*, vol. 5: *Critical Essays Edited by Noam Chomsky and Howard Zinn*, pp. 294–315.
12. David G. Marr, "The Rise and Fall of 'Counterinsurgency,' 1961–1964," *Senator Gravel*

Edition, Pentagon Papers, vol. 5, pp. 202–210; John Shy and Thomas W. Collier, "Revolutionary War," chap. 27 of *Makers of Modern Strategy: From Machiavelli to the Nuclear Age*, ed. Peter Paret (Princeton, N.J.: Princeton University Press, 1986), pp. 854–856. For a critical assessment of American performance based on a study of Vietnamese politics and strategy, see William S. Turley, *The Second Indochina War: A Short Political and Military History, 1954–1975* (New York: New American Library, 1987), pp. 194–201.

13. Douglas Kinnard, *The War Managers* (Hanover, N.H.: University Press of New England, 1977), pp. 163–164.

14. See *Study on Military Professionalism* (Carlisle Barracks, Pa.: U.S. Army War College, 30 June 1970); The BDM Corporation, *A Study of Strategic Lessons Learned in Vietnam: Omnibus Executive Summary* (1980); Richard P. Gabriel and Paul L. Savage, *Crisis in Command: Mismanagement in the Army* (New York: Hill & Wang, 1979); Robert J. Graham, "Vietnam: An Infantryman's View of Our Failure," *Military Affairs* 48, 3 (July 1984): pp. 133–139.

15. "Vietnam, Committee to Support the Administration Position," Confidential File ND 19/CO 312, Box 73, Lyndon B. Johnson Library; John P. Roche, 1966–68, Office Files of the President, Box 11, LBJ Library.

16. J. William Fulbright, *The Pentagon Propaganda Machine* (New York: Vintage Books, 1971), pp. 106–107.

17. Analyses of the role of the press are legion; it is useful to begin with "Reporting Vietnam: Eight War Correspondents Rebut S.L.A. Marshall's 'Press Failure in Vietnam,'" *New Leader*, 21 November 1966, pp. 3–16; Philip Knightley, *The First Casualty: From the Crimea to Vietnam, the War Correspondent as Hero, Propagandist, and Myth Maker* (New York: Harcourt Brace Jovanovich, 1975), chaps. 16, 17; Lawrence W. Lichty, "Comments on the Influence of Television on Public Opinion," in *Vietnam as History: Ten Years After the Paris Peace Accords*, ed. Peter Braestrup (Washington, D.C.: University Press of America, 1984), pp. 158–160; Kathleen J. Turner, *Lyndon Johnson's Dual War: Vietnam and the Press* (Chicago: University of Chicago Press, 1985); James A. Wechsler, "The Press and the War," *Progressive*, June 1967, pp. 18–19; Susan Welch, "Vietnam: How the Press Went Along," *Nation*, 11 October 1971, pp. 327–330; Jules Witcover, "Where Washington Reporting Failed," *Columbia Journalism Review* 9 (Winter 1971): pp. 7–12.

18. Michael Arlen, *Living Room War* (New York: Penguin Books, 1982), p. xiv.

19. Mueller, "Reflections on the Vietnam Antiwar Movement and on the Curious Calm at the War's End," in *Vietnam as History*, ed. Braestrup, pp. 151–157.

20. Charles DeBenedetti, "A CIA Analysis of the Anti-Vietnam War Movement: October 1967," *Peace and Change* 9, 1 (Spring 1983): pp. 31–41.

21. Mueller, "Vietnam Antiwar Movement," in *Vietnam as History*, ed. Braestrup, p. 155.

22. Russell F. Weigley, "Reflections on 'Lessons' from Vietnam," in *Vietnam as History*, ed. Braestrup, pp. 115–124; Herring, "The 'Vietnam Syndrome,'" pp. 594–612.

23. Todd Gitlin, "Seizing History: What We Won and Lost at Home," *Mother Jones*, November 1983, pp. 32–38, 48.

24. See Gettleman et al., eds., *Vietnam and America*, pp. 291–297, 335–338.

25. Gitlin, "Seizing History," pp. 38, 48.

26. DeBenedetti, *The Peace Reform in American History* (Bloomington: Indiana University Press), p. 174.

27. DeBenedetti, "On the Significance of Peace Activism: America, 1961–1975," *Peace and Change* 9, 2/3 (Summer 1983): p. 14.

28. Melvin Small, "The Impact of the Antiwar Movement on Lyndon Johnson, 1965–68: A Preliminary Report," *Peace and Change* 10, 1 (Spring 1984): p. 1.

Armed Forces and Society, Spring 1988

Tactical Victory,
Strategic Defeat

HARRY G. SUMMERS, JR.
Colonel of Infantry

One of the most frustrating aspects of the Vietnam war from the Army's   1
point of view is that as far as logistics and tactics were concerned we
succeeded in everything we set out to do. At the height of the war the
Army was able to move almost a million soldiers a year in and out of
Vietnam, feed them, clothe them, house them, supply them with arms
and ammunition, and generally sustain them better than any Army
had ever been sustained in the field. To project an Army of that size
halfway around the world was a logistics and management task of
enormous magnitude, and we had been more than equal to the task.
On the battlefield itself, the Army was unbeatable. In engagement after
engagement the forces of the Viet Cong and of the North Vietnamese
Army were thrown back with terrible losses. Yet, in the end, it was
North Vietnam, not the United States, that emerged victorious. Now
could we have succeeded so well, yet failed so miserably? That disturbing question was the reason for this book.

At least part of the answer appears to be that we saw Vietnam as   2
unique rather than in strategic context. This misperception grew out
of our neglect of military strategy in the post-World War II nuclear era.
Almost all of the professional literature on military strategy was written by *civilian* analysts—political scientists from the academic world
and systems analysts from the Defense community. In his book *War
and Politics*, political scientist Bernard Brodie devoted an entire chapter
to the lack of professional military strategic thought.[1] The same criticism was made by systems analysts Alain C. Enthoven and K. Wayne
Smith who commented: "Military professionals are among the most
infrequent contributors to the basic literature on military strategy and
defense policy. Most such contributors are civilians. . . ."[2] Even the
Army's so-called "new" strategy of flexible response grew out of civilian, not military, thinking.

This is not to say that the civilian strategists were wrong. The po-   3
litical scientists provided a valuable service in tying war to its political
ends. They provided answers to "why" the United States ought to wage
war. In like manner the systems analysts provided answers on "what"
means we would use. What was missing was the link that should have
been provided by the military strategists—"how" to take the systems
analyst's *means* and use them to achieve the political scientist's *ends*.

But instead of providing professional military advice on how 4 to fight the war, the military more and more joined with the systems analysts in determining the material means we were to use. Indeed, the conventional wisdom among many Army officers was that "the Army doesn't make strategy," and "there is no such thing as Army strategy." There was a general feeling that strategy was budget-driven and was primarily a function of resource allocation. The task of the Army, in their view, was to design and procure material, arms and equipment and to organize, train, and equip soldiers for the Defense Establishment.

These attitudes derive in part from a shallow interpretation of 5 the Army's mission. While it is true that the National Security Act transferred operational command to the Department of Defense, leaving the Army with the task to "organize, train, and equip active duty and reserve forces," the Army General Staff is still charged with "determination of roles and missions of the Army and strategy formulation, plans and application; Joint Service matters, plans, and operations. . . ."[3] In addition, Army officers assigned to the Office of the Joint Chiefs of Staff and to operations and planning positions in unified commands also have responsibility for Army (i.e., land force) strategy. Further, to argue as some do that in our democracy only the President can "make" strategy is to confuse the issue, since in most cases the President does not formulate military strategy but rather decides on the military strategy recommended to him by his national security advisors, both military and civilian.

The National Will: The People

Vietnam was a reaffirmation of the peculiar relationship be- 6 tween the American Army and the American people. The American Army really is a people's Army in the sense that it belongs to the American people who take a jealous and proprietary interest in its involvement. When the Army is committed the American people are committed, when the American people lose their commitment it is futile to try to keep the Army committed. In the final analysis, the American Army is not so much an arm of the Executive Branch as it is an arm of the American people. The Army, therefore, cannot be committed lightly.

General Fred C. Weyand
Chief of Staff, U.S. Army, July 1976[4]

One of the more simplistic explanations for our failure in Viet- 7 nam is that it was all the fault of the American people—that it was caused by a collapse of national will. Happily for the health of the Republic, this evasion is rare among Army officers. A stab-in-the-back syndrome never developed after Vietnam.

By an ironic twist of fate, the animosity of the Officer Corps was 8 drained off to a large extent by General William C. Westmoreland. On his shoulders was laid much of the blame for our Vietnam failure. According to a 1970 analysis, "For the older men, the villains tend to be timorous civilians and the left-wing press; for the younger men, they are the tradition-bound senior generals and the craven press. For one group, it is the arrogance of McNamara; for the other the rigidity of Westmoreland."[5] Those then "younger men" now make up the majority of the Army's senior officers. For example, the Vietnam experience of the Army War College Class of 1980 was mostly at the platoon and company level. As will be seen in subsequent chapters, placing the blame on General Westmoreland was unfair, but, unfair or not, it did spare another innocent victim—the American people.

The main reason it is not right to blame the American public is 9 that President Lyndon Baines Johnson made a conscious decision not to mobilize the American people—to invoke the national will—for the Vietnam war. As former Assistant Secretary of Defense for Public Affairs Phil G. Goulding commented, "In my four-year tour [July 1965–January 1969] there was not once a significant organized effort by the Executive Branch of the federal government to put across its side of a major policy issue or a major controversy to the American people. Not once was there a 'public affairs program' . . . worthy of the name."[6] Having deliberately never been built, it could hardly be said that the national will "collapsed." According to his biographer, President Johnson's decision not to mobilize the American people was based on his fears that it would jeopardize his "Great Society" programs. As he himself said:

> . . . History provided too many cases where the sound of the 10 bugle put an immediate end to the hopes and dreams of the best reformers: The Spanish-American War drowned the populist spirit; World War I ended Woodrow Wilson's New Freedom; World War II brought the New Deal to a close. Once the war began, then all those conservatives in the Congress would use it as a weapon against the Great Society. . . .

> And the generals. Oh, they'd love the war, too. It's hard to be a 11 military hero without a war. Heroes need battles and bombs and bullets in order to be heroic. That's why I am suspicious of the military. They're always narrow in their appraisal of everything. They see everything in military terms.[7]

What the military needed to tell our Commander-in-Chief was 12 not just about battles and bombs and bullets. They needed to tell him that, as Clausewitz discovered 150 years earlier, "it would be an obvious fallacy to imagine war between civilized peoples as resulting merely from a rational act on the part of the Government and to consider war as gradually ridding itself of passion."[8] They needed to tell him that it would be an obvious fallacy to commit the Army without first committing the American people. Such a commitment would require battlefield competence and clear-cut objectives to be sustained, but without the commitment of the American people the commitment of the Army to prolonged combat was impossible.

Unfortunately, this fallacy was not obvious to either the military 13 or its Commander-in-Chief, for the limited war theorists had excluded the American people from the strategic equation. With World War II fresh in their minds, they equated mobilizing national will with total war, and they believed total war unthinkable in a nuclear age.

The Vietnam war coincided with a social upheaval in America 14 where the old rules and regulations were dismissed as irrelevant and history no longer had anything to offer. There were those who proclaimed it a new age—the "Age of Aquarius." Even the term sounds banal today, but in the mid-1960s respected speakers at Leavenworth and Carlisle were warning the Army that we were entering a new phase—"post-industrial society," "Consciousness Three"—and "relevancy" was the watchword.

Like the flower children, the Army and the military establishment 15 went through its own version of the Age of Aquarius. We thought the rules for taking America to war were hopelessly old-fashioned and out of date. Like society, we became confused between form and substance. Legalistic arguments that the form of a declaration of war was out of date may have been technically correct, but they obscured the fact that this form was designed to be an outward manifestation of a critical substance—the support and commitment of the American people.

A formal declaration of war was seen as a useless piece of paper, 16 in much the same light as many saw the marriage certificate. In the 1960s and early 1970s, there were many, especially among the trendy and sophisticated, who saw marriage as an antiquated institution. By avoiding marriage they thought they could avoid the trauma of divorce, just as some thought that by avoiding a declaration of war they could avoid the trauma of war. But thousands of years of human nature and human experience are not so easily changed.

Pieces of paper *do* have value. A marriage certificate—or a decla- 17 ration of war—legitimizes the relationship in the eyes of society and announces it to the world. It focuses attention, provides certain responsibilities, and creates impediments to dissolution. While neither a marriage certificate nor a declaration of war are guarantees for staying the course, these legal forms are of immense value to society.

But in the early 1960s, we were under the delusion that we could 18 disregard not only the *form* of a declaration of war but also its *substance*—the mobilization of the American people. Secretary of Defense Robert S. McNamara was quoted as saying:

> The greatest contribution Vietnam is making—right or wrong is 19 beside the point—is that it is developing an ability in the United States to fight a limited war, to go to war without the necessity of arousing the public ire.[9]

But "right or wrong" was not beside the point and neither was 20 the intangible of "public ire." Vietnam reinforced the lessons of Korea that there was more to war, even limited war, than those things that could be measured, quantified and computerized.

.   .   .

Friction: The People

Instead of building this moral consensus and taking action to smooth 21 the natural friction that exists between the American people and their Army, Vietnam war policies tended to aggravate it. One of the most damaging aggravations was the decision to grant draft deferments for students. As General Westmoreland wrote, "The policy contributed to anti-war militancy on college campuses in that young men feeling twinges of conscience because they sat out a war while others fought could appease their conscience if they convinced themselves the war was immoral."[10]

The student draft deferments, along with the decision not to ask 22 for a declaration of war and not to mobilize our reserve forces, were part of a deliberate Presidential policy not to arouse the passions of the American people. The effect of this was that we fought the Vietnam war *in cold blood.* This cold-blooded approach to war was not unintentional. It was an outgrowth of the limited war theories that reduced war to an academic model. As we go back and read the writings of the political scientists and systems analysts on limited war, they are noteworthy for their lack of passion. But through fear of reinforcing the basic antimilitarism of the American people we tended to keep this knowledge to ourselves and downplayed battlefield realities. In order to smooth our relations with the American people we began to use euphemisms to hide the horrors of war. We became the Department of the Army (not the *War* Department) and our own terminology avoided mention of the battlefield. We did not kill the enemy, we "inflicted casualties"; we did not destroy things, we "neutralized targets."[11] These evasions allowed the notion to grow that we could apply military force in a sanitary and surgical manner. In so doing we unwittingly prepared the way for the reaction that was to follow.

We had concealed from the American people the true nature of 23 war at precisely the time that television brought its realities into their living rooms in living color. As a result, to many Americans Vietnam became the most destructive, the most horrible, the most terrible war ever waged in the history of the world. This viewpoint has persisted in the face of all historical evidence to the contrary.

There is an important lesson in this for the Army. Any future war 24 will more than likely be as bloody as the war in Vietnam. It will probably also be carried into American living rooms by television reporters, for that is the nature of their craft. As we have seen earlier, attempts to hide the realities of war from the American people only inflame the problem. Censorship is not the answer. How then do we square the circle of the battlefield and the idealism of the American people?

In his analysis of the Vietnam war General Weyand pointed out 25 the conflict arising out of American idealism and counseled what we must do in the future:

> As military professionals we must speak out, we must counsel 26 our political leaders and alert the American public that there is no such thing as a "splendid little war." There is no such thing as a war fought on the cheap. War is death and destruction. The American way of war is particularly violent, deadly and dreadful. We believe in using "things"—artillery, bombs, massive firepower—in order to conserve our soldiers' lives. The enemy, on the other hand, made up for his lack of "things" by expending men instead of machines, and he suffered enormous casualties. The Army saw this happen in Korea, and we should have made the realities of war obvious to the American people before they witnessed it on their television screens. The Army must make the price of involvement clear *before* we get involved, so that America can weigh the probable costs of involvement against the dangers of uninvolvement . . . for there are worse things than war." [12]

Notes

1. See chapter 10, "Strategic Thinkers, Planners, Decision Makers," in *War and Politics* by Bernard Brodie (New York: Macmillan, 1973).
2. Alain C. Enthoven and K. Wayne Smith, *How Much Is Enough: Shaping the Defense Program 1961–1969* (New York: Harper & Row, 1971), p. 90.
3. *US Government Manual, 1979–1980* (Washington, D.C.: USGPO, 1979), p. 202.
4. "Vietnam Myths and American Realities," *CDRS CALL* (July–August 1976); also reprinted in *Armor* (September–October 1976). General Weyand was the last commander of the Military Assistance Command Vietnam (MACV) and supervised the withdrawal of U.S. Military forces in 1973.
5. Ward Just, *Military Men* (New York: Knopf, 1970), p. 186.
6. Phil G. Goulding, *Confirm or Deny: Informing the People on National Security* (New York: Harper & Row, 1970), pp. 81–82.
7. President Lyndon B. Johnson, quoted in Doris Kearns, *Lyndon Johnson and the American Dream* (New York: Harper & Row, 1976), p. 252.

8. Clausewitz, *On War*, I: 1, p. 76.
9. Quoted in Douglas H. Rosenberg, "Arms and the American Way: The Ideological Dimensions of Military Growth," *Military Force and American Society*, edited by Bruce M. Russett and Alfred Stepan (New York: Harper & Row, 1973), p. 170.
10. William C. Westmoreland, *A Soldier Reports*, p. 297. That student draft deferment policy continues to poison U.S. civil-military relations. As Arthur T. Hadley reported in an April 1980 article, "Those who avoided Vietnam through loopholes (or more correctly, loop-highways) in the draft, being in the main honorable men, now feel guilty. They relieve these feelings either by venomous attacks on all things military, including the draft; or, becoming 200 percent American, make Attila the Hun sound like Mother Goose and advocate colossal military expenditures." (Arthur T. Hadley, "The Draft Debate: A Special Section," *Washington Post*, April 6, 1980, pp. E1–E5).
11. This tendency still persists. For example, note the use of the bland phrase "Target Servicing" in our training literature to describe the destruction of an enemy attacking force.
12. Weyand, *CDRS CALL*, July–August 1976, pp. 3, 4.

From *On Strategy: A Critical Analysis of the Vietnam War* (Novato, Calif.: Presidio Press, 1982).

Apocalypse Continued

EDWARD TICK
Writer for the New York Times

Like 17 million other men who came of age during Vietnam, I did not 1 serve in the armed forces. It was a blessing, then, to have escaped; it is a burden now. I find there is something missing in me. I have unwanted feelings that nag me in unexpected ways and at unexpected times.

Although a number of other nonveterans years ago began express- 2 ing similar problems in print and on television, I did not know that the problems applied to me. Perhaps I blocked out my feelings. In any case, I first became aware of these feelings when a man named Fred sought my psychotherapeutic services. Exactly my age, Fred wanted help for anxiety attacks and recurring nightmares. In his dreams, he was pursued by a galloping horseman determined to cut out his heart.

Through psychotherapy, we searched his past for reasons for his 3 present suffering. Nothing proved promising until, because he could bear it no longer, Fred confessed: He had fulfilled his military obligation by spending two years stateside unloading and processing body bags from Vietnam.

We had found the horseman. Fred had handled the bodies of 4
other men like so much supermarket ware, listing names and numbers and arranging transportation. He had never been in danger himself until much later, when the deaths he processed and his profound
guilt returned to haunt him.

But I, also, changed with Fred's admission. I felt uneasy, incom- 5
plete. If Fred was one step removed from the war, I was too. If he was
haunted, what was I?

I searched for clues to my discomfort. The work of the psychia- 6
trist Robert J. Lifton and others on combat veterans suffering post-
traumatic stress told me what I had not experienced. Another small
body of writing, on an elusive subject known as "Vietnam guilt," told
me that I was not the only man who had been happy to escape service
in my teens only to feel angry, confused and incomplete years later.

In high school, during the mid-1960's, I had considered enlisting 7
as a medic, not because I believed in the war, but because many of my
neighbors and classmates were fighting it. Later, my objections to the
war overrode my desire to be counted among those serving. I was prepared, during my junior year in college, to apply for conscientious-
objector status. If it were not granted, I would then decide whether I
would go to jail, flee the country or take some other course. I was un-
sure what I would do.

In the end, Lottery No. 244 rescued me from that dilemma. But it 8
plunged me into a state of permanent moral ambiguity, because part
of our heritage insists that, if there is a war to be fought, young men are
expected to fight it. War, if it exists, is a required course, and a course
with a final examination. I was, I came to feel, among those men of my
generation who had never been tested.

After learning of Fred's horseman, I began to seek out psycho- 9
therapeutic work with Vietnam veterans. They had a need to tell their
stories, and I could join them in the jungle in this way.

Ron was the first veteran of jungle combat with whom I worked. 10
"'Apocalypse Now,'" he chuckled during one session. "A picnic compared to the real thing." Ron was emotionally disabled by his combat
experiences and his reception when he came back to America. He had
been spat on, jailed and hospitalized. In the hospital, he had been
drugged into a stupor. "Why get better?" he asked. "The Government
pays me more for being disabled than I could ever make working."

Ron wanted my help to find meaning in a life whose usefulness 11
had officially ended at age 22. But, sitting across from him, I felt weak,
inadequate, physically smaller, although we were the same size. I had
to fight the urge to look at the floor instead of directly into the eyes that
were avoiding mine.

This was because I felt Ron had something over me. He had sur- 12
vived a long tour in the demilitarized zone and the decimation of his

battalion. The closest I had come to physical danger was being chased down a deserted Washington street on the night of the first moratorium against the war. The guardsman who had chased me was my age, spoke my language and, though he prodded me with his bayonet, ordered me to move with a "please."

It is not because I protested the war that I felt guilty before Ron. 13 In fact, I am even more convinced now that the war was a mistake. I think it hurt all of us in ways that linger long into adulthood. The warriors, honorable men like Ron who served in Vietnam, suffer, unlike veterans of other wars, because the correctness of what our nation did will forever be in question. Those like me who, for one reason or another, did not serve, suffer because we chose not to perform a primary and expected rite of passage. We were never inducted, not merely into the Army, but into manhood. Recently, I was contacted by Sam, a former draft resister who fled to Canada to avoid prison. He told me: "I think about Vietnam every day. I can't join in with others. Can a resister also suffer post-traumatic stress?"

I have had some of the usual rites—marriage, educational and 14 professional recognition. But no matter how many passages or accomplishments I garner, I never quite feel complete. Nor do I think that, had I served in Vietnam, I would now be enjoying the contentment I seek. A nonveteran I know says, "I cannot recall any winners at all."

I think that none of us escaped, that not one of us feels whole. All 15 our choices—service in Vietnam, service at home, freedom from service altogether—failed to provide the rite of passage that every man needs. I want to feel my own strength, worth and wholeness, and I want to belong to my country and my generation. But history got in the way. I wonder if I will forever be seeking something that cannot be.

New York Times Magazine, January 13, 1985

Different Drummers

DAVID FLEISCHAKER
*A real estate broker who frequently writes about
his family of ten for the* Louisville Courier-Journal

It's getting romantic again. The aura of serving in the armed forces has 1 returned. Patriotism is back in vogue and, after seeing movies like "An Officer and A Gentleman" and "The Right Stuff," I get pretty puffed up myself. But I have five healthy sons between 13 and 20, and this new-found feeling competes with fear.

One of the guys has already made his wishes known: to pilot 2 planes for either the Navy or Air Force after college graduation. Travel, good pay, Officer Candidate School, excitement, mission. He wants to be all that he can be, one of the select few. And now each trip to a recruiting office generates enthusiastic long-distance phone calls home.

A couple of the other kids may follow; they're proud of their 3 brother. I'm also proud of him—of them. And yet . . .

I grew up in a generation where the service was something to be 4 avoided. National policymakers assisted our escapes: deferments were given for staying in school, being the sole support of your family, working in a vital industry or having a trick knee. It was all a big wonderful game and some of my best friends practiced and pretended to be crazies so they could get 4-F classifications. We laughed.

Then came Vietnam, a bad war, and we were able to raise our 5 general fears and narrow ambitions to high principle. People fled to Canada, applied for conscientious-objector status, entered the Peace Corps. Those already in uniform were stuck. Some went AWOL, many died, most were disenchanted. I never went to the recruiting office. If I had, it would have been with placards and indictments, not questions about my future. I was sure.

Changes

I cannot see my kids without looking through the prism of my own 6 past. The possibilities of the present are bent by the experience of war in Southeast Asia and my government, which cornered itself and kept painting the corner smaller. Looking back—and it's still hard to do that even from 20 years, the focus isn't sharp enough yet—I haven't changed my mind about Vietnam. And yet . . .

Times change, and time changes us. These kids haven't forgotten 7 about Vietnam. They never knew. It's ancient history, much like the Spanish-American War is to me: a mistake, but only in the history books. However, these five young men are mine. They embody infinite investments of love. If one or more go, there is risk. The Big Risk. There is also that problem—maybe even harder—about reconciling my past to their futures.

The generation that stuffed flowers into the barrels of soldiers' 8 guns is mine. It's going to be hard to look without ambivalence at my own children carrying those guns. The generation that marched for peace is mine. To contemplate without confusion my own sons marching requires breaking some tough mental adhesions. The generation that organized the teach-ins is mine. Can I be taught?

Probably so. In fact, I have to say I'm kind of looking forward to it; 9
and that's tough to admit.

Glow

Uniforms and spit and polish for one who never made his bed. Disci- 10
pline and following orders for a guy who rebelled every single night at
bedtime. Authority and push-ups for the muscular hulk who quit
wrestling his senior year because of a disagreement with the coach.
There is even a half-embarrassed glow enveloping me. If fellows like
this are eager to enlist, we'll all be pretty well defended—if they can
wake him up before 10:30 in the morning.

I'm pretty confident, though, our boys will all wake up when they 11
have to. It's the wondering about me that catches and snags. Is Beirut
really Saigon a generation removed? Is Grenada the Dominican Republic? How much of my principled opposition two decades ago was
rooted in simple fear?

These are important questions for me, but I don't have time for 12
them. Not now. The ones I want addressed are the life-and-death
"what ifs" concerning my boys. Alas, there is no one to answer me.

One of our neighborhood's 12-year-olds was talking to his dad on 13
a recent evening. He had been caught up in the new appreciation of
military things and was thinking out loud about his future.

"Dad, when I grow up I'd like to be in the Army. As long as they 14
promise I'll never be shot at or have to shoot anybody."

That would be a good deal. But the new movies have made me 15
rethink the old truths. So have my kids. They know more about the
moon walk than I do, and the 15-year-old can now recite anything one
needs to know about the space shuttle.

Uncertain

National purpose is too big a concept, I suppose, but my children 16
somehow have settled in a place where it is their assumption that this
country is right and just, unless they are shown otherwise. The verdict
isn't in just yet, but one thing is sure: I'm not as certain as I used to be.
I'd like to believe that the flux of world politics is the culprit and that
I've remained the same, that all the old values are in place.

Yet if my kids come to me for advice, I won't know what to say. 17
There's probably no need to worry, though. The oldest one never
asked. Come to think of it, when I was his age, neither did I.

Newsweek, December 5, 1983

What Americans Think Now

ADAM CLYMER
*An assistant to the executive editor, Adam Clymer
is in charge of polling at the* Times.

Ten years after the end of the Vietnam War, the lessons it once seemed 1
to teach about placing restraints on the use of power are losing effect.
Americans are increasingly prepared to use troops, whether in El Sal-
vador or in Europe, and are about equally divided on employing the
Central Intelligence Agency to overthrow unfriendly governments, a
New York Times Poll shows.

The war itself is even less popular today than when Saigon fell, 2
but the poll of 1,533 adults last month showed that its legacy of distrust of government and the military is wearing away. The unquestion-
ing faith of the early 1960's has not returned, but there is a trend of
steadily growing trust—highest among college-age youths, 59 percent
of whom said Washington could be trusted to do the right thing all or
most of the time. Among everyone else, only 45 percent thought so.

Those same 18- to 22-year-olds were also among the most likely 3
to share President Reagan's endorsement of the Vietnam War as a
"noble cause," and to believe it "taught us that military leaders should
be able to fight wars without civilian leaders tying their hands."

Taken together, these findings strongly suggest that restraints on 4
the use of power will grow even weaker as the confident post-Vietnam
generation gains political importance. That growing trust is critical: a
general faith in government helps overcome doubt on specifics, especially in foreign affairs.

Still, there is no blank check for adventurism, in general or in spe- 5
cific situations, such as the invasion of Grenada. The 47 percent who
trusted Washington all or most of the time is notably more than the 35
percent found by the Institute for Social Research at the University of
Michigan in 1974, when the war, racial troubles and Watergate had
combined to flatten traditional faith, but it is much less than the 76
percent in 1964. Grenada is more intriguing. When those interviewed,
by telephone from Feb. 23 through 27, were asked to rate Washington's
handling of recent foreign-policy situations on a scale of 1 to 10, Grenada got an average rating of 5.66. But another kind of activism, the
Camp David Middle East negotiations of the Carter years, did even
better, at 6.45.

However far this trend ultimately goes, the mood now clearly dif- 6
fers from that of the mid-1970's. To test changes in attitude, last

month's Times Poll repeated many of the questions employed in a national poll the Chicago Council on Foreign Relations conducted in November 1974.

When asked if United States troops should be used in a list of 7 crises, support was higher in 1985 in every case. The biggest change occurred when respondents were asked about an invasion of Western Europe. In 1974, 40 percent favored using troops and 40 percent did not; this time, 54 percent were in favor and 32 percent opposed. The 18-to-29 group, presumably the fighters, now divide 55 to 37 percent in favor. In 1974, they split evenly. (Past Times polling, however, suggests that draft-age youth may become less enthusiastic if war seems less hypothetical.)

Support for using United States troops in El Salvador, if all else 8 failed to stop Communism, was not an issue in 1974. So when last month's poll found 47 percent supporting their use and 43 percent opposed, the best measuring point was a June 1983 Times/CBS News Poll that showed 32 percent in favor and 57 percent opposed.

One step short of committing troops is deploying the C.I.A., and 9 last month's poll found that 44 percent approved the C.I.A.'s working "secretly inside other countries to try to weaken or overthrow governments unfriendly to the United States." Although 46 percent disapproved, the difference is statistically insignificant, within the poll's margin of sampling error of plus or minus 3 percentage points.

As for the Vietnam generation itself, those now aged 30 through 10 38, the sense of alienation remains strong. Where 55 percent of the public, and just 48 percent of those 18 to 29, say "the government is pretty much run by a few big interests," and not for the benefit of all, 61 percent of the Vietnam generation say that. On many questions, the theme seemed to be, "Don't trust anyone, if you're over 30."

This 30-to-38 group, despite its dovish reputation, is also the 11 most hawkish. More than anyone younger or older, they support using troops in Western Europe and are convinced that the Soviet Union is a real and constantly growing threat to the United States. They are also quite favorable to using the C.I.A. to undermine unfriendly governments.

But the Vietnam generation did not get there through any revi- 12 sionist views of the war itself. Only 20 percent of its members now feel the United States "did the right thing in getting into the fighting in Vietnam," while 73 percent say it should have stayed out. As a whole, the public responded almost identically, with 19 percent saying the United States' role was right and 73 percent disagreeing. In 1972, as both war and protest wound down, the Michigan poll found 29 percent agreeing and 57 percent disagreeing.

The Vietnam experience is deeply contradictory. For example, 13 many people say the war was immoral but still believe it taught us that we must sometimes back unwholesome governments because Communist regimes are worse. One indisputable lesson is how little many in the United States know, or are willing to remember, of the searing Vietnam War. In the latest poll, just three Americans in five could say the United States sided with South Vietnam.

New York Times, March 31, 1985

ISSUE: VIETNAM

PERSPECTIVES

1. Both Kimball and Summers address the stab-in-the-back theme and the issue of public support. How does the difference in their purposes affect the way they argue for the vindication of the American people's protests?

2. Several of the articles state that the threat of nuclear weapons affected public and government response to the Vietnam war and continues to shape our view of war. Reconstruct this view into enthymeme form. You may need more than one enthymeme to represent the different viewpoints.

3. The Vietnam generation is represented as today's senior military officers in Summer's article, as civilian casualties in the "Apocalypse Continued" article, as parents in Fleischaker's column, as scholars in Kimball's work, and as statistics in Clymer's report. Describe how you believe these various views will collectively influence U.S. involvement in the event of another war. After describing your beliefs, try presenting them in the form of a syllogism.

4. During the Vietnam war years the motto "Don't trust anyone over the age of 30" was a rallying theme. From the responses of the same generation to the 1985 *Times* poll, Clymer interprets their view as "Don't trust anyone, if you're over 30." What do you infer to be the cause for this shift in attitude? Support your answer.

5. The 1985 *Times* poll characterizes the 18- to 22-year-old group as having a steadily growing trust in government and a strong support for military power. This group was also most likely to view Vietnam as a "noble cause." Fleischaker's article supports these views. What do you think accounts for these opinions? Do you believe, as Clymer suggests, that they would be less enthusiastic if war were a more immediate threat? Consider how knowledge of the Vietnam war and other wars has influenced this group's views.

6. In their respective arguments the writer of "Apocalypse Continued" uses the metaphor of war as a required course and Colonel Summers uses a marriage certificate as an analogy to a formal declaration of war. Evaluate the effectiveness of these comparisons in clarifying each writer's reasoning.

7. In the final quote in Colonel Summers' article General Weyand says we must "weigh the probable costs of involvement against the dangers of uninvolvement . . . for there are worse things than war." Compare this view with the quote from former secretary of state Shultz in George Church's article. What is the implied argument on the consequences of inaction or uninvolvement in war?

ARGUMENTS FOR INVESTIGATION

War Has No Winners

The Vietnam Memorial: Healing the Wound

Mandatory Military Service: Creating a Moral Consensus

Central America: The New Vietnam

The Effect of Vietnam Movies on Public Understanding of the War

War: How Should the Public Be Informed?

Women in Vietnam: The Forgotten Veterans

It's Not Whether You Win or Lose But How You Play the Game

CLASSIC ARGUMENTS

Arguments become classics when they give us lasting and memorable insights on universal issues. This mighty accomplishment of eloquence may be attributed to a single feature, such as the unexpected ironic persona in Swift's "A Modest Proposal" or the rich allusions and moving diction of King's "A Letter from Birmingham Jail." As time passes, these arguments continue to preserve not only important historical perspectives but also the fine art of argument.

The Allegory of the Cave

PLATO

The Greek philosopher Plato (c. 427–347 B.C.) was
a student of Socrates and founder of the Academy,
precursor to the first university. "The Allegory of the
Cave," from The Republic, *was written in the form*
of a dialogue between Socrates as the master and
Glaucon, Plato's brother, as the student.

Next, said I, here is a parable to illustrate the degrees in which our na- 1
ture may be enlightened or unenlightened. Imagine the condition of
men living in a sort of cavernous chamber underground, with an entrance open to the light and a long passage all down the cave. Here
they have been from childhood, chained by the leg and also by the
neck, so that they cannot move and can see only what is in front of
them, because the chains will not let them turn their heads. At some
distance higher up is the light of a fire burning behind them; and be-

tween the prisoners and the fire is a track with a parapet built along it, like the screen at a puppet-show, which hides the performers while they show their puppets over the top.

I see, said he. 2

Now behind this parapet imagine persons carrying along various 3 artificial objects, including figures of men and animals in wood or stone or other materials, which project above the parapet. Naturally, some of these persons will be talking, others silent.

It is a strange picture, he said, and a strange sort of prisoners. 4

Like ourselves, I replied; for in the first place prisoners so con- 5 fined would have seen nothing of themselves or of one another, except the shadows thrown by the fire-light on the wall of the Cave facing them, would they?

Not if all their lives they have been prevented from moving their 6 heads.

And they would have seen as little of the objects carried past. 7

Of course. 8

Now, if they could talk to one another, would they not suppose 9 that their words referred only to those passing shadows which they saw?

Necessarily. 10

And suppose their prison had an echo from the wall facing 11 them? When one of the people crossing behind them spoke, they could only suppose that the sound came from the shadow passing before their eyes.

No doubt. 12

In every way, then, such prisoners would recognize as reality 13 nothing but the shadows of those artificial objects.

Inevitably. 14

Now consider what would happen if their release from the chains 15 and the healing of their unwisdom should come about in this way. Suppose one of them were set free and forced suddenly to stand up, turn his head, and walk with eyes lifted to the light; all these movements would be painful, and he would be too dazzled to make out the objects whose shadows he had been used to see. What do you think he would say, if someone told him that what he had formerly seen was meaningless illusion, but now, being somewhat nearer to reality and turned towards more real objects, he was getting a truer view? Suppose further that he were shown the various objects being carried by and were made to say, in reply to questions, what each of them was. Would he not be perplexed and believe the objects now shown him to be not so real as what he formerly saw?

Yes, not nearly so real. 16

And if he were forced to look at the fire-light itself, would not his 17 eyes ache, so that he would try to escape and turn back to the things which he could see distinctly, convinced that they really were clearer than these other objects now being shown to him?

Yes. 18

And suppose someone were to drag him away forcibly up the 19 steep and rugged ascent and not let him go until he had hauled him out into the sunlight, would he not suffer pain and vexation at such treatment, and, when he had come out into the light, find his eyes so full of its radiance that he could not see a single one of the things that he was now told were real?

Certainly he would not see them all at once. 20

He would need, then, to grow accustomed before he could see 21 things in that upper world. At first it would be easiest to make out shadows, and then the images of men and things reflected in water, and later on the things themselves. After that, it would be easier to watch the heavenly bodies and the sky itself by night, looking at the light of the moon and stars rather than the Sun and the Sun's light in the day-time.

Yes, surely. 22

Last of all, he would be able to look at the Sun and contemplate 23 its nature, not as it appears when reflected in water or any alien medium, but as it is in itself in its own domain.

No doubt. 24

And now he would begin to draw the conclusion that it is the 25 Sun that produces the seasons and the course of the year and controls everything in the visible world, and moreover is in a way the cause of all that he and his companions used to see.

Clearly he would come at last to that conclusion. 26

Then if he called to mind his fellow prisoners and what passed 27 for wisdom in his former dwelling-place, he would surely think himself happy in the change and be sorry for them. They may have had a practice of honouring and commending one another, with prizes for the man who had the keenest eye for the passing shadows and the best memory for the order in which they followed or accompanied one another, so that he could make a good guess as to which was going to come next. Would our released prisoner be likely to covet those prizes or to envy the men exalted to honour and power in the Cave? Would he not feel like Homer's Achilles, that he would far sooner 'be on earth as a hired servant in the house of a landless man' or endure anything rather than go back to his old beliefs and live in the old way?

Yes, he would prefer any fate to such a life. 28

Now imagine what would happen if he went down again to take 29 his former seat in the Cave. Coming suddenly out of the sunlight, his eyes would be filled with darkness. He might be required once more to deliver his opinion on those shadows, in competition with the prisoners who had never been released, while his eyesight was still dim and unsteady; and it might take some time to become used to the darkness. They would laugh at him and say that he had gone up only to come back with his sight ruined; it was worth no one's while even to attempt the ascent. If they could lay hands on the man who was trying to set them free and lead them up, they would kill him.

Yes, they would. 30

Every feature in this parable, my dear Glaucon, is meant to fit our 31 earlier analysis. The prison dwelling corresponds to the region revealed to us through the sense of sight, and the fire-light within it to the power of the Sun. The ascent to see the things in the upper world you may take as standing for the upward journey of the soul into the region of the intelligible; then you will be in possession of what I surmise, since that is what you wish to be told. Heaven knows whether it is true; but this, at any rate, is how it appears to me. In the world of knowledge, the last thing to be perceived and only with great difficulty is the essential Form of Goodness. Once it is perceived, the conclusion must follow that, for all things, this is the cause of whatever is right and good; in the visible world it gives birth to light and to the lord of light, while it is itself sovereign in the intelligible world and the parent of intelligence and truth. Without having had a vision of this Form no one can act with wisdom, either in his own life or in matters of state.

So far as I can understand, I share your belief. 32

Then you may also agree that it is no wonder if those who have 33 reached this height are reluctant to manage the affairs of men. Their souls long to spend all their time in that upper world—naturally enough, if here once more our parable holds true. Nor, again, is it at all strange that one who comes from the contemplation of divine things to the miseries of human life should appear awkward and ridiculous when, with eyes still dazed and not yet accustomed to the darkness, he is compelled, in a law-court or elsewhere, to dispute about the shadows of justice or the images that cast those shadows, and to wrangle over the notions of what is right in the minds of men who have never beheld Justice itself.

It is not at all strange. 34

No; a sensible man will remember that the eyes may be confused 35 in two ways—by a change from light to darkness or from darkness to light; and he will recognize that the same thing happens to the soul. When he sees it troubled and unable to discern anything clearly, instead of laughing thoughtlessly, he will ask whether, coming from a brighter existence, its unaccustomed vision is obscured by the darkness, in which case he will think its condition enviable and its life a happy one; or whether, emerging from the depths of ignorance, it is dazzled by excess of light. If so, he will rather feel sorry for it; or, if he were inclined to laugh, that would be less ridiculous than to laugh at the soul which has come down from the light.

That is a fair statement.   36

If this is true, then, we must conclude that education is not what 37 it is said to be by some, who profess to put knowledge into a soul which does not possess it, as if they could put sight into blind eyes. On the contrary, our own account signifies that the soul of every man does possess the power of learning the truth and the organ to see it with; and that, just as one might have to turn the whole body round in order that the eye should see light instead of darkness, so the entire soul must be turned away from this changing world, until its eye can bear to contemplate reality and that supreme splendour which we have called the Good. Hence there may well be an art whose aim would be to effect this very thing, the conversion of the soul, in the readiest way; not to put the power of sight into the soul's eye, which already has it, but to ensure that, instead of looking in the wrong direction, it is turned the way it ought to be.

Yes, it may well be so.   38

It looks, then, as though wisdom were different from those ordi- 39 nary virtues, as they are called, which are not far removed from bodily qualities, in that they can be produced by habituation and exercise in a soul which has not possessed them from the first. Wisdom, it seems, is certainly the virtue of some diviner faculty, which never loses its power, though its use for good or harm depends on the direction towards which it is turned. You must have noticed in dishonest men with a reputation for sagacity the shrewd glance of a narrow intelligence piercing the objects to which it is directed. There is nothing wrong with their power of vision, but it has been forced into the service of evil, so that the keener its sight, the more harm it works.

Quite true.   40

And yet if the growth of a nature like this had been pruned from 41 earliest childhood, cleared of those clinging overgrowths which come of gluttony and all luxurious pleasure and, like leaden weights charged with affinity to this mortal world, hang upon the soul, bending its vision downwards; if, freed from these, the soul were turned round towards true reality, then this same power in these very men would see the truth as keenly as the objects it is turned to now.

Yes, very likely.   42

Is it not also likely, or indeed certain after what has been said, 43 that a state can never be properly governed either by the uneducated who know nothing of truth or by men who are allowed to spend all their days in the pursuit of culture? The ignorant have no single mark before their eyes at which they must aim in all the conduct of their own lives and of affairs of state; and the others will not engage in action if they can help it, dreaming that, while still alive, they have been translated to the Islands of the Blest.

Quite true. 44

It is for us, then, as founders of a commonwealth, to bring com- 45 pulsion to bear on the noblest natures. They must be made to climb the ascent to the vision of Goodness, which we called the highest object of knowledge; and, when they have looked upon it long enough, they must not be allowed, as they now are, to remain on the heights, refusing to come down again to the prisoners or to take any part in their labours and rewards, however much or little these may be worth.

Shall we not be doing them an injustice, if we force on them a 46 worse life than they might have?

You have forgotten again, my friend, that the law is not con- 47 cerned to make any one class specially happy, but to ensure the welfare of the commonwealth as a whole. By persuasion or constraint it will unite the citizens in harmony, making them share whatever benefits each class can contribute to the common good; and its purpose in forming men of that spirit was not that each should be left to go his own way, but that they should be instrumental in binding the community into one.

True, I had forgotten. 48

You will see, then, Glaucon, that there will be no real injustice in 49 compelling our philosophers to watch over and care for the other citizens. We can fairly tell them that their compeers in other states may quite reasonably refuse to collaborate: there they have sprung up, like a self-sown plant, in despite of their country's institutions; no one has fostered their growth, and they cannot be expected to show gratitude for a care they have never received. 'But,' we shall say, it is not so with you. We have brought you into existence for your country's sake as well as for your own, to be like leaders and king-bees in a hive; you have been better and more thoroughly educated than those others and hence you are more capable of playing your part both as men of thought and as men of action. You must go down, then, each in his turn, to live with the rest and let your eyes grow accustomed to the darkness. You will then see a thousand times better than those who live there always; you will recognize every image for what it is and know what it represents, because you have seen justice, beauty, and goodness in their reality; and so you and we shall find life in our commonwealth no mere dream, as it is in most existing states, where men live fighting one another about shadows and quarreling for power, as if that were a great prize; whereas in truth government can be at its best and free from dissension only where the destined rulers are least desirous of holding office.'

Quite true. 50

Then will our pupils refuse to listen and to take their turns at 51
sharing in the work of the community, though they may live together
for most of their time in a purer air?

No; it is a fair demand, and they are fair-minded men. No doubt, 52
unlike any ruler of the present day, they will think of holding power as
an unavoidable necessity.

Yes, my friend; for the truth is that you can have a well-governed 53
society only if you can discover for your future rulers a better way of
life than being in office; then only will power be in the hands of men
who are rich, not in gold, but in the wealth that brings happiness, a
good and wise life. All goes wrong when, starved for lack of anything
good in their own lives, men turn to public affairs hoping to snatch
from thence the happiness they hunger for. They set about fighting for
power, and this internecine conflict ruins them and their country. The
life of true philosophy is the only one that looks down upon offices of
state; and access to power must be confined to men who are not in
love with it; otherwise rivals will start fighting. So whom else can you
compel to undertake the guardianship of the commonwealth, if not
those who, besides understanding best the principles of government,
enjoy a nobler life than the politician's and look for rewards of a different kind?

There is indeed no other choice. 54

The Republic of Plato,
trans. Francis Macdonald Cornford
(New York: Oxford University Press, 1941)

CLASSIC ARGUMENTS: "THE ALLEGORY OF THE CAVE"

DISCUSSION

1. Plato's assumptions about human nature underlie his allegory of the cave. Identify
those assumptions and explain why you accept or reject each one.

2. Plato ends the story of the cave by stating his claim on what education is and how it
is acquired. Reread paragraph 37 and restate the claim in your own words.

3. Plato makes several assumptions about the nature of government. Identify those
assumptions and, using them as a base, reconstruct Plato's argument on the kind of
leader that is needed. Use a syllogism to express his reasoning.

4. How does Plato defend as ethical the necessity of *forcing* philosophers to rule against their will? Express his reasoning as an enthymeme and identify the warrant needed to accept his claim.

5. Except for asking one question and making one explanation, Glaucon merely agrees with the master. Why, then, did Plato choose to include Glaucon? What effect does Glaucon have on your understanding of Plato's arguments? Of the many types of people Plato analyzes, which type would Glaucon be?

WRITING SUGGESTIONS

1. It's hard to imagine a thoughtful and unambitious philosopher participating in today's media-driven election campaigns. Juxtaposing these images raises two issues: What role should the philosopher play in our society today? Do we expect our leaders to be philosophers? Choose one of these issues as the basis for an argument directed to the general public.

2. The allegory is an effective device for presenting abstract ideas and complex processes in simpler terms. Design an allegory to introduce an argument on how our political leaders should be chosen or how our education system could be made more effective.

To His Coy Mistress

ANDREW MARVELL

Andrew Marvell (1621–1678) was a Puritan patriot and political satirist who served in the English Parliament for twenty years. His poems, written for his own pleasure, were found and published after his death.

> Had we but world enough, and time,
> This coyness, lady, were no crime.
> We would sit down, and think which way
> To walk, and pass our long love's day.
> 5   Thou by the Indian Ganges' side
> Should'st rubies find: I by the tide
> Of Humber would complain. I would
> Love you ten years before the Flood,
> And you should, if you please, refuse
> 10   Till the conversion of the Jews.

My vegetable love should grow
Vaster than empires, and more slow.
An hundred years should go to praise
Thine eyes, and on thy forehead gaze:
15 Two hundred to adore each breast:
But thirty thousand to the rest.
An age at least to every part,
And the last age should show your heart.
For, lady, you deserve this state,
20 Nor would I love at lower rate.
  But at my back I always hear
Time's winged chariot hurrying near;
And yonder all before us lie
Deserts of vast eternity.
25 Thy beauty shall no more be found,
Nor in thy marble vault shall sound
My echoing song; then worms shall try
That long preserved virginity,
And your quaint honor turn to dust,
30 And into ashes all my lust.
The grave's a fine and private place,
But none, I think, do there embrace.
  Now therefore, while the youthful hue
Sits on thy skin like morning dew,
35 And while thy willing soul transpires
At every pore with instant fires,
Now let us sport us while we may;
and now, like am'rous birds of prey,
Rather at once our time devour,
40 Than languish in his slow-chapt power,
Let us roll all our strength, and all
Our sweetness, up into one ball;
And tear our pleasures with rough strife
Thorough the iron gates of life.
45 Thus, though we cannot make our sun
Stand still, yet we will make him run.

CLASSIC ARGUMENTS: "TO HIS COY MISTRESS"

DISCUSSION

1. The persona in this poem is appealing to his *mistress,* which in the seventeenth century meant *sweetheart.* Describe the context for his argument by identifying the subject, the implied occasion, and the purpose. What does the mistress's coyness convey about her level of opposition?

2. Tone reveals the writer or speaker's attitude toward the subject. Does the persona's tone differ in the three stanzas of the poem? Describe the tone in each stanza, using specific lines to illustrate and support your perception of any changes that occur.

3. How credible do you think the persona is to his audience? Identify the means by which he tries to establish his ethical appeal in each stanza and explain how you think his attempts will affect the mistress.

4. A personal argument such as this already has strong emotional overtones. How does the persona heighten the emotional appeal? Specify the emotions he appeals to most.

5. Think of each stanza in the poem as a part of a syllogism representing the persona's argument. Summarize each stanza in one sentence and label these sentences the major premise, minor premise, and conclusion. Is the conclusion valid? Are either of the premises questionable? Explain the likelihood of the mistress's accepting this logic.

WRITING SUGGESTIONS

1. "To His Coy Mistress" captures the essence of the *carpe diem* theme: *seize the day* for there may be no tomorrow. Use this theme as the driving force of an argument directed to a close personal audience.

2. The form of Marvell's poem lends itself well to imitation. Using Marvell's stanza and rhyme form, write a contemporary version of the poem.

A Modest Proposal

*For Preventing the Children
of Poor People in Ireland from Being
a Burden to Their Parents or Country,
and for Making Them Beneficial
to the Public*

JONATHAN SWIFT

*Jonathan Swift (1667–1745), an English clergyman in
Ireland, was a satirist and political propagandist. His
most famous works are* Gulliver's Travels *(1726), A*
Tale of a Tub *(1704), and "A Modest Proposal" (1729),
which was written to emphasize the consequences of
English rule over Ireland and the plight of the Irish
people.*

It is a melancholy object to those who walk through this great town,[1]   1
or travel in the country, when they see the streets, the roads, and
cabin-doors crowded with beggars of the female sex, followed by three,
four, or six children all in rags, and importuning every passenger for
an alms.[2] These mothers, instead of being able to work for their honest
livelihood, are forced to employ all their time in strolling, to beg sustenance for their helpless infants, who, as they grow up, either turn
thieves for want of work, or leave their dear native country to fight for
the Pretender in Spain,[3] or sell themselves to the Barbadoes.[4]

I think it is agreed by all parties that this prodigious number of   2
children, in the arms, or on the backs, or at the heels of their mothers,
and frequently of their fathers, is in the present deplorable state of the
kingdom a very great additional grievance; and therefore whoever
could find out a fair, cheap, and easy method of making these children
sound and useful members of the commonwealth would deserve so
well of the public as to have his statue set up for a preserver of the
nation.

But my intention is very far from being confined to provide only   3
for the children of professed beggars; it is of a much greater extent,
and shall take in the whole number of infants at a certain age who are

born of parents in effect as little able to support them as those who demand our charity in the streets.

As to my own part, having turned my thoughts for many years 4 upon this important subject, and maturely weighed the several schemes of other projectors,[5] I have always found them grossly mistaken in their computation. It is true a child just dropped from its dam may be supported by her milk for a solar year with little other nourishment, at most not above the value of two shillings, which the mother may certainly get, or the value in scraps, by her lawful occupation of begging, and it is exactly at one year old that I propose to provide for them, in such a manner as, instead of being a charge upon their parents, or the parish, or wanting food and raiment for the rest of their lives, they shall, on the contrary, contribute to the feeding and partly to the clothing of many thousands.

There is likewise another great advantage in my scheme, that it 5 will prevent those voluntary abortions, and that horrid practice of women murdering their bastard children, alas, too frequent among us, sacrificing the poor innocent babes, I doubt, more to avoid the expense than the shame, which would move tears and pity in the most savage and inhuman breast.

The number of souls in Ireland being usually reckoned one mil- 6 lion and a half, of these I calculate there may be about two hundred thousand couples whose wives are breeders, from which number I subtract thirty thousand couples who are able to maintain their own children, although I apprehend there cannot be so many under the present distresses of the kingdom, but this being granted, there will remain an hundred and seventy thousand breeders. I again subtract fifty thousand for those women who miscarry, or whose children die by accident or disease within the year. There only remain an hundred and twenty thousand children of poor parents annually born: the question therefore is, how this number shall be reared, and provided for, which, as I have already said, under the present situation of affairs is utterly impossible by all the methods hitherto proposed, for we can neither employ them in handicraft or agriculture; we neither build houses (I mean in the country), nor cultivate land: they can very seldom pick up a livelihood by stealing until they arrive at six years old, except where they are of towardly[6] parts, although I confess they learn the rudiments much earlier, during which time they can however be properly looked upon only as probationers, as I have been informed by a principal gentleman in the County of Cavan, who protested to me that he never knew above one or two instances under the age of six, even in a part of the kingdom so renowned for the quickest proficiency in the art.

I am assured by our merchants that a boy or a girl before twelve 7 years old, is no saleable commodity, and even when they come to this age, they will not yield above three pounds, or three pounds and half-a-crown at most on the Exchange, which cannot turn to account either to the parents or the kingdom, the charge of nutriment and rags having been at least four times that value.

I shall now therefore humbly propose my own thoughts, which I 8 hope will not be liable to the least objection.

I have been assured by a very knowing American of my acquaint- 9 ance in London, that a young healthy child well nursed is at a year old a most delicious, nourishing and wholesome food, whether stewed, roasted, baked, or boiled, and I make no doubt that it will equally serve in a fricassee, or a ragout.

I do therefore humbly offer it to public consideration, that of the 10 hundred and twenty thousand children already computed, twenty thousand may be reserved for breed, whereof only one fourth part to be males, which is more than we allow to sheep, black-cattle, or swine, and my reason is that these children are seldom the fruits of marriage, a circumstance not much regarded by our savages, therefore one male will be sufficient to serve four females. That the remaining hundred thousand may at a year old be offered in sale to the parents of quality, and fortune, through the kingdom, always advising the mother to let them suck plentifully in the last month, so as to render them plump, and fat for a good table. A child will make two dishes at an entertainment for friends, and when the family dines alone, the fore or hind quarter will make a reasonable dish, and seasoned with a little pepper or salt will be very good boiled on the fourth day, especially in winter.

I have reckoned upon a medium, that a child just born will weigh 11 twelve pounds, and in a solar year if tolerably nursed increaseth to twenty-eight pounds.

I grant this food will be somewhat dear, and therefore very proper 12 for landlords, who, as they have already devoured most of the parents, seem to have the best title to the children.

Infant's flesh will be in season throughout the year, but more 13 plentiful in March, and a little before and after, for we are told by a grave author,[7] an eminent French physician, that fish being a prolific diet, there are more children born in Roman Catholic countries about nine months after Lent than at any other season; therefore reckoning a year after Lent, the markets will be more glutted than usual, because the number of Popish infants is at least three to one in this kingdom, and therefore it will have one other collateral advantage by lessening the number of Papists among us.

I have already computed the charge of nursing a beggar's child 14 (in which list I reckon all cottagers, labourers, and four-fifths of the farmers) to be about two shillings per annum, rags included, and I believe no gentleman would repine to give ten shillings for the carcass of a good fat child, which, as I have said, will make four dishes of excellent nutritive meat, when he hath only some particular friend or his own family to dine with him. Thus the Squire will learn to be a good landlord and grow popular among his tenants, the mother will have eight shillings net profit, and be fit for work until she produces another child.

Those who are more thrifty (as I must confess the times require) 15 may flay the carcass; the skin of which artificially[8] dressed, will make admirable gloves for ladies, and summer boots for fine gentlemen.

As to our city of Dublin, shambles[9] may be appointed for this 16 purpose, in the most convenient parts of it, and butchers we may be assured will not be wanting, although I rather recommend buying the children alive, and dressing them hot from the knife, as we do roasting pigs.

A very worthy person, a true lover of his country, and whose virtues I highly esteem, was lately pleased, in discoursing on this matter to offer a refinement upon my scheme. He said that many gentlemen of this kingdom, having of late destroyed their deer, he conceived that the want of venison might be well supplied by the bodies of young lads and maidens, not exceeding fourteen years of age, nor under twelve, so great a number of both sexes in every country being now ready to starve, for want of work and service: and these to be disposed of by their parents if alive, or otherwise by their nearest relations. But with due deference to so excellent a friend, and so deserving a patriot, I cannot be altogether in his sentiments. For as to the males, my American acquaintance assured me from frequent experience that their flesh was generally tough and lean, like that of our schoolboys, by continual exercise, and their taste disagreeable, and to fatten them would not answer the charge. Then as to the females, it would, I think with humble submission, be a loss to the public, because they soon would become breeders themselves: and besides, it is not improbable that some scrupulous people might be apt to censure such a practice (although indeed very unjustly) as a little bordering upon cruelty, which I confess, hath always been with me the strongest objection against any project, howsoever well intended.

But in order to justify my friend, he confessed that this expedient 18 was put into his head by the famous Psalmanazar,[10] a native of the island Formosa, who came from thence to London, above twenty years ago, and in conversation told my friend that in his country when any young person happened to be put to death, the executioner sold the carcass to persons of quality, as a prime dainty, and that, in his time, the body of a plump girl of fifteen, who was crucified for an attempt to poison the emperor, was sold to his Imperial Majesty's Prime Minister of State, and other great Mandarins of the Court, in joints from the gibbet, at four hundred crowns. Neither indeed can I deny that if the same use were made of several plump young girls in this town who, without one single groat to their fortunes, cannot stir abroad without a chair,[11] and appear at the playhouse and assemblies in foreign fineries, which they never will pay for, the kingdom would not be the worse.

Some persons of a desponding spirit are in great concern about 19 that vast number of poor people, who are aged, diseased, or maimed, and I have been desired to employ my thoughts what course may be taken to ease the nation of so grievous an encumbrance. But I am not in the least pain upon that matter, because it is very well known that they are every day dying, and rotting, by cold, and famine, and filth, and vermin, as fast as can be reasonably expected. And as to the younger labourers they are now in almost as hopeful a condition. They cannot get work, and consequently pine away from want of nourishment, to a degree that if at any time they are accidentally hired to common labour, they have not strength to perform it; and thus the country and themselves are in a fair way of being soon delivered from the evils to come.

I have too long digressed, and therefore shall return to my sub- 20 ject. I think the advantages by the proposal which I have made are obvious and many, as well as of the highest importance.

For first, as I have already observed, it would greatly lessen the 21 number of Papists, with whom we are yearly over-run, being the principal breeders of the nation, as well as our most dangerous enemies, and who stay at home on purpose with a design to deliver the kingdom to the Pretender, hoping to take their advantage by the absence of so many good Protestants, who have chosen rather to leave their country than stay at home and pay tithes against their conscience to an idolatrous Episcopal curate.

Secondly, the poorer tenants will have something valuable of 22 their own, which by law may be made liable to distress,[12] and help to pay their landlord's rent, their corn and cattle being already seized, and money a thing unknown.

Thirdly, whereas the maintenance of an hundred thousand chil- 23 dren, from two years old, and upwards, cannot be computed at less than ten shillings a piece per annum, the nation's stock will be thereby increased fifty thousand pounds per annum, besides the profit of a new dish, introduced to the tables of all gentlemen of fortune in the kingdom, who have any refinement in taste, and the money will circulate among ourselves, the goods being entirely of our own growth and manufacture.

Fourthly, the constant breeders, besides the gain of eight shill- 24 ings sterling per annum, by the sale of their children, will be rid of the charge of maintaining them after the first year.

Fifthly, this food would likewise bring great custom to taverns, 25 where the vintners will certainly be so prudent as to procure the best receipts for dressing it to perfection, and consequently have their houses frequented by all the fine gentlemen, who justly value themselves upon their knowledge in good eating; and a skilful cook, who understands how to oblige his guests, will contrive to make it as expensive as they please.

Sixthly, this would be a great inducement to marriage, which all 26 wise nations have either encouraged by rewards, or enforced by laws and penalties. It would increase the care and tenderness of mothers towards their children, when they were sure of a settlement for life, to the poor babes, provided in some sort by the public to their annual profit instead of expense. We should soon see an honest emulation among the married women, which of them could bring the fattest child to the market. Men would become as fond of their wives, during the time of their pregnancy, as they are now of their mares in foal, their cows in calf, or sows when they are ready to farrow, nor offer to beat or kick them (as it is too frequent a practice) for fear of a miscarriage.

Many other advantages might be enumerated. For instance, the 27 addition of some thousand carcasses in our exportation of barrelled beef; the propagation of swine's flesh, and improvement in the art of making good bacon, so much wanted among us by the great destruction of pigs, too frequent at our tables, and no way comparable in taste or magnificence to a well-grown, fat yearling child, which roasted whole will make a considerable figure at a Lord Mayor's feast, or any other public entertainment. But this and many others I omit, being studious of brevity.

Supposing that one thousand families in this city would be con- 28 stant customers for infants' flesh, besides others who might have it at merry meetings, particularly weddings and christenings; I compute that Dublin would take off annually about twenty thousand carcasses, and the rest of the kingdom (where probably they will be sold somewhat cheaper) the remaining eighty thousand.

I can think of no one objection that will possibly be raised against 29 this proposal, unless it should be urged that the number of people will be thereby much lessened in the kingdom. This I freely own, and it was indeed one principal design in offering it to the world. I desire the reader will observe, that I calculate my remedy for this one individual Kingdom of Ireland, and for no other that ever was, is, or, I think, ever can be upon earth. Therefore let no man talk to me of other expedients: Of taxing our absentees at five shillings a pound: Of using neither clothes, nor household furniture, except what is of our own growth and manufacture: Of utterly rejecting the materials and instruments that promote foreign luxury: Of curing the expensiveness of pride, vanity, idleness, and gaming in our women: Of introducing a vein of parsimony, prudence, and temperance: Of learning to love our country, wherein we differ even from Laplanders, and the inhabitants of Topinamboo: Of quitting our animosities and factions, nor act any longer like the Jews, who were murdering one another at the very moment their city was taken: Of being a little cautious not to sell our country and consciences for nothing: Of teaching landlords to have at least one degree of mercy towards their tenants. Lastly, of putting a spirit of honesty, industry, and skill into our shopkeepers, who, if a resolution could now be taken to buy only our native goods, would immediately unite to cheat and exact upon us in the price, the measure and the goodness, nor could ever yet be brought to make one fair proposal of just dealing, though often and earnestly invited to it.

Therefore I repeat, let no man talk to me of these and the like 30 expedients, till he hath at least a glimpse of hope that there will ever be some hearty and sincere attempt to put them in practice.

But as to myself, having been wearied out for many years with 31 offering vain, idle, visionary thoughts, and at length utterly despairing of success, I fortunately fell upon this proposal, which as it is wholly new, so it hath something solid and real, of no expense and little trouble, full in our own power, and whereby we can incur no danger in disobliging England. For this kind of commodity will not bear exportation, the flesh being of too tender a consistence to admit a long continuance in salt, although perhaps I could name a country which would be glad to eat up our whole nation without it.[13]

After all I am not so violently bent upon my own opinion as to 32 reject any offer, proposed by wise men, which shall be found equally innocent, cheap, easy and effectual. But before some thing of that kind shall be advanced in contradiction to my scheme, and offering a better, I desire the author, or authors, will be pleased maturely to consider two points. First, as things now stand, how they will be able to find food and raiment for a hundred thousand useless mouths and backs? And secondly, there being a round million of creatures in human figure, throughout this kingdom, whose whole subsistence put into a common stock would leave them in debt two millions of pounds sterling; adding those who are beggars by profession, to the bulk of farmers, cottagers, and labourers with their wives and children, who are beggars in effect; I desire those politicians who dislike my overture, and may perhaps be so bold to attempt an answer, that they will first ask the parents of these mortals whether they would not at this day think it a great happiness to have been sold for food at a year old, in the manner I prescribe, and thereby have avoided such a perpetual scene of misfortunes as they have since gone through, by the oppression of landlords, the impossibility of paying rent without money or trade, the want of common sustenance, with neither house nor clothes to cover them from the inclemencies of weather, and the most inevitable prospect of entailing the like, or greater miseries upon their breed for ever.

I profess in the sincerity of my heart that I have not the least per- 33 sonal interest in endeavouring to promote this necessary work, having no other motive than the public good of my country, by advancing our trade, providing for infants, relieving the poor, and giving some pleasure to the rich. I have no children by which I can propose to get a single penny; the youngest being nine years old, and my wife past child-bearing.

Notes

1. Dublin.
2. A contemporary estimate placed the number of itinerant beggars in Ireland at 34,425.
3. Irish Catholics had been recruited to fight for Spain and France against England. One attempt in 1719 had tried to restore the "Pretender," James Stuart, to the English throne.
4. Large numbers of Irishmen emigrated to the British West Indies.
5. For Swift, a "projector" was one who proposed foolish plans.
6. Promising.
7. François Rabelais (1494?–1553), a French satirist.
8. With art or skill.
9. A meat market.
10. An imposter who in 1704 published a fictitious account of Formosa.
11. A sedan chair.
12. Subject to seizure because debts were not paid.
13. England.

CLASSIC ARGUMENTS: "A MODEST PROPOSAL"

DISCUSSION

1. "A Modest Proposal" was published anonymously, yet the piece remains one of the best-known and most memorable of all arguments. Describe the speaker or the persona, his level of authority, the characteristics he attributes to himself to establish credibility, and his tone. Refer to specific sections in the text that support your characterization.

2. Identify the occasion for the proposal and describe as specifically as possible the intended audience. Given the context, how effective do you think Swift's ironic tone is in achieving his purpose? Explain your reasoning.

3. While Swift appears to be putting forth a proposal, his real intention is to satirize the values of the English governing class and the oppressive laws under which the Irish suffered. Using specific examples of satire in the essay, reconstruct the points of criticism Swift implies. In what way does Swift use the same technique for criticizing Americans? What other groups are the target of his satire?

4. Swift chose to use statistics throughout the essay. What are these statistics used to prove and how convincing are they for the intended readers? To what values do these statistics appeal?

5. In paragraphs 21–26, Swift summarizes six arguments for accepting his proposal. Using your understanding of logic, explain why you would accept or reject each of these arguments.

6. Paragraph 29 serves a particularly important role in Swift's satire. Explain what happens in this paragraph and what Swift' strategy is in positioning this information at this point in the proposal.

WRITING SUGGESTIONS

1. Poverty, hunger, and homelessness remain problems in our society today. Try writing a satirical essay of your own to achieve one of the following purposes:
   a. to dramatize for the general public the extent of a problem
   b. to point out to a government agency the causes of a problem

2. What problem concerns you the most in our society? What attitudes and values allow that problem to exist? Using irony and exaggeration, write your own "modest proposal" ridiculing the people who hold those values.

The Cause of War

MARGARET SANGER

Margaret Sanger (1883–1966) studied nursing and contraception and is credited with having coined the term "birth control." She founded the National Birth Control League in 1917, an organization that eventually became the Planned Parenthood Federation of America. This essay is from her 1920 book, Woman and the New Race.

In every nation of militaristic tendencies we find the reactionaries de- 1 manding a higher and still higher birth rate. Their plea is, first, that great armies are needed to *defend* the country from its possible enemies; second, that a huge population is required to assure the country its proper place among the powers of the world. At bottom the two pleas are the same.

As soon as the country becomes overpopulated, these reaction- 2 aries proclaim loudly its moral right to expand. They point to the huge population, which in the name of patriotism they have previously demanded should be brought into being. Again pleading patriotism, they declare that it is the moral right of the nation to take by force such room as it needs. Then comes war—usually against some nation supposed to be less well prepared than the aggressor.

Diplomats make it their business to conceal the facts, and poli- 3 ticians violently denounce the politicians of other countries. There is a long beating of tom-toms by the press and all other agencies for influencing public opinion. Facts are distorted and lies invented until the common people cannot get at the truth. Yet, when the war is over, if not before, we always find that "a place in the sun," "a path to the sea," "a route to India" or something of the sort is at the bottom of the trouble. These are merely other names for expansion.

The "need of expansion" is only another name for overpopula- 4 tion. One supreme example is sufficient to drive home this truth. That the Great War, from the horror of which we are just beginning to emerge, had its source in overpopulation is too evident to be denied by any serious student of current history.

For the past one hundred years most of the nations of Europe 5 have been piling up terrific debts to humanity by the encouragement of unlimited numbers. The rulers of these nations and their militarists have constantly called upon the people to breed, breed, breed! Large populations meant more people to produce wealth, more people to pay taxes, more trade for the merchants, more soldiers to protect the wealth. But more people also meant need of greater food supplies, an urgent and natural need for expansion.

As shown by C. V. Drysdale's famous "War Map of Europe," the 6 great conflict began among the high birth rate countries—Germany, with its rate of 31.7, Austria-Hungary with 33.7 and 36.7, respectively, Russia with 45.4, Serbia with 38.6. Italy with her 38.7 came in, as the world is now well informed through the publication of secret treaties by the Soviet government of Russia, upon the promise of territory held by Austria. England, owing to her small home area, is cramped with her comparatively low birth rate of 26.3. France, among the belligerents, is conspicuous for her low birth rate of 19.9, but stood in the way of expansion of high birth rate Germany. Nearly all of the persistently neutral countries—Holland, Denmark, Norway, Sweden and Switzerland have low birth rates, the average being a little over 26.

Owing to the part Germany played in the war, a survey of her 7 birth statistics is decidedly illuminating. The increase in the German birth rate up to 1876 was great. Though it began to decline then, the decline was not sufficient to offset the tremendous increase of the previous years. There were more millions to produce children, so while the average number of births per thousand was somewhat smaller, the net increase in population was still huge. From 41,000,000 in 1871, the year the Empire was founded, the German population grew to approximately 67,000,000 in 1918. Meanwhile her food supply increased only a very small percent. In 1910, Russia had a birth rate even higher than Germany's had ever been—a little less than 48 per thousand. When czarist Russia wanted an outlet to the Mediterranean by way of Constantinople, she was thinking of her increasing population. Germany was thinking of her increasing population when she spoke as with one voice of a "place in the sun." . . .

The militaristic claim for Germany's right to new territory was 8 simply a claim to the right of life and food for the German babies—the same right that a chick claims to burst its shell. If there had not been other millions of people claiming the same right, there would have been no war. But there *were* other millions.

The German rulers and leaders pointed out the fact that expan- 9 sion meant more business for German merchants, more work for German workmen at better wages, and more opportunities for Germans abroad. They also pointed out that lack of expansion meant crowding and crushing at home, hard times, heavy burdens, lack of opportunity for Germans, and what not. In this way, they gave the people of the Empire a startling and true picture of what would happen from overcrowding. Once they realized the facts, the majority of Germans naturally welcomed the so-called war of defense.

The argument was sound. Once the German mothers had sub- 10 mitted to the plea for overbreeding, it was inevitable that imperialistic Germany should make war. Once the battalions of unwanted babies came into existence—babies whom the mothers did not want but which they bore as a "patriotic duty"—it was too late to avoid international conflict. The great crime of imperialistic Germany was its high birth rate.

It has always been so. Behind all war has been the pressure of 11 population. "Historians," says Huxley, "point to the greed and ambition of rulers, the reckless turbulence of the ruled, to the debasing effects of wealth and luxury, and to the devastating wars which have formed a great part of the occupation of mankind, as the causes of the decay of states and the foundering of old civilizations, and thereby point their story with a moral. But beneath all this superficial turmoil lay the deep-seated impulse given by unlimited multiplication."

Robert Thomas Malthus, formulator of the doctrine which bears 12 his name, pointed out, in the closing years of the eighteenth century, the relation of overpopulation to war. He showed that mankind tends to increase faster than the food supply. He demonstrated that were it not for the more common diseases, for plague, famine, floods and wars, human beings would crowd each other to such an extent that the misery would be even greater than it now is. These he described as "natural checks," pointing out that as long as no other checks are employed, such disasters are unavoidable. If we do not exercise sufficient judgment to regulate the birth rate, we encounter disease, starvation and war.

Both Darwin and John Stuart Mill recognized, by inference at 13 least, the fact that so-called "natural checks"—and among them war—will operate if some sort of limitation is not employed. In his *Origin of Species*, Darwin says: "There is no exception to the rule that every organic being naturally increases at so high a rate, if not destroyed, that the earth would soon be covered by the progeny of a single pair." Elsewhere he observes that we do not permit helpless human beings to die off, but we create philanthropies and charities, build asylums and hospitals and keep the medical profession busy preserving those who could not otherwise survive. John Stuart Mill, supporting the views of Malthus, speaks to exactly the same effect in regard to the multiplying power of organic beings, among them humanity. In other words, let countries become overpopulated and war is inevitable. It follows as daylight follows the sunrise.

When Charles Bradlaugh and Mrs. Annie Besant were on trial in 14 England in 1877 for publishing information concerning contraceptives, Mrs. Besant put the case bluntly to the court and the jury:

"I have no doubt that if natural checks were allowed to operate 15 right through the human as they do in the animal world, a better result would follow. Among the brutes, the weaker are driven to the wall, the diseased fall out in the race of life. The old brutes, when feeble or sickly, are killed. If men insisted that those who were sickly should be allowed to die without help of medicine or science, if those who are weak were put upon one side and crushed, if those who were old and useless were killed, if those who were not capable of providing food for themselves were allowed to starve, if all this were done, the struggle for existence among men would be as real as it is among brutes and would doubtless result in the production of a higher race of men.

"But are you willing to do that or to allow it to be done?" 16

We are not willing to let it be done. Mother hearts cling to chil- 17 dren, no matter how diseased, misshapen and miserable. Sons and daughters hold fast to parents, no matter how helpless. We do not allow the weak to depart; neither do we cease to bring more weak and helpless beings into the world. Among the dire results is war, which kills off, not the weak and the helpless, but the strong and the fit.

What shall be done? We have our choice of one of three policies. 18 We may abandon our science and leave the weak and diseased to die, or kill them, as the brutes do. Or we may go on overpopulating the earth and have our famines and our wars while the earth exists. Or we can accept the third, sane, sensible, moral and practicable plan of birth control. We can refuse to bring the weak, the helpless and the unwanted children into the world. We can refuse to overcrowd families, nations and the earth. There are these ways to meet the situation, and only these three ways.

The world will never abandon its preventive and curative sci- 19 ence; it may be expected to elevate and extend it beyond our present imagination. The efforts to do away with famine and the opposition to war are growing by leaps and bounds. Upon these efforts are largely based our modern social revolutions.

There remains only the third expedient—birth control, the real 20 cure for war. This fact was called to the attention of the Peace Conference in Paris, in 1919, by the Malthusian League, which adopted the following resolution at its annual general meeting in London in June of that year:

"The Malthusian League desires to point out that the proposed 21 scheme for the League of Nations has neglected to take account of the important questions of *the pressure of population,* which *causes the great international economic competition* and rivalry, and of the *increase of population,* which is put forward as a justification for *claiming increase of territory.* It, therefore, wishes to put on record its belief that the League of Nations will only be able to fulfill its aim *when it adds a clause* to the following effect:

"'That each Nation desiring to enter into the League of Nations 22 shall pledge itself *so to restrict its birth rate* that its people shall be able to live in comfort *in their own dominions without need* for territorial expansion, and that it shall recognize that *increase of population shall not justify* a demand either for increase of territory or for the compulsion of other Nations to admit its emigrants; so that when all Nations in the League have shown their ability to live on their own resources without international rivalry, they will be in a position to fuse into an international federation, and territorial boundaries will then have little significance.'"

As a matter of course, the Peace Conference paid no attention to 23 the resolution, for, as pointed out by Frank A. Vanderlip, the American financier, that conference not only ignored the economic factors of the world situation, but seemed unaware that Europe had produced more people than its fields could feed. So the resolution amounted to so much propaganda and nothing more.

This remedy can be applied only by woman and she will apply it. 24 She must and will see past the call of pretended patriotism and of glory of empire and perceive what is true and what is false in these things. She will discover what base uses the militarist and the exploiter made of the idealism of peoples. Under the clamor of the press, permeating the ravings of the jingoes, she will hear the voice of Napoleon, the archetype of the militarists of all nations, calling for "fodder for cannon."

"Woman is given to us that she may bear children," said he. 25 "Woman is our property, we are not hers, because she produces children for us—we do not yield any to her. She is, therefore, our possession as the fruit tree is that of the gardener."

That is what the imperialist is *thinking* when he speaks of the 26 glory of the empire and the prestige of the nation. Every country has its appeal—its shibboleth—ready for the lips of the imperialist. German rulers pointed to the comfort of the workers, to old-age pensions, maternal benefits and mininum wage regulations, and other material benefits, when they wished to inspire soldiers for the Fatherland. England's strongest argument, perhaps, was a certain phase of liberty which she guarantees her subjects, and the protection afforded them wherever they may go. France and the United States, too, have their appeals to the idealism of democracy—appeals which the politicians of both countries know well how to use, though the peoples of both lands are beginning to awake to the fact that their countries have been living on the glories of their revolutions and traditions, rather than the substance of freedom. Behind the boast of old-age pensions, material benefits and wage regulations, behind the bombast concerning liberty in this country and tyranny in that, behind all the slogans and shibboleths coined out of the ideals of the peoples for the uses of imperialism, woman must and will see the iron hand of that same imperialism, condemning women to breed and men to die for the will of the rulers.

Upon woman the burden and the horrors of war are heaviest. Her 27 heart is the hardest wrung when the husband or the son comes home to be buried or to live a shattered wreck. Upon her devolve the extra tasks of filling out the ranks of workers in the war industries, in addition to caring for the children and replenishing the war-diminished population. Hers is the crushing weight and the sickening of soul. And it is out of her womb that those things proceed. When she sees what lies behind the glory and the horror, the boasting and the burden, and gets the vision, the human perspective, she will end war. She will kill war by the simple process of starving it to death. For she will refuse longer to produce the human food upon which the monster feeds.

CLASSIC ARGUMENTS: "THE CAUSE OF WAR"

DISCUSSION

1. Although this essay was available to the general reading public of 1920, it becomes obvious to the reader that Sanger had a more specific audience in mind. Describe this audience and specify parts of the essay that support your view.

2. The occasion for the essay reinforces Sanger's tone. Explain this relationship and illustrate where this tone is most apparent in the argument. What effect do you believe this tone had on the intended audience?

3. Check the logical reasoning of Sanger's argument by using the Toulmin model. Does she oversimplify the cause of war? Is her primary audience likely to accept her warrant? Has she refuted any reservations that audience is likely to have?

4. Sanger uses several methods of establishing credibility. Look particularly at her use of pronouns and choice of evidence. Identify how she develops her ethical appeal, and discuss how it may have affected her intended audience.

5. The context for this argument (the book appeared soon after World War I ended) is especially emotional. Does Sanger heighten the emotional appeal? If so, how and where in the essay does she do this? Does her use of emotional appeal overshadow her commitment to logical reasoning or does it provide the motivation to act on the logic?

WRITING SUGGESTIONS

1. Since the publication of Sanger's essay three major wars have been waged. Is there any indication that the "militarists" and "reactionaries" at those times had the imperialistic attitudes toward higher birthrates that would support Sanger's claim? Research this issue and present an argument based on your findings.

2. By the early 1960s population growth had increased to such an extent that concerned citizen action groups like Zero Population Growth (ZPG) organized to inform the public of the problems this growth was likely to cause. An ironic twist on Sanger's argument occurred: young couples were encouraged to limit the size of their families to two children for the well-being of the country. China went several steps further by enacting criminal laws and forced abortion to curb population. These actions and those represented in Sanger's argument raise the issue of whether or not any government has the right to govern a woman's control over her own body. Construct an argument on this issue and direct it to women or the government.

Politics and the English Language

GEORGE ORWELL

George Orwell (1903–1950), an English writer of
novels, literary criticism, and political journalism, is
known for his simple, economical, and clear writing
style and his two most famous novels, Animal Farm
(1945) and 1984 *(1949).*

Most people who bother with the matter at all would admit that the   1
English language is in a bad way, but it is generally assumed that we
cannot by conscious action do anything about it. Our civilization is
decadent and our language—so the argument runs—must inevitably
share in the general collapse. It follows that any struggle against the
abuse of language is a sentimental archaism, like preferring candles to
electric light or hansom cabs to aeroplanes. Underneath this lies the
half-conscious belief that language is a natural growth and not an instrument which we shape for our own purposes.

    Now, it is clear that the decline of a language must ultimately   2
have political and economic causes: it is not due simply to the bad
influence of this or that individual writer. But an effect can become a
cause, reinforcing the original cause and producing the same effect in
an intensified form, and so on indefinitely. A man may take to drink
because he feels himself to be a failure, and then fail all the more completely because he drinks. It is rather the same thing that is happening
to the English language. It becomes ugly and inaccurate because our
thoughts are foolish, but the slovenliness of our language makes it
easier for us to have foolish thoughts. The point is that the process is
reversible. Modern English, especially written English, is full of bad
habits which spread by imitation and which can be avoided if one is
willing to take the necessary trouble. If one gets rid of these habits one
can think more clearly, and to think clearly is a necessary first step towards political regeneration: so that the fight against bad English is
not frivolous and is not the exclusive concern of professional writers. I
will come back to this presently, and I hope that by that time the
meaning of what I have said here will have become clearer. Meanwhile,
here are five specimens of the English language as it is now habitually
written.

These five passages have not been picked out because they are 3 especially bad—I could have quoted far worse if I had chosen—but because they illustrate various of the mental vices from which we now suffer. They are a little below the average, but are fairly representative samples. I number them so that I can refer back to them when necessary:

(1) I am not, indeed, sure whether it is not true to say that the Milton who once seemed not unlike a seventeenth-century Shelley had not become, out of an experience ever more bitter in each year, more alien[*sic*] to the founder of that Jesuit sect which nothing could induce him to tolerate.

Professor Harold Laski
(*Essay in* Freedom of Expression).

(2) Above all, we cannot play ducks and drakes with a native battery of idioms which prescribes such egregious collocations of vocables as the Basic *put up with* for *tolerate* or *put at a loss* for *bewilder.*

Professor Lancelot Hogben (Interglossa).

(3) On the one side we have the free personality: by definition it is not neurotic, for it has neither conflict nor dream. Its desires, such as they are, are transparent, for they are just what institutional approval keeps in the forefront of consciousness; another institutional pattern would alter their number and intensity; there is little in them that is natural, irreducible, or culturally dangerous. But *on the other side,* the social bond itself is nothing but the mutual reflection of these self-secure integrities. Recall the definition of love. Is not this the very picture of a small academic? Where is there a place in this hall of mirrors for either personality or fraternity?

Essay on psychology in Politics (New York).

(4) All the "best people" from the gentlemen's clubs, and all the frantic fascist captains, united in common hatred of Socialism and bestial horror of the rising tide of the mass revolutionary movement, have turned to acts of provocation, to foul incendiarism, to medieval legends of poisoned wells, to legalize their own destruction of proletarian organizations, and rouse the agitated petty-bourgeoisie to chauvinistic fervor on behalf of the fight against the revolutionary way out of the crisis.

Communist pamphlet

(5) If a new spirit *is* to be infused into this old country, there is one thorny and contentious reform which must be tackled, and that is the humanization and galvanization of the B.B.C. Timidity

here will bespeak cancer and atrophy of the soul. The heart of Britain may be sound and of strong beat, for instance, but the British lion's roar at present is like that of Bottom in Shakespeare's *Midsummer Night's Dream*—as gentle as any sucking dove. A virile new Britain cannot continue indefinitely to be traduced in the eyes or rather ears, of the world by the effete languors of Langham Place, brazenly masquerading as "standard English." When the Voice of Britain is heard at nine o'clock, better far and infinitely less ludicrous to hear aitches honestly dropped than the present priggish, inflated, inhibited, school-ma'amish arch braying of blameless bashful mewing maidens!

Letter in Tribune

Each of these passages has faults of its own, but, quite apart from avoidable ugliness, two qualities are common to all of them. The first is staleness of imagery: the other is lack of precision. The writer either has a meaning and cannot express it, or he inadvertently says something else, or he is almost indifferent as to whether his words mean anything or not. The mixture of vagueness and sheer incompetence is the most marked characteristic of modern English prose, and especially of any kind of political writing. As soon as certain topics are raised, the concrete melts into the abstract and no one seems to think of turns of speech that are not hackneyed: prose consists less and less of *words* chosen for the sake of their meaning, and more and more of *phrases* tacked together like the sections of a prefabricated hen-house. I list below, with notes and examples, various of the tricks by means of which the work of prose-construction is habitually dodged:

Dying Metaphors

A newly invented metaphor assists thought by evoking a visual image, while on the other hand a metaphor which is technically "dead" (e.g., *iron resolution*) has in effect reverted to being an ordinary word and can generally be used without loss of vividness. But in between these two classes there is a huge dump of worn-out metaphors which have lost all evocative power and are merely used because they save people the trouble of inventing phrases for themselves. Examples are: *Ring the changes on, take up the cudgels for, toe the line, ride roughshod over, stand shoulder to shoulder with, play into the hands of, no axe to grind, grist to the mill, fishing in troubled waters, on the order of the day, Achilles' heel, swan song, hotbed.* Many of these are used without knowledge of their meaning (what is a "rift," for instance?), and incompatible metaphors are frequently mixed, a sure sign that the writer is not interested in what he is saying. Some metaphors now current have been twisted out of their original meaning without those who use them even being aware of the fact. For example, *toe the line* is sometimes written *tow the line*. Another example is *the hammer and the anvil*, now always used with the implication that the anvil gets the worst of it. In real life it is always the anvil that breaks the hammer, never the other way about: a writer who stopped to think what he was saying would be aware of this, and would avoid perverting the original phrase.

Operators or Verbal False Limbs

These save the trouble of picking out appropriate verbs and nouns, 6
and at the same time pad each sentence with extra syllables which
give it an appearance of symmetry. Characteristic phrases are: *render
inoperative, militate against, make contact with, be subjected to, give
rise to, give grounds for, have the effect of, play a leading part (role) in,
make itself felt, take effect, exhibit a tendency to, serve the purpose
of, etc., etc.* The keynote is the elimination of simple verbs. Instead of
being a single word, such as *break, stop, spoil, mend, kill*, a verb becomes a *phrase*, made up of a noun or adjective tacked on to some
general-purpose verb such as *prone, serve, form, play, render*. In addition, the passive voice is wherever possible used in preference to the
active, and noun constructions are used instead of gerunds (*by examination of* instead of *by examining*). The range of verbs is further cut
down by means of the *-ize* and *de-* formation, and the banal statements are given an appearance of profundity by means of the *non un-*
formation. Simple conjunctions and prepositions are replaced by such
phrases as *with respect to, having regard to, the fact that, by dint of, in
view of, in the interests of, on the hypothesis that;* and the ends of sentences are saved from anticlimax by such resounding commonplaces
as *greatly to be desired, cannot be left out of account, a development to
be expected in the near future, deserving of serious consideration,
brought to a satisfactory conclusion,* and so on and so forth.

Pretentious Diction

Words like *phenomenon, element, individual* (as noun), *objective, cate-* 7
*gorical, effective, virtual, basic, primary, promote, constitute, exhibit,
exploit, utilize, eliminate, liquidate,* are used to dress up simple statements and give an air of scientific impartiality to biased judgments.
Adjectives like *epoch-making, epic, historic, unforgettable, triumphant,
age-old, inevitable, inexorable, veritable,* are used to dignify the sordid
processes of international politics, while writing that aims at glorifying
war usually takes on an archaic color, its characteristic words being:
realm, throne, chariot, mailed fist, trident, sword, shield, buckler, banner, jackboot, clarion. Foreign words and expressions such as *cul de*

sac, ancien régime, deus ex machina, mutatis mutandis, status quo, gleichshaltung, weltanschauung, are used to give an air of culture and elegance. Except for the useful abbreviations *i.e., e.g.,* and *etc.,* there is no real need for any of the hundreds of foreign phrases now current in English. Bad writers, and especially scientific, political and socio-logical writers, are nearly always haunted by the notion that Latin or Greek words are grander than Saxon ones, and unnecessary words like *expedite, ameliorate, predict, extraneous, deracinated, clandestine, subaqueous* and hundreds of others constantly gain ground from their Anglo-Saxon opposite numbers.[1] The jargon peculiar to Marxist writ-ing (*hyena, hangman, cannibal, petty bourgeois, these gentry, lackey, flunkey, mad dog, White Guard,* etc.) consists largely of words and phrases translated from Russian, German or French; but the normal way of coining a new word is to use a Latin or Greek root with the appropriate affix and, where necessary, the *-ize* formation. It is often easier to make up words of this kind (*deregionalize, impermissible, extramarital, nonfragmentatory* and so forth) than to think up the English words that will cover one's meaning. The result, in general, is an increase in slovenliness and vagueness.

Meaningless Words

In certain kinds of writing, particularly in art criticism and literary criticism, it is normal to come across long passages which are almost completely lacking in meaning.[2] Words like *romantic, plastic, values, human, dead, sentimental, natural, vitality,* as used in art criticism, are strictly meaningless in the sense that they not only do not point to any discoverable object, but are hardly ever expected to do so by the reader. When one critic writes, "The outstanding feature of Mr. X's work is its living quality," while another writes, "The immediately strik-ing thing about Mr. X's work is its peculiar deadness," the reader ac-cepts this as a simple difference of opinion. If words like *black* and *white* were involved, instead of the jargon words *dead* and *living,* he would see at once that language was being used in an improper way. Many political words are similarly abused. The word *Fascism* has now no meaning except in so far as it signifies "something not desirable." The words *democracy, socialism, freedom, patriotic, realistic, justice,* have each of them several different meanings which cannot be recon-ciled with one another. In the case of a word like *democracy,* not only is there no agreed definition, but the attempt to make one is resisted from all sides. It is almost universally felt that when we call a country democratic we are praising it: consequently the defenders of every kind of regime claim that it is a democracy, and fear that they might have to stop using the word if it were tied down to any one meaning.

8

Words of this kind are often used in a consciously dishonest way. That is, the person who uses them has his own private definition, but allows his hearer to think he means something quite different. Statements like *Marshal Pétain was a true patriot, The Soviet Press is the freest in the world, The Catholic Church is opposed to persecution,* are almost always made with intent to deceive. Other words used in variable meanings, in most cases more or less dishonestly, are: *class, totalitarian, science, progressive, reactionary, bourgeois, equality.*

Now that I have made this catalogue of swindles and perversions, 9 let me give another example of the kind of writing they lead to. This time it must of its nature be an imaginary one. I am going to translate a passage of good English into modern English of the worst sort. Here is a well-known verse from *Ecclesiastes:*

> I returned and saw under the sun, that the race is not to the swift, nor the battle to the strong, neither yet bread to the wise, nor yet riches to men of understanding, nor yet favor to men of skill; but time and chance happeneth to them all.

Here it is in modern English:

> Objective consideration of contemporary phenomena compels the conclusion that success or failure in competitive activities exhibits no tendency to be commensurate with innate capacity, but that a considerable element of the unpredictable must invariably be taken into account.

This is a parody, but not a very gross one. Exhibit (3), above, for 10 instance, contains several patches of the same kind of English. It will be seen that I have not made a full translation. The beginning and ending of the sentence follow the original meaning fairly closely, but in the middle the concrete illustrations—race, battle, bread—dissolve into the vague phrase "success or failure in competitive activities." This had to be so, because no modern writer of the kind I am discussing—no one capable of using phrases like "objective consideration of contemporary phenomena"—would ever tabulate his thoughts in that precise and detailed way. The whole tendency of modern prose is away from concreteness. Now analyze these two sentences a little more closely. The first contains forty-nine words but only sixty syllables, and all its words are those of everyday life. The second contains thirty-eight words of ninety syllables: eighteen of its words are from Latin roots, and one from Greek. The first sentence contains six vivid images, and only one phrase ("time and chance") that could be called vague. The second contains not a single fresh, arresting phrase, and in spite of its ninety syllables it gives only a shortened version of the meaning contained in the first. Yet without a doubt it is the second kind of sentence that is gaining ground in modern English. I do not want to exaggerate.

This kind of writing is not yet universal, and outcrops of simplicity will occur here and there in the worst-written page. Still, if you or I were told to write a few lines on the uncertainty of human fortunes, we should probably come much nearer to my imaginary sentence than to the one from *Ecclesiastes*.

As I have tried to show, modern writing at its worst does not con- 11 sist in picking out words for the sake of their meaning and inventing images in order to make the meaning clearer. It consists in gumming together long strips of words which have already been set in order by someone else, and making the results presentable by sheer humbug. The attraction of this way of writing is that it is easy. It is easier—even quicker once you have the habit—to say *In my opinion it is a not unjustifiable assumption that* than to say I *think*. If you use ready-made phrases, you not only don't have to hunt about for words; you also don't have to bother with the rhythms of your sentences, since these phrases are generally so arranged as to be more or less euphonious. When you are composing in a hurry—when you are dictating to a stenographer, for instance, or making a public speech—it is natural to fall into a pretentious, Latinized style. Tags like *a consideration which we should do well to bear in mind* or *a conclusion to which all of us would readily assent* will save many a sentence from coming down with a bump. By using stale metaphors, similes and idioms, you save much mental effort, at the cost of leaving your meaning vague, not only for your reader but for yourself. This is the significance of mixed metaphors. The sole aim of a metaphor is to call up a visual image. When these images clash—as in *The Fascist octopus has sung its swan song, the jackboot is thrown into the melting pot*—it can be taken as certain that the writer is not seeing a mental image of the objects he is naming; in other words he is not really thinking. Look again at the examples I gave at the beginning of this essay. Professor Laski (1) uses five negatives in fifty-three words. One of these is superfluous, making nonsense of the whole passage, and in addition there is the slip *alien* for akin, making further nonsense, and several avoidable pieces of clumsiness which increase the general vagueness. Professor Hogben (2) plays ducks and drakes with a battery which is able to write prescriptions, and, while disapproving of the every-day phrase *put up with*, is unwilling to look *egregious* up in the dictionary and see what it means. (3), if one takes an uncharitable attitude towards it, is simply meaningless: probably one could work out its intended meaning by reading the whole of the article in which it occurs. In (4), the writer knows more or less what he wants to say, but an accumulation of stale phrases chokes him like tea leaves blocking a sink. In (5), words and meaning have almost parted company. People who write in this manner usually have a general emotional meaning—they dislike one thing and want to express solidarity with another—but they are not interested in the detail of what they are saying. A scrupulous writer, in every sentence that he writes, will ask himself at least four questions, thus: What am I trying to say? What words will express it? What image or idiom will make it clearer? Is this image fresh enough to have an effect? And he will probably ask himself two more: Could I put it more shortly? Have I said anything that is avoidably ugly? But you are not obliged to go to all this trouble. You can shirk it by simply throwing your mind open and letting the ready-made phrases come crowding in. They will construct your sentences for you—even think your thoughts for you, to a certain extent—and at need they will perform the important service of partially concealing your meaning even from yourself. It is at this point that the special connection between politics and the debasement of language becomes clear.

In our time it is broadly true that political writing is bad writing. 12 Where it is not true, it will generally be found that the writer is some kind of rebel, expressing his private opinions and not a "party line." Orthodoxy, of whatever color, seems to demand a lifeless, imitative style. The political dialects to be found in pamphlets, leading articles, manifestos, White Papers and the speeches of under-secretaries do, of course, vary from party to party, but they are all alike in that one almost never finds in them a fresh, vivid, home-made turn of speech. When one watches some tired hack on the platform mechanically repeating the familiar phrases—*bestial atrocities, iron heel, bloodstained tyranny, free peoples of the world, stand shoulder to shoulder*—one often has a curious feeling that one is not watching a live human being but some kind of dummy; a feeling which suddenly becomes stronger at moments when the light catches the speaker's spectacles and turns them into blank discs which seem to have no eyes behind them. And this is not altogether fanciful. A speaker who uses that kind of phraseology has gone some distance towards turning himself into a machine. The appropriate noises are coming out of his larynx, but his brain is not involved as it would be if he were choosing his words for himself. If the speech he is making is one that he is accustomed to make over and over again, he may be almost unconscious of what he is saying, as one is when one utters the responses in church. And this reduced state of consciousness, if not indispensable, is at any rate favorable to political conformity.

In our time, political speech and writing are largely the defense 13 of the indefensible. Things like the continuance of British rule in India, the Russian purges and deportations, the dropping of the atom bombs on Japan, can indeed be defended, but only by arguments which are too brutal for most people to face, and which do not square with the professed aims of political parties. Thus political language has to consist largely of euphemism, question-begging and sheer cloudy vagueness. Defenseless villages are bombarded from the air, the inhabitants driven out into the countryside, the cattle machine-gunned, the huts set on fire with incendiary bullets: this is called *pacification*. Millions of peasants are robbed of their farms and sent trudging along the roads with no more than they can carry: this is called *transfer of population* or *rectification of frontiers*. People are imprisoned for years without trial, or shot in the back of the neck or sent to die of scurvy in Arctic lumber camps: this is called *elimination of unreliable elements*. Such phraseology is needed if one wants to name things without calling up mental pictures of them. Consider for instance some comfortable English professor defending Russian totalitarianism. He cannot say outright, "I believe in killing off your opponents when you can get good results by doing so." Probably, therefore, he will say something like this:

"While freely conceding that the Soviet régime exhibits certain 14 features which the humanitarian may be inclined to deplore, we must, I think, agree that a certain curtailment of the right to political opposition is an unavoidable concomitant of transitional periods, and that the rigors which the Russian people have been called upon to undergo have been amply justified in the sphere of concrete achievement."

The inflated style is itself a kind of euphemism. A mass of Latin 15 words fall upon the facts like soft snow, blurring the outlines and covering up all the details. The great enemy of clear language is insincerity. When there is a gap between one's real and one's declared aims, one turns as it were instinctively to long words and exhausted idioms, like a cuttlefish squirting out ink. In our age there is no such thing as "keeping out of politics." All issues are political issues, and politics itself is a mass of lies, evasions, folly, hatred and schizophrenia. When the general atmosphere is bad, language must suffer. I should expect to find—this is a guess which I have not sufficient knowledge to verify—that the German, Russian and Italian languages have all deteriorated in the last ten or fifteen years, as a result of dictatorship.

But if thought corrupts language, language can also corrupt 16 thought. A bad usage can spread by tradition and imitation, even among people who should and do know better. The debased language that I have been discussing is in some ways very convenient. Phrases like *a not unjustifiable assumption, leaves much to be desired, would serve no good purpose, a consideration which we should do well to bear in mind*, are a continuous temptation, a packet of aspirins always at one's elbow. Look back through this essay, and for certain you will find that I have again and again committed the very faults I am protesting against. By this morning's post I have received a pamphlet dealing with conditions in Germany. The author tells me that he "felt impelled" to write it. I open it at random, and here is almost the first sentence that I see: "(The Allies) have an opportunity not only of achieving a radical transformation of Germany's social and political structure in such a way as to avoid a nationalistic reaction in Germany itself, but at the same time of laying the foundations of a co-operative and unified Europe." You see, he "feels impelled" to write—feels, presumably, that he has something new to say—and yet his words, like cavalry horses answer the bugle, group themselves automatically into the familiar dreary pattern. This invasion of one's mind by ready-made phrases (*lay the foundations, achieve a radical transformation*) can only be prevented if one is constantly on guard against them, and every such phrase anaesthetizes a portion of one's brain.

I said earlier that the decadence of our language is probably curable. Those who deny this would argue, if they produced an argument at all, that language merely reflects existing social conditions, and that we cannot influence its development by any direct tinkering with words and constructions. So far as the general tone or spirit of a language goes, this may be true, but it is not true in detail. Silly words and expressions have often disappeared, not through any evolutionary process but owing to the conscious action of a minority. Two recent examples were *explore every avenue* and *leave no stone unturned*, which were killed by the jeers of a few journalists. There is a long list of flyblown metaphors which could similarly be got rid of if enough people would interest themselves in the job; and it should also be possible to laugh the *not un-* formation out of existence,[3] to reduce the amount of Latin and Greek in the average sentence, to drive out foreign phrases and strayed scientific words, and, in general, to make pretentiousness unfashionable. But all these are minor points. The defense of the English language implies more than this, and perhaps it is best to start by saying what it does *not* imply.

To begin with it has nothing to do with archaism, with the salvaging of obsolete words and turns of speech, or with the setting up of a "standard English" which must never be departed from. On the contrary, it is especially concerned with the scrapping of every word or idiom which has outworn its usefulness. It has nothing to do with correct grammar and syntax, which are of no importance so long as one makes one's meaning clear, or with the avoidance of Americanisms, or with having what is called a "good prose style." On the other hand it is not concerned with fake simplicity and the attempt to make written English colloquial. Nor does it even imply in every case preferring the Saxon word to the Latin one, though it does imply using the fewest and shortest words that will cover one's meaning. What is above all needed is to let the meaning choose the word, and not the other way about. In prose, the worst thing one can do with words is to surrender to them. When you think of a concrete object, you think wordlessly, and then, if you want to describe the thing you have been visualizing you probably hunt about till you find the exact words that seem to fit. When you think of something abstract you are more inclined to use words from the start, and unless you make a conscious effort to prevent it, the existing dialect will come rushing in and do the job for you, at the expense of blurring or even changing your meaning. Probably it is better to put off using words as long as possible and get one's meaning as clear as one can through pictures or sensations. Afterwards one can choose—not simply *accept*—the phrases that will best cover the meaning, and then switch round and decide what impression one's words are likely to make on another person. This last effort of the mind cuts out all stale or mixed images, all prefabricated phrases, needless repetitions, and humbug and vagueness generally. But one can often be in doubt about the effect of a word or a phrase, and one needs rules that one can rely on when instinct fails. I think the following rules will cover most cases:

(i) Never use a metaphor, simile or other figure of speech which you are used to seeing in print.
(ii) Never use a long word where a short one will do.
(iii) If it is possible to cut a word out, always cut it out.
(iv) Never use the passive where you can use the active.
(v) Never use a foreign phrase, a scientific word or a jargon word if you can think of an everyday English equivalent.
(vi) Break any of these rules sooner than say anything outright barbarous.

These rules sound elementary, and so they are, but they demand a deep change in attitude in anyone who has grown used to writing in the style now fashionable. One could keep all of them and still write bad English, but one could not write the kind of stuff that I quoted in those five specimens at the beginning of this article.

I have not here been considering the literary use of language, but merely language as an instrument for expressing and not for concealing or preventing thought. Stuart Chase and others have come near to claiming that all abstract words are meaningless, and have used this as a pretext for advocating a kind of political quietism. Since you don't know what Fascism is, how can you struggle against Fascism? One need not swallow such absurdities as this, but one ought to recognize that the present political chaos is connected with the decay of language, and that one can probably bring about some improvement by starting at the verbal end. If you simplify your English, you are freed from the worst follies of orthodoxy. You cannot speak any of the necessary dialects, and when you make a stupid remark its stupidity will be obvious, even to yourself. Political language—and with variations this is true of all political parties, from Conservatives to Anarchists—is designed to make lies sound truthful and murder respectable, and to give an appearance of solidity to pure wind. One cannot change this all in a moment, but one can at least change one's own habits, and from time to time one can even, if one jeers loudly enough, send some wornout and useless phrase—some *jackboot, Achilles' heel, hotbed, melting pot, acid test, veritable inferno* or other lump of verbal refuse—into the dustbin where it belongs.

Notes

1. An interesting illustration of this is the way in which the English flower names which were in use till very recently are being ousted by Greek ones, *snapdragon* becoming *antirrhinum, forget-me-not* becoming *myosotis*, etc. It is hard to see any practical reason for this change of fashion: it is probably due to an instinctive turning-away from the more homely word and a vague feeling that the Greek word is scientific.
2. Example: "Comfort's catholicity of perception and image, strangely Whitmanesque in range, almost the exact opposite in aesthetic compulsion, continues to evoke that trembling atmospheric accumulative hinting at a cruel, an inexorably serene time-lessness. . . . Wrey Gardiner scores by aiming at simple bull's-eyes with precision. Only they are not so simple, and through this contented sadness runs more than the surface bittersweet of resignation." *(Poetry Quarterly.)*
3. One can cure oneself of the *not un-* formation by memorizing this sentence: *A not unblack dog was chasing a not unsmall rabbit across a not ungreen field.*

CLASSIC ARGUMENTS: "POLITICS AND THE ENGLISH LANGUAGE"

DISCUSSION

1. What assumptions does Orwell make about his audience's relationship to the subject of the essay? State those assumptions and write a profile of Orwell's intended audience.

2. Does Orwell fulfill the title's commitment to the reader by establishing a relationship between politics and language? Explain the connection in your own words and state the warrant the audience must believe to accept that connection.

3. Writing about the effective and ineffective use of language places Orwell in an especially vulnerable position. How does Orwell establish his credibility through his own style? Does he ever violate his own standards? Reread Orwell's rules before evaluating his style.

4. Orwell devotes the majority of the essay to illustrating and analyzing the ways language is abused. What is his claim and what motivation does he provide for the audience to continue reading?

5. Orwell writes in the first person singular *I* and refers to the writers he hopes to inform as *one* and *he.* How does this use of pronouns affect the distance between Orwell and his audience? How does his use of *you* in the concluding paragraph change that effect?

WRITING SUGGESTIONS

1. Write an update of Orwell's argument using examples from current sources. The examples you select should be specifically designed for your intended audience.

2. Choosing pronouns to avoid sexist language has become a controversial matter. For example, should we use *he or she, she or he, he/she,* or *s/he*? Explore the issues of this controversy and present an argument defending your views, with your English teacher as the intended audience.

Letter from Birmingham Jail

MARTIN LUTHER KING, JR.

Martin Luther King, Jr. (1929–1968) was an American clergyman who advocated nonviolence and racial brotherhood. He won the Nobel Peace Prize in 1964 for his work to secure civil rights for black Americans, an effort that caused him to be jailed several times.

April 16, 1963

My Dear Fellow Clergymen:

While confined here in the Birmingham city jail, I came across 1
your recent statement calling my present activities "unwise and untimely." Seldom do I pause to answer criticism of my work and ideas. If
I sought to answer all the criticisms that cross my desk, my secretaries
would have little time for anything other than such correspondence in
the course of the day, and I would have no time for constructive work.
But since I feel that you are men of genuine good will and that your
criticisms are sincerely put forth, I want to try to answer your statement in what I hope will be patient and reasonable terms.

I think I should indicate why I am here in Birmingham, since you 2
have been influenced by the view which argues against "outsiders

coming in." I have the honor of serving as president of the Southern Christian Leadership Conference, an organization operating in every southern state, with headquarters in Atlanta, Georgia. We have some eighty-five affiliated organizations across the South, and one of them is the Alabama Christian Movement for Human Rights. Frequently we share staff, educational, and financial resources with our affiliates. Several months ago the affiliate here in Birmingham asked us to be on call to engage in a nonviolent direct-action program if such were deemed necessary. We readily consented, and when the hour came we lived up to our promise. So I, along with several members of my staff, am here because I was invited here. I am here because I have organizational ties here.

But more basically, I am in Birmingham because injustice is here. 3 Just as the prophets of the eighth century B.C. left their villages and carried their "thus saith the Lord" far beyond the boundaries of their home towns, and just as the Apostle Paul left his village of Tarsus and carried the gospel of Jesus Christ to the far corners of the Greco-Roman world, so am I compelled to carry the gospel of freedom beyond my own home town. Like Paul, I must constantly respond to the Macedonian call for aid.

Moreover, I am cognizant of the interrelatedness of all commu- 4 nities and states. I cannot sit idly by in Atlanta and not be concerned about what happens in Birmingham. Injustice anywhere is a threat to justice everywhere. We are caught in an inescapable network of mutuality, tied in a single garment of destiny. Whatever affects one directly, affects all indirectly. Never again can we afford to live with the narrow, provincial, "outside agitator" idea. Anyone who lives inside the United States can never be considered an outsider anywhere within its bounds.

You deplore the demonstrations taking place in Birmingham. But 5 your statement, I am sorry to say, fails to express a similar concern for the conditions that brought about the demonstrations. I am sure that none of you would want to rest content with the superficial kind of social analysis that deals merely with effects and does not grapple with underlying causes. It is unfortunate that demonstrations are taking place in Birmingham, but it is even more unfortunate that the city's white power structure left the Negro community with no alternative.

In any nonviolent campaign there are four basic steps: collection 6 of the facts to determine whether injustices exist; negotiation; self-purification; and direct action. We have gone through all these steps in Birmingham. There can be no gainsaying the fact that racial injustice engulfs this community. Birmingham is probably the most thoroughly segregated city in the United States. Its ugly record of brutality is widely known. Negroes have experienced grossly unjust treatment in courts. There have been more unsolved bombings of Negro homes and churches in Birmingham than in any other city in the nation. These are the hard, brutal facts of the case. On the basis of these conditions, Negro leaders sought to negotiate with the city fathers. But the latter consistently refused to engage in good-faith negotiation.

Then, last September, came the opportunity to talk with leaders 7 of Birmingham's economic community. In the course of the negotiations, certain promises were made by the merchants—for example, to remove the stores' humiliating racial signs. On the basis of these promises, the Reverend Fred Shuttlesworth and the leaders of the Alabama Christian Movement for Human Rights agreed to a moratorium on all demonstrations. As the weeks and months went by, we realized that we were the victims of a broken promise. A few signs, briefly removed, returned; the others remained.

As in so many past experiences, our hopes had been blasted, and 8 the shadow of deep disappointment settled upon us. We had no alternative except to prepare for direct action, whereby we would present our very bodies as means of laying our case before the conscience of the local and the national community. Mindful of the difficulties involved, we decided to undertake a process of self-purification. We began a series of workshops on nonviolence, and we repeatedly asked ourselves: "Are you able to accept blows without retaliating?" "Are you able to endure the ordeal of jail?" We decided to schedule our direct-action program for the Easter season, realizing that except for Christmas, this is the main shopping period of the year. Knowing that a strong economic-withdrawal program would be the by-product of direct action, we felt that this would be the best time to bring pressure to bear on the merchants for the needed change.

Then it occurred to us that Birmingham's mayoral election was 9 coming up in March, and we speedily decided to postpone action until after election day. When we discovered that the Commissioner of Public Safety, Eugene "Bull" Connor, had piled up enough votes to be in the run-off, we decided again to postpone action until the day after the run-off so that the demonstrations could not be used to cloud the issues. Like many others, we waited to see Mr. Connor defeated, and to this end we endured postponement after postponement. Having aided in this community need, we felt that our direct-action program could be delayed no longer.

You may well ask, "Why direct action? Why sit-ins, marches, and 10 so forth? Isn't negotiation a better path?" You are quite right in calling for negotiation. Indeed, this is the very purpose of direct action. Nonviolent direct action seeks to create such a crisis and foster such a tension that a community which has constantly refused to negotiate is forced to confront the issue. It seeks so to dramatize the issue that it can no longer be ignored. My citing the creation of tension as part of the work of the nonviolent-resister may sound rather shocking. But I must confess that I am not afraid of the word "tension." I have earnestly opposed violent tension, but there is a type of constructive, nonviolent tension which is necessary for growth. Just as Socrates felt that it was necessary to create a tension in the mind so that individuals could rise from the bondage of myths and half-truths to the unfettered realm of creative analysis and objective appraisal, so must we see the need for nonviolent gadflies to create the kind of tension in society that will help men rise from the dark depths of prejudice and racism to the majestic heights of understanding and brotherhood.

The purpose of our direct-action program is to create a situation 11 so crisis-packed that it will inevitably open the door to negotiation. I therefore concur with you in your call for negotiation. Too long has our beloved Southland been bogged down in a tragic effort to live in monologue rather than dialogue.

One of the basic points in your statement is that the action that I 12 and my associates have taken in Birmingham is untimely. Some have asked: "Why didn't you give the new city administration time to act?" The only answer that I can give to this query is that the new Birmingham administration must be prodded about as much as the outgoing one, before it will act. We are sadly mistaken if we feel that the election of Albert Boutwell as mayor will bring the millennium to Birmingham. While Mr. Boutwell is a much more gentle person than Mr. Connor, they are both segregationists, dedicated to maintenance of the status quo. I have hoped that Mr. Boutwell will be reasonable enough to see the futility of massive resistance to desegregation. But he will not see this without pressure from devotees of civil rights. My friends, I must say to you that we have not made a single gain in civil rights without determined legal and nonviolent pressure. Lamentably, it is an historical fact that privileged groups seldom give up their privileges voluntarily. Individuals may see the moral light and voluntarily give up their unjust posture; but, as Reinhold Niebuhr has reminded us, groups tend to be more immoral than individuals.

We know through painful experience that freedom is never vol- 13 untarily given by the oppressor; it must be demanded by the oppressed. Frankly, I have yet to engage in a direct-action campaign that was "well timed" in the view of those who have not suffered unduly from the disease of segregation. For years now I have heard the word "Wait!" It rings in the ear of every Negro with piercing familiarity. This "Wait" has almost always meant "Never." We must come to see, with one of our distinguished jurists, that "justice too long delayed is justice denied."

We have waited for more than 340 years for our constitutional 14 and God-given rights. The nations of Asia and Africa are moving with jetlike speed toward gaining political independence, but we still creep at horse-and-buggy pace toward gaining a cup of coffee at a lunch counter. Perhaps it is easy for those who have never felt the stinging darts of segregation to say, "Wait." But when you have seen vicious mobs lynch your mothers and fathers at will and drown your sisters and brothers at whim; when you have seen hate-filled policemen curse, kick, and even kill your black brothers and sisters; when you see the vast majority of your twenty million Negro brothers smothering in an airtight cage of poverty in the midst of an affluent society; when you suddenly find your tongue twisted and your speech stammering as you seek to explain to your six-year-old daughter why she can't go to the public amusement park that has just been advertised on television, and see tears welling up in her eyes when she is told that Funtown is closed to colored chidren, and see ominous clouds of inferiority beginning to form in her little mental sky, and see her beginning to distort her personality by developing an unconscious bitterness toward white people; when you have to concoct an answer for a five-year-old son who is asking, "Daddy, why do white people treat colored people so mean?"; when you take a cross-country drive and find it necessary to sleep night after night in the uncomfortable corners of your automobile because no motel will accept you; when you are humiliated day in and day out by nagging signs reading "white" and "colored"; when your first name becomes "nigger," your middle name becomes "boy" (however old you are) and your last name becomes "John," and your wife and mother are never given the respected title "Mrs."; when you are harried by day and haunted by night by the fact that you are a Negro, living constantly at tiptoe stance, never quite knowing what to expect next, and are plagued with inner fears and outer resentments; when you are forever fighting a degenerating sense of "nobodiness"—then you will understand why we find it difficult to wait. There comes a time when the cup of endurance runs over, and men are no longer willing to be plunged into the abyss of despair. I hope, sirs, you can understand our legitimate and unavoidable impatience.

You express a great deal of anxiety over our willingness to break 15 laws. This is certainly a legitimate concern. Since we so diligently urge people to obey the Supreme Court's decision of 1954 outlawing segregation in the public schools, at first glance it may seem rather paradoxical for us consciously to break laws. One may well ask: "How can you advocate breaking some laws and obeying others?" The answer lies in the fact that there are two types of laws; just and unjust. I would be the first to advocate obeying just laws. One has not only a legal but a moral responsibility to obey just laws. Conversely, one has a moral responsibility to disobey unjust laws. I would agree with St. Augustine that "an unjust law is no law at all."

Now, what is the difference between the two? How does one de- 16
termine whether a law is just or unjust? A just law is a man-made code
that squares with the moral law or the law of God. An unjust law is a
code that is out of harmony with the moral law. To put it in the terms
of St. Thomas Aquinas: An unjust law is a human law that is not rooted
in eternal law and natural law. Any law that uplifts human personality
is just. Any law that degrades human personality is unjust. All segregation statutes are unjust because segregation distorts the soul and
damages the personality. It gives the segregator a false sense of superiority and the segregated a false sense of inferiority. Segregation, to use
the terminology of the Jewish philosopher Martin Buber, substitutes
an "I-it" relationship for an "I-thou" relationship and ends up relegat-
ing persons to the status of things. Hence segregation is not only politically, economically, and sociologically unsound, it is morally wrong
and sinful. Paul Tillich has said that sin is separation. Is not segregation an existential expression of man's tragic separation, his awful es-
trangement, his terrible sinfulness? Thus it is that I can urge men to
obey the 1954 decision of the Supreme Court, for it is morally right;
and I can urge them to disobey segregation ordinances, for they are
morally wrong.

Let us consider a more concrete example of just and unjust laws. 17
An unjust law is a code that a numerical or power majority group
compels a minority group to obey but does not make binding on itself.
This is *difference* made legal. By the same token, a just law is a code
that a majority compels a minority to follow and that it is willing to
follow itself. This is *sameness* made legal.

Let me give another explanation. A law is unjust if it is inflicted 18
on a minority that, as a result of being denied the right to vote, had no
part in enacting or devising the law. Who can say that the legislature of
Alabama which set up that state's segregation laws was democratically
elected? Throughout Alabama all sorts of devious methods are used to
prevent Negroes from becoming registered voters, and there are some
counties in which, even though Negroes constitute a majority of the
population, not a single Negro is registered. Can any law enacted
under such circumstances be considered democratically structured?

Sometimes a law is just on its face and unjust in its application. 19
For instance, I have been arrested on a charge of parading without a
permit. Now, there is nothing wrong in having an ordinance which requires a permit for a parade. But such an ordinance becomes unjust
when it is used to maintain segregation and to deny citizens the First-
Amendment privilege of peaceful assembly and protest.

I hope you are able to see the distinction I am trying to point out. 20
In no sense do I advocate evading or defying the law, as would the
rabid segregationist. That would lead to anarchy. One who breaks an
unjust law must do so openly, lovingly, and with a willingness to ac-

cept the penalty. I submit that an individual who breaks a law that conscience tells him is unjust, and who willingly accepts the penalty of imprisonment in order to arouse the conscience of the community over its injustice, is in reality expressing the highest respect for law.

Of course, there is nothing new about this kind of civil dis- 21 obedience. It was evidenced sublimely in the refusal of Shadrach, Meshach, and Abednego to obey the laws of Nebuchadnezzar, on the ground that a higher moral law was at stake. It was practiced superbly by the early Christians, who were willing to face hungry lions and the excruciating pain of chopping blocks rather than submit to certain unjust laws of the Roman Empire. To a degree, academic freedom is a reality today because Socrates practiced civil disobedience. In our own nation, the Boston Tea Party represented a massive act of civil disobedience.

We should never forget that everything Adolf Hitler did in Ger- 22 many was "legal" and everything the Hungarian freedom fighters did in Hungary was "illegal." It was "illegal" to aid and comfort a Jew in Hitler's Germany. Even so, I am sure that, had I lived in Germany at the time, I would have aided and comforted my Jewish brothers. If today I lived in a Communist country where certain principles dear to the Christian faith are suppressed, I would openly advocate disobeying that country's anti-religious laws.

I must make two honest confessions to you, my Christian and 23 Jewish brothers. First, I must confess that over the past few years I have been gravely disappointed with the white moderate. I have almost reached the regrettable conclusion that the Negro's great stumbling block in his stride toward freedom is not the White Citizen's Counciler or the Ku Klux Klanner, but the white moderate, who is more devoted to "order" than to justice; who prefers a negative peace which is the absence of tension to a positive peace which is the presence of justice; who constantly says, "I agree with you in the goal you seek, but I cannot agree with your methods of direct action"; who paternalistically believes he can set the timetable for another man's freedom; who lives by a mythical concept of time and who constantly advises the Negro to wait for a "more convenient season." Shallow understanding from people of good will is more frustrating than absolute misunderstanding from people of ill will. Lukewarm acceptance is much more bewildering than outright rejection.

I had hoped that the white moderate would understand that law 24 and order exist for the purpose of establishing justice and that when they fail in this purpose they become the dangerously structured dams that block the flow of social progress. I had hoped that the white moderate would understand that the present tension in the South is a necessary phase of the transition from an obnoxious negative peace, in which the Negro passively accepted his unjust plight, to a substantive and positive peace, in which all men will respect the dignity and worth of human personality. Actually, we who engage in nonviolent direct action are not the creators of tension. We merely bring to the surface the hidden tension that is already alive. We bring it out in the open, where it can be seen and dealt with. Like a boil that can never be cured so long as it is covered up but must be opened with all its ugliness to the natural medicines of air and light, injustice must be exposed, with all the tension its exposure creates, to the light of human conscience and the air of national opinion, before it can be cured.

In your statement you assert that our actions, even though 25 peaceful, must be condemned because they precipitate violence. But is this a logical assertion? Isn't this like condemning a robbed man because his possession of money precipitated the evil act of robbery? Isn't this like condemning Socrates because his unswerving commitment to truth and his philosophical inquiries precipitated the act by the misguided populace in which they made him drink hemlock? Isn't this like condemning Jesus because his unique God-consciousness and never-ceasing devotion to God's will precipitated the evil act of crucifixion? We must come to see that, as the federal courts have consistently affirmed, it is wrong to urge an individual to cease his efforts to gain his basic constitutional rights because the quest may precipitate violence. Society must protect the robbed and punish the robber.

I had also hoped that the white moderate would reject the myth 26 concerning time in relation to the struggle for freedom. I have just received a letter from a white brother in Texas. He writes: "All Christians know that the colored people will receive equal rights eventually, but it is possible that you are in too great a religious hurry. It has taken Christianity almost two thousand years to accomplish what it has. The teachings of Christ take time to come to earth." Such an attitude stems from a tragic misconception of time, from the strangely irrational notion that there is something in the very flow of time that will inevitably cure all ills. Actually, time itself is neutral; it can be used either destructively or constructively. More and more I feel that the people of ill will have used time much more effectively than have the people of good will. We will have to repent in this generation not merely for the hateful words and actions of the bad people, but for the appalling silence of the good people. Human progress never rolls in on wheels of inevitability; it comes through the tireless efforts of men willing to be co-workers with God, and without this hard work, time itself becomes an ally of the forces of social stagnation. We must use time creatively, in the knowledge that the time is always ripe to do right. Now is the time to make real the promise of democracy and transform our pending national elegy into a creative psalm of brotherhood. Now is the time to lift our national policy from the quicksand of racial injustice to the solid rock of human dignity.

You speak of our activity in Birmingham as extreme. At first I was 27 rather disappointed that fellow clergymen would see my nonviolent efforts as those of an extremist. I began thinking about the fact that I stand in the middle of two opposing forces in the Negro community. One is a force of complacency, made up in part of Negroes who, as a result of long years of oppression, are so drained of self-respect and a sense of "somebodiness" that they have adjusted to segregation; and in part of a few middle-class Negroes who, because of a degree of academic and economic security and because in some ways they profit by segregation, have become insensitive to the problems of the masses. The other force is one of bitterness and hatred, and it comes perilously close to advocating violence. It is expressed in the various black nationalist groups that are springing up across the nation, the largest and best-known being Elijah Muhammad's Muslim movement. Nourished by the Negro's frustration over the continued existence of racial discrimination, this movement is made up of people who have lost faith in America, who have absolutely repudiated Christianity, and who have concluded that the white man is an incorrigible "devil."

I have tried to stand between these two forces, saying that we 28 need emulate neither the "do-nothingism" of the complacent nor the hatred and despair of the black nationalist. For there is the more excellent way of love and nonviolent protest. I am grateful to God that, through the influence of the Negro church, the way of nonviolence became an integral part of our struggle.

If this philosophy had not emerged, by now many streets of the 29 South would, I am convinced, be flowing with blood. And I am further convinced that if our white brothers dismiss as "rabble-rousers" and "outside agitators" those of us who employ nonviolent direct action, and if they refuse to support our nonviolent efforts, millions of Negroes will, out of frustration and despair, seek solace and security in black-nationalist ideologies—a development that would inevitably lead to a frightening racial nightmare.

Oppressed people cannot remain oppressed forever. The yearn- 30 ing for freedom eventually manifests itself, and that is what has happened to the American Negro. Something within has reminded him of his birthright of freedom, and something without has reminded him that it can be gained. Consciously or unconsciously, he has been caught up by the *Zeitgeist*, and with his black brothers of Africa and his brown and yellow brothers of Asia, South America, and the Caribbean, the United States Negro is moving with a sense of great urgency toward the promised land of racial justice. If one recognizes this vital urge that has engulfed the Negro community, one should readily understand why public demonstrations are taking place. The Negro has many pent-up resentments and latent frustrations, and he must release them. So let him march; let him make prayer pilgrimages to the city hall; let him go on freedom rides—and try to understand why he must do so. If his repressed emotions are not released in nonviolent ways, they will seek expression through violence; this is not a threat but a fact of history. So I have not said to my people, "Get rid of your discontent." Rather, I have tried to say that this normal and healthy discontent can be channeled into the creative outlet of nonviolent direct action. And now this approach is being termed extremist.

But though I was initially disappointed at being categorized as 31 an extremist, as I continued to think about the matter I gradually gained a measure of satisfaction from the label. Was not Jesus an extremist for love: "Love your enemies, bless them that curse you, do good to them that hate you, and pray for them which despitefully use you, and persecute you." Was not Amos an extremist for justice: "Let justice roll down like waters and righteousness like an everflowing stream." Was not Paul an extremist for the Christian gospel: "I bear in my body the marks of the Lord Jesus." Was not Martin Luther an extremist: "Here I stand; I cannot do otherwise, so help me God." And John Bunyan: "I will stay in jail to the end of my days before I make a butchery of my conscience." And Abraham Lincoln: "This nation cannot survive half slave and half free." And Thomas Jefferson: "We hold these truths to be self-evident, that all men are created equal. . . ." So the question is not whether we will be extremists, but what kind of extremists we will be. Will we be extremists for hate or for love? Will we be extremists for the preservation of injustice or for the extension of justice? In that dramatic scene on Calvary's hill three men were crucified. We must never forget that all three were crucified for the same crime—the crime of extremism. Two were extremists for immorality, and thus fell below their environment. The other, Jesus Christ, was an extremist for love, truth, and goodness, and thereby rose above his environment. Perhaps the South, the nation, and the world are in dire need of creative extremists.

I had hoped that the white moderate would see this need. Per- 32 haps I was too optimistic; perhaps I expected too much. I suppose I should have realized that few members of the oppressor race can understand the deep groans and passionate yearnings of the oppressed race, and still fewer have the vision to see that injustice must be rooted out by strong, persistent, and determined action. I am thankful, however, that some of our white brothers in the South have grasped the meaning of this social revolution and committed themselves to it. They are still all too few in quantity, but they are big in quality. Some—such as Ralph McGill, Lillian Smith, Harry Golden, James McBride Dabbs, Ann Braden, and Sarah Patton Boyle—have written about our struggle in eloquent and prophetic terms. Others have marched with us down nameless streets of the South. They have languished in filthy, roach-infested jails, suffering the abuse and brutality of policemen who view them as "dirty nigger-lovers." Unlike so many of their moderate brothers and sisters, they have recognized the urgency of the moment and sensed the need for powerful "action" antidotes to combat the disease of segregation.

Let me take note of my other major disappointment. I have been 33 so greatly disappointed with the white church and its leadership. Of course, there are some notable exceptions. I am not unmindful of the fact that each of you has taken some significant stands on this issue. I commend you, Reverend Stallings, for your Christian stand on this past Sunday, in welcoming Negroes to your worship service on a non-segregated basis. I commend the Catholic leaders of this state for integrating Spring Hill College several years ago.

But despite these notable exceptions, I must honestly reiterate 34 that I have been disappointed with the church. I do not say this as one of those negative critics who can always find something wrong with the church. I say this as a minister of the gospel, who loves the church; who was nurtured in its bosom; who has been sustained by its spiritual blessings and who will remain true to it as long as the cord of life shall lengthen.

When I was suddenly catapulted into the leadership of the bus 35 protest in Montgomery, Alabama, a few years ago, I felt we would be supported by the white church. I felt that the white ministers, priests, and rabbis of the South would be among our strongest allies. Instead, some have been outright opponents, refusing to understand the freedom movement and misrepresenting its leaders; all too many others have been more cautious than courageous and have remained silent behind the anesthetizing security of stained-glass windows.

In spite of my shattered dreams, I came to Birmingham with the 36 hope that the white religious leadership of this community would see the justice of our cause and, with deep moral concern, would serve as the channel through which our just grievances could reach the power structure. I had hoped that each of you would understand. But again I have been disappointed.

There was a time when the church was very powerful—in the 37 time when the early Christians rejoiced at being deemed worthy to suffer for what they believed. In those days the church was not merely a thermometer that recorded the ideas and principles of popular opinion; it was a thermostat that transformed the mores of society. Whenever the early Christians entered a town, the people in power became disturbed and immediately sought to convict the Christians for being "disturbers of the peace" and "outside agitators." But the Christians pressed on, in the conviction that they were "a colony of heaven," called to obey God rather than man. Small in number, they were big in commitment. They were too God-intoxicated to be "astronomically intimidated." By their effort and example they brought an end to such ancient evils as infanticide and gladiatorial contests.

Things are different now. So often the contemporary church is a 38 weak, ineffectual voice with an uncertain sound. So often it is an arch-defender of the status quo. Far from being disturbed by the presence of the church, the power structure of the average community is consoled by the church's silent—and often even vocal—sanction of things as they are.

But the judgment of God is upon the church as never before. If 39 today's church does not recapture the sacrificial spirit of the early church, it will lose its authenticity, forfeit the loyalty of millions, and be dismissed as an irrelevant social club with no meaning for the twentieth century. Every day I meet young people whose disappointment with the church has turned into outright disgust.

Perhaps I have once again been too optimistic. Is organized reli- 40 gion too inextricably bound to the status quo to save our nation and the world? Perhaps I must turn my faith to the inner spiritual church, the church within the church, as the true *ekklesia* and the hope of the world. But again I am thankful to God that some noble souls from the ranks of organized religion have broken loose from the paralyzing chains of conformity and joined us as active partners in the struggle for freedom. They have left their secure congregations and walked the streets of Albany, Georgia, with us. They have gone down the highways of the South on torturous rides for freedom. Yes, they have gone to jail with us. Some have been dismissed from their churches, have lost the support of their bishops and fellow ministers. But they have acted in the faith that right defeated is stronger than evil triumphant. Their witness has been the spiritual salt that has preserved the true meaning of the gospel in these troubled times. They have carved a tunnel of hope through the dark mountain of disappointment.

I hope the church as a whole will meet the challenge of this de- 41 cisive hour. But even if the church does not come to the aid of justice, I have no despair about the future. I have no fear about the outcome of our struggle in Birmingham, even if our motives are at present misunderstood. We will reach the goal of freedom in Birmingham and all over the nation, because the goal of America is freedom. Abused and scorned though we may be, our destiny is tied up with America's destiny. Before the pilgrims landed at Plymouth, we were here. Before the pen of Jefferson etched the majestic words of the Declaration of Independence across the pages of history, we were here. For more than two centuries our forebears labored in this country without wages; they made cotton king; they built the homes of their masters while suffering gross injustice and shameful humiliation—and yet out of a bottomless vitality they continued to thrive and develop. If the inexpressible cruelties of slavery could not stop us, the opposition we now face will surely fail. We will win our freedom because the sacred heritage of our nation and the eternal will of God are embodied in our echoing demands.

Before closing I feel impelled to mention one other point in your 42 statement that has troubled me profoundly. You warmly commended the Birmingham police force for keeping "order" and "preventing violence." I doubt that you would have so warmly commended the police force if you had seen its dogs sinking their teeth into unarmed, nonviolent Negroes. I doubt that you would so quickly commend the policemen if you were to observe their ugly and inhumane treatment of Negroes here in the city jail; if you were to watch them push and curse old Negro women and young Negro girls; if you were to see them slap and kick old Negro men and young boys; if you were to observe them, as they did on two occasions, refuse to give us food because we wanted to sing our grace together. I cannot join you in your praise of the Birmingham police department.

It is true that the police have exercised a degree of discipline in 43 handling the demonstrators. In this sense they have conducted themselves rather "nonviolently" in public. But for what purpose? To preserve the evil system of segregation. Over the past few years I have consistently preached that nonviolence demands that the means we use must be as pure as the ends we seek. I have tried to make clear that it is wrong to use immoral means to attain moral ends. But now I must affirm that it is just as wrong, or perhaps even more so, to use moral means to preserve immoral ends. Perhaps Mr. Connor and his policemen have been rather nonviolent in public, as was Chief Pritchett in Albany, Georgia, but they have used the moral means of nonviolence to maintain the immoral end of racial injustice. As T. S. Eliot has said, "The last temptation is the greatest treason: To do the right deed for the wrong reason."

I wish you had commended the Negro sit-inners and demon- 44 strators of Birmingham for their sublime courage, their willingness to suffer, and their amazing discipline in the midst of great provocation. One day the South will recognize its real heroes. They will be the James Merediths, with the noble sense of purpose that enables them to face jeering and hostile mobs, and with the agonizing loneliness that characterizes the life of the pioneer. They will be old, oppressed, battered Negro women, symbolized in a seventy-two-year-old woman in Montgomery, Alabama, who rose up with a sense of dignity and with her people decided not to ride segregated buses, and who responded with ungrammatical profundity to one who inquired about her weariness: "My feets is tired, but my soul is at rest." They will be the young high school and college students, the young ministers of the gospel and a host of their elders, courageously and nonviolently sitting in at lunch counters and willingly going to jail for conscience' sake. One day the South will know that when these disinherited children of God sat down at lunch counters, they were in reality standing up for what is best in the American dream and for the most sacred values in our Judeo-Christian heritage, thereby bringing our nation back to those great wells of democracy which were dug deep by the founding fathers in their formulation of the Constitution and the Declaration of Independence.

Never before have I written so long a letter. I'm afraid it is much 45 too long to take your precious time. I can assure you that it would have been much shorter if I had been writing from a comfortable desk, but what else can one do when he is alone in a narrow jail cell, other than write long letters, think long thoughts, and pray long prayers?

If I have said anything in this letter that overstates the truth and 46 indicates an unreasonable impatience, I beg you to forgive me. If I have said anything that understates the truth and indicates my having a patience that allows me to settle for anything less than brotherhood, I beg God to forgive me.

I hope this letter finds you strong in the faith. I also hope that 47 circumstances will soon make it possible for me to meet each of you, not as an integrationist or a civil-rights leader but as a fellow clergyman and a Christian brother. Let us all hope that the dark clouds of racial prejudice will soon pass away and the deep fog of misunderstanding will be lifted from our fear-drenched communities, and in some not too distant tomorrow the radiant stars of love and brotherhood will shine over our great nation with all their scintillating beauty.

Yours for the cause of Peace and Brotherhood,
Martin Luther King, Jr.

CLASSIC ARGUMENTS: "LETTER FROM BIRMINGHAM JAIL"

DISCUSSION

1. King's letter is a direct response to the eight Alabama clergymen who spoke out against him for breaking the law, but there are indications that King intended his letter to be read by a larger, more general audience. Illustrate how King addresses both audiences.

2. King carefully explains how the occasion affects the purpose and even the length of his letter. Why does he acknowledge this, at what strategic points does he acknowledge it, and what effect does he hope to have on his immediate audience?

3. The clergymen implicitly criticized King and his actions in a public statement. How does King establish himself as a man of good will who is saying something worth listening to? Do you think he convinced his primary audience? The general public? Use specific quotations from the letter to support your opinion.

4. King's letter is considered a well-reasoned defense of civil disobedience as a means of securing civil liberties. Outline his argument using either a syllogism or the Toulmin model. Explain how King refutes the clergymen's likely objections to his claim.

5. The last three paragraphs do not advance King's argument. What is their purpose and which type of appeal do they represent? Overall, which appeal—logical, ethical, or emotional—is the most persuasive in King's argument? Explain your opinion.

WRITING SUGGESTIONS

1. King argues that there is a difference between just and unjust laws (paragraphs 15–20). Do you agree? Write an argument to an audience in your age group advocating the need to make this distinction and act accordingly, or asserting that the procedure for making laws ensures that they are just.

2. In paragraphs 21 and 22 King cites several historical examples of civil disobedience, and in other writings he acknowledges the influence of Mahatma Gandhi and Henry David Thoreau on his work. What instances of civil disobedience have occurred during your lifetime? Have they been successful in effecting change? Write an argument in defense of civil disobedience and direct it to an organization representing a cause you believe in.

The Importance of Work

BETTY FRIEDAN

Betty Friedan (1921–) was the first president and a founder of the National Organization for Women. This essay is drawn from her 1963 book The Feminine Mystique, *which anticipated many important issues of the women's movement for the next two decades.*

The question of how a person can most fully realize his own capacities   1
and thus achieve identity has become an important concern of the philosophers and the social and psychological thinkers of our time—

and for good reason. Thinkers of other times put forth the idea that people were, to a great extent, defined by the work they did. The work that a man had to do to eat, to stay alive, to meet the physical necessities of his environment, dictated his identity. And in this sense, when work is seen merely as a means of survival, human identity was dictated by biology.

But today the problem of human identity has changed. For the 2 work that defined man's place in society and his sense of himself has also changed man's world. Work, and the advance of knowledge, has lessened man's dependence on his environment; his biology and the work he must do for biological survival are no longer sufficient to define his identity. This can be most clearly seen in our own abundant society; men no longer need to work all day to eat. They have an unprecedented freedom to choose the kind of work they will do; they also have an unprecedented amount of time apart from the hours and days that must actually be spent in making a living. And suddenly one realizes the significance of today's identity crisis—for women, and increasingly, for men. One sees the human significance of work—not merely as the means of biological survival, but as the giver of self and the transcender of self, as the creator of human identity and human evolution.

For "self-realization" or "self-fulfillment" or "identity" does not 3 come from looking into a mirror in rapt contemplation of one's own image. Those who have most fully realized themselves, in a sense that can be recognized by the human mind even though it cannot be clearly defined, have done so in the service of a human purpose larger than themselves. Men from varying disciplines have used different words for this mysterious process from which comes the sense of self. The religious mystics, the philosophers, Marx, Freud—all had different names for it: man finds himself by losing himself; man is defined by his relation to the means of production; the ego, the self, grows through understanding and mastering reality—through work and love.

The identity crisis, which has been noted by Erik Erikson and 4 others in recent years in the American man, seems to occur for lack of, and be cured by finding, the work, or cause, or purpose that evokes his own creativity. Some never find it, for it does not come from busy-work or punching a time clock. It does not come from just making a living, working by formula, finding a secure spot as an organization man. The very argument, by Riesman and others, that man no longer finds identity in the work defined as a paycheck job, assumes that identity for man comes through creative work of his own that contributes to the human community: the core of the self becomes aware, becomes real, and grows through work that carries forward human society.

Work, the shopworn staple of the economists, has become the 5 new frontier of psychology. Psychiatrists have long used "occupational therapy" with patients in mental hospitals; they have recently discovered that to be of real psychological value, it must be not just "therapy," but real work, serving a real purpose in the community. And work can now be seen as the key to the problem that has no name. The identity crisis of American women began a century ago, as more and more of the work important to the world, more and more of the work that used their human abilities and through which they were able to find self-realization, was taken from them.

Until, and even into, the last century, strong, capable women 6 were needed to pioneer our new land; with their husbands, they ran the farms and plantations and Western homesteads. These women were respected and self-respecting members of a society whose pioneering purpose centered in the home. Strength and independence, responsibility and self-confidence, self-discipline and courage, freedom and equality were part of the American character for both men and women, in all the first generations. The women who came by steerage from Ireland, Italy, Russia, and Poland worked beside their husbands in the sweatshops and the laundries, learned the new language, and saved to send their sons and daughters to college. Women were never quite as "feminine," or held in as much contempt, in America as they were in Europe. American women seemed to European travelers, long before our time, less passive, childlike, and feminine than their own wives in France or Germany or England. By an accident of history, American women shared in the work of society longer, and grew with the men. Grade- and high-school education for boys and girls alike was almost always the rule; and in the West, where women shared the pioneering work the longest, even the universities were co-educational from the beginning.

The identity crisis for women did not begin in America until the 7 fire and strength and ability of the pioneer women were no longer needed, no longer used, in the middle-class homes of the Eastern and Midwestern cities, when the pioneering was done and men began to build the new society in industries and professions outside the home. But the daughters of the pioneer women had grown too used to freedom and work to be content with leisure and passive femininity.

It was not an American, but a South African woman, Mrs. Olive 8 Schreiner, who warned at the turn of the century that the quality and quantity of women's functions in the social universe were decreasing as fast as civilization was advancing; that if women did not win back their right to a full share of honored and useful work, woman's mind and muscle would weaken in a parasitic state; her offspring, male and female, would weaken progressively, and civilization itself would deteriorate.

The feminists saw clearly that education and the right to partici- 9 pate in the more advanced work of society were women's greatest needs. They fought for and won the rights to new, fully human identity for women. But how very few of their daughters and granddaughters have chosen to use their education and their abilities for any large creative purpose, for responsible work in society? How many of them have been deceived, or have deceived themselves, into clinging to the outgrown, childlike femininity of "Occupation: housewife"?

It was not a minor matter, their mistaken choice. We now know 10 that the same range of potential ability exists for women as for men. Women, as well as men, can only find their identity in work that uses their full capacities. A woman cannot find her identity through others—her husband, her children. She cannot find it in the dull routine of housework. As thinkers of every age have said, it is only when a human being faces squarely the fact that he can forfeit his own life, that he becomes truly aware of himself, and begins to take his existence seriously. Sometimes this awareness comes only at the moment of death. Sometimes it comes from a more subtle facing of death: the death of self in passive conformity, in meaningless work. The feminine mystique prescribes just such a living death for women. Faced with the slow death of self, the American woman must begin to take her life seriously.

"We measure ourselves by many standards," said the great 11 American psychologist William James, nearly a century ago. "Our strength and our intelligence, our wealth and even our good luck, are things which warm our heart and make us feel ourselves a match for life. But deeper than all such things, and able to suffice unto itself without them, is the sense of the amount of effort which we can put forth."

If women do not put forth, finally, that effort to become all that 12 they have it in them to become, they will forfeit their own humanity. A woman today who has no goal, no purpose, no ambition patterning her days into the future, making her stretch and grow beyond that small score of years in which her body can fill its biological function, is committing a kind of suicide. For that future half a century after the child-bearing years are over is a fact that an American woman cannot deny. Nor can she deny that as a housewife, the world is indeed rushing past her door while she just sits and watches. The terror she feels is real, if she has no place in that world.

The feminine mystique has succeeded in burying millions of 13 American women alive. There is no way for these women to break out of their comfortable concentration camps except by finally putting forth an effort—that human effort which reaches beyond biology, beyond the narrow walls of home, to help shape the future. Only by such a personal commitment to the future can American women break out of the housewife trap and truly find fulfillment as wives and mothers—by fulfilling their own unique possibilities as separate human beings.

CLASSIC ARGUMENTS: "THE IMPORTANCE OF WORK"

DISCUSSION

1. The title of Friedan's book received much attention in 1963 when it was published. Describe the book's initial audience. Do you think both men and women were included in that group? Did their beliefs match Friedan's assumptions about the roles of men and women in society? Were they offended by her characterizations?

2. Although Friedan uses the terms *men, women,* and *humanity* to make distinctions in roles, some of her use of language, especially in the first sentence, reflects the sexist terminology society is trying to eliminate today. Did this language undermine Friedan's credibility with her 1963 audience? How does it affect her credibility with you? How could Friedan revise her essay to eliminate sexist expressions?

3. What arrangement strategy does Friedan use to reach her audience? What is the progression of subject matter? Why does she delay applying her argument directly to women?

4. What premises lead to Friedan's claim that women need meaningful careers? Were her readers likely to accept these premises in 1963? Do you accept these premises today? Explain your answers.

5. Friedan relies on the philosophies of several men and only one woman for support. Does this imbalance undermine her credibility or does it indicate the need for women's identity? Explain.

WRITING SUGGESTIONS

1. Much has changed for women since the publication of *The Feminine Mystique,* but many problems still exist. Write an argument defining the feminine mystique of the 1990s for your general age group.

2. Two natural extensions of Friedan's advocacy of meaningful careers for women are equal opportunity and comparable worth. Choose one of these issues as the basis for an argument directed to an employer.

Why I Want a Wife

JUDY SYFERS

Judy Syfers (1937–) is an American writer whose work includes essays on abortion, union organizing, and the role of women in society. Since "Why I Want a Wife" appeared in Ms. *magazine in 1971, the essay has been reprinted many times.*

I belong to that classification of people known as wives. I am A Wife. 1
And, not altogether incidentally, I am a mother.

Not too long ago a male friend of mine appeared on the scene 2
fresh from a recent divorce. He had one child, who is, of course, with
his ex-wife. He is obviously looking for another wife. As I thought about
him while I was ironing one evening, it suddenly occurred to me that I,
too, would like to have a wife. Why do I want a wife?

I would like to go back to school so that I can become econom- 3
ically independent, support myself, and, if need be, support those dependent upon me. I want a wife who will work and send me to school.
And while I am going to school I want a wife to take care of my children. I want a wife to keep track of the children's doctor and dentist
appointments. And to keep track of mine, too. I want a wife to make
sure my children eat properly and are kept clean. I want a wife who
will wash the children's clothes and keep them mended. I want a wife
who is a good nurturant attendant to my children, who arranges for
their schooling, makes sure that they have an adequate social life with
their peers, takes them to the park, the zoo, etc. I want a wife who
takes care of the children when they are sick, a wife who arranges to be
around when the children need special care, because, of course, I cannot miss classes at school. My wife must arrange to lose time at work
and not lose the job. It may mean a small cut in my wife's income from
time to time, but I guess I can tolerate that. Needless to say, my wife
will arrange and pay for the care of the children while my wife is
working.

I want a wife who will take care of *my* physical needs. I want a 4
wife who will keep my house clean. A wife who will pick up after me. I
want a wife who will keep my clothes clean, ironed, mended, replaced
when need be, and who will see to it that my personal things are kept
in their proper place so that I can find what I need the minute I need

it. I want a wife who cooks the meals, a wife who is a *good* cook. I want a wife who will plan the menus, do the necessary grocery shopping, prepare the meals, serve them pleasantly, and then do the cleaning up while I do my studying. I want a wife who will care for me when I am sick and sympathize with my pain and loss of time from school. I want a wife to go along when our family takes a vacation so that someone can continue to care for me and my children when I need a rest and change of scene.

I want a wife who will not bother me with rambling complaints 5 about a wife's duties. But I want a wife who will listen to me when I feel the need to explain a rather difficult point I have come across in my course of studies. And I want a wife who will type my papers for me when I have written them.

I want a wife who will take care of the details of my social life. 6 When my wife and I are invited out by my friends, I want a wife who will take care of the babysitting arrangements. When I meet people at school that I like and want to entertain, I want a wife who will have the house clean, will prepare a special meal, serve it to me and my friends, and not interrupt when I talk about the things that interest me and my friends. I want a wife who will have arranged that the children are fed and ready for bed before my guests arrive so that the children do not bother us. I want a wife who takes care of the needs of my guests so that they feel comfortable, who makes sure that they have an ashtray, that they are passed the hors d'œuvres, that they are offered a second helping of the food, that their wine glasses are replenished when necessary, that their coffee is served to them as they like it. And I want a wife who knows that sometimes I need a night out by myself.

I want a wife who is sensitive to my sexual needs, a wife who 7 makes love passionately and eagerly when I feel like it, a wife who makes sure that I am satisfied. And, of course, I want a wife who will not demand sexual attention when I am not in the mood for it. I want a wife who assumes the complete responsibility for birth control, because I do not want more children. I want a wife who will remain sexually faithful to me so that I do not have to clutter up my intellectual life with jealousies. And I want a wife who understands that *my* sexual needs may entail more than strict adherence to monogamy. I must, after all, be able to relate to people as fully as possible.

If, by chance, I find another person more suitable as a wife than 8 the wife I already have, I want the liberty to replace my present wife with another one. Naturally I will expect a fresh, new life; my wife will take the children and be solely responsible for them so that I am left free.

When I am through with school and have a job, I want my wife to 9 quit working and remain at home so that my wife can more fully and completely take care of a wife's duties.

My God, who *wouldn't* want a wife? 10

CLASSIC ARGUMENTS: "I WANT A WIFE"

DISCUSSION

1. Syfers' essay appeared in the first issue of *Ms.* in December 1971, a time when many people were actively petitioning for change—in the Vietnam war, civil rights, and women's rights. Describe how Syfers could expect her intended audience of feminist women to react to her definition of *wife.* How would more traditional women respond? What would men's reaction be?

2. The pronoun *I* often conveys the credibility of firsthand experience. Is this the case with Syfers' use? Are the details she includes personalized or generalized? Explain how Syfers develops an ethical appeal in her argument.

3. List the order in which the wife's expected services are identified. Describe this sequence with respect to Syfers' purpose as you see it and evaluate the effect of the sequence on readers.

4. Tone creates perhaps the strongest appeal in this argument. How would you characterize Syfers' tone? Consider her use of italics, repetition, hyperbole, parenthetical expressions, and pronouns in your analysis. How does the tone help achieve her purpose?

5. In her attack on sexual stereotyping in marriage does Syfers make any assumptions or include details that limit the stereotyping to an economic class or to an ethnic or racial group? Use specific examples in your answer.

WRITING SUGGESTIONS

1. Is Syfers' definition of a wife still valid today? Are husbands abused in ways analogous to Syfers' "wife"? Write your own version of "I want a wife" or "I want a husband" to an audience of your general age group.

2. Before people marry they often formulate in their minds an ideal relationship between husband and wife. Write an argument defining this ideal to your general age group. Choose a tone that demonstrates a practical understanding of the realities of achieving such an ideal relationship.

INVITATIONS

The visual impact of a graph, a list, the results of a poll, or an editorial cartoon is immediate. Information in these forms can punctuate an argument more directly than in a
series of paragraphs, but it relies on the reader to supply the details and the emotional
response. Visual presentations often evoke new connections and prompt investigation
of related issues.

The documents, charts, polls, and cartoons that follow invite the reader to participate, to join a dialogue on an issue. The questions after each selection react to the
specific argumentative point being portrayed. If you respond to the selections as part of
a group, that collaboration should evoke more questions. When you exchange answers
to those questions, the dialogue that occurs will lead to discussion of larger, more universal issues and a fuller understanding of the argument. With further investigation you
or your group should be able to develop a problem-solving proposal.

Who Are the Homeless?

The New York Times/CBS News Poll: Perceptions of the Problem

*Do you personally see homeless people around your community or on your
way to work, or is the problem only something you have seen on television or
have read about?*

	January 1986	January 1989
See the homeless first hand	36%	51%
Know about them only from watching TV or reading about them	59%	48%

How much of the blame for homelessness do you think should be put on:

. . . local governments for failing to take care of people in need?
A lot: 30%   Some: 52%   Hardly any: 14%

. . . homeless people for being unwilling to work?
A lot: 37%   Some: 50%   Hardly any: 11%

. . . mental institutions for releasing patients who aren't able to lead normal lives?
A lot: 44%   Some: 38%   Hardly any: 12%

. . . the domestic policies of the Reagan Administration?
A lot: 24%   Some: 52%   Hardly any: 18%

. . . alcohol and drug abuse by the homeless?
A lot: 50%   Some: 40%   Hardly any: 7%

Based on telephone interviews with 1,533 people nationwide, conducted Jan. 12–15. Those with no opinion are not included.

New York Times, January 29, 1989

INVITATIONS: WHO ARE THE HOMELESS?

IMMEDIATE RESPONSES

The number of people who see the homeless firsthand appears to have increased. Is this because there are more homeless people to see or because society is more aware of their existence?

Are the majority of homeless people alcohol and drug abusers who are unwilling to work?

What policies have the local and federal governments instituted to assist the homeless?

Who is to blame for this problem?

EXTENDED ARGUMENTS

Does the existence of such a large number of homeless people indicate an erosion of democracy?

What is the cause of this problem? When did it start? How did it grow to be such a pervasive national problem?

Should we fear the homeless? Why?

Who is responsible for aiding the homeless?

Housing the Homeless

FEIFFER*

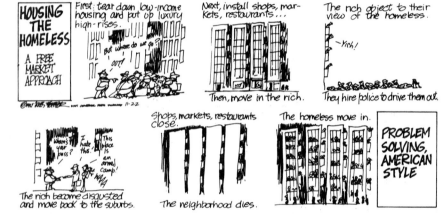

Washington Post, November 22, 1987

INVITATIONS: HOUSING THE HOMELESS

IMMEDIATE RESPONSES

What are the priorities of a free market approach?

What happened to the people living in the low-income housing?

Who, if anyone, benefits from this problem-solving approach?

Why does Feiffer characterize the free market approach as an American style of solving problems?

EXTENDED ARGUMENTS

Is providing housing for the homeless a real solution to the problem?

In his article "Let's Stop Punishing the Homeless—and Ourselves" (Chapter 9),

Tom Simmons asserts that "the homeless could become a contributing part of our social structure." Is this a real possibility?

True or false: In America the rich get richer and the poor get poorer.

Are the homeless a problem only in America? If so, why? If not, do other countries offer a solution we can follow?

Homelessness occurs only in inner cities. Therefore, city governments should be responsible for solving the problem.

The Politics of Toothpaste

From Rating America's Corporate Conscience: A Provocative Guide to the Companies Behind the Products You Buy Every Day, *by Steven D. Lydenberg, Alice Tepper Marlin, Sean O'Brien Strub, and the Council on Economic Priorities. The council, a New York–based public-policy group, evaluated the "social responsibility" of more than 125 major corporations, organizing its findings by company and, to help consumers, by product category.*

TOOTHPASTES

Size of charitable contributions	Women directors and officers	Minority directors and officers	Social disclosure	Brand name	Company	Involvement in South Africa	Conv. weapons-related contracts	Nuclear weapons-related contracts	Authors' company of choice
$	♠	?	No	Colgate Ultra-brite	Colgate-Palmolive	Yes A/B	No	No	
$	♠	♠	✍	Crest	Proctor &	No	No	No	✔
$		♠	✍	Gleem	Gamble				
$			✍						
$	No	No	No	Aim Close-up Pepsodent	Unilever	Yes ?	No	No	

? = No information available
Single figure (**$, ♠**) = Minimal
Double figure (**$$, ♠♠, ✍✍**) = Moderate
Triple figure (**$$$, ♠♠♠, ✍✍✍**) = Substantial

No = No involvement or participation
Yes = Involvement or participation, A, B, C in the South African column reflect the degree of compliance with Sullivan Principles and/or involvement in strategic industries.

Harper's Magazine, February 1987

IMMEDIATE RESPONSES

Is politics connected to everything we buy?

How does what I buy characterize my social responsibility?

Are there additional indicators of social responsibility that should be used as criteria for evaluating corporations?

Do many people think about these issues when they buy products?

EXTENDED ARGUMENTS

Ignorance is no excuse *or* ignorance is bliss.

Products should be displayed in stores according to the social responsibility level of the corporations that produce them.

Boycotting products is/is not an effective means of effecting change.

There should be federal tax penalties levied on corporations that are not socially responsible.

Understanding Women

From "Recruiting and Selection Standards," a memorandum distributed by the Ortho Pharmaceutical Corporation to its divisional managers. The 1980 document, which includes sections on the interviewing, assessment, and hiring of women, was introduced as an exhibit in a sex-discrimination suit filed by a Texas woman who was fired by the company after she became pregnant.

Female Applicant Profile

The female sales rep we are looking for is not the stereotypical twenty-seven-year-old beautiful, blue-collar daughter of an electrician. She can be any age and from any background. We are only concerned that her *attitude* toward "work"—an attitude toward that combination of "job" and "career"—be such that she will be able and interested enough to function as an employee for approximately *five years.*

The hiring manager should not try to hire someone with the executive potential to become a president, a vice president, or a regional manager. In fact, a candidate who shows strong presidential potential at the entry level is not likely to last long enough to get the promotion.

Appearance

She's not "pretty," she's not sexy; she should be neat, clean, and without frills. She should have neither excessive jewelry nor long fingernails. Her clothes should be practical, not high fashion. Her heels should be made for walking, not modeling. She should have the look of someone who might clean her bathroom or kitchen on her hands and knees. If you went to school together, she would be likable—a friend. She wouldn't look like someone who found new boyfriends in singles bars.

Education

She went to a state college, not a private university, and not recently. She probably had a part-time job. She probably didn't belong to a sorority. She was a C or a B student and had to work for it. Ideally, she prepared for a business career. If she had a car, it was practical; you could not even imagine her in a Corvette.

Personality

Conscientious, thorough, completes what she starts; persistent, down-to-earth, friendly, likable. She's also independent, competitive. Financial security would rank high on her value scale. She's not waiting to get married to solve her financial problems. Open and candid, often to her disadvantage. Strong sense of right and wrong.

Early Work History

Her background before college should indicate a need to earn her own spending money: after-school jobs, summer jobs. Some of the jobs were probably boring, but they were the best she could get.

Family Background

Blue-collar. Her father, and perhaps her mother, worked in and chose occupations that provided good, steady incomes.

Work History

No glamour jobs.

Harper's Magazine, April 1987

INVITATIONS: UNDERSTANDING WOMEN

IMMEDIATE RESPONSES

Reject beauty? It's still discrimination!

Require a college education, but don't let her use it?

So you want someone who is competent but who doesn't have a commitment to work?

What in the world is a "glamour job"?

Anyone who passed the personality requirements would be too competent to pass the interview!

Do *any* women work at this company?

Is there an applicant profile for males?

EXTENDED ARGUMENTS

There is planned obsolescence in both people and job positions.

You can fight discrimination with laws, but how do you make sure those laws are enforced?

How can people protect themselves against discrimination?

Levying stricter punishments for discrimination would eliminate it sooner.

Delicacy of Prevention

Boston Globe, February 7, 1987

INVITATIONS: THE DELICACY OF PREVENTION

IMMEDIATE RESPONSES

Does the network really value feelings more than health?

Who does the network think its audience is?

What segment of the audience would be offended by the word *condom*? Why?

What criteria are used to determine the acceptability of a word for the television audience?

Who makes this policy? Is it used consistently?

Is this censorship?

EXTENDED ARGUMENTS

Is AIDS a health issue first and a moral issue second?

In an attempt to protect, how does policy often censor?

What are the ethics of keeping people informed?

Policy and laws should be determined by the greatest good for the greatest number.

In advertising, the end justifies the means.

GLOSSARY

Abstract: a brief summary that often appears at the beginning of a paper to allow readers to survey the content; a *descriptive abstract* explains the paper's purpose and method, and an *informative abstract* tells what a paper says (Chapter 12).

Abstract language: words and phrases expressing ideas and qualities in broad concepts (for instance, *honor*) apart from a specific event or object; contrast with *Concrete language* (Chapter 10).

Acknowledgement phrase: a phrase attributing the name of the source when incorporating a paraphrase or introducing a quotation (for example, "According to Harris,") (Chapters 5 and 11).

Allusion: a comparison to a well-known historical, news, literary, or mythological figure or event (Chapter 10).

Amplification: a technique used in the conclusion to emphasize and enlarge the importance of the main points of the argument (Chapter 9).

Analogy: an extended comparison (Chapter 7). See also *Connotation* and *Definition*.

Annotation: creating an active dialogue with the writer while reading a selection by making marginal comments and asking questions; compare with *Critical reading* (Chapter 5).

Appeals: methods of reaching an audience with the information and motivation it needs to accept a new or opposing view (Chapters 7 and 8):

Appeal to ethics: appealing to the audience through the credibility and good character of the writer.

Appeal to logic: appealing to the intellect and reasoning of the audience (see *Induction* and *Deduction*).

Appeal to emotions: appealing to the values and psychological needs of the audience.

Argument: a process of reasoning presented to an audience to persuade them to accept a specific claim (Chapters 1 and 2).

Assertion: an idea the writer proposes for the reader's acceptance; assertions should be followed by supportive evidence and logical reasoning (Chapter 2).

Assumption: an idea or belief you accept to be true without verification; in an *enthymeme*, the implied premise the writer uses as the basis for developing a reason for accepting a conclusion (Chapters 6 and 7).

Audience: the people to whom a writer or speaker addresses an argument; potential audiences range from known and personal to unknown and public and generally fall into one of these categories: self, known peer, general age group, known authority, teachers, unknown authority, and general public (Chapter 1).

Authority: a credible source used as support for a conclusion (Chapter 2).

Backing: the support or authority on which a warrant or assumption is based (Toulmin model, Chapter 2).

Bibliography: a list of sources consulted in conducting research (Chapter 12).

Categorical argument: in deductive argument, reaches a logical conclusion on the state of being of a particular member within a general category or class (Chapter 7).

Categorical proposition (CP):   See *Claim of fact*.

Claim: the *proposition* or *thesis* of an argument; the assertion based on verifiable evidence; what the arguer is trying to prove (Chapter 2).

Claim of fact: also called a *categorical proposition* (CP); responds to the questions "What is it?"; "Does it exist?"; "Does it happen?"

Claim of cause or effect: responds to the questions "Why is it that way?"; "How does it happen?"; "What are the consequences?"

Claim of value: responds to the questions "Is it good or bad?" and "Is it right or wrong?"

Claim of policy: responds to the question "What should be done?"

Cliché: a worn-out expression or idea, no longer capable of creating a convincing image (for instance, cool as a cucumber) (Chapter 10).

Climactic order: a sequence of argumentative points leading to and ending with the strongest point (Chapter 9).

Cluster: a brainstorming diagram that places the research subject or question at the center and branches out to related potential sources; used in planning research possibilities for interviewing, observation, and surveys (Chapter 3).

Conclusion: the result of a line of reasoning; in a *syllogism*, the inevitable consequence of the major and minor premises (Chapter 7).

Concrete language: specific detail and precise diction used to characterize a real thing or experience; contrast with *abstract language* (Chapter 10).

Confirmation: the main argument and proof presented to substantiate the thesis (Chapter 9).

Connotation: the emotional implication of words; evokes associations with values and beliefs and conveys approval or disapproval (Chapter 10).

Content note: also called an *explanatory note;* a method of signaling the reader that you have additional information to provide on a topic; use an asterisk (*) or superscript number (Chapter 11).

Context: the environment for discourse: the people (producer and receiver), the subject, the purpose, and the occasion (Chapter 1).

Credibility: the trustworthiness of the writer or speaker's character as conveyed to the audience (Chapter 7, Appeal to Ethics).

Critical reading: reading with a discriminating eye for logical reasoning and the quality of sources supporting the information presented (Chapter 5).

Data: the verifiable evidence that supports the claim in the Toulmin model of deductive reasoning (Chapter 2).

Deduction: reasoning composed of two premises that, if accepted as true, lead to an inevitable conclusion; expressed formally in the form of a *syllogism* (Chapter 7, Appeal to Logic). See also *Categorical argument, Disjunctive argument,* and *Hypothetical argument.*

Definition: an explanation of what a word or concept means or signifies; several methods may be used or combined to develop an *extended definition:* synonym, etymology, stipulation, example, negation, figurative comparison, function, comparison and contrast, and analogy (Chapter 2).

Diction: the word choice the writer uses to clarify meaning and convey *tone* or attitude (Chapter 10).

Discourse: language in use, spoken or written (Chapter 1).

Discourse community: a group of people bound by its use of language and the role language plays in its activities (Chapter 1).

Disjunctive argument: in deductive argument, states a major premise that presents alternative possibilities introduced by *either/or* (Chapter 7).

Documentation: the full acknowledgement of sources used in paraphrase or quotation (parenthetical, footnote, or endnote form) (Chapter 11).

Enthymeme: in deductive reasoning, an abbreviated form of a syllogism that combines a conclusion and a reason connected by the implied assumed beliefs of the audience; based on a condition of probability (Chapter 7).

Euphemism: a substitution of pleasant words for a perceived offensive situation; often less accurate because it is less direct (Chapter 10).

Extenuation: a technique used in the conclusion to reduce the significance of the opposition's points (Chapter 9).

Fallacy: faulty reasoning that presents an argument built on false or deceptive relationships between the premises and the conclusion (Chapter 7).

Hyperbole: an elaborate exaggeration, often intended to be humorous or ironic (Chapter 10).

Hypothetical argument: in deductive argument, states a conditional major premise in an *if/then* clause (Chapter 7).

Induction: the examination of evidence about specific individual cases to discover and predict what generalizations *probably* apply to all those cases; the probability is dependent on the quantity and quality of the examples (Chapter 7).

Interview question sequence: a planned order of questions that move from the literal, factual level to application to evaluation to make the best use of the source's expertise (Chapter 3).

Jargon: a specialized professional language that when used in a different context causes confusion for the reader (Chapter 5).

Logic: the study of orderly thinking; the sequence and connection of thoughts and ideas (Chapter 7).

Metaphor: an implied comparison that equates two things or qualities without using an explicit connecting word (Chapter 10).

Metonymy: the representation of an object, an institution, or concept by something associated with it (Chapter 10).

Monroe's motivated sequence: an organizational structure for a presentation that includes five parts: attention, need, satisfaction, visualization, and action (Chapter 9).

Observation: looking with an open attitude and planned focus at something for the purpose of making new discoveries; observations are notated in logs, journals, and diaries (Chapter 3).

Occasion: the *when* of an argument; often the event that provoked the conflict of the argument (Chapter 1).

Opinion scale: range of attitudes an audience may have toward a given issue: unconditionally opposed, conditionally opposed, undecided, ambivalent, conditional support, unconditional support (Chapter 6).

Paraphrase: presentation of material from a source, in the writer's own words; follows the original source point by point, resulting in a similar length; must be properly documented (Chapters 5 and 11).

Persona: the writing voice and character the writer chooses to present the information and develop a relationship with the reader; identified through diction and use of personal pronouns *I, you, we, they* (Chapter 7).

Personification: giving human qualities to inanimate or nonhuman objects (Chapter 10).

Plagiarism: presenting someone else's ideas and words as your own; the unacknowledged use of another writer's words and ideas (Chapters 7 and 11).

Précis: a concise summary of essential points (Chapter 12).

Premise: the statement upon which an argument is based (Chapter 7).

Primary source: original documents and eyewitness, firsthand experience that provides authentic, specific details and personal testimony (Chapter 3).

Purpose: the *why* of an argument; the relationship the writer hopes to develop between the audience and the subject (Chapter 1).

Qualifier: a limitation placed on the claim in the Toulmin model of deductive reasoning; changes the formality of the claim from absolute to probable (Chapter 2).

Readability: how writing is presented to ease the reader's access to information and understanding; length of paragraphs, complexity of sentence structure, clear documentation, legibility, headings, and illustrations (Chapter 5).

Reasoning: in a syllogism, the sequence of thought that connects the premises to the conclusion (Chapter 7).

Refutation: anticipates and answers any objections the readers have to the thesis of the argument (Chapter 9).

Reservation: a rebuttal; a limitation placed on the warrant indicating the conditions that must be met in order for the warrant to establish the necessary connection between the data and the claim; used in the Toulmin model (Chapter 2).

Rhetorical context: See *Context.*

Rhetorical question: a question that implies its own answer, one the writer assumes will be answered uniformly by members of the audience (Chapter 7).

Rogerian argument: a nonthreatening approach using neutral language and an objective presentation of both sides to build trust and understanding in the reader (Chapter 9).

Secondary sources: print or on-line sources that interpret and evaluate information and can lead to the primary sources of others, including encyclopedias, dictionaries, biographies, indexes, bibliographies, abstracts, computer data bases, books, periodicals, and government publications (Chapter 4).

Sexist language: the use of pronouns and terms that fail to recognize the identity of women in a respectful and equal way; the use of labels to stereotype either gender (Chapter 10).

Simile: a direct comparison using the connecting words *like* or *as* (Chapter 10).

Summary: presentation of a condensed version of a source in the writer's own words; summaries should be brief, comprehensive, and objective, with no editorializing; they should be properly documented (Chapters 5 and 11).

Survey: the use of polls or questionnaires to elicit public opinion from a representative sample (Chapter 3).

Syllogism: a form of deductive thinking that includes a major premise, a minor premise, and a conclusion that to be considered valid should be the inevitable consequence of the two premises (Chapter 7).

Systematic notation: a uniform method of recording observations (Chapter 3).

Tone: the writer's attitude toward subject and audience—personal, impersonal, humorous, or ironic (Chapter 10). See also *Diction* and *Persona*.

Toulmin model: a model of deductive reasoning containing three primary elements: the data, the warrant, and the claim (Chapters 2 and 7).

Uncertainty: a necessary ingredient of an arguable claim; the higher the level of uncertainty, the greater the degree of evidence and verification the audience requires (Chapter 2).

Warrant: a general principle or assumption that establishes a connection between the data and the claim in the Toulmin model of deductive reasoning; the major assumption the writer expects to share with the audience (Chapter 2).

   Authoritative warrant: an assumption based on shared respect for an authority or expert.

   Motivational warrant: an assumption based on shared needs and values.

   Substantive warrant: an assumption based on shared confidence in the reliability of the evidence presented.

Working bibliography: a beginning list of available resources the writer consults in conducting research (Chapter 12).

Works cited: a list of the sources cited in a research paper; also referred to as *References* (APA style) (Chapter 12).

Working outline: a beginning plan used to sequence the main points of an argument from notes; revised as sources are evaluated and new emphases emerge (Chapter 12).

ACKNOWLEDGEMENTS

Chapter 2

pp. 17–19: Curtis J. Sitomer, "Courting Clients: What Limits on Ads for Lawyers?" *The Christian Science Monitor,* February 25, 1988. Copyright © 1988 The Christian Science Publishing Society. All rights reserved. Reprinted with permission of *The Christian Science Monitor.*

pp. 22–23: Adam Smith, "Everyday Drugs," *Powers of Mind.* Copyright © 1975 by Adam Smith. Reprinted with permission of Random House, Inc.

pp. 27–29: Robert M. Pirsig, "Gumption: The Psychic Gasoline," *Zen and the Art of Motorcycle Maintenance.* Copyright © 1974 by Robert M. Pirsig. Reprinted with permission of William Morrow and Company, Inc.

pp. 30–32: Robert C. Solomon, "Culture Gives Us a Sense of Who We Are," *Los Angeles Times,* January 25, 1981. Reprinted with permission of Robert C. Solomon.

pp. 33–36: J. B. Priestley, "Wrong–Ism," *Essays of Five Decades,* edited by Susan Cooper (New York: The Atlantic Monthly Press, 1968). Copyright © 1968 by J. B. Priestley. Reprinted with permission of Sterling Lord Literistic, Inc.

pp. 40–41: Carll Tucker, "Fear of Dearth," *Saturday Review,* 1979. Reprinted with permission of Omni Publications International Ltd.

pp. 43–45: Pico Iyer, "How Paradise Is Lost—and Found," *Time,* June 9, 1986. Copyright © 1986 Time Inc. All rights reserved. Reprinted with permission of Time Inc.

pp. 49–50: Richard Corliss, "Sea Shepherd from Outer Space," *Time,* December 8, 1986. Copyright © 1986 Time Inc. All rights reserved. Reprinted with permission of Time Inc.

pp. 52–54: Arthur Ashe, "No More Zero-sum Game," *The New York Times,* August 31, 1986. Reprinted with permission of Arthur Ashe.

pp. 56–60: Fred Powledge, "Let's Bulldoze the Suburbs," *Penthouse,* June 1981. Reprinted with permission of Penthouse.

pp. 62–64: Lewis Thomas, "How to Fix the Premedical Curriculum," *The Medusa and the Snail.* Copyright © 1978 by Lewis Thomas. All rights reserved. Reprinted with permission of Viking Penguin, a division of Penguin Books USA, Inc.

Chapter 3

pp. 68–69: "Do You Think College Tuition Costs Are Too High?" Voices Across the USA column, *USA Today,* March 3, 1987. Copyright 1987 *USA Today.* Reprinted with permission of *USA Today.*

pp. 72–75: Cyril Zaneski interview with Diane Harmon, "An Issue That Radiates Confusion," *The Virginian-Pilot and The Ledger-Star,* June 8, 1987. Reprinted with permission of *The Virginian-Pilot and The Ledger-Star.*

p. 131: Knight-Ridder News Service, "Parents Recall Happily Child's First Steps, Fear Substance Abuse," July 12, 1987. Reprinted with permission of Knight-Ridder News Service.

pp. 132–136: Jack C. Horn, "Bigger Pay for Better Work," *Psychology Today,* July 1987. Copyright © 1987 PT Partners, L.P. Reprinted with permission of *Psychology Today.*

pp. 136–138: Associated Press, "College Costs Expected to Climb 6% to 8%, Top $18,000 at Some Schools," August 7, 1987. Reprinted with permission of the Associated Press.

pp. 138–140: Mark Solheim, "The Pain and the Gain," *Changing Times,* August 1987. © 1987 Kiplinger Washington Editors, Inc. Reprinted with permission of The Kiplinger Washington Editors, Inc.

pp. 141–142: "Attitudes About AIDS" and "View on AIDS" charts, *Los Angeles Times,* July 31, 1987. Copyright © 1987 *Los Angeles Times.* Reprinted with permission of the *Los Angeles Times.*

pp. 144–153: "Fact File: Attitudes and Characteristics of This Year's Freshmen," *The Chronicle of Higher Education,* January 11, 1989; originally from Alexander W. Astin, "The American Freshman: National Norms for Fall 1988," published by the American Council on Education and the University of California at Los Angeles. Reprinted with permission of *The Chronicle of Higher Education.*

Chapter 4

pp. 170–178: Phillip Knightley, "The First Televised War," from "War Is Fun 1954–1975," *The First Casualty.* Copyright © 1975 by Phillip Knightley. Reprinted with permission of Harcourt Brace Jovanovich, Inc.

pp. 179–187: Susan Fraker, "Why Women Aren't Getting to the Top," *Fortune,* April 16, 1984. Reprinted with permission of *Fortune.*

pp. 189–193: Walter Isaacson, "History Without Letters," *Time,* August 31, 1987. Copyright © 1987 Time Inc. All rights reserved. Reprinted with permission of Time Inc.

Chapter 5

p. 198: Jeannette Harris, "Student Writers and Word Processing: A Preliminary Evaluation," *College Composition and Communication,* October 1985. Copyright © 1985 by the National Council of Teachers of English. Reprinted with permission of the NCTE.

pp. 199–200: James Trefil, "Quantum Physics' World: Now You See It, Now You Don't," *Smithsonian,* August 1987. Reprinted with permission of James Trefil.

pp. 201–202: Galen Rowell, "Baltistan," *National Geographic,* October 1987. Reprinted with permission of the National Geographic Society.

pp. 203–206: Stanley N. Wellborn, "Life in a Greenhouse," *U.S. News & World Report,* September 29, 1986. Copyright 1986 *U.S. News & World Report.* Reprinted with permission of *U.S. News and World Report.*

pp. 208–209: James S. Newton, "What's New in Music Technology," *The New York Times,* March 1, 1987. Copyright © 1987 by The New York Times Company. Reprinted with permission of The New York Times Company.

p. 211: Figure 1, a biographical entry on Robert Creeley from James D. Hart, *The Oxford Companion to American Literature,* Fifth Edition. Copyright © 1983 by Oxford University Press, Inc. Reprinted with permission of Oxford University Press.

pp. 211–214: Meg Gerken, "Battle of the Sexes," *Women's Sports & Fitness* magazine, 1981. Reprinted with permission.

pp. 216–217: Jeff Meer, "Winter Depression: Day for Night," *Psychology Today,* June 1987. Copyright © 1987 PT Partners, L.P. Reprinted with permission of *Psychology Today.*

pp. 217–220: Margaret Mead, "One Vote for This Age of Anxiety," *The New York Times,* May 20, 1965. Copyright © 1965 by The New York Times Company. Reprinted with permission of The New York Times Company.

p. 296: Figure 14, Travelers advertisement. 1988. Reprinted with permission of The Travelers Insurance Company.

p. 297: Figure 15, SunTour bicycle components advertisement. 1989. Reprinted with permission of SunTour USA, Inc.

pp. 298–302: Richard M. Restak, "The Other Difference Between Boys and Girls," *The Brain: The Last Frontier.* Copyright © 1979 by Richard M. Restak. Reprinted with permission of Doubleday, a division of Bantam, Doubleday, Dell Publishing Group, Inc.

pp. 308–310: Mike Royko, "A Faceless Man's Plea," *Chicago Daily News,* December 10, 1973. Reprinted with permission of Tribune Media Services.

p. 311: Figure 16, Stanley H. Kaplan Educational Center Ltd. advertisement. 1988. All trademarks and copyrights on this ad are owned by Stanley H. Kaplan Educational Center Ltd. All rights reserved. Reprinted with permission of the Stanley H. Kaplan Educational Center Ltd.

pp. 313–315: L. Bruce Laingen, "In Search of Public Servants," *Christian Science Monitor,* March 11, 1988. Reprinted with permission of L. Bruce Laingen.

p. 317: Figure 17, An American Symbol advertisement. 1985. Reprinted with permission of Ross Roy Advertising Inc.

p. 318: Figure 18, Smith Corona advertisement. 1988. Reprinted with permission of the Smith Corona Corporation.

p. 319: Figure 19, SunTour bicycle components advertisement. 1989. Reprinted with permission of SunTour USA, Inc.

pp. 320–321: Ellen Goodman, "From Voters to Passive Viewers," March 10, 1988. © 1988 The Boston Globe Newspaper Company/Washington Post Writers Group. Reprinted with permission of the Washington Post Writers Group.

Chapter 8

pp. 323–327: Ed Henry, "Air Bags vs. Seat Belts," *Changing Times,* March 1988. © 1988 Kiplinger Washington Editors, Inc. Reprinted with permission of The Kiplinger Washington Editors, Inc.

pp. 329–331: Frank Trippett, "A Red Light for Scofflaws," *Time,* January 24, 1983. Copyright © 1983 Time Inc. All rights reserved. Reprinted with permission of Time Inc.

p. 333: Figure 1, "A message from those who don't to those who do," and "A message from those who do to those who don't." © 1984 R.J. Reynolds Tobacco Co. Reprinted with permission of the R.J. Reynolds Tobacco Company.

p. 334: Figure 2, "The most inflammatory question of our time." © 1985 R.J. Reynolds Tobacco Co. Reprinted with permisson of the R.J. Reynolds Tobacco Company.

Chapter 9

pp. 345–347: Lance Morrow, "A Holocaust of Words," *Time,* May 2, 1988. Copyright © 1988 Time Inc. All rights reserved. Reprinted with permission of Time Inc.

pp. 349–352: Arthur M. Schlesinger, Jr., "The Challenge of Change," *The New York Times,* July 27, 1986; adapted from the book *Cycles of American History.* Copyright © 1986 by Arthur M. Schlesinger, Jr. Reprinted with permission of Houghton Mifflin Company.

pp. 353–355: Mark Kleiman, "Grant Bachelor's Degrees by Examination," *The Wall Street Journal,* September 6, 1985. Reprinted with permission of Mark Kleiman.

pp. 355–357: Lester C. Thurow, "Why Women Are Paid Less Than Men," *The New York Times,* March 8, 1981. Copyright © 1981 by The New York Times Company. Reprinted with permission of The New York Times Company.

pp. 363–365: Rachel Richardson Smith, "Abortion, Right and Wrong," *Newsweek,* March 25, 1985. Reprinted with permission of Rachel Richardson Smith.

pp. 367–369: Patricia Taylor, "It's Time to Put Warnings on Alcohol," *The New York Times,* March 20, 1988. Copyright © 1988 by The New York Times Company. Reprinted with permission of The New York Times Company.

pp. 369–371: James C. Sanders, "We Need Role Models, Not Labels," *The New York Times,* March 20, 1988. Copyright © 1988 by The New York Times Company. Reprinted with permission of The New York Times Company.

pp. 371–373: Tom Simmons, "Let's Stop Punishing the Homeless—and Ourselves," *The Christian Science Monitor,* March 10, 1988. Reprinted with permission of Tom Simmons.

Chapter 10

p. 380: *Hagar* cartoon, "Barbarian's Block," April 25, 1988. Reprinted with permission of King Features Syndicate.

p. 385: *Hagar* cartoon, "Profit-Sharing Plan," July 29, 1986. Reprinted with permission of King Features Syndicate.

pp. 386–389: Willie Morris, "A Love That Transcends Sadness," *Parade,* 1981. © 1981 by Willie Morris. Reprinted with permission of Sterling Lord Literistic Inc.

pp. 391–393: Roger Angell, "A View from the Upper Deck," *The Summer Game.* Copyright © 1971 by Roger Angell. All rights reserved. Reprinted with permission of Viking Penguin, a division of Penguin Books USA, Inc.

pp. 393–394: Jeffrey Pasley, "The Idiocy of Rural Life," *The New Republic,* December 8, 1986. Reprinted with permission of *The New Republic.*

pp. 395–396: Henry Fairlie, "The Idiocy of Urban Life," *The New Republic,* January 5, 1987. Reprinted with permission of *The New Republic.*

pp. 397–399: William Safire, "Curbing Lie Detectors," from "The Sweat Merchants," *The New York Times,* February 29, 1988. Copyright © 1988 by The New York Times Company. Reprinted with permission of The New York Times Company.

p. 399: Conrad cartoon, "Public Affairs," August 18, 1987. © 1987 The Times. Reprinted with permission of the Los Angeles Times Syndicate.

Chapter 11

pp. 418–420: Studs Terkel, "Carey Edwards, 25," *American Dreams: Lost and Found.* Copyright © 1980 by Studs Terkel. Reprinted with permission of Pantheon Books, a Division of Random House, Inc.

pp. 424–429: Thomas Murray, "The Growing Danger from Gene-Spliced Hormones," *Discover,* February 1987. © Discover, Family Media, Inc. Reprinted with permission of Discover, Family Media, Inc.

pp. 430–433: Martha Lear, "The Pain of Loneliness," *The New York Times,* December 20, 1987. Reprinted with permission of Martha Weinman Lear.

p. 432: Daniel W. Russell et al., "Quantifying the Emotion," from the U.C.L.A. Loneliness Scale, 10-Question Version, in the *Journal of Personality Assessment,* June 1978, pp. 290–294. Reprinted with permission of Lawrence Erlbaum Associates, Inc.

Debates

pp. 489–497: William Bradford Reynolds and Richard Wasserstrom, "Two Views of Affirmative Action," *Report from the Center for Philosophy and Public Policy,* Winter 1985. Reprinted with permission of the Institute for Philosophy and Public Policy.

pp. 499–501: Allen L. Sack, "Random Tests Abuse Dignity," *The New York Times,* May 29, 1988. Copyright © 1988 by The New York Times Company. Reprinted with permission of The New York Times Company.

pp. 501–503: James C. Puffer, "N.C.A.A. Plan Is Deterrent," *The New York Times,* May 29, 1988. Copyright © 1988 by The New York Times Company. Reprinted with permission of The New York Times Company.

pp. 505–511: Robin Wilson, "Many College Officials Oppose Plan That Would Require National Service as a Prerequisite for Federal Student Aid" and "But Some Student Leaders Approve of the Idea of Public Service," *The Chronicle of Higher Education,* February 15, 1989. Copyright 1989 The Chronicle of Higher Education. Reprinted with permission of The Chronicle of Higher Education.

pp. 518–522: Linda M. Ewing, "Moral Considerations for Combat Assignment," *Minerva,* Winter 1986. Reprinted with permission of Linda M. Ewing.

Issues

pp. 524–531: Lawrence R. Krupka and Arthur M. Vener, "College Student Attitudes Toward AIDS Carriers and Knowledge of the Disease," *College Student Journal,* Fall 1988. Reprinted with permission of Project Innovation.

pp. 532–534: Michael Kinsley, "Moral Anemia," *The New Republic,* December 1, 1986. Reprinted with permission of *The New Republic.*

pp. 535–537: Mark Robichaux, "Safety vs. Civil Rights," *The Wall Street Journal,* September 18, 1987. © 1987 Dow Jones & Company, Inc. All rights reserved. Reprinted with permission of *The Wall Street Journal.*

pp. 537–541: Matt Clark, "Doctors Fear AIDS, Too," *Newsweek,* August 3, 1987. © 1987 Newsweek, Inc. All rights reserved. Reprinted with permission of *Newsweek.*

pp. 541–545: Willis B. Goldbeck, "AIDS and the Workplace," *The Futurist,* March–April 1988. Reprinted with permission of the World Future Society.

pp. 545–555: Kenneth R. Howe, "Why Mandatory Screening for AIDS Is a Very Bad Idea," from Christine Pierce and Donald VanDeVeer, eds., *AIDS: Ethics and Public Policy* (Belmont, CA: Wadsworth, 1988). Reprinted with permission of Kenneth R. Howe.

pp. 557–559: Alfredo J. Estrada, "Quietly Keeping Them Out," *Harper's Magazine,* August 1987. Copyright © 1987 by *Harper's Magazine.* All rights reserved. Reprinted with permission of *Harper's Magazine.*

pp. 560–561: Richard Lacayo, "Storming the Last Male Bastion," *Time,* July 4, 1988. Copyright © 1988 Time Inc. All rights reserved. Reprinted with permission of Time Inc.

pp. 562–565: George M. Anderson, "Defending the Poor: A Harder Task," *America,* January 14, 1989. Published by America Press, Inc., 106 West 56th Street, New York, NY 10019. © 1989. All rights reserved. Reprinted with permission of George M. Anderson.

pp. 565–567: Les Payne, "Myth of White Supremacy Is Segregation's Legacy," *Los Angeles Times,* August 3, 1987. Copyright © 1987 Los Angeles Times Syndicate. Reprinted with permission of the Los Angeles Times Syndicate.

pp. 567–570: John Schwartz, George Raine, and Kate Robins, "A 'Superminority' Tops Out," *Newsweek,* May 11, 1987. © 1987 Newsweek, Inc. All rights reserved. Reprinted with permission of *Newsweek.*

pp. 570–575: Rick Weiss, "Predisposition and Prejudice," *Science News,* January 21, 1989. Copyright 1989 by Science Service, Inc. Reprinted with permission of *Science News,* the weekly newsmagazine of science.

pp. 577–579: Isaac Asimov, "A Cult of Ignorance," *Newsweek,* January 21, 1980. Reprinted with permission of Isaac Asimov.

pp. 579–581: William Raspberry, "Two Kinds of Illiteracy," *The Washington Post,* September 5, 1987. © 1987 Washington Post Writers Group. Reprinted with permission of the Washington Post Writers Group.

AUTHOR/TITLE INDEX

SUBJECT INDEX

Abstract
  as a reference source, 160, 162–163
  as a section in a research paper, 451,
    456, 470
Abstract language
  in a claim, 21
  effects on tone; diction, 379–392
Accommodation, 65–66
Acknowledgement phrase, 223
  to introduce a paraphrase, 223
Ad hominem, 281
Ad populum, 284
Allusion, 390
Ambiguity, 286
American Psychological Association
    (APA) style, 407–412
  sample paper, 468–485
Amphiboly, 287
Amplification, 358
Analogy
  as a definition strategy, 26
  as an inductive structure, 266–267
Annotation, 202–206
APA style, 407–412
Appeals
  to authority, 48
  to consequence, 48, 55
  to emotion, 302–307
  to ethics, 255–261
  to ignorance, 285
  to logic, 261–292
  purpose, 254–255
  kinds of, 255–307
  recognizing, 310–316
  arranging, 322–337

Arguability, in claim of fact, 21–22
Argument
  definition, 1, 14
  importance of, 12
Aristotle, 245, 262, 303
Assertion, 15
Assimilation, 65–66
Assumptions
  anticipating audience, 47
  identifying, 243
  and warrant, 15–17
Audience
  categories of
    general public, 7
    known peers, 5
    known authority, 6
    specialists, 6
    unknown authority, 6
  definition, 4, 5
  discovery of, 9
  distance features, 5, 6, 7
  information needs, 11–12, 196, 251–
    253
  opposition levels, 249–250
  related characteristics, 9–10
  shaping argument for, 322–337
Authoritative warrant, 16
Authority, 16–17, 48

Backing, definition, 16
Begging the question, 278
Bibliography
  as a part of research paper, 409–412
  as a reference source, 159–162
Bibliography cards, 435–437

Explanatory notes, 407
Extenuation, 359
External documentation, 409–412

Fallacies, 274–289
  ad hominem, 281
  ad populum, 284
  ambiguity, 286
  amphiboly, 287
  appeal to ignorance, 285
  begging the question, 278
  either/or, 276
  equivocation, 288
  false analogy, 280
  false cause or post hoc, 275
  hasty generalization, 275
  non sequitur, 286
  slippery slope, 280
False analogy, 280
False cause, 275
Feasibility, 55–56
Figures, 452
Focus
  on audience assumptions, 47–48
  discovering, 8–11
  in interviews, 69
  in observations, 93

Generalization, 263
  statistical, 264
  universal, 264

Hasty generalization, 275
Hayakawa, S. I., 380
Headings, 452–454
Humorous tone, 394
Hyperbole, 390
Hypothetical argument, 271

Impersonal tone, 394
Indexes, 160–162
Induction
  argument structures
    based on samples, 264–265
    from analogy, 264–267
  assessing support for, 289–292
  definition, 262
  reasoning, 262–267

Internal documentation, 406–409
Interview, 71–82
  design, 71
  establishing objectivity, 77
  establishing persona, 76
  presenting data, 81–82
  question sequence, 75
Introduction, 343–348
Ironic tone, 395

Jargon, 226, 384–385
Journal
  definition, 101
  examples, 101, 103

Log
  definition, 99
  examples, 99–100, 101, 102–103,
    104–105
Logic, 262
  See also Logical appeal
Logical appeal
  assessing support, 289–292
  common fallacies, 274–289
  purpose, 261
  reasoning, 262–272, 310–312, 315
  testing logic, 272–274
Logos. See Logical appeal

Maslow, Abraham, 304
Mean, 127
Median, 127, 129
Metaphor, 390
Metonymy, 390
Mitchell, Arnold, 305
MLA style, 407–412
Mode, 127
Modern Language Association (MLA)
    style, 407–412
  sample paper, 455–467
Monroe, Alan, 365
Monroe's motivated sequence, 365–367
Motivational warrant, 17

Non sequitur, 286
Nonsexist language, 383
Note cards, 437–440